Economics and Economic Change

On the CD enclosed in the back of the book you will find valuable **student** learning material including:

- Thirteen interactive tutorials on fundamental economic models and concepts, as well as statistical skills and techniques
- Interactive check-your-understanding quiz for each part of the book
- Guide to using SPSS
- 18 SPSS data sets for use in practical statistical exercises

The Open University course DD202 team

Paul Anand, Reader in Economics

Brenda Barnett, Course Secretary

Penny Bennett, Project Leader

Pam Berry, Compositor

Karen Bridge, Software Designer

Michael Brogan, Course Manager

Vivienne Brown, Professor of Intellectual History

Stephen Clift, Editor

Lene Connolly, Print Buyer

Neil Costello, Associate Director, SQW

Sarah Crompton, Graphic Designer

Graham Dawson, Course Team Chair and Senior Lecturer in Economics

Sue Dobson, Cartoonist

Christopher Downs, Software Course Team Chair and Senior Lecturer in Economics, University College, Chichester

Wilf Eynon, Audio Visual

Ian Fribbance, Staff Tutor

Phil Gauron, Series Producer, BBC

Janis Gilbert, Graphic Artist

Richard Golden, Production and Presentation Administrator

Mark Goodwin, Editor

Celia Hart, Picture Researcher

Martin Higginson, Staff Tutor

Susan Himmelweit, Professor of Economics

Steve Hoy, Producer, BBC

Andrew Law, BBC

Damian Lewis, Software Developer, BBC

Avis Lexton, Secretary

Maureen Mackintosh, Professor of Economics

Ione Mako, BBC

Paul Manners, BBC

Mariana Mazzucato, Professor of Economics

Vicki McCulloch, Graphic Designer

Judith Mehta, Lecturer in Economics

David Morris, Software Developer

Jonathan Owen, Graphic Artist

Anne Paynter, Course Secretary

Carlton Reeve, BBC

Roberto Simonetti, Senior Lecturer in Economics

Hedley Stone, Staff Tutor

Andrew Trigg, Senior Lecturer in Economics

Chris Wooldridge, Editor

Tutor consultants

Michelle Jenkins

Maureen Le Roi

Alistair Young

External authors

Suma Athreye, Reader in International Business and Strategy, Brunel Business School, Uxbridge

Nick Crafts, Professor of Economic History, London School of Economics and Political Science

Guiseppe Fontana, Lecturer in Economics, University of Leeds

Francis Green, Professor of Economics, University of Kent at Canterbury

Diane Perrons, Senior Lecturer in Economics, London School of Economics and Political Science

Malcolm Sawyer, Professor of Economics, University of Leeds

David Spencer, Lecturer in Economics, University of Leeds

Andrew Stevenson, Honorary Senior Research Fellow, Department of Economics, University of Glasgow

Anthony J. Venables, Professor of Economics, London School of Economics and Political Science

External assessor

John Vint, Professor of Economics, Manchester Metropolitan University

External consultant

Dr Terry O'Shaughnessy, Tutor and Fellow in Economics, St Anne's College, Oxford

Economics and Economic Change

Second edition

Edited by
Graham Dawson, Paul Anand, Suma
Athreye, Susan Himmelweit, Maureen
Mackintosh, Malcolm Sawyer and
Terry O'Shaughnessy

FT Prentice Hall
FINANCIAL TIMES

The Open University

An imprint of **Pearson Education**
Harlow, England • London • New York • Boston • San Francisco • Toronto • Sydney • Singapore • Hong Kong
Tokyo • Seoul • Taipei • New Delhi • Cape Town • Madrid • Mexico City • Amsterdam • Munich • Paris • Milan

Pearson Education Limited
Edinburgh Gate
Harlow
Essex CM20 2JE
England

and Associated Companies throughout the world

Visit us on the World Wide Web at:
www.pearsoned.co.uk

The Open University
Walton Hall
Milton Keynes
MK7 6AA
www.open.ac.uk

First published 2006

© The Open University 2006

ISBN-13: 978-0-273-69351-2
ISBN-10: 0-273-69351-4

British Library Cataloguing-in-Publication Data
A catalogue record for this book is available from the British Library

Library of Congress Cataloging-in-Publication Data
A catalog record for this book is available from the Library of Congress

10 9 8 7 6 5 4 3 2 1
10 09 08 07 06

Typeset in 10/12pt Minion by 35
Printed and bound in Great Britain by Ashford Colour Press, Hampshire

The publisher's policy is to use paper manufactured from sustainable forests.

Contents

Macroeconomics

Part 4   National economies

Chapter 14   Investment and capital accumulation   374

David A. Spencer

Part 5   Winners and losers from globalization: the international economy

Chapter 15   International trade and production   397

Anthony Venables

Chapter 16   Globalization, inequality and economic growth   426

Suma Athreye

Chapter 17   National currencies and international money markets   453

Andrew Stevenson

Part 6   Looking into the long term

Chapter 18   Unemployment and inflation   483

Graham Dawson

Chapter 19   Macroeconomic performance and stabilization   515

Nicholas Crafts

Chapter 20   Environmental sustainability   548

Graham Dawson

Supporting resources

For students

The CD enclosed in the back of the book contains valuable learning resources

- Thirteen interactive tutorials on fundamental economic models and concepts, as well as statistical skills and techniques
- Interactive check-your-understanding quiz for each part of the book
- Guide to using SPSS
- 18 SPSS data sets for use in practical statistical exercises

For instructors

Visit **www.pearsoned.co.uk/dawsonetal** to find valuable online resources

- Complete, downloadable Instructor's Manual with selected answers to end-of-chapter questions for discussion and review
- Downloadable PowerPoint slides of figures and tables from the book

For more information please contact your local Pearson Education sales representative or visit **www.pearsoned.co.uk/dawsonetal**

Preface

Economics and Economic Change is a new introductory economics text intended mainly for students on courses which are components of multi- and inter-disciplinary degree programmes as distinct from more traditional single honours economics degrees. These degree programmes include business studies, social sciences, social policy and public policy. The book contains the core teaching of an Open University course of the same title, which consists of *Microeconomics* and *Macroeconomics*. More and more students in higher education are studying independently, in part because part-time and distance provision are expanding and in part because large classes create difficulties in providing adequate individual attention for full-time students. Economics principles texts can be hard going for students without the support of seminars and discussion. In contrast, *Economics and Economic Change* mixes critical debate, ethical reflection and discussion of current economic issues with the exposition of theoretical analysis. Together with the interactive style of teaching drawn from The Open University's long experience of open supported distance education, the text offers, we believe, an engaging introduction to an important social science for full-time and part-time students alike.

Economics and Economic Change is one of a 'new generation' of economics courses that reflects the economic and social impact of information and communication technologies. While the text teaches students how to analyse the effects of new technologies on the economy, the accompanying CD-ROM enables students to see themselves as taking part in the economic processes they are learning to understand. In presenting a range of teaching materials in this way – real-world case studies, 'test your understanding' quizzes, a statistical package and 'virtual tutorials' on diagrammatic analysis – *Economics and Economic Change* 'enacts' the changes that are taking place and enables students to develop ICT skills.

This book is based upon an Open University course and is therefore a product of collective working. The course team, listed on p.ii, includes both Open University academics and outside contributors. The academic editors are grateful to our external contributing authors for giving the considerable time this enterprise requires. We would particularly like to thank Malcolm Sawyer for his collaboration in planning and editing *Macroeconomics*.

An Open University course team also includes many essential contributors besides academic authors. The academic editors of this book are very appreciative of the outstanding professional effort and expertise contributed by the course manager and project leader, the secretarial staff, the publishing editors, the designers and artists, the software designers and the BBC producers. The external assessor for the course as a whole, John Vint, has been a source of wise advice on structure, content and the accessibility of the course. Finally, the members of our panel of Open University tutors have put a great deal of effort into trying to ensure that the course content is appropriate for students and have always contributed to the conviviality of course team meetings.

Finally, Justinia Seaman, her colleagues at Pearson Education and their reviewers have contributed much valuable advice about turning an Open University course text into an introductory economics textbook for all students who approach economics as a social science or through business studies.

July 2005

Introduction

Graham Dawson

As a child in Birkenhead, I was regularly taken to visit my great aunt Adelaide. For her, the problem was how to occupy the seven-year-old boy while she and my mother brought each other up to date on news and gossip from their branches of the family. (It seemed to be part of my younger sister's early socialization that she was expected to sit in on the exchange.) The solution lay in a large glass-fronted bookcase. The only book I still remember was a very old one called *The Romance of Business*. Within its dark-blue cloth covers I discovered biographies of major nineteenth-century industrialists and entrepreneurs and indeed the 'life stories' of the firms they created. As far as I can recall, Mr Bryant and Mr May got together to manufacture safety matches, Jesse Boot started out with a stall in Nottingham market and our local hero (albeit born in Bolton) Mr Lever established Port Sunlight as the supplier of the nation's soap.

These narratives gave me an early inkling of two ideas, which I think I understand a little more clearly now. First, there was a sense of the risks these businessmen had taken in being so innovative, bringing new products to market with no certainty that they would 'catch on' with people. The book's title did not lie; there was adventure and glamour about their economic exploits, creating industrial empires and family fortunes out of what proved to be good ideas. Second, in making their own way in the world, they transformed it. Soap and safety matches are now so ubiquitous that we do not give them a second thought, but there was a time when they were innovative 'high-tech' products, perhaps encountering consumer resistance before transforming the daily habits of the population.

Thanks to my great aunt 'Addie', I received an early introduction to the importance of innovation and to the idea of economic change. Economics came later. As an undergraduate I discovered that the standard methods of analysing the activities of firms involved diagrams, tables of statistical data and a rather formal and abstract way with verbal explanation. It was much more like physics than a biography. Nevertheless, the models of consumer demand, perfect competition and monopoly, once applied to the real world of buying and selling, of production and trade, were just as illuminating as the old blue book, although the light they cast was more austere.

Economics and Economic Change is an attempt to bring you both the romance and the physics of economic life, to reflect the rapid pace of economic change and to capture the enduring structures that shape it. However, there is another dimension of economic change that the course addresses: the moral or ethical dimension. Economic change is not only beneficial, liberating and exciting in its impact on the lives of the people who shape it and are in turn shaped by it. There are casualties as well as victorious generals. Indeed, the military metaphor is appropriate, because economic change has been and continues to be at the heart of a struggle between social classes, ethnic groups and nations that sometimes bursts out into violent conflict. On a less spectacular level, economic change brings with it for many people dislocation and upheaval, the loss of traditional liveli-hoods and accustomed ways of life and the reality of material deprivation and hardship. Throughout the course there is an engagement with the implications, both beneficial and damaging, of economic change for people's lives and for their well-being.

As the title suggests, *Economics and Economic Change* combines an exploration of some major aspects of economic change in the international and national economies with an introduction to economic theory. You will, therefore, find two 'storylines' interwoven throughout the text. One is about economic change: what is innovation, how does economic change occur and what are the most important economic problems that arise? The other storyline is about economic analysis: the exposition of economic ideas and economic debates. Describing the two main strands of the text in this way acknowledges that they are closely related. We need economic concepts and ideas in order to understand economic change and to identify and analyse economic problems. But changing economic events also feed back upon and influence the ideas and preoccupations of economists.

In emphasizing the interaction of ideas and events, this book – like all texts in social science – is very much a child of its time and place. Written in Britain, in the West, and from within the Anglo-American tradition in economics, the text reflects a number of early twenty-first century uncertainties. This is perhaps most evident in the themes we have chosen for the 'economic change' strand. Among the contemporary economic issues the book explores are the following: Are we living through a new Industrial Revolution, led by information and communication technologies? Why is the intensity of work effort increas-ing? What should be done about increasing inequalities in some economies, including inequality in access to adequate health care? Why have capitalist economies tended to go through booms and slumps, causing inflation and unemployment? What do we know about the economic outcomes of globalization? Is capitalism environmentally sustainable?

Models and voices

In the 'economics' strand, too, *Economics and Economic Change* reflects early twenty-first century questioning, for example of the benefits and limits of both markets and govern-ment and of the ways in which they complement each other. The 1990s saw the long US boom, heralded by some as the 'new economy' inaugurated by information technology and welcomed by some as the reward for political confidence in the benefits of the unfettered market. This context has strengthened a renewed interest among economists in innovation and the role it plays in industrial revolutions. It has also triggered an interest in economic institutions, reflected here in the discussions of market institutions and of the economics of policy and governance.

Over many years economics has been exploring the consequences of how markets go wrong, or 'fail' – a concern which has been rekindled by the failure of some Western market systems to re-employ all the unemployed. This text picks up this renewed concern with the imperfections of markets, treating markets that work imperfectly as the dominant case in analysing markets and the national economy.

There is a further sense in which the approach to economics in this text is clearly the product of its time. Economics is a social science, though one which makes considerable claims to precision and prediction. In broad terms, recent social science has been marked by a systematic focus on what might be summarized as standpoint and language. There has been intensive questioning of whether there is necessarily a diversity of understanding of the social world structured by the points of view of those undertaking the theorizing. Related to this, there has been a renewed awareness of the importance of language and metaphor in social science.

These concerns with language and method in social science have until recently largely passed economics by. However, the last few years have seen a new interest among economists in the rhetoric of the subject, in the basis of its claims to knowledge about economies, and in its fundamental assumptions. In this text we have tried to reflect some of these concerns in our approach to teaching economics.

One of the main ways in which economists seek to understand economies is by constructing economic 'models'. These models are rather formal statements of how different elements of the economy interact: what influences what and how. Economic models can be stated in words, visually in diagrams or by using mathematics. In an introductory text such as this, the main media are words and diagrams. Like all textbooks in economics, this book sets out to explain how economists construct models to try to understand how economies work.

Economics and Economic Change uses models drawn from some rather different theoretical perspectives. There is a pluralist feel to the text. It uses models that engage with the historical narrative of economic change, with the 'life cycles' of industries that follow, for example the car industry, from a 'new dawn' of innovation through maturity and into decline – and, in that particular case, renewal. This text also uses models that are expressed in geometrical diagrams and in equations to 'stop the action' and examine the properties of market structures, to investigate the balance of the forces of supply and demand at a particular moment.

This book is also a child of its time in reflecting contemporary engagement with ethical issues, with questions of right and wrong, and even with questions of what is ultimately good for people. Questions in ethics are on many people's minds, provoked by a range of issues from cloning and euthanasia through the responsibility for climate change and other environmental damage to the importance of trust and integrity in corporate life and the afflictions of sleaze, scandals and spin in political affairs. In this text we introduce ethical questions by thinking about well-being, or what is ultimately good for people, and how economic activity can contribute to it. We return to ethical issues at several points, for example when examining the ethics of the environment.

Another activity encompassed within 'economics' is the examination of economic data and the use of models and data together to explore economic change. This activity, its theory and practice, is the specialism of a branch of economics called econometrics. While this text does not teach econometrics, it recognizes that understanding economics requires some understanding of the excitements and difficulties of trying to confront models with data.

Finally, a word about styles of writing. Economists speak in many different 'voices', reflecting personalities, subject matter, aims and audiences. They write both to analyse and to persuade, and hence do both in a cool and abstract tone and in emotive prose. Economics makes strong claims to clarity and exactitude while being a highly political subject: the stuff of public debate.

Unusually, this text contains some of this flavour of many voices. It is written by a variety of different authors, all professional economists but with different specialisms and approaches to economics. The aim of the editors has been to ensure that the presentation of the theory and arguments proceeds logically through the text, but not to suppress differences in style and approach. Style and content are deeply interrelated, and we hope to provide a feel for the variety and range of what is called economics.

Using the text

This book has been developed from a distance-learning text and we have retained two key features of the original text: it was designed to be studied independently, and it is written in a style addressed to you, the student. We believe that there are significant advantages in retaining these features. Using a textbook is a solitary activity and it is important not to increase the sense of isolation by adopting the impersonal style that is familiar from so many texts. We hope that we can reward the interest in economic issues and events that sparked your interest in the subject by constantly emphasizing the application of theory to economic issues, not only through formal case studies but in the integration of real-world examples into the main text. The text is also designed to be studied in the order in which the material is presented. The presentation builds up logically from Chapter 1, with cross-referencing between chapters throughout.

The course is divided into two books. In *Microeconomics*, the first book, Chapter 1 considers four ways in which some social scientists have claimed that there might be a 'new economy' coming into being: the switch from manufacturing to services, globalization, new technology and flexible labour markets. The good and bad points of economic change, its benefits and costs, are discussed. For example, what does it mean for people trying desperately to balance the urgent demands of work and life? Chapter 2 takes one aspect of the debate concerning the new economy – innovation in the form of the introduction of information and communication technologies – and places it in the historical context of industrial revolutions. Is the new economy really new or 'just another' industrial revolution? This highlights the role of innovation in creating industries, a theme that is picked up in Chapter 3. The main focus is on firms and how the costs of producing output change as they increase the scale of production and introduce new technology into the production process. Chapter 3 also introduces the diagrammatic analysis of firms' costs and of consumer demand. These chapters introduce the range of activities that constitutes economics: formulating theories, modelling, debate and persuasion, analysis of data, understanding the behaviour of economic institutions such as companies and households, and analysing economic processes. These chapters seek to show how all of these economic techniques can be used to build up a rich understanding of innovation and economic change.

This approach is taken up and developed by Chapters 4, 5 and 6, which explore the behaviour of firms within markets and the different forms that competition can take, such as competition on price as well as competition through innovation. Theory is combined with practical case studies and examples. Chapter 4 is built around a case study of Microsoft, the US software company that was accused by the US authorities of misusing its power to block competition. UK and EU legislation also seek to curb the power of large companies because it may be used to harm the interests of consumers, for example by charging prices that are 'too high'. The role of large companies, or monopolies, in innovation, in bringing new products to consumers, is also analysed. However, not every market is marked by product innovation, rapid technical change and monopoly power. Think of buying fresh fruit and vegetables in the sort of market that takes place in many towns on 'market day'. Or think of buying second-hand goods, anything from a house or a car to a baby buggy or guitar, through the classified ads in a local newspaper. Chapter 5 examines markets where competition among a large number of sellers provides one way of securing for consumers the lowest possible prices. Markets of this sort have been seen by some politicians and economists as an ideal way of organizing economic life, as 'free markets', and their role as a benchmark in economic theory will be further discussed in

Chapter 8. Chapter 6 analyses competition in markets with a few firms, each of which takes its rivals' behaviour into account in determining its own competitive strategy. In this situation competition can be understood as a war, involving alliances and collusion as well as supermarket 'price wars'. A new technique, game theory, is introduced to model firms' decision-making in markets where we might imagine each firm trying to guess what its competitors are going to do.

Microeconomics concludes with four chapters that are more directly about people rather than firms, markets and industries. Chapters 7, 8, 9 and 10 explore issues to do with the well-being of the people who make economies work, as producers and consumers. Do flexible labour markets provide good jobs? Why is the intensity of work effort increasing? How do material wealth, happiness and sustainability measure up as different interpretations of well-being? How is the role of government in furthering people's well-being changing? Do governments still have the will to redistribute income and wealth for the sake of reducing inequality? What can governments do to secure equal access to adequate health care?

Chapter 7 analyses the distinctive features of the labour market, paying particular attention to differences in skill, minimum wage legislation and trade unions. This provides the background for a discussion of issues of special contemporary relevance, including the flexible labour market and increasing work intensity. Chapter 8 introduces the ethical dimension of economic analysis. The national income accounts, which measure the value of the output of goods and services available for consumption, are explained and their limitations as an estimate of people's well-being exposed. This chapter also examines the underlying theory that equates well-being with the satisfaction we enjoy as consumers. Alternative concepts and measures of well-being are explored. These include 'green' national income intended to measure environmental damage and repair, the claim that people have rights to essential goods, and psychological approaches to well-being as happiness. Chapter 9 turns to the contributions that governments and, in particular, welfare states make to well-being. The chapter outlines the standard economic arguments for government intervention in markets that left to themselves, or only minimally regulated, would 'fail', that is, fail to ensure that people are as well off as they might be. The examples discussed are wide ranging, from environmental degradation to unemployment benefits. The chapter also introduces techniques for measuring the degree of inequality in the distribution of income among a national population. Chapter 10 applies these techniques to the measurement of an especially important aspect of inequality: inequality in access to appropriate and effective health care. The chapter also analyses the ways in which market failure would occur if the finance of health care and its delivery were to be left to lightly regulated markets. One response to health-care market failure is the UK National Health Service and the chapter includes a case study of NHS reform.

Macroeconomics, the second book of *Economics and Economic Change*, develops further the twin 'storylines' of economic change and economic analysis that ran through the first book. We have chosen three main themes for the economic change strand in this book. Why do capitalist economies tend to go through booms and slumps, and how do policy makers try to cope with the resulting inflation and unemployment? What do we know about the economic outcomes of globalization? Why has the performance of some economies been so much better than that of others, and is their growth environmentally sustainable?

Macroeconomics is the branch of economics that analyses the economy as a whole, or the 'aggregate economy', by looking at the relationship between key aggregates such as the overall level of output, unemployment and inflation. Chapter 11 opens with a brief survey of contemporary macroeconomic stability; that is, the relative steadiness of inflation, growth and unemployment in most industrial economies over the last decade or so. This 'snapshot' of current macroeconomic successes and failures in the older industrial economies is used to place current debates in macroeconomic analysis and policy in historical context. The idea of analysing the economy as a whole in this way was the core theoretical innovation of *The General Theory of Employment, Interest and Money*, published in 1936 by John Maynard Keynes, probably the most influential economist of the twentieth century.

Before the *General Theory*, the prevailing belief among economists was that markets work automatically in a self-adjusting manner. According to this view, the price mechanism works by allocating resources to where they are most needed. If a good is in short supply, then its price is too low and it will rise; if a good is in oversupply, then its price is too high and it will fall. In so far as aggregates were thought about at all, they were assumed to behave similarly to the particular goods whose markets were analysed using the techniques of microeconomics. So, according to this view, unemployment must be the result of wages – the price of employing labour – being too high, and a labour market free from interference would in time see a reduction in wages to balance demand and supply at full employment. Keynes argued that this view was wrong and that the labour market is not able to adjust automatically to eliminate unemployment.

According to Keynes, the aggregate markets of the macroeconomy are fundamentally interconnected, so that it is inappropriate to use the methods that one would use for analysing demand and supply in a single unconnected market. For this reason, the fault with the argument that the labour market is self-adjusting is that it ignores the relationship between employment and the aggregate economy, between the labour market and the goods market. Widespread unemployment can emerge because there is a problem at the level of the aggregate economy that prevents the labour market from adjusting. In particular, Keynes focused on the role of 'aggregate demand' – the total demand for goods and services in the aggregate economy – as a key determinant of the level of unemployment. If aggregate demand for goods is low and firms cannot sell all their output, they will cut back production and workers will lose their jobs.

Keynes's *General Theory* was revolutionary in providing economic analysis with this new notion of the 'aggregate economy'. The aggregate economy refers to the national economy as a structured set of economic relations between economic agents. Chapter 12 builds on the model of the circular flow of income (Chapter 8) to explain some of the interdependencies in a national economy where one agent's expenditure is another's income. To analyse this flow, it is necessary to group economic agents into different aggregate types. There are *workers* who sell their labour. There are *firms* that produce the national output and *households* that consume it. There is also the *government*; and there is the *rest of the world*. Understanding the outcome of these different types of agents' planned expenditures enables us to clarify the conditions for equilibrium of the aggregate economy.

Thinking of the aggregate economy in this way also implies a process of aggregating across markets. Chapter 13 analyses the three aggregated markets that comprise the aggregate economy: the goods market, the labour market and the money market. The chapter examines the components of aggregate demand in the goods market, in terms of the different types of economic agents and the type of demand they provide. There is consumption demand from consumers and investment demand from firms. Government expenditure provides another source of demand, as does the rest of the world in the demand for exports. All these different types of demand have different causes and therefore depend on a different set of factors, some of which can be influenced by policy. Adding up the demand for final goods and services in all the markets in the economy gives aggregate demand. If supply, the capacity to produce output, is not a problem, the level of aggregate demand determines the equilibrium level of national output. Relating this level of output to the labour needed to produce it shows that aggregate demand may be lower than is required to ensure full employment. If so, the government may intervene to raise aggregate demand, perhaps by changing its tax and spending plans, to influence consumer demand and government demand, or perhaps by changing interest rates in the money market, to influence investment demand.

Chapter 14 discusses investment, picking up the link between interest rates and investment and hence aggregate demand that Chapter 13 established. The importance of the level of investment to policy makers derives from both its role in achieving and sustaining economic growth and its volatility. Investment is the most volatile element of aggregate demand, yet it is also the one with the greatest significance for the rate of economic growth in the long run. The chapter analyses the factors that influence investment decisions in order to identify the sources of this volatility.

Analysis of the aggregate economy requires a notion of the national economy. In the analysis of Chapters 12 to 13 the aggregate or macroeconomy is defined by national boundaries. The government that intervenes to reduce unemployment is the national government, which has a particular responsibility for the performance of its own national economy. Thus, Keynesian macroeconomics also helped to identify the national economy as a distinct set of economic relationships that are amenable to systematic analysis and the particular concern of the national government.

Chapters 15 to 17 take the understanding of national economies a stage further by considering trade and production in open economies; that is, national economies that are open to international trade. First, Chapter 15 makes a return to microeconomic theory and Chapter 16 examines empirical evidence on the application of this theory to globalization. The return to microeconomics is necessary because the microeconomic analysis of international trade between particular industries in different national economies provides an important foundation for understanding international trade and its effects on the performance of national economies. The analysis of international trade used in Chapter 15 is microeconomic because it looks at the gains from trade in markets for two specific goods, where the industries supplying the market may be located in different national economies. The economic relationships between national economies as such, mediated by the exchange rates of national currencies, are examined in Chapter 17.

Chapter 15 considers how international trade arises from the differential endowments of resources among national economies. It shows how international trade can improve the consumption possibilities of economies, increase world output and make everyone better off. There are substantial benefits from participation in international trade. However, there are losers as well as winners. Although the consumers in a national economy may benefit from international trade, the theory of international trade suggests that this may be at the expense of some producers who cannot compete with foreign producers. This leads once again to a consideration of policy issues, in particular the circumstances in which the imposition of a tariff may be preferable to allowing completely free trade.

In considering the population's well-being, therefore, much depends on the distribution of the gains from trade. The acceleration of international trade and production is usually referred to as 'globalization'. Chapter 16 investigates the extent to which theoretical predictions about the gains from trade, and who the winners and losers are, can be observed in the contemporary global economy. This largely empirical chapter finds that globalization has in practice been confined to a relatively small number of economies. Some low-income countries appear to have benefited from globalization to the extent of catching up with living standards in high-income countries. However, globalization seems also to be associated with increasing inequality both between and within national economies.

Chapter 17 examines 'open economy macroeconomics', the macroeconomic analysis of economies that are open to trade, by bringing together Chapters 15 and 16's discussion of economic relations between national economies with the macroeconomics of Chapters 12 and 13. This involves integrating a new element into the analysis, the exchange rate, and investigating how it is determined under fixed and floating exchange systems. The chapter examines the impact of the exchange rate on macroeconomic variables including inflation, interest rates and aggregate demand. It finds that, in a world economy with a high degree of international capital mobility where funds can be moved easily across national borders to buy and sell national currencies, fixed exchange systems are unsustainable. However, floating exchange rates bring a risk of volatility and unexpected impacts on the national economy. The alternative is for a group of countries, most of whose trade is with each other, to set up a single currency, as some European Union member states have done by adopting the euro.

Macroeconomic performance in the long run is the main theme of Chapters 18 to 20. We hope that, as you approach the end of this text, you will be both looking back over the central themes of preceding chapters and wondering how to continue your study of economics. Similarly, to review the core ideas of *Macroeconomics* and to think about future prospects or to ask 'What next?' seem to be equally fitting themes with which to conclude this introduction to economics. The first task is to manage the transition from the short-run macroeconomic analysis of Chapters 11 to 14 to the discussion of macroeconomic performance in the long run. What influence do short-run policy decisions have on performance in the long run? Why have some economies grown so much more quickly than others? Is economic growth sustainable, or is it using up environmental and other resources faster than it replaces them?

Chapter 18 examines the limitations of government policy to boost aggregate demand in the short run in order to reduce unemployment. In the Keynesian model examined in Chapter 13, there are no supply constraints because it is assumed that there are unemployed workers and unused capacity and resources. Inflation in the 1970s persuaded many policy makers to temper their commitment to adjusting aggregate demand with the aim of reducing unemployment in the short run. The experience of the deleterious effects of inflation suggested that greater weight should instead be given to price stability as a necessary condition for long-run growth.

Chapter 19 reviews the macroeconomic performance of selected economies in the light of the theoretical insights that have been developed earlier in this book. The aim is to clarify the relationship between the use of macroeconomic policy designed to stabilize the economy in the short run and economic growth in the long run. Comparisons of macroeconomic policy and performance in different national economies suggest that policy can influence long-run outcomes, although a major factor in explaining growth, namely technological change, is not controlled by policy makers. The chapter argues that macroeconomic policy-making has improved in recent years, in part through the delegation of monetary policy to the central bank (such as the Bank of England in the UK). Nevertheless, the performance of any national economy is always potentially at risk to 'shocks' from elsewhere in the world, such as the oil price rises of the 1970s.

Chapter 20 takes a more reflective look at some of the issues raised by economic growth. Using climate change as a case study, the chapter discusses the limits to growth. Ecological economists argue that the physical environment sets limits to growth and the economic activity should be redirected towards sustainable development. The chapter also discusses ethical or social limits to growth, building on Chapter 8's discussion of theories of human well-being that go beyond material living standards. The policy dimension is again prominent in a discussion of emissions trading, an attempt at the international level to use markets to achieve environmental objectives set through the political process.

Throughout the text, we have used two conventions to assist your studying:

Questions

You should stop and try to find answers to these before reading the commentary that follows in the text. They are designed to help you find out how well you have understood the preceding material, and to get you to pause and think for yourself.

Exercises

The exercises allow you to test your understanding of concepts and techniques by applying and practising them. The answers are at the back of the book. You should not give in to the temptation to skip these, since they are an important part of the teaching. Sometimes you will only understand the following section if you have worked through an earlier exercise.

Questions for discussion and review

At the end of each chapter you will find a number of questions of different kinds that together give you an opportunity to review and test your understanding of the contents of the chapter and to develop answers to essay questions of the sort you are likely to encounter in formal examinations. You might think of these questions as a bank of resources to draw upon as you prepare term-time assignments and end-of-course examinations.

These questions come from three sources. Some are printed from the 'test yourself' quizzes at the end of each Part of the text on the CD-ROM. Some are from the end-of-course examinations for each year since the Open University course DD202 Economics and Economic Change was launched in 2003. And the rest are taken from the continuous assessment component of the OU course. All the questions have therefore been 'tried and tested' by hundreds of Open University students. We hope that you find them helpful and appropriately challenging in your own studies.

In addition to the material in the book itself, you will find a CD-ROM in the back of the book. This CD-ROM contains a number of useful learning resources to aid your studies, including:

Interactive tutorials

These tutorials complement the text's teaching of fundamental economic models and concepts (those denoted by <e>), as well as provide guidance on statistical skills and techniques (denoted by <s>). The tutorials found on the CD-ROM relate to the chapters in the book as follows:

Microeconomics

Part 1: Are we living through a new industrial revolution?

Chapter 1: Living and working in the 'new economy'
Tutorial 1 <s>: Understanding tables and graphs
Tutorial 2 <s>: Using SPSS to present and describe data

Macroeconomics

Check-your-understanding quizzes

For each part of the book there is an interactive quiz on the CD-ROM so you can check your understanding of the concepts and ideas that have been introduced. Feedback is provided as you go along to help you deepen your understanding.

Guide to using SPSS

SPSS is a statistical software package that is commonly used for the analysis of economic data. You may well make use of this software during your studies. This guide gives you useful tips on using SPSS.

SPSS data sets

18 sets of economic data are provided, in SPSS format. These data sets will be useful to those with a licence for SPSS, to practice statistical exercises.

Welcome to *Economics and Economic Change*. We hope that you enjoy this invitation to what we regard as the fascinating subject of economics.

Microeconomics

1

Living and working in the 'new economy'

Diane Perrons and Graham Dawson

Concepts

- the switch from manufacturing to services
- globalization
- information and communication technologies (ICT)
- the weightless economy

Objectives

After studying this chapter you should be able to:

- appreciate different understandings of the new economy
- understand claims about the benefits and costs of the new economy.

1.1 Introduction

10 p.m. Friday evening

Sunil, in India, has just received an email from Claire in Brighton, England, who runs a micro enterprise from her front room, clarifying details of some programming she has just subcontracted.

Tom is at a wine bar celebrating news of a £1 million investment of venture capital in his company.

Stephen has just begun the night shift in a call centre.

Joyce has just left her cleaning job, one of three jobs she currently holds. She is also a part-time office administrator and runs her own small enterprise designing and selling cushions.

These people reflect the varied dimensions of what it has become fashionable to call the 'new economy'. In emailing Sunil, Claire is using the Internet to run an enterprise from her own home. Tom represents one of the successes of the new economy and illustrates how some dot.com companies attract the interest of venture capitalists, financial institutions that invest in new enterprises. Stephen demonstrates how routine jobs underpin the workings of the new economy and Joyce illustrates how workers lower down the employment hierarchy often have to become entrepreneurial and construct their own work patterns in order to survive. The examples also illustrate how jobs are more likely to be in the service sector rather than manufacturing, as likely to be done by women as men and how the working day has lengthened, all characteristics of the new economy.

These are real examples but are they typical? Recently, academics from a range of disciplines and journalists have used the term 'new economy', but their understandings of it differ. This chapter considers some of these different understandings. What is the role of information and communication technologies (ICT) thought to be in the new economy? Section 1.2 suggests that they are a major feature of the economic changes currently taking place but globalization and the shift from manufacturing to services are also important. Should we welcome the new economy for the opportunities it brings or feel threatened by its disruption of ways of economic and social life to which we are accustomed? Section 1.3 discusses the benefits and problems of the new economy and examines the possibility that the opportunities and threats embodied in the new economy are two sides of the same coin.

This chapter examines a debate about the new economy; it does not investigate the new economy directly or take it for granted that there ever was such a thing. The important point is that the debate highlights some of the causes and effects of economic change, a central theme of this book.

1.2   Understanding the new economy

Reflecting upon the economic activities mentioned in '10 p.m. Friday evening' suggests three possible ways of understanding what is actually happening to the economy, how it is changing. First, it is widely believed that we live in an increasingly globalized economy in the sense that economic activity in different countries is more interdependent and more integrated than it used to be. Second, this interdependence is connected to the fact that ICT plays a greater role in economic activity nowadays. For example, as Sunil in India and Claire in England demonstrate, the Internet brings people closer together in space and time and has created new ways of organizing business transactions. Third, the nature of work has changed, with new jobs in high-income countries tending to be in the service sector rather than in manufacturing. These changes – globalization, greater role of ICT and the shift from manufacturing to services in industrialized economies – have been linked together to characterize the new economy. In examining these changes we will discover that working patterns have also undergone significant change, adding a fourth dimension to the new economy. The typical worker is now as likely to be female as male and to work with a computer whether they are gas boiler engineers or travel agents. They are also much less likely to work a standard working week than even ten years ago. In Sections 1.2.1–1.2.3 we examine these three changes in turn and in Section 1.2.4 reflect on their implications for subsequent chapters.

▨ ▥ ■ 1.2.1   The shift from manufacturing to services in industrialized economies

There was a profound restructuring of economic activity in 'older' industrialized countries in the last quarter of the twentieth century from manufacturing to service activities. There are several reasons for this restructuring. First, the long-established industrialized countries such as Germany, the USA, Japan and the UK have faced increasingly intense competition as more countries have industrialized. Second, productivity, or output per worker, has increased in manufacturing industries, enabling the same output to be produced by a smaller number of employees. Third, many people in the richer countries already possess a wide range of the consumer goods that manufacturing industry supplies, but are short of time. So there has been a growth in personal consumer services, such as leisure, including holidays and fitness training.

Service sector work, however, is far more diverse than manufacturing, particularly in the USA and the UK. There are highly skilled and highly paid producer service jobs in information systems, marketing, design and finance, in which most workers are male and white. At the bottom of the hierarchy are people engaged in private consumer services, often in cleaning, catering, security, leisure and personal care work, who are low-paid, rarely earning more than the minimum wage in the UK. Many of these lower-status jobs, for example those referred to in '10 p.m. Friday evening', are directly related to the activities of the time-pressed high-status workers who rely heavily on marketed services.

This restructuring of economic activity from manufacturing to services in part contributes to rising wage inequality. In the period following the Second World War, manufacturing employment provided many working-class people, especially men, with an opportunity to earn regular and relatively high wages in industries such as cars and steel. Earnings were concentrated quite narrowly around a relatively high average wage and maintained through trade unions, which ensured that workers obtained a share of the benefits of productivity increases. Earnings in the service sector, by contrast, are characterized by a lower average wage and a higher dispersion, that is, a greater difference between higher and lower wages. There is also a much wider range of employment opportunities in service industries (Harrison and Bluestone, 1990). The restructuring of employment from manufacturing to services can in part explain the increases in earnings inequality in the UK and US economies.

The result of these changes is that a much smaller proportion of the population in the long-established industrialized economies are directly involved in the production of physical goods in either agriculture or industry. Restructuring, however, rarely takes place as smoothly as some economic models might predict. As the Cambridge (UK) economist Joan Robinson – one of the most important economic theorists of the twentieth century – once said, the real world is not made of plasticine, and neither people nor buildings can be instantly remoulded. Not all factories can be converted into telephone call centres, although this does happen, and people may be unwilling, unable or not given a chance to change their skills.

▦ ▨ ■ 1.2.2   Globalization

Economic globalization may be defined as the increasing interdependence and integration of economic activity in different countries (Thompson, 2000, p.92). Interdependence means that the production of goods in one country is affected by the production of goods in another. For example, the import of Japanese cars into the UK has affected the UK car industry by taking sales away from it. Integration is a closer relation than interdependence, implying that production processes in different countries are so closely co-ordinated that they are best understood as parts of a single complex production process. An example is the manufacture of Honda car engines in Swindon, UK, for installation into cars assembled elsewhere.

Economic globalization has been facilitated by the development of ICT. One outcome of ICT-assisted globalization is that some leading companies, especially in clothing and footwear, no longer play any direct role in manufacturing the goods they sell; Nike, for example, does not manufacture any shoes. Similarly, many of the well-known clothing labels do not manufacture their clothes because they can make more profit from branding and marketing products. Production takes place in a range of companies in both rich and poor countries, which are variously owned and often connected through complex subcontracting arrangements. Each firm seeks to minimize risk in the highly competitive and volatile global market. Underpinning these developments has been the evolution of ICT which, somewhat paradoxically, has facilitated the location of modern factories in poorer countries and the re-emergence of small-scale producers in richer ones.

In the case of clothing, some production takes place 'offshore' in low-wage countries, but some remains in rich countries. For example, Los Angeles, often thought to be the heart of the US new economy, has the highest number of manufacturing jobs in the USA: 663 400 in 1997, which is nearly 6000 more than Chicago and 200 000 more than the third largest manufacturing city, Detroit (Bonacich and Appelbaum, 2000, p.28). These jobs are found in both the new 'high-tech' manufacturing industries and also in the old-style garment industry where over 100 000 workers, many recent migrants, work in the growing number of sweatshops (Bonacich and Appelbaum, 2000).

One reason why sweatshops have re-emerged is the increased power of brand marketers and retailers. Their ability to subcontract production to offshore producers and small-scale local producers enables them to maximize flexibility and so minimize their own risk, which is especially important owing to the transient nature of fashion. It also means that they can absolve themselves of responsibility for the working conditions of producers, although by no means all do so. These conditions can be particularly desperate owing to the global nature of the competition. The corresponding downward pressure on wage costs is intensified by the uncertainty of fashion, leading to long working hours, largely by women, especially in the rush to meet deadlines, and low pay, both offshore and in local sweatshops. The wide choice we as consumers have between different fashion products is paid for by the working conditions of the people who make them.

At the same time the increased economic integration of different countries has increased labour mobility. Many economic migrants to 'older' industrial countries from low-income countries end up working in low-productivity manufacturing, for example as home-workers or as owners of or workers in sweatshops in the clothing industry or in the low-paid jobs expanding in the service sector. Indeed, one of the ironies of globalization is that while many women workers in Bangladesh are working outside the home for the first time in new clothing factories, their compatriots, who migrated to London, are more likely to find themselves working at home (Kabeer, 2000). Women and minority ethnic groups are often over-represented in all of these low-paid activities which are often characterized by part-time work with unsociable hours.

In other industries, such as cars, the shift in manufacturing from the UK and the rest of Europe, far from creating sweatshops, has raised incomes and living standards, for example in east Asia. The shift in manufacturing is by no means complete; cars are produced in large numbers in the UK and Europe, while also being made by a largely male workforce overseas.

■ ■ ■ 1.2.3 Information and communication technologies

The new economy is much more than a shift from manufacturing to services and the increased integration of economies on a global scale. It is also strongly linked to the development of ICT, which has facilitated the development of new processes and products, especially 'knowledge goods' which are described below.

The Internet has increased the 'connectivity' or interconnectedness between economies by making textual communication possible in real time as well as providing a new means of disseminating new products and services. For example, ideas can be transmitted across the globe far more quickly than ever before and product obsolescence is much faster. The speed-up in communications means that events in one part of the globe can very quickly affect the fortunes of people living thousands of miles away. For example, the financial crisis in south-east Asia in 1998 led to a worldwide restructuring of the microchip industry. This restructuring resulted in the closure of a firm in Sedgefield in north-east England, which in turn affected the incomes of bar workers and taxi drivers in and around that locality as well as those who were made redundant by the closure itself.

The Internet also allows organizations to take advantage of different time zones and different wage cost zones in order to make cost savings. For example, you may book airline tickets or make enquiries at any time, but if you do so at night your connection is likely to be routed to a different time zone. In this way, companies can provide a 24-hour service, without having to pay higher night-time wage rates. Small firms, micro enterprises and even sole traders as well as multinational organizations can subcontract work globally. As in '10 p.m. Friday evening' a worker in the new media sector in Brighton can subcontract work to a programmer in India whom she had 'met' through the Internet (Perrons, 2001).

In terms of changing patterns of work, the Internet has also facilitated the development of the 24-hour economy. Longer opening and operating hours require flexible working patterns, which in turn allow people to fit paid work around other activities, such as caring or education. But, at the same time, they disrupt collective norms and rhythms of work. As the working day becomes more flexible, many salaried workers are expected to work long hours to demonstrate commitment to their organization (Hochschild, 1997) and to match the working hours of different time zones. In this way, new, more flexible working patterns have complex and diverging implications for other aspects of life.

Knowledge has always been central to competitive economies, to production processes and to selling commodities, but in the new economy a lot more knowledge, intelligence and 'style' is embedded within existing products such as cars, cameras and washing machines. Cars, for example, may have electronic windows and automatic windscreen wipers and headlights, which are programmed to respond to rain and light conditions. More significantly, there has also been an expansion of goods consisting almost entirely of knowledge and for Quah (1996) this represents the hallmark of the new economy. Software is the classic example. The cost of producing the actual physical product – the game or software package – is minuscule. However, the research and development costs going into its production are massive. In other words, the cost of the first product is enormous but the costs of replicating it many times over are then comparatively small.

We will take a closer look at 'knowledge products' in Section 1.3.3 but now it is time to reflect briefly on the significance of the new economy for the economic analysis to be explored in Chapters 2–6.

■ ■ ■ 1.2.4 Looking ahead: understanding economic change

Section 1.2 has looked at different ways of understanding the new economy, of understanding what is actually happening.

Question	Look back over the different understandings of the new economy. Is there really a new economy, just one, or are there three 'new economies'?

There is no single obviously right way of answering this question. Three distinct processes seem to be going on: the switch from manufacturing to services, globalization and the development of ICT. Changes in working patterns seem to be associated with all three processes. Thinking about economic change in terms of the new economy may be helpful in organizing our inquiries. The academics and commentators whose different interpretations will be examined in Section 1.3 certainly think so. They tend to see themselves as interpreting the 'new economy', just as those whose work we referred to in this section see themselves as debating different understandings of the new economy. It is therefore convenient to continue to use this terminology. However, it is worth remembering that the term 'new economy' can be used to pick out any or all of the three changes that are taking place in economic activity. Some of the differences in interpretation may reflect the way in which economists are focusing on different aspects of the new economy – on new economies or simply on economic change.

Now that we are stepping back from the different understandings of the new economy to take, very briefly, a more detached look at them, it seems a good moment to broach another critical question.

Question	Is the 'new economy' really new? Or we might ask, *how* new is the 'new economy'?

There is no simple answer to this question either. It seems reasonably clear that the different changes described above are not all equally new. For example, the shift from manufacturing to services in industrialized economies has been researched and debated for 30 years, while the widespread use of the Internet by consumers is no more than five years old.

Focusing on one dimension of change, the development of undeniably new technologies, economists try to understand what is happening by asking whether a new industrial revolution is taking place. What parallels are there in the past for today's rapid technological change and what do such episodes tell us about contemporary economic change? The next chapter explores these questions through a comparison of the early stages of the US automobile industry and the personal computer industry. Both industries exhibit a common pattern of development or 'life cycle' and Chapter 3 looks more deeply into the economics of the technological innovations underlying them.

Chapters 3–6 take up the theme of innovation and examines the ways in which firms use innovation to compete for sales and profits. Firms also compete in other ways, for example by trying to match or even undercut the prevailing price at which the product is sold. In trying to understand the new economy, and how new it really is, economists therefore look closely at the behaviour of firms and the industries and markets to which they belong. They also debate these issues energetically, because there are different understandings of the behaviour of firms, industries and markets.

1.3 The benefits and costs of the new economy

As well as looking at the behaviour of firms and the industries and markets to which they belong, economists also engage in a different style of inquiry, thinking about what economic change means for the lives of the people involved. Once again there is a variety of interpretations and different ideas but this time they concern the desirability of economic change. What benefits does the 'new economy' bring and what costs, or negative effects, does it impose on people? In analysing these benefits and costs, different economists will be guided by different priorities and values. Some economists may place greater weight on material rewards as against health and happiness. Some may prioritize the well-being of workers over that of consumers. Others may assume that the interests of entrepreneurs are paramount and overlook the needs of people with caring responsibilities.

In the late 1990s some economists, especially in the USA, emphasized relationships between 'headline' economic indicators such as inflation, wages, productivity and growth (which are analysed in Chapters 11–20). For these economists, such as Alan Greenspan (1998), the Chairman of the Federal Reserve (the US central bank), what was new about the new economy was the almost unprecedented coexistence of economic growth and low inflation. The combination of 'tight' labour markets (where employers have difficulty in finding enough workers to fill all the job vacancies) and hence low unemployment with low pressure for wage rises was also unusual. The coexistence of these factors challenged the conventional economic theory that tight labour markets lead to wage rises and more generally that rapid growth – a boom – will lead to inflation and then to 'bust'. This view is encapsulated in the extract from *Business Week Online*:

The New Economy
It works in America. Will it go global?

It seems almost too good to be true. With the information technology sector leading the way, the US has enjoyed almost 4% growth since 1994. Unemployment has fallen from 6% to about 4%, and inflation just keeps getting lower and lower. Leaving out food and energy, consumer inflation in 1999 was only 1.9%, the smallest increase in 34 years.

This spectacular boom was not built on smoke and mirrors. Rather, it reflects a willingness to undertake massive risky investments in innovative information technology, combined with a decade of retooling US financial markets, governments, and corporations to cut costs and increase flexibility and efficiency. The result is the so-called New Economy: faster growth and lower inflation.

(Business Week Online, 31 January 2000)

In fact it *was* too good to be true. US economic growth slowed during 2001, the terrorist attacks on the World Trade Center on 11 September undermined consumer confidence and by the end of the year the US economy was in recession. This raises the question, 'was the spectacular boom built on smoke and mirrors after all?' In other words, was it a unique historical episode or is it reasonable to believe that the economy will be seen nevertheless to have undergone a lasting change?

There are understandings of the 'new economy' that emphasize longer-lasting changes in the nature and organization of firms and employment patterns. The development of information and computing technologies is emphasized because they can potentially revolutionize business organization and therefore have implications well beyond the high-technology sector itself. Changes in the composition of the workforce, such as the increasing participation of women and the development of new, more flexible patterns of employment, affect how people can manage their work/life balance. The role of the state in creating a deregulated environment, which promotes flexibility in financial markets and working practices, has also been emphasized. All of these changes are claimed to be deep-seated and widespread and therefore unlikely to be reversed, despite short-term ups and downs in the economy.

The benefits that are claimed for the new economy arise from the development of high-technology and knowledge which offer new products and processes and new forms of high-level employment as well as opportunities for entrepreneurs. These are some of the real changes that are thought to underlie the unprecedented levels of inflation-free growth in the late 1990s in the US economy as referred to in the extract (above) from *Business Week Online*.

By contrast, the negative aspects of the new economy are highlighted by writers such as Ulrich Beck (2000) and Richard Sennett (1998), who link rapid economic change with increasing inequality, risk and insecurity, family breakdowns, falling fertility and the fragmentation of communities.

Some economists link the positive and negative effects of the new economy. For example, Danny Quah (1996) argues that the positive and negative dimensions of the new economy are opposite sides of the same coin and form part of an emerging digital divide. That is, some of the essential characteristics of the knowledge-based economy which contribute to economic growth also increase economic inequality and put increasing pressure on balancing the claims of work and life.

▪ ▪ ▪ 1.3.1 The benefits of the new economy

The benefits claimed for the new economy are mainly concerned with technological change, productivity and economic growth. Manuel Castells (2001) argues that we have entered a new technological paradigm centred around microelectronics-based information/communication technologies. The development of the Internet, in particular, is said to have profound implications for the organization of economic activity and for increasing productivity.

The Internet provides a new communication medium between businesses and between businesses and consumers and facilitates new ways of organizing the production, distribution and exchange of existing goods and services. It can reduce transaction and search costs between buyers and suppliers in a wide range of areas and allows the development of new products and services. These developments arguably underlie the unprecedented growth in the US economy in the second half of the 1990s.

Internet business-to-consumer sales are expanding rapidly but nowhere do they account for even 1 per cent of retail sales – being highest in Sweden at 0.68 per cent followed by the USA (0.48 per cent) and the UK (0.37 per cent) (OECD, 2000). Evidence on the comparative costs of Internet sales is mixed. In principle, consumers can save on search and travel costs by comparing prices and purchasing directly from home. They have immediate access to world markets, which could stimulate competition and bring about increases in efficiency at a global level. Suppliers would also save on showrooms but their overall delivery costs could rise as distribution would switch from high- to low-density routes, that is instead of journeys from warehouses to shopping centres more diverse journeys from factories to residential areas would need to be made (OECD, 2000). This problem would not arise in the case of 'weightless' or digitized products, which can be distributed very cheaply and incur minimal storage and inventory costs.

A further potential efficiency gain for producers is that they can target their marketing much more effectively as it is easy for them to build up a profile of their clients, allowing a form of mass customization. Amazon.com, for example, recommends new purchases to clients by comparing their purchase records with other clients. A firm called Babycenter.com tailors their information to parents according to the stage of pregnancy or age of the children (Borenstein and Saloner, 2001). Thus, by using their electronic databases, constructed in part by the consumers, firms can provide individualized and what appear to be personalized services far more efficiently than by traditional face-to-face contact, as Reich, a former Secretary of Labour in the Clinton administration, notes:

> I'm all of four feet ten inches tall, with a waistline significantly larger than that of a ten-year-old boy, which means that if I'm to look even vaguely respectable, anything I wear has to be custom-tailored. It is a royal pain, and often I don't bother. But recently I discovered the Web site of a clothing manufacturer on which I can enter all my size specifications and select the shirts and trousers (along with fabrics and styles) I want. Within days the garments arrive at my front door. When I first ordered, I expected the tailor who received my improbable measurements to assume they were mistaken, and change them (this had happened before). But the shirt and trousers fit perfectly. And then it hit me: I wasn't dealing with a tailor. I was transacting with a computer that had no independent judgement.
>
> *(Reich, 2001, pp.11–12)*

Thus, there are some advantages for consumers, even though the technology potentially allows sophisticated forms of price discrimination as prices could in principle be varied according to the individual customer profile (OECD, 2000). Consumers can also organize auctions and exchange products on the Internet, as in the case of the Napster music system, which essentially allows users to download each other's CDs. At the time of writing the legality of this system is being challenged in the courts. Consumers and protesters, for example the anti-sweatshop movement, can also exchange knowledge about the actions of companies very quickly, thereby enabling more effective monitoring of the ethics of trade (Klein, 1999).

Companies involved in training, marketing and public relations have also begun to provide these services through the Internet. These activities have generated a range of new firms and new employment. The jobs include the computing technologies themselves (hardware and software) for managing web-based transactions and have created a whole new range of activities from web-based graphic design, web system/database management, video installations through to programming. Because many of these activities are at the boundaries of new technologies, it has led to the development of small firms and micro enterprises which fuelled the so-called dot.com boom of 1999–2000.

The Women's Unit of the UK government has argued that ICT represents 'one of the biggest opportunities for women in the twenty-first century to earn more, have more flexible working practices and adapt their current business or try a business start-up'. Thus, they maintain that 'self-employment and enterprise offer women a real alternative means of earning good income and achieving greater flexibility in their working lives' (Women's Unit, 2000). That is, given the way that contemporary technologies extend the range of working opportunities both temporally and spatially, they potentially provide a means of redressing current gender inequalities. 'Family friendly' working patterns, if not quantity of work, can be constructed by entrepreneurs, homeworkers and freelancers who can manage their own routines. In some ways they may realize the vision of the 'electronic cottage' (Toffler, 1980), although the problems of social isolation and family tensions also have to be recognized (Perrons, 2001). However, women also face constraints. In the UK, for example, they are under-represented on ICT courses, the proportion of women working in these areas has fallen and they have more problems obtaining access to capital. The limited evidence suggests that the gender balance has not changed.

One of the reasons why it might be difficult to establish statistical associations between productivity growth and ICT is that they are general purpose technologies so their effects are wide ranging (see Chapter 2). E-commerce can potentially increase efficiency, as discussed above, but the physical delivery of products, where necessary, remains a labour-intensive activity. Thus, it is very difficult to gather data that might adequately describe the complex and diverging nature of the new economy.

Changes in the organization of economic activity also lead to employment changes at both ends of the employment hierarchy. At the upper end, highly skilled specialists in computer programming, systems analysis and web design are employed in setting up systems to facilitate Internet transactions. At the lower end, people are employed in warehouses and call centres. So the high-technology side of the new economy remains dependent on some labour-intensive work in delivering products and in all forms of personal services. Aggregate statistics bury these divergent trends.

Even the OECD (2000) report effectively predicts an emerging duality in the work-force as well as the disappearance of some jobs altogether. It points out that:

> a retail sale via the Internet probably does not require the same intensity of sales staff, but it requires people with IT skills to develop and program software, operate and maintain computer servers and networks and people skilled in graphics design to keep the web site attractive *and others to dispatch orders* [emphasis added]. In addition, firms will implement modifications to their production processes in order to exploit the potential of B2B [business-to-business] and B2C [business-to-consumer] commerce over the Internet. Certain jobs, especially those characterized by the transfer of information from one party to another such as travel agents, insurance and stock brokers are likely to be redefined and become less common.
>
> *(OECD, 2000, p.208)*

▪▪▪ 1.3.2 The downside of the new economy

During the US boom of the 1990s, some economists attributed the paradox of economic growth, rising productivity, but stable or only modestly rising wage costs, to the growing sense of insecurity in the labour force (Greenspan, 1998). Employment insecurity is also emphasized by sociologists such as Ulrich Beck (2000) and Richard Sennett (1998). This section outlines some of their arguments because they are central to those who take a critical view of the new economy. Their arguments also contain implications for the social sustainability of the new economy that is emerging in Europe and the USA.

Ulrich Beck, the German sociologist, argues in *The Brave New World of Work* (2000) that in the new economy work at all levels is characterized by insecurity and increasing inequality. Fernando Flores and John Gray (2000, p.24) speak of the 'death of the career' and argue that life-long identities are giving way to 'brief habits'. They suggest that 'the lives of wired people are more like collections of short stories than the narrative of a bourgeois novel'. These writers all suggest that work in the new economy is organized around pro-jects and is therefore very fluid or changeable. This is especially so in the high-technology sector where teams of people with necessary skills are constructed for particular projects and then dissolved as the project is completed. People change – or are required to change – their employer and their geographical location frequently. Consequently, connections between individuals, firms and communities are fragile. If this view is correct, these pro-cesses could undermine the social sustainability of the new economy.

The empirical evidence for claims about increasing insecurity is, however, rather mixed. There is fairly strong evidence for a growing sense of insecurity but at the same time aggregate statistics on job duration indicate little change. In a five-country European study (Ireland, Norway, Portugal, Sweden and the UK) a survey of people between the ages of 18 and 30 perceived jobs to be episodic and insecure, even though those in work tended to work long hours (Lewis and Brannen, 2000).

There has been a considerable restructuring of economies and companies have also been downsizing, which may be responsible for the sense of insecurity and 'skill obsolescence'. In these circumstances employees may be willing to accept low wages in return for job security, possibly accounting for the coexistence of economic growth and moderate increases in wage costs. A study of people in low-paid work by the Institute for Public Policy Research (IPPR, 2000), a left-of-centre policy think-tank, found that the security of a full-time job and a long-term contract superseded all other 'quality of work' concerns for older workers who had experienced periods of unemployment, but was less important to younger respondents. An illustrative comment came from a male airport worker aged between 40 and 50 at Hounslow: 'I'm just happy to have work, to have some security and to be earning a living.' In the mid to late 1990s only a small proportion of new jobs coming onto the labour market in the UK were full time and permanent (Gregg and Wadsworth, 1999).

Data on employment duration, however, may not be an adequate measure of insecurity. People are sometimes more likely to stay with an employer if they are uncertain about their prospects of re-employment. By contrast, in the high-tech sector, short-term contracts may reflect employee strength rather than weakness. That is, what some workers might conceive as insecurity, an independent contractor might welcome as the freedom to move between contracts to build up their skill portfolio. Security can mean different things to people at different levels in the employment hierarchy and these different dimensions will be conflated in aggregate statistics for employment as a whole; thus, insecurity is difficult to test empirically.

A further downside of the new economy is the emerging duality in the labour force, referred to in the quotation from the OECD (2000) at the end of Section 1.3.1, and increasing income inequality. Middle-class well-educated men are over-represented in high-technology jobs in firms while women, including some who have arrived in the country only recently, are over-represented in the less highly rewarded jobs that provide services more directly for people, such as care work for children and the elderly. Boyd *et al.* (1995) have referred to this as a division between the high-tech and the high-touch occupations. Both types of work are very much part of the new economy and share characteristics of insecurity, but they are very different in nature and in financial reward.

The development of the personal care and personal services sector depends on whether people are willing to work for low wages. These jobs are typically labour intensive and the scope for productivity increases is limited. In some sectors, such as retail and call centres, students are employed, but this group rarely finds work in personal care attractive.

Employment in call centres is growing. Estimates suggest that there are (in 2001) the equivalent of about 400 000 full-time jobs in UK call centres – about 1.8 per cent of the workforce. Some estimates suggest that this figure will double in the next five years. But newer technologies, such as voice recognition software and direct use of the Internet by consumers, could also displace these workers. Call centres deal with telephone enquiries, usually about banking, ticket bookings and billing, but especially for services such as electricity, gas and telephone, or with mail order sales. The size of the workforce in call centres varies from 20 to over 300 people. Often they are completely separate from other activities of the firms to which they belong, which means that career opportunities are limited. Typically, there are four tiers, from an operator (the lowest level) to team leader, supervisor and manager. Promotion to supervisor can be rapid, partly because of the high level of turnover. Pay varies between different types of call centre and by the level of wages in the locality, but generally it is considerably above the minimum wage, though still well below average pay (Incomes Data Services, 2001). Thus, opportunities are limited within call centres and there are no career routes from call centres to the wider organizations whose calls are processed.

These jobs are important because they are the archetypal 'footloose' form of employment sought after, for example, by Local Economic Development Agencies in the UK, who emphasize that low pay is prevalent in their areas in order to attract companies. Even though these are part of the new economy, many old-style working practices remain. The employees are closely monitored, their conversations are constantly recorded and employees often work from scripts designed to keep the calls as short as possible. When they have finished one call, another call can be automatically directed to them.

▦ ▩ ■ 1.3.3 The weightless economy

In this subsection we want to look at one attempt to link some of the positive and negative aspects of the new economy. Danny Quah is an economist at the London School of Economics who has studied the new economy over a number of years. He refers to the new economy as the weightless or *dematerialized* economy and he examines its economic implications and also why it has a tendency to lead to increasing economy inequality.

According to the 'weightless economy' argument, the fact that current economic expansion has been inflation-free may be because it places less pressure on physical resources than earlier episodes of rapid industrial and technological change. One reason is that new materials and microcomputers have led to a reduction in the size and weight of goods. For example, we have as much computing power on our desk as would have filled several rooms in 1980. The argument is that without a huge increase in demand for resources such as raw materials, their prices have not increased dramatically.

However, it is perhaps the nature of 'knowledge goods' that has the most profound economic implications. Knowledge goods are infinitely expansible and non-rival, which means that their consumption by one individual does not reduce the amount available to another. Thus, as Quah illustrates, several people can be using the same word processing package but they cannot all eat the same chocolate biscuit (Quah, 1999). The weightless form of knowledge goods together with the Internet creates a disrespect for physical distance, and therefore potentially these products also have infinite global reach.

A whole new range of goods and services are made up of bits and bytes, rather than bricks or steel, and can be downloaded directly from the Internet. Computer software is one example, sometimes freely provided, and the practice is spreading to books and films. There are also entirely new products coming onto the market, such as interactive digital media. For example, the Channel 4 programme *Big Brother* was broadcast 24 hours a day on the Internet, and the pop group Gorillaz had a top ten hit record despite having only a virtual existence. Similarly, some computer games can be downloaded from or played directly on the Internet.

Quah points out that although not everyone would consider a Britney Spears recording a 'knowledge good', the fact that it can be directly downloaded from the Internet gives it the same economic properties of being replicable or infinitely expansible and non-rival. For Quah (2001) these properties represent the defining feature of the new economy: that an increasing range of goods and services, from business computer software to computer games and films, has become like knowledge.

Two main economic implications of knowledge goods and the weightless economy can be identified. First, weightlessness opens up the prospect of *sustainable* growth, insofar as it enables economies to grow without depleting stocks of natural resources. To the degree that the economy is weightless, 'international trade becomes not a matter of shipping wine and textiles from one country to the next, but of bouncing bits off satellites' (Quah,

1996, p.7). Critics of the weightless economy argument, such as Lutz (1999, p.231), observe that PCs and other hardware still have to be manufactured and transported all over the world, using up resources including oil. However, according to Quah (1999), consumer hardware accounted for only one-third of IT (information technology) and 'in the foreseeable future it will likely become a progressively smaller fraction of the total' (Quah, 1999, p.10). This issue will be taken up again in Chapter 20.

Second, in theory, knowledge goods create a more egalitarian world (Quah, 2001). Suppose that consumption does not reduce the amount of knowledge goods available for other consumers, that knowledge goods are sometimes freely provided and should have an infinite global reach, and that they are replicable at almost no cost. In principle, ensuring equal access to them should therefore be easier than ensuring equal provision of physical goods and resources. In reality, however, the opposite trends can be observed, with increasing inequalities on a global scale and also within countries. Furthermore, it is the economic properties of knowledge goods that paradoxically contribute towards increasing economic inequality.

For example, the existence of dematerialized products contributes to the 'superstar effect', which helps to explain increasing income polarization, particularly marked in the USA and the UK. Quah (1996) demonstrates this by asking why the income differential between opera singers is greater than that between workers in many other occupations, such as shoemakers.

In the case of opera, it makes little difference to the singer, in terms of the effort involved, whether they are singing to 2 or 200 000 people. Consumers, however, generally prefer to listen to more famous singers than ones of lesser renown even though they may be of minimal perceptible difference to the majority of listeners. The almost costless replication of products such as CDs means that market size is unlimited by conventional barriers such as distance.

Consequently, the market share taken by superstars is huge, limited mainly by competition from other superstars. Therefore, in these cases, 'the winner takes all', which explains why the gap between high and low incomes is greater for singers than it is for shoemakers. The spread of incomes is much wider for knowledge goods than for products where such dematerialized replication is not possible.

Quah (1996) points out that the income differential is not simply a question of differential returns being given to differential natural endowments. Whose voice is replicated or who becomes a superstar depends on the selection decisions made by companies and so superstars are to a considerable extent *made* rather than born. Given this recognition, the comparison with the shoemaker becomes slightly more questionable. Branding and style have also made some shoes much more 'desirable' than others, making the returns to the owners of popular brands (although not the shoemakers themselves) much more wealthy than those of similar products but with 'no logo' as Naomi Klein (1999) puts it.

One reason why people accept widening inequalities, Quah argues, is increasing social mobility. That is, the poor tolerate the rich because they can see a greater opportunity for becoming rich themselves. However, there are also specific features, including gender stereotyping, associated with the restructuring of economic activity and the work of lower-paid workers that make their chances of becoming rich through their current work remote.

▨ ▨ ■ 1.3.4 Looking ahead: economic change and human well-being

There are different interpretations of the new economy and its impact on human well-being, on whether the changes sometimes labelled the 'new economy' are desirable or beneficial. It is time to review the benefits and costs of the new economy.

What do you think are the main points for and against the new economy in its impact on human well-being? A list of points is all that is required, although you may want to add your own comments or responses.

This is our list. It is not definitive in any sense and there is no intention either to find 'matching' good and bad points or to place them in order of importance. The idea is simply to initiate discussion.

Arguments for the new economy	Arguments against the new economy
Faster growth and low inflation	Social isolation
Personalized services	Family tensions
Efficiency gains	Employment insecurity
Flexible working patterns	Flexible working patterns
Environmental sustainability	Social unsustainability
Access to knowledge from remote locations	Income inequality increasing

Our first impression is that positive things about the new economy seem to be mainly economic, while the negative aspects are largely social. This brings to mind a picture of economic change disrupting established patterns of social life. It also suggests that the greater material well-being that economic growth brings may be bought at the cost of increasing threats to health, happiness and security. The general principle that emerges from these thoughts is that human well-being has a number of different components or dimensions, social as well as economic, and psychological or spiritual as well as material. Sifting these different senses of well-being is one of the tasks of Chapters 7–10.

However, qualifications soon occur. There is, above all, the danger of excessive generalization, of assuming that everyone wants the same things. For example, the fragility of communities and the fluidity of relationships might suit some, perhaps many, people. Not everyone wants to live their lives within a set of permanent relationships or in what can easily be experienced as the stifling atmosphere of a close-knit community. This is why 'flexible working patterns' appears in both columns. For many women with caring responsibilities who have been denied access to good jobs by traditional assumptions about gender roles, flexibility increases opportunities for paid work. On the other hand, there are many middle-aged male workers, such as the airport worker from Hounslow, who would probably prefer a 'job for life'.

In this case it seems possible to identify groups of winners and losers systematically on the basis of employment status, gender, age and other social characteristics. This is not quite the same as recognizing differences in personal preferences, such as wanting to be left alone. Taking this thought further reveals some tensions within the more 'economic' positive aspects of the new economy. For example, personalized services through computer ordering is a benefit for consumers, which, in an overall assessment of the desirability of economic change, must be weighed against adverse effects on other economic groups such as increasing insecurity and lower wages for some workers.

Following this line of thought further raises questions about the efficiency gains from the widespread use of ICT: who benefits and who should benefit? To what extent do consumers benefit as efficiency gains bring lower costs that might be passed on as lower prices? Should more of the efficiency gains from ICT be passed on to consumers in this way? This issue is raised as early as the discussions of competition policy in Chapters 4–6.

The policy dilemma is how to ensure that enough of the cost reductions from ICT are passed on to consumers while allowing enough to be kept as profits to provide adequate incentive for firms to keep on innovating.

Increasing inequality introduces another dimension in our thinking about economic change and well-being. It might seem that we can simply say that this is just another situation of winners and losers. Increasing inequality of incomes is unfortunate if you work in personal care or a call centre but it is fine if you are an opera superstar. However, while some people might accept or even welcome inequality as the foundation of aspirations to material success that motivate many people's lives, others find it unacceptable, unfair or unjust. Among them are people whose views about income inequality are independent of their own income position, that is, independent of the outcome of economic activity for themselves. When people become interested in other people's well-being, they are engaging in ethical inquiry. Ethics is concerned with questions about what is good for people, about what the good life for a person is and about how we ought to live. This includes the issues of what economic and social arrangements are desirable and on what basis we should make such decisions. For example, is there a conflict between inequality and efficiency? Without some (how much?) inequality, would we lack adequate incentives to engage in economic activity to the best of our abilities? On the other hand, does a sense of social justice suggest that income inequality has gone too far, devaluing relatively low-paid but socially valuable work, such as jobs in the personal care sector?

Ethical questions such as these lie at the heart of Chapters 7–10, which explore key issues concerning the well-being of the people who make economies work as producers and consumers. Do flexible (or competitive) labour markets provide good jobs? Why is the intensity of work effort increasing? This part critically examines material wealth, happiness and human capabilities as different interpretations of well-being. How is the role of government in furthering people's well-being changing in the twenty-first century? What can be done to reduce inequalities, not only in income, but in health status and in access to health care?

1.4 Conclusion

Every era defines for itself its most pressing economic problems. They emerge from a complex public dialogue, involving ideas and experience, theories and political pressures. Economists influence and take part in that dialogue but they certainly do not control it. Are we living through a new industrial revolution powered by ICT? Should we be grateful to big companies such as Microsoft and Nike for their new products or try to curtail their power? Does more material well-being always make people happier? Do poor countries gain from international trade and globalization? Is continued economic growth environmentally sustainable? Assumptions about what is economically possible and desirable influence the answers that politicians and commentators as well as academics give to these questions. John Maynard Keynes, perhaps the twentieth century's most famous economist, wrote at the end of his best known book:

> the ideas of economists and political philosophers, both when they are right and when they are wrong, are more powerful than is commonly understood [...] Practical men [and women – *authors*], who believe themselves to be quite exempt from any intellectual influences, are usually the slaves of some defunct economist.
>
> *(Keynes, 1936, p.383)*

The tone may be rather self-congratulatory and reflects the sexist attitudes of the time, but the point has as much force now as in the 1930s. Economic issues change but economic ideas continue to matter.

The variety of understandings of the new economy and of interpretations of its desirability illustrate how economic theory is as much a debate as the public dialogue to which it contributes. The presentation of theory as debate carries the most general message of this chapter, namely that economic theory is not a fixed body of knowledge but, like all social sciences, an arena of research and dispute. Economists, like other social scientists, develop differing and distinctive ways of thinking about the world, or broad conceptualizations within which they work. These different visions of the world are influenced by the issues which economists regard as important. In other words, how economists think depends in part on what they think about.

Hence, as economies and economic issues change, so does economics. We hope you will enjoy your exploration of this endlessly debatable subject.

Questions for review and discussion

Question 1 The 'new economy' is differently understood by different economists, but over certain features there is broad agreement. Tick the letters corresponding to the three statements below that command this broad agreement:

A ❑ It is likely to be easier to find work in a call centre than in a car assembly plant.
B ❑ Productivity in manufacturing is likely to be low or falling.
C ❑ Incomes across occupations are likely to be tending towards greater equality.
D ❑ The rate of inflation is likely to be low or falling.
E ❑ Research and development costs are likely to be high as many new products incorporate a lot of 'knowledge'.

Work changes us as people

The workplace of people in professional, managerial and administrative jobs is being transformed. The routines of the traditional office are being replaced by working on the move, working at home and working in a new type of office.

These changes have profound implications for skills, managerial strategies and team working. They are changing the kind of people we are.

Work is now done electronically using mobile phones, email, laptops, PCs and similar devices. As long as we are in touch with the 'electronic envelope' we can work anywhere and at any time.

Although these developments may bring benefits, they also pose challenges.

Nick Jewson (Centre for Labour Market Studies, University of Leicester),
The Sunday Times (Appointments)

Question 2 Using evidence from the above extract, and from the course text, discuss the nature of the changes brought about by the 'new economy'. To what extent is it true to say that the benefits are largely economic, while the challenges are largely social?

2

Information technology: a new era?

Mariana Mazzucato

Concepts	Objectives
■ industrial revolution ■ technological change ■ productivity ■ industry structure ■ industry life cycle ■ information technology ■ new economy	After studying this chapter you should be able to: ■ understand the relationship between technological change and industrial revolutions ■ appreciate the pervasive effect that new technologies can have on the economy and, in particular, on productivity ■ understand how industry dynamics can be analysed using the 'industry life cycle' model ■ use data and historical examples to support economic arguments.

2.1 Introduction

> Everything that can be invented has been invented.
> *(The Commissioner of the United States Office of Patents, **1899**, recommending that his office be abolished, quoted in* The Economist, *2000, p.5)*

> There is nothing now to be foreseen which can prevent the United States from enjoying an era of business prosperity which is entirely without equal in the pages of trade history.
>
> *(Sutliff, **1901**)*

The rise of information and communication technologies (ICT) – that is, computers, software, telecommunications and the Internet – and the large impact that these new technologies are having on the way that society functions, have prompted many to claim that we have entered a new era, often referred to as the 'Third Industrial Revolution', the 'information age' or the 'new economy'. Previous industrial revolutions were also linked to the rise of new technologies: the First Industrial Revolution, concentrated in Britain from around 1760 to 1850, introduced Cort's puddling and rolling process for making iron,

Crompton's mule for spinning cotton and the Watt steam engine; the Second Industrial Revolution, from around 1890 to 1930, witnessed the development of electricity, the internal-combustion engine, the railway and the chemical industry. In each of these cases, the new technologies allowed new industries to develop and economic growth to increase.

The concept of the 'new economy' is thus a claim that the emergence of new information technology (IT) was responsible for the economic prosperity (e.g. rising incomes, rising employment) experienced by most Western countries in the 1990s. This was the decade in which personal computers (PCs) were diffused throughout the economy, and the decade which saw the commercial rise of the World Wide Web. The PC reached a 50 per cent household penetration rate in the USA only in 1999, while before 1990 the Internet was used mainly by the US Defense Department, not for commercial purposes.

However, as the two introductory quotations indicate, proclamations that we have entered a 'new' era are not new. In fact, the advent of electricity, the internal-combustion engine and the radio telegraph witnessed similar proclamations about the future. They too emerged during periods of prosperity; for example, electricity and the automobile diffused through the economy during the prosperous and 'Roaring' 1920s. So how can we tell whether we are really entering a qualitatively new era or whether recent changes have simply been a quantitative extension of the past?

This chapter uses tools and frameworks from economics to study this question. It focuses on the historical and theoretical relationship between changes in technology, productivity and economic growth. The key driving force discussed will be *technological change*: that is, organizational and technical changes in the way that societies organize production and distribution. As in the previous chapter, the question is: what exactly is so *new* about the 'new economy'? But whereas in Chapter 1 the focus was on the effect of new technologies and work practices on the way that people live and work, here the focus is on the organization and evolution of firms and industries.

In each industrial revolution (including the current one), important *non-technological* factors have influenced industry dynamics and growth. Socio-political factors have been particularly prominent. For example, the rise of industrial trade unions in the Second Industrial Revolution greatly affected firm-level, industry-level and country-level growth. In this chapter, however, the analysis is limited to the role of technology.

We shall conduct our investigation by focusing on two related questions, neither of which has a clear-cut answer. The goal of the chapter is to help you to think about these questions using concepts and tools from economics.

First, after a brief overview of the concept of the industrial revolution, I shall ask whether the rise of IT has significantly affected economic growth, as new technologies did in previous eras. Focusing on the effect of technology on economy-wide growth implies that the perspective is a macroeconomic one. Macroeconomics looks at the functioning of the economy as a whole.

Second, I shall take a more microeconomic perspective. Microeconomics looks at the functioning of individual elements of the economy, whether they be consumers, firms, industries or markets. I shall ask whether the rise of new information technologies has fundamentally changed the way that individual firms and industries operate. To do this, I shall compare the patterns that characterized the early phase of a traditional industry with those that characterized the early phase of a relatively new industry. The traditional industry (one that is today considered to be relatively 'mature', not high growth) is the US automobile industry from 1900 to 1930, while the relatively new industry is the personal computer industry from 1975 to 2000. The similarities will lead us to ask whether we are really in a 'new economy' or simply in an economy driven, as in some past eras, by the development of new industries.

2.2 Technological change and economic growth

In this section I shall look at the way that technological innovations in previous eras, such as the invention of electricity in the early 1900s, radically affected the way society organized production and at how these changes spurred general economic growth. In many instances, the changes were so large that they defined an entire period, just as the rise of information technologies has led some to call the current era the 'information age'.

▓ ▨ ■ 2.2.1   Industrial revolutions and technological change

Industrial revolution

An industrial revolution occurs when technological change fundamentally transforms the way in which a society carries out the production and distribution of goods.

The way that technological change can fundamentally alter society is best viewed through the lens of previous industrial revolutions. The term **Industrial Revolution** usually refers specifically to the series of technological changes that occurred in England between 1760 and 1850 (such as steam power). More generally, the term refers to eras when rapid and significant technological changes fundamentally alter the way that production is carried out in society, affecting not only how people work but also how they live their lives. Consider the impact that electricity in the Second Industrial Revolution had not only on factories but also on the lives of families in their homes. Thus an industrial revolution occurs when new technological inventions and innovations fundamentally transform the production processes of goods and services to such an extent that all society is affected.

For our purposes the words 'invention' and 'innovation' can be used interchangeably. More specifically, however, the term 'invention' refers to the discovery of new products or processes, while 'innovation' refers to the commercialization (bringing to the market) of new products or processes. Furthermore, we can distinguish between *product* innovations and *process* innovations. Product innovations result in the production of a new product, such as the change from a three-wheel car to a four-wheel car, or the change from LP records to CDs. Process innovations increase the efficiency of the methods of production of existing products, for example the invention of the assembly-line technique.

The inventions and innovations that form industrial revolutions are those that open new doors and create new ways of doing things, not simply those that fill gaps in existing ways of doing things (Mokyr, 1997). The core of the First Industrial Revolution in the eighteenth century was a succession of technological changes that brought about material advances in three basic areas: (1) the substitution of mechanical devices (such as machines) for human labour; (2) the substitution of inanimate sources of power (such as steam) for animate sources of power (such as horse power); and (3) the substitution of mineral raw materials for vegetable or animal substances, and in general the use of new and more abundant raw materials (Landes, 1972).

These changes in technology and equipment occurred simultaneously with changes in *organizational* arrangements. For example, at the end of the nineteenth century the rise of electricity and the internal-combustion engine allowed the factory system to emerge, which radically changed the organization of work. The factory system, used first for the production of cotton but then extended to other industries, created a new, unified system of production which replaced the craft labour carried out in individual workshops. The main innovation of this new system was that it allowed workers to be brought together for the first time under common supervision with strict discipline, and it also introduced the use of a central, usually inanimate, source of power. The factory system enabled production to become more efficient as it allowed the company to spread its costs over a much larger output, a dynamic called 'economies of scale' which you will study in Chapter 3.

Economists interested in the pervasive effects of technological change in different industrial revolutions have devised the concept of a **general purpose technology** (GPT). A GPT is a technology that is general enough to be used in various industries and has a strong impact on their functioning. There are four main characteristics of a GPT (Lipsey *et al.*, 1998). As you read the list, consider how a new technology such as electricity or information technology fulfils each criterion.

1 It must have a wide scope for improvement and elaboration. This means that the technology does not appear as a complete and final solution, but as a technology that can be improved through the different opportunities for technological change that surround it.

2 It must be applicable across a broad range of uses. This means that its use is not restricted, for example, to only one industry but open to many different types of industries and consumers.

3 It must have a potential use in a wide variety of products and processes. This means that the new technology should not result in the creation of only one set of products (such as a computer), but a wide set of products (such as complex new air-traffic control systems or new inventory controls).

4 It must have strong complementarities with existing or potential new technologies. This means that the technology does not only replace existing methods but also works with them, ensuring an even broader impact on the systems of production and distribution.

Examples of GPTs include different power delivery systems (water-wheel, steam, electricity, internal-combustion engine), transport innovations (railways and motor vehicles), lasers and the Internet. The invention of the internal-combustion engine not only made possible personal automobiles, motor transport and air transport, but also created 'derivative' inventions such as the suburb, the motorway and the supermarket. Electricity allowed the work day to be extended (allowing for different shifts in a 24-hour period), gave a huge impetus to the entertainment industry, and greatly enhanced manufacturing process technologies. (We shall also see how it created the conditions for 'mass production' via the moving assembly line.)

GPTs are important because they spur technological change in different areas (and this effect is behind the first three characteristics of GPTs listed above). In fact, radical technological changes are often **cumulative changes**: change in one area leads to change in another area. David Landes is an economic historian and his account of the way in which the invention of the steam engine caused changes in many different industries has become well known. He calls this process 'technological interrelatedness'.

In all this diversity of technological improvement, the unity of movement is apparent: change begat change. For one thing, many technical improvements were feasible only after advances in associated fields. The steam engine is a classic example of this technological interrelatedness: it was impossible to produce an effective condensing engine until better methods of metal working could turn out accurate cylinders. For another, the gains in productivity and output of a given innovation inevitably exerted pressure on related industrial operations. The demand for coal pushed mines deeper until water seepage became a serious hazard; the answer was the creation of a more efficient pump, the atmospheric steam engine. A cheap supply of coal proved a godsend for the iron industry, which was stifling for lack of fuel. In the meantime, the invention and diffusion of machinery in the textile manufacture and other industries created a new demand for energy, hence for coal and steam engines; and these engines, and the machines themselves, had a voracious appetite for iron, which called for further coal and power. Steam also made possible the factory city, which used unheard-of quantities of iron (hence coal) in its many-storied mills and its water and sewage systems. At the same time, the processing of the flow of manufactured commodities required great amounts of chemical substances: alkalis, acids, and dyes, many of them consuming mountains of fuel in the making. And all of these products – iron, textiles, chemicals – depended on large-scale movements of goods on land and on sea, from the sources of the raw materials into the factories and out again to near and distant markets. The opportunity thus created and the possibilities of the new technology combined to produce the railroad and steamship, which of course added to the demand for iron and fuel while expanding the market for factory products. And so on, in ever-widening circles.

(Landes, 1972, pp.2–3)

Question	Can you think of new industries that have grown out of the PC and the Internet?

You may have thought of online shopping, Internet banking, digital cameras, information services (such as online recipes) and computer desks. Having reflected on the nature of technological change and its role in defining industrial revolutions, we shall now examine how technological change affects the efficiency of firms and hence general economic growth.

▪ ▪ ▪ 2.2.2 The effect of technology on productivity

In each industrial revolution, new inventions radically changed the way that production and distribution were organized, and often led to large and rapid increases in the efficiency of production. The rise of electricity, for example, allowed US productivity to increase in the manufacturing sector (as opposed to the agricultural or service sector) by more than 5 per cent per annum throughout the 1920s.

Productivity

Productivity is an indicator of the efficiency of production or distribution. Labour productivity can be measured as output produced per hour of labour.

Let us pause a moment and consider what this means. The term **productivity** refers to the amount of output that a given amount of inputs (such as hours of labour) can produce. For example, consider an automobile factory that is able to produce 10 cars per day using 100 hours of labour. If a new invention permits those same workers to produce 20 cars in the same amount of time, their productivity has been doubled.

The productivity of a whole economy, such as the UK economy – as opposed to a particular factory – is measured by first calculating the total output produced by the economy in one year. This is called the GDP or gross domestic product, and the calculation will be explained in Chapter 8. Total output divided by total labour hours in the year gives us a measure of labour productivity. A 5 per cent growth in UK productivity over a year means that the UK economy has become 5 per cent more productive than it was in the previous year. This should mean that the economy can produce 5 per cent more output (GDP) with the same amount of inputs.

Question	Stop here and check your understanding of percentages and growth rates. They are quite simple, but it is important to get them clear. If a group of workers produces 10 000 units of output in one year, and 12 000 units the next year, how would you calculate the percentage increase in productivity?

You want to know the percentage increase represented by the second year's output, 12 000, over the first year's output, 10 000. Subtracting 10 000 from 12 000 gives us the increase. Divide the answer by 10 000 to calculate the increase relative to the first year. Then multiply by 100 to turn the answer into a percentage (the dot '·' means 'multiplied by').

$$12\,000 - 10\,000 = 2000$$

$$\frac{2000}{10\,000} \cdot 100 = 20$$

So, output increased by 20 per cent. As the number of workers stayed the same, this is also the increase in productivity.

Exercise 2.1

If you want to check your understanding of percentages, calculate the percentage increase in productivity if the output expands from 12 000 in year 2 to 15 000 in year 3.

In plumbing, for example, productivity would increase if the use of new materials enabled plumbers to fix broken pipes more quickly. This would free up more time for plumbers to work on other operations and hence increase their output per hour, that is, their productivity. Productivity can increase either when work methods are made more efficient without (necessarily) the introduction of new technology, perhaps from a better organization of the factory floor, or when new methods are introduced to the production process through the introduction of new technology – for example, when new machinery allows work to be done more quickly and with fewer mistakes. Adam Smith (1723–90), one of the founders of modern economics, claimed that increases in productivity lie at the heart of economic growth and prosperity. In his influential book *The Wealth of Nations* (first published in 1776), Smith uses the example of pin making to describe the process by which productivity can increase through a rise in the division of labour, that is, the degree to which workers divide tasks between themselves. The rest of his classic text is dedicated to describing the effect of increasing productivity on the development of markets and economic growth:

> The greatest improvement in the productive powers of labour, and the greater part of the skill, dexterity, and judgement with which it is anywhere directed, or applied, seem to have been the effects of the division of labour . . . To take an example, therefore, from a very trifling manufacture; but one in which the division of labour has been very often taken notice of, the trade of the pin-maker; a workman not educated to this business . . . nor acquainted with the use of the machinery employed in it . . . could scarce, perhaps, with his utmost industry, make one pin a day, and certainly could not make twenty. But in the way in which this business is now carried on not only the whole work is a peculiar trade, but it is divided

into a number of branches, of which the greater part are likewise peculiar trades. One man draws out the wire, another straightens it, a third cuts it, a fourth points it, a fifth grinds it at the top for receiving the head; to make the head requires two or three distinct operations; to put it on, is a peculiar business, to whiten the pins is another, it is even a trade by itself to put them into the paper; and the important business of making a pin is, in this manner, divided into about eighteen distinct operations, which, in some manufactories, are all performed by distinct hands, though in others the same man will sometimes perform two or three of them. I have seen a small manufactory of this kind where ten men only were employed, and where some of them consequently performed two or three distinct operations. But though they were very poor, and therefore but indifferently accommodated with the necessary machinery, they could, when they exerted themselves . . . make among them upwards of forty-eight thousand pins in a day.

(Smith, 1937, pp.65–6)

Question	What are the different tasks, outlined by Smith, involved in pin making? Why does productivity increase when these tasks are divided between workers instead of all being done by one worker, that is, when the division of labour increases?

Division of labour

The division of labour refers to the degree to which the various tasks involved in the production of a good or service are divided among different workers.

The **division of labour**, as described here by Smith, increases the productivity of workers by allowing them to concentrate on a fixed and simple task, and hence to become more efficient at that task over time. (Smith also warned of the negative effect that this repetition could have on the workers' intelligence and morale.)

The division of labour, and hence productivity, increased with the emergence of the factory system, in which many workers were brought together under one roof for the first time and each worker was responsible for a small part of the final product. This was very different from the craft manufacture system, in which each worker was responsible for producing the entire product.

Increases in productivity, even if just in one industry, can be transmitted throughout the economy for several reasons. First, increases in productivity can lead to higher incomes for an economy's citizens. All output must be transformed, through the process of production and sale, into someone's income (e.g. the boss's profits and the workers' wages). Hence, increases in productivity, which allow more output to be produced by a given amount of inputs, also lead to more income per head, that is, greater wealth for society. For example, if more cars can be produced due to increases in the productivity of car production, more cars are sold, which means that the car manufacturers' revenues increase. Furthermore, if, as is sometimes the case, increases in wages are linked to increases in productivity, then workers' wages may also rise (or, at least, their employment prospects may be more secure).

Second, increases in productivity diffused throughout the economy have an effect on prices. Increases in productivity tend to lower the cost of production, precisely because more output can be produced with the same amount of inputs. Since cost reductions tend to be translated into price reductions, increases in productivity eventually tend to reduce prices. Indeed, the introduction of assembly lines made a substantial contribution to the affordability of consumer durables such as the car. The increase in income per head and the reduction in prices allow consumers to be better off. This potential increase in the wealth of manufacturers, workers and consumers is the reason Adam Smith's book, which focused on the links between productivity and economic growth, was titled *The Wealth of Nations*.

Productivity may also increase for reasons not related to technological change, for example if workers are simply 'exploited' more (with or without new technology). Output per worker may increase if workers are forced to work more quickly or for longer hours, prevented from taking lunch breaks, or given no holidays. These are all conditions that still persist today in some low-income countries, as well as in some industries in those Western countries in which workers are not unionized and/or work in 'sweatshops', that is, factories that operate illegally in terms of international standards for wages and working conditions.

For a new technology to affect economy-wide productivity it must be widely adopted across industries instead of being restricted to a narrow domain. For example, full electrification of factories did not occur until the 1920s. Prior to that, from the 1890s to the beginning of the 1920s, most factories simply added electric motors to existing (older) equipment. Until the 1920s power transmission in factories was still operated through the 'group drive' system, in which only parts of the factory were electrified and electric motors turned separate shafts. The 'unit drive' system did not appear until the boom period of the 1920s, which opened up the potential for new, fully electrified plants (David and Wright, 1999). The switch from group to unit drive transmission allowed individual electric motors to run machines and tools of all sizes. The new unit drive not only allowed huge savings in fuel and energy efficiency, but also allowed the factory layout to be more amenable to the assembly-line system, which spread throughout the economy in the 1920s (although it had first been used by Ford Motors in 1910). The new technology facilitated the circulation of materials, made workers more productive and reduced downtime, as the entire plant no longer had to be shut down to make changes in just one department.

Exercise 2.2

Write a short paragraph (of not more than 100 words) describing the impact of technological change on economic growth. You should use the key concepts introduced in Section 2.2, although you do not have to define them.

2.3 Information technology, productivity and growth

Having discussed the radical and pervasive effect that inventions in previous eras have had on economy-wide productivity, and how they have even defined entire periods, we shall now ask how the rise of information technology compares to these previous revolutions. During the early growth phase of PC use, a leader article in *Fortune* magazine did not hesitate to compare the rise of the PC to previous technological revolutions.

> The chip has transformed us at least as pervasively as the internal-combustion engine or electric motor.
>
> *(Fortune, 8 June 1988, pp.86–7)*

In fact, the debate about the 'new economy' is a debate about whether the computer and the Internet have had an impact on the economy as great as that of other GPTs in previous eras.

Question	Would you say that the personal computer is a GPT? (Hint: in what ways is it applicable across a broad range of uses?)

The personal computer (PC) qualifies as a GPT due to the wide-ranging and pervasive effect it has had on the economy. Given the four characteristics of GPTs, consider how it: (1) has continued to experience radical improvements, such as the doubling of processor speed every 18 months (known as 'Moore's Law'), (2) is applicable across a wide variety of industries, from online trading to inventory control in factories, (3) has created the need for new products and processes, such as the production of portable printers, and (4) is often used alongside older technologies, such as the use of computer-aided design/manufacturing (CADCAM) to reduce inventory alongside traditional assembly lines. Furthermore, as happened with electrification, for many years the PC did not break free from its predecessor, the mainframe, but served mainly to support it (as display terminals). Only in 1990, with the emergence of the Wintel platform, that is, the interaction between the Windows operating system and the Intel processor, did the PC break free from IBM's grip on the mainframe computer market.

The emergence of IT has created new products, processes and distribution systems. New products include the computer, the Internet and digital TV; new processes include Internet banking, automated inventory control and automated teller machines; and new distribution systems include cable and satellite TV. But the evidence does not fully support the claim that IT has affected economy-wide productivity in the same way as technological change in previous eras. In the late 1980s Robert Solow, a Nobel prize-winning economist from the Massachusetts Institute of Technology, summarized the problem as follows: 'Computers appear everywhere but in the productivity statistics' (Solow, 1987). The 'Solow Paradox', as this is often called, addresses the fact that the wave of inventions based on the microprocessor and the memory chip failed to generate the economy-wide increases in productivity that previous technological revolutions had produced. Only in the mid 1990s did productivity growth seem to be on a rebound: between 1975 and 1995 the annual average productivity growth for the business sector in the USA (i.e. non-agricultural production) was only 1.4 per cent per annum; after 1996 the annual average rose to 2.9 per cent. In the first two quarters of 2000 the figure reached 5.2 per cent, putting it on a par with the productivity increase that occurred after the electrical revolution. In the past, new technologies such as electricity began to affect economy-wide productivity only once they had reached the 50 per cent penetration rate (i.e. when 50 per cent of households and/or businesses used the technology). For electricity, this occurred in the 1920s. Since PCs reached the 50 per cent mark in the USA only in 1999, it might still be too early to ask whether the computer is showing up in the productivity statistics.

Are the recent increases in productivity *sustainable*? The answer to this question, and the crux of the debate concerning the effect of IT, centres on distinguishing whether recent increases in productivity are just *cyclical*, and hence temporary, or whether they are the beginning of a new and long-lasting *trend*. If the increase in productivity in the USA in the late 1990s was cyclical, this means that it occurred simply because the US economy as a whole was undergoing a boom in the latter half of the 1990s, and the increases will disappear now that (as I write) the boom is over. All economies fluctuate in a **business cycle**. For a few years, growth is quite rapid, output and incomes rise, and unemployment falls. This is the 'boom'. Then the cycle turns. Growth slows, and in a true recession the total output of the economy falls. This is the down-turn of the cycle. The cycle is driven by changes in consumer spending and business investment and, historically, a boom or recession tends to last three to eight years.

Business cycle

The business cycle refers to the periods of boom and recession that succeed each other in market economies.

27

However, if the productivity increases of the late 1990s, especially in the USA, were a *trend* increase, this means that the rise in productivity was independent of the business cycle and resulted from the characteristics of new technologies or specific government policies. For example, if a new technology allowed the productivity of many industries to increase permanently, it would create a trend increase in productivity. If the rise in productivity persisted during a recession, it would be further evidence of a trend. Indeed, the word 'new' in the 'new economy' implies that the increase was a trend related to the characteristics of the new technologies (otherwise it would not be new).

IT can affect productivity by increasing the efficiency of the IT-producing sectors, such as computer manufacturers, and/or by increasing the productivity of the IT-using sectors, such as the service industries that process data using computers. There is really no debate at all on the former point: all agree that industries such as the computer and software industries have experienced great productivity increases due to the radical and rapid nature of technological change in these industries. In the 1990s the average productivity growth in the IT-producing sectors was 24 per cent per year, well above that of the other manufacturing sectors. The disagreement, therefore, is about the effect of IT on the rest of the economy.

The optimists in this debate, including Alan Greenspan, Chairman of the US Federal Reserve Bank, argue that the rise of IT has allowed most advanced capitalist economies to achieve a *permanent* (trend) higher level of productivity, because of the ways in which the new technologies have improved efficiency, for example through better control of inventories and cheaper access to information. They argue that IT has caused firms to increase their investment in capital equipment per worker and that this has occurred simultaneously with large increases in the productivity of other inputs, both machinery and labour, two-fifths of which has come from efficiency gains in computer production alone. These optimists argue that productivity increases will persist into the future, due to the rise in research and development spending and the rise in investments in business capital, including computers. Such investments, argue the optimists, should allow productivity to keep growing.

Pessimists, such as the US economist R.J. Gordon, claim that recent productivity gains have been only cyclical, that is, a result of the fact that the US economy has been experiencing a boom. A boom can cause productivity to increase because there is more work to be done during prosperous periods and hence there is a greater incentive for employers to work employees harder, making them more productive – and leading to an increase in productivity. To support his point, Gordon (2000) provides data showing that most of the productivity gains have been limited to the IT-*producing* sectors (such as the personal computer industry) and have not spread out to other sectors, including the IT-*using* sectors. In fact, after excluding the manufacture of durable goods and computers (12 per cent of the economy), and after adjusting for the business cycle, the statistics do not show any productivity increases in the remaining portions of the economy! And to make things even worse, it is in those sectors where IT has been used the most, such as financial services, that productivity increases show up the least.

Gordon (2000) claims that it is not so surprising that the rise of the Internet has not affected productivity to the same degree as the development of electricity did. Unlike electricity, the Internet has not produced new products; it has simply substituted for existing products (e.g. the substitution of online purchasing for mail-order catalogues). Likewise, most of the changes are in terms of market shares not productivity: what one company wins the other loses, as is evidenced by the effect that Amazon.com is having on the profitability of the big bookshop chains Borders and Waterstones. Electricity, however, made possible the invention of many *new* products such as the vacuum cleaner and

Figure 2.1
The Internet
increases
productivity at work
(or does it?)

the refrigerator. The electric motor, the aeroplane, the telephone and even the indoor
flush toilet, invented by the Englishman Thomas Crapper in 1886, have had more effect
on productivity than the Internet. Surfing the Internet may be fun and is often useful, but
can its impact on production be compared to the effect of electricity on the illumination
of factories and the rise of the assembly line? Some go as far as to say that, if anything, the
Internet has *reduced* productivity by distracting people from serious work, a claim that is
behind the popular joke that IT stands for 'insignificant toys' (Figure 2.1). Gordon (2000)
quotes the finding by Active Research Inc., a San Francisco Internet-based market research
company, that online shopping does not peak in the evening when workers are at home,
but in the middle of the day when they are in the office!

Other sceptics point to the possibility that the rise in US productivity has been due more
to the increased flexibility of the US labour market than to any specific characteristics of
information technology. OECD studies comparing the US experience with that of other
developed countries have found that the high US productivity growth in the mid 1990s was
followed only in Australia, Finland and Canada, and not at all in Germany, Italy, France
and Japan, which have less 'flexible' labour markets (Colecchia and Schreyer, 2002). Flexible
labour markets are defined as those in which there are fewer government (and trade union)
regulations concerning working conditions and pay scales and in which industrial trade
unions are weaker or non-existent. For example, it is well known that in the USA workers
can be fired much more easily (often indiscriminately) than in European countries. Hence,
a lesson that may be drawn from the OECD reports, although it is not stated directly, is that
the higher productivity of the 'flexible' countries might be due, not to IT, but to the fact
that workers in those countries can be worked harder, paid less and fired more easily.

However, Gordon's (2000) findings have been criticized in turn for not taking into
account the difficulty of measuring productivity in an economy characterized by rapid

technological change. The issue here is that the traditional measurements of output used to calculate productivity figures do not take into consideration changes in the quality of output, such as improved product quality, choice, time savings and convenience. This is a big problem for productivity calculations as it means that if more change occurs on the quality side than on the quantity side, that is, better products rather than more products, the total change in output will be severely underestimated.

This problem is even greater in the service sector as most service improvements come in terms of not more services but better services. For example, output in the health-care industry will be underestimated if all that is counted is patient throughput or treatment episodes, without accounting for the extent to which consumers enjoy better treatment. Quality improvements in health care include better diagnosis, new medical equipment and less invasive treatments. Another example is provided in a study cited by *The Economist* (2000). This study claimed that when changes in the quality of output are not recognized, output in the US banking industry appears to have grown by only 1.3 per cent between 1977 and 1994. If quality changes are included, for example by taking into account the rise of automated teller machines and online banking, the study argued that output appears to have grown by 7 per cent!

Another way in which consumer satisfaction is not recognized in traditional productivity accounts is by neglecting the wider *choice* that people have in the products they buy. In the extreme case, if the same amount of output is produced in one year as in the previous year, but the choice of products has doubled, the official measures would not pick that up as a change in output. These are not problems in a world of mass production, where the point is to produce a lot of standard goods for the general consumer, but they are problems in the world of mass customization, where the point is to produce the 'right' goods for the specific consumer. Nonetheless, economists have devised methods to tackle these problems, some of which will be discussed in Section 2.4.

A summary

I have shown that, while IT has no doubt had an impact on productivity, it is not clear whether this goes beyond the IT-producing sector, or whether the gains will outlast the boom period of the business cycle. With so much debate, whom should we believe? Perhaps, as is often the case, the truth lies somewhere in the middle. The optimistic view highlights the way that IT has transformed society, and how this transformation has in many instances led to growth through the productivity-enhancing aspects of IT. The pessimistic view reminds us to be cautious in attributing such growth solely to the rise of IT, given that the rise in productivity has occurred during the boom period of the business cycle. Others argue that perhaps the productivity increase has occurred as a result of influences unrelated to IT, such as the rise of flexible labour markets. If the increase continues, it would appear that the productivity increases have been trend increases. If they fall, it would appear that they are more cyclical in nature.

Exercise 2.3

List two or three things that could happen in the US economy in the future that would go some way towards settling the debate between optimists and pessimists on the impact of IT.

2.4 'Garage tinkerers': new economy or industry life cycle?

As you have now seen, the concept of the 'new economy' has inspired a number of studies that compare the effect that new technologies have had on economy-wide productivity in previous eras with the effect that IT has – or has not yet – had in the current era. I shall now ask another question, still along the lines of 'what's new in the new economy?', but this time from a more microeconomic perspective, which focuses on the individual firm and industry rather than on the whole economy. (Look back at the distinction made in Section 2.1 between microeconomics and macroeconomics.) I shall ask whether the information revolution, that is, the emergence of IT as a new GPT, has changed the way that firms and industries evolve.

Why should we ask this question? Well, just as there is a debate about whether the 'new economy' has changed the dynamics of productivity, there is also a debate about whether the 'new economy' has changed the way that firms and industries operate and evolve. For example, some claim that the 'new economy' has made technological change and entrepreneurial activity more important to company survival than it was before, and hence has heightened the role of small, flexible and innovative firms. Others claim that technological change, new ideas and entrepreneurial activity were just as important in the early phase of industries that emerged before the 'new economy' era. Rather than investigating this debate through the views of optimists and pessimists, as we did above, we can dive right in by comparing an old-economy industry, the US automobile industry, which has been around for 100 years, and a new-economy industry, the US personal computer industry. The goal is to see whether patterns that are claimed to be characteristic of new high-tech industries were just as common in the early development of a traditional industry. These patterns include the role of small entrepreneurial firms ('garage tinkerers'), the rapidity with which firms rise and fall, and the importance of technological change for company survival.

■ ■ ■ 2.4.1 The industry life cycle

The comparison between the automobile industry and the PC industry makes sense only if we concentrate on similar periods in their evolution. We will concentrate here on the 'early' development of both industries, in what will be called the 'introductory' and 'early growth' phases in their life cycles. This is the period running from 1900 to 1930 in the automobile industry and from 1975 to 2000 in the PC industry. The automobile industry refers here to all firms producing cars and trucks, and the PC industry refers to all firms producing personal computers (i.e. laptops and desktops rather than mainframes or workstations). To make the comparison as tight as possible, only the *US* market of each industry is studied, that is, US and foreign firms selling in the US market. Looking at the international market would inevitably cause us to consider other factors independent of industrial dynamics, such as different countries' business cycles and politics. We will not keep referring to US industries in what follows, but to help you to remember what we are discussing we will use the American term 'automobile' throughout this section rather than the British 'car'.

We will use the 'industry life cycle' framework to study the two industries side by side, highlighting similarities and differences in their development over time. The industry life-cycle framework, which you will study in more detail in Chapter 3, focuses on those economic mechanisms that cause firms to be born (to 'enter' an industry), to grow, and possibly to die (to 'exit' an industry). It also examines how these mechanisms affect changes in the industry structure. Industry structure refers to the characteristics of an industry, such as the number of firms operating in it, the distribution of power between them (whether some are very large and others very small, or whether they are all very large), and the degree to which new firms find it easy to enter the industry. Mechanisms affecting industry structure include the dynamics of entry and exit, technological change and falling prices. It is, therefore, on mechanisms such as these that we will focus.

The industry life cycle is characterized by different phases.

- A *pre-market* or *hobbyist phase*, in which the product is produced more as a hobby or luxury than for commercial purposes. This phase is characterized by much variety in the characteristics of both firms and the product versions they produce.

- An *introductory phase*, in which the product begins to be produced more for commercial purposes than for hobby reasons. This phase is characterized by the rapid entry of many new firms which seek to take advantage of the new profit opportunities. Entry occurs principally through technological change, that is, each firm enters with a different version of the product, so this phase is the one characterized by the most product innovation.

- A *growth phase*, in which the industry grows rapidly due to the emergence of a standardized product. A standardized product refers to the convergence of industry production around a product with a given set of characteristics (e.g. a four-wheeled car with a roof). Efficiency in the industry increases, as the standardized product can be mass produced (not possible if the product is undergoing too much change), and demand for the product rises as consumers learn more about it. Those firms not able to produce the standardized product efficiently are forced to 'exit' the industry (more on this below).

- A *mature phase*, in which demand slackens and fewer technological opportunities are available. If a new product innovation is introduced in the mature phase of the industry (e.g. the replacement of LP records with CDs in the music industry) the industry life cycle may start anew as new firms enter to profit from the new technological opportunities provided by the new product. However, whether the existing leaders remain the leaders will depend on whether the new innovations build on the leaders' existing capabilities and hence strengthen their position, or make those capabilities obsolete and hence threaten their position.

I shall now review these different phases in more detail through an analysis of the evolution of the US automobile and PC industries. We will see that there are some remarkable similarities in the early development of these two industries.

2.4.2 Live fast, die young

Both the automobile and PC industries were characterized by a great deal of turbulence in the first 20 to 30 years of their existence. In both cases, many new firms entered the industry, introduced new varieties of the product, and soon left the industry, leaving only a few dozen firms to compete during the growth phase. By 1926 only 33 per cent of the firms that had started producing automobiles during the previous 22 years had survived. In the case of PCs, by 1999 only 20 per cent of the firms that had started producing PCs had survived. In both cases, the majority of firms did not last more than five years! This turbulent 'live fast, die young' period of great entry and exit is characterized by a lot of technological change. Let us look at this in more depth.

Figure 2.2
Some early
automobiles
Source: Epstein,
1928, pp.29, 48

The *hobbyist* period in the automobile industry lasted approximately from 1885 to 1900. The first internal-combustion engine was invented in 1877 by Nikolaus Otto in Germany, and the first car (three-wheeled!) was invented in 1885 by Karl Benz, also in Germany. The first four photographs in Figure 2.2 show that between 1893 and 1899 automobiles were simply 'horseless carriages'. They were the products of experiments carried out by 'tinkerers' in their homes or workshops. Carroll and Hannan (2000) document 3845 'pre-production' organizing attempts in the US automobile industry, of which only 11 per cent reached the market place.

The *introductory* period, in which cars began to be manufactured commercially, started in 1900. Before this date the automobile industry was not even listed in the census of manufacturers under a separate heading, yet by 1926 it had already attained an equal importance to shipbuilding and railroads (Epstein, 1928, p.30). In 1901 Oldsmobile produced the world's first mass-produced automobile, and in 1910 the Ford Motor Company used the industry's first branch-assembly plant, that is, an assembly-line system for mass-producing cars, to produce the Model T, which soon became close to an industry standard. The period between 1900 and the end of the 1920s witnessed the most variety in product versions ever experienced in the industry. The second set of four photographs in Figure 2.2 shows some of the automobiles that emerged from this period of experimentation and tinkering.

Before 1973, the computer industry was formed around the production of the *mainframe* computer, dominated by IBM since the 1960s, and the *minicomputer*, the embryonic form of today's PC, dominated by Digital Equipment Corporation (whose computer was called the PDP-8). The first mass-produced computer was introduced by Micro Instrumentation and Telemetry Systems in 1974 (the MITS Altair 8800). As in the automobile industry, in the early years (up to 1980) demand was concentrated among hobbyists. The new start-ups were very similar to the early 'tinkerers' in the automobile industry: production was often organized out of a structure that looked like a garage, and the producers were driven by creativity and a passion for the product. As in the automobile industry, entry occurred mainly through product innovation. Figure 2.3 illustrates the wide range of product designs in these early years.

The *introductory period* in the PC industry, in which real commercial growth began, occurred only after IBM introduced the IBM 'PC' in 1981, initiating the phase of IBM 'compatibility' (both hardware and software) which later allowed economies of scale to operate in the industry. Three further developments markedly increased the growth of the PC industry: (1) Intel's introduction of the 32-bit 386 processors in 1985, which

Apple Lisa

Amstrad PPC640D

Addressgraph-Farrington
1680

AT&T 3B2/300

Bondwell B2

Atari 800

Amstrad CPC464

MITS Altair 8800

Imsai 8080

AT&T PC 6300

Figure 2.3
Some early PCs

allowed graphical interfaces and hence a more user-friendly environment; (2) the introduction of Windows 3.0 in 1990, which standardized the PC on the Windows operating
systems, allowing 'cloning' of the IBM PC; and (3) the rise of the World Wide Web in
the 1990s. All three developments contributed to a rapid increase in sales and, later, to a
rapid fall in prices.

Hence, in both industries the early years were characterized by a great deal of turbulence:
new firms entering the industry with new product innovations, and industry growth taking off. Figure 2.4 depicts this turbulence graphically as the rise and fall of firm numbers
(i.e. how many firms exist in the industry in a given year) for the first 30 years or so of
each industry. The vertical axis shows the number of firms; the horizontal axis shows the
age of the industry for its first 27 years.

Question	Look at Figure 2.4. What was similar about the early years of the US automobile and PC industries?

The two industries experienced a remarkably similar pattern of growth: both industries
went from infancy to just below 300 firms in only 10 to 15 years. The peaks of the curves
in Figure 2.4 illustrate that there was a maximum of 271 automobile firms in 1909 and
a maximum of 286 PC firms in 1987. After this point, the industries experienced a
'shake-out', that is, the elimination of a large number of firms, which in the case of the
US automobile industry culminated in the survival of only three domestic firms.

What caused the great number of exits, or 'shake-outs', from the two industries? As
predicted by life-cycle theory, most of the firms left the two industries at around the time
the product became standardized, that is, when the great experimentation with different

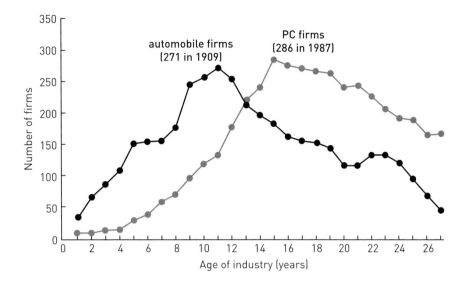

Figure 2.4
Number of firms in the US automobile industry (1899–1925) and the US PC industry (1973–99)

product types had ended and the industry had consolidated around a particular standard. In the automobile industry this occurred around 1910, soon after the Model T was introduced. In the PC industry it occurred around 1990, soon after the new Wintel platform emerged (the combination of the Windows operating system and the Intel processor), which set a new standard for the industry.

Once the product had become standardized, companies focused on increasing the efficiency of production through process innovations. For example, greater efficiency was achieved by introducing mass-production techniques, which allowed economies of scale. The term 'economies of scale', which you will learn more about in Chapter 3, refers to the dynamic by which an increase in the quantity produced allows the firm to spread its costs over a larger output, which lowers the cost of producing each unit of output. Mass production also allows improvements in efficiency from 'learning by doing': the more that is produced, the more that is learned, from experience, about how to make production more efficient. As large firms, by definition, achieve a higher scale of production ('scale' is measured by level of output), small firms are forced out of the market in the phase in which scale matters the most.

▨ ▣ ■ 2.4.3 Prices and industrial change

Many of the new entrants entered by introducing a new variation of the product. In fact, the early period in both industries was characterized by much technological change in the form of product innovation. Once a product standard emerged, product and process innovations around that standard led to a drastic fall in the product price in both industries. We will now look at some of the indicators of this turbulence in technology and prices.

How can we look at price changes over time in industries in which the product undergoes so many changes, especially in the early stages? Economists have devised a way to do just that, called 'hedonic prices'. These are quality-adjusted prices, that is, prices that keep certain quality characteristics constant. In the case of automobiles over the last decade or so, the price might try to exclude changes such as the emergence of anti-lock brakes, the availability of engines with improved fuel consumption and reduced CO_2 emissions, airbags, stronger safety shells, traction control and central locking. In the PC industry, the

Figure 2.5
Hedonic prices in
the US automobile
industry
(1906–1926) and
the US PC industry
(1980–2000)
Source: Raff and
Trajtenberg, 1997;
Bureau of Economic
Analysis, 2000

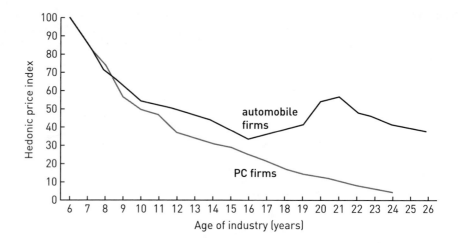

characteristics to be held constant might include available RAM, processor speed, screen size and weight.

Figure 2.5 illustrates the evolution of quality-adjusted hedonic prices in both industries. You can see that in both industries prices fell drastically over the first three decades. Between 1906 and 1940, quality-adjusted prices in the automobile industry fell by 51 per cent (i.e. they halved), with most of the change occurring between 1906 and 1918 (Raff and Trajtenberg, 1997). (The quality-adjusted price calculation also removes the effect of inflation, something that will be explained in Chapter 8.) This fall in price reflects the radical changes in technology, the spread of mass production and the general expansion in the market for cars.

The prices of personal computers were also greatly affected by technological advances. Berndt and Rappaport (2000) found that PC quality-adjusted hedonic prices fell by an average of 18 per cent between 1983 and 1989, 32 per cent between 1989 and 1994, and 40 per cent between 1994 and 1999. Prices began to drop significantly after Intel's introduction of the 32-bit 386 processors in 1985 and the introduction of Windows 3.0 in 1990. The latter allowed the production of PCs to be standardized (via cloning of the IBM PC). The rise of the Internet also increased sales and decreased prices. In recent years, quality-adjusted prices have fallen at an average annual rate of 24 per cent (Bureau of Economic Analysis, 2000).

Before we interpret what Figure 2.5 tells us about prices in the two industries, let me explain the meaning of the numbers on the vertical axis, which shows an *index* of (hedonic) prices. The concept of an index (plural indices) may be familiar to you. In case it is not, here is an explanation. It is worth getting this clear, as indices are used a lot in economics. They are basically a simple way of measuring change. The most widely used method of constructing an index is based on the notion of the percentage, as discussed earlier in this chapter (Section 2.2.2).

Suppose that the price of a product is €5 in 2000, €7.50 in 2001 and €10 in 2002 (just to keep the arithmetic simple). We want to start our index in 2000. So the price in that year is set equal to 100 per cent.

So €5 is the index base = 100

Then we compare all the other prices with the index base, using percentages. So to find the index for 2001, we divide the price in 2001 by the price in 2000, and multiply the result by 100 to give us a percentage.

Table 2.1

Year	Actual price of product €	Price index (base 2000)
2000	5.00	100
2001	7.50	150
2002	10.00	200

€7.50 as an index (base 2000) is €7.50/€5 · 100 = 150

For 2002, we do the same calculation, always comparing it with the *base year* (2000 in this example).

€10 as an index (base 2000) is €10/€5 · 100 = 200

So Table 2.1 shows the price index for the three years.

Question   Look carefully at Figure 2.5. What does it tell you about prices in the first three decades of both industries?

Focus on the slope of the curves, which indicates how prices are changing: a steep downward slope shows rapid price reductions. Figure 2.5 clearly indicates that in both industries prices fell drastically during the first three decades. One difference, however, between the two industries is that prices fell for a longer time in the case of PCs. We will examine the reasons for this difference after we have looked at the patterns of innovation.

Exercise 2.4

Complete Table 2.2.

Table 2.2

Year	Actual price of product €	Price index (base 2003)
2003	12.00	100
2004	16.00	
2005	19.00	
2006	21.00	

▨ ▨ ■ 2.4.4 Technological change

In both industries the fall in prices was driven by radical changes in the production of the products. How might we investigate the technological changes and the changes in quality that occurred in both industries simultaneously with the drastic fall in prices? There are various methods used by economists to measure technological change. Some methods focus on the 'inputs' into the innovation process, such as the spending on research and development by firms. But this is not ideal as it does not indicate whether the spending

Figure 2.6
Product and
process innovations
in the US
automobile industry

Source: Abernathy
et al., 1983

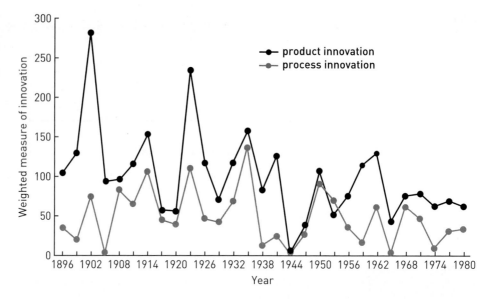

was successful, that is, it does not look at the output of the process, just at the intention. Some methods look at innovative output in terms of the numbers of patents issued by the firms. But this is not ideal either as it does not discriminate between patents which barely affect production and patents which cause major change to the industry. We will use two alternative methods here. One takes into account a list of innovations produced in the automobile industry, where each innovation is given a score according to its effect on the production process of automobiles. The other measures quality change and is derived from the quality-adjusted measure of prices explained above.

For the automobile industry, Abernathy *et al.* (1983) compiled a list of all the product and process innovations from 1893 to 1987 and gave each innovation a score on a scale from 1 to 7. This scale is similar to that used by market researchers who enquire how much you like a product on a scale from 1 to 5. The score is called a 'weight'. A weight of 1 means that the innovation affected the automobile very little (e.g. a new type of colour spray), while a weight of 7 means that it affected it a lot (e.g. the introduction of the assembly line or a new type of engine). The number of innovations per year and their weight produced a score for the year, which indicated the degree to which technological change had occurred. Product and process innovations were listed separately. Figure 2.6 illustrates this data by plotting the weighted measure of innovation in three-year intervals. The fact that both lines fall over time on average indicates that most product and process innovations occurred in the early years, when the industry experienced a high rate of new firm entry.

Although we do not have the same data for the PC industry, our second measure of innovation can be applied to both industries. This second measure looks at the degree to which the *quality* of the product has changed over time, a good proxy for innovation as innovation changes the quality of products and processes. To derive this measure of quality change, you start from the index of actual prices of a car or a PC. This is, in essence, the average price of each product sold in stores, turned into a price index as explained above. That is divided by the quality-adjusted hedonic price you have already studied. The first index shows the prices for goods of changing quality; the second, prices for goods of unchanged quality. Dividing the first by the second gives you a quality index: it will be high if there is a lot of quality improvement and low if there is little quality improvement.

Figure 2.7
Quality improvements in the US automobile industry
Source: Raff and Trajtenberg, 1997

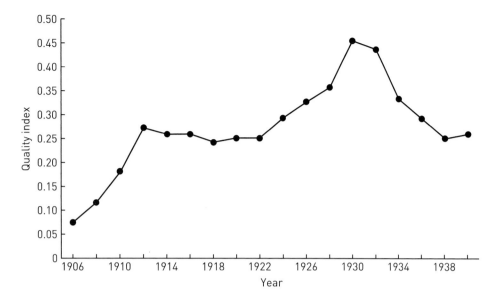

Figure 2.8
Quality improvements in the US PC industry
Source: Filson, 2001

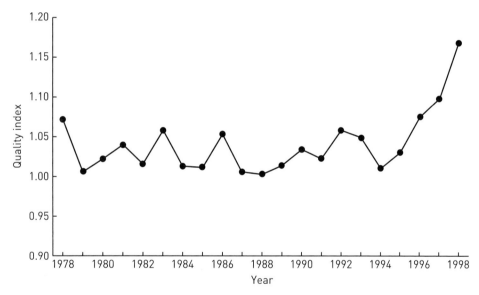

Question Look carefully at Figures 2.7 and 2.8. How do quality changes compare at similar stages in the two industries' life cycles?

As in Figure 2.5, it is the slope of the lines that is important: how the quality index changes over time. A steep upward slope indicates a period of great increase in quality.

One difference between the two industries that you can see if you compare Figures 2.7 and 2.8 is that, whereas in the automobile industry the degree of quality change was greatest in the very early years (1906–12), in the PC industry it was greater during the third decade of its existence. This difference is due to the fact that the PC industry emerged from the existing mainframe and minicomputer industry, in which firms such as IBM and DEC controlled the industry and hence had little competitive stimulus to innovate. The reason is that a firm's goal when innovating is to out-perform its competitors; so if it is not being challenged by those competitors, it has less incentive to innovate. Radical innovation was not unleashed in the industry until those firms that had a technical lead lost their control of the innovation process. Innovation up until 1990 was to a large extent controlled by IBM, as everything had to be IBM compatible. Only once the Wintel standard (the combination of the Windows operating system and the Intel processor) replaced the IBM standard, did the industry experience the kind of turbulence experienced in the very early years of the automobile industry. Therefore, although there was a lot of entry into the PC industry during its first fifteen years (as seen in Figure 2.4), it took longer than that for the new firms to eliminate the lead of the giants that preceded them. Below we shall see the implications of this for the industry structure.

Furthermore, Bresnahan (1998) holds that the reason that technological change in the PC industry lasted into the third decade of its existence, instead of dying off as often happens during the growth stage of the industry life cycle (as in automobiles), is that technological leadership in this industry is not dominated by one firm or a set of firms but divided among firms in different parts of the computer industry. These firms are the makers of PCs themselves (e.g. IBM, Dell, Compaq); the makers of the microprocessors (e.g. Intel); the makers of the operating systems (e.g. Microsoft); and the makers of application software (e.g. Lotus, WordPerfect, Ashton-Tate). This divided technical leadership has ensured rapid advances from specialists and a very competitive market, as PC firms are forced to compete not only with other firms that produce PCs but also with firms that produce parts or complementary products that work with another firms' products.

■ ■ ■ 2.4.5　Changes in industry structure

How did the turbulence caused by new firms entering and leaving the industry, radical technological change and falling prices affect the overall industry structure? The term 'industry structure' refers mainly to the way in which power is distributed among firms. This can be described by factors such as the number of firms in the industry and the distribution of **market shares**.

Market share

The market share of a firm is its share of total industry production expressed as a percentage.

An industry that has one firm with 50 per cent of the market and 50 other firms with only 1 per cent of the market (market shares must total 100 per cent) has a very different industry structure from an industry in which 10 firms each have 10 per cent of the market. An industry is described as 'concentrated' when a few firms have large market shares. Economists are interested in industry structure because it has implications for consumers. One of the issues is the extent to which the existence of very large firms in the industry will prevent a competitive environment, for example whether they inhibit other firms from entering the industry and discourage innovation. This issue was at the heart of the Microsoft trial, which you will read more about in Chapter 4, in which a very large software firm, with almost complete domination of the market, was accused of hindering competition in the industry.

In both industries, the periods of greatest technological advance were also the periods in which market shares were the most unstable and industry concentration at its lowest. Market share dynamics are important because unstable market shares mean that the status quo in the industry is being disrupted: the leaders' lead is being challenged. When market shares are stable the existing leaders are not challenged by outsiders. Incremental technological change tends to be less disruptive to the leaders' position than radical technological change, which is often carried out by outsiders. In fact, some have argued that competition should be measured, not by the level of 'concentration' (i.e. whether market share gives some firms too much power), but by the level of market share instability. As long as there is some instability the existing leaders cannot relax and are thus forced to compete.

Case study: Cars – from technological change to marketing and back?

In the automobile industry, market share instability was especially strong during the period from 1910 to 1925, which witnessed not only high entry/exit rates but also some of the most radical innovations in the industry. Market share instability then decreased as entry fell and innovation became less important. The strong economies of scale that developed in the 1920s, when most of the industry (not only Ford) began to use mass-production techniques, alongside the fall in prices, caused the industry to become increasingly concentrated. The 'Big Three' US automobile producers (Ford, GM and Chrysler) have dominated the US industry for most of the post-Second World War period. Concentration stopped increasing in the 1970s when the entry of foreign firms into the US market created a more competitive market. Foreign firms especially profited from the opportunity to satisfy the high demand for small cars during the oil crisis of the 1970s, an area in which they had more experience. Since the 1970s, competition has been carried out principally via advertising wars and price wars. As the twenty-first century opens, however, the automobile industry stands on the brink of a new round of technological innovation, as hydrogen looks set to replace petroleum as the standard fuel (Chapter 3, Section 3.4.2).

Question

Do you think there are any economic factors underlying the varying importance of technological change over time? Is this pattern of structural change over time likely to be replicated in other industries (e.g. the PC industry)?

In the PC industry, market shares were the most stable and industry concentration the highest in the early years when IBM dominated the industry. During the late 1980s and early 1990s, the end of the IBM-compatibility era (with the rise of Wintel) and the emergence of the World Wide Web caused some disruption to the status quo, which resulted in unstable market shares and a fall in concentration. Concentration later rose again in the 2–3 year period up to the time of writing in 2001, because companies such as Dell were focusing less on innovation and more on simple measures to cut costs and hence prices so as to increase market share.

> Dell computers is vowing to remain on the offensive in an ongoing PC price war, sacrificing profits in a bid to gain market shares – a strategy that the company's founder admitted could ultimately kill off a competitor.
>
> *(Popovich, 2001)*

> A price war is hitting PC makers hard. Many well-known names could disappear from the high street . . . But not all the problems are due to the downturn in the economy or the bursting of the internet bubble. Much of the suffering has been caused by Dell computer which started a price war to gain market share.
>
> *(Schofield, 2001, p.1)*

You will study the concept of a price war in Chapter 6. For the present let us simply note that this recent trend has, in fact, been seen by many industry analysts as a threat to the industry. Unless the PC industry goes back to the era of competing via innovation (as in the early 1990s) it is bound to end up as a traditional, stagnant industry run by a few firms that are more interested in protecting their market shares (through price reductions and advertising wars) than in the future technological growth of the industry.

■ ■ ■ 2.4.6   The future?

In the USA, the automobile reached the 50 per cent household penetration rate in 1923, about 23 years into the industry's development. The PC reached that threshold rate in 1999, also about 23 years into its development. Given the discussion in Section 2.3, this suggests that the economy-wide effects of the PC have yet to be fully seen. And given the arguments in this section, it also suggests that the PC is now starting to reach the end of its growth phase. In fact, in 2001 PC sales fell for the first time. As a report in the *Financial Times* noted: 'Shipments of personal computers have suffered their first quarterly fall in at least 15 years' (Kehoe, 2001).

Given the similarities in the early development of the two industries, it is likely that some of the patterns that have characterized the mature phase of the automobile industry will also characterize the future of the PC industry, which is only now entering its mature phase. Using this logic we might expect the PC industry to be characterized by higher levels of concentration (already happening with the recently proposed merger between HP and Compaq, and with the price war led by Dell), more market share *stability* between the incumbents, and more focus on process innovation and advertising than on product innovation.

However, if future competition is carried out more through product innovation than through price wars and economies of scale (as it is currently), then this drift into stagnation may not occur. Instead, if innovations allow new firms to come forward and displace the old leaders, the characteristics of the early phase may reappear and the life cycle will start up again. We may witness new entries and exits and renewed market share instability. The future market structure of the PC industry will also be influenced by the nature of innovation in another sense: whether new innovations will continue to allow the technical leadership to be divided among firms, a situation which in the past has allowed new entry to occur and smaller firms to survive.

2.5   Conclusion

This chapter has enabled you to think about the essential role of technological change in determining economy-wide growth and the growth of firms and industries. We have seen that many issues surrounding the new economy are really issues around the dynamics of technological change: rapid increases in productivity, the emergence of many small firms, new products and new processes, and so on. The main lesson of the chapter has been to provide a historical perspective to the introduction of new technologies. Without such a historical perspective, patterns may falsely appear to be new: we have just forgotten!

Questions for review and discussion

Question 1   Suppose a firm uses 200 hours of labour per day and produces 4000 mobile phones. It then reduces its labour inputs to 100 hours per day and finds it can produce 3000 phones. Which one of the following is a correct statement about the change in the firm's productivity? Tick the letter corresponding to the correct statement from the list below.

A ❑ The firm now produces 25% fewer phones, so its productivity has fallen by 25%.
B ❑ The firm has cut its labour hours by 100 but its output has fallen by 1000, so its productivity has fallen.
C ❑ The firm employs 50% of the labour hours it employed before and produces 75% of its previous output, so its productivity has risen by 25%.
D ❑ The firm has increased its output per labour hour from 20 units to 30 units, so its productivity has risen by 50%.

Question 2 Some of the following features of industrial revolutions belong to a microeconomic perspective (as opposed to a macroeconomic perspective). Select the ones you think belong (there is more than one correct statement).

A ❑ There will be a rise in the level of productivity across the economy.
B ❑ There is rapid entry into and exit from a new industry in its growth phase.
C ❑ You will see cumulative technological change resulting from the birth of new general purpose technologies.
D ❑ There is an increase in the level of income per head.
E ❑ There will be a sustained fall in the price of a new product once a product standard has emerged.

Question 3 Which one of the following characteristics is most typical of an industry in its growth phase?

A ❑ There will be rapid entry of new firms, each producing a different version of the product.
B ❑ There will be firms of many kinds producing in a pre-commercial way.
C ❑ The emergence of a standardized product will be followed by the exit of firms unable to produce it efficiently.

Question 4 The table below is designed to give information about the price of a product in two years, 2000 and 2005. Write the correct values into the spaces in the table.

Year	Actual price of product (£ per unit)	Price index (base year 2000)
2000		
2005	£30	75

Question 5 Explain briefly using examples:

(a) how productivity may increase with the introduction of new technology;
(b) how the characteristics of a general purpose technology help us to understand industrial revolutions;
(c) how technological progress may increase economic growth.

3

Innovation, markets and industrial change

Graham Dawson and Judith Mehta

Concepts

- the market demand curve
- increasing and diminishing returns to a factor of production
- the short-run average cost curve
- the long-run average cost curve
- increasing and decreasing returns to scale; economies and diseconomies of scale
- the industry life cycle
- the learning curve
- network externalities

Objectives

After studying this chapter you should be able to:

- appreciate the importance of technological change, costs of production and consumer preferences to the changing organization of production
- understand the relation between the quantity demanded of a good and its price as represented by the demand curve
- understand economic models of the relation between firms' costs and output
- analyse the role of technology and costs in influencing industry structure over the life cycle.

3.1 Technological change, demand and costs

The new economy

Over the past 40 years global computing power has increased a billionfold. Number-crunching tasks that once took a week can now be done in seconds. Today a Ford Taurus car contains more computing power than the multimillion-dollar mainframe computers used in the Apollo space programme. Cheaper processing allows computers to be used for more and more purposes. In 1985, it cost Ford $60,000 each time it crashed a car into a wall to find out what would happen in an accident. Now a collision can be simulated by computer for around $100. BP Amoco uses 3D seismic-exploration technology to prospect for oil, cutting the cost of finding oil from nearly $10 a barrel in 1991 to only $1 today . . .

Thanks to rapidly falling prices, computers and the Internet are being adopted more quickly than previous general-purpose technologies, such as steam and electricity. It took more than a century after its invention before steam became the dominant source of power in Britain. Electricity achieved a 50% share of the power used by America's manufacturing industry 90 years after the discovery of electromagnetic induction, and 40 years after the first power station was built. By contrast, half of all Americans already use a personal computer, 50 years after the invention of computers and only 30 years after the microprocessor was invented. The Internet is approaching 50% penetration in America 30 years after it was invented and only seven years since it was launched commercially in 1993.

(The Economist, *23 September 2000, pp.5, 10*)

That is how *The Economist* discussed the issue you studied in Chapter 2: the role of information technology as a general purpose technology.

Question	How would you summarize the argument about prices, costs and information technology put forward in *The Economist*?

It seems to us that the argument is that improvements in information technology caused a decline in the costs that firms face in producing goods. Falling prices have in turn encouraged a rapid take-up by consumers of products embodying information technology. Economists place costs on the supply side of markets, where firms produce and sell goods such as cars, oil, personal computers and Internet access. Take-up by consumers is on the demand side of the market. The quotation suggests that new information technology *causes* a decline in costs and hence in prices that enables large numbers of consumers to buy safer cars, personal computers and so on. Technological change, a supply-side phenomenon, is seen as a prime cause of economic change.

In the previous chapter, Mariana Mazzucato looked at the impact of newly introduced technologies in the early phase of the US auto industry and the PC industry, highlighting the similarities between what we are observing today in the IT-based industries and what we observed 100 years ago in an industry we now consider mature. As we write, technological change continues to be very rapid, and two particular technological developments will be used in this chapter to illustrate our discussion of the forces shaping the organization of industrial production. The dilemma faced by car manufacturers in adjusting to the 'hydrogen economy' of the future will be discussed in Section 3.4. We also discuss digital technology, which has revolutionized sound reproduction as well as the capture and transmission of visual images in DVD, digital television and digital cameras. Car manufacturers are also exploiting its potential. For example, the Citroën C5 'bristles with the latest digital technology to improve your motoring experience' (see Figure 3.1). An advertisement for the C5 alludes to the origins of digital technology, showing instructions as sequences of 'switches' in a computer as being 'on' or 'off', or set to '1' or '0'.

In this chapter we will introduce the use of economic models of markets, firms and industries to examine the relationships among consumer demand, technological change and costs. Section 3.2 develops the idea expressed in *The Economist* extract that falling prices were responsible for the rapid take-up of new products by consumers. This is an example of a widely observed relation between the quantity demanded of a good by consumers and the price of the good: the lower the price, the greater the quantity demanded. However, there are other influences on market demand. For example, consumers are likely to buy more goods if their incomes increase. So Section 3.2 explains how economists analyse the interaction between price and other influences. This analysis is the first part of the theory of consumer demand, which will be further developed in Chapter 8.

Figure 3.1
An advertisement
for the Citroën C5

Technology as it should be. 100% useful.

The rest of the chapter focuses mainly on the supply side of the market, exploring the role of costs and technological change in the organization of production. The objective is to understand the process by which a firm – initially one among many similar firms jostling for position – emerges ahead of the pack to achieve an advantage over its competitors, as Ford did in the US automobile industry (Chapter 2). What was so special about Ford? More generally, how can we account for the change in structure that so many industries seem to undergo? Why do most of the many small firms so common in the early years of new industries disappear to leave an established industry dominated by a few large firms? Why does the heterogeneity or extreme variety of those small firms in new industries give way to a much greater degree of similarity, indeed standardization, among the few survivors?

In exploring these questions, economists use models of the relation between the output, technology and costs of firms. In Section 3.3, we define technology in an economic model of a firm, and use it to explore the link between technology and costs. We begin from a model in which firms take technology as given and their ability to change their costs is severely constrained, and then build in progressively more decision-making flexibility over the adoption and use of technology.

Section 3.4 links this analysis of technology and costs to the model of the industry 'life cycle' introduced in Chapter 2, Section 2.4.1. The life-cycle model represents an industry as if it were a biological organism going through the stages of birth, growth, maturity and decline, and is used to consider the interaction of demand and technology in shaping industrial structure. This section further extends the analysis of firms, technology and costs to include models where firms' freedom to learn and create is one driver of technological change itself. This helps us to understand how a particular firm can become the 'leader of the pack' through innovation and how it can then gain an advantage over competitors by reducing its costs through large-scale production.

3.2   Market demand

Case study: Digital outsells film

Sales of digital cameras have overtaken traditional 35 mm cameras for the first time. According to monthly figures collated by national electric and photo retailer Dixons, digital camera sales outstripped 35 mm cameras during the month of April. 'This is a sea change in consumer photography,' said Dixons marketing director Ian Ditcham. 'As a leading photographic retailer, Dixons is a clear barometer of consumer trends,' he said. The main reasons for the popularity of digital cameras are falling prices, the growth of home PC and internet usage and the instant delivery of images without the need for processing.

(Adapted from Outdoor Photography, *August 2001, no.15, p.4)*

Questions

1   What do you think are the main similarities between the arguments in this case study and the second paragraph of 'The new economy' quotation discussed in Section 3.1?

2   Figure 3.2 illustrates a number of different makes of digital camera. What other products do you normally associate with the manufacturers of these cameras?

The quotation and the case study describe the take-up by consumers of new products embodying innovations in information technology. Both link the popularity of new technology among consumers with falling prices and draw attention to the rapidity of consumer take-up. There is something new for Dixons and other retailers to sell and for consumers to buy. A new product, the digital camera, has created a new market. Figure 3.2 shows that this market is supplied by a number of manufacturers normally associated with the production of a range of other consumer goods. Nikon and Olympus make traditional cameras. Epson is a well-known brand of personal computers and printers. Sony is probably best known for the Walkman, the first personal audio-cassette player. Casio puts its name on watches and calculators. Fuji is particularly interesting as a manufacturer not only of cameras but also of film, the medium under challenge from digital.

Industry

An industry is a group of firms producing a broadly related range of goods using similar technologies.

Market

A market is constituted by the buying and selling of goods or services.

It seems natural to us to say that these firms from different **industries**, including computers, electronics and optical equipment, have together created a new **market**, that is, a market for a new product, the digital camera. This suggests that industries can be thought of as being about the production of a range of broadly related goods, and markets are about the sale and purchase of a more narrowly defined set of goods. For example, the optical equipment industry produces cameras, photocopiers, microscopes, telescopes and so on in order to supply different markets. There are consumer markets for disposable cameras, entry-level compact cameras or cameras for the serious amateur and so on. There are industrial markets for cameras for professionals or microscopes for specialist use in medical and scientific research. So markets can be identified in terms of their consumers and the purposes for which those consumers are buying goods, as well as in the more familiar terms of the goods themselves. Phrases such as 'the market for medium format

47

Figure 3.2
A selection of digital cameras from the buyer's guide of *What Camera?* magazine
Source: *What Camera?*, winter 2001, pp.16–20

cameras' are common. But a medium format camera might appeal to the serious, and affluent, amateur as well as the professional. It is not easy to say where one market ends and another begins.

Precisely where we draw the line between 'industry' and 'market' depends on which aspect of economic activity we want to analyse. Producing and selling are both stages in a single complex process of making profits from the *supply* of goods by turning inputs into outputs that consumers are willing and able to buy. It is helpful to use the term 'industry' if we want to direct attention towards suppliers (as producers) and the technologies they are using. Most countries use a system known as the Standard Industrial Classification to assign organizations to industries. Under this system, each organization is assigned to an industrial category according to the principal goods or services it produces. The system is essential to the collection of statistics that enable us to estimate the relative contributions of the different industries to national income, and to detect which parts of the economy are growing or contracting over time.

To speak of a market directs attention towards the relations between suppliers (as sellers) and buyers of a particular good. It is usually taken for granted that buyers and sellers are engaged in *voluntary* exchange, of money for goods, and that buyers are able to exercise *choice* (to buy or not to buy, to buy this good rather than that one). 'Market' is therefore a politically charged term, unlike 'industry', shown, for example, by the prevalence in political debate of the expression 'free market'. (The nature of markets, including this political dimension, is also discussed in Chapter 5, Section 5.1.)

The focus in Section 3.2 will be on consumer demand for products and in particular the price at which they are offered for sale. It is therefore appropriate to use the term 'market' in this section, reserving 'industry' for later sections where our attention is directed towards the costs incurred by firms in producing goods.

Figure 3.3
A market demand curve for electronic personal organizers

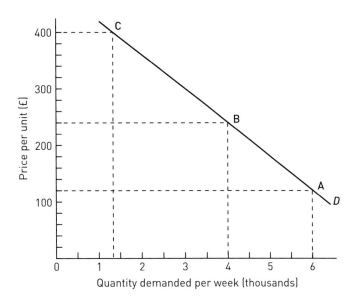

▨▨■ 3.2.1   Market demand and price

This subsection will explore the widely observed relationship between the quantity demanded of a good by consumers and the price of the good: the lower the price, the greater the quantity demanded. This relationship underlies the way in which falling prices are responsible for the rapid take-up of new products by consumers, as reported in the quotations above. We focus on the market demand curve, which represents the demand of all the consumers in a given market. However, as well as the price of the good, there are other influences on market demand, discussion of which will be postponed until Section 3.2.2. This makes it possible to take a step-by-step approach and to begin by considering the influence of price alone.

The relationship between demand and price can be represented in different ways: in words, in a diagram or by using algebra. We expressed it in words in the preceding paragraph: the lower the price, the greater the quantity demanded. This relationship can also be shown in a diagram, known as a demand curve (always by convention a 'curve' though it may be drawn as a straight line). Figure 3.3 shows a demand curve, and we look at it in detail in a moment. Note first that as part of the step-by-step approach, the demand curve is drawn on the assumption that the price of the product is the only relevant variable influencing demand for the product. A 'variable' is a precisely defined aspect of the economy, such as the price of a good, that can take a range of values (such as £1, £2, £3, ...).

All the other influences on market demand are held constant while we look at the relationship between demand and price. This procedure is usually known by the Latin phrase *ceteris paribus*, which means 'other things being equal'. It is the foundation for constructing economic models, which abstract from the complexities of real economic life to concentrate on one or two variables that seem to be important. Once we have understood how two variables are related – how a change in one affects the other, *ceteris paribus* – it is possible to move on, dropping the assumption that other things have remained equal. We can introduce other variables, gradually making the model more complex by considering the effects of changes in them.

An economic model therefore provides a systematic way of thinking about causal relationships. We can use them to formulate hypotheses about cause and effect, such as 'lower prices caused the increase in sales'. That puts us in a position to look for evidence that might lead us to accept or reject the hypothesis.

The market demand curve is a very simple economic model in that it abstracts from the many things going on in a market to focus on only two: the quantity demanded of the good and its price. Look at Figure 3.3, and notice that the vertical and horizontal axes are 'anchored' at the zero point, called the origin. As with all such diagrams, movements up the vertical axis, and along the horizontal axis to the right, represent higher values. Each point on the curve D shows the quantity demanded (measured on the horizontal axis) at a particular price (measured on the vertical axis). The market demand curve therefore shows the quantity demanded at each and every price by all the consumers in a particular market. We say 'each and every price' to draw attention to the fact that in drawing the market demand curve as a continuous line, economists are making estimates. The good may not have been offered for sale at 'each and every' price but only a small number of selected prices. Drawing the market demand curve as a continuous curve on a diagram such as Figure 3.3 shows estimates of what demand would be at other prices.

Figure 3.3 shows a hypothetical market demand curve for electronic personal organizers (hypothetical because it is not based on actual sales figures but is being used purely as an illustration of market demand curves in general). Electronic devices are particularly good at storing files, allowing them to be used in different ways, and have come to dominate the market for portable information storage. The market demand curve depicts the quantity consumers demand, depending on price. This 'quantity demanded' is not necessarily the number of electronic personal organizers that people need, but what they are willing and able to purchase at different prices.

The demand curve in Figure 3.3 shows that with a price of £120, the quantity demanded of electronic personal organizers is 6000 units per week (point A). For a higher price at, say, £240, *ceteris paribus*, we can find out how many units will be purchased by moving along the demand curve to point B, where the quantity demanded is only 4000. If the price was as high as £400 smaller quantities would be purchased; we move along the demand curve to point C, and see that the quantity demanded is only 1300 units. This inverse relationship between the price of a good (or service) and the quantity demanded (shown by the market demand curve sloping downwards and to the right) is known as 'the law of demand'.

So economic models can be stated in words and represented in diagrams. They can also be represented by using algebra. The claim that demand depends on – or changes in response to – price can be written as:

$D = f(P)$, *ceteris paribus*

which is read as demand (D) *is a function of* price (P), all other influences held constant. Both demand and price vary in this model; quantity demanded is the *dependent* variable, since it changes in response to price, the *independent* variable. So this algebraic statement makes clear the causal relation proposed by the model, while the diagram, Figure 3.3, showed the *negative* relationship it proposes between demand and price: a higher price results in a lower quantity demanded (*ceteris paribus*).

However, there may be some exceptions to this 'law' of demand. Early in the twentieth century, Thorstein Veblen, an American institutional economist, analysed cultural influences on consumption. In *The Theory of the Leisure Class* (Veblen, 1912) he suggested that it can be important to show off your wealth by means of conspicuous consumption. The rich can demonstrate their wealth by buying goods that are widely known to be very expensive and beyond the reach of most consumers. The term *Veblen goods* is used to denote luxury items, such as exclusive jewellery, cars or designer clothes which may therefore be in greater demand at higher prices.

At the lower end of the income scale, consumers in very poor countries may actually buy less of a very basic good, such as rice, when its price falls. This is because they can use the spending power released by the fall in the price of the basic foodstuff to replace some rice with a greater variety of foods. Such goods are called *Giffen* goods because the influential economist Alfred Marshall, apparently in error, gave Sir Robert Giffen credit for discovering this exception to the general law of demand.

■ ■ ■ 3.2.2 Other influences on market demand

What about other variables which may affect demand? Let us consider four such variables. As is often the case in economics, the first two points involve understanding some rather formal relationships between variables, in this case price and income.

1 *The price of other goods.* Two goods x and y are known as *substitutes* if the quantity demanded of good x increases after a *rise* in the price of good y. The rise in the price of good y causes consumers to switch to good x. For example, if the quantity demanded of electronic personal organizers increases after a rise in the price of (print) diaries, these goods are substitutes. On the other hand, two goods x and y are *complements* if the quantity demanded of good x increases after a *fall* in the price of good y. The fall in the price of good y causes consumers to buy more and also to buy more goods that are used with it, such as good x. For example, if the quantity demanded of electronic personal organizers increases after a fall in the price of desktop computers (to which data can be downloaded), these goods are complements.

2 *The incomes of consumers.* The amounts of income consumers have at their disposal determines the absolute level of consumption: people with high incomes tend to purchase more of most goods and services than people with low incomes. But the level of income also influences the kind of things that people buy. If a country's national income goes up, households have more total purchasing power, and more goods and services of most types will be bought. A *normal good* is one for which the quantity demanded increases when incomes rise. In countries where the average level of income is relatively high, most goods are normal goods (e.g. refrigerators, cars, haircuts, houseplants and electronic personal organizers). Studies of households in poverty show their very limited purchases. There are some products, such as basic foodstuffs, or black and white television sets, of which fewer items will be purchased as income rises. For example, if poor households in low-income countries get richer, they are able to substitute beans, meat or fish for part of their basic grain diet of rice, maize or millet. Less rice will therefore be purchased. When demand for a commodity falls as incomes go up, the commodity is called an *inferior good*.

3 *Socio-economic influences.* J.S. Duesenberry, an American economist, suggested that demand for particular commodities, as well as consumption expenditure in general, is affected by a 'demonstration effect', where people feel social pressures to purchase what others have. J.K. Galbraith, another American economist, talks of a dependence effect, where wants are dependent on the very process by which they are satisfied, since producers use advertisements and sales people to persuade us to purchase what they are making. Many commentators suggest that for a wide range of goods 'consumption to be' has replaced 'consumption for use'. That is, the consumption of many goods and services has become an expression of identity and self-definition, with less emphasis

placed on the use value of the product. As more people turn to shopping for entertainment and leisure, and as the phrase 'retail therapy' increasingly enters into everyday language in high-income countries, it becomes more difficult to understand the demand side of the economy without taking account of society's norms and values.

4   *The expected future price of the good.* Expectations about future prices may affect demand. People may buy non-perishable goods now because they think that prices will be higher in the future or delay purchases in the belief that price cuts are imminent.

We can use algebra to express very concisely what it will take us a paragraph to say in words. A demand function is an algebraic expression of the idea that the demand for a good depends on its price and on the other variables discussed above. We can now write the demand function for a commodity, *x*, in the following expanded form:

$$D_x = f(P_x, P_r, Y, Z, P_e)$$

This demand function states that the market demand for commodity x D_x is a function of, or depends on, five variables. P_x is the price of commodity x itself, while P_r stands for the price of related goods, that is, substitutes and complements. Y is the standard symbol in economics for the income of all consumers or households together. Then there are socio-economic variables, labelled Z. Finally, P_e stands for expected future prices. The number of variables on the right-hand side of the equation shows that the complete market demand function for a good is quite complex.

So far we have looked at a hypothetical market demand curve for electronic personal organizers on the assumption that while the price of the good changes other things remain equal. What happens if we relax the *ceteris paribus* assumption? In other words, supposing that commodity *x* is electronic personal organizers, what happens if any of the items on the right-hand side of the demand function change? A change in any of the variables other than the price of electronic personal organizers can be shown by a *shift* in the whole demand curve, because the *ceteris paribus* assumption, on which the original curve was drawn, has been dropped. The shift may be to the left or right, depending on the cause of the change.

Figure 3.4 shows such a shift in demand. This figure does not have a numerical scale on the axes, as in Figure 3.3. Instead, the axes are just labelled 'Price' (*P*) and 'Quantity'

Figure 3.4
A shift in a market demand curve

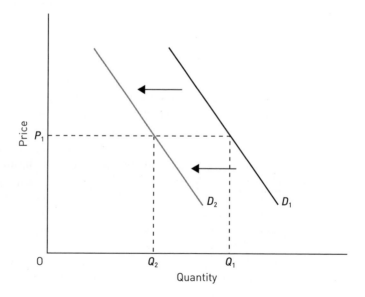

(Q). 'Quantity' should be understood as 'quantity per period of time', such as a day, a week or a year. Diagrams such as this allow us to focus on the direction of change of variables and their implications, rather than exact magnitudes. Let us suppose that consumer incomes fall, so that everyone has less to spend on normal goods. The quantity demanded will therefore decrease at all prices. For example, at price P_1 quantity demanded falls from Q_1 to Q_2. This means that we now have a new relationship between quantity demanded and price, and this is shown by the new market demand curve D_2 in Figure 3.4 lying to the left of the original one, D_1.

The key points about movements along and shifts of the market demand curve are:

■ If the price of the good changes while all other variables remain the same, this is reflected in a movement *along* the market demand curve.

■ If a variable other than the price of the good itself changes, the whole curve shifts, showing that after the change in the variable more (or less) is now demanded at each price.

Here is an exercise to help you think about shifts in the market demand curve.

Exercise 3.1

Think for a few minutes about how other things besides price may *not* remain equal in the market for electronic personal organizers. Work out what effect each will have on the demand curve. Then see if you can complete Table 3.1 below.

Table 3.1
Shifts in the market demand curve for electronic personal organizers

Change in variable	Effect on demand curve
Decrease in income	Decrease in quantity demanded at all prices Demand curve shifts to the left
Increase in income	
Rise in price of a substitute	
Fall in price of a substitute	
Rise in price of a complementary good	
Fall in price of a complementary good	
Change in socio-economic influences in favour of electronic personal organizers	
Change in socio-economic influences away from electronic personal organizers	

3.3 Firms, costs and technology

In this section the focus turns towards the supply side of the market, towards firms and industries, exploring the importance of costs and technological change in the organization of production. The objective is to understand the kinds of change in industrial structure discussed in Chapter 2, that is, changes in the number and size of firms in an industry. One such change saw the emergence of Ford, initially one among many similar firms jostling for position in the US automobile industry, as the industry 'leader'. What was so special about Ford? Henry Ford was the first car maker to introduce an innovative assembly-line production technology. This gave him a competitive advantage over firms using more traditional and, for that reason, more expensive processes. Since consumers were unwilling to pay higher prices for broadly similar products, Ford's rivals were forced to take up the same new methods of production if they wanted to compete.

This story raises some important questions about competition, technology and costs. How do firms respond to changing conditions in their industry? What can a 'typical' firm do to cut its costs? What are the main constraints on its behaviour? Economists use models of the relationships between technology, costs and output of firms to explore these questions. This section examines these relationships in a basic economic model of a firm. It explores the scope the firm has for cutting its costs in the short and long run, and the impact of changing technology on the firm's costs. The distinction between the short run and the long run is important because it is based on assumptions about how much room to manoeuvre the firm has in responding to changing market conditions and draws attention to the role of investment in the firm's response. It is in the short run that the firm's actions are subject to the greatest constraint. In the analysis in this section, firms take technology as given. In Section 3.4 we remove this constraint, restoring to firms some influence in shaping technology and hence their costs to their own advantage.

■ ■ ■ 3.3.1   Technology and costs in the short run

Advertising leaflets are dropping through letter boxes around the UK, as we are writing this chapter, from cable suppliers trying to attract new customers for their services. They promise to provide a telephone line, a bundle of television channels, an Internet connection, home shopping and movies-on-demand, all at a 'bargain price'. These leaflets raise some interesting questions. How does expanding output of cable services by selling to new customers make it possible to offer them for sale at a lower price? What happens to the costs of producing cable services as the firm increases its output of them?

In analysing the costs, technology and output of firms, economists create a model of the typical or representative **firm**. A firm is an organization that buys inputs, such as land, labour and capital, and transforms them into output for sale. We call these inputs to the firm's production process *factors of production*.

A firm that wants to expand output is likely to need more inputs. For example, in order to increase output the cable supplier would probably recruit more workers, such as the technicians who install cable boxes in customers' homes and the telephonists who respond to customer enquiries. It might also need to buy in more of the equipment used by these workers, such as telephones, computers and engineering tools, and it might need to rent more office space. In other words, the firm increases its input of factors of production, namely labour (the technicians and telephonists), capital (telephones, computers and engineering tools) and land (office space). The firm is assumed to have done this by purchasing the additional inputs it needs from the relevant factor markets, for example by recruiting new workers in the labour market.

The firm can combine factors of production in various ways to create output, but is limited by the technology available to it. The best production methods available to the firm are summarized in its **production function**, which identifies the maximum output a firm can produce from each available combination of inputs. We can write it out using algebra in exactly the same way as we wrote out the demand function in Section 3.2:

$$Q = f(F_1, F_2, \ldots, F_n)$$

The firm

The firm is an organization that transforms inputs of land, labour and capital into an output of goods and services for sale.

Production function

The production function specifies the maximum output a firm can obtain from each available combination of inputs.

This says that the firm's output (Q) (the dependent variable) is a function of the various factors of production (the different Fs, up to any number 'n' of them) such as land, different types of labour and machinery (the independent variables). This production function is the firm's *technology*. The firm is assumed to do the best it can with its inputs, without waste. If there is technological change, the firm can get more output from its inputs, that is, increase their productivity (Chapter 2, Section 2.2.2). In the models we discuss in this section all firms have access to the same technology.

The firm's objective is not to produce maximum output, but rather to make as much profit as possible. However, reducing costs is an important competitive tool in the search for profits, as the cable supplier's offer of a 'bargain price' to new customers illustrates. So how do firms' costs change as output changes? What makes it possible to supply more customers at a lower price? Are there any limitations to this process? The distinction between the short run and the long run helps to answer these questions.

Question	We referred above to the cable supplier recruiting new workers. Can you think of any employers or industries that have found this difficult?

In 2001 in the UK the health and education industries were beset with staff shortages and in some areas recruited from overseas. It is likely to take most employers longer to increase the quantity of skilled than unskilled labour. Skills may not be available in the locality and workers may have to be enticed to move from other jobs, involving periods of notice. New workers may have to be trained and the training period may well be lengthy. BBC television reported on 4 September 2001 that Arriva, a UK train and bus operator, had announced the cancellation of up to a hundred services a day because of a shortage of train drivers. Arriva had the capital equipment, the trains, to run the services but could not do so until it had increased the amount of skilled labour at its disposal by training new drivers. In this example the firm is constrained in its response to the demand for rail services because the quantity of one factor of production, labour, is fixed.

The short run

A firm is operating in the short run when it is unable to change the quantity it uses of at least one of its factors of production.

Economists describe the situation in which Arriva finds itself as **the short run**. In the short run the firm can vary the quantity it uses of some of its factors of production but there is at least one which is fixed. The term denotes this constraint on the firm's behaviour rather than a particular period of historical time. The firm's actions take place in actual or historical time and so the short run will eventually come to an end, in Arriva's case when the drivers have been trained in a matter of months. Therefore, the short run, understood as the condition of being unable to change the quantity used of at least one factor, refers to different periods of historical time, depending on the circumstances of each particular firm. Another example from transport illustrates this variety. London's Heathrow, Stansted and Gatwick airports are constrained in responding to rising demand for air travel from London and south-east England by the planning process required before new runways or terminals can be constructed. In this case the fixed factor is capital and the short run is measured in years, perhaps even decades.

Heathrow Terminal 5 to get go-ahead

After an inquiry that began in 1995, the government is poised to give the go-ahead for Heathrow's Terminal 5. It is due to open in 2007, subject to final approval.

(Adapted from The Sunday Times, *4 November 2001, p.2)*

In the short run, therefore, the firm has one or more variable factors of production but at least one fixed factor. How does the firm's output change in the short run as it increases the amount of a variable factor? For example, let us suppose that the cable supplier recruited more labour, such as technicians and telephonists, while using unchanged quantities of both capital and land. Hiring more labour allows it to increase output. Initially, output may rise faster than the inputs of labour. Each additional worker may not need a computer all to themselves and, up to a point, extra workers can share the same office space. So initially increases in the amount of labour may generate larger 'returns' in the form of increases in output. At this stage in its expansion of output in the short run, therefore, the firm is experiencing increasing returns to a factor of production, in this case labour.

However, this fortunate situation has its limits. If the firm continues to expand output by increasing the input of labour with unchanged inputs of capital and land, a point will be reached after which the employment of even more workers brings successively smaller increases in output. For example, there may be so many workers that each one spends some time idle in the queue waiting to use a computer. The input of labour is rising faster than output, and the firm is now experiencing diminishing returns to a factor of production. Diminishing returns pose a serious constraint on the expansion of a firm in the short run.

These relationships between inputs and outputs in the short run influence the firm's costs. Returning to the cable supplier, it is now possible to frame a more precise question: what happens to the costs of producing these services as the firm increases its output of them in the short run? To analyse this, we need to distinguish **total costs** (TC) and the **average cost** (AC) of production. A firm's total costs are the expenses incurred in buying the inputs necessary to produce the firm's output. Average cost is the cost per unit of output. Average cost (AC) is therefore the total cost of production (TC) divided by the number of units produced (Q):

Total costs

The total costs of the firm are the expenses incurred in buying the inputs necessary for production.

Average cost

The average cost of production is the total cost of production divided by the number of units produced.

$$AC = \frac{TC}{Q}$$

We can draw a short-run average cost ($SRAC$) curve that models the relationship between different levels of output and average cost (AC) in the short run (Figure 3.5). Each point on the $SRAC$ curve represents the average cost in the short run (measured on the vertical axis) of producing a quantity of output (measured on the horizontal axis). Output (Q) is measured per time period, such as a year. The $SRAC$ curve is expected to be 'U'-shaped, as shown in Figure 3.5. The downward-sloping section of the $SRAC$ curve indicates that as output expands from a low level, average costs in the short run fall. Eventually, however, the $SRAC$ curve begins to slope upwards, showing that at output levels above Q_1 average costs rise as output increases.

The shape of the $SRAC$ curve arises from the technical constraints on short-run output expansion just described. We assume that the price of inputs is constant. As output expands the fixed cost of the fixed factors of production, such as the cable system itself, is being spread over an expanded number of customers. Increasing returns to a factor of production means that output rises faster than the variable input, so the cost of the variable factor per unit of output falls too. So initially the average cost of production (AC) falls as output rises.

Eventually, however, diminishing returns to the variable factor of production sets in. Output starts to rise more slowly than the variable input so the additional cost required to produce additional units of output starts to rise. Eventually total cost (fixed plus variable costs) will start to rise faster than output: that is, average costs will start to rise. On Figure 3.5 this happens as output rises above Q_1.

Figure 3.5
A short-run average
cost (*SRAC*) curve

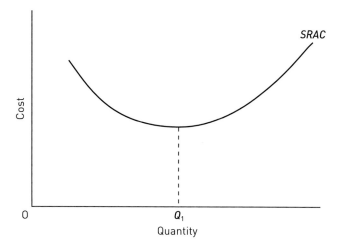

To sum up, in the short run the firm's ability to reduce costs as output rises is constrained by diminishing returns. In the long run, opportunities to invest in factors such as plant and machinery mean that the quantity of all factors of production can be varied. How does that affect the firm's costs?

■■■ 3.3.2 Long-run costs and economies of scale

What makes it possible to offer more output for sale at a lower price? That was one of the questions with which Section 3.3.1 opened. Part of the answer is that the firm's cost curves, which reflect the technology it is using, may display falling average cost as output increases over a range of output levels. The other part of the answer is that market demand must be sufficient to justify successive expansions of output. A firm such as the cable supplier seeking to increase sales by offering 'bargain prices' to its new customers is making an assumption about the size of the market. This section examines the relation between output and average cost on the assumption that the size of the firm's market is sufficiently large to justify increases in its input of all factors of production.

The long run

In the long run
the firm is able
to change the
quantity of all of
its factors of
production.

There is greater scope for cutting costs in **the long run**. In the long run the firm can increase inputs of all factors of production: labour, capital and land. This corresponds in reality to firms making investments. Firms invest in labour by training key personnel such as train drivers, technicians and telephonists. They may invest in items of capital equipment from telephones and computers to new factories or warehouses. They may invest in land by buying more office space or, literally, perhaps by buying a 'greenfield' site for a new runway. In modelling firms in the long run, it is still assumed that they are operating with given technology available to all firms.

How exactly do economists analyse the effects of investment of this kind on the firm's costs? The long-run average cost (*LRAC*) curve models the relationship between changes in output and average cost (*AC*) in the long run (Figure 3.6). Each point on the *LRAC* curve represents the average cost, in the long run, of producing a given quantity of output. The shape of the *LRAC* curve varies with the technology in use by firms in a particular industry. An increase in output in the long run is described as an increase in the *scale* of production, the phrase reflecting the implications of investment in plant and equipment. In the long run, a firm can adjust the quantities of all its factors of production to produce its desired level of output at the lowest possible cost. To achieve higher levels of output, a firm will need to buy more factors of production. How will costs change?

Figure 3.6
Long-run average cost (*LRAC*) curves.
(a) *LRAC* curve displaying increasing, constant and decreasing returns to scale;
(b) 'L'-shaped *LRAC* curve; and
(c) downward-sloping *LRAC* curve

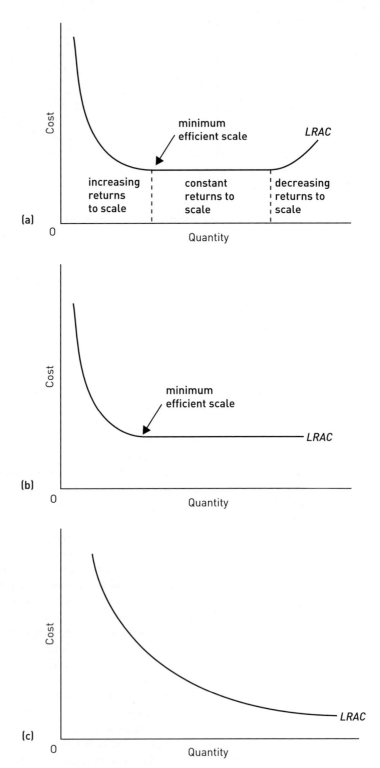

Figure 3.6 shows three possible shapes for the firm's long-run average cost (*LRAC*) curve. All three have a downward-sloping section: in (a) and (b) this occurs at low output levels; in (c) *LRAC* slopes down continuously over the whole output range. If the *LRAC* slopes downwards, the firm is benefiting from **increasing returns to scale or economies of scale** over the relevant range of output. We will use these two terms interchangeably. They imply that as output increases, long-run average costs fall.

Increasing returns to scale arise within the firm from the firm's production function. Increased output may allow a firm to use inputs more productively. If doubling all the firm's inputs more than doubles output, there are increasing returns to scale. This may be because there are economies of increased dimensions. For example, enormous oil tankers and very large lorries can transport goods at lower cost per unit than smaller ships and vehicles because their capacity rises faster than the materials needed to make and run them. Industrial plant displays the same effect: building a factory extension that doubles the output capacity of the firm may be possible without doubling the costs of using and maintaining it. Furthermore, larger scale may also allow the more efficient use of inputs through specialization of tasks that was described in Chapter 2, Section 2.2.2.

The firm may also benefit from economies of scale that arise from sources outside the firm. These are reductions in a firm's average costs arising from the expansion of the industry to which it belongs. For example, the first IT firms which located in what has become known as Silicon Valley in the USA – or in Silicon Fen as the area around Cambridge, UK, is sometimes called – gained economies of scale when the industry began to expand. The concentration of numerous, closely related high-tech companies in a single geographical area meant that highly specialized factors of production (e.g. computer technicians and silicon chips) were available to them more cheaply and easily than they were to firms located elsewhere.

Firms may find that there is a limit to the economies of scale that they can achieve, a situation shown in Figure 3.6(a). They will reach a level of output after which no further reductions in average cost can be obtained. This level of output is known as the **minimum efficient scale (MES)**. The MES marks the size of the firm beyond which there are no cost advantages to be reaped from operating at a larger scale; it is the point at which all economies of scale have been taken up. As Henry Ford's smaller rivals discovered, once large-scale assembly-line production had been developed serious cost disadvantages were incurred by a firm operating below the MES, where average cost is higher than it would be if all scale economies were to be exploited. The MES is located at the beginning of the flat section of the *LRAC* curve, over which average cost is constant in Figure 3.6(a). The firm is experiencing **constant returns to scale** over this range of output.

The *LRAC* curve depicted in Figure 3.6(a) rises at high levels of output. Average costs increase as output increases. The firm is now experiencing **decreasing returns to scale or diseconomies of scale**. Decreasing returns to scale or diseconomies of scale arise from the disadvantages that large-scale production may entail. The major source of diseconomies of scale is the co-ordination problems that beset management in large bureaucratic organizations. The rapid expansion of an industry may also cause external diseconomies of scale, if labour costs increase as more and more firms chase scarce supplies of specific skills. For example, firms in some 'new economy' industries find wages are being bid up because of a shortage of workers with the appropriate IT skills.

The 'U'-shaped *LRAC* curve shown in Figure 3.6(a) is only one of three possible shapes that are usually distinguished. If the technology of the industry in which the firm is active is different from that of another industry, this will be expressed in a different *LRAC* curve. In Figure 3.6(b) the *LRAC* curve is 'L'-shaped, indicating that the firm continues to experience constant returns to scale across its output range once output is above the MES. This

Increasing returns to scale/ economies of scale

Increasing returns to scale/economies of scale exist when long-run average cost falls as output increases.

Minimum efficient scale (MES)

Minimum efficient scale refers to the output at which long-run average costs first reach their minimum level as output rises.

Constant returns to scale

Constant returns to scale exist when long-run average cost remains unchanged as output increases.

Decreasing returns to scale/ diseconomies of scale

Decreasing returns to scale/ diseconomies of scale exist when long-run average cost rises as output increases.

might correspond to a firm that can continue to replicate its production processes, for example by adding additional assembly lines, each one exactly like the others.

A third possibility is depicted in Figure 3.6(c), where the firm enjoys economies of scale right across its output range. There is, therefore, every incentive, in the form of ever lower average costs, for firms to continue to expand output. A single firm can supply the whole market at a lower cost than could be achieved by a number of firms in competition with each other. Network industries such as gas, water and electricity distribution, fuel retailing, railway track and cable networks in telecommunications are examples of industries where firms are appropriately modelled by the *LRAC* curve shown in Figure 3.6(c) (see Chapter 4, Section 4.4.2).

The three *LRAC* curves in Figure 3.6, considered together, imply that the technology of an industry is expressed in the shape of the particular *LRAC* curve used in modelling that industry. There is a further implication, which is that technology, reflected in costs, shapes the structure of the industry. If, for the moment, the 'structure' of an industry is understood to mean the number and size of firms that are active in it, this point can be illustrated in a number of ways. You have already seen that the US automobile and PC industries experienced a 'shake-out' of small firms as product standardization enabled the exploitation of economies of scale.

In industries in which firms experience constant returns to scale there will be a minimum level of output, the MES, at which constant returns set in, that firms must be able to sustain if they are to remain competitive. The MES varies with the particular technologies characteristic of different industries. For many parts of the clothing, footwear and furniture industries, all economies of scale may be exploited at relatively low levels of output and so the MES is low relative to market size. By contrast, in industries such as automobiles and chemicals where economies of scale are available over much greater ranges of output, the MES is much higher in relation to the size of the market.

Question	What does this suggest to you about the number and size of firms in the clothing, footwear and furniture industries compared with those in automobiles and chemicals?

There are likely to be fewer but larger firms in the automobile and chemical industries compared with the clothing, footwear and furniture industries. In the former, the exploitation of economies of scale up to high output levels relative to market size leaves room for only a few large firms in the market. In the latter, increasing returns to scale are exhausted at lower output levels relative to market size so there is room for more firms. In automobiles and chemicals the model predicts greater pressure for mergers and acquisitions as firms seek to expand output by taking over rival firms.

The existence in some industries of a level of output beyond which decreasing returns are experienced sets a limit to the size of firms and hence to the pressure for mergers and acquisitions. In fact, decreasing returns to scale can lead to the break-up of very large firms so that management can focus on making the 'core' business more competitive. The break-up of the chemicals firm ICI into ICI and Zeneca in 1993 can be interpreted as an example of this kind of behaviour.

If increasing returns are available across the whole output range required to supply the market, this has dramatic implications for industry structure. A single producer can supply the entire market at a lower cost than two or more competing firms. This is because a single firm avoids the cost of duplicating distribution networks such as gas, water and electricity pipes, railway track and telecommunications cables; its consequences for consumers are discussed in Chapter 4.

Figure 3.7
A downward shift in
the *LRAC* curve

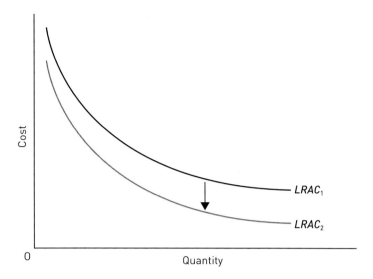

The technology of an industry, expressed in the shape of the *LRAC* curve of its firms, is therefore a major influence on the structure of that industry. However, in modelling firms' costs in the short run and the long run, it has been assumed that firms are operating with given technology. It is now appropriate to relax this assumption and investigate the role of technological change in shaping industrial structure.

As Section 3.3.1 explained, a firm's production function embodies its technology. The model assumes that technology is given and is available to all firms in an industry. We can therefore think of technological change as a change in each firm's production function. Particular input combinations now become more productive, producing more output. What effect does this have on the long-run average cost curve?

The *LRAC* curves in Figure 3.6 were drawn on the assumption of given technology. Technological change can therefore be understood as a *shift* in the average cost curve. Figure 3.7 shows a downward shift in an *LRAC* curve like that shown in Figure 3.6(c). The shift of $LRAC_1$ downward to $LRAC_2$ in Figure 3.7 shows that long-run average costs have fallen at each and every level of output, or scale of production.

Technological change may not affect average costs at all levels of output. Henry Ford's introduction of moving assembly-line production methods is an example of a technological change that changed the shape of the *LRAC* curve for firms in the industry, shifting it downwards at high levels of output. The new methods hugely extended the range of output over which firms could benefit from increasing returns to scale. In this way, technological change, and its associated cost changes, exert a major influence on industrial structure. We explore this further in Section 3.4.

Exercise 3.2

A revision exercise before you move on.

1 Explain the meanings of the concepts listed below and how the items in each pair of concepts are related:
   (a) increasing and diminishing returns to a factor of production
   (b) economies of scale and increasing returns to scale
   (c) decreasing returns to scale and diseconomies of scale.
2 Why do short-run average costs differ from long-run average costs?

3.4 Technological change and industrial structure

This section will explore the interaction of technology and costs with market demand in shaping industrial structure throughout the industry life cycle. Many industries begin as a numerous and turbulent group of firms jostling for position, experimenting with new and idiosyncratic products, and turn into a much smaller, more stable number of firms, making standardized products by routine methods. In this section we add a rather different view of firms to that developed in Section 3.3, modelling firms as dynamic agents engaged in a learning process and an active search for technological innovation. The term 'dynamic' signifies that the model constructs firms and industries as acting and undergoing change in historical time. The technology available to firms is no longer being assumed to be given from outside the firm. The industry life cycle, outlined in Section 3.4.1, provides a theoretical framework for identifying general patterns of structural change across different industries. Section 3.4.2 discusses some additional concepts used in modelling the dynamics of industrial structure.

▪ ▪ ▪ 3.4.1 The industry life cycle

The model of the industry life cycle outlined in Chapter 2 represents an industry as if it were a biological organism going through the stages of birth, growth, maturity and decline. This helps us to understand how a particular firm can become the 'leader of the pack' through innovation. In Section 3.2 it was explained that an economic model is a deliberate simplification of the world, which helps to provide a systematic way of thinking about causal relationships. The industry life cycle is a rather different type of model. The aim is still to provide a systematic way of thinking about economic activity but not by analysing particular interactions between variables. The industry life cycle is instead a systematic way of thinking about general patterns of structural change across different industries. In this sense, the industry life cycle is an 'ideal type', enabling us to bring order to the complexity of historical events by classifying them as belonging to this or that phase of an identified pattern of industrial change.

The industry life cycle models industries as following a similar pattern of development as industry output changes, moving from many small and different firms to a few large and similar firms. This change in industrial structure is driven by the interplay between consumer demand and technology throughout the industry life cycle. Section 3.2 examined some of the influences on market demand and the particular importance of price. In fact, price and non-price factors are of varying importance at different phases of the life cycle. Section 3.3 analysed the firm's *SRAC* and *LRAC* curves, which reflect the technology available to the firm. Costs are of crucial importance to the firm at each phase of the industry life cycle but firms are driven to focus on costs in different ways at different phases.

The model of the industry life cycle is depicted in Figure 3.8. The curved line traces how the total output of a typical industry changes over time. In this diagram, the total output of the industry is measured along the vertical axis. The horizontal axis shows the passage of time.

The introductory phase is characterized by *product innovation*, that is, the introduction of novel products for which there are no close substitutes. At this stage the scale of production is low, costs are high and demand for the new industry's products is limited to relatively few consumers. There will be considerable variety among firms in the industry, ranging from small firms that are as new as the industry to large firms with established products in other industries that are diversifying into the new one. Some firms will have entered the industry

Figure 3.8
The industry life cycle

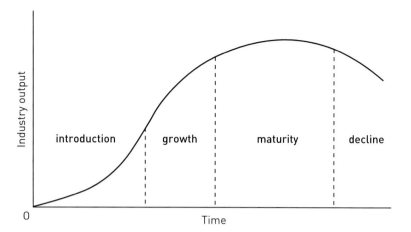

right at the start, while others enter more gradually as the profit opportunities created by the original 'pioneers' become clear. This 'heterogeneity' among firms, that is, their variety, will be reflected in differences in the technology they use and hence in the costs that they face. Hence technology is no longer understood as 'given' and common to all. The experimental nature of production at this stage favours firms that can learn quickly and are therefore able to be more flexible and better able to adjust output rapidly in response to changing conditions. In the introductory phase of the industry life cycle, production is a risky business and firms cannot be sure that their product is exactly what consumers want.

You can see, in Figure 3.8, that, as the industry moves from the introductory phase into the growth phase, the size of the industry, measured in terms of its output, increases. Firms will be able to exploit economies of scale. There is, however, a condition. The selection of 35 mm SLR film cameras and digital cameras shown in Figure 3.9 holds a clue about the condition for achieving economies of scale.

Question	What do you think is the main difference between the appearance of the 35 mm SLR film cameras and that of the digital cameras in Figure 3.9?

There is considerable variety among the digital cameras. At first glance the Fuji Finepix 6800 resembles a hand-held computer; the Fuji Finepix 40i looks to us like a portable CD player and is in fact an MP3 player as well as a digital camera; and the Nikon Coolpix 950 is perhaps too radical a design to be mistaken for anything else. On the other hand, the Fuji Finepix 4900 looks much more like a 35 mm SLR film camera. This variety and sense of experiment is consistent with the digital camera industry being in its introductory phase. Manufacturers seem undecided whether a digital camera should look like a computer with a lens or a camera with some data-processing software. By contrast, it seems to us that the 35 mm SLR cameras are remarkably similar in appearance and they are also similar in technical specification. Standardization is evidently lacking among digital cameras. Product standardization is symptomatic of a move to the growth phase of the industry life cycle. Once firms have standardized the product, they can also standardize the manufacturing process and move to production on a large scale.

Question	What advantages will this move to production on a large scale confer on firms in the growth phase of the industry life cycle?

Figure 3.9
A selection of 35 mm SLR film cameras and digital cameras

Source: *What Camera?*, winter 2001, pp.17–24, 47, 48

Film cameras

Digital cameras

The advantages of large-scale production, summed up in the concept of economies of scale, or increasing returns to scale (Section 3.3.2), generate a revolution in industrial structure once the expansion of demand gets under way. On the supply side, increasing returns to scale at the growth stage of the cycle can be exploited by the largest and most efficient firms as they compete and survive. Those firms that have failed to keep pace with changing opportunities exit from the industry; that is, a 'shake-out' takes place. This contraction in the number of firms means that the industry exhibits a greater degree of concentration as a few large firms dominate the industry. If you look back at Chapter 2, Figure 2.4 you can see that from 1909 to the mid 1920s the number of firms in the US automobile industry fell from 271 to approximately 50 and the number of firms in the US PC industry showed an equally dramatic decline during the years from 1973 to 1999.

How might this be explained? On the demand side, the fall in average costs resulting from increasing returns makes it possible for the firm to reduce the price it charges for the new product. This sequence of events was encountered in the extract from *The Economist*'s survey of the new economy at the beginning of Section 3.1. The suggestion was that new technologies are a major cause of the decline in costs and hence in prices that enables large numbers of consumers to buy safer cars, personal computers and so on. In terms of the model of market demand explained in Section 3.2, the fall in price leads to a movement along the market demand curve, bringing the product into the range of many more consumers. This is reinforced by a shift in the market demand curve caused by a change in socio-economic influences, in particular the demonstration effect that describes the tendency of people to imitate the consumption decisions of those who have already bought the product (Section 3.2.2).

The phase of maturity is reached as the market approaches saturation and replacement demand becomes important. By now there are many similar products for consumers to choose from, as they replace their first car or washing machine – or 35 mm SLR camera – and price exerts a major influence on demand. By the mature phase, the product has become well established and most of the consumers who would like one have already acquired it. The quantity demanded is therefore relatively stable and this is reflected in a flattening of the curve in Figure 3.8. Firms now have to work hard to reach those consumers who still have not bought the product and to create a demand for replacement purchases. The UK domestic appliance industry provides a good example of this phase. Most of the consumers wanting to own a refrigerator now have one and so the main source of market demand lies with consumers setting up home for the first time, and those needing to replace old equipment. Since there are plenty of very similar products available, price is a key determinant in deciding which one to buy.

On the supply side the focus of the firm's attention therefore shifts to *process innovation* aimed at securing reductions in the average cost of production. For example, Henry Ford found that the way to drive down costs is through the introduction of innovative new manufacturing processes. The firm that fails to innovate and to adopt industry best-practice technologies of production soon finds that it cannot compete with the lower prices offered by its rivals and is forced to exit the industry. In these circumstances the aim of investment may be to enable a firm to 'catch up' with its competitors by introducing the best available technology already in use elsewhere. A good example of this is provided by the German car manufacturer BMW when it took over the Longbridge car plant in the UK. BMW brought the factory up to date with the technologically advanced methods of car production introduced into the UK when the Japanese firms Nissan and Toyota set up new factories near Sunderland and Derby respectively.

Finally, the industry enters into decline when new industries with new products embodying superior technology render the old industry's products obsolete. This phase may be brought on by further product innovation giving rise to a new industry with its own introductory phase so that radically new products replace the obsolete ones. For example, the development of synthetic materials in the 1960s meant that a wide range of industries using 'natural' materials went into decline. Some of the firms in these industries, such as carpet manufacturers, were able to draw on the new materials to reinvent their products, but others disappeared altogether as demand for their products dissolved.

Each stage of the model of the industry life cycle presented above is fixed and distinct. In reality, the boundaries between stages in the development of an industry are blurred and can be difficult to observe in a short time horizon. The length of the life cycle also varies with the extent to which the products it makes can be reinvented. The personal stereo industry offers an example. By the 1980s, many consumers already owned a personal stereo that played audio-cassettes. With the arrival of new technologies for recording music on CDs, consumers shifted from cassettes to CDs in order to benefit from better recording quality. This stimulated a replacement demand for personal stereos that could play CDs, extending the life cycle of the personal stereo industry.

■ ■ ■ 3.4.2   Industrial dynamics: knowledge and network industries

This final subsection introduces two more concepts that develop further our analysis of the dynamics of industrial structure, with particular reference to the 'new economy' industries. A dynamic approach to industrial change places considerable emphasis on innovation and learning, seeing firms as actively searching out innovative products and processes and learning how to produce and sell them. Some of the novelty of the new economy is reflected in the concepts used in trying to understand it, which are applied here to a brief analysis of network industries.

Knowledge and learning in the industry life cycle

In Section 3.3 we described technology as 'given' to firms. Now let us reflect on that idea. We can think of technology as consisting in bodies of knowledge necessary to produce artefacts. An appreciation of the importance of knowledge to economic activity is not new, for it was recognized by the eminent economist Alfred Marshall, who wrote that 'Capital consists in a great part of knowledge and organisation' (Marshall, 1925, p.138). What Marshall meant can perhaps best be understood by considering two 'thought experiments' broadly similar to those conducted by the philosopher Sir Karl Popper. In the first, all human artefacts, and hence all capital equipment, are wiped out in an extraordinary natural disaster. Human beings survive unharmed and set about constructing their capital stock, and other artefacts, all over again. This is an immense task but in a decade or so the job is done. In the second thought experiment we imagine once again that all capital equipment is destroyed. The difference is that this time human knowledge is also lost. All memories of how to build lathes, computers, robots, cars, combine harvesters and all the other machines the human race has ever invented are annihilated and so too are all the skills acquired in learning how to use them. The human race effectively returns to a much earlier period in its evolution when the capital stock consisted perhaps of stone tools. Even supposing that history repeats itself and people eventually reinvent the technologies leading up to the capital stock of twenty-first century humanity, it would take thousands of years to get back to where we were. The hardware is important but it is human knowledge that really matters. Learning how to use the hardware most effectively is therefore a crucial capacity for firms.

The 'learning curve' captures the idea that turning technological change to competitive advantage is a skill that has to be learned like any other. Figure 3.10 depicts this idea. It shows a fall in average cost that occurs as learning takes place over time after the firm starts up in production. This figure looks rather like the *LRAC* curve in Figure 3.6(c) but depicts a different relationship between output and costs. The horizontal axis, labelled

Figure 3.10
A learning curve

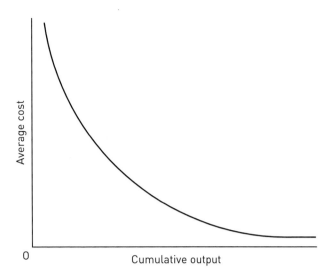

'cumulative output', shows the output a firm produces each year *added together* over time. This contrasts with the *SRAC* and *LRAC* diagrams in Section 3.3, where output was measured per time period, such as a year, and the diagrams picture the firm's costs at any given output per year. In Figure 3.6, a firm might move left or right, depending on its output decisions for the year. However, in Figure 3.10 you should think of the firm as moving rightwards over time, since each year it continues in business cumulative output will necessarily increase.

Learning-by-doing

Learning-by-doing refers to a fall in unit costs and cumulative output increases.

When a firm benefits from **learning-by-doing**, it is said to be 'moving along the learning curve' or gaining from 'experience effects'. Imagine that the production process involves the use of a new machine. When a worker first starts to operate the machine, lack of familiarity means that mistakes are made and progress is slow. However, the worker learns from these mistakes and as the hours spent operating the machine increase, productivity improves, that is, more units of output are produced per unit of input. The more cumulative output is produced, the more efficiently it is produced. The cost of producing a unit of output therefore declines as cumulative output increases, as Figure 3.10 shows.

Learning effects are not confined to assembly-line tasks but can occur throughout the firm wherever repetition gives rise to experience. Their significance in the industry life cycle is greatest when firms are learning how to use new technology. This occurs both in the introductory phase, as firms experiment with new products, and in the mature phase, as firms learn how to use new processes to improve the manufacture of a standard product. As the point is reached when all the cost savings derived from experience have been extracted, there is a flattening of the learning curve (Figure 3.10). From then on the firm diverts its attention to other ways of reducing its costs as a means of gaining an advantage over rivals.

A firm's capacity for learning how to use new technology depends in part on whether innovations build on its existing strengths or render them obsolete. Many historical studies have documented how technological change (process or product innovation) does not evolve in a continuous and smooth manner but discontinuously. A long period of incremental change may be punctuated by episodes of radical change. These discontinuities that are introduced by technological innovation can be classified as either 'competence enhancing' or 'competence destroying' (Tushman and Anderson, 1986).

To understand this, we need to recognize that once we allow firms to learn and innovate individually, we have moved away from the model of the firm presented in Section 3.3.

That section modelled a 'representative' firm among very similar firms. Once firms can learn, we move away from this approach, towards modelling firms as diverse organizations that develop distinct capabilities or competencies over time (Chapter 4 develops this idea further). Competence-enhancing innovations are innovations that develop new products, or improvements to existing products, which build on a firm's existing competence and strengthen its market position. This cumulative 'success begets success' dynamic causes the market structure to become more concentrated, stable and less friendly for new firms:

> Existing firms within an industry are in the best position to initiate and exploit new possibilities opened up by a discontinuity if it builds on competencies they already possess . . . the rich are likely to get richer.
>
> *(Tushman and Anderson, 1986, p.444)*

Competence-destroying innovations have the opposite effect. They develop new products or changes in existing products which require completely new skills and knowledge to be developed. These innovations disrupt industry structure, rendering current capabilities obsolete. Existing firms, set in the old way of doing things, are often not quick or ready enough to adapt to this radical change, allowing new flexible firms (not always small) to enter, remaking industry structure – and perhaps starting a whole new life cycle. Innovation can therefore either stabilize or destabilize industrial structure.

Network externalities and increasing returns to scale

> The reader should ask herself the following question: Would I subscribe to a telephone service knowing that nobody else subscribes to a telephone service?
> The answer should be: Of course not! What use will anyone have from having a telephone when there is no one to talk to?
>
> *(Shy, 2001, p.3)*

Network externalities

Network externalities arise when the value to one consumer of joining a network depends on the number of other consumers joining the network.

The uncertainty surrounding production in the introductory phase, which places such importance on the ability of the firm to secure quick benefits from learning effects, is particularly acute in 'network industries', such as telecommunications, computers, video players, banking services, fuel retailing and many others. On the demand side, the example of a telephone service shows that the benefit (or 'utility', see Chapter 8) that people get from consuming such goods depends on the extent to which other people also use these goods. These goods are said to display **network externalities**, because the value one consumer gets from, say, a telephone depends on factors external to their own consumption of it. The idea of externalities is widely used in economics (see Chapter 9). Network externalities (which can also be referred to as 'network effects') thus 'arise when the attractiveness of a product to customers increases with the use of that product by others' (Fisher and Rubinfeld, 2000, p.13). The more people who subscribe to the same standardized system, the more services and people the user can access, and so the greater the value of that system to each individual user. The implication is that firms that are in the introductory phase of a network industry life cycle face huge rewards from establishing an early lead for their product. Even if competing products have more useful features, the product with the largest network will be difficult to dislodge simply because the number of its subscribers make it the most attractive option for new subscribers.

On the supply side there is considerable scope for the firm with the largest network to achieve increasing returns to scale. The firm faces the cost of developing and maintaining a single network, and that cost can be spread over a large and rising quantity of output, reducing average cost (*AC*). The industry life cycle models the transition to the growth phase as depending in part on product standardization (Section 3.4.1). A stronger version of standardization is present in network industries. The cost advantages are particularly dramatic for a firm that can establish its own network, or a technical component essential to the functioning of a network, as the industry standard.

Network industries have in common a number of characteristics including *complementarity*, *compatibility* and *standards* (Shy, 2001, pp.1–3). A network industry produces complements, such as trains and railway tracks, cameras and film, computers and software, CD players and CDs, and cars and fuel. These complementary products must be compatible with one another in the sense that trains are no use unless they fit the tracks, film is needed if you want to use a film camera and so on. In other words, complementary products must operate on the same standard. For example, in the nineteenth century it was impossible for regional railway companies in the UK to run rolling stock on each other's tracks until a national gauge or width was established. This gauge is an example of an industry standard. Without a standard gauge or film size or computer operating system, product standardization cannot take place and economies of scale are unobtainable. Establishing an industry standard may involve a struggle between competing would-be standards. When video players were first introduced in the 1980s, two different recording formats appeared on the market, VHS and Betamax. It was some years before VHS was established as the industry standard.

Case study: BMW wants to make internal-combustion engines that run on hydrogen

One way that global warming might be reduced is by powering cars with something that does not release carbon dioxide when it is burned. That is part of the idea behind a 'hydrogen economy' – a future in which hydrogen, which can be produced from renewable sources, takes over from hydrocarbons as the world's principal fuel.

Several of the world's car makers – notably Ford, DaimlerChrysler and Honda – are studying fuel cells. These react hydrogen and oxygen together to produce electricity. Fuel cells certainly work but they are still some years from commercial viability in cars. There is, however, an alternative: burn the hydrogen in a conventional internal-combustion engine. And that is what BMW proposes to do.

Converting an engine to run on hydrogen is relatively simple. There are, however, two catches. The first is that fuel cells are a far more efficient way to use hydrogen than burning it ·

in a conventional engine. The second is that, gram for gram, hydrogen contains significantly less energy than petrol. Performance will reflect that, unless those clever engineers at BMW can somehow overcome the difference. If they cannot, then BMW, whose prestige and independence rely largely on its engine-making ability, may be in trouble. Were fuel cells to become the standard, the firm's future could be bleak.

(Adapted from The Economist, *21 July 2001, p.86)*

Question

This case study describes the situation facing car manufacturers as they develop new technology for the 'hydrogen economy' of the future. How does BMW's decision to use hydrogen in an internal-combustion engine illustrate the uncertainties confronting firms in network industries in the introductory phase of the industry life cycle?

The new network industry in this case is hydrogen fuel production and retailing. A means of propulsion, such as an internal-combustion engine or a fuel cell, and a fuel, such as petrol or hydrogen, are complementary goods. The means of propulsion and the fuel must be compatible, in the sense that a conventional internal-combustion engine is compatible with petrol and a fuel cell with hydrogen. The industry can progress to the next phase of the life cycle only if an industry standard can be agreed upon. There seems to be a consensus that hydrogen will become the standard fuel. Beyond that, however, there is uncertainty. Ford, DaimlerChrysler and Honda are investing in fuel cell technology in the belief that it will become the industry standard in the 'hydrogen economy', while BMW take the view that the internal-combustion engine will retain that position in the new circumstances. The industry dilemma highlights the role of technological change in shaping industrial structure. If BMW have 'backed a loser' and invested in a technology that fails to become the industry standard, they may, as the case study suggests, lose their independence. The number of firms in the industry will decrease if BMW's destiny is to fail, as part of the process by which technological change shapes a new industrial structure.

Network externalities on the demand side and increasing returns on the supply side may interact in what is colloquially termed a 'double whammy' to produce a dramatically different industrial structure as an industry moves into the growth phase. A firm that benefits from such a double whammy will secure monopoly power in its industry. The economic analysis of monopoly power is the subject of Chapter 4.

3.5 Conclusion

The idea of the double whammy brings together the two driving forces behind changes in industrial structure, with which the chapter opened and now closes. The use of a new technology causes a decline in the costs of production, which in turn encourages a rapid take-up by consumers of products embodying the new technology. The chapter has explored the factors affecting consumer demand. While the price of the product was found to be of crucial importance, socio-economic influences such as culture and identity were seen to have an important role to play, especially in the introductory phase of the industry life cycle. Chapter 8 will explain the foundations of consumer demand with an account of utility theory and its role in understanding individual choice and equilibrium.

On the supply side the firm's cost curves reflect the technology it uses to produce goods and services. An analysis of cost curves showed the constraints imposed by technology on the firm's development and how technological change creates new opportunities. Technology is ultimately a matter of knowledge and technological change can best be modelled in dynamic terms, as firms search creatively for new products and processes and learn how to make and employ them.

In the network industries, prominent in the new economy, the demand- and supply-side factors interact in particularly striking ways. Network externalities and industry standards combine to push the industry from a turbulent crowd of heterogeneous firms to a small number of similar firms. In Chapter 4 we put together the analysis of demand, costs and technology into a study of firms' decision-making and of the behaviour of firms in industries where one firm is big enough to wield monopoly power.

Questions for review and discussion

Question 1 Complete the following sentences by selecting the correct word or phrase from the list below to fill in the spaces:

Independent   dependent   positive   negative   Giffen   Veblen
slope downwards from left to right   slope upwards from left to right
are horizontal   are vertical   are indeterminate

A market demand curve shows the relationship between quantity demanded (the . . . variable) and price (the . . . variable). According to the 'law of demand', this relationship will be a . . . one. Some luxury goods called . . . goods, and some very basic goods, called . . . goods, are exceptions to the 'law of demand', and their market demand curves . . .

Question 2 Figure 3.11 shows a hypothetical demand curve for cartridge pens. Draw a shift in the curve leftwards or rightwards as appropriate to illustrate the likely effect of each of the following:

(a) An increase in the price of fibre-tipped pens
(b) An increase in the price of ink cartridges

Figure 3.11
Hypothetical
demand curve for
cartridge pens

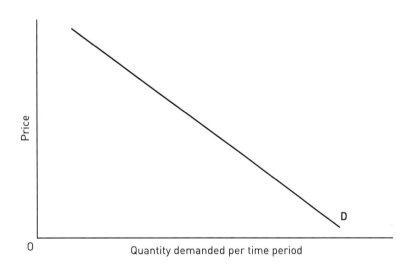

Question 3 Say which is the most appropriate phrase to complete the sentence below:

A firm is operating in the short run when

A ❑ It cannot change the quantity it uses of any of the factors of production, so some inputs are being wasted.
B ❑ It is suffering diminishing returns to its fixed and variable factors.
C ❑ There is not sufficient time for it to raise its output.
D ❑ It cannot change the quantity it uses of at least one of its factor inputs.

Question 4 Figure 3.12 shows a short-run average cost curve for a firm. Select *two* statements from the list below. The statement you mark '1' should state what happens as output rises from Q_1 to Q_2. The statement you mark '2' should state what happens as output rises from Q_2 to Q_3.

Note: 'average' means 'per unit of output'.

A ❏ Average fixed cost falls, average variable cost falls then rises.
B ❏ Falling average variable cost outweighs rising average fixed cost.
C ❏ There are diminishing returns to the variable factors throughout.
D ❏ Average fixed cost and average variable cost both rise.
E ❏ There are increasing returns to the variable factors throughout.

Figure 3.12
Short-run average
cost curve

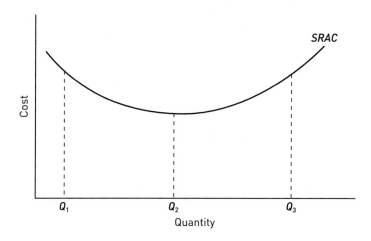

Questions 5 Figure 3.13 shows long-run average cost curves for two firms, A and B, each in a different industry. Select from the list of statements below the one that is consistent with what is shown in the diagram.

A ❏ Firm A attains minimum efficient scale (MES) at a lower level of output than Firm B.
B ❏ Both firms experience diseconomies of scale at the highest levels of output shown.
C ❏ Firm A operates in an industry where there is great pressure to expand output, for example by merger.
D ❏ Firm B has higher fixed costs than Firm A.

Figure 3.13
Long-run average
cost curve

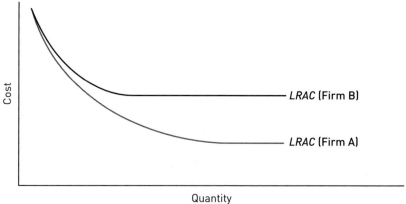

Question 6   Figure 3.14 shows a learning curve for a firm. The curve is similar in shape to a long-run average cost (*LRAC*) curve, but the relationship it depicts is different. Select from the list below the *three* statements that correctly identify differences between curves of these two kinds:

A ❑ The horizontal axis of the learning curve shows cumulative output; that of the *LRAC* curve shows output per time period.

B ❑ The costs shown by the learning curve exclude capital costs; those shown by the *LRAC* curve include capital costs.

C ❑ The firm moves rightwards along its learning curve over time; the firm may move leftwards or rightwards along its *LRAC* curve.

D ❑ At some points on the learning curve, factor inputs are being wasted owing to mistakes and inexperience; at all points on the *LRAC* curve, the firm uses all inputs to their full potential and there is no waste.

Figure 3.14
Learning curve

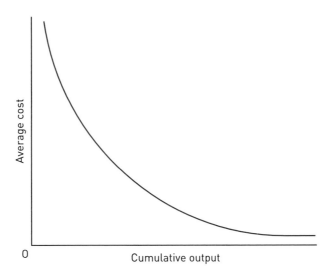

Question 7   Complete the following sentences by selecting words or phrases from the list below.

Representative   competence-enhancing   mature   distinct competencies
competence-destroying   manufacturing   network   reproduce competencies

In analysing the costs, technology and output of firms, we can use a model of a . . . firm. But when thinking about innovation, we need to model firms as diverse organizations that develop . . .

. . . innovations tend to cause market structure to become more concentrated. The need to secure quick benefits from learning effects is particularly acute in . . . industries.

Question 8   The table below gives information about a firm's costs in the short and long run.

	Output (000s)					
	1	2	3	4	5	6
Short-run average cost (£)	18	9	9	11	14	14
Long-run average cost (£)	18	6	5	5	5	6

(a) Draw a diagram showing each of the above curves and explain briefly what distinguishes the short run from the long run.

(b) With reference to the diagram, explain how (i) diminishing returns and (ii) diseconomies of scale affect the production costs of a firm.

(c) With reference to the diagram, give an example of a change which can cause (i) a movement along the long-run curve and (ii) a shift of the long-run curve.

Question 9   Essay: Using examples, explain how network externalities and economies of scale interact to determine industrial structure.

4

Monopoly power and innovation

Neil Costello and Maureen Mackintosh

Concepts

- the firm's demand curve
- average and marginal revenue
- marginal cost, average cost and total cost
- profit maximization
- price elasticity of demand
- a firm's capabilities or competencies
- barriers to entry and contestability of a market

Objectives

After studying this chapter you should be able to:

- understand, and apply to cases, economic models of pure monopoly and monopolistic competition
- explain how monopoly power may be sustained over time and how it may be undermined by competition
- examine the relationships between monopoly power and innovation
- discuss some implications for competition policy of high rates of innovation.

4.1 Monopoly, innovation and competition

Case study: Breaking up Microsoft?

It was an interesting week for the 'New Economy'. On Monday, federal Judge Thomas Penfield Jackson declared that Microsoft had violated the antitrust laws by engaging in predatory tactics that discouraged technological competition. On Wednesday, the White House staged a conference that credited the New Economy's technological advances for raising living standards . . . Connections and contradictions here beg to be explored.

Among the panelists at the White House conference was Microsoft Chairman Bill Gates. Presumably, he was not invited because he is a corporate thug, which is – by inference – how Jackson depicted him. What are we to think of Gates? A larger contradiction looms. If Microsoft is such an anticompetitive monster, how has the New Economy become (at least by reputation) so competitive that it raises efficiency and lowers inflation? . . .

Case study continued

Because Microsoft's operating systems (Windows and its offspring) control roughly 90 percent of personal computers, it's hard to separate the company from this larger transformation [of the economy]. Microsoft's central contribution was (and is) standardization. This meant that applications programs – from spreadsheets to photo processing – didn't have to be written for multitudes of operating systems. Software markets expanded, so writing programs became more profitable. Computer networks could be more easily constructed. People who learned computer skills at one company wouldn't lose them by moving elsewhere . . .

The question posed by the Microsoft case is whether antitrust laws can cope with technological competition. When Congress passed the Sherman Antitrust Act – under which Microsoft was convicted – in 1890, the evils of monopoly power seemed obvious. A monopolist might restrict supply and prop up prices. Competitors might conspire to do the same thing. Competition meant price competition; the antitrust laws aimed to preserve it.

But today's most significant competition doesn't involve identical products sparring over price. It involves rival technologies struggling for superiority. Cable TV competes against satellite TV. Wireless communication competes with land lines. The Linux operating system is beginning to challenge Windows. For most technologies, standards are vital. Without them, mass markets are impossible. Sometimes standards arise by voluntary agreements among firms; sometimes they result from the triumph of one or a few firms. The check on this dominance – if there is a check – is the threat of a new technology.

Source: Robert J. Samuelson, Washington Post,
11 April 2000

Question

Why was the United States government trying to break up one of the most successful companies in the world?

Microsoft was at the time one of the world's largest firms. In its financial year to June 2000 it had net income of US$9.42 billion and in July 2001 employed nearly 44 000 people worldwide. It claimed to be 'Building on the popularity of the Windows operating system and the Office productivity suite, [and] on developing technology for the next-generation Internet' (www.microsoft.com, 6 July 2001).

The US 'antitrust' authorities – what in Europe are called the competition authorities – took the opposite view, arguing in court that Microsoft was misusing its dominance in computer operating systems to try to become dominant in the market for Internet browsers. Judge Thomas Penfield Jackson recommended that Microsoft should be broken up into two companies. Microsoft immediately launched an appeal.

A number of the themes of this chapter and this part are raised in the *Washington Post*'s commentary on these events. Microsoft, a big winner in the consolidation of the computing industry, is a firm with great monopoly power; that is, it can greatly influence a whole market by its behaviour. The Microsoft court case turned on the effects of its monopoly power: was it developing its products to the benefit of users, the industry and the economy, or was it merely defending its own huge profits by blocking beneficial competition and innovation?

Journalists, government agencies, firms and judges draw on economic theory in trying to answer questions like that; in this chapter you will study some of those theories. The central theme of the chapter is the interaction of monopoly power with competition, especially competition through innovation.

Figure 4.1
The *New Yorker*
pictures the
proposed break-up
of Microsoft

Question	Look back at the *Washington Post* commentary. It contrasts two kinds of competition. What are they?

Robert Samuelson contrasts 'technological competition' – what we call competition through innovation – with 'price competition'. Price competition occurs when firms gain customers by selling goods more cheaply than their competitors. Competition through innovation occurs when firms introduce new products and improve old ones. The distinction between them is not quite as sharp as the article seems to suggest: as Chapter 3 showed, innovation can also reduce costs and allow firms to lower prices and increase their market share.

In this chapter we look more closely at how firms compete for monopoly power, how they behave when they have it, and how market dominance is undermined. Section 4.2 defines monopoly power in terms of the demand for a firm's products. Section 4.3 builds up, based on the analysis of costs in Chapter 3, the economic model of 'pure monopoly' that is frequently employed by governments attacking monopoly power. Section 4.4 turns to competition between firms with monopoly power, and the ways in which dominant firms fight to sustain market dominance. Section 4.5 analyses innovation as a competitive weapon of market dominance, and introduces an alternative economic model of the firm that pays attention to firms' internal organization and capabilities. Section 4.6 pulls together some implications of these theories for the Microsoft case and for the general issue of appropriate government policy towards big powerful companies in innovative market contexts.

4.2 Monopoly power and the firm's revenues

■ ■ ■ 4.2.1 Pure monopoly and monopoly power

The extent to which a firm can exercise influence over its market – as Microsoft clearly did at the time of the court case discussed in the *Washington Post* – depends both on the nature of the demand for its products and on the kind of competition it faces in that market. This section and the next introduce some economic theory that gives a rather precise meaning to those statements, and hence helps us to begin to define and assess the extent of a firm's monopoly power.

In Sections 4.2 and 4.3 we analyse the decisions a firm will make in an economic model of a firm and a market. Some basic elements of this model were introduced in Chapter 3: market demand for a product, a firm's costs and market price. Economic models that simplify markets and firms right down to interactions of demand, costs and price can, as we hope to show, produce strong results that are influential in policy making.

However, these models do contain a rather 'transparent' notion of a firm, reducing it, as Graham Dawson and Judith Mehta explained in Chapter 3, Section 3.3.1, to a set of specified relationships between inputs and outputs. In the simplest versions of these models, with which we begin, firms compete solely on the basis of price. The models can also be used, as in Sections 4.4 and 4.5, to analyse competition through innovation and what the *Washington Post* called, above, 'predatory' behaviour. However, the models seem to miss something: they offer little understanding of why particular firms, propelled by large personalities such as Bill Gates, are so successful in pursuing monopoly power. Chapter 3, Section 3.4 introduced models that help us to understand how a particular firm can gain an advantage over its competitors through innovation. Section 4.5 builds on these models to analyse the role of individual entrepreneurs and the organizational basis for particular firms' competitive success.

Monopoly power or market power

A firm has monopoly power (market power) if it has some choice in setting the price of its product and its decision about how much to supply influences the price it can charge.

Economic models of the interaction of demand, costs and price give us a clear initial definition of **monopoly power or market power**. These two terms are often used interchangeably, and will be throughout this text. A firm with monopoly power (market power) has some influence over its market; in particular it has some discretion about the price it charges for its product. Firms are particularly likely to exercise such monopoly power if they are large relative to the size of the market as a whole. That is, firms in relatively concentrated industries can be expected to have more monopoly power than firms in industries that contain many small firms.

Question | You met the concept of industry structure in Chapter 2, Section 2.4.5. Look back at that now. What are the two ways of measuring industry structure?

Industry structure can be measured in terms of the number of firms in an industry or in terms of the market share of the largest firms expressed as a percentage of total industry production. The smaller the number of firms or the greater the market share of a few large firms in an industry, the greater the degree of industrial concentration. The most extreme concentration – hence on this measure the greatest market power – occurs when a single firm supplies the whole market. This is called a **pure monopoly**.

Pure monopoly

A pure monopoly exists when a single firm is the sole supplier in a market.

Chapter 3, Section 3.2 discussed some of the difficulties of defining 'industry' and 'market'. For the purposes of this chapter, we are going to assume that each industry, composed of one or more firms, supplies a single market. This means that a 'pure monopoly' is therefore both the sole firm in an industry and the sole supplier to its market.

Question Look back at the *Washington Post*'s commentary on Microsoft in 2000. Did the firm fit the definition of a pure monopoly?

Microsoft held in 2000 something close to a pure monopoly in the market for Intel-compatible operating systems for personal computers: around 90 per cent of sales worldwide. Personal computer (PC) manufacturers, the most important direct customers for operating systems, testified at Microsoft's trial that they believed there were no reasonable substitutes: they had to buy and install Windows (Fisher and Rubinfeld, 2000).

■ ■ ■ 4.2.2 The demand curve of a firm with monopoly power

We now look in more detail at the way demand conditions influence market power. Graham Dawson and Judith Mehta introduced the market demand curve for a good or service in Chapter 3, Section 3.2.1. They explained that this is a model of the relationship between quantity demanded by consumers of a particular good and the market price of that good. If all other influences on demand are held constant, then normally quantity demanded will rise as price falls.

Question Can you draw a market demand curve and distinguish the causes of movements along the curve from the causes of shifts in the curve? If not, revise Chapter 3, Section 3.2 before reading on.

The demand curve for the output of a pure monopolist is the market demand curve, since the firm has the market to itself. However, most firms do not have a market to themselves, not even Microsoft: only some of the market demand is typically demand for a particular firm's product. If a market is supplied by several firms with market power, then each firm faces a downward-sloping demand curve for its product.

In markets for many familiar products, each firm develops a specific profile or 'brand' for its product, to differentiate it from competing products and attract customers. Kellogg's, for example, promotes its breakfast cereals as distinctively different to those of other companies, and is at pains to point out that it does not provide breakfast cereals under 'own label' brands for supermarket chains. One of the company's advertising slogans has been 'if it doesn't say Kellogg's on the box, it isn't Kellogg's in the box'; the implication is that its products are superior in some way. This is known as *product differentiation*.

Question Try to think of some more examples of product differentiation before reading on.

Product differentiation is characteristic of markets where the products are broadly similar and a firm wants to make sure that its own product is easily recognized by consumers. Examples include detergents, cigarettes, soft drinks, instant coffee and petrol. In all of these markets the products are seen by consumers as quite close substitutes, but not identical. For example, if Kellogg's put its prices up by 20 per cent some consumers would still buy Kellogg's.

We can therefore model each firm as facing a downward-sloping demand curve for its products. Figure 4.2 shows the demand curve facing a supplier of a product in a market where firms have some monopoly power: it might be, as shown, a supplier of PCs.

Figure 4.2
A demand curve for
PCs supplied by a
single firm with
market power

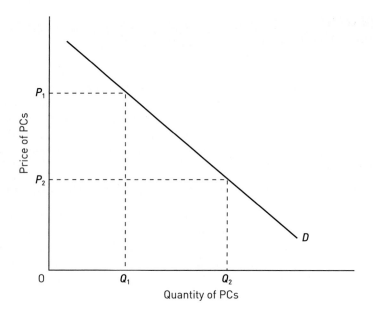

Question | **Explain carefully what Figure 4.2 shows.**

The demand for the firm's PCs is assumed to be a function of the price of the PCs. The model abstracts from, or 'holds constant', every other influence on the demand, such as people's incomes and the price of other companies' PCs. If price rises, quantity demanded (in a given time period) will fall. Conversely, if the firm reduces its price from P_1 to P_2, the quantity of its PCs demanded will increase from Q_1 to Q_2. Both the quantity demanded and price vary in this model; the quantity demanded is the dependent variable, since it changes in response to price, the independent variable.

▪▪▪ 4.2.3   Average revenue and marginal revenue

We defined a firm with monopoly power in Section 4.2.1 as a firm with some choice in setting the price of its product. This is reflected in the downward-sloping demand curve faced by such a firm, showing that if the firm sets a lower price it can increase the quantity demanded. The demand curve for a firm's goods determines the *total revenue* the firm would earn at each price it might set. With price P_1 in Figure 4.2, the firm's total revenue (TR) is P_1 multiplied by the quantity demanded Q_1. More generally, a firm's total revenue is the quantity of its goods demanded times price:

$$TR = P \cdot Q$$

It follows that the demand curve (D) of the firm is also its *average revenue* (AR) curve. The average revenue is the revenue per unit sold: in Figure 4.2 it is the firm's revenue per PC. Average revenue is therefore total revenue divided by quantity demanded, and is equal to the price per PC. That is:

$$AR = \frac{TR}{Q} = P$$

Marginal revenue

Marginal revenue is the change in total revenue resulting from the sale of an additional unit of output.

which reads, average revenue is total revenue divided by quantity demanded, which is equal to price. Each point on the demand curve therefore shows the average revenue (equals price) of the firm for each quantity demanded.

This analysis of a firm's revenue is a building block for analysing a firm's decision about the price it should charge for its goods. To complete it we need one more concept, **marginal revenue** (*MR*). Marginal revenue is the change in total revenue resulting from the sale of an additional unit of output.

> **Question** Look again at Figure 4.2. Suppose that demand is currently Q_1 at price P_1. Now the firm wants to sell an extra PC. How will price and total revenue change?

If the firm wants to increase demand by one PC it will have to reduce its price. And that means it will receive a lower price for all the PCs it sells, not just the additional one. That is the snag about a downward-sloping demand curve. So the marginal revenue – the change in total revenue – the firm receives from selling an extra PC is positive if the extra revenue from selling one more PC outweighs the drop in revenue from reducing the price of all the others.

'Marginal' concepts such as marginal revenue identify the effects of small changes in one variable (such as quantity demanded) on another variable (such as total revenue). Marginal concepts are used quite a lot in economics because they offer a useful way of analysing decision-making, as this chapter will illustrate. Section 4.3 introduces another marginal concept: marginal cost. Section 4.4 brings marginal cost and marginal revenue together to analyse a firm's decision on what price to set for its goods. Make sure you have got to grips with the revenue concepts by doing Exercise 4.1 before moving on.

Exercise 4.1

Suppose that our computer firm has a demand for only one PC at €1000, and has to reduce the price steadily to increase demand for PCs. Complete columns 3 and 4 on Table 4.1, using the data in the first two columns. Look back at the explanations of average, total and marginal revenue to help with your calculations.

Table 4.1
Price, quantity demanded and revenue of a computer firm

(1) Price (P) = average revenue (AR) €	(2) Quantity (Q) of computers demanded	(3) Total revenue (TR) €	(4) Marginal revenue (MR) €
1000	1	1000	–
950	2	1900	900
900	3	2700	
850	4		
800	5		

> **Question** Look at your completed Table 4.1, and state carefully the relationship that it shows between marginal revenue, average revenue and total revenue as price falls.

Figure 4.3
Average revenue
and marginal
revenue curves of a
firm with monopoly
power

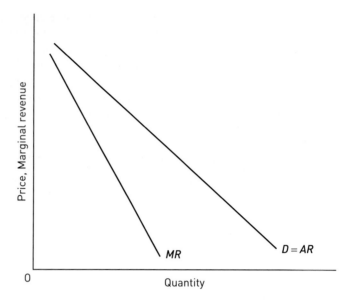

As price (average revenue) falls (column 1), quantity demanded rises (column 2). Total revenue increases as demand rises (column 3). The addition to total revenue from each additional unit of demand is the marginal revenue (column 4). Marginal revenue falls as quantity demanded rises. Furthermore, if you compare marginal with average revenue, you will see that marginal revenue is less than average revenue at each quantity demanded.

This relationship between marginal and average revenue is implied by the downward slope of the demand curve. Average revenue (price) declines as quantity rises. Marginal revenue must therefore (arithmetically) be less than average revenue for the reason explained above: the marginal revenue is the price (average revenue) of the extra PC *less* the revenue lost by reducing the prices of all the others in order to raise demand.

A marginal revenue (*MR*) curve traces the marginal revenue received by the firm at each price set and each quantity demanded. A downward-sloping demand curve is therefore always associated with a marginal revenue curve that lies below it, as in Figure 4.3.

■■■ 4.2.4 The price elasticity of demand

Suppose that our computer firm decides to reduce its price in order to increase the quantity of its PCs demanded. The number of extra PCs sold will depend on how steeply the demand curve for its PCs slopes downwards. A shallower (flatter) slope means that a given price reduction (e.g. from €1000 to €950) will sell more extra PCs than would be sold if the demand curve sloped more steeply at that point.

The firm's most important concern, however, is likely to be with the effect of the price decrease on its total revenue. This will depend, as we saw in Section 4.2.3, on the balance between the loss of revenue from lower prices and the gain in revenue from extra sales. This section shows that the effect of a given price change on a firm's total revenue varies as the firm moves along a straight line demand curve.

If the firm finds that a small percentage drop in price produces a large percentage increase in sales, then it will see its total revenue increase. However, if a large percentage price reduction is needed to sell just one more PC, the marginal revenue might be negative, and total revenue would fall.

Figure 4.4
Average revenue
(demand) curve for
a computer firm
with monopoly
power

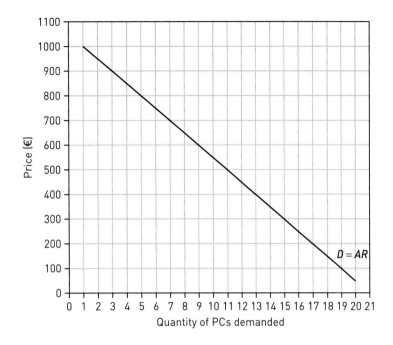

Question Explain that last statement to yourself, looking back at Section 4.2.3 if necessary.

Marginal revenue will be negative if the revenue raised by selling the extra PC is less than the revenue lost by reducing the price for all other units that could previously be sold at a higher price.

Hence, the firm's revenue prospects as its price changes depend on the responsiveness of demand to price changes. Economists call this responsiveness the **price elasticity of demand**. It is measured by dividing the proportionate change in quantity demanded by the proportionate change in price that brought it about:

Price elasticity of demand.

The price elasticity of demand measures the responsiveness of the quantity demanded of a product to changes in its price.

$$\text{price elasticity of demand} = \frac{\text{proportionate change in quantity demanded}}{\text{proportionate change in price}}$$

You can express the proportions as percentages. Exercise 4.2 asks you to review your understanding of percentages (see Chapter 2, Section 2.2.2) and also gives you practice in calculating elasticities.

Exercise 4.2

Figure 4.4 shows our computer firm's average revenue curve, plotted from the data on Table 4.1 and extended to price = €50.

The firm reduces price from €800 to €600.

1 What is the percentage decline in price?
2 What is the resultant percentage increase in quantity demanded?
3 What is the price elasticity of demand when price falls from €800 to €600?

Price elasticities of demand are generally negative, as Exercise 4.2 showed, because price and quantity demanded move in opposite directions. In practice we calculate and compare elasticities by ignoring the minus sign and just looking at the number. So we say that an elasticity of -4 is greater than an elasticity of -0.5. If quantity demanded is very responsive to price, so that the percentage change in quantity is greater than the percentage change in price, then demand is price **elastic**. If highly unresponsive, so that the percentage change in quantity is smaller than the percentage change in price, it is **inelastic**.

Elastic and inelastic demand

Demand is price elastic if the price elasticity is greater than 1.
Demand is unit elastic if the price elasticity = 1.
Demand is price inelastic if the price elasticity is less than 1.

So you found in Exercise 4.2, that between €800 and €600 per computer, demand was price elastic since the elasticity is (minus) 3.2. However, on Figure 4.4, if price falls from €250 to €200 (-20 per cent) quantity demanded rises from 16 to 17 (only 6.25 per cent). So the price elasticity of demand is

$$\frac{6.25}{-20} = -0.3125$$

which is inelastic. We can conclude from this example that price elasticity is not constant along a straight line demand (average revenue) curve but declines as we move from left to right.

Question	Did you understand the last paragraph fully? Calculate the price elasticity of demand between different points on the $D = AR$ curve in Figure 4.4, in order to check your understanding.

A firm's output decision will be influenced by its elasticity of demand. To see why, consider what happens if a firm lowers its price in the face of inelastic demand. The proportionate increase in demand will be less than the proportionate change in price (the elasticity is less than 1). If price falls by 10 per cent, quantity demanded rises by less than 10 per cent. Result, total revenue falls, and marginal revenue is therefore negative. A wise firm with monopoly power will not expand output to the point where each additional unit of output sold reduces its total revenue in this way. That is, the firm will not operate on the inelastic part of its demand curve.

Finally, what influences a firm's elasticity of demand? Look back at the earlier discussion of product differentiation. The price elasticity of demand is strongly influenced by the ease with which consumers can substitute a firm's good with another. For example, to Neil Costello's unsophisticated culinary eye, one bag of salt seems to be exactly the same as any other bag of salt. Thus he would always buy a cheaper bag of salt rather than a more expensive one. Conversely, to his gullible(?) eye, one medium-sized car is not exactly the same as any other, so he is prepared to pay more for particular cars which he sees as superior in some way. What this means is that in a world of consumers with Neil's characteristics the price elasticity of each brand of salt is high. A price increase for one brand results in a big shift to other brands. But the price elasticity of each brand of medium-sized car in a world of Neil lookalikes is not so high. A price increase in one brand does not produce such a big shift to alternatives. The extent to which goods are substitutes for each other is a major determinant of price elasticity of demand.

However, this does not mean that the price elasticity of demand cannot be influenced by the firm. Firms try to differentiate their brands through advertising in markets where there is monopoly power; that is, they try to reduce the extent to which their products are perceived as similar to other products. There are other ways too for a firm to reduce the price elasticity of demand for its product, such as tying its use to complementary products the firm also supplies. Microsoft, for example, sought to tie users of Windows software into using the Internet Explorer browser rather than alternative methods of browsing the Internet such as Netscape's Navigator. PC manufacturers that installed Windows could neither remove Internet Explorer nor feature a rival browser more prominently. Microsoft also offered Internet service providers, including America Online, a feature in its operating system to make it easy for users to establish an account, but only if the service provider denied most of its subscribers an alternative browser. One effect would be to make it more likely that consumers would continue to use the Microsoft browser if its price went up, since switching to another browser became more difficult.

4.3 Pure monopoly

The Microsoft court case pitched two economics professors against each other: Franklin Fisher from the Massachusetts Institute of Technology, expert witness for the government, and Richard Schmalensee on behalf of Microsoft. Both employed in their arguments the economic model of pure monopoly presented in this section. The model is useful because it examines an extreme case of monopoly power. Studying it can allow us to draw some conclusions, not only about how monopolies are likely to behave if unconstrained, but also about the conditions that sustain monopolies and the implications for policy.

To construct the model, we bring together the analysis of a firm's costs developed in Chapter 3 with the analysis of revenues in the last section, in order to study the pricing and output decisions of a pure monopolist.

▨ ▩ ■ 4.3.1 Marginal and average costs

In Chapter 3 Graham Dawson and Judith Mehta argued that the shape of firms' cost functions is of considerable relevance to understanding how industries change over time. The average cost curve traces average or unit costs of production at different levels of output, in the short and long run (Chapter 3, Section 3.3). From the shape of the average cost curve, whether downward sloping, 'U'-shaped or horizontal, we can deduce the pattern of the firm's total costs and marginal costs (just as a pattern of marginal and total revenues were implied by the downward-sloping average revenue curve).

The firm's total cost (TC) at each level of output is, by definition, the quantity produced (Q) multiplied by average cost (AC):

$$TC = AC \cdot Q$$

Marginal cost

Marginal cost is the change in total cost incurred as a result of producing an additional unit of output.

Marginal cost (MC) is then the change in total cost incurred when the firm produces an extra unit of output. The shape of the marginal cost curve is closely related to the shape of the average cost curve. Figure 4.5 shows the shape of the marginal cost curve associated with a 'U'-shaped average cost curve.

At levels of output below Q_1 on Figure 4.5, average cost falls as output increases. Marginal cost is therefore less than average cost. This is the same arithmetical relationship as we explained above between marginal revenue and average revenue. If average cost is declining, the addition to total cost as a result of producing the last unit must be less than average cost, because as output rises the cost of producing each unit declines. At

Figure 4.5
Marginal cost curve
with a 'U'-shaped
average cost curve

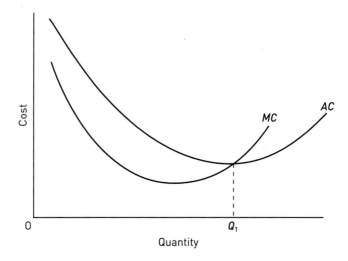

Q_1, average cost has reached its minimum. As output rises above Q_1, average cost starts to rise. Marginal cost is therefore now above average cost. This is because an increase in output raises the average cost of producing each unit, so the addition to total cost required to produce an extra unit must be larger than average cost. It follows that the marginal cost curve crosses the average cost curve at its lowest point.

Exercise 4.3

A numerical exercise may help to understand this. Table 4.2 shows output and average cost for a hypothetical firm. Complete the last two columns and graph the average and marginal cost curves on a single diagram.

Figure 4.5 showed a 'U'-shaped average cost curve. This might be a short-run or a long-run curve. Short-run average cost curves will be 'U'-shaped, since the firm cannot alter its fixed costs such as investment in plant and machinery. In the long run the firm can invest in additional plant, and, unless prevented from doing so, new firms can also invest and enter an

Table 4.2
A firm's average
and marginal costs

Units of output (Q)	Average cost (AC)	Total cost (TC)	Marginal cost (MC)
1	100	100	–
2	90	180	80
3	80	240	60
4	75	300	
5	72	360	
6	72	432	
7	75	525	
8	80		
9	92		
10	115		

Figure 4.6
Horizontal long-run
average and
marginal cost
curves of a firm

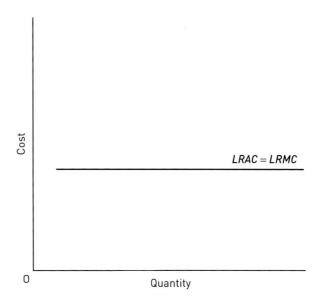

industry. Chapter 3, Section 3.3 noted that long-run average cost curves may be 'U'-shaped, or may decline continuously over the output range relevant to a particular market.

Question | What is the shape of the marginal cost curve associated with a continuously declining long-run average cost curve?

The marginal cost curve will lie below the average cost curve at all levels of output. This answer follows directly from the discussion of the relationship between average and marginal revenue curves. Look back at Section 4.2.3 if you were not sure of the answer.

A firm may also have long-run average costs that are constant over a large output range. This would mean that the long-run average cost (*LRAC*) curve was horizontal at these output levels (Figure 4.6). In this case, long-run marginal costs (*LRMC*) will be equal to average costs: each additional unit of output adds the same amount to total cost.

■■■ 4.3.2 The profit-maximizing monopolist

We can now analyse the pricing and output decisions of a pure monopolist. We will assume that the firm has a sole objective, to maximize its profits. This is not an unrealistic assumption, though it is unlikely to be the only aim firms pursue. Firms whose shares are quoted on the stock market have constantly to chase higher profits in order to satisfy shareholders' desire for maximum returns. Even firms with no competitors in their product markets need to try to keep their share prices buoyant in this way, in order to be able to continue to attract investors and raise funds.

The profits our firm is seeking to maximize are the difference between its total costs and its total revenues. It can alter profits by altering output and hence the price at which it must sell. A pure monopolist faces no competition, so it does not have to worry about other firms' responses to its pricing and output decisions. Its constraint is the demand function for its product. The monopolist can choose the price at which it sells its output, and that will determine the quantity sold. Alternatively, it can choose its desired output

Figure 4.7
Profit maximization
by a pure
monopolist

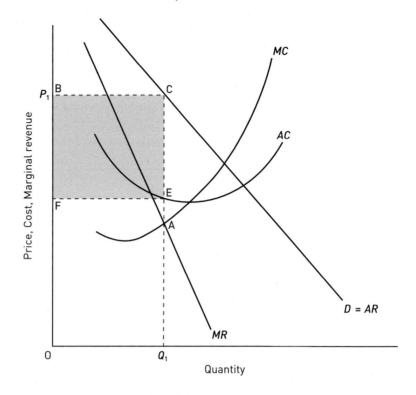

(sales) level, and that will determine the price that can be charged. Its aim is to choose the price/quantity combination that maximizes profits.

A firm that is seeking to maximize profit will choose the level of output (sales) that maximizes the difference between total cost and total revenue. To get an intuitive grasp of how it might do this, think of a firm gradually increasing output. Each additional unit produced and sold increases total revenue, so long as marginal revenue is positive. Producing the additional unit also adds to total cost so long as marginal cost is greater than zero.

If the marginal revenue is higher than the marginal cost, the addition to total revenue is larger than the addition to total cost and profit rises. Total revenue has increased by more than total cost. Conversely, if marginal cost is larger than marginal revenue, then producing and selling the additional unit has reduced profits. Where marginal revenue and marginal cost are equal, profit is maximized. This **condition for profit maximization** applies to firms in all market structures, not just to pure monopolists.

Now let us apply this condition to the monopolist. Figure 4.7 puts the firm's cost and revenue curves (Figures 4.3 and 4.5) together on a single diagram. What output will the monopolist choose in order to maximize profits? On Figure 4.7, the marginal revenue curve MR crosses the marginal cost curve MC at point A with output Q_1. Suppose the monopolist chooses to produce Q_1. What price will have to be charged to sell the whole of that output?

The monopolist's demand curve (average revenue curve) is $D = AR$. If the firm wishes to sell Q_1 it will charge P_1. A higher price will leave it with unsold goods, while a profit-maximizing firm will not charge a lower price, since that would reduce revenue.

The firm will make total profits equal to the shaded area BCEF on Figure 4.7. The vertical distance BF (= CE) measures the profit per unit, that is, the difference between the price P_1 and average cost. The horizontal distance BC (= FE) is equal to Q_1, the

The condition for profit maximization

Profit is maximized at the level of output at which marginal revenue = marginal cost: $MR = MC$

Equilibrium

In an economic model, an equilibrium is a situation from which there is no incentive for change.

output produced. Total profits are therefore BF times BC, the area of the rectangle BCEF.

At output levels below Q_1 the marginal revenue curve MR is above the marginal cost curve MC. So increasing output towards Q_1 will add to profits. At output levels above Q_1 marginal revenue is below marginal cost, so reducing output will reduce costs more than it reduces revenue, hence profits will rise. It follows that Q_1 is the firm's profit-maximizing output. Once it is producing Q_1 it has no incentive to change its output. Q_1 is therefore the firm's **equilibrium** output in Figure 4.7, and P_1 the equilibrium price.

■■■ 4.3.3 Market dominance and supernormal profits

The rewards of market dominance can be large. The model of pure monopoly shows that a monopolist may be able to make high profits. Furthermore, these are not just short-run profits. The model rules out by assumption the possibility that other firms can enter the market, attracted by those profits, and compete away the monopolist's customers by charging a price for the product lower than P_1 in Figure 4.7. Hence a pure monopolist may be able to earn supernormal profits in the long run.

Opportunity cost

The opportunity cost of using a resource is the amount it would have earned in its best alternative use.

To see what this means, consider the firm's decision to invest, for example, in more machinery. This investment will only be worthwhile if the return on the investment is as good as, or better than returns available if the funds had been invested elsewhere. So the cost of making the investment is the return from the alternative activity forgone, which might, for example, be the profit from investing in another industry. This alternative return forgone is the **opportunity cost** of the investment. You will meet this concept of opportunity cost often in economics.

The opportunity cost of investment determines the profit that would be just sufficient to keep the firm in the industry. This level of profit, called *normal profit*, is included in the economic definition of a firm's costs, odd though it may seem to call a profit a cost. The average cost curve of the monopolist thus includes normal profit because it is considered an (opportunity) cost. If average cost equals average revenue, only normal profits are being made; if average revenue exceeds average cost, as in Figure 4.7, the firm enjoys *supernormal profits*.

We now have another possible indicator of monopoly power, in addition to concentration ratios: the extent to which a firm can set price above average cost. Section 4.4 will show how competition even in markets with some monopoly power can drive out supernormal profits. Furthermore, a pure monopolist will always set a price above marginal cost. You can see this in Figure 4.7, where P_1 is greater than marginal cost (MC) at point A. Chapter 5 explores a model of competition without monopoly power, where price is forced down to marginal cost. So a further indicator of the extent of monopoly power in a market is the mark-up of price over marginal cost. This can be measured as:

$$\frac{P - MC}{P}$$

a measure sometimes called the 'degree of monopoly'.

Lest all this seems too detached from the real world, note that these indicators of monopoly power were at issue in the Microsoft court case. Expert witnesses for the government argued that Microsoft was exploiting its market power to earn supernormal profits by charging consumers more than they would pay if there were more competition in the market for computer operating systems. They pointed to the high observed levels of company profitability as evidence that Microsoft was using market power to raise prices significantly above long-run average costs (Gilbert and Katz, 2001, p.29).

Furthermore, the economists for both sides tried to calculate whether the observed gap between Microsoft's marginal cost and price was at the level to be expected if Microsoft was behaving like a profit-maximizing monopolist. To do this, they started from precisely the model of monopoly behaviour outlined in Section 4.2.2. They made estimates of marginal costs and of the elasticity of demand for Windows software; and from these they estimated the price a pure monopolist would be expected to charge.

From these calculations they drew opposing conclusions. Schmalensee, for Microsoft, argued that the short-run monopoly price for Windows should have been at least 16 times the price actually charged. Fisher, for the government, argued that Microsoft was charging a long-run monopoly price for the software. The argument turned in part on the distinction between short and long run, and in part on the objectives of the firm. The government argued that Microsoft's price for Windows reflected monopoly pricing tempered by the broader objectives of the firm, including expanding the installed base of Windows, encouraging the use of complementary products such as applications software and discouraging software pirating (Gilbert and Katz, 2001, p.29).

The model of pure monopoly described in this section is a *static* model, in a number of senses. First, it holds many things constant: technology, for example, and the way the firm organizes production. Most crucially, it rules out competition by assumption, thus removing the main force for change in industrial markets. Second, the model is designed to explore the firm's *equilibrium* price and quantity; it is a model of a firm at rest, not one that is changing. Models of this kind can be used to analyse change – we will do so in the next section – but there is no doubt that they miss the sense of turbulence and continuous change conveyed by Mariana Mazzucato in Chapter 2 when discussing the automobile and computer industries over time. Sections 4.4 and 4.5 reintroduce competition and technological change to our analysis.

4.4   Contestability and barriers to entry

Economists have long recognized that almost all monopolists face potential competition, and that this will influence their behaviour. Joseph Schumpeter was an influential economist working in the first half of the twentieth century. He was deeply interested in social relations and social philosophy and is particularly well known for his theory of economic development. He was an early critic of the model of monopoly just outlined, arguing that its emphasis on profit maximizing with given technology (Section 4.3.2) focused too much on 'data of the momentary situation', rather than being concerned, as firms were, with the past and the future and 'the competition from the new commodity, the new technology' (Schumpeter, 1942, p.84).

Schumpeter's arguments seem highly contemporary. He emphasized innovation and the destruction of sections of the economy and whole ways of life by new techniques of production and new products. Firms that hold strong monopoly power in one era can find that their markets disappear through industrial transformation. Schumpeter's examples included transport: canal companies driven out of business by the railways; the railways threatened by the motor car. In the current era, a comparable transformation has come in information technology. The large producers of mainframe and midi computers who once exercised enormous market power, seemingly invulnerable, disappeared or were completely transformed at the end of the twentieth century with the advent of the personal computer. For example, during the late 1970s IBM dominated the market for large mainframe computers. In 1981 it launched the IBM personal computer – a relatively late entrant into the market for small portable machines. Its relationship with Microsoft, then a small 32-person company supplying the DOS operating system, and the successful marketing of its new range saved it from extinction, though it has never regained the dominance it held in earlier decades and the changes of the 1980s 'fundamentally rocked' the business (www.ibm.com, 3 October 2001).

In this section and the next, we respond to Schumpeter's critique in two stages. We first drop the assumption that a monopolist faces no competition, and instead assume that in the long run – that is, once firms are able to invest in new capacity – firms can enter new markets. Indeed, they can create whole new markets for innovative products. We explore in this section the barriers that can be established, by technology and by the conduct of established or 'incumbent' firms, to the entry of new firms into an industry, and some consequences of lowering barriers to entry, drawing on the model of the profit-maximizing firm developed in Sections 4.2 and 4.3. In Section 4.5 we then look specifically at competition through innovation, drawing on an alternative model of firms as evolving institutions with specific skills or 'capabilities'.

■ ■ ■ 4.4.1 Economies of scale and barriers to entry

Graham Dawson and Judith Mehta analysed in Chapter 3 one of the most important sources of monopoly power: economies of scale. If there are economies of scale in an industry, firms' long-run average cost ($LRAC$) curves are downward sloping: average cost falls as output rises. If a firm expands ahead of its rivals it can take advantage of these economies of scale in such a way that it can dominate the industry. The firm's combination of low average costs and high output become a *barrier to entry* to other firms. This means that other firms, attracted to the industry by the profits they see the existing firm making, find that they cannot profitably enter and supply part of the market.

Let us look a little more closely at why not. Figure 4.8 shows the long-run average cost curve and the demand curve for a single firm that currently monopolizes its market. Average costs fall as the scale of the firm's operation is increased, up to the point of minimum efficient scale A at output level Q_1. Beyond A, costs per unit of output are constant. The market demand curve is D, the firm supplies the whole market. For simplicity

Figure 4.8
Barriers to entry under economies of scale

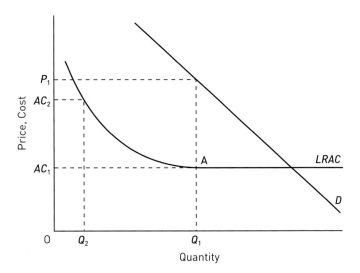

we have omitted the marginal cost and marginal revenue curves. Let us just assume that Q_1 and P_1 are the profit-maximizing price and quantity for the monopolist.

Now consider the position of another firm trying to muscle in on the market. All firms in the industry have (by assumption) the same cost curves. Suppose that a new firm sets up production sufficient to supply a small part of current demand (Q_2). You can see that at that level of output its average costs are considerably higher (AC_2) than those of the established firm (AC_1).

However, the new firm's average cost AC_2 is less than the market price P_1. So surely it can come in and make a profit. What is the problem?

Natural monopoly

A natural monopoly exists if, as a result of economies of scale, a single firm can supply the market at a lower average cost than a number of smaller firms.

There are two problems. First, there is additional output in the industry from the new firm. To sell the new output, the new firm will have to drive down the price, undermining its own profitability. Second, the incumbent firm is making supernormal profits per unit equal to $(P_1 - AC_1)$. It is likely to be willing to sacrifice some of those profits for a while, reducing price to make entry unprofitable, in order to sustain its monopoly power. (You will study 'strategic' behaviour by firms, of which this is an example, more systematically in Chapter 6.)

There is room for only one firm in this market, since a single firm can supply the market at lower average cost than any combination of smaller firms. Industries of this kind are called **natural monopolies**. The barrier to entry to the market characterized by natural monopoly is therefore the downward-sloping part of the average cost curve.

Question To reinforce this conclusion, study Figure 4.9. This is identical to Figure 4.8 except that each firm now has constant average costs. Assume again that the incumbent firm produces output Q_1. Could a second firm now come in and compete for part of the market by producing Q_2?

Yes. The new firm's average costs are identical to those of the incumbent firm, at AC_1. Because there are no economies of scale, the larger firm has no cost advantage over the

Figure 4.9
Barriers to entry under constant average costs?

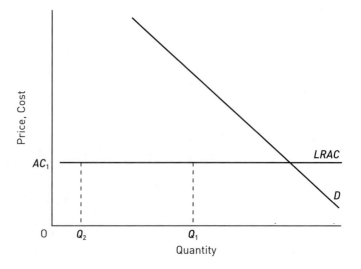

new entrant, and the market will be divided between a number of competing firms. There is no cost barrier to entry.

There are many areas of the economy where the cost conditions generate strong barriers to entry. Software, Microsoft's product, is a good example. The initial cost of producing software is very high. IBM, for example, is reported to have spent US$1 billion to develop, test and market its OS/2 operating system as a (failed) alternative to Windows (Gilbert and Katz, 2001, p.28). Once software is produced, the marginal duplication costs to produce additional copies are close to zero, as Microsoft's chief economic witness assumed in his calculations. Major pieces of software, such as PC operating systems, therefore exhibit very large economies of scale, and this is a major source of Microsoft's monopoly power. One economic commentator (Klein, 2001) described Microsoft as operating in a 'natural monopoly market'.

However, the phrase 'natural monopoly' suggests a permanency that economic history belies. The industries that most closely fit the natural monopoly model are the 'network industries' (Chapter 3, Section 3.4.2). There are a number of 'old economy' industries where economies of scale are generated by physical infrastructural supply networks that are inefficient to duplicate, such as gas pipes, water pipes and cabling. Even in these industries, however, technology can undermine the economies of scale. Perhaps the best example is telecommunications, where mobile telephony has destroyed the natural monopoly characteristics of the supply of telephone services.

▪ ▪ ▪ 4.4.2 Network externalities and market contestability

There are also barriers to entry on the demand side of some markets. A key characteristic of a number of 'new economy' industries, explained in Chapter 3, Section 3.4, is network externalities. These imply that the value of an item – such as a particular computer operating system – to consumers rises as the use of the product by others increases.

From the point of view of firms supplying computer operating systems, for example, these network externalities operate as a barrier to entry in a way that is comparable to economies of scale. The first firm into the market can rapidly build up a customer base, since the more people buy in, the greater the incentive for others to do so too. Once there is an established incumbent firm, the barrier to other firms' entry is formidable: it will be hard to persuade existing customers to switch supplier, since they will lose key network benefits. This effect of network externalities is called 'lock-in': once consumers are integrated into a network it is expensive to shift them.

Microsoft dominated the operating systems market in this way. The more users adopted the Microsoft operating system (MS-DOS and Windows), the more it became advantageous for other users to do the same, so that they could communicate easily with existing users, share files and learn from each other. Microsoft was able to benefit from these network externalities to establish its operating system as the standard system, even though a number of other operating systems, notably Apple, were seen as superior by many commentators and users. Because Windows was widely used, there were strong incentives for new computer users to purchase machines operating with that system. Software developers wrote additional programs for the operating system – such as specialist software used by economists – and users became 'locked-in' to Microsoft's systems and products. In these circumstances, even if better software had existed, the costs of training staff in the new systems and changing hardware could have been prohibitive, and the inconvenience of using a different system from others reinforced the incentive to stick with Microsoft products. The government labelled this, in the Microsoft case, the 'applications barrier to entry'.

Network externalities and 'lock-in' on the demand side thus pose a barrier to entry even in industries where there are not large economies of scale. They become formidable barriers when they are associated with economies of scale, as in the Microsoft case.

Firms wishing to compete with Microsoft in the operating systems market thus faced a dual barrier to entry: economies of scale on the supply side and network externalities on the demand side. As a result, the PC operating systems market displayed a particularly severe lack of **contestability**.

Complete or 'perfect' contestability is very rare since virtually all industries and markets display some entry barriers, although they vary greatly in severity.

Contestable market

A market is perfectly contestable if entry and exit are costless.

Question	If you were setting up your own business, which of the following ideas would you consider to be the most viable? Note down, for each, one barrier you would face in setting up such an undertaking. ■ a sandwich shop ■ selling antiques via the Internet ■ brain surgery.

It may be very difficult to set up a sandwich shop without approvals from the relevant health and safety authorities. *Regulations* thus affect the ease with which firms can enter markets or operate once they have established themselves. In addition, it may be the case that you do not have the necessary *skills* to operate in some sectors of the economy. Brain surgery is an obvious example. Thus barriers to entry can be related to ownership of particular skills or *resources*. If you wanted to use the Internet to sell antiques you would need the skills to establish and run a website. You would also need to be able to source and deliver antiques, perhaps requiring the creation of a network of antique dealers. So you would already need to have resources such as a good knowledge and set of contacts in the trade. If a firm was already undertaking this kind of e-commerce in antiques, dealers might be tied into it by exclusive deals that prevented you working with them.

■ ■ ■ 4.4.3 Artificial barriers to entry

The last example illustrates a general point: barriers to entry may be 'natural' in the sense that they are inherent in the product or service, or they may be deliberately created by firms in a deliberate attempt to prevent competition. The more a firm can prevent other firms from entering a market, the more freedom it will have to exercise monopoly power to the detriment of consumers, by charging high prices and making supernormal profits. If a market is contestable, incumbent firms realize that any monopoly profits will be short lived, because new firms will come in and compete them away. Section 4.4.4 analyses that process. Competition authorities are particularly concerned to ensure that firms do not create artificial barriers to contestability.

However, effective competition does not necessarily require firms actually to enter a market. Firms already in a market will be aware that if they make high profits they will create strong incentives for competitors to move in. Hence, they may be prevented from exercising monopoly power by fear of generating entry by competitors where barriers to entry are low. Hence, an industry with few firms may display competitive behaviour, so long as barriers to *potential* competitors are low.

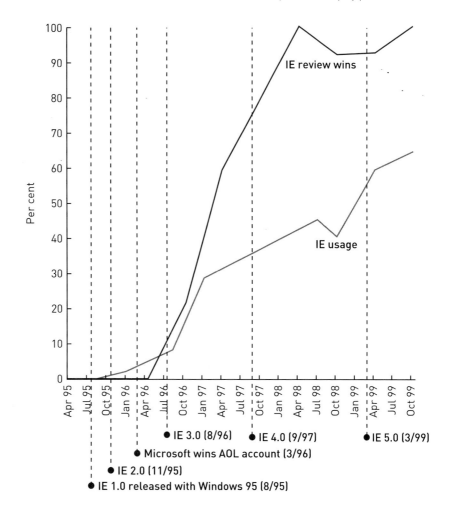

Figure 4.10
Trends in Internet Explorer's share of review 'wins' and usage, from April 1995 to October 1999

Source: Klein, 2001, p.48

The debate in the Microsoft case turned in part on the extent of contestability of its market. The government argued that the reason Microsoft was putting so much effort into gaining market share for their Internet Explorer browser was that Netscape represented a source of potential competition for Windows. The reason for this was that Netscape had the potential, along with the Java language, to grow into a layer of 'middleware' – software that lies between the operating system and the applications software – that would separate the software applications of interest to users from the underlying operating system. This would break the link, described above, between the network externalities on the demand side and the economies of scale in operating system software, and hence largely remove the 'applications barrier to entry'.

Microsoft put more than US$100 million per year during 1995–97 into improving its browser Internet Explorer. It also gave away Internet Explorer for free, and paid Apple to use the browser (Klein, 2001). Figure 4.10 illustrates the effects of these efforts on market share. Internet Explorer started to win approval from reviewers by comparison with other browsers ('IE review wins') and market share ('IE usage') increased.

Economists differ on the implications of these effects for users. Nicholas Economides argues that the direct benefits to the consumer of cheaper and higher quality net access were very large; he emphasizes the benefits to users of the shared software standards created by Microsoft operating systems software. Fisher and Daniel Rubinfeld, for the government, argued that Microsoft's actions were 'predatory'. That is, they were making investments and charging prices that were only profitable in the long run taking into account the super-normal profits that could be earned once the competition was eliminated (Fisher and Rubinfeld, 2000). The government emphasized the long-term potential damage to users from eliminating future competitive pressure on prices and quality (Gilbert and Katz, 2001).

■■■ 4.4.4 Monopolistic competition

Given the central role of competitive pressure in the case against monopoly, let us look more closely at the effects of competition in contexts where firms have monopoly power but markets remain contestable. This section examines competition on the basis of price. Section 4.5 turns to competition through innovation.

The model of monopolistic competition builds on the pure monopoly model, but drops the assumption that new firms cannot enter the market. It shows that entry of new firms can result in the disappearance of supernormal profits, but there are some less satisfactory effects on costs.

Look back at Figure 4.7, and think of this now as the short-run profit-maximizing position of a firm holding a temporary monopoly in a market open to entry. In the long run, new firms can freely enter the industry by investing in their own plant, and the incumbent firm can also invest in new plant and equipment.

Question	What happens to the demand curve of the original or 'incumbent' firm when others come in?

There is now a distinction between the demand curve facing the firm and the market demand curve. The firm's demand curve lies to the left of the market demand curve, since only part of the market demand is now demand for its product. This is a market where (by assumption) firms have market power. There will be product differentiation (Section 4.2), and we can picture the new firms coming in with a similar but slightly different product. Consumers can choose between them. The slightly different product may also attract some new consumers, but as new firms enter the market, the original firm's demand curve is likely to shift to the left.

How far left will the demand curve shift? This is a question about the *equilibrium* of the firm in an industry where firms have monopoly power. Section 4.3 analysed the equilibrium for a pure monopoly. Once firms can enter the industry, they will continue to move into it so long as there are supernormal profits being made, since supernormal profits mean, by definition, profits higher than the return available elsewhere. Figure 4.11 shows the point of long-run profit-maximizing equilibrium of a firm in a monopolistically competitive industry after entry has ceased.

We have drawn the firm's long-run average cost curve as 'U'-shaped but flatter than the short-run cost curve in Figure 4.7. The demand curve $D = AR$ is the *firm's* demand curve. As other firms have come in, the demand curve has shifted left. At the same time, the firm has moved leftwards along its long-run average cost curve: it may have disinvested as demand has decreased at each price for its product. The firm's equilibrium is at the point where there are no longer any supernormal profits to be made. This happens at point A on Figure 4.11, where the demand curve is tangent to the average cost curve, that is, it just touches it. At this point with output Q_E the firm maximizes profits by setting $LRMC = MR$ (point B). Supernormal profits have fallen to zero because price equals average cost. There is therefore no longer any incentive for new firms to move into the industry.

Figure 4.11
The equilibrium of a firm in monopolistic competition in the long run

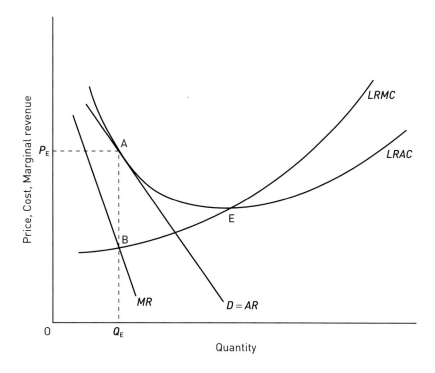

This model is only relevant to cases where the minimum efficient scale of firms is such that there is room for a number of firms in the market. Notice, however, that at output Q_E and price P_E the firm is not operating at the point of minimum efficient scale E. Average costs are higher than they would be if the firm was supplying a larger part of the market. So monopolistic competition can drive up costs above their minimum level, and although there are no supernormal profits, consumers may not be getting the best possible deal. On the other hand, competition has brought product diversity to the market.

4.5 Competition through innovation

In the model of monopolistic competition firms compete on price, and by product differentiation. However, as Schumpeter pointed out, firms also compete by creating radically new products, changing consumers' lives in the process. This process of product innovation may be particularly marked at the early stage of an industry life cycle. Later, as an industry consolidates, process innovation may sustain a firm's grip on the market. Being first into a market can have benefits, as discussed in Chapter 3, Section 3.4; they are further explored in Chapter 6. This section analyses competition through innovation, drawing on a rather different theory of the firm from the one we have used so far in this chapter.

▪ 4.5.1 Capabilities, resources and the entrepreneurial firm

A company producing a new product has to create a market for it, and the more innovative the product is, the more the firm has to work to persuade customers to understand it and to buy it. For example, TranscenData was at the time of writing in 2001 a small high-tech company based near Cambridge, England. It was built up by an academic engineer, Geoff Butlin, on the basis of his research interests. Geoff's attempts to commercialize his ideas had mixed success but he learned from his experiences and in the middle of the 1990s began to develop a new product which he realized had potentially a global market. The product was about data exchange. In building other products earlier, Geoff had used his complex technical ideas to produce computer-aided design tools. To do that he had to learn how to move data from one computer design system to another and he recognized that his small company had a world lead in that area.

TranscenData decided to develop this new product and finally gave it a name, CADfix, which the market loved. The name was very expressive of what the product was doing – fixing computer-aided design (CAD) models. Geoff was taking a new product to market. He also knew, from hard-earned previous experience, that excellent technical solutions were not a guarantee of commercial success and that other companies, with perhaps greater commercial acumen, were only too ready to run with new ideas. He was very much aware of the potential competition from new entrants, though initially there were no close substitutes so he enjoyed considerable monopoly power.

What kind of economic model would help us to analyse the chances of a particular firm building on and holding on to monopoly power? The question creates particular problems for the model of the firm studied so far, because this is a question about how particular firms *differ* from each other in ways that gain some potential advantage. The model used so far in this chapter has, however, assumed that competing firms are the *same*: they have the same technology, and react in standard ways to market conditions. Chapter 3 described the model, for this reason, as analysing a 'representative firm' (Section 3.3.1). The moment we look at innovation we clearly have to drop that assumption, and consider individual firms as innovators. Technological change in the model becomes uneven, and particular firms can build up a dominant market position – or disappear.

There is an alternative tradition in economics of modelling the behaviour of firms, one that has recently taken on a new lease of life as innovation has again become a central concern. This approach sees individual firms as evolving organizations – as TranscenData evolved – that develop particular resources and capabilities over time. You can think of 'capabilities', or 'competencies' as they are also known (Chapter 3, Section 3.4), as the things a firm is good at. Two influential theorists in the evolutionary tradition, Nelson and Winter (1982), model these organizational capabilities as embedded in the 'routines' of a company. Routines are practices in which firms engage in a taken-for-granted way. A firm's routines are acquired in the same way as skills are acquired by individuals, by learning or sometimes by accident. When organizations become 'skilful', they respond to situations effectively through taken-for-granted patterns of behaviour, without thinking each situation through from scratch, rather as a skilful sports star performs.

Particular firms can thus become good at certain activities, such as spotting the next technological breakthrough early, or providing good customer service, and reproduction of those skills and capabilities becomes part of the firm's way of operating. Alongside organizational skills, firms also develop particular organizational resources: for example, networks of suppliers they can rely on; particular highly skilled groups of staff; or large investments in specialized plant. This model of firms is 'evolutionary' in the sense that firms develop distinct capabilities over time, and those most effective in current market contexts win the competitive battle – for a time. This approach assumes firms may pursue a range of objectives, one of which is chasing enlarged market share.

So in an evolutionary model history matters. Joseph Schumpeter, cited at the beginning of the last section, argued that models based on price and quantity, where all firms have the same technology, lack a sense of past and future. An evolutionary model overcomes that: it analyses how particular firms build on their past to create scope for future success – or to drive the firm to bankruptcy by being unable to change. TranscenData is an example of a firm that built on past skill and experience to create a market niche for a new product.

■ ■ ■ 4.5.2 Innovation and monopoly power

Successful product innovation is particularly characteristic of 'entrepreneurial' firms, led by individuals and reflecting their character. The evolutionary model allows space for considering the impact of the personality of a firm's founder on its fortunes. Microsoft was a firm still run and part-owned by a dominant entrepreneurial founding figure, Bill Gates. These issues too find their way into policy debate: part of the debate around Microsoft was about what *kind* of firm Microsoft had become. Was it one that, through its own organizational culture and routines, was constantly searching for improvement, responding to competitive threat with better products? Or had it, as it gained monopoly power, stopped innovating and gone over to defensiveness, trying to prevent competition through innovation rather than winning through innovating?

For Microsoft, Schmalensee argued that, whatever the arguments about the extent of the threat from competitors, Microsoft 'behaves as if it faces . . . intense dynamic competition', and presented evidence of 'relentless innovation to improve its operating system'. He concluded that

> despite what would appear to be an ironclad monopoly, the evidence based on real world observations is that Microsoft does not *behave* like a firm with monopoly power.
>
> *(www.microsoft.com, September 2001, Microsoft's emphasis)*

Here Schmalensee is contrasting the evidence relevant to the standard pure ('ironclad') monopoly model with evidence of the behavioural characteristics of the firm, relevant to the evolutionary model. Fisher and Rubinfeld (2000) for the government agreed that behavioural evidence was also relevant. They used company emails to support their argument that Microsoft displayed the opposite behavioural tendency: an organizational focus on suppressing competition to the detriment of product improvement and consumer choice.

So there is no single answer to the question, do firms with monopoly power continue to innovate? A firm's behaviour will depend on its history and its current competitive challenges. Firms with monopoly power may continue to face competition through product innovation. In that case, a highly concentrated industry – one containing very few firms – may continue to behave competitively in a dynamic sense: the incumbent firms innovate constantly, since they perceive barriers to entry through product innovation as low, and entry always a potential threat. Schmalensee argued that Microsoft faced constant competitive threats of this kind.

As industries consolidate, some large firms may shift from product to process innovation (Chapters 2 and 3). Process innovation involves producing existing products more efficiently, using new production technology, or merely organizing production more efficiently using existing technology. Process innovation can therefore shift a firm's long-run average cost curve downwards (Chapter 3, Section 3.3.2).

Figure 4.12 analyses such an innovation by a profit-maximizing monopolist. For simplicity, we have this time drawn the firm's *LRAC* curve to display only the range where constant returns to scale exist ($LRAC = LRMC$). The monopolist's profits are maximized

Figure 4.12
The effect of a
monopolist's
innovation on price
and costs

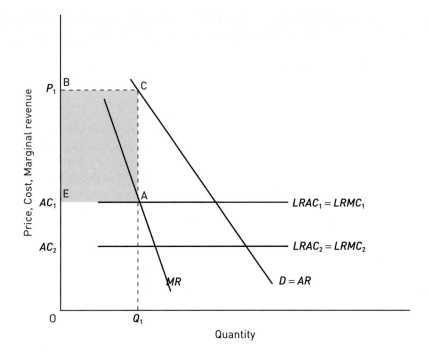

initially where $LRMC_1 = MR$ at point A. Output is Q_1 with an average cost per unit of AC_1 and price P_1. Supernormal profits are initially shown by the rectangle BCAE. The process innovation shifts the long-run cost curve downwards to $LRAC_2$.

Exercise 4.4

Indicate on Figure 4.12 the monopolist's new profit-maximizing price and quantity after the innovation. What has been the effect on price?

Your answer should show that even a pure monopolist, as defined in Section 4.3, will charge a lower price after the innovation than before; the innovation benefits consumers.

Schumpeter argued in the 1940s that large firms with monopoly power may be particularly likely to pursue this and other kinds of innovation. They are more likely than firms with little market power to be able to obtain financial backing from banks for risky innovation, and they may have a flow of supernormal profits to be reinvested. Furthermore, large firms with monopoly power have incentives to innovate since they can hope to benefit from their innovations by reaping further monopoly profits, hence monopoly power can drive industrial growth and create cheaper products for consumers.

These benefits of innovation can be threatened by contestability. In highly contestable markets, there is little incentive for a firm to innovate, if imitators will quickly compete away the market advantage gained by the innovator. Thus for policy purposes contestability has to be tempered with the opportunity for firms to make adequate returns. This is the key argument for allowing firms to take out patents on inventions that are the basis for innovation, allowing them to protect and exploit for profit the intellectual property rights in their ideas for a limited period. Competition authorities are increasingly concerned to get the policy framework right to promote and sustain competition through innovation.

4.6 Monopoly power and competition policy dilemmas

We can now draw together some implications of our study of monopoly power for competition policy. The antitrust prosecutors in the United States, like the competition authorities in Europe, including the UK's Competition Commission, have as their objective the prevention of the abuse of monopoly power to the detriment of consumers. The theory in this chapter helps to identify some central dilemmas policy makers face, especially when dealing with firms in highly innovative and rapidly changing industries. We start with another look at the Microsoft case, concentrating this time not on the economic analysis presented but on the remedies proposed by the government.

4.6.1 Structure and conduct

Appeals court rules against Microsoft break-up

Microsoft on Thursday won its battle against being broken up when a US appeals court threw out a lower court ruling that split the company in half, and closed almost all doors for another try at a break-up.

But the seven-judge panel, in a unanimous decision, also upheld many of the key charges in the government's landmark lawsuit, finding that Microsoft was a monopoly that acted illegally in an attempt to maintain its dominance in personal computer operating systems.

Bill Gates, Microsoft chairman, said he was 'pleased' with the court's decision, which had removed the threat of break-up. 'We feel very good about what the court has written here. The decision is consistent with our ability to go forward with our new products.' . . .

In a 125-page ruling, the appeals court found that Microsoft had not illegally tried to monopolise the internet browser market, as the government had charged. It also asked a lower court to reconsider a ruling that Microsoft's practice of including its web browser, Internet Explorer, in its Windows operating system was illegal 'tying' . . .

The court did find many of Microsoft's business practices to be unlawful, particularly contracts it signed with a wide array of companies in the industry – including computer manufacturers, internet service providers, and independent software vendors – that shut rival browsers out of the market.

Source: Peter Spiegel and Paul Abrahams, http://www.financialtimes.com,
28 June 2001

Government authorities who are considering acting against a firm for abuse of monopoly power will investigate both market *structure* – the extent of monopoly power enjoyed by the firm – and market *conduct* – the behaviour of a firm with monopoly power. In the Microsoft case, as in others on both sides of the Atlantic, the assessment of the extent of market power is the 'initial step' in tackling the problem, since a firm without monopoly power cannot abuse it. Gilbert and Katz list the methods used by the US courts to assess the extent of market power: they first define

the relevant market(s) affected by the firm's conduct. A market is a set of products that consumers consider to be reasonably close substitutes for each other [then] the assessment of market power moves on to the calculation of market share, examination of competitive interactions, determination of the conditions of entry and analysis of other pertinent structural features of the market.

(Gilbert and Katz, 2001, pp.29–30)

The 'structural' features of the market that determine the assessment of monopoly power cover a broad range, including barriers to entry and the pattern of interaction with actual and potential competitors. In many cases, a pertinent issue is the size of the relevant market: an industry dominated by a single firm in one country may operate in and face competition in integrated international markets.

The analysis then moves on to the *market conduct* of the firm. Here, the behaviour of the firm is scrutinized for abuse of monopoly power, such as monopoly pricing and deliberate blocking of competition by 'predatory' behaviour against the interests of consumers. European Union legislation bans the abuse of a 'dominant position' in a market by a monopolist, and that wording was brought into UK law by the Competition Act of 1998. In the USA, similarly, for the courts to act against Microsoft, they needed to be convinced *both* that the firm held monopoly power and that it had abused it to the long-term detriment of computer users. The possession of monopoly power alone is not an offence; as Gilbert and Katz (2001, p.30) put it: 'Indeed it would not make economic sense to punish a firm that possesses market power solely as a consequence of its having developed a superior product, because doing so would erode the incentives for innovation.'

The structure/conduct distinction is a fuzzy one: evidence of conduct can be and is used to assess the competitiveness of a market structure. But the distinction between the extent of monopoly power and its abuse is central to policy options. Competition authorities, whether in the USA or Europe, once convinced that a firm is abusing monopoly power, can seek to remedy the situation by *structural remedies*, that is, reducing the extent of market power by, for example, breaking up a dominant firm into two or more smaller ones. Alternatively, they can seek to impose *conduct* (or *behavioural*) *remedies* that seek to change market conduct by directly prohibiting or penalizing particular forms of conduct. Policies in both Europe and the USA typically mix structural and behavioural remedies, but there are nevertheless different policy traditions on the two sides of the Atlantic.

The US policy stance has displayed, since the Sherman Act cited at the beginning of this chapter, a greater emphasis on 'structural' remedies. This was the type of remedy that Judge Thomas Penfield Jackson sought to impose on Microsoft, breaking it up into two companies. One company would have held the Windows operating system, and the other all the applications and Microsoft's other lines of business. The Appeals Court, in June 2001, overturned that order (see above), arguing (among other points) that it was not clear that splitting the company would prevent the behaviour by Microsoft that the court found anti-competitive. In September 2001 the US Justice Department announced it was abandoning the effort to break up the company. Instead, it sought to address conduct through imposing penalties to prevent certain types of behaviour it regarded as designed to exclude competitors from its market.

The European Union approach, and the UK policy tradition, both permit structural remedies. However, there is greater emphasis on conduct remedies for the abuse of market power. The UK Competition Commission investigates cases referred to it by the Office of Fair Trading (OFT) and focuses on the *effects* of firms' behaviour on a case by case basis. Conduct remedies, when firms have been found to be abusing market power (e.g. through monopoly pricing) or acting to create artificial barriers to entry by competitors, have included price reductions and changes in pricing structure. For example, in October 1999, following an OFT investigation, football clubs in the UK agreed that licensing contracts with shirt manufacturers would include a requirement that retailers would not be prevented from discounting replica kits. A number of Premiership clubs had used their dominant position to encourage manufacturers to withhold supplies to retailers who were selling at a discount. The OFT ruled that where contracts were already in place, manufacturers had to tell dealers that they could sell kits at whatever price they chose. The OFT's intention was that supporters and parents of young fans would benefit from lower prices for replica kits.

4.6.2 Monopoly power and competition policy in dynamic markets

Highly innovative industries with fast changing market structures pose very particular dilemmas for competition policy, and the analysis in this chapter helps to identify some of these dilemmas and their implications.

Perhaps the sharpest dilemma relates to the incentive to innovate. It is hard for competition authorities to distinguish between high profits from innovations that benefit consumers, on the one hand, and high profits that result from short-run profit extraction against consumers' interests, on the other. Policy needs to protect the incentive to make profits through innovation, while attacking monopoly profits of the type identified in the static model.

This is not an easy balance to achieve. In a famous phrase, John Hicks, a British economist writing in the 1930s, said 'The best of all monopoly profits is a quiet life' (Hicks, 1935, p.8). Schmalensee, for Microsoft, picked that up:

> Far from living the quiet life of a monopolist immune from entry, Microsoft perceived itself as being in a constant struggle to maintain its leadership in computer operating systems.
>
> *(www.microsoft.com, 5 September 2001)*

The key word is 'leadership'. As we have argued above, Microsoft was operating in a market where a high level of concentration was 'natural'. The market for operating systems was likely to have one 'leader' at a time. A difficult question for policy was, how serious was the competitive threat that it faced? There was room for a huge amount of debate on this question, not least because it turned in part on what might happen if Netscape software developed in particular directions.

This in turn makes it hard in highly innovative markets to distinguish vigorous competition from deliberate creation of barriers to entry. In markets with economies of scale and network externalities, the common standards created by a dominant supplier such as Microsoft, and the low costs associated with high volume, benefit consumers. Entry by competitors is very difficult, and when it happens it is 'catastrophic entry' – catastrophic, that is, for the incumbent firm. A new firm grabs the leadership. It is hard for policy makers to spot the moment when the old market leader tips over from innovator to blockage on progress. If government tries to force entry too soon, it may just slow innovation; if it lets an incumbent block entry through tactical behaviour, it may have the same effect. Hence the importance of the issues raised by the evolutionary models of the firm: the extent to which innovation is built into the incumbent firm's culture and organizational style.

We can draw a few tentative conclusions. In innovative markets, barriers to entry remain important policy issues: competition through innovation can be shut out by artificial entry barriers, and there needs to be a very strong argument why such barriers should persist. One such argument, however, is the effect on incentives for innovation. Firms need to know that if they spend on developing new products they can gain a return: but not one that prevents the next wave of innovation. Furthermore, there are industries where monopoly power is highly transitory. New firms pick up the new technologies in months, and the initial firm's market power disappears: in these markets, there may be no role for competition policy, however monopolized the markets (briefly) appear. Geoff Butlin's experience showed that TranscenData was operating in a market constantly threatened by new entry. And, finally, innovation is expensive: large firms have a continuing role to play in generating investment in innovation, but there also need to be sources of funds for the next set of innovative firms.

4.7 Conclusion

Competition policy is an area of government policy strongly built on economic analysis. The focus of this chapter has been competition in innovative markets in which firms have monopoly power. We have argued that the static models of monopoly and monopoly power have a lot to teach us – and policy makers – still. But they miss crucial issues relevant to dynamic market environments. The evolutionary models of the firm address different questions, notably about the role of innovativeness and entrepreneurial behaviour in competition, that are particularly relevant in dynamic markets. The next chapter turns from markets where firms have market power to markets where they do not.

Questions for review and discussion

Question 1 The table below shows data for a firm selling watches. The firm's marginal revenue from the sale of the thirteenth watch is (tick the letter corresponding to the correct amount):

A ❑ £155
B ❑ £–25
C ❑ £2015
D ❑ £–15

Quantity of watches sold	Price of a watch (£)
10	200
11	185
12	170
13	155

Question 2 Figure 4.13 shows cost and revenue for a firm. Complete the following explanatory statement by placing in the spaces the most appropriate words from the list below:

Total revenue   marginal revenue   average revenue   average cost   total cost
marginal cost   output

At output level Q_1, the . . . . . . earned by the firm is P_1. Since . . . . . . is greater than . . . . . . at output Q_1, the firm could increase profits by increasing . . . . . .

Figure 4.13
Cost and revenue
curves

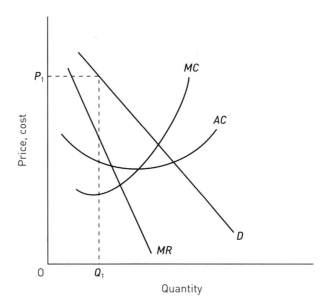

Question 3 The graph (Figure 4.14) shows the demand curve and the marginal revenue curve for a firm. At which point on the demand curve (Q_a, Q_b or Q_c) is demand price inelastic?

Figure 4.14
Demand and
marginal revenue
curves

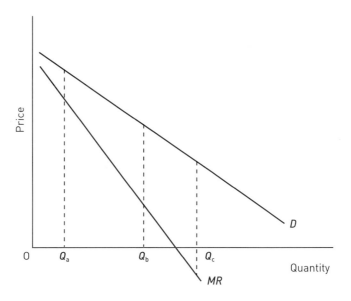

Question 4 Figure 4.15 represents the initial cost and revenue curves of a monopolist producer of low-fat ready meals.

(a) Assuming profit maximization, redraw the diagram and indicate and explain the output level 'Q_1', the price at which this output is sold 'P_1', and the area of profit.

(b) Given the level of demand, use the concept of price elasticity of demand to explain why the monopolist will not necessarily maximize output.

(c) If the monopolist was required to charge a price equal to marginal costs, mark on your diagram the new output level.

(d) Explain why the above decision would be advantageous to consumers.

Figure 4.15
Initial cost and
revenue curves
of a monopolist
producer of low-fat
ready meals

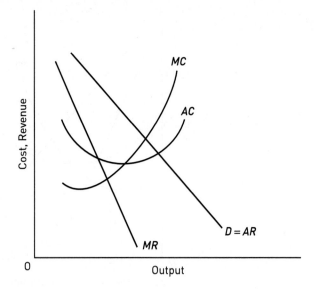

Question 5   Essay: Explain the distinction between 'structure' and 'conduct' in the study of
industry. How do these features of the industry landscape influence competition
policy?

5

Competitive markets

Judith Mehta

Concepts

- perfect competition
- perfect information, homogeneous products and freedom of entry and exit
- equilibrium of the perfectly competitive firm
- supply curves of the firm and industry in the short and long run
- market equilibrium

Objectives

After studying this chapter you should be able to:

- analyse the behaviour of firms and industries in the model of perfect competition
- understand how demand and supply interact to establish market equilibrium in perfect competition
- appreciate the significance of the model of perfect competition as a policy benchmark.

5.1 Introduction

Article 81

1. The following shall be prohibited as incompatible with the common market: all agreements . . . which have as their object or effect the prevention, restriction or distortion of competition within the common market, and in particular those which:

    (a) directly or indirectly fix the purchase or selling prices . . . ;
    (b) limit or control production, markets, technical development or investment;
    (c) share markets or sources of supply;
    (d) apply dissimilar conditions to equivalent transactions with other trading parties, thereby placing them at a competitive disadvantage;
    . . .

3. [Paragraph 1 may be inapplicable if an agreement] contributes to improving the production or distribution of goods or to promoting technical or economic progress, while allowing consumers a fair share of the resulting benefit . . .

(Treaty of Amsterdam, 1997)

In Chapter 4 it was suggested that highly innovative industries pose an acute dilemma for policy makers (Section 4.6.2). What is this dilemma and how is it reflected in the extract from the Treaty of Amsterdam (1997), which sets out the framework for European Union competition policy?

The policy dilemma is how to protect the incentive to make profits through innovation, while seeking to curb monopoly profits of the kind identified in the static model of monopoly. The influence of the static model is evident in Article 81, paragraph 1's prohibition of agreements (among firms that wield market power) which 'directly or indirectly fix the purchase or selling prices' and 'limit or control production'. You will recall that the model predicts that a monopolist will restrict output to sustain a higher price. However, paragraph 3 acknowledged the importance of dynamic considerations concerning innovation, stipulating that paragraph 1 may be inapplicable if an agreement 'contributes to . . . promoting technical or economic progress'.

At the root of this policy dilemma is an ambiguity in the concept of competition: does competition consist in selling as much output as possible at the lowest possible price or in bringing new products to market? If the former, it seems logical that policy should be guided by the objective of securing the market structure that is as far removed from pure monopoly as possible. In economic theory this is perfect competition and it is the subject of this chapter.

The model of perfect competition is also a source of ideas that inform political as well as economic discussion. You may be familiar with debates in the media in which the advantages and disadvantages of 'the market system', or 'free markets', are discussed. These terms describe a particular way of organizing economic activity. Under the market system, firms are free to decide what to produce and how to produce it, while households are free to decide which to buy of the consumption goods available to them. The plans of all the millions of individual firms and households in the economy are co-ordinated through the adjustment of prices which takes place when buyers and sellers come together in competitive markets.

There are, of course, other ways of organizing an economy. One example is the system of 'central planning', sometimes described as the 'command economy' because it is the government that decides on the level and kind of production and consumption, and the government that determines prices. That is, production and consumption take place 'by command' rather than through voluntary transactions in markets.

In practice, most Western economies (e.g. the US and the UK) are 'mixed economies'. A mixed economy is one in which for the most part firms and households are free to pursue their plans through free market transactions. However, the government exerts some control over production and consumption through taxation and the transfer of payments to those with low incomes, and through the provision of certain goods and services, such as defence, health care and education. It is conventional to refer to this kind of economy as a market economy, while recognizing that it is not a pure case of the market system.

Since the 1980s there have been three contexts in which the market system has featured heavily in public debate. First, many of the erstwhile socialist countries of eastern Europe have moved away from central planning and towards the market system. Second, a programme of privatization has been taking place in the UK and elsewhere under which many organizations previously owned by the government are being transferred into private ownership. In both these cases the idea has been to reduce the role of government in decision-making in favour of a greater role for free markets; you may have seen this idea expressed rather grandly as 'rolling back the frontiers of the state'. Third, as the market system has reached out to almost every corner of the globe, pressure groups have formed to express concern at the impact of free markets on the natural environment and on the world's poorer countries. At the time of writing, these concerns were being expressed under the banner of 'the anti-capitalist and anti-globalization movement'.

Given the intense debate which the market system engenders, why is this particular way of organizing economic activity seen as desirable by so many politicians and economists?

Policy is informed by the belief that markets – or, more specifically, *perfectly competitive markets* – are good for us. It is argued that when consumers are free to 'shop around' for the best bargains, and when firms must compete with rivals selling similar goods and services, then there is pressure for resources to be used efficiently, for goods and services to be produced of the kind and quality that consumers want, and for prices to reach the lowest possible level. These virtues are reflected in the assumptions of the model of perfect competition. When compared with other types of market structure (say, monopoly) and other forms of economic organization (say, central planning), perfect competition leads to better outcomes for consumers. The fact that in reality few, if any, markets in a modern market economy can be characterized as perfectly competitive all of the time does not reduce the relevance of perfect competition as something to aim for.

Because the idea of perfect competition has come to provide such an important, if sometimes contentious, policy benchmark, we need to look carefully – and critically – at how perfectly competitive markets are depicted in the economic models which inform policy decisions. That is the task of this chapter. We will be developing models of the perfectly competitive firm and the perfectly competitive industry, and showing how, according to economic theory, the activities of the supply side of the economy (i.e. producers or sellers) and the demand side (consumers or buyers) are co-ordinated. We will then compare the outcomes of firm behaviour under perfect competition with monopoly and question the realism of this approach to the competitive process: is the model of perfect competition a 'well-designed machine', or does it merely describe a 'special case' where 'its sleek design is too smooth to grasp more than a smaller and smaller fraction of what economists regard as market behavior' (Makowski and Ostroy, 2001, p.531)? By the conclusion of the chapter, you will have acquired deeper insights into competitive market structure; you will also be sensitive to some of the limitations of this approach and, hopefully, feel eager to join the debate.

5.2 The perfectly competitive firm

Do you remember what a model is and what its purpose is in economics? A model is a deliberate simplification of some part of the real world. It is always underpinned by some simplifying assumptions so that we may focus our attention on a clearly defined set of circumstances. The value of models is that they help to develop insights into relations of cause and effect. In order to do this, models emphasize some facets of the real world while playing down or omitting others.

Decisions about what to leave in and what to leave out of a model can be highly contentious, because the insights we get out of a model are sensitive to the assumptions we put into it: change these assumptions and the model will generate different results. This may be an unsettling thought if we would like economics to deliver 'hard and fast' truths. However, it is also an exciting thought because there is the potential to use models to engage in debates about the way the economy works. Perhaps, like me, you are one of those who are attracted to economics for exactly this reason.

There are four simplifying assumptions that underpin the perfectly competitive model. These are that all firms and consumers are price-takers, that buyers and sellers are fully informed, that products are homogeneous, and that there is free entry into and exit from the market. These assumptions are explained in the next section.

■ ■ ■ 5.2.1   The assumptions of the model of perfect competition

The reliance of the model of perfect competition on simplifying assumptions is sometimes understood to imply that it need not be taken very seriously. As I suggest in Section 5.5, there is some force in the claim that the model is unrealistic. However, new communications technologies, such as the Internet, have enhanced the potential realism of the perfectly competitive model.

> Visionaries of the 'new economy' tend to present it as getting closer than ever to the universal free market, letting perfectly informed buyers confront perfectly competitive sellers. On the demand side, the new 'friction-free capitalism' promises consumers access to perfect information about all comparable products and their prices. On the supply side, production becomes sufficiently competitive to meet new demand because: (a) there are no economies of scale, so that every product has many competing suppliers; (b) there is costless entry and exit, so that even suppliers with no obvious rivals must set competitive prices to avoid having sales snatched by new arrivals; and (c) there are generic processes and products, giving consumers a wide choice among products that are essentially identical.
>
> *(Adapted from Shipman, 2001, pp.334–5)*

Let us keep these points in mind as we examine the assumptions of the perfectly competitive model.

All firms and consumers are price-takers

You saw in Chapter 4 that under pure monopoly the industry consists of a single firm supplying the whole market for a product. This firm can exercise monopoly or market power because there are no substitutes for the goods or services it supplies. In contrast, a competitive industry is one in which all firms and consumers are small *relative* to the size of the market, so that none of them wields any market power.

The relation of the firm's size to the market is crucial: a 'small' firm in this context may have a very large turnover but still counts as 'small' if it is unable to influence the market price. For example, a city may support many large general music stores but only one small seller of classical music appealing to specialist tastes. The latter is large relative to the local market for such specialized tastes (and hence has monopoly power in the local market) while the general music stores compete with each other despite their greater size. By the same token, a large steel firm may be small compared with the world market for the product.

In determining whether a firm counts as 'small' we therefore have to pinpoint the relevant market. There are general music stores all over the world, but the relevant market is highly localized geographically because consumers will not want to travel far for relatively low-value purchases. In contrast, the relevant market for steel is global; because of the high value of transactions, and the importance to buyers of getting the right kind and quality of steel, the proximity of the firm to the buyer is of less importance.

In a perfectly competitive market, no firm has any monopoly power. What precisely does this mean? One way to model this idea is to suppose that each firm's impact on their market is too small to influence the market price. While a monopolist has to reduce price to sell more, a perfectly competitive firm knows it can sell as much as it likes at the market price. It is so small relative to the market that price reductions are unnecessary even to sell additional quantities that seem large by the firm's standards. And if the firm were to try to raise its price above the market level, it would simply lose sales to rivals who continued to sell at the lower price. Such a firm is described as a **price-taker**. Under these conditions, firms can only choose how much output to sell, rather than being able to choose from among the range of combinations of quantity and price. As a consumer you are probably aware of what it means to be a price-taker in this way; most of us demand quantities which individually are so small relative to the entire market (say, for clothes, CDs or stereo systems) that we are used to taking the market price as given and do not expect to be able to negotiate a lower price. Similarly, many firms are also so small in their market that they must sell what they produce at the 'going rate'.

Price-taker

A price-taker is a firm or consumer whose output or demand is so small relative to the market that it has no effect on the market price.

Question | What examples can you identify of goods or services that can only be sold at a price determined by the market?

Many markets contain large numbers of price-taking firms. In the area where I do my shopping, for example, there are many small independent retailers selling eggs whose revenues are determined by market conditions; I can go to any one of them and the price of a box of six medium-sized white eggs will be the same. Similarly, individual operators on the foreign exchanges sell euros for dollars and other currencies at a price dictated by overall market conditions. The clothing industry also contains many small producers who can exercise little individual influence on market prices. The perfectly competitive model supposes a market composed entirely of such small 'actors' with no dominant operators.

Buyers and sellers have perfect information

The significance of this second condition is best illustrated by considering what might happen if it were *not* true. If buyers are poorly informed about the range of prices available and are unable to 'shop around', they have no way of judging whether the particular price being offered by one particular seller is reasonable. Consider a traveller visiting a town for the first time and needing a local guide book. They will be poorly informed about the price of local guide books and the location of shops selling them. A seller who is aware of the customer's lack of knowledge (say, a vendor located immediately outside the railway station) can exploit the situation by raising the price of guide books above the market level; under these conditions, we would say that the seller has a degree of monopoly power.

Local fruit and vegetable markets (see Figure 5.1) are often regarded as highly competitive. They fit the information requirement very well because of the ease of price comparisons: by wandering around the stalls, buyers can easily discover the different prices and qualities on offer. This example shows how important it is for information to be easily available. If it is very difficult to find the price which different suppliers might charge (e.g. for a non-standard car repair), then gathering information becomes costly and consumers may not be prepared to pay these 'search costs'.

Figure 5.1
Price comparisons
are easily made in
fruit and vegetable
markets

Question Can you think of examples of markets in which information about the range and price of products is easily available to buyers and sellers? What mechanisms exist to improve the amount of information available?

In recent years the amount of information available to buyers and sellers has increased because of easier and cheaper access to the Internet. Anyone with access to a computer can log on to any of the many websites provided by suppliers which describe their product range and menu of prices, while suppliers can make themselves known through 'email marketing'.

> We're in a very competitive environment where we're up against huge companies like Mr Kipling and McVities . . . Email has brought us new customers but more importantly it has done the awareness thing for us. If people do not think you exist, they are not going to buy your product.
>
> (The Guardian, *4 October 2001*)

There is evidence that the impact of the Internet on competitive conditions is strongest either where the good or service has very precise characteristics, as in the transactions in stocks and shares, or where it is extremely simple, such as plastic cups or paper napkins, and that it is especially in business-to-business markets that these effects are being felt. Other areas of potential competitive gain are where information between buyers and sellers was previously poorly matched, such as consumer durables, and in the online job market where job posting has grown spectacularly. While it is too soon to be certain about what is happening, it is possible that the information flows generated by new technologies may be leading to more competitive trading conditions, making 'real world' markets more closely resemble the perfectly competitive model (Graham, 2001, pp.145–58).

Products are homogeneous

This is the third assumption. Shopping around by customers is a more effective discipline on the pricing behaviour of firms when the products of the various firms are more similar, or 'homogeneous', in the perceptions of buyers. Moreover, if prospective buyers can see nothing to differentiate one firm's product – say, detergent – from another's, individual suppliers of the product have little room to manoeuvre with respect to price because buyers will simply opt for the cheapest product available. Conversely, if it is believed that the detergent produced by firm A gets clothes cleaner than the detergents produced by all the other firms, firm A will be able to charge more, even if its product is manufactured to the same formula as all the others. Firm A is not then a price-taker. This example tells us that if firms are to be price-takers, products must be regarded as homogeneous in the markets in which they sell.

The discussion of the industry life cycle in Chapter 3 showed that trading conditions can change over time. Consider the market for eggs again. At one time this market could be characterized as perfectly competitive. After all, eggs are easy to standardize (by size and colour), leading buyers to regard one egg of a given grade as the same as another. Moreover, there were many retailers selling this homogeneous product at the prevailing market price. But then some consumers developed a preference for free-range eggs. Eggs are no longer regarded as homogeneous and so we may say that the market has split into two market segments. For a short while, these market segments had different market structures. The original market remains competitive but, because there were only a few suppliers of free-range eggs, each one had an element of market power and was able to command a large premium for its products. As more retailers entered this new market, market power was dissipated. Free-range eggs still cost a little more than those produced using the cheaper intensive-farming methods but, since all of the many retailers of free-range eggs have no choice but to charge the prevailing market price, the market in free-range eggs resembles the model of perfect competition.

There is freedom of market entry and exit

In Chapter 4, you saw that barriers to entry are crucial to the establishment and retention of monopoly or market power. Conversely, for there to be no market power, it must be the case that potential entrants are free to enter the market. This is most likely to be the case when minimum efficient scale is small; set-up costs are then likely to be relatively low, and economies of scale will not pose an entry barrier.

This condition does not require that new entry actually does take place; what matters is that the threat of new entry is real, that is, that the market is *contestable*. There is then no opportunity for existing firms to restrict supply so as to raise prices and profits above the competitive level. Firms already in the market will know that prices and profits would simply be bid downwards by the entry of new firms until each firm is once again earning normal profits; at this point there is no longer any incentive for new entry.

It must also be the case that firms can exit the market at zero cost in the event that production is no longer profitable. The firm which is making a loss (e.g. because it is using outmoded and hence more costly production techniques) then has an incentive to leave the market rather than continuing to produce. As the number of firms falls, and total industry output is reduced, price is bid up until the point is reached at which all remaining firms are making normal profits and there is no longer any incentive to exit. In the model of perfect competition, the firm faces the greatest pressure to use efficient production processes and to produce the kind and quality of products that consumers want to buy.

These four assumptions that underlie the perfectly competitive model are quite tough conditions and few actual markets will satisfy all of them. However, there *are* real-world markets in which monopoly power is very limited. A model of perfect competition, based on price-taking firms exercising no monopoly power, can provide some useful insights into market competition.

■ ■ ■ 5.2.2 The competitive firm's demand curve

The demand curve facing the individual perfectly competitive firm reflects its position as a price-taker. Let me remind you of what is being represented when we graph a demand curve. The vertical axis measures price, while the horizontal axis measures the quantity demanded per time period. Each point on the demand curve therefore indicates the quantity demanded per time period at a particular price. In Chapter 3, you saw that the *market* demand curve slopes downwards, indicating that a lower price is required to sell a greater quantity of goods (Chapter 3, Figure 3.3).

The demand curve for the market as a whole slopes downwards whatever the market structure (e.g. monopoly or perfect competition). But for the individual firm in the market, the shape of the demand curve for its own product depends crucially on the structure of the market in question. The shape of the demand curve facing a *price-taking* firm is different from the market demand curve.

Question	What do you think the demand curve facing a price-taking firm will look like? Think about a market you are familiar with in which there are numerous rival suppliers. What do you think would happen if just one supplier were to raise its price while all the others maintained the same lower price?

Let us return to the market for eggs in my locality. Because there are many different suppliers of eggs, if one shop raises the price of eggs while all the others maintain a lower price, I will simply make my purchase at one of the many rival outlets selling identical eggs for less. Since we may expect my neighbours to behave in the same way, the expensive shop will soon find its customer base has dissolved. It will either have to restore the price of eggs to the original lower level or close down.

The greater the choice the consumer has between competing suppliers, the more responsive a firm's demand will be to changes in the price of its own product. This implies that a firm with many competitors will face a fairly flat demand curve; the flatness of the curve indicates that a small price rise will choke off demand. So we can conclude that the price responsiveness of the firm's demand curve tends to increase with the degree of competition, because consumers have plenty of alternative sources of supply if the price is raised. In the extreme case the firm is left with no discretion about price at all. If it raises its own price above the market price, all sales are lost to competitors. At the same time, there is no point in lowering its own price because it can sell as much as it wants at the market price and need not reduce price to sell more. In such a case the firm observes the prevailing market price, and then decides how much to produce. This quantity decision will depend on the firm's costs, as we will discuss below.

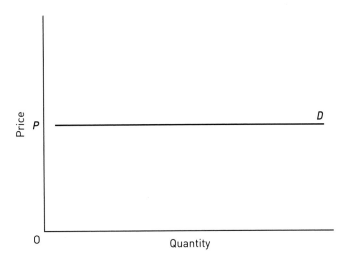

Figure 5.2
The horizontal demand curve facing a perfectly competitive firm

The firm's demand curve gets flatter and flatter as more and more competition is introduced. The perfectly competitive model represents the limiting case, in which there is such a large number of firms selling identical products that the individual firm has no influence on price at all. The perfectly competitive firm's demand curve is therefore horizontal, indicating that it has no discretion at all about what price to charge and is a price-taker (Figure 5.2).

What is the price elasticity of demand of a horizontal demand curve? Recall that its definition is: the price elasticity of demand (ε_D) = proportionate change in quantity demanded divided by the proportionate change in price. As the demand curve gets flatter and flatter, the top part of the equation increases enormously. The proportionate change in quantity demanded becomes very large, for a small proportionate change in price. In the limiting case of a horizontal demand curve, ε_D becomes infinitely large, and the firm's horizontal demand curve is said to be infinitely elastic.

The firm producing in such a market realizes that its actions are insignificant in their effect on price. The market itself determines at what price the product or service should be traded, and the firm determines only how much to sell. Because the individual firm is so small relative to the market, it can sell as little or as much as it likes without affecting market price. But remember: the horizontal demand curve is the demand curve facing the price-taking *firm*. The market demand curve will still be downward sloping.

▨ ▦ ■ 5.2.3 The competitive firm's output decision

Not all industries are the same. Some industries see the rapid entry and exit of firms as conditions change and market prices fluctuate. This is particularly likely in the early stages of the industry life cycle when the market has yet to be established. Other industries, particularly those that have reached maturity, are relatively stable. The behaviour of the firm will be modelled under both circumstances. We will therefore begin with the output decision of the firm at a single moment holding market conditions constant, and then move on to discuss events taking place as market conditions change and entry and exit occur. Throughout this chapter 'industry' means all the firms supplying a particular homogeneous product to a competitive market.

In modelling perfect competition, firms are assumed to choose their actions so as to maximize profits. We have seen that the perfectly competitive firm has no room to manoeuvre with respect to price. What factors determine the quantity of output produced, given that the firm can sell as much as it wants at the market price? Like the firm with a degree of monopoly power, the perfectly competitive firm will expand output as long as the extra benefits of doing so exceed the extra costs, that is, until marginal revenue is exactly equal to marginal cost. Let us revisit the horizontal demand curve to see what this means and how we can represent it.

Question	Look back at Figure 5.2. Can you draw onto it the marginal revenue curve for the firm facing a horizontal demand curve?

Chapter 4, Section 4.2.3 explained the relationship between the total, average and marginal revenue of a firm. The marginal revenue is the change in total revenue as a result of the sale of an additional unit of output. A firm with monopoly power faces a downward-sloping demand curve. It will therefore find that its marginal revenue curve will be *below* the demand curve because, to sell one more unit, the firm not only has to lower the price of that unit but of all the other units which could otherwise have been sold at a higher price.

However, the relation between demand and marginal revenue looks different for the perfectly competitive firm. With a horizontal demand curve, the price is dictated by the market. The perfectly competitive firm can sell as many units as it likes at the market price and therefore the addition to total revenue from selling one more unit is simply the price for that unit. That is, marginal revenue equals price. For the perfectly competitive firm, marginal revenue does *not* change as output expands. We can now add the marginal revenue curve to the first diagram of the chapter. As Figure 5.3 shows, in perfect competition a single horizontal line represents both the demand (D) and marginal revenue (MR) curves.

What is implied when the demand and marginal revenue curves can be represented by a single curve? You will remember from Chapters 3 and 4 that the demand curve traces the firm's average revenue (AR) at each level of output. As we have just seen, for the perfectly competitive firm, marginal revenue equals price ($MR = P$). Since the firm faces a given market price (P), and since marginal revenue equals price, we have our first conclusion from the model. In perfect competition:

$$AR = MR = P$$

Figure 5.3
Demand and marginal revenue for the firm in perfect competition

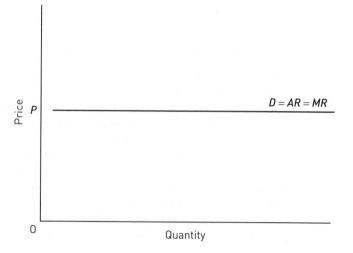

The profit-maximizing output

We can now identify the level of output that will maximize profits for the firm. Intuitively, the argument is as follows. For a given market price, the firm should produce the quantity of output at which the marginal cost of production is equal to marginal revenue; that is, where:

$$MC = MR$$

The argument here is the same as for firms with market power. That is, if marginal revenue is above marginal cost, the firm will increase profits by producing and selling more output. Conversely, if marginal revenue is below marginal cost, the firm can increase its profits by reducing output.

As just noted, for a competitive price-taking firm, marginal revenue is equal to the market price at all levels of output. So for the competitive firm, the condition for profit maximizing reduces to:

$$MC = P$$

This condition is illustrated in Figure 5.4. The only difference between this diagram and the previous one is the introduction of the marginal cost curve, which you will recognize from Chapter 4. Q is the profit-maximizing output. This is the equilibrium output because the firm has no incentive to change its output. To see this, compare Q with Q_1 and Q_2. At Q_1, marginal revenue is above marginal cost, so increasing output will increase profits. Conversely, at Q_2, marginal revenue is below marginal cost, so output should be reduced. There is only one profit-maximizing level of output, Q, which is where $MC = MR = P$, represented by the intersection of the two curves.

Figure 5.4
Profit-maximizing output of a firm in perfect competition

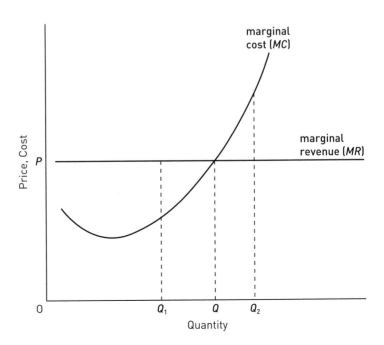

Table 5.1
Output and total cost of a shirt manufacturer

Output (shirts/day)	Total cost £
0	12
1	17
2	20
3	21
4	24
5	29
6	36
7	45
8	56

In order to reinforce these ideas, it will help to work through a numerical example, which will be developed further below. Suppose that the firm is a small owner-managed shirt manufacturer operating in a perfectly competitive market. Table 5.1 shows the firm's total cost for different levels of production.

From these figures you can derive the firm's marginal cost for the different levels of output shown. Marginal cost enables the profit-maximizing output to be identified.

Exercise 5.1

1 Derive the marginal cost for each level of output from the data in Table 5.1.
2 If the market price is £7, what output of shirts maximizes the firm's profits?

Exercises like this are not meant to suggest that firms think in terms of marginal revenue and marginal cost curves when deciding on the amount of output to produce. Terms like 'marginal revenue' and 'marginal cost' are parts of the economist's apparatus for modelling decisions, but they may not be part of the vocabulary of the firm. Perhaps it is helpful to imagine a discussion at a board meeting between the marketing director and the production controller along the following lines. If the marketing director believes that the revenue from increased sales will be more than the extra costs which the production manager says would be incurred, the firm will decide to produce more output; conversely, if the revenues from increased sales would be less than the extra costs, the firm will decide not to increase output. The discussion taking place between these individuals is the same as the decision process described by economists but the argument is framed in different terms.

▨▨■ 5.2.4 The supply curves of the perfectly competitive firm

Supply curve

The supply curve of a firm indicates how much it will supply at each market price.

Section 5.2.3 concluded that under perfect competition, the firm produces where price is equal to marginal cost:

$$MC = P$$

With a little more analysis of a firm's decision-making we can use this information to derive a supply curve for the firm. The **supply curve** is analogous to the demand

Figure 5.5
The supply
decisions of
the perfectly
competitive firm as
price changes

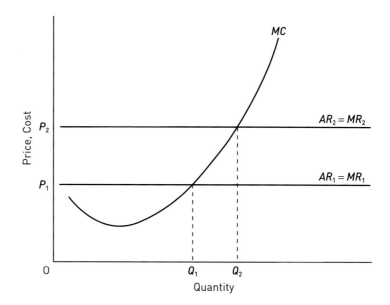

curve in that it provides information about how much the firm will supply at each price, just as the demand curve shows how much consumers will buy at each price. To trace out the firm's supply decisions as prices change, we need to look at the firm's marginal cost curve.

Figure 5.5 shows the profit-maximizing output quantities, Q_1 and Q_2, for a perfectly competitive firm facing two different market price levels, P_1 and P_2. When the price rises from P_1 to P_2, the firm will supply more since the profit-maximizing output has risen. Given the shift of the marginal revenue curve, from MR_1 to MR_2, the extent of the increase in output is determined by the shape of the marginal cost curve. As you know from Chapter 3, the firm's costs depend on the time period specified, whether it is the short run or the long run, so I will look at each of these in turn.

Short-run supply

In order to examine the firm's costs more closely, it is helpful to review the distinction between fixed (or overhead) costs and variable costs (Chapter 3, Section 3.3.1). Fixed costs are those costs which are unavoidable and which do not vary with the level of output in the short run; they include things such as the rent on factory buildings. Variable costs are the costs of those factors of production that vary with the level of output, such as the price of raw materials and the wages paid to labour. The firm's total costs comprise both of these elements.

Figure 5.6 shows the cost curves of the perfectly competitive firm in the short run. We have distinguished between variable and total costs, since this distinction is important to the firm's short-run supply decision. The firm's short-run average cost (*SRAC*) is calculated by dividing the firm's *total* cost in the short run by the number of units produced, for each level of output. The short-run average variable cost (*SRAVC*) is the *variable* cost per unit at each level of output. The two curves converge because a fixed overhead cost is averaged over a larger number of units as output rises. At a market price of P_1 the output level at which marginal cost equals price is Q_1.

Figure 5.6
The short-run cost curves and supply curve of the perfectly competitive firm

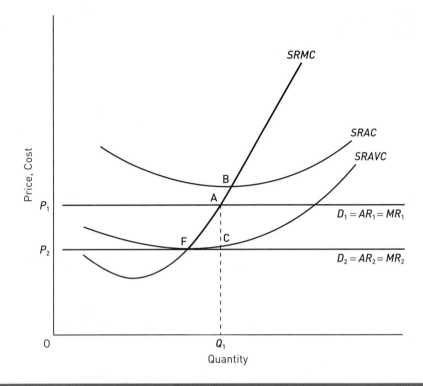

Exercise 5.2

This exercise consolidates your understanding of short-run cost curves. Table 5.2 builds on Table 5.1. We now assume that the shirt manufacturer is operating in the short run. Total cost (and therefore your calculations of marginal cost) remain as before. We assume that the owner-manager of the shirt factory incurs £12 per day in fixed costs for renting premises and equipment. By subtracting £12 from total cost at each output level, Table 5.2 adds a column for short-run variable cost of labour, materials and equipment maintenance to produce each level of output.

Calculate short-run *average* total cost (*SRAC*) and short-run *average* variable cost (*SRAVC*) from Table 5.2. Then draw, using graph paper, the marginal cost, average variable cost and average total cost curves of the firm. Check that the marginal cost curve cuts the average total and average variable cost curves at around their minimum point.

Table 5.2
Output, variable and total costs of a shirt manufacturer in the short run

Output (shirts/day)	Short-run total cost £	Short-run variable cost £
0	12	0
1	17	5
2	20	8
3	21	9
4	24	12
5	29	17
6	36	24
7	45	33
8	56	44

Question Now look again at Figure 5.6. At price P_1, $MC = MR$ at point A, with output Q_1. Will the firm in fact choose to produce Q_1 or will it prefer not to produce at all?

The firm's decision to produce or not to produce depends on the relation between costs and revenues. At Q_1 on Figure 5.6, the price the firm receives for its goods, P_1, is high enough to cover its average variable costs at that output (point C). But P_1 is not high enough to cover its average total costs ($SRAC$) at any output. However, each unit sold is making a contribution to its fixed costs of a size represented by the distance AC on Figure 5.6. The firm is therefore making a loss at Q_1: it is not covering total costs. But its fixed costs are unavoidable in the short run. So in the short run, as long as price is above average variable costs, the firm is better off continuing to produce rather than ceasing production altogether. Q_1 is the loss-minimizing output and the best the firm can do in the short run. The excess of price over variable costs at least makes some contribution to fixed costs.

In the financial pages of the press, you will often come across reports of firms that are operating at a loss. At the time of writing, examples include several airlines, a number of 'dot.com' companies and a football club. Now why would a firm want to continue production in these circumstances rather than simply close down?

Short-run supply curve

The short-run supply curve of the perfectly competitive firm is that part of the short-run marginal cost curve above the short-run average variable cost curve.

We can now identify the **short-run supply curve** of the perfectly competitive firm. The short-run marginal cost curve in Figure 5.6 cuts the short-run average variable cost curve at its minimum point, which is F. If market price falls below price P_2, then the firm is not covering even its average variable costs. This creates a loss which can be avoided if the firm stops producing altogether. At any point on the marginal cost curve between F and B (where B is the point of minimum average total costs) the firm will continue to produce in the short run despite an overall loss. At any point above B, price is above average total costs and the firm will be making supernormal profits. It follows that the emphasized bold part of the firm's short-run marginal cost curve, above point F in Figure 5.6, is also its supply curve.

In order to illustrate these ideas, let us return to the example of the shirt manufacturer appearing in Exercises 5.1 and 5.2. Look again at the marginal cost data that you calculated from Table 5.1. At each price, the firm will supply the quantity at which price equals marginal cost. If the market price is £7, six shirts will be produced per day; if £9, seven shirts.

You can also use your answer to Exercise 5.2 to check the minimum point of average variable costs below which the shirt manufacturer will cease production. When the price is £5 per shirt the manufacturer will make five shirts per day; average variable cost at this output is £3.4 per shirt, leaving a contribution of £1.6 per shirt to fixed costs. So the firm will continue to produce in the short run. As prices fall, the firm will cease production once the revenue from output does not cover the variable costs. For example, at a price of £1, the best the firm can do is to produce three shirts, but to do so it incurs variable costs of £3 per shirt. The firm will do better by producing nothing, forgoing £1 per shirt in revenue but saving £3 per shirt in variable costs. In the short run the minimum price which covers average variable costs is £3. At prices lower than this the firm stops production.

Long-run supply

So far, the analysis has identified the outcome of the supply decision in the short run when the firm's fixed costs are unavoidable. In the long run, the firm has more options available to it.

Question	What distinguishes the long-run from the short-run cost curves of firms?

In the long run, the firm is able to vary all its inputs. There are no fixed costs. Chapter 3 showed that the long-run average cost curve varies in shape depending on the technology the firm is using (Section 3.2, Figure 3.6). The persistence of many small competitive firms in an industry suggests that the minimum efficient scale (MES) is small relative to the size of the market and that economies of scale are limited. Otherwise a dominant firm would emerge. In these circumstances the firm will face a 'U'-shaped long-run average cost curve, the upward-turning portion showing that diseconomies of scale (or decreasing returns to scale) set in at a scale that is small relative to the size of the market.

Let us now derive the long-run supply curve of the perfectly competitive firm just as we did for the short run. Once again, the firm's supply decisions as prices change are traced out by its marginal cost curve. However, the long-run marginal cost (*LRMC*) curve, and hence the *LRAC* curve, is flatter than the short-run curves. The reason is that costs can be reduced in the long run by adjusting capacity as output rises or falls towards the lowest point on the average cost curve (point A in Figure 5.7). This is the MES and marks the level of output at which long-run costs are minimized. The firm will produce where price equals long-run marginal cost provided that price is not below long-run average costs. This means the firm's *long-run supply curve* is traced by that part of the *LRMC* curve which is above minimum average costs, that is, the emphasized bold part of the *LRMC* curve above point A in Figure 5.7.

Before leaving this model of the firm, it is worth noting a further assumption on which it is based, that the firm is endowed with complete information about its own costs, and about trading conditions in the market. A look at the financial pages of any national daily newspaper shows that the real world is characterized by change and uncertainty, which in some cases includes uncertainty about the prevailing market price of a product, or the cost of the inputs required to make that product. For example, a recent press report pointed to the finding that firms can seriously underestimate total costs when venturing into the use of computers by failing to understand what is involved in maintenance and repairs. As a consultant observed, 'Small and medium-sized enterprises generally don't have anyone in-house who can offer them a detailed explanation of all the issues' (*The Guardian*, 4 October 2001).

Figure 5.7
The long-run supply curve of the perfectly competitive firm

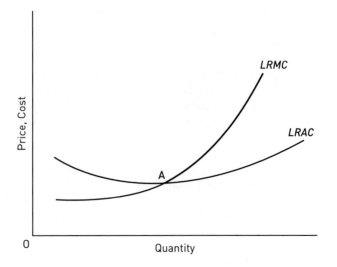

In ignoring the uncertainty that characterizes much of the real world, we are following a practice that is common in economic modelling. We omit certain factors from our analyses, not because they are unimportant, but because they allow the simplest set of circumstances to be examined. Within these limitations, the model has provided answers to three questions faced by the perfectly competitive firm: how much to produce, whether to produce in the short run, and whether in the long run to remain in the industry.

5.3   The perfectly competitive industry

It is nearly 10 years since Body Shop was at its peak [. . .] Since then, the only way for the chain that revolutionised the beauty business with raspberry bath bubbles sold in refillable urine sample bottles has been down [. . .] the real damage has been done by the big corporations, such as Boots in Britain and Bath & Bodyworks in the US, which saw a good idea and decided to do the same. When Body Shop was flavour of the month on the stock exchange, there were no similar products or green-tinged outlets [. . .] Now there are 'natural' products on every supermarket shelf [. . .] Boots was first to copy the formula and now there are new competitors like Lush, that make Body Shop look like a member of the establishment [. . .] Shoppers, meanwhile, are going to supermarkets.

(Julia Finch, The Guardian, *3 October 2001)*

The entry of new firms into a market is a common feature of economic activity, as the newspaper article illustrates. When we turn our attention from the competitive *firm* to the perfectly competitive *industry* as a whole, we therefore have to add to the model the entry and exit of firms. Recall that an industry consists of the firms supplying the market for a particular product. The perfectly competitive industry therefore consists of a large number of price-taking firms. Each supplies only a small part of total industry supply and is hence unable individually to influence the market price. In the perfectly competitive model, as in monopolistic competition (Chapter 4, Section 4.4.4), the entry of firms is explained as a response to the existence of supernormal profits, building on the assumption that firms have a single goal, to maximize profits. This is an abstraction from motivations such as 'seeing a good idea and deciding to do the same', which is justified on the grounds that it enables us to construct a systematic model, not trying to explain everything at once but isolating one factor at a time.

Supply by a perfectly competitive industry is determined by two variables: the supply decisions of each firm within the industry, and whether there are new entries or exits. In the short run there is a fixed number of firms in the industry, each deciding on a short-term basis how much to produce according to their marginal costs and the market price. At each market price we can deduce how much each firm will produce and sell, and we can add up these outputs to find the total supplied. The firms' marginal cost curves, and therefore the industry short-run supply curve, will be relatively steep, since some of the factors of production are fixed (e.g. firms can increase output only by more intensive use of existing capital equipment).

In the long run, existing firms can change the scale of their operation, moving along their long-run average cost curve, and firms may enter or leave the industry. The role of supernormal profits in this process can be understood by considering a perfectly competitive industry in which the market price has recently risen sharply. Perhaps the product has suddenly become fashionable. As a result, in the short run, firms in the industry are making supernormal profits, as depicted in Figure 5.8.

Figure 5.8
Short-run
supernormal profits
of a perfectly
competitive firm

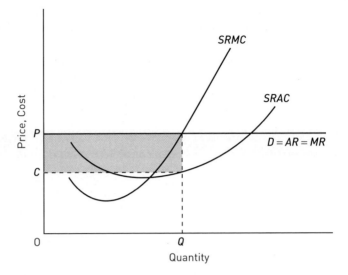

Recall that one of the assumptions of the perfectly competitive model is that firms and consumers are perfectly informed, so the profitability of firms, and their costs and market conditions, are common knowledge. The objective of the firm is to maximize profits – and supernormal profits are, of course, higher than normal profits. The firm depicted in Figure 5.8 will produce output Q at the ruling market price P. It is making supernormal profits equivalent to the shaded area, that is, the difference between price P and average total cost C, multiplied by the number of units of output produced Q.

Question What effect will supernormal profits have on firms within the industry and those outside it?

Supernormal profits entice existing firms to expand in the long run when all factors can be adjusted, including those which are fixed in the short run. And they attract new firms into the industry. Perfect competition assumes there are no barriers to new entry (Section 5.2.1). If the industry's products call for readily available standardized inputs (e.g. unskilled labour and non-specialized components) then new firms will be able to reproduce the conditions of the existing firms at the same cost levels without any difficulty.

Question Assuming there are no barriers to entry, what will happen to market price as new firms enter the industry?

As new firms come in, prices are likely to be bid downwards by the increased competition for sales. The supernormal profits depicted in Figure 5.8 will be squeezed. If we assume that firms continue to enter the industry until there are no more supernormal profits to be made, then prices will fall until firms are in the situation depicted in Figure 5.9. It is possible for falling prices to have dramatic effects on the industry. If eager entrants find they have together driven prices below long-run average costs, many firms will fail. This may allow prices to rise again until the remaining firms can cover costs. One example of expansion and new entry occurred in the late 1990s when it became fashionable in the

Figure 5.9
The perfectly
competitive firm
in long-run
equilibrium

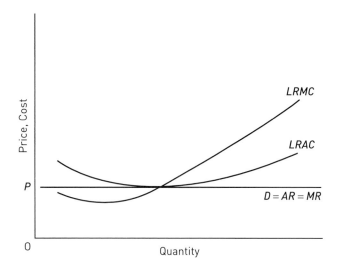

UK to take a break from work or shopping in one of the new-style coffee shops. Existing chains of coffee shops expanded and new firms moved into the market to take advantage of the profits to be made. It is now the case that most large towns and cities have so many alternative coffee shops that it is difficult to see how profitability can be maintained.

Figure 5.9 supposes that the firm shown is representative of the whole industry. However, if all the firms in the industry were exactly identical, using the same technology of production and, hence, with the same cost curves, we would have an 'all or nothing' situation in which all firms would leave the industry when price was below the minimum average cost, or all would enter for prices above this cost level. This does not seem realistic. It is perhaps more reasonable to think of this firm as the *marginal* firm in the industry, where its normal profits represent the best new entrants can expect. Some older firms may be doing rather better, say, as a result of being the first to enter the industry.

What shape is the industry supply curve in the long run? Industry supply is likely to be more price-elastic (**price elasticity of supply**) in the long run than in the short run, as illustrated in Figure 5.10. (Price elasticity of demand was explained in Chapter 4, Section 4.2.4.) If prices rise from P_1 to P_2, supply will increase in the short run to Q_2. In

Price elasticity of supply

Price elasticity of supply is a measure of the responsiveness of supply to changes in price.

Figure 5.10
Short-run and long-run supply curves of a perfectly competitive industry

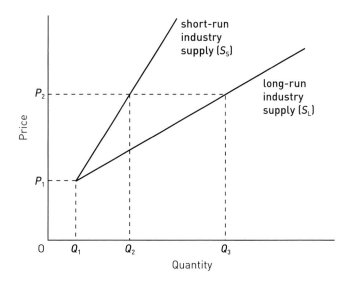

the long run it will rise further from Q_2 to Q_3 as new firms come in. The long-run supply curve (S_L), however, is still likely to be upward-sloping. New firms may be less efficient than older firms and the industry as a whole may experience cost constraints on expansion. For example, the labour needed by firms entering an expanding industry may not be attracted away from other industries except at increased wages. The industry supply curve then slopes upward, showing the higher price needed to coax in additional factor inputs and, hence, the rise in costs as total industry output increases.

The model of perfect competition thus allows us to construct short- and long-run supply curves for the perfectly competitive industry. These industry supply curves are the supply curves for a product in a perfectly competitive market. We can draw these supply curves independently of the particular demand conditions obtaining at any moment in the market as a whole.

This completes the analysis of supply under perfect competition. In the next section we will draw together the supply side and the demand side of the market.

5.4 Market demand, supply and equilibrium

In a competitive market, prices of goods and services can change with some rapidity, and people react to price changes. The model of the perfectly competitive market assumes that buyers as well as sellers are price-takers. Individual consumers make their buying decisions in response to the prevailing market price, and market demand is the sum of their decisions. As you know, for the market as a whole the demand curve is downward sloping, implying larger total demand at lower prices. This section brings together market demand and supply curves to show the results of the interactions between a great many price-taking individuals.

5.4.1 Reinterpreting demand

The downward-sloping market demand curve can be thought of as the sum of many individual consumers' demand curves for an industry's product. As Chapter 3 noted, *ceteris paribus* (all other things being equal) people can be expected to buy less of a product as its price rises. If we take the *ceteris paribus* qualification seriously, and set aside the socio-economic influences on consumption discussed in Chapter 3, we can interpret the demand curve in a way that will be useful for evaluating perfect competition in Section 5.5.

We can consider each consumer as an independent decision maker, and make similar assumptions about self-interest as we made for firms. Just as the firm is assumed to pursue the maximum possible profits, so the consumer is assumed to pursue the maximum possible satisfaction, or 'utility'. (The concept of utility will be explained in Chapter 8.) Consumers are assumed to know what is in their own best interests and to make choices consistent with these interests, given the income at their disposal. Within such a framework we can analyse how a consumer will choose between the different products available. It quickly becomes clear that it is purchases at the *margin*, that is, the last music CD or the last can of cola purchased, that are particularly important in influencing market prices. This is similar to the earlier analysis of the firm where it is the cost of the *marginal* unit, that is, of the last unit produced, which is relevant to the decision about how much to produce.

Like the firm, the consumer in a perfectly competitive market is a price-taker, facing market prices over which she or he has no control. To allocate income so that utility is maximized, she or he must spend it in such a way that the last euro's worth of each product provides her or him with equal utility. If this was not the case, the consumer could still transfer a euro from a product which provides less utility, to one which provides more, thereby increasing total utility. Without such adjustment the consumer would not be acting in the rational way which this model of decision-making requires (as Chapter 8, Section 8.3.2 explains in more detail).

The implication of this line of thought is that, in allocating income among competing possible purchases, the consumer will adjust consumption until the ratio of the utility derived from the last or marginal euro spent on a good to the price paid for that good is the same for all the goods the consumer purchases. So, for example, if a new stereo system costs twice as much as the cost of the last improvement made to your home, then it must have been worth twice as much to you. If that stereo system was worth any less, you could have maximized your satisfaction by buying a cheaper system and spending more on home improvements.

There are two assumptions that are important to this analysis of demand. The first is that more consumption increases satisfaction. The second is that the more we buy of something, the less the last or marginal unit is worth. So as we buy more of something, the price we are willing to pay for it falls. For example, when I am ravenously hungry I am willing to pay a great deal for a bar of chocolate which provides some satisfaction. A second bar provides extra satisfaction but by an amount which is less than the first bar because the edge has been taken off my appetite; as a consequence, I'm willing to pay less for it. The amount of extra satisfaction I gain from a third bar is even less, and so on.

This approach enables us to interpret the demand curve in a new way. The demand curve is not only a description of how much is bought at each price, but for each individual it represents the *willingness-to-pay* for the last unit of each good bought. Under this interpretation we can see that price-taking consumers both contribute to total market demand and at the same time determine their own demand depending on the given market price.

How, then, is market price determined in an environment in which no single actor has any influence? We need to bring the information about supply and demand curves together.

■ ■ ■ 5.4.2 Market equilibrium

The individual firm, the individual consumer and the industry can be brought together in a three-part diagram, Figure 5.11. Figure 5.11(a) shows a typical price-taking consumer, with a downward-sloping demand curve. This curve shows how much this individual will buy of the good in question at each price. Total market demand is the horizontal addition of individual demand. That is, if there are a million consumers just like this one, the total demand for the good will be one million times that quantity at each price. This aggregate demand is described by the market demand curve in (b). Notice that the units of measurement of output on the horizontal axis of (b) must be much larger than those on (a) (or (c)).

Similarly, Figure 5.11(c) shows the marginal cost curve of a typical price-taking firm. The firm maximizes profit at the point where (horizontal) marginal revenue is equal to marginal cost, so at levels of marginal cost above minimum average costs, this becomes the firm's supply curve. The industry supply curve *is* the market supply curve. Therefore if there are 500 such firms in the industry, the supply to the market will be 500 times the supply from each individual producer. Total market supply is the horizontal addition of the individual supply curves and is shown in (b).

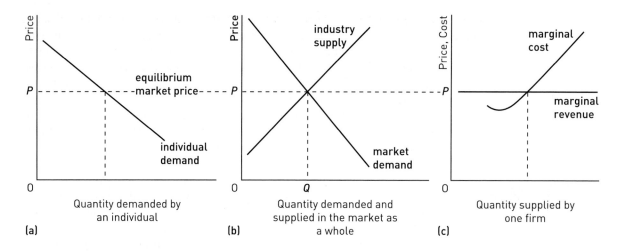

Figure 5.11
Consumer's
demand (a), market
equilibrium (b), and
firm's supply (c)

Figure 5.11 (a) and (c) therefore represent the equilibrium for each price-taking consumer and producer, that is, the best position they can achieve given the market price.
Figure 5.11(b) shows how the individual decisions of consumers and producers interact in
the market to determine the equilibrium price, P. The point of intersection of the market
demand and supply curves identifies the point at which the market is in equilibrium, that
is, the price at which quantity supplied equals quantity demanded. By following the dashed
line across to the vertical axis, you can read off the equilibrium price, P; and by following
the line down to the horizontal axis, you can read off the equilibrium quantity, Q. At this
point there is no pressure for change from within the market: given the market price, P,
no consumer wishes to purchase any more or less, and no producer wishes to supply any
more or less. So this is the *market equilibrium*.

The market price that each consumer observes determines the amount they choose
to buy (represented by their individual demand curves); by the same token, the market
price also determines both the quantities supplied by individual producers and how
many producers choose to be in the market. There is thus a constant interaction between
buyers and suppliers in the market: the market sends price signals which are in turn
translated into quantity decisions by individual actors, which feed back into the market
to determine the equilibrium price.

▪▪▪ 5.4.3 Changes in market conditions

We know from earlier analysis that the slope of the supply curve depends on whether we
are considering the short or long run. Similarly, consumers will be able to make a fuller
response to price changes (say, changing the type of heating system if there is a change in
the price of a fuel) over a longer period. Once the time period is established, supply can
be analysed in the same way as demand. The same distinction between shifts in the curves
and movement along them is valid.

Question	Which types of change would cause a shift in a supply curve, and which a move-ment along it?

The important distinction, again, is between responses to price changes (movements
along the supply curve) and to changes in other factors (shifts of the curve). Variables

that affect the amount a firm is prepared to supply at a particular price are reflected in the marginal cost curves from which the supply curve is derived. Changes in these variables therefore cause the supply curve to shift. The effect on the industry supply curve depends on whether the cost changes are particular to the firm or experienced across the industry as a whole. For example, fluctuations in the world price of oil are a common occurrence and have an industry-wide effect where oil and oil-based products are a significant factor input. When the oil price rises, all airlines find their operating costs rising, and may 'ground' a proportion of their aircraft. Conversely, a single airline may find itself in trouble for firm-specific reasons, such as poor management.

Question	A virulent disease destroys a high proportion of the year's crop of coffee beans. What effect will this have on the market supply curve for coffee beans and on the equilibrium price? What will be the wider effects of this event? What would you expect to happen in the long run? Assume that the market for coffee is perfectly competitive.

The drop in output of coffee beans as a result of the disease reduces market supply at each price, shifting the short-run supply curve to the left. Figure 5.12 shows this leftward shift of the supply curve from S_1 to S_2. At the old equilibrium price, P_1, there is now *excess demand*. At P_1, people still wish to buy Q_1, but only Q_3 is now on offer. The price will have to rise to P_2 before the supply of and demand for coffee beans are back in equilibrium at output Q_2. The effect of the shift of the supply curve is to raise the market price.

Events taking place in this market will have a knock-on effect in other markets. For example, at higher coffee prices, we would expect consumers to buy more of cheaper substitutes such as tea, increasing the demand for tea and hence its price. We cannot say precisely what will happen in the long run. Firms which are badly hit by higher coffee prices may decide to exit from the industry, particularly if the disease proves difficult to eradicate and expectations of future profits are diminished.

Figure 5.12
A shift in the market supply curve for coffee beans

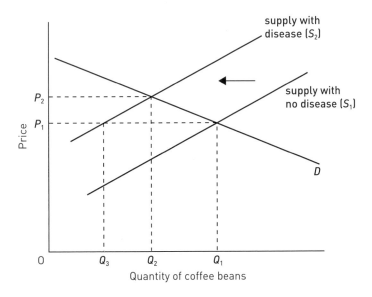

Question	A new technology for the transmission of electric power is developed. Only 7 per cent of the energy originally generated is lost in transmission, and one super-conductive cable can transmit the same quantity of electricity as three of the old-style copper cables. What effect will this have on the supply curve and the equilibrium price?

This is a rather trickier case to analyse. This innovation has already taken place and at the time of writing new super-conductive cables are beginning to be laid in Detroit in the USA. The new technology will reduce costs once electricity suppliers have had time to invest in the new distribution process. Assuming for the sake of argument that the market is perfectly competitive, we can speculate on what will happen to the price of electricity on the assumption that the technology is widely adopted by the industry.

Assume that the new technology reduces the average cost of production of power at all levels of output. The effect is to shift each firm's cost curves downwards. As a result, each firm will be willing to supply more output at the current market price and also at all other market prices that allow profitable operation; that is, the firm's supply curve shifts to the right.

Exercise 5.3

This exercise will ensure that the last point is clear. Look back at Figure 5.4, which is the same as Figure 5.11(c). Copy the *MC* and *MR* curves and then sketch on your diagram the effect of the new technology on the marginal cost curve. Show the new profit-maximizing output, assuming market price remains constant.

Adding up the firms' new supply curves implies that the market supply curve shifts to the right. Firms already in the industry will together supply more at each market price. Figure 5.13 shows the shift in supply from S_1 to S_2. At the old equilibrium price, P_1, there is *excess supply*: people still want to buy Q_1 but Q_2 is available. Price will have to fall to P_2 before the supply and demand for electricity are back in equilibrium at Q_3.

Figure 5.13
A shift in the supply
of electricity

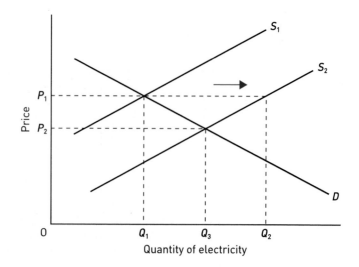

This analysis has identified the characteristics of market equilibrium; it does not tell us anything about the process by which the market moves from one equilibrium to another but compares two equilibrium positions. This kind of analysis is called a *comparative static* analysis of changing market conditions. The results of the analysis can be very useful when applied to real market situations. For example, they can be fed into the calculations of electricity suppliers to help them decide if it would be worthwhile to invest in the new transmission technology.

Exercise 5.4

Suppose that unexpectedly warm weather has a beneficial effect on Florida's orange groves leading to an increase in the supply of orange juice. Assuming that the market is perfectly competitive, what will happen to the equilibrium price? Illustrate your answer with a diagram, and comment on the way in which the market might shift from the old equilibrium to the new one.

In each example of a change in market equilibrium, shown in Figures 5.12 and 5.13, the initial disturbance was caused by a shift in the supply curve. The new equilibrium was found at another point along the demand curve, which did not shift. In the real world, there are continuous shifts in both demand and supply, as tastes and preferences change, new technologies are introduced and unexpected events take place. As the coffee bean case demonstrates, the effect of a change is unlikely to be restricted to a single market. Under these conditions, long-run equilibrium really does seem like a distant horizon – always in sight but never quite reached!

Case study: An economic history of chocolate

The story of chocolate can be traced backed at least as far as the Mayan Indians who described cocoa as 'the food of the gods'. Thought to contain chemicals that, when consumed, stimulate the production of natural opioids in the brain, the cocoa bean was revered also by the later Aztecs who used it as a form of currency. Around 1500, Spanish explorers were the first to bring cocoa beans to Europe where they were used to make drinks until the mid nineteenth century when an English company introduced the first solid bar, a product subsequently refined by Swiss candle-maker, Daniel Peter, who gave the world its first taste of 'milk' chocolate.

For most of the twentieth century (1910–79), Ghana was the world's largest supplier of cocoa beans, though trade with the outside world was heavily influenced by companies who used their market power to buy beans from producers at the lowest prices possible. During the late 1920s and 1930s a number of Ghanaian farmers boycotted these trading companies who had tried to avoid increasing prices to producers. Much later, towards the end of the 1970s, as cocoa prices plunged, many Ghanaian farmers cut down trees for timber and planted other food crops in their place.

Like many other commodities, cocoa prices have oscillated dramatically during the past 30 years. High market prices during the 1970s encouraged an expansion of production to the point where, by the end of the 1980s, world production had reached 2.4 million tonnes. Prices fell in response to this increase in supply and consumption rose too, but only slowly. As a result, stocks of cocoa accumulated, and prices began to fall again.

This behaviour illustrates two important aspects of market behaviour. First, both supply and demand are subject to long-term changes. Second, there is a lag between crop planting and production which means that, when prices are high, producers invest in more plants but the effect on supply has

Case study continued

to wait for the plants to mature. At that time, the market becomes flooded and prices plummet.

By 2004, the USA was still the largest consumer of cocoa in the world, taking up 22 per cent of the world's production each year. In recent years, Brazil's demand has grown dramatically and new markets in Asia, where there has been little tradition of cocoa consumption in the past, are expected to develop rapidly.

On the production side, supplies have benefited from a range of government policies in a number of countries. In Brazil and the Côte d'Ivoire, development and rehabilitation programmes encouraged farmers to use modern hybrid plants. Indonesia also promoted cocoa production as a means of generating economic growth in rural areas.

In 2005, the Head of Economics and Statistics in the International Cocoa Organization concluded that the future for cocoa was 'bright' as demand was expected to exceed supply in the medium term while promotional campaigns and scientific advances in production were thought likely to have effects on the market over the longer term.

Questions

1   What factors have encouraged the growth in demand for chocolate?

2   How would you represent a shift in demand on a price–quantity diagram?

3   Do you think the demand for chocolate will continue to grow in future?

4   What impact will changes in demand have on the equilibrium price of chocolate?

Figure 5.14
Scene from the film *Chocolat*

5.5   Monopoly and perfect competition compared

Just one task remains to complete our analysis of competition within a comparative static framework and this is to compare the outcome of perfect competition with the outcome of pure monopoly for a particular industry. The only difference under consideration is a difference in the number of firms from just one to 'very many'. This means we can compare

Figure 5.15
Monopoly and
perfect competition
compared

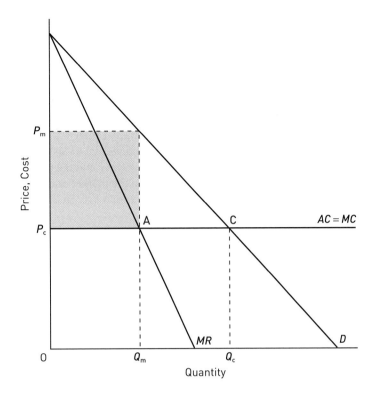

the behaviour of the *same* industry under monopoly and perfect competition. All the components of the analysis will be familiar to you; it is simply a case of bringing them together.

Figure 5.15 shows a firm, a monopolist, producing for a market that is *potentially* perfectly competitive. Let us imagine that government regulations have protected the industry from new entry. D is the market demand curve; because the firm is a monopolist, D is also the demand curve facing the firm. MR is the monopolist's marginal revenue curve. Notice that MR is downward sloping and lies below the demand curve at every point. This indicates that, in contrast to the perfectly competitive firm, the monopolist must reduce price in order to sell more output (and must reduce output in order to set a higher price). As a consequence, marginal revenue falls as output increases. $AC = MC$ is the firm's average cost and marginal cost curve, showing that the firm faces constant returns to scale across the output range.

Question | Think back to Chapter 4. How does the monopolist decide on the quantity to produce and the price to charge? What is the size of the monopolist's profits?

The profit-maximizing level of output for any firm, whether in monopoly or perfect competition, is found where marginal cost is equal to marginal revenue. For the monopolist, this is Q_m in Figure 5.15 (follow the dashed line down from point A). The market demand curve shows that at output Q_m the price is P_m (follow the dashed line up from Q_m, through point A, to where it just meets the demand curve). The size of the monopolist's profits is represented by the shaded rectangle in the diagram. The supernormal element is measured by the excess of price over average cost, multiplied by the quantity sold:

$$(P_m - AC) \cdot Q_m$$

What happens under perfect competition? Let us suppose that the government has deregulated the industry, allowing in new entrants. The market is now supplied by a large number of broadly similar price-taking firms. The cost conditions in the industry are being held constant, and so the constant returns to scale experienced under monopoly are carried over into perfect competition. The line $AC = MC$ is therefore the industry supply curve in the long run as industry output expands. You can think of the industry as composed of many small firms, all operating at minimum long-run average cost as in Figure 5.9. Industry output expands at price P through the entry of new firms operating at the same cost. The effect is a horizontal industry supply curve.

The intersection of that supply curve and the market demand curve D at point C gives the equilibrium level of output in the market under perfect competition. This is Q_c at the equilibrium price P_c. Since price equals average cost, the firms in the industry are making normal profits.

Question What does Figure 5.15 tell you about consumer satisfaction under monopoly and perfect competition?

The monopolist charges a higher price and produces a lower quantity than the market price and quantity under perfect competition. Consumers are therefore worse off under monopoly than under perfect competition. Not only do they face higher prices under monopoly, they are not able to buy the quantity of output given by $Q_c - Q_m$. The introduction of competition therefore benefits consumers in these two important respects.

The result of the comparison of the models of monopoly and perfect competition is an important one. It is often called upon to justify the use of perfect competition as a benchmark for industrial policy.

Question To see what this might mean, look back at the quotation from the European Union's Treaty of Amsterdam in Section 5.1. Can you see an influence of the model of perfect competition in these clauses?

The prohibition on activities that prevent, restrict or distort competition reflects a belief that competition is the most important safeguard of consumers' interests. The particular prohibition on limiting production and on creating competitive disadvantage for particular firms reflects the comparison you have just studied between monopoly and perfect competition: free entry of firms and competition on equal terms defines competition in these documents. Article 81, paragraph 3 picks up the model in another way. Competition is desirable – as the comparison between models suggests – because it produces benefits for consumers. Hence paragraph 3 permits exceptions to competition regulations only where, as a result of agreements to promote innovation, it is clear that consumers still reap 'a fair share of the resulting benefit'. Chapter 6 will further analyse competition policy and agreements between firms.

As a result of these considerations, European competition policy has frequently promoted market conditions that bring markets closer to meeting the assumptions of the model of perfect competition. This is what we mean by the model being used as a 'benchmark' for industrial policy. For example, the European Commission – like the UK competition authorities – has blocked mergers between firms that would reduce the total number of firms in the market. More generally, the effort to integrate the European economies to create the single European market is aimed, in part, at creating competition among firms that previously held protected positions in national markets. A larger integrated market implies more competing firms. The presumption underlying these policies is that a larger number of firms in a market implies more competition and benefits for consumers. This presumption is rooted in the economic comparison outlined in this section between monopoly and perfect competition.

While the perfect competition model has in this way influenced industrial policy, the model is nevertheless the subject of considerable criticism from economists. A particularly severe critic of the realism of the perfect competition model was offered by Friedrich Hayek, an economist who thought of competition not in terms of models of market equilibrium but as a dynamic process:

> The theory of perfect competition has little claim to be called 'competition' at all. If the state of affairs assumed by the theory ever existed, it would not only deprive of their scope all the activities which the very verb 'compete' describes but would make them virtually impossible.
>
> Advertising, undercutting, and improving ('differentiating') the goods and services are excluded by definition – 'perfect competition' means the absence of all competitive activities.
>
> *(Hayek, 1976)*

The model of perfect competition provides one interpretation of competition. The perfectly competitive firm is a price-taker and cannot survive unless it can maintain its costs at a level that allows it to earn normal profit by selling its output at the prevailing market price. This is certainly a form of competition many of us encounter when we go shopping at the fruit and vegetable stalls illustrated in Section 5.2. However, as the quotation from Hayek (1976) reminds us, this form of competition is only one way in which firms may compete. In concentrating exclusively on it, the perfect competition model fails to accommodate competition through differentiating goods and services in the manner discussed in Chapter 4, Section 4.2.

Furthermore, although the effects of widely available technological change can be analysed in the model, as in Section 5.4.3, the concept of perfect competition cannot easily accommodate competition through innovation. The industry life cycle, explained in Chapter 3, suggested that individual firms often compete through innovation, by introducing new products or new technologies of production. This form of competition lies beyond the perfect competition model and calls for a different kind of analysis of industrial dynamics, moving away from the models of representative firms to models that allow firms to be very different. This theme from Chapters 2 and 3 is taken up again in Chapter 6.

The policy implication is that an industry consisting of many small firms cannot necessarily be relied upon to remain in that condition. If it is an industry in the introductory phase of its life cycle, the likeliest prospect is of increasing concentration and the emergence of a dominant firm. Competition policy must therefore be sensitive to the particular characteristics of each market.

> There are rather few examples of market structures or conduct which we can condemn unambiguously as not being in the public interest. Similarly, there are few market practices to which we can give a definitive assent. In most examples, 'it all depends' on the particular circumstances under consideration.
>
> *(Hay and Morris, 1991, p.609)*

5.6 Conclusion

The general result of the model of perfect competition is that in a market where firms and consumers are price-takers, we are more likely than in a monopolized market to observe low prices, higher output and profits at no more than the normal level. There are markets in the real world which satisfy, or very nearly satisfy, the conditions for perfect competition. Under these conditions, the model generates some real insights into the outcomes of a competitive market structure. Many markets are, however, as we have discussed in earlier chapters, far removed from the ideal described by 'perfect competition'. These markets are supplied by industries that supply differentiated rather than homogeneous products; they are characterized by poor information, a high level of instability and change, competition over non-price aspects of products, barriers to entry and exit, and a tendency towards a small number of large firms rather than a large number of small firms. This does not mean that competition is absent from such markets. However, under these very different conditions a different approach to the modelling of competition is required. In the next chapter, Vivienne Brown will develop an approach to competition that can shed more light on the behaviour of firms in these markets.

Questions for review and discussion

Question 1 Complete the following sentence:

For a market to be highly contestable, there must be

A ❏ a large number of firms already in the market.
B ❏ extensive network externalities.
C ❏ virtually costless entry to and exit from the market.
D ❏ significant economies of scale in production.

Question 2 Complete the following sentence:

A firm in perfect competition

A ❏ unlike a monopolist, can increase its marginal revenue by increasing output.
B ❏ that is maximizing profits in the short run must be producing at a level of output where $MR = SRAC$.
C ❏ may be able to lower its average costs to a limited extent in the long run by adjusting its capacity.
D ❏ that is maximizing profits in the short run should increase its output in response to a fall in the price of its product in order to continue to make maximum profits.

Question 3 Figure 5.16 shows cost curves and revenue curves for a firm in perfect competition and currently making normal profit.

Label the diagram correctly by inserting appropriate labels, from the selection provided below, on the graph.

LRMC   AFC   SRAVC   SRAC   SRMC   AR   LRAC   MR

Figure 5.16
Cost and revenue
curves for a firm in
perfect competition
and making a
normal profit

Question 4 Figure 5.17 shows cost and revenue curves for a firm in perfect competition. Which of the following is true?

A ❑ The firm would do better not to produce at all rather than produce output Q_1, as revenue at output Q_1 is not sufficient to cover total costs.

B ❑ The firm is making supernormal profit in the short run, as price is greater than average variable costs.

C ❑ The firm could raise its profit/reduce its losses in the short run by increasing output to bring in higher revenue.

D ❑ The firm cannot raise its profit/reduce its losses in the short run by increasing output to bring in higher revenue.

E ❑ The firm cannot raise its profit/reduce its losses in the short run by adjusting output.

Figure 5.17
Cost and revenue
curves for a firm in
perfect competition

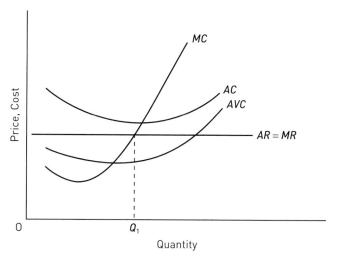

Question 5 Figure 5.18 shows cost and revenue curves for a Firm A, a firm newly attracted into a perfectly competitive market by the availability of supernormal profits. Draw a shift in the AR curve as necessary to illustrate each of the following:

Figure 5.18
Cost and revenue
curves for Firm A

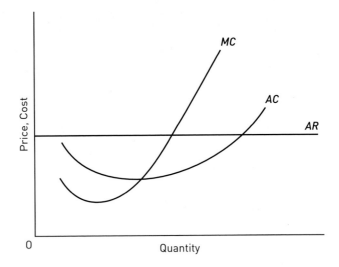

(a) More new firms enter the industry, reducing but not eliminating Firm A's
supernormal profit.
(b) The entry of new firms continues, leading to a situation in which Firm A will decide
to leave the industry.

Question 6   Figure 5.19 shows the cost curves of a firm operating in a perfectly competitive market.

Use the letters on the diagram in answering the questions below:

(a) Indicate the short-run supply curve of the firm.
(b) Assuming a marginal firm in long-run equilibrium, redraw the diagram and mark
in the average and marginal revenue curves.
(c) Indicate on your diagram as 'Q' the level of output and as 'P' the price charged.
What is the level of profit? Explain your answer.
(d) Assume the demand for the product of this industry declines. Using a diagram,
illustrate the effect of this on the industry price and output, and briefly discuss the
wider effects of this change.

Figure 5.19
Cost curves of a
firm operating
in a perfectly
competitive market

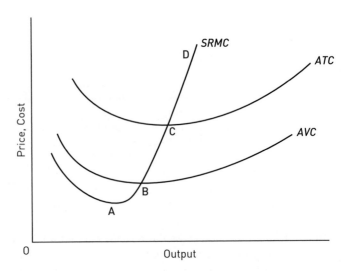

6

Strategic competition: conflict and co-operation

Vivienne Brown

Concepts

- strategic competition
- oligopoly
- duopoly
- game theory
- dominant strategy
- commitment
- cartel; explicit collusion
- implicit collusion

Objectives

After studying this chapter you should be able to:

- understand what is meant by strategic competition and how this may include elements of conflict and co-operation
- understand what is meant by game theory and be able to apply the prisoners' dilemma game and first-mover advantage game
- analyse issues in strategic competition such as advertising, output cartels, price fixing, price wars and strategic alliances
- understand some issues concerning competition policy as applied to strategic competition.

6.1 Introduction: strategy matters

Competitive behaviour between firms is sometimes described in the language of 'war'. We read in the newspapers of a 'price war' among firms when prices are reduced aggressively to try to boost market share by taking sales away from rival firms. This happens from time to time in many sectors of the economy, including the major retailing sectors and the markets for specific consumer goods or services. Rival supermarket chains keep a close watch on their market shares and periodically battle for customers by slashing prices. In 2001, at a moment when four supermarket chains – Tesco, Sainsbury's, Asda and Safeway – controlled half of the grocery sector in the UK, another price war seemed to be under way. Claims and counterclaims were made about price reductions, and some of these were even taken to the Advertising Standards Authority. In price wars of this sort, firms seem to have opposing interests.

At other times, relations between firms competing in the same market seem to go to the opposite extreme; instead of the language of 'war', it is now the language of 'alliance' and 'partnership' that provides the keywords. For example, in 1999 an alliance was formed between France's Renault and Japan's Nissan when Renault took a 36.8 per cent stake in Nissan. At that point Nissan was ailing, but within two years Nissan's loss had been turned into a profit, and the success of the Renault–Nissan alliance had become the subject of numerous books and business-school case studies, including one by the Harvard Business School (*The Economist*, 2001a). Here, corporate profits had been given a boost by the formation of an alliance with a rival firm rather than by attempting to wage war against it. In cases of this sort, firms seem to have mutual interests.

Although these two types of firms' behaviour – waging war and forming alliances – are so different, there is one thing that they have in common: firms are *interdependent*, in that each firm's actions will affect rival firms, whose reactions will in turn affect their rivals. A firm in this situation will have to take into account the expected reactions from rivals in making its own plans, and if a firm is really smart it will prompt rivals into reacting in ways that are beneficial to it. In such cases the simple contrast between opposing interests and mutual interests seems to break down, and what we see are various mixes of conflict and co-operation. Competition between firms that is characterized by interdependence is known as **strategic competition**. This type of competition is different from both perfect competition and monopolistic competition, and we are going to be analysing it in detail in this chapter.

Strategic competition

Strategic competition means that firms need to take account of expected reactions by rivals when making their plans.

In the perfect competition model, which you studied in Chapter 5, firms take the market price and technology as given and so do not go in for price cutting or innovation. In the monopolistic competition model, that is, competition between firms with monopoly power (Chapter 4), firms typically compete through product differentiation or innovation. But in neither of these types of models do firms take into account the expected reactions of rivals when deciding what to do. So these models miss a key feature of many important markets, including the grocery sector, the motor industry, the airline industry, commercial banks and the markets for many basic household items, including foods, soft drinks, cigarettes . . . the list goes on and on.

Firms in these markets certainly find it profitable to cut prices, or to innovate, or to advertise. In so doing, however, they may well take into account their interdependence with rivals, and the smartest of them will choose their actions to ensure a favourable reaction from other firms. Sometimes, firms compete globally, as in the case of automobile producers, but they could be competing for a national market, as in the case of supermarket chains, or even a local market, as in the case of two restaurants facing each other across a town square.

Oligopoly

An oligopoly is a market supplied by only a few firms.

Duopoly

A duopoly is a market supplied by two firms.

The practical examples of strategic competition are thus extremely wide-ranging, encompassing both markets supplied by a very few firms and those supplied by a sizeable number of firms. The term for a market comprising a few firms is **oligopoly** and a firm operating in an oligopoly market is known as an *oligopolist*. If there are only two firms, the market is known as a **duopoly** and the two firms are *duopolists*. Oligopolistic markets typically display strategic competition, but the crucial point about strategic competition is the interdependence of the firms not the number of them. Strategic competition is less likely if the number of firms is large, but the number of firms that may compete strategically depends on the characteristics of specific markets.

Strategic competition is the subject of this chapter, and we shall study it using a new modelling technique: *game theory*. The policy implications of strategic competition will be considered briefly in the final section of the chapter.

6.2 Introducing game theory

■ ■ ■ 6.2.1 Game theory

The analysis of strategic competition uses *game theory* because it provides some of the conceptual tools required for modelling interdependence. Game theory has applications beyond economics, including the modelling of war, politics, business and personal and family relations. In an introductory book on game theory entitled *Thinking Strategically: The Competitive Edge in Business, Politics, and Everyday Life*, the authors Avinash Dixit and Barry Nalebuff compare game theory with planning a war.

> [T]hink of the difference between the decisions of a lumberjack and those of a general. When the lumberjack decides how to chop wood, he does not expect the wood to fight back; his environment is neutral. But when the general tries to cut down the enemy's army, he must anticipate and overcome resistance to his plans. Like the general, you must recognize that your business rivals, prospective spouse, and even your child are intelligent and purposive people. Their aims often conflict with yours, but they include some potential allies. Your own choice must allow for the conflict, and utilize the co-operation.
>
> *(Dixit and Nalebuff, 1991, pp.1–2)*

Dixit and Nalebuff explain that the general must think strategically in planning ahead and anticipating the enemy's reactions. So, if the general's objective is to win the war, not just the next battle, he has to have a forward-looking strategy. The general needs to look ahead to where he wants to be at some point in the future, and then think backwards to the present from that desired point. The same follows for a firm: if a firm wants to increase its market share or eliminate a rival, it has to look ahead to that future, and then think back to the present and plan accordingly. This implies that the environment facing the firm is not neutral, as firms' actions produce feedback effects that influence their environment. Thus theories of strategic competition emphasize that the business environment – the market or industrial structure – within which firms operate is not simply given to them as a natural part of the landscape, but may be constructed by their own actions. This is something we shall examine later in this chapter.

Dixit and Nalebuff argue that life is itself a 'game', and that strategic thinking is required in just about all aspects of life; just as a general calculates his best strategy vis-à-vis the enemy, so business rivals, spouses and parents calculate the best course of action. You may think this claim is inappropriate (or offensive) but the thinking behind it has been extensively applied in economics. Notice, too, how Dixit and Nalebuff incorporate both conflict and co-operation in the passage. They recognize that players will not always have aims that conflict, and they advise them to utilize the potential for mutually bene-ficial co-operation as well as allow for conflict. Just as a general needs to cultivate allies as well as to isolate the enemy, so a firm sometimes needs to establish co-operative relations with others as part of its overall competitive strategy to advance its own aims. Here again we see the combination of conflict and co-operation that is so typical of strategic competition.

It is worth pausing a moment here to note some of the basic terms you will need in this chapter.

- A *game* is a situation involving interdependence.
- The *players* in a game are decision makers.
- A *strategy* is a plan of action available to a player.
- *Strategic decisions* recognize the mutual interdependence.
- A *pay-off* is a player's gain (or loss) from particular strategies. A pay-off can be anything that is valued (or disvalued) by the players. In economic games, the pay-off will be an economic variable such as profit, revenue or sales.

Game theory

Game theory is a technique for modelling strategic choice as a game between players.

These terms help to define what is meant by **game theory**, which analyses the range of 'best moves' available in a situation of mutual interdependence such as strategic competition. Thus game theory is the study of *strategic decision-making*.

Game theory assumes that players are self-interested in that they try to maximize their own *pay-off* from the game. In economic games, the pay-off is usually taken to be profits, output or sales, but there is no restriction on the form the pay-off can take. A game may be a one-off game or it may be a repeated game played again and again.

The behavioural assumptions of game theory are:

1 *individualistic* – the pay-off is calculated individually for each player without recourse to wider notions of collective well-being; and
2 *rationalistic* – players are deemed able to calculate pay-offs correctly and then select the one that will maximize individual pay-off.

In presenting a game, the range of potential pay-offs are presented in a *pay-off matrix*, which is a tabular array showing all the various possible outcomes on the basis of which the players individually select their own preferred strategy. The actual values of the pay-offs are normally selected arbitrarily to illustrate particular outcomes of a game and are not intended to represent realistic values for actual games played out in real situations. This means that it is the structure of pay-offs that is important rather than their absolute levels.

■ ■ ■ 6.2.2 Introducing the prisoners' dilemma

Have you ever wondered why there is so much advertising, and whether it would be better for firms if they spent less on it? If all firms were to reduce their advertising, then perhaps each would increase its profits; if sales are unaffected and costs are lower, the profits should be greater. Why don't firms try this? One answer to this question is derived from game theory using one of the most famous of all games: *the prisoners' dilemma*.

The prisoners' dilemma game has been applied to many different situations. The interest of the game lies in the paradox that it highlights, namely that individual decision-making can lead to an inferior outcome for the players in comparison with joint decision-making. The name of the game comes from a story that illustrates the nature of the paradox. This story involves two prisoners who are held for questioning concerning a crime which they are alleged to have committed together. The prisoners would each do better if they were both to deny the crime, but when they are interrogated separately each one confesses. How can such an apparently paradoxical result happen?

In this game the prisoners (the players) are faced with just two options (the strategies): to deny having committed the crime, or to confess and thereby implicate the other player. Each prisoner must decide individually which strategy to choose. The terms of the game are such that the prisoners have no experiences beyond the game, so that only the pay-offs matter; there are no shared norms of behaviour, for example, or enforcement agencies.

In addition, assume for the moment that the game is played just once; this kind of game is called a 'one-shot' game. The pay-offs for the prisoners take the form of years of imprisonment, so the objective of each prisoner is to minimize their individual pay-off. The question is: which strategy – confess or deny – will each prisoner choose? Any moral considerations (e.g. the virtues of telling the truth) are set to one side.

As each of the two players faces two options, there are four possible strategy combinations or strategy pairs: each prisoner confesses; each prisoner denies; the first prisoner confesses and the second denies; and the first prisoner denies and the second confesses. The structure of the pay-offs is such that individual decision-making leads each prisoner to confess, as this yields a lower pay-off whether the other prisoner confesses or denies. But if each of the prisoners confesses, they both end up worse off than if each had denied.

The significance of this result is that it shows how individual decision-making can, in certain circumstances, lead to an inferior outcome for each player in comparison with joint decision-making. If the prisoners are indeed guilty, you might think that it is good that they are not able to achieve a better outcome for themselves by falsely denying the crime – but the result of the analysis also applies if the prisoners are innocent! There are many situations in the real world in which the details of the 'story' are different but the structure of the problem is the same.

■ ■ ■ 6.2.3   The prisoners' dilemma game

I said above that it is the particular structure of the pay-offs in the prisoners' dilemma game that results in the paradox. Let us now see how this works. The prisoners' pay-offs are set out in Figure 6.1, in a form called a pay-off matrix. Take some time to look at Figure 6.1 carefully. There are two prisoners, A and B. Each of the prisoners has a choice of two strategies: 'confess' or 'deny'. There are $2 \times 2 = 4$ possible strategy pairs: A and B deny, A and B confess, A denies and B confesses, and A confesses and B denies. These four possible strategy pairs are represented by the four cells in the pay-off matrix; inside each cell is written the prisoners' pay-offs to each strategy pair. The pay-offs are given in terms of years of imprisonment. A's pay-offs are the first entry in each of the four cells, followed by B's.

The aim of the game for each of the players is to minimize the period of imprisonment. The actual values in this matrix have been chosen to illustrate the structure of the pay-offs (i.e. the relationship among the pay-offs) that is characteristic of the prisoners' dilemma. To keep the arithmetic simple, each of the players here faces the same pay-offs as the other player; this means that the matrix is symmetrical. The game does not depend on this, however, and you will meet a matrix that is not symmetrical in Exercise 6.1.

Figure 6.1
Pay-off matrix showing the prisoners' dilemma

		Prisoner B	
		confess	deny
Prisoner A	confess	3, 3	1, 4
	deny	4, 1	2, 2

Dominant strategy

A dominant strategy is a strategy that has the better pay-off for a player irrespective of the other player's strategy.

Which strategy will each prisoner choose? Let us start from A's point of view. If B confesses (reading down the first column of Figure 6.1), A would get 3 years for 'confess' and 4 years for 'deny'. So it is better for A to confess. If B denies (reading down the second column), A would get 1 year for 'confess' and 2 years for 'deny'. So again it is better for A to confess. Thus, whether B confesses or denies, it is better for A to confess. In the terms of game theory, 'confess' is the **dominant strategy** for A, as this is better for A no matter what B's strategy is.

Question	Now try it for yourself. What is B's dominant strategy?

The analysis here is symmetrical with that for A. If A confesses (reading across the first row), B's pay-off is 3 years for 'confess' and 4 years for 'deny', so B would be better off confessing. If A denies (reading across the second row), B's pay-off is 1 year for 'confess' and 2 years for 'deny'. Again, 'confess' is the dominant strategy for B.

It follows that, in the prisoners' dilemma game, each player has a dominant strategy: 'confess'. This is the outcome of the game. According to the matrix in Figure 6.1, if each prisoner confesses then each receives 3 years' imprisonment (top left-hand cell). But if each denies, each one receives only 2 years' imprisonment (bottom right-hand cell)! Individually choosing the best strategy leads to an outcome that is inferior for both of the players. It follows that a better outcome requires the prisoners individually to choose a strategy that appears to be worse for them. That is the paradox of the prisoners' dilemma.

Exercise 6.1

Another example of a prisoners' dilemma game is shown in Figure 6.2. The strategies are expressed quite generally as 'co-operate' and 'not co-operate'. The pay-offs here can be anything that is valued by the players; this implies that the players are trying to *maximize* their pay-offs. Note too that in this example the two players are not facing the same pay-offs, so the matrix is not symmetrical.

What is the outcome of the prisoners' dilemma game shown in Figure 6.2?

Figure 6.2
A prisoners' dilemma game

		Player B	
		co-operate	not co-operate
Player A	co-operate	3, 5	1, 6
	not co-operate	4, 3	2, 4

■■■ 6.2.4 Advertising as a one-shot prisoners' dilemma game

Now we are ready to go back to the issue of advertising. How can the one-shot prisoners' dilemma game help us to understand why firms spend so much on advertising? Figure 6.3 presents an advertising game. In this, we assume that there are two duopolists, A and B,

Figure 6.3
An advertising game

Firm B

		high advertising	low advertising
Firm A	high advertising	4, 4	12, 2
	low advertising	2, 12	10, 10

each producing mobile phones, and that each has a choice of two strategies: 'high advertising' or 'low advertising'. The economics behind the matrix is as follows. If A goes for high advertising expenditure and B goes for low advertising expenditure, then A has greater profits than B because B loses business to A. But if each firm chooses high advertising each one receives lower profits than if each firm chooses low advertising, since in the latter case each is spared the expense of advertising and the sales are largely unaffected. In the pay-off matrix in Figure 6.3, the pay-offs are the individual firms' profits. Note that in this case each firm is trying to *maximize* its pay-off.

Question	What is the dominant strategy for each firm in the advertising game in Figure 6.3?

In this game the dominant strategy for each firm is high advertising, as whatever the other firm's strategy, there is a greater pay-off individually to high advertising than to low advertising. Consider A. If B's strategy is high advertising, then high advertising is better for A than low advertising (4 > 2). If B's strategy is low advertising, then high advertising is better for A than low advertising (12 > 10). So A goes for high advertising. The same holds for B. Thus each firm goes for high advertising and the pay-off is 4 for each firm (top left-hand cell).

Of course, the firms would have been better off with the strategy of low advertising, with a pay-off of 10 each (bottom right-hand cell). Modelling the choice of advertising strategy as a prisoners' dilemma game may thus explain why each firm individually chooses a high-advertising strategy, even though a low-advertising one would have been more profitable for both.

■■■ 6.2.5 The paradox resolved?

Commitment

Commitment binds players to a joint agreement by making individual decisions coincide with the joint decision.

Surely, you might say, intelligent players can find a way to resolve the paradox illustrated by the prisoners' dilemma? If individual decisions do not lead to the co-operative outcome, why don't the players abandon individual decision-making in favour of joint decision-making, and thereby jointly choose the 'co-operative' outcome: the prisoners could agree jointly to deny and the firms could agree jointly to choose low advertising? In the prisoners' dilemma game, however, decisions are made *individually*, not jointly; and what the one-shot prisoners' dilemma game shows is that an agreement will not be kept in the presence of individual decision-making unless that agreement coincides with individual choices. In other words, individual decision-making will not support an agreement unless there is some **commitment** that binds players to a joint agreement by making individual decisions coincide with the joint decision.

145

A fundamental point about the one-shot prisoners' dilemma game is that commitment is absent: there are no mechanisms for committing individuals to a joint decision by making individual decisions coincide with the joint one. This is why agreements collapse and the co-operative outcome eludes the players. As an illustration of this, consider a slight variation to the one-shot prisoners' dilemma story. Suppose the authorities allow the prisoners to meet beforehand to discuss their strategy. The prisoners promise to deny when the time comes. The trouble, however, is that there is nothing to bind the players to this promise. When the prisoners return to their cells, the decision to be taken is still an individual decision, not a joint decision. Individually, the pay-offs are still such that A and B each works out that, whether or not the other player keeps to the promise, confessing is the better strategy. This follows from the terms of the one-shot game: decisions are made individually by the players; only the pay-offs matter to the players; and the game is played once. In these circumstances, when they are back in their cells, each player still confesses. It turns out that having a meeting and agreeing beforehand makes no difference to the outcome of the game: the co-operative outcome is as far off as it was before.

This analysis shows that players cannot resolve the paradox of the one-shot prisoners' dilemma game within the terms of the game as stated above. As the paradox follows strictly from the terms of the game, however, we can work out how the paradox could be resolved if those terms were different. If the pay-offs are not all that matters to the players, or if the game is repeated, then it may be possible for the players to achieve the co-operative outcome even when the strategies are chosen individually. We will consider each of these situations separately.

If the pay-offs are not the only thing that matters, then there might be shared norms or practices that could provide commitment and so ensure that individual promises are kept. For example, returning to the prisoners, if shared norms strongly proscribe implicating others (honour among thieves), or if the prisoners are members of a gang and know that other gang members will harm them for confessing after their imprisonment is over, these norms and practices could provide commitment by ensuring that the prisoners individually choose to deny.

However, if the norms and practices *themselves* ensure commitment, making a promise beforehand may be redundant! The reason for this is that if the norms and practices that provide commitment do not depend on the existence of a promise, then the promise is not necessary. For the prisoners, this implies that if the norm of honour among thieves is an unspoken norm, or if gang members know about the likelihood of reprisals, then either of these could be sufficient to ensure commitment without the need for a promise beforehand. What emerges from this analysis is that an agreement without commitment is ineffective, but commitment may not require an agreement. We shall return to this result when we consider implicit collusion.

The story of the prisoners was presented above as a one-shot game, but the prisoners' dilemma game may be played repeatedly. When the prisoners' dilemma game is repeated, players need to look ahead and take the pay-offs in further rounds into account. In this case, each prisoner wants to minimize imprisonment over the repeated rounds of the game, not just the current round. Looking ahead in this way over many rounds of the game may result in individual decisions that lead to the co-operative outcome. Thus, in repeated prisoners' dilemma games, commitment may be provided by the individual incentive to minimize imprisonment over repeated plays of the game.

These two basic approaches to resolving the paradox of the prisoners' dilemma can be applied to cases of strategic competition. The next two sections consider different types of strategic competition: Section 6.3 examines output restrictions and Section 6.4 examines pricing and strategic competition.

Exercise 6.2

It was emphasized above that it is the structure of the pay-offs, not their absolute levels, that is significant. To see more clearly what this means, try to construct your own version of the one-shot prisoners' dilemma game using your own numbers. Try this for yourself before looking at the answer to this exercise. The answer presents a general form of the pay-off matrix for a one-shot prisoners' dilemma game, showing the relationships among the pay-offs, which you can use to check your own matrix.

6.3 Collusion to restrict output

■ ■ ■ 6.3.1 Cartels and the prisoners' dilemma

Cartel

A cartel is a group (of firms, countries) which makes joint decisions with a view to increasing the combined profits of its members by suppressing competition between them. This behaviour is also known as (explicit) collusion.

During the late 1990s and early 2000s the price of unprocessed coffee fell sharply because increased world production was outstripping sales. This sharp fall in price hit coffee producers, including the many small family producers of unprocessed coffee in countries such as Tanzania, Columbia and Brazil. Individual producers of unprocessed coffee are too numerous and too small relative to the world market to have any impact on the world price, and in this respect the world market for unprocessed coffee can be modelled in terms of a perfectly competitive market (Chapter 5). But if the producing *countries* could get together perhaps they could jointly decide on market supply; this would help to smooth out fluctuations in market price and possibly maintain a more remunerative price over the longer period. This would involve suppressing competition between them and jointly exercising some monopoly power (Chapter 4). The countries might thus be able to achieve a better outcome by forming a **cartel**, which could take joint decisions on behalf of its members.

Ideally for the members (although not necessarily for consumers), a cartel could function as a monopolist in trying to maximize combined profits for the cartel, although it might also try to use its regulatory power to improve the functioning of the industry. It would be up to the individual members to negotiate their output quotas and their shares of the profits. In practice, cartels are unlikely to control all the output in an industry and so cannot aspire to a pure monopoly; the question is whether they can control sufficient output to meet their objectives.

This is what the Association of Coffee Producing Countries (ACPC) tried to do. In 2000 a Retention Plan was agreed in which members would reduce their exports of coffee by 20 per cent in order to increase (and stabilize) the world price. An earlier scheme to buttress the price of coffee by reducing the quantity coming onto the market had broken down in 1989, but in 2000 the ACPC had high hopes that its plan would work.

We can use the analysis in Section 6.2 to model the problems that cartels face in sustaining agreements of this sort. Member countries have a joint incentive to keep to the agreement, but each individual country has an incentive to break it. If all member countries break the agreement, however, the agreement collapses. This is a classic example of the tensions between conflict and co-operation that can be modelled using the prisoners' dilemma game.

Assume that there are two countries which produce good *x*, country A and country B. The two strategies are 'restrict output' and 'default' (by not restricting output). These options are shown for A and B in the pay-off matrix in Figure 6.4, which represents a one-shot prisoners' dilemma game. The pay-offs are the individual countries' profits. The economics behind this matrix is that if each country restricts exports, the price rises and

Figure 6.4
Cartel to restrict
output

		Country B	
		restrict output	default (not restrict output)
Country A	restrict output	200, 200	100, 250
	default (not restrict output)	250, 100	150, 150

so the pay-offs increase for each country. If neither country restricts, the price falls and so the pay-offs fall for each country. If one restricts and the other defaults, the restricting country has a lower pay-off and the defaulting country has a higher pay-off, because the restricting country suffers from the price fall caused by the other country without the benefit of the defaulting country's extra sales. Will the cartel be successful?

Question Will the cartel be successful according to the pay-off matrix in Figure 6.4?

Consider A's strategy. If B restricts output it is better for A to default, as this gives a pay-off of 250 rather than 200. If B defaults it is better for A to default, as this gives a pay-off of 150 rather than 100. So A goes for the 'default' option. As this game is symmetrical, the same holds for B. The outcome of the game is that each player defaults with pay-off of 150 (bottom right-hand cell).

The outcome of the game is inferior to one in which each country restricts output with a pay-off of 200 (top left-hand cell). Although the best outcome for the players (not the consumers!) is that each should keep to the agreement, deciding on output levels individually means that both countries default. Again, deciding on strategy individually results in an inferior outcome for the players.

Thus, although it might seem that a cartel could achieve a better outcome for the players, this is not possible if there is no commitment to the joint decision; and cartel members cannot be committed to the joint decision if each has an individual incentive to break it. If default remains on a small scale, the cartel may survive but, as soon as default becomes sizeable, the cartel will collapse as the increased output drives down the price. This is what happened to the ACPC in 2001 when the Retention Plan was formally abandoned in the face of a failure to reduce exports. The ACPC is an example of a country cartel but the same analysis holds for a cartel of firms.

Exercise 6.3

There are two firms. If each one increases output, the pay-off for each firm is 300. If each one reduces output, the pay-off for each firm is 500. If one increases output and one reduces output, the pay-off for the increasing firm is 600 and the pay-off for the reducing firm is 200.

1 Draw the pay-off matrix and fill in the pay-offs for the two firms to the strategies 'increase output' and 'reduce output'.
2 If the pay-offs are all that matter to the firms, explain whether they could successfully collude to reduce output.

▨ ▨ ■ 6.3.2 Successful cartels

Not all cartels collapse. OPEC (Organization of Petroleum Exporting Countries) is one of the best-known of all output cartels. OPEC monitors a reference basket of crude oils and seeks to maintain price (and an orderly market) by means of output quotas for member countries. There are three main problems for OPEC in doing this. The first problem is controlling the members' output of oil. The second problem is forecasting demand, as the demand for oil is sensitive to world economic growth (which in turn responds, with a time lag, to the price of petrol). The third problem is that OPEC members do not account for all oil production and OPEC has little influence over non-OPEC oil production; at the time of writing in 2001, OPEC members accounted for about 40 per cent of world oil output.

In spite of the ups and downs it has experienced, OPEC has not broken up as ACPC has. This implies that in spite of the difficulties involved, especially the second and third problems just mentioned, OPEC is managing to control its members' output of oil to some degree. How can this be explained? Remember that, in the prisoners' dilemma game, only the pay-offs matter, and in the one-shot version the game is played only once. Both of these features of the game may be unrealistic in real-world applications.

In a real-world application of the game, whether repeated or not, the pay-offs may not be all that matter. This means that norms of behaviour, institutional practices and non-economic factors extending beyond the pay-offs may also influence behaviour. Furthermore, for many real-world situations it is more appropriate to think of the game as being played repeatedly. Output is always measured over a period of time, but this time element is missing from the matrix in Figure 6.4. The matrix needs to be reinterpreted in terms of output produced over a specified period of time, say a day, a week or a month, so that the game would be played repeatedly, every day, week or month. This implies that players would need to look ahead and take into account not only the current pay-offs but also those in further rounds. This in turn requires that players consider the reaction of the cartel or of other members if they default in the current play of the game. It is the presence of both these factors that helps to account for the fact that some cartels achieve a measure of success.

A cartel is successful only if members are individually committed to a course of action that supports it, so the question is: what provides commitment to the agreement? As we know from the analysis in Section 6.2 of the one-shot prisoners' dilemma game, players may be bound to the agreement if there is something beyond the pay-offs that matters to the players. This 'something' may be rooted in the experiences, relationships, practices or cultures beyond the game that provide norms, social sanctions or incentives for the players in deciding on their strategy. For example, a cartel composed of countries may punish cheating by political means, or there may be ways in which the cartel can exert other forms of economic pressure on members to conform. A cartel composed of firms is unlikely to be able to exert non-economic forms of pressure against defaulting members, but it may have different ways of exerting economic pressure against firms that default on the agreement.

Furthermore, we know that commitment may also be secured by players individually maximizing their pay-offs in a repeated prisoners' dilemma game as they look ahead and think back. In this case, the strategies chosen individually by players over many repetitions of the game may lead to a co-operative outcome for the players. For example, a cartel could create incentives for individual members to keep to the agreement if it imposed penalties for default in the form of lower pay-offs in future rounds of the game, such that overall pay-offs were lower for default than for keeping to the agreement. If the cartel members look ahead and realize this fact, the threat of punishment by the cartel might provide commitment. Changing the pay-offs by punishing default would thus provide commitment by ensuring that the strategies chosen individually by players coincide with those that are needed to maintain the agreement.

For commitment of any sort to be effective, defaults have to be detected. This may be easier if the number of players (countries or sellers) is small and the game (setting output or price) is repeated frequently, or if information about the members is readily available. Furthermore, influences beyond the pay-offs or further repetitions of the game have to matter for present choices. If players do not care about anything beyond the pay-offs or about what happens in further rounds of the game, then the pay-off in the present game is all that matters. For the threat of punishment in repeated games to have an effect, it is also necessary for the game to be played indefinitely without a known end-point. The reason is that there must always be a further round of the game in which the punishment can be carried out, but a known end-point undermines this. Finally, the punishment has to be certain; this implies that the threat of punishment has to be 'credible', that is, players must believe that they will indeed be punished if they default. If the threat is not credible, players will ignore it.

Thus cartels may sometimes be able to achieve greater combined profits (or greater stability of market shares) by means of explicit collusion in the form of agreements over, say, output levels or prices. As we found out in Section 6.2, an agreement without commitment is likely to be ineffective. This implies that a successful cartel needs to provide some means of binding players to the agreement by making players' individual decisions coincide with the joint decision (e.g. by punishing defaulting firms). But we also saw in Section 6.2 that commitment may not require an agreement as such; and this implies that commitment may not depend on the cartel's activities at all. This brings us to the paradoxical secret of successful collusion: if the commitment necessary for successful collusion does not depend on the *explicit* collusion provided by a cartel, successful collusion may not require a cartel at all! In this case, the players are said to be engaged in *implicit* collusion. This is an important point, because it implies that explicit collusion may not be necessary for collusive behaviour. Implicit collusion is the subject of the next section.

■ ■ ■ 6.3.3 Implicit collusion

Implicit collusion

Implicit collusion occurs when firms behave as if they are colluding but there is no agreement to do so.

Implicit collusion occurs when players individually choose strategies that lead to those outcomes that would have been agreed jointly by the players, although agreement has not in fact taken place.

Implicit collusion also requires commitment. Mechanisms that might provide commitment for implicit collusion may be provided by the practices of the market; even though each player decides on strategy individually and there is no collusive agreement, the market context may provide commitment to collusive behaviour. We shall examine an example of this in connection with pricing in the next section.

Implicit collusion may also be sustained in repeated prisoners' dilemma games by players individually learning which strategies promote the collusive outcome. For example, strategies that punish defaulting firms in a repeated game may emerge without joint agreement. A big player may come to assume the role of 'enforcer' in punishing defaulting firms by flooding the market and letting prices fall. Small defaults may be tolerated, but if they become widespread the big player punishes the others by itself defaulting. The big player may thus periodically have to reinforce the point that pay-offs in further rounds of the game will be severely reduced if players default in the current round. Such a punishment strategy works by making default less profitable to players individually over repeated games.

Another strategy is known as 'tit-for-tat': a player follows another player's default with default but follows co-operative play with co-operation. Cheating is punished and good play is rewarded. As the game is repeated indefinitely, players come to learn that it is not in their interests as individuals to cheat on others, even though there is no joint agreement. Players need to implement some 'forgiveness', so that co-operative play is reinstated and another's default is not punished for too long, otherwise the players would get stuck in default mode with no one backing down. The strategy of a 'forgiving' version of tit-for-tat has been found to be very effective in securing the co-operative outcome in simulated prisoners' dilemma games (Axelrod, 1990).

Returning to OPEC, it is possible that different kinds of co-operative behaviour may help to explain its continued existence, if the cartel is modelled as a repeated-play prisoners' dilemma game. There may be a sense of common cause that helps to bind members to the joint decision, but individual incentives to co-operate are based on each member's realization that cheating (or, at least, too much cheating) reduces individual pay-offs over repeated plays. Furthermore, Saudi Arabia with its high output and large reserves has functioned as the big player that is prepared to flood the market and punish default by smaller countries.

Similarly, in a cartel of firms, shared activities such as trade associations or social inter-connections may help to promote implicit collusion. Firms may also learn over repeated plays that it is not in their individual interests to cheat, and, again, large firms may function as the enforcer of last resort in maintaining discipline even in the absence of any explicit agreement to do so.

This section has shown that explicit agreement is not necessary for collusive behaviour. Section 6.4 examines the possibilities for implicit collusion over pricing.

6.4 Pricing and strategic competition

We saw in Section 6.1 that price wars sometimes take place. But one puzzle is why price wars do not occur more frequently. This section presents a game theory approach to price wars and non-price competition.

6.4.1 Price wars

In 2001 a price war hit PC makers. This was partly a defensive reaction to poor sales growth, as the PC market was reaching saturation just as the global economy was thought to be sliding into recession. The headlines of such price wars make dramatic reading, and consumers benefit from the low prices, but out-and-out price wars are relatively rare. We will build on the argument of the previous section to show how implicit collusion can enable firms to escape from the prisoners' dilemma that can lead to a price war.

The extent to which price cutting increases a firm's profits depends partly on the elasticity of the firm's demand curve and partly on how rival firms react. For any given demand conditions, we can model price cuts for two firms by supposing that there are two strategies: 'leave price unchanged' and 'cut price'. The pay-offs are the firms' profits and these are shown in Figure 6.5. The economics behind this matrix is that if one firm cuts price and the other does not, then the price-cutting firm gains. If each firm cuts price they both lose out; there may be some increase in the total quantity demanded at the lower price, but it is not enough to compensate for the reduction in price.

Figure 6.5
A price war:
Round 1

		Firm B	
		leave price unchanged	cut price
Firm A	leave price unchanged	100, 100	80, 110
	cut price	110, 80	90, 90

Question Start with B this time, and identify the firm's dominant strategy.

As in the earlier one-shot prisoners' dilemma games, each player has a dominant strategy. B will note that whether A leaves price unchanged (top row) or cuts price (bottom row), B's best strategy is to cut price. A's dominant strategy is the same. The outcome is that each firm has a pay-off of 90. But each firm would have been better off leaving its price unchanged, with a pay-off of 100! Each firm calculated individually that it was better to cut price, but when they both did so they simply spoilt the market for themselves. Again, individual decision-making yields an inferior outcome for the players.

What can each firm do now? Should each fight to the finish? To answer this we need to consider what would happen if a similar game were played again, that is, we need to model what would now be Round 2 of a price war. This is shown in Figure 6.6. Starting from the end of the first round of the price war with pay-offs of 90, the economics behind the matrix is the same as in Figure 6.5 but the price at which firms start the game is lower. So 'leave price' in Figure 6.6 refers to the 'cut price' in Figure 6.5, which is where the firms finished in Round 1.

Question Is there a dominant strategy in the game shown in Figure 6.6?

The game in Figure 6.6 is similar to the one in Figure 6.5. Each firm has a dominant strategy which is to cut price and so each firm ends up with a pay-off of 80, although both firms would have been better off if each had left price unchanged. What we now have is a price war that is harming both firms.

The two rounds of the price-cutting shown in Figures 6.5 and 6.6 illustrate the cumulative nature of change as firms interact with each other over time. But could there

Figure 6.6
A price war:
Round 2

		Firm B	
		leave price unchanged	cut price
Firm A	leave price unchanged	90, 90	70, 100
	cut price	100, 70	80, 80

Firm B

Figure 6.7
An alternative
round 2: Reversing
the price war?

		leave price unchanged	increase price
Firm A	leave price unchanged	90, 90	110, 60
	increase price	60, 110	100, 100

have been a different Round 2 in which firms reversed the price cuts of Round 1 and put the pay-off back to 100 from 90, instead of further reducing it from 90 to 80 as we saw in Figure 6.6? Let us consider an alternative scenario for Round 2 by considering two strategies 'leave price unchanged' and '*increase* price'. This is shown in Figure 6.7. If each firm leaves price unchanged then each has a pay-off of 90; this was the outcome at the end of Round 1. The strategy 'increase price' for one firm with 'leave price' for the other firm would result in profits of 60 for the former and 110 for the latter, as customers switch to the firm with lower prices. If each firm raises price then each would have a pay-off of 100. The question is: can the firms reverse the price war on the basis of individually choosing their strategies?

Question To see whether the firms can reverse their price war, consider the outcome of the game in Figure 6.7.

Each firm has a dominant strategy of 'leave price unchanged' with a pay-off of 90. Neither firm individually has an incentive to raise price as doing this will cause sales to be lost to the rival firm, even though each would be better off if they were both to do so. The lesson is that once a price war has started it is not easy for firms individually to return to the pre-war situation.

If firms are forward-looking, however, they can look ahead and see this too! Firms can thus recognize that destructive price wars may be the outcome of current price cutting. Once we move from a one-shot game to the idea that similar games may be played indefinitely, players need to look ahead and anticipate the consequences of their actions. As we saw earlier, just as an army general needs to look ahead and then think back to the present and plan accordingly, so too does a firm. This suggests that firms individually may well learn how *not* to engage in price wars, that is, they learn to co-operate.

Exercise 6.4

Two rival airlines, FlyingHigh and HighFlights, with similar levels of quality and service, are each considering whether to introduce a discounted fare below the current standard fare. With present standard fares, each airline has a profit of £60 million. If each of the airlines introduces the discounted fare, each would have a profit of £40 million. If one airline introduces the discounted fare and the other does not, then the profit of the former is £80 million and the profit of the latter is £30 million.

Using a pay-off matrix, explain the firms' dominant strategies.

■ ■ ■ 6.4.2 Price fixing

Implicit collusion may also result from the practices of the market. The ready availability of information on rivals' prices facilitates implicit collusion by enabling firms to monitor each others' prices without explicit agreements, and this makes it easier for firms to keep prices in line – or to fix prices – without formally agreeing to do so. This openness may be brought about by such apparently innocuous activities as the publication of trade price lists, consumer magazines or online information. The practice of making 'meet competition' promises to customers may also facilitate collusion by providing commitment. This is the subject of this section.

Some shops offer a 'meet competition' promise to their customers: if a buyer finds another seller who can offer the same goods at a lower price, then the first seller is obliged to sell at that price too. Buyers generally see this promise as a sign of intense competition, but it can also be seen as a form of commitment in a strategic game that makes credible the threat of punishment against a player who cuts prices. Price cutting by a 'rogue' store now has to be matched by the other stores; this functions as a commitment to punish default by matching the price cut, and so commitment is secured by removing the individual incentive to reduce price. Furthermore, detection of default is now easier for the firms as price-conscious customers provide it free of charge by informing a seller whose product can be bought more cheaply elsewhere.

Note, though, that the punishment hurts the non-defaulting stores that have to match the price cuts as well as the rogue stores that are cutting prices. This is where the credibility of the threat of punishment comes into play. Rogue stores know that punishment will hurt the non-defaulting firms, and so the threat of punishment is credible only if the non-defaulting firms are bound to administer the punishment and reduce their prices too. The 'meet competition' promise thus binds the non-defaulters to administer the punishment. As all firms know this, however, there is no individual incentive for any firm to reduce price. As we saw earlier, the essence of commitment is that it binds players individually to adhere to what would be the joint decision.

In terms of a prisoners' dilemma game, the effect of the 'meet competition' promise is that it eliminates the strategy combinations in which just one player cuts price. So, returning to the pay-off matrix in Figure 6.5, the bottom-left and top-right cells are effectively eliminated. What remains of the pay-off matrix is shown in Figure 6.8.

The strategy of undercutting a rival is now eliminated. Given the choice of leaving the price unchanged with a pay-off of 100 and cutting the price with a pay-off of 90, each firm chooses to leave the price. The game is no longer a prisoners' dilemma game and price competition is eliminated! The 'meet competition' promise thus resolves the prisoners' dilemma for the firms, and so the game is no longer a prisoners' dilemma game.

Figure 6.8
'Meet competition'

		Firm B	
		leave price unchanged	cut price
Firm A	leave price unchanged	100, 100	
	cut price		90, 90

Exercise 6.5

Assume that there is a 'meet competition' promise by each firm in the airline industry. What difference would this make to your answer in Exercise 6.4? Use a pay-off matrix to explain your answer.

■ ■ ■ **6.4.3 Non-price competition**

The absence of price competition does not imply that there is no competition between firms. Instead of cutting prices, firms may engage in *non-price competition*. This suggests that firms are limiting the area of conflict by co-operating to prevent a potentially ruinous type of competition while competing in other areas. Firms thus use non-price competition to enhance their competitiveness even if – perhaps especially if – the product is fairly standardized.

Firms may improve services as a form of non-price competition, but the dividing line between the product and the service is often fuzzy. Airline competition was once strongly characterized by non-price competition focusing on improved service for business travellers, such as better in-flight meals, more comfortable seats, on-board massages, free gifts, executive lounges with office machines and so on. Classic airline policy was to offer these improved services to the front-of-cabin passengers who provide most of the revenue, and reserve their price cutting for the largely leisure travellers at the back of the plane. This traditional airline policy has been dramatically challenged by budget airlines, however, as pioneered by easyJet and Ryanair, which slash prices by cutting out all unnecessary costs and offering a strictly no-frills service. At the time of writing it is too early to say whether this budget approach will transform air travel, although the increased security provisions and fall in consumer demand following the terrorist attacks in the USA in September 2001 look set to prompt some rethinking of airline policy and a restructuring of the industry in response to sharp falls in profitability.

Non-price competition also includes advertising to heighten the effects of product differentiation and promote brand loyalty for what might otherwise appear to be similar products, such as breakfast cereals, detergents, confectionery, cigarettes and soft drinks, which are the focus of extensive advertising (Chapter 4, Section 4.2). For example, the cola market has some features of a classic duopoly with heavy advertising expenditures by the two leading brands, Coca-Cola and Pepsi-Cola. In addition, there may be inducements such as free gifts, stamps or coupons to buy particular brands. Competition between petrol stations, where there is relatively little scope for product improvement, may take the form of free gifts or shopping and restaurant facilities. Non-price competition between rival supermarkets is often linked to the quality of the service, such as the width of the shopping aisles, the speed of the check-out and customer loyalty cards. It may also involve extensions in the product range, including delicatessen items, in-store bakery items and non-food products such as consumer durables, clothing and banking facilities. More recently, retailing has included online customer services.

Sometimes design factors and designer labelling are an important element in non-price competition, especially as higher prices can then be charged for products with a superior design or brand image, thus moving even further away from a potential price war in which firms try to maintain competitiveness by cutting prices. This may be seen in the fashion industry, for example, not only in exclusive fashion shops but also in high-street stores.

■ ■ ■ 6.4.4 Explaining price wars

The analysis in the previous sections helps to explain why price wars are not more frequent and why non-price competition is important. But price wars do sometimes occur and so it is worth pausing to consider why this happens.

There is some evidence to suggest that price cutting is linked to the cyclical state of the economy: if the economy is in recession and sales are depressed, there may be more of an incentive for firms to reduce prices aggressively. In terms of our game theory model, this may be explained by saying that the time period of the analysis is suddenly shortened, such that the model of repeated plays of the prisoners' dilemma game becomes less relevant: in a recession there is often a fear that there may be no tomorrow! As we have seen, in 2001 price wars were taking place in UK supermarkets and in the PC industry at a time when the global economy was sliding into recession. Similarly, if an economy is shortly expected to come out of a recession, firms may cut prices as an aggressive policy to try to improve market share and establish new customer loyalties in preparation for the coming up-turn.

Another factor is that different firms may be able to offer different levels of price cuts because they have different capabilities and different costs (Chapter 4, Section 4.5.1). If a firm has lower costs than its rivals then it can potentially make price reductions that the others cannot match. This would yield high pay-offs to the more efficient firm. An example of this situation is provided by discount stores. Another example is provided by budget airlines such as easyJet and Ryanair, which have slashed costs compared with conventional airlines by rethinking the economics of air travel. As we saw in Section 6.4.1, however, these budget airlines would be ill-advised to get into a price war with each other.

On the other hand, firms may be reluctant to change prices in response to small changes in costs for fear of setting off the unfavourable reactions of their rivals. When cost changes are significant, however, aggressive price cutting may be based on falling costs over time, and this is likely to be more important when there is dynamic competition (Chapter 3, Sections 3.3 and 3.4; Chapter 4, Section 4.5). The race to cut costs can therefore very easily turn into an aggressive price war as firms desperately try to sell their increasing output. In a dynamic industry where firms have increasing returns to scale, the competition between them can become a fight to the death, as the market may be too small for them all when they are producing at their lowest-cost output levels. This is illustrated by the microchip industry which has experienced enormous shake-outs. (See Chapter 2, Section 2.4 on the consolidation of the PC industry.) This situation can also be analysed using the first-mover advantage game, which we'll be considering in the next section.

As in the conduct of war, some moves in a price war may be aggressive or aggressively self-defensive; others may be exploratory, testing the other side, and testing the market, too, to see how responsive consumers are to price and quality changes. In these cases, the price cuts are part of the learning process for firms that are exploring the limits of their rivals' responses. Sometimes, too, a price war is initiated as a retaliatory move to punish other firms who have defaulted on a collusive agreement to fix prices (see Section 6.3). Furthermore, some firms may take a long-term view of these skirmishes in an attempt to drive out weaker rivals. For example, a firm may temporarily reduce price to the absolute minimum to try to drive out weaker firms that it thinks will be unable to bear the short-term losses. If the price is reduced below costs, this behaviour is known as 'predatory pricing'; the objective is to force weaker firms out of the industry, and then increase prices and take advantage of reduced competition in the future. In many countries, predatory pricing is illegal. (Chapter 4 discusses the court case against Microsoft, which was accused of predatory behaviour towards its competitors.)

In Sections 6.2 to 6.4 we have been examining forms of strategic competition in which there are different mixes of conflict and co-operation. In Sections 6.5 and 6.6 we will consider two different models which lie at opposite ends of the spectrum: the first-mover advantage game in Section 6.5 concerns conflict, and the discussion of strategic alliances in Section 6.6 concerns co-operation.

Exercise 6.6

In this section we have seen that firms may engage in non-price competition to avoid price wars, and that this may include advertising or improvements in product quality or service. In Section 6.2.4, however, we saw that advertising may itself be modelled using the prisoners' dilemma game. It follows from this that improvements in product quality or service may also be modelled in this way. Similarly, investment in innovation in processes or products may also be modelled as a strategic choice using the prisoners' dilemma game.

Two firms, LeadTheWay and FastForward, produce state-of-the-art electronic goods. Each knows that it needs to innovate ahead of its rival to increase its profit, but engaging in extensive R&D is very expensive and risky. If neither goes for a new R&D project, each has existing profits of £100 million. If one goes for the R&D project ahead of the other and the other does not, the more innovative firm has profits of £180 million and the less innovative firm has profits of £10 million. If each one goes for a new R&D project, each has profits of £80 million.

Using a pay-off matrix to model this as a one-shot prisoners' dilemma game, explain whether the firms will opt for the new R&D project.

6.5 First-mover advantage

If an industry has substantial increasing returns to scale this may limit the number of firms which can survive (Chapters 2 and 3). Strategic competition tends to be most applicable in cases where the number of firms is relatively small, so it follows that industries with substantial increasing returns, in which firms' optimal scale of production is large relative to market demand, may also be those for which models of strategic competition are particularly relevant.

Firms may gain market advantage by exploiting economies of scale with given technology (Chapter 3, Section 3.3.2), or dynamic cost reductions as technology progresses, especially when production methods are being transformed as the scale of production increases (Chapter 3, Section 3.4.1). Particular firms may gain market dominance through learning-by-doing where the technology is new and firms work out cheaper ways of implementing new technology as they become more experienced (Chapter 3, Section 3.4.2). Network externalities are another source of market dominance by particular firms (Chapter 3, Section 3.4.2). As noted earlier, examples of industries where increasing returns generate high degrees of market concentration include the motor industry, chemicals, personal computers and microchips.

In these industries it may matter a great deal which firms start out first because the early firms have a *first-mover advantage*. This advantage may arise from learning-by-doing or from any of the other cumulative advantages that can be exploited by getting into the market early (Chapter 3, Section 3.4). This situation can be modelled strategically using a quite different game from the prisoners' dilemma: the first-mover advantage game.

Figure 6.9
First-mover
advantage

		Firm B	
		produce	not produce
Firm A	produce	−100, −100	100, 0
	not produce	0, 100	0, 0

Like the prisoners' dilemma game, the first-mover advantage game assumes individual decision-making and that players seek to maximize individual pay-offs. The structure of the pay-offs is different, however, and so the first-mover advantage game is a different kind of game. Suppose that there are two firms, A and B, and that the market is large enough for only one of them working at full capacity. The game is shown in Figure 6.9. The firms' strategies are 'produce' and 'not produce'. If each of the firms produces they make losses of 100 each (i.e. profits of −100 each). If only one firm produces it has a pay-off of 100.

> **Question** Study Figure 6.9 carefully. What is the better strategy for A?

Figure 6.9 is not a prisoners' dilemma game. Here the better strategy for A depends on B's strategy. If B produces, it is better for A not to produce with a zero pay-off. If B does not produce, A's best strategy is to produce with a pay-off of 100. A symmetrical analysis applies to B. There is therefore *no* dominant strategy because the better strategy for each firm depends on the strategy of the other. There are therefore two possible outcomes to this game: either A produces or B produces.

What will be the outcome? The game implies that if one firm is sure the other will produce, then its best strategy is to stay out. A firm that successfully occupies the market first will therefore scoop the whole available return. Hence the name of the game. The example of Microsoft, which you studied in Chapter 4, illustrates the point. Producing software is characterized by extensive increasing returns to scale and by huge network externalities generated by the benefits to users of compatible systems. By establishing Windows as the market standard, Microsoft gained overwhelming dominance over the operating systems market. Others were then deterred from entering because of the scale of the investment required and the difficulty of establishing a new standard. The Microsoft court case turned in part on whether Microsoft was using Internet Explorer to fight off a prospective challenge from Netscape to this dominance.

In any real situation, what is likely to determine which of the rival firms survives in this fight to the death? It may not be the first firm into the market that survives, but it may well be the firm that manages to achieve the first sustained cost advantage and sustained market coverage. If a firm is early in the market, it can start travelling along its learning curve; it becomes familiar with the technology, it can build on its initial customer loyalty, it can benefit from network externalities, it can buy up relevant patents, it can establish its distribution network and so on. Cumulatively, a market leader emerges and then is hard to compete out – until the next major technological change.

Perhaps this explains why existing firms are eager to keep their options open in developing new market opportunities, even rashly so. For example, many firms in 1999 and 2000 were keen to move into dot.com industries for fear of being left behind on new economy developments. As it turned out, the dot.com expansion proved to be a speculative bubble ready to burst and many firms lost heavily, but their instinct not to be left behind is indicative of the acknowledged benefits of first-mover advantage. Once a firm loses contact with a new market, it is often harder to gain a presence there in the face of established competition.

6.6 Strategic alliances

The pervasive metaphor of game theory is that of 'war', but as we have seen firms facing strategic competition may develop co-operative forms of behaviour as well as engage in conflict with rival firms. As noted above, a strategy to limit the potential destructiveness of all-out war may require co-operative behaviour. This implies again that firms cannot always be thinking in terms of conflict with their rivals but must also think in co-operative terms.

In recent years, many firms have begun to experiment with a further type of co-operation in the form of strategic alliances, an idea that was pioneered by Japanese firms but widely adopted by others. Toshiba Corporation was one of the pioneers in developing strategic alliances as a way of securing global growth by sharing the costs and the risks with other firms.

> When you consider the severe economic environment today in Japan and the unsettled nature of most major overseas markets, you can understand our desire to try to turn yesterday's competitors into tomorrow's partners. We still compete with most of the companies with whom we have formed alliances. But we have found that co-operation is often more sensible in certain markets where it involves creating a new business opportunity.
>
> *(Fumio Sato, President of Toshiba, quoted in* Fortune International, *1993, p.S5)*

According to this view, strategic alliances allow the partners to develop into areas that would otherwise have been inaccessible, and so they help to promote competition in such areas. This context for strategic alliances is thus one of a dynamic and global competition in which only the most efficient and innovative firms can prosper (Chapter 4, Section 4.5). This view sees strategic competition as a journey into unknown territory, but a journey that is becoming increasingly specialized and expensive, and one on which travellers are ill-advised to venture alone. It is also a journey that is becoming increasingly risky, as Exercise 6.6 illustrates, although the returns to successful innovation may be considerable. In this context, a large, established firm may form a partnership with a small, specialist start-up; or traditional rivals find that they can co-operate in a specific area of their activities so that each may enhance its competitiveness on a global basis; or a global corporation needs a local partner in exploring foreign markets. As noted in *The Economist*: 'At a time of rapidly developing technologies, alliances provide a way to dip a toe in the water with minimum risk' (*The Economist*, 2001b). This raises two sorts of questions: the first concerns the kind of co-operative behaviour that is implied by alliances; the second concerns whether such alliances are beneficial.

We have so far met co-operative behaviour among firms that are colluding over output or price. The colluding firms have separate interests, although these interests are

Figure 6.10
Strategic alliances can be important in the growth phase of new knowledge-based industries . . . and in the mature phase of older manufacturing industries

Left: Nick Winton of UK eUniversities Worldwide and Greg Stroud of Sun Microsystems sign a strategic alliance in the British Library Reading Room

Right: Suzuki and Kawasaki co-produce motor bikes to cut costs

interdependent. The interests are separate in the sense that Firm A's interest is to increase Firm A's profits and Firm B's interest is to increase Firm B's profits. They are inter-dependent in that an increase in A's profits depends on what B does, and vice versa. In the case of strategic alliances, firms also have *mutual* interests, that is, Firm A's interest includes directly increasing B's profit as well as its own, and Firm B's interest includes directly increasing A's profit as well as its own. The degree of interdependence and of co-operation between the firms is thus of a higher order than in the case of collusion.

One example of a strategic alliance is provided from the new-economy side of retailing (or 'e-tailing'). In 2001 Tesco (UK)'s online deliveries system was adopted by Safeway (USA) in California to support its GroceryWorks online channel. Tesco was said to be contributing its technology and US$22 million of a US$35 million refinancing of GroceryWorks, taking a 35 per cent stake in the business in return. The partnership was seen as giving a boost to 'old-economy' Tesco's more economical system of in-store 'picking' for the online deliveries (i.e. the online orders are picked off the shelves in the supermarkets), whereas other online grocery businesses had invested in costly warehous-ing for storing the online goods (Voyle and Edgecliffe-Johnson, 2001; *Financial Times*, 2001). What is significant from the point of view of our discussion of co-operation is that both Tesco (UK) and Safeway (USA) had a mutual interest in the success of Safeway's adoption of Tesco's online delivery system in that Tesco (UK) had a financial stake in Safeway (USA).

Another example is provided by the motor industry alliance of France's Renault and Japan's Nissan referred to in Section 6.1. In 1999 Renault took a 36.8 per cent stake in Nissan and Carlos Ghosn moved from Renault to Nissan to overhaul its manage-ment practices. The fruit of this managerial rethink was not only to turn a loss into a profit for Nissan, but also to design a new fleet of cars for Nissan based on ten basic platforms which would be shared with Renault. The mutual advantage for the firms thus included a sharing of floorpans and basic body parts which was expected to provide enormous cost savings for both firms in producing their separate fleets of cars, which would look different although based on identical platforms. As Ghosn reportedly remarked, the alliance depended on 'managing the contradiction between synergy and identity' (*The Economist*, 2001a).

Strategic alliances are often looked upon more favourably by economists than cartels or collusion, and this is reflected in the use of terms such as 'alliance' or 'virtuous collusion'. The reason is that alliances are thought to improve the efficiency of the firms, either managerially or in terms of innovation, production, distribution or the develop-ment of shared networks, such that costs are reduced and consumers benefit. In the case of cartels and collusion, however, costs remain unchanged but prices are increased and the firms are thought to benefit at the expense of consumers.

Alliances are thought to be beneficial to consumers if they are directed at promoting innovation. Economists agree that there tends to be an under-investment in innovation and insufficient dissemination of information on innovation. Investment in innovation is very expensive, risky and long-term, and firms calculate the profitability of such investment only by taking into account the impact on their own profits individually, without regard to wider benefits. To the extent that sharing the costs and risks of such investment encourages firms to do more of it than they would otherwise, and to share or exchange the information that they have, strategic alliances are thought to be beneficial not only to the firms involved but also to consumers. Alliances are also thought to be beneficial if they bring together complementary activities and capabilities rather than competing ones. Even if the partners are competing directly in the same market, complementary capabilities – such as skills, knowledge, facilities or networks – may provide the basis for a beneficial alliance. Where the partners are not competing directly, mutually beneficial inter-firm co-operation may come from technology licensing, supply arrangements, joint ventures, research agreements, mutual training schemes or the exchange of people and ideas. Thus strategic alliances tend to be most successful between firms that have complementary strengths.

So, returning to our examples: the alliances between Tesco (UK) and Safeway (USA) and between Nissan and Renault were based on enhanced investment and complementary inputs from the two partners. The Tesco/Safeway alliance promoted e-tailing by allowing Tesco to share its expertise with Safeway, and the Nissan/Renault alliance promoted the sharing of better management and larger economies of scale in car production. Both alliances were expected to be financially beneficial to the individual firms, but appraisal by economists tries to look beyond the individual firms' profitability to assess the likely impact on costs and, hence, the benefits to consumers. Sharing investment and production in some areas is thought to provide one way of improving efficiency in production while maintaining competitition for the benefit of consumers.

It is recognized that strategic alliances may not last very long and sometimes raise difficult issues associated with different corporate cultures. Sustained co-operation may thus not be feasible over long periods because of different business cultures, different objectives of the partners or changing external circumstances, or because the initial objectives of the alliance have been more or less fulfilled. It may be that part of the synergy of such alliances arises precisely because of the interaction of two different corporate cultures, but that this arrangement will often be short-lived. As Ghosn remarked, there is a tension between creating synergies between firms and maintaining their sense of individual identity. Strategic alliances also raise the more delicate question of the cultural context in which such partnerships are viable, and this in turn sometimes requires a different conception of business ethics and inter-firm relations. This issue has been the subject of considerable interest recently among economists trying to learn about best practice in firms from different cultural contexts.

6.7 Strategic competition policy

This section briefly considers some of the implications of our analysis of strategic competition for competition policy. You have already met some of the difficulties involved in framing competition policy (Chapter 4, Section 4.6). In this section we shall see that reframing policy questions in strategic terms leads to some unusual – and sometimes counterintuitive – results.

▪ ▪ ■ 6.7.1 Collusion

Competition policy tries to put an end to anti-competitive behaviour. The analysis in Sections 6.3 and 6.4, however, underlines just how difficult this can be in practice. Collusion may be sustained not only by explicit agreements but also by implicit collusion resulting from practices which, on the face of it, might not appear to be anti-competitive. We have seen that apparently competitive practices such as 'meet competition' promises may provide the commitment that sustains collusive behaviour.

What has emerged from the analysis of strategic competition is that anti-competitive behaviour does not necessarily imply secret agreements in smoke-filled rooms – or even discreet gentlemen's agreements in exclusive clubs – but may be the result of ordinary practices of day-to-day trading or trade association activities. This makes it harder for governments and regulatory authorities to establish whether behaviour is collusive. In the case of explicit collusive agreements there is the possibility of finding clear evidence, but in the absence of this all that can be done is to examine whether the outcomes in terms of prices and output are more consistent with collusion than with competition. To establish whether price fixing has taken place, for example, it is necessary to look at the relation between firms' costs and prices, and to try to establish whether there is evidence of 'parallel' pricing across firms, that is, whether firms' prices tend to move together. But if the firms are facing similar costs, it is hard to know whether parallel prices follow from the similar costs faced by the firms or whether the firms are colluding over price.

In spite of these difficulties there have been some successful crackdowns on cartels over the years, and some of these suggest that large numbers of firms may be involved, showing that collusive behaviour is not the preserve of markets with few firms. For example, it was reported in *Fair Trading*, the magazine of the Office of Fair Trading, UK, that in 2000 the German competition authority undertook its largest ever cartel prosecution against 62 companies in the ready-mixed concrete industry, which were fined DM 320 million for operating an output cartel. In Denmark the discovery of an alleged cartel in electrical wiring was expected to lead to 200 to 300 firms being prosecuted (*Fair Trading*, Issue 29, February 2001, p.12).

In the UK, the Office of Fair Trading was given enhanced powers in the Competition Act 2000 and is planning new competitive measures under its new Director General, John Vickers, previously Chief Economist and Executive Director at the Bank of England and Professor of Economics at Oxford. These include a new 'leniency' policy, influenced by the US policy, which offers leniency, that is, total immunity from legal penalties, to the first cartel member to provide information on other cartel members (plus some discretionary limited leniency for other cartel members), together with the imposition of financial penalties of up to 10 per cent of a company's UK turnover for the period of infringement (up to a maximum of three years). It was reported that in the USA over the last five years such a leniency policy 'has been responsible for detecting and cracking more international cartels than all of our search warrants, secret audio and videotapes and FBI interrogations combined' (Scott Hammond, Director of Criminal Enforcement for the US Department of Justice's Antitrust Division, speaking at the International Cartels Workshop hosted by the Office of Fair Trading in November 2000, which was attended by over a hundred international cartel busters, as reported in *Fair Trading*, Issue 29, February 2001, pp.13–14).

In 2000 the UK government announced a proposal to make it a criminal offence for individuals to engage in cartels, thus also threatening to jail business executives who take part in price-fixing cartels rather than simply impose fines on their companies, and bringing UK legislation more in line with the USA rather than the EU. Explicit cartel

Case study: From collusion to art wars

A dramatic example was the explicit collusion between the auction houses Christie's and Sotheby's between 1993 and 1999 to fix prices by agreeing on the commission that clients were charged for selling their fine art, jewellery and furniture. The prosecution alleged that clients were cheated of as much as $400 million during the period. Sotheby's pleaded guilty to price fixing and was fined $45 million; and the former chairman, Alfred Taubman, was liable to up to three years' imprisonment as well as a large fine. Christie's, on the other hand, received immunity for being the first to provide evidence of the collusion, and its former chairman, Sir Anthony Tennant, could not be extradited from Great Britain

to the USA and so remained free. The trial in New York during 2001 held the elite art world transfixed, and there were reportedly plans to make a Hollywood movie based on the price fixing and the ensuing humiliation of two of the most prestigious auction houses in the world (Eunjung Cha, 2001).

Question

What factors aided the identification of collusion in this case? Do you think implicit collusion would have been possible for the auction houses and, if so, how difficult would the practice have been to uncover?

agreements and implicit concerted practices which are anti-competitive in their objectives or effects are prohibited under Article 81(1) of the Treaty of Amsterdam (previously Article 85(1) of the Treaty of Rome) (see also Chapter 5, Section 5.1). It is widely thought, however, that the European Commission has been hampered in cracking down on cartels by lack of resources, legal restraints and bureaucratic delays. The Commission also lacks the threat of jail for convicted price-fixing executives; and observers have noted that the threat of claims for damages by consumer groups against convicted companies which are present in the USA is not available in the EU. During 2000 and 2001, however, partly helped by new rules to reward 'whistle-blowers', Mario Monti, the European Competition Commissioner, launched a new offensive against cartels. During 2001 the competition department reportedly raised €1.8 billion in fines on cartels, and these included illegal agreements on Nordic airline routes, graphite electrodes, sodium gluconate, vitamins, brewing, citric acid, zinc phosphate, carbonless paper and euro bank charges. The euro bank charges cartel involved five German banks which operated a price-fixing cartel on foreign exchange transaction charges in order to compensate for the anticipated loss of revenue caused by reduced opportunities for foreign currency speculation with the introduction of the euro. The banks were fined £63 million (Guerrera, 2001; Osborn, 2001).

■■■ 6.7.2 Strategic alliances

As was argued in Section 6.6, there are some sound economic arguments in favour of strategic alliances, so policy makers accept and even encourage those alliances while being wary of alliances that do not offer these benefits. In principle, this implies that alliances promoting the production and diffusion of innovation and/or involving complementary skills and resources are regarded as beneficial. It also implies that alliances involving co-operation other than at the R&D stage (e.g. marketing and distribution stages), and those co-operating over non-complementary activities, are more likely to be regarded as anti-competitive.

Although, in principle, the issues might seem straightforward, in practice it is often not clear how to keep these various aspects separate. First, in practice it is sometimes difficult to separate the different stages of research, product development, manufacturing and marketing. Second, given the risks and long-term nature of investment into new products and processes, the co-operating firms might want to argue that they also need to co-operate at the manufacturing and marketing stages to make the investment financially attractive. Third, applying these principles to the complexities of real circumstances can be extremely difficult. Thus finding the right balance between beneficial alliances and anti-competitive collusion is often difficult in practice.

As we saw above, agreements and practices are prohibited by Article 81(1) of the EC Treaty if they are held to be anti-competitive, but there are exemptions from this under Article 81(3) if the agreements and practices contribute to 'improving the production or distribution of goods or to promoting technical or economic progress, while allowing consumers a fair share of the resulting benefit'. The grounds for exemption thus reflect our economic analysis of strategic competition that, although such agreements and practices are harmful if their effects are solely anti-competitive, on balance they may be beneficial if there are improvements in efficiency that outweigh the negative effects arising from the reduction in competition.

■■■ 6.7.3 Picking winners?

The first-mover advantage game in Section 6.5 highlights the importance of being in at the start of new developments. Should government policy try to anticipate this by picking winners? This policy question is illustrated in Figure 6.11, which is the same as Figure 6.9 except that A, the preferred firm, is now subsidized by 150 to produce when it would otherwise make a loss (top left-hand cell).

A receives a subsidy of 150 if it would otherwise make a loss, that is, the negative pay-off of −100 is converted into a positive pay-off of 50 if both firms produce. It follows that A now has a dominant strategy 'produce' as this has the better pay-off whatever B's strategy. But in this case, B's best strategy is 'not produce' (0 as opposed to a negative pay-off).

Question	Does the government actually have to pay the subsidy for its policy to work?

This is an interesting question as it depends on how we are modelling the government. At one time, in the UK at least, the answer to this question would have been 'yes'. An issue might have been whether or when the government should or could put an end to the payment. This kind of case is similar to the 'infant industry' argument, which asserts that new industries should be supported while establishing themselves, particularly in the context of low-income countries. The problem is deciding when the moment has come for the industry to become independent of government support.

Figure 6.11
Picking the winner

		Firm B	
		produce	not produce
Firm A	produce	50, −100	100, 0
	not produce	0, 100	0, 0

In strict game theory terms, however, if the government's subsidy policy is a credible policy that is made known in advance, B's best strategy is not to produce. In which case the government does not actually have to pay any subsidy! This is the equivalent of the credible threat already discussed, and it raises the question of how the government's promise could be made credible.

But if we are considering how the government's policy is to be made credible, we are now treating the government as a player in the game.

■ ■ ■ 6.7.4   The government as player?

Once we conceive of the government as a player in a strategic game we need to specify its pay-offs too. What are its interests? Does the government have its own pay-offs, or does it identify with the pay-offs of particular players? And how well informed can the government be? If everyone is acting strategically, how can the government gain independent information about which firm is likely to be better in the long run? The firms concerned are not going to be truthful but will present information to their own advantage, and why should the government know better than firms in the market what will be the better bet in the long run?

Once the government and its authorities – and even its appointed regulators and commissioners – are seen as players in a game, their interests, their credibility and their pay-offs have to be taken into account. But this changes the nature of the policy analysis in ways that become highly complicated and not fully understood. As we saw above, the UK government has recently proposed that the Competition Commission should be free of political control and that stiffer penalties should be introduced for company executives found to be engaged in collusive behaviour. It remains to be seen whether these proposals find their way onto the statute book, but perhaps they will be seen as a credible commitment on the part of the government to change the structure of the pay-offs facing firms.

6.8   Conclusion: why strategy matters

This chapter has examined different kinds of strategic competition and has introduced game theory as a way of modelling this competition. One of the interesting results to emerge from this analysis of firms' interdependence is that conflict and co-operation are not necessarily opposites, as firms may be faced with situations that include a mixture of conflict and co-operation. As in many situations in social life, firms need to handle both the conflict and the co-operation, but an implication of this is that it may sometimes be harder to identify anti-competitive practices. Game theory can help us to understand firms' co-operative and conflictual behaviour, complementing the models you studied in Chapters 2 and 3.

Questions for review and discussion

Question 1   Complete the following by placing in the first space a phrase from the left-hand column and in the second space a phrase from the right-hand column.

superior to	the worst individually
inferior to	the best individually
the same as	between the best and the worst individually

In the prisoners' dilemma game, if each player chooses their dominant strategy, the outcome will be . . . that resulting from each player going against their dominant strategy. If player A chooses a dominant strategy and player B goes against his, this will result in an outcome that is . . . for player B.

Question 2 In Figure 6.12, A and B are firms; X and Y are the strategies available to them. The pay-offs represent profits, and we assume that each firm wishes to make as much profit as possible. Insert the numbers from the list to fill in the blank spaces in the matrix in such a way that the two firms, A and B, are faced with the prisoners' dilemma. The pay-offs should be symmetrical for the two firms. Also, if both firms choose the same strategy, each should receive the same amount of profit. Each number needs to appear twice on the matrix. One number is filled in for you.

3 5 5 8 8 10 10

Figure 6.12
Game strategy
matrix

Question 3 Rearrange the numbers from the answers to question 2 in Figure 6.13 so that each player has the same dominant strategy as before but there is no prisoners' dilemma. Once again, pay-offs for the two firms should be symmetrical. One number is filled in for you (note there is more than one combination that is correct).

3 5 5 8 8 10 10

Figure 6.13
Game strategy
matrix

Question 4 This question has five True/False statements associated with it.

The matrix in Figure 6.14 shows pay-offs to each of two firms, A and B. Each prefers higher profit to lower profit. The two firms choose their strategies simultaneously.

For each part of the question, indicate whether the statement is true or false.

Figure 6.14
Game matrix
showing possible
pay-off

	B	
	produce	not produce
A produce	−50, −75	70, 0
not produce	0, 80	0, 0

(a) Firm A has a dominant strategy.
(b) Firm B does not have a dominant strategy.
(c) (0, 80) is a possible equilibrium solution, since with this outcome neither firm has an incentive to change strategy.
(d) The offer of a subsidy of 65 to firm B if both firms produced would be sufficient to ensure that firm A would not produce.
(e) The offer of a subsidy of 60 firm A would be sufficient to ensure that firm B would not produce.

Question 5   Read the following extract:

> This week, two of Monopoly's biggest players landed on a square they were hoping to avoid. A throw of the enforcement dice by the Office of Fair Trading (OFT) left Argos and Littlewoods with a £22 million fine for fixing the price of toys. The £22 million fine is the OFT's biggest yet. Its investigation uncovered correspondence between the companies individually and 'Hasbro' the toy maker about an agreement not to sell below the recommended retail price. Hasbro managed to use the game's famous 'get out of jail' card, by telling the OFT about the secret arrangement. The admission meant that Hasbro escaped punishment for its part in the scheme.
>   The fine is part of an OFT plan to concentrate on eliminating price-fixing above all other anti-competitive practices.
>
> *(The Sunday Times, Business Section, 23 February 2003)*

(a) With the aid of the prisoners' dilemma game, explain why the firms colluded to fix the price of toys.
(b) What are the problems faced by firms when they act as a cartel?

7

What makes an
economy successful? Work,
well-being and the state

Part 3

The labour market

Francis Green

Concepts

- the perfectly competitive model of the labour market
- marginal revenue product
- human capital
- imperfectly competitive models of the labour market
- marginal factor cost
- institutional interventions in labour markets
- minimum-wage legislation
- trade unions
- segmentation and segregation
- efficiency wages
- the worker discipline effect

Objectives

After studying this chapter you should be able to:

- understand the scope and limits of the perfectly competitive model of the labour market
- appreciate the greater explanatory power of imperfectly competitive models of the labour market incorporating institutional factors
- explain recent changes in the UK labour market by applying models of the labour market
- explain some general characteristics of labour markets by applying models of the labour market.

7.1 Introduction

Some salient changes have taken place in labour markets throughout the industrial economies in recent years. The UK, for example, has seen an increase in the relative wages of skilled workers, a rise in the proportion of skilled workers, an increase in the intensity of work effort and the introduction of minimum-wage regulation. In this chapter we will examine these recent changes in the UK labour market and some other, more lasting, features of labour markets in general.

7.1.1 Relative wages, skilled workers and work effort

Three recent changes in the UK labour market – an increase in the relative wages of skilled workers, a rise in the proportion of skilled workers and an increase in the intensity of work effort – are illustrated by the evidence given in Table 7.1. The first row of Panel A shows

Table 7.1
British jobs have
become more
intensive and more
skilled

Panel A	1979–81	1993–95
Ratio of the average wage for university-educated workers to the average wage for workers with no qualifications		
Males	1.63	1.93
Females	1.92	2.11
Ratio of university-educated workers to workers with no qualifications		
Males	0.19	0.71
Females	0.07	0.43

Panel B	1992	1997
Proportion of workers who strongly agree with the statement: 'My job requires that I work very hard'		
Males	30	38
Females	33	42

Source: Machin, 1999; Green, 2001

that the average wage of workers who have a degree rose, relative to the wages of workers with no qualifications, by about 30 percentage points for men and 19 percentage points for women from 1979–81 to 1993–95. In other words, the value of a degree increased during this period. Over the same period, those with degrees became more numerous in the workforce than those with no qualifications. For example, in 1979–81 there were roughly two men with a degree in the workforce for every ten with no qualifications at all. By 1993–95 the ratio had risen to more than seven degree-holders for every ten with no qualifications.

Panel B of Table 7.1 gives evidence about the increasing intensity of work effort, although effort is difficult to measure objectively. A representative sample of the British workforce was asked an identical question in 1992 and 1997. The interviewees were asked whether they agreed with the statement: 'My job requires that I work very hard.' The proportion of men and women strongly agreeing with the statement rose between 1992 and 1997.

Employers often describe jobs as 'more demanding' than they used to be. Although this term is rather vague, if we interpret it as a statement that jobs are becoming more skilled, and require workers to work more intensively than they used to do, then we can see from Table 7.1 why employers hold this view. The employers' view seems to be accurate in this case.

An important factor driving the changes shown in Table 7.1 is the nature of modern technology. The computer and a range of other new technologies, such as biotechnology, are thought to generate an increase in the demand for skilled workers. Actually, the effect in many industries may be a sharp decrease in the demand for less-skilled workers, because routine work is the most easy to automate. For example, in the 1990s large numbers of non-manual back-office staff in the financial industry lost their jobs in this way. But whether new technologies increase the number of highly educated workers in an industry or decrease the number of less-educated workers, the effect is to raise the *relative* demand for the more highly educated workers.

A similar argument suggests that the new technologies of the modern age demand the sort of worker who is prepared to put in high levels of effort. For example, the technologies to be found in call centres – which grew from nothing to become an industry employing more than 400 000 workers by the end of the 1990s – are widely thought to both enable and demand high levels of effort. Each call can be delivered instantaneously to workers, and their effort can be monitored with great precision. The system offers rewards to workers who are prepared to endure the high pace of the work.

■■■ 7.1.2 The labour market

A financially starved student goes into town one day, knocks on a factory door and asks if there is any work going: perhaps there is a half-day's labouring to be done, perhaps not. On the other side of the globe, a 40-year-old man goes to work in an office in one of the large Japanese corporations: he has been working there for 20 years already and confidently expects to do so for 20 more. These two people are doing the same thing in one general respect: they are both participating in a labour market.

They seem poles apart. The student works just a few hours in return for equivalent wages and may never again have any relationship with the company. The Japanese worker benefits from the 'nenko system', which guarantees lifetime employment in the firm for a proportion (largely male) of the Japanese workforce. The relationship between the worker and the firm is still an exchange of work for wages, but the implications of its long-term character are very different from those of the 'casual' labour market of the student.

Most workers participate in labour markets that lie between the poles of the casual labour market and the nenko system. Some jobs are more stable and secure, and are regarded as long-lasting or even as 'permanent', in contrast to others which are subject to a greater likelihood of closure and are typically more short term. But of course many 'permanent' jobs cease to exist in the event of dismissals for misconduct or, more commonly, redundancy. Even the seemingly 'safe' IBM, which for a century or so had never made any workers redundant anywhere in the world, found itself declaring massive redundancies in the 1990s' shake-out of the computer industry (Chapter 2).

So, while it is correct, if somewhat trite, to define a labour market as the place where wages are exchanged for labour, it is already clear that one striking feature of labour markets is that jobs vary so much in their length and degree of security. What else is special about labour markets that merits our exclusive attention in this chapter? You can probably think of a number of factors in answer to this question, but for the purposes of this chapter we need to emphasize three significant points.

First, in a labour market the money that is being exchanged is wages (or salaries), and these form a very large part of most people's income. On average about 60 per cent of income in the UK is derived from the reward for labour (*Economic Trends*, April 2001). Hence the factors that determine wages have a great effect on income distribution. Moreover, our welfare is directly linked to our employment prospects. When unemployment looms as the result of a failure of the labour market it is a matter of great concern.

A second reason why the analysis of labour markets is special is that the wages paid to an employee do not automatically guarantee that a satisfactory job is done from the firm's point of view. When we buy apples from a street seller it is relatively easy to see if any are rotten and insist on replacements if necessary. By contrast, to motivate workers to work in return for their wages requires that they be managed somehow. The economic analysis of labour markets cannot properly be considered completely separately from the issue of worker motivation. Later on in the chapter we will consider a model which highlights the consequences of this link between wages and worker motivation.

The third reason why labour markets are different from many others in the modern world is that their scope is geographically far less wide than other important markets. We have become accustomed to thinking in global terms in relation to the money market or to many product markets: UK-based banks, for example, by no means confine their operations to UK lending. Yet firms based in a particular country or area largely recruit their workforces from that area. For many types of work, and those below the highest grades, that area is usually taken to be the town and its surroundings; the UK Department of Employment delineates them as 'Travel-To-Work Areas' on maps. For other types of work, such as senior management, the market may be national in scope. International recruitment occurs in a relatively small number of cases, with the important exception of the large-scale migration of labour. Yet despite occasional mass migration, the fact that labour markets remain distinctly national is evident, if only from the different wages paid to the same type of labour in different countries. In developing countries, wages are typically a small fraction of even unskilled manual workers' wages in the industrialized world. And between countries of the advanced industrialized world there remain distinct differences in wages and conditions of work.

In this chapter we will primarily, although not exclusively, draw examples from the UK labour market. The relatively high economic, social and political barriers to mass migration mean that this remains a sensible region to examine.

In the light of these special characteristics of labour markets, the aim of this chapter is to address two broad questions about how they operate.

1 What are the determinants of wages and employment? Why do some workers get paid more than others?

2 How do institutional interventions in the free operation of labour markets affect their performance? By 'institutions' here we mean anything other than individual workers or firms (e.g. trade unions, employer organizations, or the various arms of government).

We will begin the analysis of these questions by elaborating on the 'perfect competition' or 'competitive' model of the labour market. The chief reason for beginning with this is that many official policy analyses and positions have traditionally emerged from this approach. For example, it used to be assumed that minimum-wage legislation tended to raise wages at the expense of employment. A related policy has been to reduce the power of trade unions, which are also thought to contribute to inefficiency and to high wages at the expense of potential jobs for the unemployed. All of these conclusions can be drawn from the perfect competition model. Minimum-wage legislation and trade unions are two distinct but related themes, which we will examine in detail later in this chapter.

As the chapter proceeds you will see that, although there are useful insights to be gained from the perfect competition model, most of the assumptions that underpin this model are unrealistic. Nevertheless, the model can serve as a benchmark against which to contrast the assumptions of other models based on imperfect competition, which are regarded as the normal or most widespread structure of the labour market. You may judge these assumptions for yourselves.

7.2 The perfectly competitive labour market

The perfect competition model is primarily an analysis of a 'spot market' in which an amount of labour (e.g. measured in hours) in the present is sold for wages. Both the price of labour – the wage rate – and the level of employment are determined by the intersection of demand and supply, just as in many commodity markets. A number of assumptions form the starting point of this model.

A1 Buyers and sellers of labour are price-takers: they cannot individually alter wages.

A2 All participants are perfectly informed: workers know the available job and wage opportunities, while firms know the potential workers in the labour market.

A3 Workers can move freely between jobs or in and out of work.

A4 Labour hours, once purchased from the workers, are used without problem as effective labour to produce output.

A5 Firms aim to maximize profits.

■■■ 7.2.1 The demand for labour

The demand for labour is the demand for a factor of production. It is commonly referred to as a 'derived demand' since the labour is wanted not for itself but for the profits which it brings to the company. Let us consider how the demand for labour is determined in principle by a firm using just this one variable factor, labour, to produce an output, that is, to maximize its profits. The marginal physical product of labour (MPP_L) is the extra output produced by utilizing an extra unit of labour. The MPP_L declines as labour increases, in accordance with diminishing returns to a factor of production (Chapter 3, Section 3.3.1). In the analysis here we are particularly concerned with the **marginal revenue product** (MRP), which is related to the MPP_L.

Marginal revenue product

The marginal revenue product is the extra revenue obtained by the firm from employing an extra unit of labour.

If P is the price of the product we can write:

$$MRP = P \cdot MPP_L$$

Because we assume that in perfect competition the firm is a price-taker, the decline in MPP_L means that the MRP curve is also declining. The MRP curve is illustrated in Figure 7.1.

Suppose that the market wage rate is given by W. The theory of the firm's demand for labour may now be simply stated: the firm that maximizes profits will demand labour up to the point at which the wage equals the marginal revenue product, or:

$$W = MRP$$

Figure 7.1
The firm's demand for labour, under perfect competition

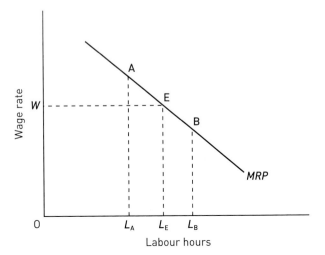

Demand for labour

The demand curve for labour in a perfectly competitive model is given by the marginal revenue product curve.

This is illustrated by the point E on Figure 7.1, where employment is L_E. How do we know this is the optimal amount to employ? We can reason by considering alternative points. At A, with only L_A employed, the MRP is above W. This means the firm could get extra profits by employing one more unit of labour, since the extra revenue, MRP, is greater than the cost, W. Conversely, at B, with MRP below W, the firm could get more profits by cutting a unit of labour, since the cost saving, W, is more than the lost revenue, MRP. Thus, neither A nor B is a point at which profits are maximized; but at E, no change in employment could raise profits further.

If the wage rate were raised or lowered, the profit-maximizing firm would simply alter its employment according to its MRP curve. The curve thus traces out the **demand for labour**.

Not all firms are the same, of course, and so their labour demand curves may have different slopes and shapes, but they are expected to be downward sloping. Hence, when we aggregate all firms to obtain the market demand for labour, we would also have a downward-sloping demand curve. This is a key conclusion emerging from the analysis and it will be used again, below. But before leaving this topic we must consider some loose terminology we have been using so far: in talking about labour we have not discussed different types of labour, such as carpenters, labourers, managers and so on. Implicitly, we have been assuming that all labour is the same. Nevertheless, the same arguments can apply to any specific type of labour, leading to the conclusion that there are downward-sloping demand curves for each type.

Exercise 7.1

The proposition that the demand for labour rises when the wage rate falls is widely believed. Can you trace the steps in the argument leading to that conclusion?

▨ ▨ ■ 7.2.2 Labour supply

We turn next to look at the underlying determinants of labour supply. These can be divided into: (a) the factors determining overall labour supply, and (b) the factors determining the supply of a particular type of labour, relative to alternative types of labour. Let us look at each in turn.

Overall labour supply

In any country the ultimate boundary affecting labour supply is population. Table 7.2 contains some summary data for the UK. You will see that although there are nearly 60 million people, only just under half are in the workforce (meaning that they are either employed or officially unemployed). A number of factors play a part in determining this overall figure. There are social and demographic factors, such as the proportion of people of normal working age and society's attitudes towards women or younger or older people working, which have changed gradually over the years. There are technical factors, such as the availability of washing machines, which have made work in the home more productive than in earlier times, thereby in principle freeing up time for paid work. There are also political factors, such as the availability of state-financed child-care facilities or

Table 7.2
UK population and
labour statistics,
2001

	Thousands
Population	59 954[1]
Workforce	29 619
Workforce in employment	28 142

1 Mid-year projection.
Source: *Annual Abstract of Statistics*, 2001; *Labour Market Statistics*,
June 2001

the provision of full-time education or higher education. And there are private economic factors, such as the availability of private sources of income, that may alter the incentive to work. Someone with a large private income will be able to afford the cost (in terms of lost wages) of not going to work.

Labour supply to a particular line of work

Now we have considered the overall supply of people wishing to work, we need to consider the supply of potential workers to particular kinds of work. It is this supply, together with the demand for particular types of labour, that provides an explanation of relative wages – that is, wages in one job relative to those in another. This is crucial both for reasons of distribution and for reasons of economic incentives.

For the moment we shall set aside the question of different skill requirements for different jobs. Suppose we consider two jobs, A and B, with the same skill requirements but with different conditions of work: job A has poorer conditions than job B. This might mean more risky or less pleasant work surroundings in some way. Job B might, for example, be window cleaning, while job A is window cleaning on high-rise buildings. The supply of high-rise window cleaners is going to depend on the wages and riskiness of the high-rise jobs *relative to* those for the ordinary window cleaners. A typical supply curve might look like the one in Figure 7.2.

Figure 7.2
Labour supply for
high-rise window
cleaning

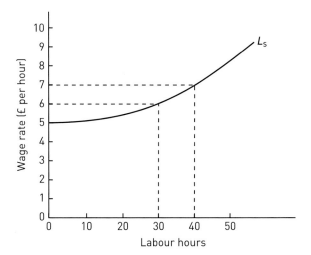

Figure 7.3
The determination
of wages and
employment in
high-rise window
cleaning under
perfect competition

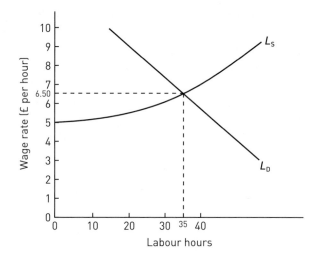

Suppose that workers could get £5 per hour for ordinary window cleaning. Assuming no one prefers the extra risks of high-rise work, the labour supply L_S will be zero for any wage at or below £5. At £6, however, a certain number (30) are prepared to accept the risks of high-rise work. At a wage of £7, more workers (40) are induced to forgo the safer job for the extra rewards. The variation in workers' attitudes towards the risk causes the relative supply curve to be upward sloping.

■ ■ ■ 7.2.3 Labour supply and demand and 'compensating wage differences'

Let us now put our supply and demand curves together. Pursuing the same example, the market demand for high-rise window cleaners will be downward sloping, as for any labour. The determination of wages and employment is shown in Figure 7.3.

It is assumed in this figure that a process of free-market bidding will sooner or later lead to a market equilibrium with supply equal to demand at a level of 35, with a wage rate of £6.50 per hour. There is thus a wage premium of £1.50 or 30 per cent compared with ordinary window cleaning, which is the 'compensating wage difference', representing the market valuation of what it takes to induce workers to assume the extra risk of high-rise work.

Exercise 7.2

Show, using a demand and supply diagram, what would happen to high-rise window cleaners' wages and employment on the completion of a new high-rise office block in town.

■ ■ ■ 7.2.4 Human capital

One over-simplification in the model of labour markets so far is that we have ignored the effect of differences in skill. Yet skill differences account for a good proportion of wage differences, for the simple reason that the supply of workers with specialized skills is restricted. It could be argued that a few jobs require rare abilities that can be developed

Figure 7.4
Age–wage profiles
and the investment
in human capital

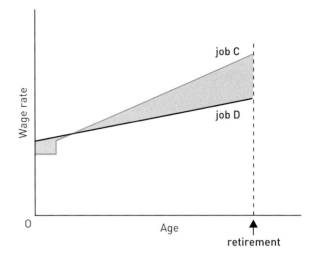

but not acquired if not already present – not everyone can acquire the skill to participate in professional tennis, for example. Nevertheless, most jobs use skills that require greater or lesser amounts of education and training. The theory of human capital states that people will have an incentive to acquire skills (or 'human capital') if it gives them access to high-paying jobs. Suppose that we consider two further jobs, C and D. Job C pays more than job D but it requires an extra year's training. The pay differential thus 'compensates' for the disadvantage of having to take an extra year's training, in a way analogous to our window cleaner example, where the high-rise worker is compensated for the extra risk.

But what is the precise disadvantage of this training? We can picture this by looking at how wages might hypothetically alter over a lifetime of work, as shown in Figure 7.4.

In job D a steady increase in wages is expected through to retirement. In job C only a low income is received in the year spent training (perhaps from a government grant). But while the starting wage for job C is the same as for job D, only a year behind, it is pictured as increasing more rapidly over the lifetime. The differentials of job C over job D increase over time. The total blue area represents the benefit of the extra training. The cost, however, is the grey area. This cost represents the lost wages during the early period. To be added to this are the fees incurred for the training and any other 'out-of-pocket' costs, and the total costs represent the 'disadvantage' of the training.

Put in this way, this is really a theory of investment, similar to any investment in physical capital. A firm buys a machine and thereby incurs costs in the present. It expects that the machine will produce extra revenues and profits in the future, these being the pay-off to the investment. Similarly, the pay-off to the individual of undergoing education or training is the extra wages to be gained later on. There will also, in the case of training, be a pay-off to the firm that provides the training for its workforce, in the form of greater productivity from that workforce. The only difference, then, between investment in physical capital and investment in human capital is that, whereas physical capital could be sold off to another user, it is difficult or impossible to sell human capital once acquired, except in a slave society.

Monetary advantage is not the only reason for education and training. The theory of human capital stresses the monetary rationale but this need not exclude other 'non-pecuniary' factors. These must include the satisfaction of studying (I hope you agree) and the potential future rewards of being more educated or trained, or perhaps a more satisfying job.

Exercise 7.3

What are the costs and benefits, as you see them, of studying on a distance-learning course, such as an Open University course? When are they likely to occur? Which of them might, in principle, be quantifiable?

In thinking of the acquisition of human capital as an investment, the particular case of training presents a problem that has proved vitally important in the UK economy and other economies. The problem is that much training, to be effective, needs to be done in and by firms rather than schools. The basic question this poses is: who pays for the training?

One way for the individual to pay for firm-based training is to work for the firm but receive lower wages during the training period. At the extreme, trainees might receive no wages, or even pay the firm for the training received. The underlying assumption here is that the trainees (or their families) own sufficient funds to cover living expenses during the training period or can gain access to funds through the capital market. You might want to judge for yourself how realistic that assumption is.

■ ■ ■ 7.2.5   Summary and implications of the perfect competition model

The analysis began with five economic assumptions, A1 to A5, to which we now add another:

A6   Potential trainees have access to perfect capital markets.

Question   What answers are given by the perfect competition model to the two broad questions in Section 7.1.2?

Taking the first question, wage differentials are explained as the outcome of the individual choices underlying the supply of and demand for labour. In sum, the wages of one job may be more than another's because:

1   there is a 'compensating difference' in the conditions of work (e.g. risk or unpleasantness);

2   the job requires particular skills which are costly to acquire. Workers must incur these costs through undergoing education or training. Only those that choose to do so receive the compensating rewards of better-paid jobs.

As for the second question, the only aim of government intervention in this view should be to support free-market processes. For example, within such a framework it is easy to rationalize the case that is sometimes made against minimum-wage legislation. This issue is taken up in Section 7.3.

7.3   From perfect to imperfect competition: minimum-wage legislation

In 1999 the then recently elected Labour government introduced a national minimum wage for the first time in the UK. Such legislation is an example of the institutional structures that make labour markets imperfectly competitive. This section uses the example of minimum-wage legislation to effect a transition from the perfectly competitive labour market to imperfectly competitive labour markets. Minimum-wage legislation is examined, first, from the perspective of the perfectly competitive model, and then from within an imperfectly competitive framework. The policy implications of the models are very different.

▨ ◼ ◼ 7.3.1 The perfectly competitive labour market and minimum-wage legislation

This section begins with an illustration of the general argument against intervention fore-shadowed at the end of Section 7.2. It examines the case that is made against the state attempting to raise the wages of the low-paid. In most industrialized countries there is a national minimum wage that applies to all jobs. Economists basing their arguments on the demand and supply framework have usually argued that this must reduce employment in those jobs where the minimum wage is above the market wage.

The argument is illustrated in Figure 7.5, which gives the supply and demand for labour hours in the low-pay sectors of the economy. If the government imposes a wage W_M, where the market would otherwise settle on a wage W_E, the hours of work in these jobs are restricted to L_M. The benefit to workers who keep their jobs is the increased wage rate, but $L_E - L_M$ labour hours are no longer available. The extent of this shortfall is determined by the size of the wage rise and the elasticity of labour demand.

On the basis of this analysis it is commonly argued that minimum-wage legislation is detrimental to economic efficiency even if it reduces inequality. It could also be argued that the legislation might exacerbate inequality: if large numbers of people were to be made unemployed and they all received low state benefits, this could more than outweigh any benefits to equality from raising the pay of those in work.

The development of UK government policy during the 1980s and early 1990s was consistent with these general conclusions. In the UK, until recently, minimum-wage legislation applied to only a minority of the workforce – those in industries thought to be unprotected by trade unions and covered instead by Wages Boards and Councils. The chief areas covered were clothing, agriculture, retail trades and catering. In 1986 protection was limited to those over 21 years of age, and holiday pay was excluded from the regulations even for adults. This was a precursor to the eventual abolition of all the councils in 1993 except the one for agricultural workers.

Figure 7.5
The effect of minimum-wage legislation on employment under perfect competition

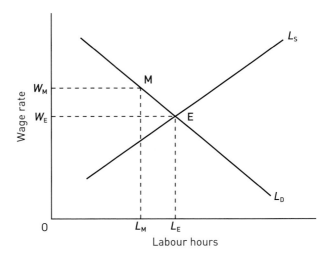

The reintroduction of minimum-wage legislation in 1999 clearly reflected policy makers' reliance upon a different economic model of the labour market.

▦ ▪ ■ 7.3.2 Minimum-wage legislation in imperfectly competitive labour markets

For the rest of this chapter we will dismantle the perfect competition model, by considering what happens in a number of cases when the assumptions are dropped and new ones inserted. This will bring us to a more detailed examination of the policy issues we have highlighted, starting with minimum-wage legislation.

With this issue fresh in mind from the previous section, it is appropriate to begin with assumptions A1 and A2, two assumptions that were crucial to deriving the policy conclusion that argued against intervention. In particular, we should question the proposition that firms cannot individually alter wages. This proposition is illustrated by the horizontal curve L_{S1} in Figure 7.6, which shows an infinitely elastic supply of labour hours to a firm at the going wage rate. For two related reasons this assumption may be false. Let us assume that a firm offers to employ workers at a wage less than W. Would anybody work for the firm? The answer is yes. First, there may be many workers who lack information about what jobs and wages are available elsewhere – so they accept the job or, simply, continue working for the firm if they already work there. Second, even if they have information about better-paying jobs they may face transport and other costs that make it detrimental to switch jobs. Some workers may leave the company, or fewer workers apply, so on balance the firm that offers lower wages will get some labour but less than before. In other words, the supply curve of labour to a particular firm is likely to be upward sloping. This is illustrated by the curve L_{S2} in Figure 7.6.

The fact that the labour supply curve L_{S2} slopes upwards means that we must now reconstruct the analysis of the firm's employment decision. This is done in Figure 7.7.

We start with a labour supply curve L_S which is upward sloping like the curve L_{S2} in Figure 7.6. Under perfect competition the upward-sloping labour supply curve was a *market* supply curve and the profit-maximizing level of employment was determined to be $MRP = W$. The curve L_S in Figure 7.7, on the other hand, is the supply curve for a single firm under imperfect competition, taken from Figure 7.6. The profit-maximizing level of employment is no longer where $MRP = W$.

Figure 7.6
Labour supply curves of a single firm. L_{S1}: labour supply to a firm under perfect competition; L_{S2}: labour supply to a firm under imperfect competition

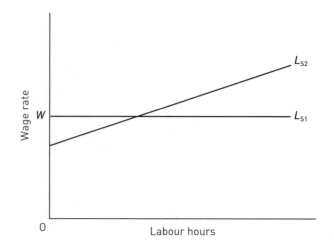

Figure 7.7
The determination
of wages and
employment under
imperfect
competition

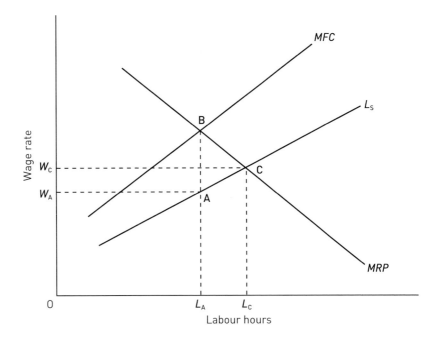

**Marginal
factor cost**

The marginal
factor cost of
labour is the extra
cost of employing
an extra unit of
labour.

The firm which aims to maximize profits would be failing to do so if it set labour hours at the point C, where $MRP = W_C$ on the supply curve. Why is this? To answer this question, we must recognize that the **marginal factor cost** (*MFC*) of labour, that is, the cost to the firm of employing one extra hour of labour, is not identical to the wage rate if the firm faces an upward-sloping labour supply curve.

In Figure 7.6 the horizontal labour supply curve to the firm under perfect competition, L_{S_1}, implies that the *MFC* is equal to the wage rate (which is why we did not need to distinguish them in Section 7.3.1). Because the supply curve of labour is upward sloping for the firm under imperfect competition, the *MFC* is equal to the wage rate (the cost attributed to the one extra hour) *plus* the small change in the wage bill of all the other hours worked. That is, the *MFC* must be *above* the wage rate. A numerical example will serve to illustrate this point. Suppose a firm employs 100 hours of labour for £5 per hour. Its total wage bill is therefore £500. If it were to increase the hours to 101, it would need to raise its wage rate to, say, £5.25 in order to attract the extra hour of labour. The new wage bill is $101 \times £5.25 = £530.25$. Hence the cost of the extra hour is £30.25, greater than the wage rate for one hour's work.

Figure 7.7 shows the relationship between L_S, which traces out the wage rate the firm must offer to attract each level of labour supply, and the *MFC* curve, which traces out the marginal cost to the firm of employing successively greater amounts of labour.

We can now answer the question posed above. Why will the firm fail to maximize profits if it sets labour hours at point C in Figure 7.7? Suppose that the firm were to set employment at point C, where $W = MRP$. If it lowers labour hours by one unit, the amount of labour cost saved equals the wage rate, W_C, plus the reduction in the wage bill of its remaining workers. This is shown by the *MFC* curve, which lies above L_S. Hence the amount saved is greater than the revenue lost (*MRP*) and the firm's profits will rise.

Only when *MFC* equals *MRP* will profits be maximized – as illustrated by point B on Figure 7.7. Why? If labour hours were lower than at B, profits could be raised by increasing them, since $MRP > MFC$. Conversely, if labour hours were higher than at B, profits could be raised by lowering them, since $MFC > MRP$.

Figure 7.8
Minimum wages
under imperfect
competition

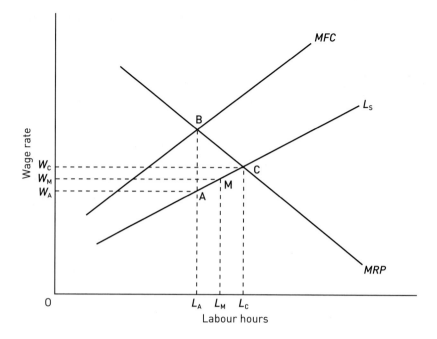

Note, however, that when hours worked are determined in this way the wage rate is W_A, given by the relevant point on the supply curve – that is, A. It is evident that both wages W_A and employment L_A are *lower* than at C, where $W = MRP$, the equilibrium position that would apply if the imperfectly competitive firm were replaced by a number of perfectly competitive firms collectively facing the market labour supply curve L_S.

Consider, now, the impact of minimum-wage legislation where the minimum wage is set at W_M, above the level W_A that the firm would otherwise choose. Figure 7.8 repeats Figure 7.7 but adds a minimum wage of W_M. In this case we can say that the firm would employ labour hours L_M, greater than L_A. Why? Because there is no advantage for the firm in employing fewer labour hours. At M the *MRP* is greater than the minimum wage rate W_M, so any cut-back in hours would lead to a fall in profits. The point is that the minimum wage prevents the employer from reducing the wage bill for the remaining workers, which would otherwise have been the reason for lowering the hours worked. To the left of point M, the *MFC* facing the employer is equal to W_M however many labour hours employed, since the existence of the minimum wage makes this section of the supply curve horizontal. On the other hand, the firm would not raise hours worked because that would mean raising wages above W_M and, the *MFC* being above *MRP* at that point and all points rightwards, this would lower profits. Hence M must be the profit-maximizing point under the minimum-wage legislation.

Question	How does this conclusion differ from that obtained in the perfect competition model?

The conclusion is in striking contrast to that obtained in the perfect competition model. Up to the value W_C, any increase in the minimum wage brings unequivocal benefits to workers, in the form of both higher wages and greater employment levels, while removing some of the profits of the companies. Once W_C has been reached, however, any further rises in the minimum wage would lead to falls in employment, in line with the perfect competition model.

As a result of this analysis, we can only conclude that the effect of minimum-wage legislation on employment is uncertain from the point of view of economic theory. If the perfect competition model is correct, or if the minimum wage is pushed too high (above W_C), we would expect a reduction in employment. But if the imperfect competition model with an upward-sloping labour supply is correct, and the minimum wage is not pushed excessively above the free-market level W_A, we would expect an increase in employment. Only careful empirical investigation will be able to show us which effect is valid, and the conclusion could be different for different countries. Most empirical studies have been done for the US labour market, where there is currently no consensus as to the impact on employment. A number of recent studies have shown little or no effect in either direction.

Case study: Should Florida introduce a minimum wage?

On 2 November 2004, Florida voters overwhelming approved new minimum-wage legislation that would apply throughout the state. This meant that Florida was the thirteenth state to introduce a minimum wage that was higher than the federal minimum which applied across the United States. In a report designed to evaluate the impacts, Pollin, Brenner and Wicks-Lim (2004) suggest that the economic case in favour of the higher minimum was strong. In the first instance, the federal minimum-wage level had fallen by nearly 40 per cent, in real terms, from its peak in 1968. At a minimum wage of $5.15 per hour in 2004, a significant number of families supposedly well above the official poverty line were facing hardships such as missing meals, housing evictions and disconnection of utilities.

In their evaluation, Pollin *et al.* suggested that the overall cost to business of the increased minimum would be $406 million, which amounted to 0.04 per cent of total sales revenues. The main reaction of businesses would, the researchers argued, be to increase prices by a small amount, part of which would be offset by productivity gains as workers would be expected to become slightly more committed to their

jobs. On the other hand, their analysis showed little reason to be concerned about 'unintended' consequences. The implications for costs were small while layoffs and relocations were themselves costly suggesting that the effect on unemployment levels might be minimal. Indeed, the fact that the disposal income of low-wage workers and families would increase by $500 to $600 per household would not only bring about an opportunity to improve their own quality of life but also raise the turnover of retail stores in low-income neighbourhoods. Indexing the minimum wage to changes in the cost of living as measured by the retail price index would be an important part of making this change valuable to low-paid workers over the medium to long term.

(Source: adapted from Pollin *et al.*, 2004)

Question

Would you expect to see similar conclusions for different countries? In this case, do we need the imperfect competition model to provide an economic justification for Florida's increased minimum wage? If not, why not?

This conclusion is consistent with the recent UK experience. Following the change of government in 1997 to a Labour administration, a national minimum wage was introduced for the first time on 1 April 1999, set at an hourly rate of £3.60 for adults (with a reduced rate of £3.00 for 18–21 year olds). Roughly 1.3 million workers became eligible for wage rises, of whom 7 out of 10 were women. The nation's wage bill rose by about 0.35 per cent on average, but much more in the low-paying industries. Yet, according to the Low Pay Commission, there were no discernible effects on employment. The groups most affected saw rises in their levels of employment both before and after the introduction of the minimum wage. Reassured by the absence of adverse employment effects, the government annually revised the level of the minimum wage upwards: thus the adult rate is £5.05 (October 2005).

7.4 Imperfectly competitive labour markets: trade unions and segmentation

Two aspects of the unrealistic nature of the perfectly competitive model of labour markets are its assumption that firms and workers are independent agents (assumption A1) and its failure to correspond to the observed realities of labour markets. Assumption A1 is contradicted by the existence of trade unions in many industries. The observed reality of wages in many labour markets is that differentials seem to reflect a 'segmentation' of labour markets into 'good' and 'bad' jobs rather more than skill differences and compensating differences in work conditions.

7.4.1 Trade unions and the labour market

Perhaps the most unrealistic aspect of the model of perfect competition in the labour market is the view that labour-market actors – firms and workers – all act independently and are unable to influence prices or wages (assumption A1). This may be a fair approximation in a few minor sectors of the economy, but for the most part in many countries wages and conditions are the subject of collective negotiations between trade unions and employers, or sometimes between groups of unions and employers. If wages and conditions are not the subject of collective bargaining, they are often regulated by explicit legal or implicit customary codes. In addition, many millions of people in Europe are employed by governments whose behaviour cannot simply be likened to a profit-maximizing firm. In all these cases, the simple notion of labour supply and labour demand under perfect competition, as outlined in Section 7.2, is inapplicable.

We will look here at some of the ways in which the presence of trade unions changes the picture. Table 7.3 gives an approximate idea of the potential influence of unions in some different countries. It gives the union density, defined as the number of union members as a percentage of potential union members. While it might be reasonable as a first approximation to disregard unions in the USA (it has a union density of only 16 per cent), an analysis of labour markets in most of Europe, especially in Scandinavia, would be seriously unrealistic. Nevertheless, UK unions have been substantially cut down to size in the last 20 years. The union density of 34 per cent for 1994 in Table 7.3 is actually a point on a slope, as the density has steadily fallen from over 50 per cent in 1980. This fall occurred in the context of adverse economic conditions (high unemployment) and a series of anti-union pieces of legislation, starting with the 1980 Employment Act, which successfully limited the ability of unions to recruit new members and reduced their power in relation to management.

The perfect competition theory essentially regards the impact of unions on the market as detrimental; hence the evident policy conclusion is to reduce their influence. There are two main bases for the argument. First, it is assumed that unions raise wages, thus moving the firm up its labour demand curve to point M in Figure 7.8, thereby displacing employment from the unionized to the non-unionized sector of the economy. What is

Table 7.3
Union density in
1994

Country	Union density %
Australia	35
Canada	38
France	9
Germany	29
Italy	39
Japan	24
Netherlands	26
Spain	19
Sweden	91
UK	34
USA	16

Source: *OECD Employment Outlook*, 1997, p.71

not clear is how far up the curve the unions would want to force wages. It is hardly reasonable to think of unions aiming to push wages up indefinitely. Assuming they had the power to raise wages, but assuming also that they were aware of the downward-sloping labour demand curve, they would want to limit the use of that power so as not to sacrifice too much employment. But how much is 'too much'? This is not an easy question, because it depends on what sorts of workers have power in unions – is it the older workers with relatively secure jobs who would want to raise wages substantially, or is it the more marginal younger workers whose jobs are less safe?

Empirical estimates of unions' impact on wages are hard to obtain, but what economists can find is an estimate of a union/non-union wage differential for otherwise similar workers. In Britain, the best estimates of this lie in the 10–15 per cent range for manual workers, though these are subject to quite wide margins of error.

For non-manual workers the estimated impact on wages is much lower, and arguably zero. In most countries (including Britain) the evidence is that trade unions tend to reduce wage inequalities because they are better at raising the wages of lower-paid workers. For policy makers who wish to allow market forces always to have sway, this evidence is one reason for the introduction of policies to reduce the bargaining power of unions.

Second, policy makers might want to reduce unions' influence because they may slow down innovation and lower productivity by enforcing restrictive practices within companies. Here the argument is that, in order to protect jobs, unions prevent the introduction of labour-saving innovations, and hinder the substitution of one kind of labour for another.

Set against these negative connotations for the economic effects of unions, there are also reasons to expect that unions might have a positive impact on productivity. American writers Freeman and Medoff (1984) argue that unions provide a collective 'voice' to speak to management, and that this can improve productivity. Without a union an aggrieved worker may have little choice but to remain unhappy or to quit the firm. A union helps sort out the grievance and hence lowers labour turnover. Lower labour turnover reduces the costs of hiring replacements and provides more incentives for firms to train their employees. Moreover, unions acting in co-operation with management can find ways to improve efficiency that are eventually beneficial. In so far as unions do raise wages, this can also keep up worker morale and hence worker effort (Section 7.5). Finally, it is often recognized that upward pressure on wages may stimulate efficiency gains from improved management. In the short run, higher wage demands from a newly organized union can 'shock' a sleepy management into better performance. But perhaps more important is the long-run effect attributed to unions that have been successful in keeping wages high in Germany. The result has been to force management to adopt strategies for high skills and high productivity. Arguing that managers given the choice will often opt for a low-wage route to competitiveness, the high wages that unions impose could act as a barrier to this route. Instead, management will opt for high value-added products that require high levels of ongoing research and development, sustained investment and continued training for the workforce.

For all these reasons it is theoretically possible that the presence of unions can raise the marginal physical product of labour (MPP_L) and hence the marginal revenue product, which is the basis of the demand for labour curve. A conceivable scenario is then illustrated by Figure 7.9. Our initial point is E, the intersection of the labour supply curve L_S and the marginal revenue product curve in a perfectly competitive labour market in the absence of unions. Now examine the impact of unions. On the one hand they may raise the wage rate, which in the absence of any changes in efficiency would lower employment accordingly, as shown by a movement along the MRP curve to point M. However, where unions also raise the MRP, shifting the MRP curve rightwards, this would in itself raise employment. Putting the two effects together results in an ambiguous effect. As drawn at point N the net result is no impact on employment, but depending on the extent of unions' impact on the MPP_L, the employment effect could be positive or negative.

In view of the theoretically conflicting theories about unions' impact on productivity, economists have sought to estimate the empirical effects. The results are not clear-cut, but the balance of evidence suggests that in a significant number of cases the impact on productivity is positive. That does not mean to say that it always is or will be positive: this is one of those many areas in economics when the answer cannot be predicted by theory and may differ empirically from circumstance to circumstance.

Thus far we have considered the impact of unions on wages and on productivity in companies. In addition, unions can have an effect on other aspects of the labour market. For example, it has been found quite consistently in a number of studies that unions tend to compress wage differentials. That this is so should not be too surprising, because much

Figure 7.9
Unions' impact
on wages and
employment

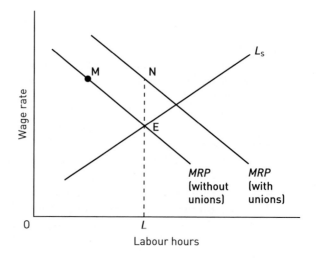

of the union movement has been historically rooted in an ideological commitment to equality. This means that a complete assessment of unions should not rest simply on the theoretical and empirical issues looked at here, even though they are important for our analysis of labour markets.

▣ ▣ ■ 7.4.2 Segmentation and segregation in the labour market

Segmentation and wage differentials

While the perfect competition model suggests to us that wage differentials in the economy reflect skill differences or 'compensating' differences in work conditions, such a conclusion has often seemed at odds with the reality observed by empirical labour economists. Starting in the USA in the late 1960s, observers began to notice an intransigent 'segmentation' of jobs – initially a dual system of two segments. In one segment, the primary labour market, were 'good jobs' – ones with reasonably high wages, some prospects for improvement (including access to training), relative job security, high fringe benefits and long job tenure. In the secondary labour market were 'bad jobs' with the converse, that is, low pay, high turnover and relative insecurity, with few other benefits. Such segmentation has also been observed in other countries. One way of seeing this in Britain is to note the considerable differences in average wages in different industries, as shown in Table 7.4. It is apparent that jobs in, say, the energy and water supply industries pay well, while the hotel and catering industry is an area of low pay. Thus male manual workers in the former industry receive on average 81 per cent more in wages than their equivalents in the latter industry. Other wage differences are less extreme, but still substantial.

There are many empirical studies by economists which attempt to explain differences in wages. It is common for such studies to focus on differences in skill levels and on compensating factors, as suggested by the perfectly competitive model of the labour market. But although such considerations do play a role, the studies almost invariably leave

Table 7.4
Average hourly pay (excluding overtime) of full-time employees, Great Britain, 2000

Industry	Men		Women	
	manual £	non-manual £	manual £	non-manual £
Agriculture, forestry and fishing	5.62	–	5.23	6.65
Energy and water supply	10.31	15.66	–	10.22
Mining	8.01	–	–	–
Manufacture of basic metal and fabricated metal products	7.92	12.48	5.24	7.95
Manufacture of transport equipment	9.40	14.61	6.68	10.00
Other manufacturing industries	6.75	11.65	5.67	7.94
Construction	7.68	13.00	–	8.47
Hotels and catering	5.71	9.97	4.68	7.50
Transport and communications	7.60	13.08	7.66	9.14
Banking, finance, insurance, etc.	9.39	18.41	5.71	10.46
Other services (including government)	6.72	13.47	5.20	9.52

Source: *New Earnings Survey*, 2000

unexplained some of the variation in wages between industries. The remaining variation may be thought to reflect elements of segmentation, wherein there are notable barriers to entry preventing workers in less good jobs from transferring to the better ones. This implies a rejection of assumption A3: perfect labour mobility. Here are three factors preventing such mobility that economists have looked at.

1 There may be barriers to obtaining the necessary skills for a primary-sector job.
2 Groups of workers may seek to protect their privileged status by erecting artificial barriers around their occupation. Professional workers may use artificially high qualifications standards; trade unions may use industrial muscle to protect their craft status.
3 Discrimination on the grounds of sex, race or disability is sometimes associated with such barriers and is used to keep certain groups out of an occupation by rejection or, more usually, by discouragement.

Exercise 7.4

Can you think of any other factors preventing labour mobility?

Occupational segregation and male/female differentials

An enduring and striking feature of labour markets in all countries is the lower pay received by female workers. This is evident in every industry in Britain, as you can see from taking another look at Table 7.4. Table 7.5 shows that the ratio of female to male earnings is less than 100 per cent in all the countries listed. However, there is considerable variation in the extent to which women are disadvantaged: of the countries shown, female workers fare best in Australia and worst in Japan. This variation suggests that women's disadvantages in the labour market are linked to the social and economic environment, which varies from country to country.

One of the major explanations that writers have given for the low pay of women is their concentration into relatively few occupations. As women's labour is over-supplied to

Table 7.5
Ratio of female to male weekly earnings of full-time workers

Country	Ratio of female to male weekly earnings %
Australia	87
Sweden	84
Switzerland	75
Spain	71
UK	75
Japan	64
USA	76

Source: Blau, 2000, pp.75–99

Table 7.6
Proportion of
female workers,
Great Britain, 1992

Occupation	Proportion of female workers %
All workers	47
Managers and professionals	30
Intermediate non-manual workers	62
Junior non-manual workers	76
Personal service workers	82
Foremen and supervisors	17
Skilled manual workers	10
Semi-skilled manual workers	41
Unskilled manual workers	64

Source: *Labour Force Survey*, 1992

these occupations there is no market pressure for a rise in pay. This unbalanced supply of female labour comes from the exclusion of women from many high-paying occupations. This is a process I like to refer to as *horizontal segregation*. Horizontal segregation is an instance of labour market segmentation, where the host of social and economic forces limiting the access of women to the high-paying occupations constitutes the source of labour immobility. Note, however, that segmentation can occur independently of such segregation and is conceivably quite separate.

The horizontal segregation of women is supplemented by *vertical segregation*, whereby males are disproportionately found in higher grades and females in lower grades, within any particular occupation or industry. This is a most obvious source of pay inequality. The reasons for the disparity range from overt discrimination to more subtle limitations placed upon women via their role in domestic labour. Some idea of how extensive horizontal and vertical segregation is in Britain can be gleaned from looking at Table 7.6. Note the predominance of female workers among the lower-ranking occupations (in terms of expected pay levels), such as personal service workers and unskilled manual workers. Nearly three-quarters of women workers are to be found either in these occupations or among junior and intermediate non-manual workers. Moreover, these figures conceal further concentrations of women among the detailed occupations subsumed within each group of the table.

Both segmentation and segregation are contributory causes of inequality in the labour market. Moreover, artificial barriers to labour mobility and the under-use of women in many areas of the labour market are evident aspects of inefficiency. The case for government intervention, contrary to the perfect competition model, is strong. Some policies directed at these features of the labour market are:

1 To subsidize the acquisition of skills through education and training.
2 To prevent the artificial use of barriers into the professions by ensuring that qualifications used as entry criteria are justified – that is, to regulate the profession from outside.
3 To use education and training to counteract forms of socialization that support the gender-identification of jobs.
4 To proscribe acts of direct discrimination in selecting on grounds of sex or other characteristics. Into this category in Britain, for example, come the 1970 Equal Pay Act and the 1975 Discrimination Act.

▨ ▧ ■ 7.4.3 Recent changes in the UK labour market revisited

We are now in a position to use some of the ideas already developed to try to understand two of the recent changes to the UK labour market observed in Section 7.1.1. These are the increase in the relative wages of skilled workers and the rise in the proportion of skilled workers. The analysis begins with the perfectly competitive model and then introduces institutional factors.

An application of supply and demand analysis

We can begin to make analytical sense of these changes by making use of the ideas and tools we have developed in this chapter. It is useful to start with the competitive model, represented in Figure 7.3, but we are now going to change the framework to the relative supply and demand for skilled workers.

In Figure 7.10 the line L_D represents the relative demand for skilled workers. By the word 'relative' I am referring to the ratio of skilled to unskilled workers. It slopes downwards because firms want to minimize the costs of producing each unit. If skilled workers became relatively more expensive, firms would want to substitute cheaper workers where possible. L_S represents the relative supply of skilled workers. A higher wage induces more people to undergo the necessary training to become skilled. Note that we are assuming a certain time-lapse here: new skilled workers cannot be found instantaneously. Rather the line says that, following a wage rise and after time for the training and education to have taken place, there will be more skilled workers.

Suppose now that new technology leads to an increase in the relative demand for skilled workers (for any given relative wage). There will be an outward shift from L_{D1} to L_{D2}. If nothing else happens, the effect will be to raise both the relative wage (from w_1 to w_2) and the relative quantity (from n_1 to n_2). This is precisely what we have observed in Table 7.1.

The story, however, is far from complete, because we ought to ask whether changes have also been occurring in the relative supply of skilled labour. The answer is patently yes: over recent decades great efforts have been made by UK governments (and other governments) to open up access to education and training in many ways. We can represent this change by a shift in the supply curve of skilled labour from L_{S1} to L_{S2}. Note, however,

Figure 7.10
Relative supply and demand for skilled workers

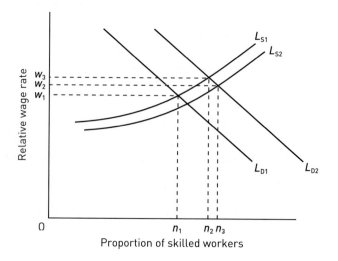

Proportion of skilled workers

the way I have drawn the diagram: the rightward shift in the supply curve is smaller than the rightward shift in the relative demand curve. The significance of this assumption is that the resulting new equilibrium still has both higher relative wages for skilled workers and a higher relative stock of skilled workers, consistent with Table 7.1.

Institutional factors

Although a supply/demand framework has got us some way in understanding the observed directions of change, this does not mean that we are relying on a perfectly competitive model. There are several ways in which institutions are important components of a full analysis. We will now discuss two of them.

First, a crucial aspect of the above analysis is that the growth of the supply of skilled workers was seen to lag behind the growth of demand. The supply of skilled workers depends partly on the decisions of individuals (and their families) but also, fundamentally, on the decisions of governments, which control and largely fund the education and training institutions that generate the skills. If skills supply is failing to keep up with the growth in demand, this could be because government and individuals have failed to anticipate the changes and to devote sufficient resources to the necessary investment in schools and colleges. Thus the politics of education, over a long period, are important to understanding the relative shifts in skilled labour supply. A traditional accusation levied against British education was that for too long it was elitist, caring for the needs of the brightest and wealthiest but neglecting to develop the skills of the majority (by comparison with other countries). A corollary of this analysis is that, should government become more successful in accelerating the supply of skills faster than demand, an equalizing tendency could develop in the labour markets, in which the relative pay of skilled workers would fall.

Second, an institutional feature that needs to be incorporated into the analysis is the role of trade unions. However, they have been going through a period of declining density (Section 7.4.1), so their direct sphere of influence has become a smaller part of the overall economy. Declining union power helps to explain why wage inequality has increased especially fast in Britain since the 1970s. In other countries, presumably experiencing a similar increase in demand for skills, the rise in the skilled wage premium was much less than in Britain. In principle, this cross-country difference can be explained in terms of our analysis in two ways. First, in other countries governments may have been more successful in keeping the supply of skills up with the rising demand (as in the above example). Second, union power persisted longer or even grew in the other countries, modifying the competitive forces to sustain greater equality. As we saw above (Section 7.4.1), this power has traditionally been used to support a somewhat lower wage dispersion between workers.

7.5 Imperfectly competitive labour markets: efficiency wages

Section 7.5 continues the application of supply and demand analysis and institutional factors to recent changes in the UK labour market by turning to the third change: increased work intensity. This introduces the main topic of the section, which is the analysis of worker motivation and management.

Question	How could one adapt the analysis of the relative supply and demand of skilled workers (Figure 7.10) to explain the increased proportion of workers with high levels of work effort?

The answer is fairly straightforward. A similar analysis could be used to understand the increased work effort, if we were to redraw Figure 7.10 but label the axes as 'Wage rate' and 'Number of high-effort workers relative to low-effort workers'. If the technology changes lead to a demand for higher effort, we would expect to see both higher effort on average and greater relative rewards. Table 7.1 shows the higher effort, but we do not have evidence about how the relative wages of high-effort and low-effort workers have changed.

Part of the answer may lie in the reduced influence of trade unions. Trade unions have traditionally attempted to resist pressures to intensify work. However, they have been going through a period of declining density (Section 7.4.1), so their direct sphere of influence has become a smaller part of the overall economy. Moreover, even where they are present, unions are likely to be less able to influence events than they were when there were fewer restrictions on their activities, including their ability to use the strike weapon. The fact that trade unions have declined faster in Britain than elsewhere in Europe may be a factor in making Britain the place where effort has increased the most in Europe (Green and McIntosh, 2001).

This brief discussion of increasing work intensity in the UK labour market opens up the more general issue of worker motivation. An important economic approach to this issue links wages and productivity, arguing that higher wages can increase productivity.

▪▪▪ 7.5.1   Efficiency wages and the worker discipline effect

We have already alluded briefly, in discussing the role of unions (Section 7.4.1), to the possible effect of higher wages in eliciting greater effort through improved 'morale' and hence motivation of workers. This effect is one example of a range of models for labour market analysis entitled, a bit misleadingly, **efficiency wage models**.

Efficiency wage models

Efficiency wage models recognize that higher wages raise productivity by increasing the efficiency with which labour is managed and motivated.

The common conclusion of efficiency wage models is that higher wages can raise productivity. In each case, we shall, in effect, be dropping assumption A4. So far in this chapter I have looked at the complications that arise when assumptions A1, A2 and A3 are replaced by various alternatives. Turning to assumption A4 shows why it too plays a crucial role in the perfect competition model. We shall address the fact that, once the labour contract has been agreed, it is impossible for employers to monitor the effort that is put in during every minute of the day. Some way of *managing and motivating labour* has to be found.

There are three such models. In the first model, it is argued that better wages may lead to improved relations between employers and workers. The 'morale' effect arises when the employer pays wages above the minimum that would be necessary to keep employees from quitting the firm, and workers respond by exceeding the production targets that management sets for them. Thus, up to a point, it pays the employer to pay a 'good' wage, above the basic minimum: the improved morale results in greater productivity that more than covers the extra expense.

A second model of how higher wages might improve productivity applies primarily in low-income countries. In fact it was here, in the context of agriculture in low-income countries, that economists first noticed the relationship between wages and productivity. The argument is that higher wages enable a better standard of living for the workforce, which leads to stronger and healthier workers. Where a firm's workforce is largely manual, keeping it healthy will increase productivity.

There are obvious limits to this model. It could not apply where there is a high turn-over of workers – it is no good from the firm's angle to create a healthy workforce for other firms. It would not apply where there is a reasonable level of welfare benefits or other sources of income that allow good nourishment independent of wages from work. For this reason it is not a model we would expect to be relevant in the industrial world, except perhaps in pockets of extreme poverty.

The worker discipline effect

A third, and more general, argument builds from the proposition that work itself is disliked by workers, and that the only reason people go to work is for the wages. This proposition underlies the approach of most economists. We can immediately object that many workers gain satisfaction from their jobs. Nevertheless, there is a large class of work which is essentially alienating or unpleasant. Moreover, it remains a reasonable starting point to suggest that if workers could have the same wages without having to put in the effort, they would frequently choose to do so.

In 1915, Henry Ford instituted a further dramatic change in his automobile factory near Detroit. I say 'further' because he had only recently introduced his revolution-ary assembly-line techniques to car production. Now he suddenly raised the wages of shop-floor workers from $3 to $5 a day. Furthermore, he maintained this would increase his profits. From the point of view of much conventional economics based on the simple perfect competition model this makes little sense. But it is possible to see Ford's reasoning in the context of the theory of efficiency wages. Part of the story was prob-ably to do with the morale effect outlined above. It may also be due to the 'worker discipline effect'.

The idea behind the worker discipline effect is that workers cannot be monitored closely every minute. They must be induced to continue supplying effort when not observed by a manager or supervisor. But if work is unpleasant and disliked, why work? In such circumstances, the 'rational' worker would choose to minimize his or her effort, except for one thing: the risk of being caught shirking and consequently dismissed. From the firm's point of view, this discipline must be sufficiently strong to motivate effort from the workforce. This necessitates the following measures.

1 There must be some chance of workers who are not working properly being caught. In other words, there must be some supervisors to direct and monitor workers in their daily tasks. These supervisors add to the costs of production.
2 The threat to dismiss shirking workers (or otherwise penalize them) must be serious.

It is in the latter point that the importance of wages comes in. Suppose that wages are low – at or not much above the income that workers would get easily from elsewhere, either from state benefits or from other easily available employment. In these circumstances, there is not much to lose from being dismissed. The 'cost of job loss' – the difference between wages and the income that could be obtained if dismissed – must be sufficient to make dismissal a real danger. Otherwise, why would workers work? The problem Henry

Ford found among his workforce prior to his raising wages was that there was a great deal of disenchantment with the work itself, and consequently a low level of effort and high turnover (either from dismissal or from workers simply leaving). By upping the stakes, Ford made the 'cost of job loss' considerable for his workforce. His confidence in the profit-increasing reason for his move lay in his expectation that at $5 a day he would have a more loyal, harder-working workforce, whose overall productivity would increase by more than the extra wage cost.

Having looked at these three models of how high wages can lead to higher productivity, we will now ask: what implications do they have for our analysis of labour markets? We will look at two answers to this question: the first leads to a modification of our analysis, while the second introduces the subject of unemployment.

■■■ 7.5.2 Implications of efficiency wage models

First implication: the elasticity of demand for labour

Recall that the marginal revenue product of labour (MRP) curve is the basis of the derived demand for labour, because the profit-maximizing condition for the firm is to employ workers up to the point at which the MRP equals the wage rate. This proposition remains true. But we must now recognize that firms could change the MRP, for any value of L, by changing the wage rate. The higher the wage rate the greater the effort and productivity of the marginal worker (and, also, of the average worker). Thus the marginal physical product of labour (MPP_L) could shift when the wage is changed.

In Figure 7.11, the wage rate is initially W_0. The curve labelled MRP $(W = W_0)$ is the appropriate marginal revenue productivity curve for that wage rate. Profits are therefore maximized at labour hours L_0. Notice that, in this analysis, we are working with a model in which profit maximization occurs at $W = MRP$, as in perfect competition, but dropping the assumption that firms cannot individually alter wages. The firm could choose to raise wages to W_1, but if so it would be incorrect to say that hours would fall to the point B. Rather, since at each level of hours the MPP_L is higher due to the efficiency wage effect, the whole MRP curve shifts upwards. In Figure 7.11, maximum profits would instead be obtained at point C and labour hours L_1.

Figure 7.11
Demand for labour, with efficiency wages

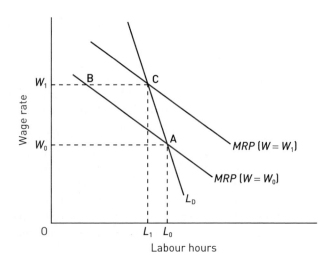

Figure 7.11 thus illustrates that the demand for labour curve in this case (joining points A and C) is less elastic than the *MRP* curve as a result of the efficiency wage effect. Indeed, if you reflect a little, you will see how the *MRP* curve could conceivably have shifted up sufficiently to ensure *no* cut in hours worked or even a rise coincident with the wage rise. Whether that would happen depends on the strength of the efficiency wage effect, which would differ according to circumstances.

Question	At this point it is worth checking your understanding of the above analysis against a possible confusion that sometimes occurs. Consider the following two statements:

1 The basic model tells us that the marginal revenue product of labour is equal to the wage.
2 The efficiency wage model tells us that the marginal revenue product of labour (as well as the marginal physical product of labour) is affected by the wage.

These two statements are both valid, but are making different propositions. Can you see how they are different?

The answer is that the first proposition is a condition that ensures the firm is maximizing its profits. It would be true, under competitive conditions, whether or not efficiency wage forces were important. The second is a causal statement about what determines marginal productivity: the fact that wages are thought to have an impact is the hallmark of efficiency wage models. The statement would be true even if the firm were not at its profit-maximizing position.

Second implication: a rationale for unemployment

For our second implication, we introduce the topic of unemployment, in order to examine an interesting conclusion that follows from efficiency wage models in contrast to the perfect competition model. Recall that, in the latter, it was assumed that labour markets cleared by means of wage adjustments which equate supply and demand. Figure 7.3 depicted one particular cleared labour market. The same arguments apply to the labour market as a whole. In the perfect competition model, then, there is no explanation of why unemployment occurs, other than to imply that if unemployment exists, wages must have failed to adjust to the market-clearing rate. In brief: unemployment could always be eliminated by lowering wages sufficiently.

Consider now the impact of the worker discipline effect. This tells us that, in a world where work is disliked and supervision less than perfect, it would be impossible to motivate workers to work if there were no unemployment. Workers would see that there is little or no cost to being dismissed, because with full employment they could immediately get a job elsewhere at the same wage. Only if there is a risk of spending some time unemployed, with a consequent reduction in income, would workers be induced to work rather than shirk.

This basic insight can be used to show that there must be a certain amount of unemployment to keep the economy at work – perhaps a rather surprising conclusion.

Figure 7.12 is an adaptation of the demand/supply framework applied to the aggregate labour market, but amended to account for the worker discipline effect.

Figure 7.12
Unemployment
from the worker
discipline effect

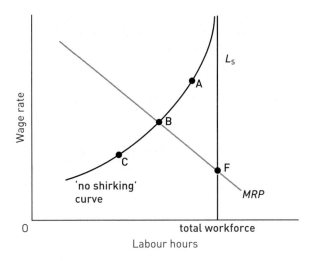

We assume for simplicity a fixed workforce, depicted by the vertical line L_S. The *MRP* is the marginal revenue product of labour curve which is drawn in the usual way, assuming that workers once employed put in the required effort. In terms of the perfect competition model, equilibrium would occur at point F with everyone employed.

However, the argument above has shown that the trouble is that *no worker would choose to work at the wages paid at point F*. Instead, we can plot a relationship between the level of wages and the level of employment as follows.

For a relatively high level of employment (for example, point A) a dismissed worker would experience a relatively short spell of unemployment. Hence a high wage level is needed to motivate workers – a low wage and workers would choose to shirk.

By contrast, at a low level of employment (for example, point C) the consequence of dismissal could be a long period out of work. Therefore a much lower wage level is needed to get people to work. Joining up points such as A and C gives us the 'no shirking curve', meaning that this gives us the wage that employers must pay to elicit proper effort from their workers for each level of employment and unemployment. There is, in other words, a trade-off between high wages and unemployment: lower one of them and it becomes necessary to raise the other in order to secure sufficient employee motivation.

Point B, the intersection of the 'no shirking curve' with the *MRP* curve, is the point at which employers will be maximizing their profits. Hence B is the equilibrium point for the economy. Firms will have no incentive to employ more (or fewer) workers since the wage equals the *MRP*.

Exercise 7.5

At point B, the equilibrium, there are unemployed workers. Why can they not offer to work for lower wages than the existing workers and so get jobs?

This equilibrium with unemployment has been arrived at without assuming that trade unions or governments or any other outside agent manipulates wages. The only departure from the perfect competition model is to drop assumption A4 and replace it with a simple model of worker motivation.

Intervention: could government eliminate unemployment?

The perfect competition model counselled no intervention, owing to its conclusion that full employment was the normal outcome from unfettered market processes. The rather striking conclusion of the model we have just looked at is that it may be counterproductive for government to attempt to reduce or eliminate unemployment, when that unemployment functions as a threat or discipline for those in work. Assume, for the moment, that government policies can alter the level of employment on Figure 7.12. Ask what would be the consequence of raising employment beyond the point B. Answer: a considerable disruption of effort. In a prescient paper written not long after the depression years of the 1930s, the Polish economist Kalecki questioned whether big businesses or the governments under their influence would ever want to eliminate unemployment entirely, even if they would try to reduce it below the levels of the depression years (Kalecki, 1943). In the middle 1960s, when the British economy seemed to operate successfully enough with only a few hundred thousand unemployed, Kalecki's fear appeared misplaced. It was widely assumed then that Keynesianism could ensure full employment. Two decades later, no one was so sure after a prolonged period of high unemployment. It seems likely that the risk of months, even years, on the dole was a motivating factor for many workers in Britain and elsewhere.

But we should not necessarily conclude that it is government's job to maintain a suitable level of unemployment in support of business enterprise, even if the model helps to explain the relaxation of the objective of full employment which no government could fail to emphasize in the 1950s and 1960s. First, there is no suggestion that the currently very high levels of unemployment across Europe are necessary for worker motivation. Nothing in the current argument speaks against aiming for a reduction in these levels. Second, it must be remembered that the model is built on an assumed world of alienating, disliked work, where motivation to work comes primarily through the fear of lost wages. But there are many lines of work where this is not the case, and there are other, more positive forms of motivation, including the provision of more challenging and satisfying work. Encouraging and enabling these other routes to worker motivation would also be a valid form of government intervention. If successful, it would open the door to macroeconomic policies aimed not just at reducing unemployment but also at genuine full employment.

7.6 Conclusion

If nothing else, this chapter will have shown how complex labour markets are in reality, far from the simple perfect competition model of supply and demand. As a general rule, though with exceptions, each time an element of complexity was introduced, questioning the assumptions of the perfect competition model, we developed an alternative model designed to capture some known feature of actual labour markets. Moreover, with each new model we arrived at a rationale for government intervention in one form or another on the grounds of economic efficiency. To take some examples, governments have a case for intervening to remove or minimize barriers to labour mobility between sectors of the labour market, or to impose a wage minimum on the labour market.

Despite the complexity, we have also seen how some far-reaching changes in the labour market can be analysed using a combination of models of supply and demand in the labour market, and an understanding of the institutional features that impinge upon and modify the forces of supply and demand.

Questions for review and discussion

Question 1 Figure 7.13 shows a firm in an imperfectly competitive labour market. Say which wage rate(s) (e.g. W_1, W_2) is/are identified by each of the following descriptions. Note that there may be more than one of the wage rates that satisfies some of the descriptions.

Note:
MFC = Marginal Factor Cost
MRP = Marginal Revenue Product

(a) The wage rate that will be set by the firm if it maximizes its profits in a free market.

$W_1 \; W_2 \; W_3 \; W_4 \; W_5 \; W_6 \; W_7$

(b) The equilibrium wage rate that would result if the imperfectly competitive firm were replaced by a number of perfectly competitive firms collectively facing the market labour supply curve L_S.

$W_1 \; W_2 \; W_3 \; W_4 \; W_5 \; W_6 \; W_7$

(c) A statutory minimum wage rate that would result in the profit-maximizing imperfectly competitive firm employing *fewer* labour hours than it would in a free market.

$W_1 \; W_2 \; W_3 \; W_4 \; W_5 \; W_6 \; W_7$

(d) A statutory minimum wage rate that would result in the profit-maximizing imperfectly competitive firm employing *more* labour hours that it would in a free market.

$W_1 \; W_2 \; W_3 \; W_4 \; W_5 \; W_6 \; W_7$

Figure 7.13
Firm in imperfectly competitive labour market

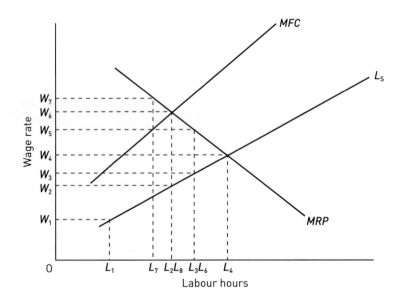

Question 2   Say which statement correctly completes this sentence:

If males are disproportionately found in higher grades and females in lower grades within an occupation, this is an example of

A   ❏   labour market segmentation.
B   ❏   vertical segregation.
C   ❏   horizontal segregation.
D   ❏   efficiency wages.

Question 3   Assume that students pay for their own tertiary education and that the market for tertiary education is perfectly competitive. Assume also that students undertake tertiary education only in order to obtain employment afterwards. We may depict such a market as in Figure 7.14 (this is the same as Figure 10.1 in Chapter 10).

(a) Make a copy of the diagram. Identify the private market equilibrium and label this equilibrium quantity as Q_p and equilibrium price as P_p. Also, label the social optimum output as Q_s and the market price required to induce suppliers to supply that quantity as P_s. Explain with the aid of the diagram the concept of positive externalities and why this might apply to the market for tertiary education. Give some examples of the positive externalities you might observe.
(b) Briefly explain how the analysis in (a) could be used to make the case that tertiary education should be subsidized by government.
(c) In 1998 the government required students to pay a flat-rate fee of £1000 a year for their university tuition. From 2006 the government will enable universities to charge top-up fees of up to £3000 a year more. In the light of your analysis of the private and social benefits of tertiary education, comment briefly on the government's policy of making students pay part of the cost of their tuition.

Figure 7.14
Private and social
benefits in the
market for
education

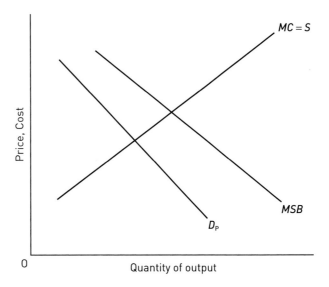

8

Welfare: from income to well-being

Paul Anand

Concepts

- welfare economics
- national income
- indices
- circular flow (CF) model
- marginal utility and total utility
- Pareto optimality and Pareto improvements
- allocative efficiency
- capabilities

Objectives

After studying this chapter you should be able to:

- understand the measurement of national income, and appreciate its limits as an approach to the measurement of welfare
- understand the concept of utility as used in consumer behaviour theory and in welfare economics
- understand some concepts and evidence associated with well-being.

8.1 Introduction: Socrates and the Pot Noodle

Chief: A Pot Noodle is the most beautiful thing on Earth. It is a new way of making money. A way of making money . . . *where no money existed before*: the very definition of excitement.

Philip: Look, I'm probably being thicker than a middle manager's Filofax here Chief, but I'm just not in an 'understanding you' mode at all. Uhm . . . what *is* a Pot Noodle? . . .

Chief: The most unlikely food stuff in history . . . Only the British could market Pot Noodle, because only the British would eat them . . . Anyone worth their company BMW can carve a bigger share of an existing market, but show me the person who can make a pound where there was no pound to be made. That's the fellow who's going to be sitting alongside me and the board in the executive Jacuzzi whirlpool bath.

Philip: The executive Jason Chief, that's a mightily big carrot!

Chief: Find me a Pot Noodle and you're in it Philip, what's more you can sit on one of the jets . . . Make an old man happy!!

(Ben Elton, Gasping, 1990, pp.9–11)

What makes you happy? In what ways does the economy contribute to your welfare? Can happiness be measured or modelled? What role do markets play in providing for people's happiness?

Throughout history, humanity has pondered these questions. Socrates, the Greek philosopher, born to a midwife and sculptor in 469 BC, thought particularly hard about them. A small man, known for his wit and conversation, he was never slow to share his thoughts with others. He gave lessons without charge, falling into poverty as a result, and he became known throughout the city of Athens for his habit of interrogating complete strangers on matters they would otherwise have taken for granted. Socrates believed he could help people improve their lives by reason alone, although enough people found his directness sufficiently threatening that he was eventually tried for corrupting the social fabric of the city and failing to worship the city's gods. 'I have neglected the things that concern most people – making money, managing an estate, gaining military or civic honours . . . I tried to persuade each of you not to think more of practical advantages than of his mental and moral well-being' (Plato, 1993).

It was the practice in Athens for major decisions to be made by a show of hands from an electorate comprising all free adult males. Of the 500-strong jury of citizens at Socrates' trial, 280 voted for conviction, to which Socrates is said to have quipped that he 'didn't think the margin would be so narrow'. Socrates seemed less concerned about his fate than the others around him were, and stated that he would hold steadfast to his views about the relative importance of philosophy and material concerns. After that, 360 of the 500 jury members voted for the death penalty.

Socrates' life and death and Ben Elton's satirical attack on the 1980s are examples of different approaches to the relationship between money and happiness.

Perhaps you are surprised that economists are even concerned with such things. They are not the sort of issues that economic journalists cover on the evening news; they seem to be questions that belong more to the realms of philosophy or psychology. You have seen in previous chapters that economics, like other social sciences, is concerned with *explanation*, *prediction* and *description*, but in this chapter and the next we are going to emphasize the importance of *normative* questions – that is, questions about what *should* be done to improve people's lives. Such judgements are central to economics. For example, whenever the government investigates anti-competitive behaviour in a particular industry, it does so largely because our models of market behaviour show that a monopoly can give rise to *inferior* outcomes. And as you will see in Chapter 9, governments are intimately involved in questions about the best distribution of income and wealth within societies. In these situations economists are concerned with welfare, that is, with the consequences of economic activity for people's lives. Welfare has been interpreted in a range of different ways, from a materialistic emphasis on access to and control over money and material goods to a wider view that encompasses physical, mental and spiritual well-being. Economics *is* intimately concerned with welfare, and it is here that we shall begin to focus on the significance of welfare in economic analysis.

So what does welfare imply for economic analysis? In this chapter we will consider three different perspectives.

In Section 8.2 we will look at income and an economic model of national income known as the 'circular flow' (CF) model. In most countries around the world, income in the form of money is vital to people's everyday existence, and the CF model provides us with a framework for understanding changes in income at a national level. In recent years, however, economists working on environmental issues and low-income countries have been critical of national income as a measure of welfare, and we will look at some of these criticisms.

Section 8.3 deals with the utility approach to welfare. Utility offers us a way of thinking about individual choice, and you will see that it helps us to understand, among other things, why the demand curves you have been using since Chapter 3 often slope downwards. This application of utility to individual choice completes the theory of consumer demand introduced in Chapter 3. Returning to the welfare implications of the utility approach, the idea of Pareto improvements, changes from which nobody loses and some gain in terms of utility, will be introduced. We will look at the argument that Pareto optimality is an appealing idea and that it plays a significant role in helping us to understand the merits of competitive market structures; but we will also see that it has some significant limitations.

Finally, in Section 8.4 we will consider a third approach, one that looks at different aspects of well-being, a topic which draws on ideas from psychology and philosophy. This section will look at empirical evidence on the relationship between happiness and income. We will then move on to explore the idea that well-being depends not only on outcomes, but also on how those outcomes are achieved, and examine Sen's capabilities theory, which has been used to develop measures of well-being based on individuals' own accounts of what matters to them. We will conclude by suggesting that Sen's theory provides, or at least implies, an interesting, and in many ways persuasive, answer to questions about the nature of individual happiness in public policy.

8.2 The economic wealth of nations

'Money doesn't talk, it shouts.'

A paraphrase of Bob Dylan (1965)

■ ■ ■ 8.2.1 The circular flow (CF) model of income

How is it that individuals and societies come to be wealthy in economic or material terms? There are various answers to this question, but an important part of the story has to do with trade. If human beings did not engage in exchange, the specialization and division of labour that Adam Smith highlighted in his famous book, *The Wealth of Nations* (first published in 1776), would not be possible. Were everyone forced to provide for all their own needs, the technological and material cultures that distinguish humanity could not have emerged and spread. Today, in most economies around the world, most exchanges depend upon the use of money.

Economists analyse such exchanges using a circular flow (CF) model of income (Figure 8.1).

The basic CF model strips the economy down to some bare essentials. We can think of the economy as comprising a set of exchanges. Firms pay wages to households in exchange for labour. Firms also pay other forms of income (dividends and interest, rent) to households in return for the supply of other factors of production (capital, land). Households pay firms for the goods and services they consume. So there are two flows. The first is a 'physical' flow of goods and services from firms to households and of the services of factors of production such as labour from households to firms. The second is a money flow in the opposite direction, from firms to households in the form of income for the factors of production they supply and from households to firms in the form of consumption expenditure for the purchase of goods and services. The physical flow

Figure 8.1
The basic CF model
of income

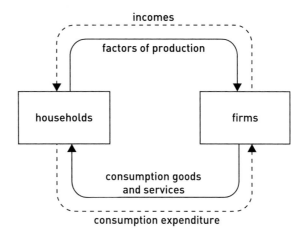

comprises all the goods and services, including the services of factors of production, involved in the different economic interactions that are made between households and firms. The financial flow records these transactions. In Figure 8.1 the dotted lines are financial flows, and the solid lines show flows of real goods and services.

This version of the CF model is sometimes referred to as the 'spendthrift' economy, because the households spend all their income. Another aspect of its being a very basic model is the omission of the government sector and international trade. We will therefore make some additions to the model, and explore how this more sophisticated model can be used to measure economic activity using the national income accounts.

■ ■ ■ 8.2.2 Extensions to the CF model

A more realistic version of the CF model is represented in Figure 8.2, which shows three extensions of the basic model. To keep Figure 8.2 uncluttered, we will concentrate on the *financial* flows, but you should remember that these are always balanced by physical flows of goods and services. One important extension to the basic CF model incorporates savings by households and investment by firms. Householders do not typically spend all their income; rather they save some of it. But what do they do with their savings? Unless

Figure 8.2
The CF model with
injections and
withdrawals

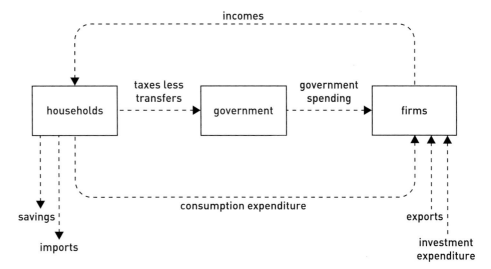

they simply keep them at home in the form of idle cash balances, they deposit them in a financial institution such as a bank or a building society. It is common usage to describe funds deposited in this way as 'investments'. In economic terms, this behaviour is known as 'financial investment'. Financial institutions play a crucial role in collecting up savings (i.e. financial investments) and lending to firms so that physical investment can take place (i.e. investment in directly productive assets). Financial institutions thus act as intermediaries between financial investment and physical investment.

In this CF model, savings reduce consumers' expenditure below their incomes, and can therefore be envisaged as a withdrawal from household spending. This creates a potential imbalance between the flow of money and the flow of goods and services around the system. If there are savings, consumption expenditure will be less than incomes and so the production of consumption goods and services cannot generate all the incomes in the economy. Some income must be generated by production for other purposes. In addition to producing consumer goods, firms produce capital goods, that is, goods such as machinery that are used in making consumer goods to purchase from each other. We can schematically picture two kinds of firm, one producing consumption goods and the other producing capital or investment goods. The firms sector as a whole purchases capital goods from itself. Purchases of these investment goods are financed in this model by borrowing from financial institutions, and this borrowing for investment can be envisaged as an 'injection' of finance into firms.

Our CF model has now become more complicated, but it is still an economy without a government sector. Typically, the most significant sources of government revenue are direct taxes such as income tax, indirect taxes levied on consumption such as value added tax (VAT), so-called 'sin' taxes on alcohol and tobacco products, and corporate taxes levied on businesses. Some of this tax revenue goes straight back to recipients of financial support in the form of pensions and social security. These payments are known as *transfer payments* and are not included in the CF model because there is no corresponding flow of goods and services. So tax revenue, minus transfers, is another withdrawal from the circular flow of income. The corresponding injection is the money that the government spends on goods and services in defence, health, education and so on.

We can also use the CF model to calculate the implications of international production and trade. Goods or services we bring into the country are known as 'imports' and goods and services we sell abroad are referred to as 'exports'. The physical flow of goods and services is always matched by a financial flow in the opposite direction when people pay for the goods and services they buy. So what happens to national income when we introduce exports and imports into the model? Any goods and services sent out of a country will be accompanied by a corresponding payment of money to factors of production in that country. This is the economic argument for believing exports to be a good thing.

The argument about imports is just the reverse of that for exports. If we increase our imports, then we have to increase the amount we pay to foreign factors of production, resulting in a withdrawal from the circular flow of income. Buying a foreign holiday results in a financial flow out of the country to pay for goods and services produced in another country, so this is an import.

▪ ▪ ▪ 8.2.3 Measuring national income using the CF model

Question	Look back at Figure 8.1. How many ways of measuring income do you think it suggests?

National income

National income
is the value of the
goods and services
available in a
national economy
over a given period
of time, usually
a year.

Even the basic CF model suggests that there might be more than one way of measuring **national income**. First, we could try to measure the values of the 'physical' flow of goods and services from firms to households, that is, national output. Second, we could try to measure the money flow moving in the opposite direction, that is, national expenditure. Third, we could try to measure the money flow from firms to households, in return for the services of factors of production, that is, in a literal sense, national income. Because of the ways in which economic transactions are recorded, these three methods are all commonly used, and all of them should give the same result. Why?

There are two reasons. The first is that the two money flows, income and expenditure, must be equal. In any transaction there is a buyer and a seller, and the buyer's expenditure *is* the seller's income. The second is that the physical flow, output, can be measured or valued in terms of either of the money flows, as expenditure incurred in producing it or as income received from selling it.

The more realistic CF model in Figure 8.2 is more complicated in two ways. First, households receive incomes as sellers of labour and other factors of production, but as potential buyers they do not spend all their incomes on the output of the national economy; some is saved, some is paid to the government in taxes and some is spent on imports. Second, these withdrawals of expenditure from the circular flow of income are balanced by injections of expenditure on national output by other sectors. Firms buy capital goods; the government buys capital goods (e.g. aircraft carriers, schools and hospitals); and consumers from overseas (as well as foreign firms and governments) buy the nation's exports.

The CF model in Figure 8.2 is more realistic than the basic model in Figure 8.1, but it is by no means a complete representation of all the transactions in an economy. For example, in the interests of simplicity we have omitted the income flow from government to households that corresponds to the labour services of public sector employees. Calculating national income is complicated, but remember that it is based on the simple identity of income and expenditure whenever money changes hands in an economic transaction.

Output measurement

The output approach involves collecting data on output through surveys of firms. To avoid double counting, economic statisticians focus only on the value added by each firm, that is, the value of each firm's output minus the value of intermediate goods, those that were used up in producing it. For example, a firm buys steel and adds value to it by using it in the manufacture of a car; double counting would occur if the national accounts included the value of both the steel and the car. Totalling up the value added by each firm in the economy gives a figure for the gross domestic product (GDP), that is, the value of all the output produced by factors of production located in the national economy. The main advantage of this method is that it provides a breakdown of the output value of each industry, which is useful if one wants to monitor the performance of specific areas of an economy.

Figure 8.3 shows the gross value added at basic prices for the main sectors of the UK economy in 1999. The term 'gross' means that no deduction has been made to reflect the fact that capital equipment depreciates, that is, that it loses value, becoming worn out or obsolete until it must be replaced. The qualification 'at basic prices' means that the figures exclude taxes on goods and services, such as value added tax (VAT), and include subsidies, in order to reflect the cost of the factors of production used in producing the goods and services.

Figure 8.3
Gross value added
at basic prices,
UK 1999

Source: Office for
National Statistics,
2001, Table 2.1,
p.109

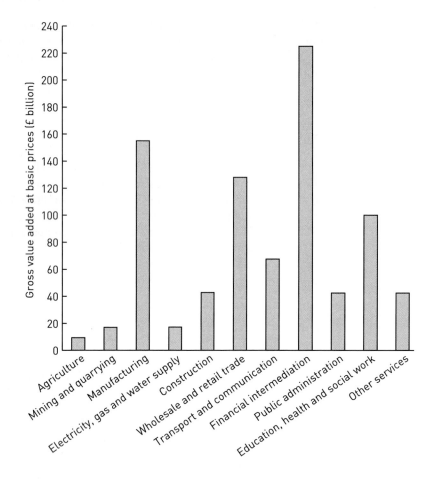

Figure 8.3 underlines the status of the UK economy as a 'service economy' (Chapter 1). The largest contribution to the value added was made by financial services. Adding finance to the other major service industries – wholesale and retail, education and transport – shows that the value added by services (very approximately £490 billion) is more than three times greater than the value added by manufacturing (approximately £155 billion). This may strike you as surprising in an economy that was once renowned (not necessarily accurately) as 'the workshop of the world'. The small contribution made to value added by agriculture is also striking. The contribution of electricity, gas and water supply appears to be smaller than the impact of domestic bills might suggest.

These are the only figures we shall look at that are expressed in terms of basic prices; all the others are shown at market prices. This adjustment is necessary to prevent inconsistency between the results of the output and expenditure methods of calculating national income. Market prices are the prices consumers actually pay in the shops and supermarkets, and these prices are affected by taxes on goods and services such as VAT and subsidies such as those on agricultural produce. It is therefore necessary to add taxes on products (goods and services) to output at basic prices and to subtract subsidies from

Table 8.1
UK gross domestic product (GDP), 2000: the output approach

	£m
Gross value added, at basic prices	831 053
Value added taxes (VAT) on products	64 906
Other taxes on products	54 271
Less subsidies on products	−6 818
GDP at market prices	943 412

Source: Office for National Statistics, 2001, Table 1.2, p.39

output at basic prices in order to arrive at the gross domestic product (GDP) at market prices. Table 8.1 shows this adjustment to give UK GDP at market prices for 2000.

Expenditure measurement

Question Look back at Figure 8.2, which shows the CF model with injections and withdrawals. What are the four sources of expenditure on firms' output?

The components of aggregate (i.e. total) expenditure are consumption expenditure, investment expenditure, government spending and exports. The *expenditure* method of measuring national income relies on surveys and data collection centred on the final expenditures of the various agents in the economy engaged in expenditure. The qualification 'final' is necessary to avoid double counting, which would occur if, to adapt the example used earlier, expenditure by a car manufacturer on steel was added to consumption expenditure on the car (including the value of the steel used in making it). We should also subtract the spending on imports that forms part of each component of expenditure. It is easier in practice to subtract import expenditure as a whole and therefore just treat net exports (i.e. exports minus imports) as a component of aggregate expenditure. Household data are collected through the Household Expenditure Survey; government data through its accounts; data on investment expenditure or 'gross capital formation' from surveys of firms; and net exports or the 'external balance' through figures collected by the government for goods and services sold abroad (exports) minus goods and services bought from overseas. Adding all these final expenditures together gives a second measure of national income. As is shown in Table 8.2, GDP at current market prices measured by the

Table 8.2
UK gross domestic product (GDP) at current market prices, 2000: the expenditure approach

	£m
Consumer expenditure	617 648
General government final consumption	174 791
Gross capital formation	167 099
External balance	−15 719
Statistical discrepancy	−407
GDP at current market prices	943 412

Source: adapted from Office for National Statistics, 2001, Table 1.2, p.39

expenditure approach provides estimates of the components of aggregate expenditures in the economy. These estimates are widely used in formulating economic policy.

Income measurement

The *income* approach tries to measure incomes directly from the returns lodged with the tax-collecting branch of the government – the Inland Revenue in the UK. If economic activities were reported correctly, this method would give a third estimate of national income. The advantage of this approach is that it could provide statistics on the distribution of incomes, between different social groups or between different factors of production.

From Table 8.3 we can begin to see how the UK economy is constituted using data from the income approach. Income from employment, including self-employment, accounts for just over half of total GDP. If we look at gross trading profits, we can see that they account for just over a quarter of total GDP. This item includes the operating surpluses (excess of revenue over costs) of some governmental organizations as a rather minor component.

Table 8.3
UK gross domestic product (GDP) at current market prices, 2000: the income approach

	£m
Income from employment	521 443
Profits	237 051
Mixed income	54 442
Taxes on production and imports	137 955
Less subsidies	−7 724
Statistical discrepancy	245
GDP at current market prices	943 412

Source: adapted from Office for National Statistics, 2001, Table 1.2, p.39

So far we have focused on GDP as the measure of national income. You may also hear commentators refer to gross national income (GNY), which is the value of the final output produced by nationally owned factors of production, wherever that production takes place (Table 8.4). If a UK supermarket owns a mango plantation in Peru, then the profit from that farm's output is part of the UK's GNY (but not its GDP). Alternatively, the output produced by a Japanese car company located in Derbyshire is part of the UK's GDP, because it is output produced in the UK's domestic economy. It is not part of the UK's GNY, because the profits do not accrue to factors owned by UK companies or individuals. In sum, GNY measures income relating to factors *nationally owned* (wherever they are); GDP measures income due to factors *domestically located* (whoever owns them).

Table 8.4
UK gross national income (GNY) at current market prices, 2000

	£m
GDP at current market prices	943 412
Net income from the rest of the world	3 036
GNY at current market prices	946 448

Source: adapted from Office for National Statistics, 2001, Table 1.2, p.39

National income accounting, as we saw above, is based on an economic model, the circular flow of income. Remember that, in principle, all three approaches to national income measurement should give the same result. The practicalities of data gathering, however, mean that methods vary in their accuracy and so in practice, as you have seen in Tables 8.2 and 8.3, there are generally small discrepancies between the measures.

Like most economic models, the CF model has some important insights as well as a few significant limitations. On the positive side, it helps us to understand how the economy changes over time and to estimate the standard of living, which is one important measure of welfare.

Real and nominal income

Economic change is the guiding theme of this book, and economists use national income statistics to obtain a sense of how an economy is changing. If we were to use data expressed in '£ million', the results could be misleading. Suppose, for example, that a country's GDP increased by 25 per cent between 1990 and 2000. Were its consumers 25 per cent better off in 2000 than in 1990? Did they have 25 per cent more goods and services to buy? Not necessarily.

Question | Can you think of a reason why not?

Inflation

Inflation refers to a rise in the general level of prices in a country.

Inflation rate

The inflation rate measures the rate at which prices are rising, and is expressed as a percentage increase in the general level of prices from one year to the next.

The reason is a familiar facet of economic experience: **inflation**. Inflation refers to a rise in the general level of prices in a country, and the **inflation rate** measures the rate at which prices are rising, usually expressed per year. So the answer to my two questions above would be 'Yes, definitely' only if the inflation rate during the 1990s had been exactly 0 per cent, that is, if there had been no inflation at all, a situation known as 'price stability'. At the other extreme, if the inflation rate had been 25 per cent, the apparent increase in output would have been illusory; there would have been no increase at all in the quantity of goods and services available for consumption, only a rise in the prices at which an unchanged quantity of output was sold. In reality, the truth usually lies somewhere between these two extremes, and an increase in a country's GDP reflects both an increase in the quantity of output and the effects of inflation.

Suppose we want to compare real output in different years. If we can find a way of adjusting for inflation, or removing its influence, we would be left with the actual increase in the quantity of output, that is, real output. Nominal or money output is the value of output expressed in the prices prevailing at the time it was sold; so it can also be referred to as GDP in current market prices. In order to strip away the effect of inflation, we want output for each year to be expressed in prices that have not changed over the period, that is, GDP at constant market prices or real output. The way in which this is done can be illustrated using the UK national income accounts, which express the national income of the UK in terms of both current market prices and constant 1995 market prices (Table 8.5).

The only figures that are the same in the two rows are those for 1995. The figures in the top row – GDP measured in the prices current in the years in question – have all been adjusted for inflation in the bottom row, taking 1995 prices as the 'base year' for the adjustment.

Table 8.5
UK GDP in current market prices and constant market prices, 1985–2000

	1985 £m	1990 £m	1995 £m	2000 £m
GDP at current prices	354 952	557 300	719 176	943 412
GDP at constant 1995 prices	560 255	659 171	719 176	826 144

Source: Office for National Statistics, 2001, Table 1.2, pp.38–9 and Table 1.3, pp.40–1

Let us see how the calculation of real income works by taking a hypothetical example. Let us suppose that money GDP at market prices for Utopia in 1995 was equivalent to £400 million and it increased to £430 million in 1996. The inflation rate between 1995 and 1996 was 5 per cent. What was Utopia's real income in 1996 expressed in terms of 1995 prices? This can be calculated as follows.

1 First, we can think of the 1995 prices as equivalent to 100. These are the 'base year' prices. In effect, we are making the 1995 income represent 100 per cent, and then thinking of any change from one year to the next as a percentage change. To do this we derive an index of inflation between 1995 and 1996 expressed in terms of this figure of 100. With 5 per cent inflation the price index for 1996 will be 105.

2 We then need to 'deflate' the 1996 money GDP of £430 million using the inflation index. This is done by dividing 430 by 105 and then multiplying the result by 100.

$$\frac{430}{105} \cdot 100 = 409.5 \text{ (to one decimal place)}$$

This result is equivalent to dividing 430 by 1.05.

So, the real value of 1996 GDP is £409.5 million, which is considerably less than the nominal GDP of £430 million.

Exercise 8.1

Suppose that the inflation rate had been 7.5 per cent between 1995 and 1996. What would have been Utopia's real GDP, or GDP at constant market prices, in 1996?

The figures in the bottom row of Table 8.5 have been recalculated using this method to provide 'real' values expressed in terms of 1995 prices. Clearly, the figures for the years before 1995 have been recalculated to 'inflate' them forward to 1995 prices, but the same principles apply. In fact, the UK national income accounts provide a quick way to calculate these real changes in the national income totals by the use of the 'GDP deflator'. The GDP deflator expresses the ratio of GDP at current prices to GDP at constant prices:

$$\text{GDP deflator} = \frac{\text{GDP at current prices}}{\text{GDP at constant prices}} \cdot 100$$

Data for this index are shown in Table 8.6.

If we have the GDP deflators we can calculate real GDP from money GDP using the following formula:

$$\text{real GDP} = \frac{\text{money GDP}}{\text{GDP deflator}} \cdot 100$$

Table 8.6
GDP deflator
(1995 = 100), 1985,
1990, 1995 and 2000

	1985	1990	1995	2000
GDP deflator	63.3	84.6	100.0	114.2

Source: Office for National Statistics, 2001, Table 1.1, pp.36–7

This is a reorganization of the above definition of the GDP deflator, as you can see if you remember that money GDP is GDP at current prices and real GDP is GDP at constant prices.

Exercise 8.2

You can check the way this is done by taking the figure for 2000 UK GDP at current market prices from the top row of Table 8.5 and calculating 2000 UK GDP at constant market prices using the GDP deflator from Table 8.6. Your answer should coincide with the figure for 2000 UK GDP at constant market prices in the bottom row of Table 8.5.

Have a go at this calculation now.

Now we turn to the second application of the CF model: estimating the standard of living.

The standard of living interprets welfare in terms of access to material goods and services. GDP estimates the value of the total output of goods and services produced in an economy. It tells us how big the economy is. If we want to know the share of output available to the average person in the economy, however, we need to divide GDP by the number of people living in the economy. This adjustment yields a figure for GDP per head (of the population). From Tables 8.1, 8.2, 8.3 and 8.5 we know that UK GDP (for 2000 at current market prices) was £943 412 million. The UK population in 2000 was 59 756 000.

Question What was GDP per head for the UK in 2000?

The answer is:

$$\frac{£943\ 412\ 000\ 000}{59\ 756\ 000} = (\text{approximately})\ £15\ 788$$

This means that the average person (woman, man and child) had a share of goods and services worth £15 788. This highlights one limitation of national income accounts as a measure of welfare: GDP per head tells us nothing about the actual distribution of goods and services. Is the value of the goods and services available to most individuals approximately £15 788, just a little above or a little below? Or do the majority of people get by on substantially less than that, with relatively few individuals having access to much more? Chapter 9 discusses the distribution of income and methods of measuring it.

The CF model tells us little about other issues that might have an effect on well-being. It is not explicitly concerned with individual people's preferences, the availability of employment or the quality of the environment. But economists, and those in related disciplines, do have things to say about all of these issues, and it is to those issues that we will now turn.

▦ ▨ ■ 8.2.4   An alternative approach: sustainable economic welfare or 'green income'

National income is not a perfect measure of welfare. For many years, economists used to point out that national income would go down if a person married their housekeeper. This is because the standard measure of national income measures only output that is sold in a market transaction and so produces a money income. The presumption was that after the marriage the work would still be done but the market transaction would disappear, and the conclusion was that national income was defective as a measure of the value of output. This somewhat old-fashioned story highlights a real problem: namely, that there are many valuable activities – such as work in the home – that are simply invisible to measures of national income based on market transactions. In 2002 the Office for National Statistics started to publish a separate Household Satellite Account, which gives an estimate of the output of all unpaid work. It showed that the total value of the output of unpaid work was almost as much as that of GDP in 2002.

There are other problems too. Let us take three that illustrate the range of issues that have been discussed by critics of national income accounting. First, there are questions of distribution. We have seen that national income measures are well suited to summarizing the total amount of activity in an economy, but even GNY per head does not tell us about the distribution of income within countries. This is a serious omission if policy makers think that economic growth will alleviate poverty.

Second, as labour economists have noted, national income accounts fail to make allowance for changes in human capital. Human capital comprises the skills and abilities that people have as a result of education or experience, and its importance to individual earnings means that it will be relevant to national income (Chapter 7, Section 7.2.4). Changes in physical capital through investment and depreciation are measured in national income accounts, but changes in human capital are not. The fact that they are much harder to measure is probably the reason, but the omission is serious nonetheless.

Third, it is now widely accepted that many environmental issues are not handled well by national income accounts. For example, the current and future costs of climate change and rising sea levels are a direct consequence of previous economic activity that led to the emission of greenhouse gases. At the time of these emissions, however, no charge was made against the national income accounts to reflect these future losses. Furthermore, when we come to spend money on preventing or repairing damage done by climate change in the future, it will be entered in the national income accounts as an increase in economic activity. The problem is that the accounts are not accompanied by a statement of what is happening to the value of our national assets, such as the climate and low-lying land on the coast.

Environmental economists have attempted to deal with just these issues. One of the more influential attempts can be found in a publication by Herman Daly, a World Bank economist, and John Cobb, an academic theologian (Daly and Cobb, 1994). Their approach involves making some 20 adjustments to consumption (as measured in GDP) in order to derive an index of what they call 'sustainable economic welfare' (ISEW).

The first adjustment involves dividing consumption by a measure of inequality. The ISEW assumes that greater inequality in the distribution of income reduces welfare, because an extra $100, for example, would have no effect on the welfare of a millionaire but would be much appreciated by someone living in poverty (see Section 8.3.1 on the diminishing marginal utility of income, and Chapter 9 on measuring inequality and poverty). In Table 8.7, column B gives an index of inequality and indicates that inequality has increased since 1951, which implies that column A overstates the contribution of consumption to welfare.

Table 8.7 A simplified calculation of the index of sustainable economic welfare (ISEW) for the USA, 1990

Consumption	Distributional inequality[1]	Weighted consumption	Services[2]	Environmental impacts[3]	Other	ISEW
A	B	C (= A/B)	D	E	F	= C + D + E + F
1265.6[4]	1.087	1164.3	807.8	−1149.3	−4.6	818.2

1 Distributional inequality measured by an index set to 1 in 1951.

2 Includes services such as household labour, benefits from consumer durables and improvements in health and education that are not reflected in national income.

3 Includes environmental impacts such as car accident costs, loss of wetlands and farmland, long-term environmental damage and ozone depletion.

4 Currency: 1972 US dollars.

Source: adapted from Daly and Cobb, 1994, pp.462–3

Dividing column A by column B corrects this overstatement, as shown in column C. This constitutes a major departure from just using figures such as GNP, the US equivalent of UK GNY, which reflect only an *average* level of economic welfare, something that most people do not actually receive. There are more people who live below the average income than live above it, because a few very rich people pull the average up.

Next, Daly and Cobb add to 'weighted consumption' the value of services that are excluded from national income, including items such as the value of unpaid work done in the home. The deductions made in the next column reflect the omission from GNP of environmental impacts, including health expenditures (e.g. treatment of asthma caused by worsening air pollution), the loss of wetlands, ozone depletion and other forms of long-term environmental damage. This approach is illustrated in Table 8.7 with US data for the year 1990.

Daly and Cobb used their approach to calculate an index of SEW (ISEW) for the USA, which they then compared with per capita GNP, 'per capita' being a Latin term meaning 'per head' (see Figure 8.4).

Question From Figure 8.4, what can you say about the relationship between GNP and 'green national income' (ISEW) over time?

Figure 8.4
A comparison of ISEW and GNP per capita for the USA
Source: Daly and Cobb, 1994, p.464

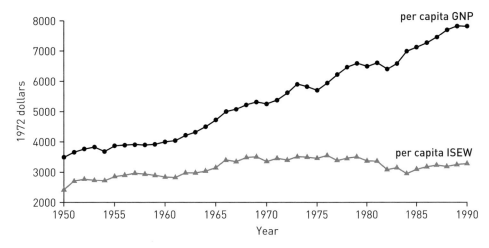

One point to note is that from 1950 to 1990 both GNP and ISEW increased in the USA, although the increase in ISEW was noticeably smaller. Perhaps a more important difference is that ISEW and GNP moved in opposite directions in the 1980s: GNP rose but ISEW declined. Looking at the reasons behind these changes, it seems that inequalities in consumption changed quite dramatically over the period. Inequalities were at their lowest in the latter half of the 1960s, after which the trend was towards greater inequality. And although efforts to reduce pollution and accidents were largely successful in the 1970s and 1980s, the impact on total ISEW was modest.

Daly and Cobb concluded their study by reflecting on the purpose and nature of such measurements:

> The purpose of an index that strives to measure economic well-being is not simply to show us how we are presently faring . . . It should also reveal the kinds of policies that would enable a nation to improve its welfare . . . Are the policies of our government going to be guided by GNP, or by ISEW or some other measure of sustainable welfare?

(1994, p.507)

Question	To what extent do you think Daly and Cobb's ISEW is an improvement over GNP or GDP as a measure of welfare?

Let us consider three points. First, Daly and Cobb's analysis shows that environmental costs are large and growing. Because this environmental damage is not included in US GNP or GDP, one might conclude that these will be seen as increasingly flawed measures of national income. Second, while acknowledging that ISEW performs an important service by reflecting the value of environmental damage, one might ask what it is that ISEW measures. Does it really indicate how sustainable economic welfare is? It seems that just incorporating environmental costs tells us very little, if anything, about how likely it is that these levels of economic welfare can persist into the future if that is what 'sustainability' means. Third, the ISEW includes a measure of inequality. While distributional issues are important, they enter the formula for ISEW in a particular way. Other approaches are equally plausible. For instance, the weight or importance ISEW attributes to inequality appears to be arbitrary.

8.3 Utility, welfare and markets

For money can't buy me love.

(Paul McCartney)

You have seen, in Chapters 4 to 6, that the analysis of different kinds of market structures plays a central role in economics. In this section, we will examine in a bit more detail how the analysis of markets is related to views about what people want. Traditionally, economists have used the concept of *utility* (rather than money income) in this analysis. Utility expresses the idea that the welfare derived from consumption is a subjective concept, in the sense that the satisfaction one person gets from consuming a given amount of a particular good may be quite different from the satisfaction another person gets from

Utility

Total utility is the satisfaction derived from consuming a given amount of a good.

consuming the same amount of the same good. Think, for example, of the UK television commercials for Marmite – one person loves it, another hates it. Or think of the saying that one person's meat is another's poison. The idea of utility also captures the idea that the satisfaction from consumption varies with the amount of the good consumed: too much of good thing can make you bored, sick or drunk. And, finally, many economists have argued that if society wants to maximize welfare, it should aim to maximize the **utility** enjoyed by consumers.

■ ■ ■ 8.3.1   Consumption and diminishing marginal utility

Marginal utility

Marginal utility refers to the change in total satisfaction derived from consuming a good when the amount consumed changes by one unit.

One of the oldest ideas in utility theory is the concept of diminishing **marginal utility**, something first discussed by mathematicians in the early 1700s. The idea is that the more units of something that are consumed, the less valuable are successive units to the consumer. For instance, you might consider how much coffee you need to drink in order to complete the next essay. Perhaps one cup would help keep you awake, but two cups would make you alert as well. A third cup might have no further effect, and a fourth cup might begin to produce undesirable effects. The fact that the value of cups of coffee declines the more we consume is an example of what economists refer to as 'diminishing marginal utility'. If we could imagine the utility or satisfaction derived from each cup of coffee as a number, we might represent the coffee example as shown in Table 8.8, where utility is measured in units called 'utils'.

The first two columns of Table 8.8 show a particular cup of coffee and the utility derived from that particular cup. These figures depict the marginal utility of coffee. In this case, the first cup of coffee gives 5 utils, and the fourth cup gives −2 utils. Each successive cup provides less utility than the one before. For most goods and services we expect that, eventually, successive units of consumption will produce smaller and smaller additions to the consumer's total utility. In such cases, marginal utility is said to be diminishing. In last pair of columns, we have the total number of cups drunk and the total utility derived from drinking those cups. The total and marginal utility figures are related: in mathematical terms, marginal utility represents the change in total utility. Conversely, total utility is just the sum of all the marginal utilities. In our example, total utility increases until the third cup of coffee, but by a declining amount. Drinking the fourth cup of coffee has a negative marginal utility that reduces the total utility.

Exercise 8.3

If marginal utility is positive, does the total utility rise or fall?

Table 8.8
The utility of coffee

Cup of coffee	Marginal utility	Total number of cups drunk	Total utility
0	–	0	0
1st	5	1	5
2nd	4	2	9
3rd	0	3	9
4th	−2	4	7

Where do these marginal utility numbers come from? Historically, the idea comes from work by experimental psychologists which shows that, in many fields, our response to stimuli tails off as the intensity of the stimulus increases. For example, we might detect minor changes in volume at low levels of sound but are unable to detect similar changes at much higher sound levels. And you might find that your essays get better the more work you do, but that diminishing returns set in, until a point is reached at which further effort seems to add very little.

Question	Diminishing marginal utility has been used by economists to argue for income and wealth redistribution – that is, a tax and benefit system that redistributes income or wealth from the rich to the poor. Can you think in what way?

Economists generally assume that one person's 'utils' cannot be compared to another's. However, the argument in favour of redistribution involves making a comparison between consumers. If it is true of most consumers that the marginal utility of income declines the more one has, and people have similar levels of utility from similar levels of income, then people on low incomes will have the highest marginal utility from additional income. Redistribution from rich to poor amounts to shifting income from people for whom it produces little utility, at the margin, to people capable of using it to produce more utility, at the margin. Whatever the motive, most countries do have redistributive tax and benefit systems. Of course, income taxes are difficult to avoid, so they represent an infringement of personal liberty, one that some cultures find more acceptable than others.

■ ■ ■ 8.3.2 Individual equilibrium

An important use of utility theory is in describing equilibrium conditions for consumers. This application of utility theory enables us to complete the theory of consumer demand that was introduced in Chapter 3. When economists say that a consumption pattern is in equilibrium, they mean that the consumer could obtain no more utility from any other consumption pattern and therefore has no reason to deviate from that pattern. You will recall from Chapters 4 and 5 that the profit-maximizing firm, in equilibrium, sets output levels so that marginal cost equals marginal revenue ($MC = MR$). Similar insights apply to the equilibrium of the consumer. Suppose that there are two goods, videos and takeaways.

A necessary condition for equilibrium in consumption is that the marginal utility of the last £1 spent on videos equals the marginal utility of the last £1 spent on takeaways. Why? If not, that is, if the consumer is getting more utility from one good at the margin (e.g. videos), then it pays to shift consumption away from the other good (takeaways). For example, suppose the last £1 you spend on videos brings you 30 utils, while the last £1 you spend on takeaways brings you 10 utils. You would not be in equilibrium, that is, you would not be maximizing your utility, in that situation. Assuming videos and takeaways display diminishing marginal utility, suppose you buy more videos and fewer takeaways. You could continue to switch your spending in this way until the last £1 you spend on (more) videos brings you 20 utils and the last £1 you spend on (fewer) takeaways also brings you 20 utils. At this point you cannot increase your utility by changing your consumption of videos and takeaways; you get the same number of utils whether you spend your last £1 on videos or takeaways. So your consumption is in equilibrium.

We can restate the condition for equilibrium as follows:

$$\frac{\text{marginal utility of videos}}{\text{price of videos}} = \frac{\text{marginal utility of takeaways}}{\text{price of takeaways}}$$

Put informally, this equation asserts that, in equilibrium, the consumer should get the same 'bangs for their bucks' in different areas of expenditure. Economists have also used this equation to explain why demand curves slope downwards. Suppose that the utility from additional consumption of videos and takeaways is positive but declining, that is, that diminishing marginal utility applies to both goods. What happens if the price of videos goes up? The quantity on the left-hand side of the equation will be less than that on the right-hand side, indicating that the consumer is not in equilibrium. To compensate, the consumer must increase the marginal utility they receive from consuming videos, and this requires the consumption of fewer videos and more takeaways. Alternatively, if the price of videos were to fall, then the ratio on the left-hand side of the equation would be larger than that on the right-hand side. To restore equality between the two sides of the equation, the consumer would need to decrease the marginal utility of videos which, given diminishing marginal utility, means consuming more videos. So diminishing marginal utility implies that, to maximize utility, the consumer's demand curve should be downward sloping.

Let us work through a more formal derivation of the consumer's demand curve from information about utility. To see how this can be done, assume that the consumer buys one cup of coffee, at a price of £1. If one cup is the right quantity for the consumer at this price, then this price–quantity point represents equilibrium for the consumer. Using the ratio condition for equilibrium above, we can calculate that in this equilibrium the ratio of marginal utility to price must be equal to 5 (ignoring units). Furthermore, this ratio should be the same for all goods and their prices, that is, 5. As more coffee is consumed, the marginal utility is ultimately likely to fall, but we could reasonably assume that as a person's equilibrium bundle of spending moves from one to two cups of coffee, the ratio stays approximately the same – as coffee takes a rather small proportion of a person's total income. Given these assumptions, we can use information on utility to say how much the consumer is willing to pay for different quantities of coffee; in other words we can derive their demand curve.

So, if we consider the demand for two cups of coffee, we see, from Table 8.8, that the marginal utility of a second cup is 4 utils. From the equilibrium condition and the information above, 4/£price = 5, so the £price of coffee must be 4/5 (by simple algebraic rearrangement) or 80 pence. In other words, the consumer needs the price of coffee to fall by 20 pence in order to justify buying two cups. We now have two price–quantity points on the consumer's demand curve (Figure 8.5(a)); we can obtain more points by repeating this process and, where it makes sense, we might join these points together to give the familiar, continuous downward-sloping curve that is generally used to represent demand (Figure 8.5(b)). Traditionally, it has been important to economists to argue that a consumer's demand curve can be derived from their underlying preferences for goods measured by the utilities they enjoy from their consumption. So this derivation shows how the theory of consumer demand is grounded in utility theory.

We can, and do, apply the above equation well beyond its application to the analysis of consumer demand. Some of these uses seem to be more important than the application to consumption might suggest. For instance, the economist-philosopher John Broome (1993) has used this equation to argue that governments should distribute expenditure so that the marginal utility of life-saving expenditures is the same in different areas of

Figure 8.5
Deriving a demand
curve from utility
information

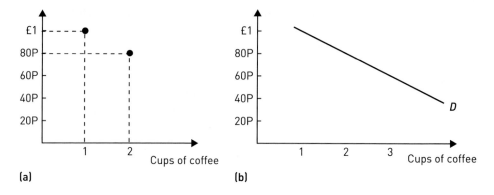

(a)   (b)

government expenditure. If it costs much less to save lives by spending money on environmental programmes than it does to save lives and thereby increase utility by spending money on health care, then we should divert resources from health to environment. Or to put it another way, we should expect to see equal value for money in different areas of expenditure on consumption.

Case study: The value of life and government policy

An interesting exercise in quantifying the different benefits in various areas of expenditure was conducted by the Harvard-based economist Kip Viscusi, who looked at the cost per life saved for risk and safety legislation in the USA.

Table 8.9 indicates a number of areas in which regulatory legislation has been passed, the sponsoring agency and the cost per life saved for each regulation. These cost figures may not be exact, but they illustrate the range of costs that different agencies impose. It is worth pointing out that we are assuming that the average cost per

life figure is closely related to the marginal cost per life figure. In practice, these figures will be different, so we should regard this assumption as an approximation.

Question

Suppose that you were in a position to make marginal changes to the expenditure decisions of the organizations in Table 8.9. Examine the data in the table and decide what changes you would make to increase utility by saving more lives.

Table 8.9
Cost of saving lives by regulation and agency

Regulation	Agency	Cost per life saved $m[1]
Unvented heaters	Consumer Product Safety Commission	0.1
Seat belts	National Highway Traffic Safety Administration	0.3
Alcohol and drugs	Federal Railroad Administration	0.5
Servicing wheel rims	Occupational Safety and Health Administration	1.2
Grain dust	Occupational Safety and Health Administration	5.3
Asbestos	Environmental Protection Agency	104.2
Land disposal	Environmental Protection Agency	3 500.0
Formaldehyde	Occupational Safety and Health Administration	72 000.0

[1] Currency unit is 1984 US dollars.
Source: adapted from Viscusi, 1998, p.98

Viscusi's analysis (see case study above) suggests that the regulations sponsored by the Environmental Protection Agency tend to have a higher cost per life saved. We might therefore say that to get more lives saved per unit of expenditure we should be moving regulatory effort and resources from issues such as formaldehyde to issues such as heater design and seat belts. If one were able to make marginal changes to the budgets of these organizations, one could use the necessary conditions for equilibrium to argue that expenditure should be shifted to those agencies and regulations that save more lives per dollar. The fact that regulations relating to formaldehyde cost a staggering $72 billion to save one life, a sum approximately equivalent to the entire national income of some low-income countries, suggests that a redirection of resources, assuming it were possible, would lead to outcomes that saved more lives and so increased utility.

▨ ▨ ■ 8.3.3 Pareto optimality and the utility possibility frontier

Welfare economics

Welfare economics is the study of the effect on well-being of different allocations of resources among individuals.

An important use of the concept of utility arises from its application to **welfare economics**, the study of the effect on well-being of different allocations of goods and services between individuals. In this simple example, we will assume that we have a variety of goods and services that can be shared out in numerous ways between two people, Alice and Ben. We can also assume, for simplicity, that each person derives utility only from the goods they are allocated, and that both have a maximum level of utility beyond which they cannot be any happier. Under these assumptions (both of which might be challenged), we can draw what is called a utility possibility frontier for Alice and Ben (Figure 8.6).

In Figure 8.6, the horizontal and vertical axes represent the utilities of Alice and Ben respectively. At the origin, in the left-hand corner, both parties obtain zero utility. The wavy line on the right-hand side, the utility possibility frontier (UPF), represents the most utility that could be obtained by Alice and Ben from the goods and services available. The points U_{Alice}^{max} and U_{Ben}^{max} show the maximum levels of utility for Alice and Ben respectively. In this case, both parties obtain maximum utility when the other party has zero utility. (The waviness represents the difficulty of measuring the individual utilities of Alice and Ben. This being the case, one could have drawn a smoother curve, while noting that the line cannot be measured precisely in practice.)

Many economists have argued that the utilities of different people cannot be compared. This is often referred to as 'the problem of interpersonal comparisons'. Suppose there is

Figure 8.6
Utility possibility frontier for Alice and Ben

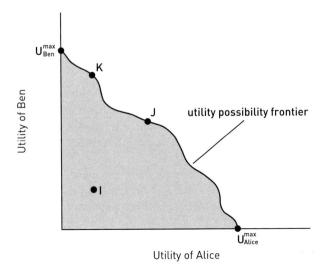

only one kidney machine to treat two patients. One might allocate the machine to the patient who would get more utility from being treated, but it is difficult to see how anyone could tell which of the two patients this would be. In some sense, most people are probably attracted to the principle that both patients have an equal right to treatment, so it is not even clear that any measure of utility differences should play a policy role in determining access to health.

These problems of interpersonal comparisons have led many economists to focus on comparisons between distributions or states of affairs in which *everyone* is better or worse off. Each possible allocation of goods will give rise to a utility level for Alice and a utility level for Ben, which we can plot as points on the two-dimensional graph in Figure 8.6. Point I is one such point, and the set of all feasible distributions of utility is given by the shaded area. If we move to points above I, Ben gets more utility; if we move to points to the right of I, Alice's utility increases. Moving to points north-east of point I, towards point J, represents increases in the utility of Alice and Ben, changes known as *Pareto improvements*. The term comes from the Italian economist, Vilfredo Pareto, who noted the importance of allocations in which the welfare of everyone improves. A weak Pareto improvement is a change in which some people are better off but no one is worse off.

All points on the north-eastern boundary of the shaded area represent allocations of utility from which no further Pareto improvements can be made. At point J, for example, it is possible to increase Ben's utility (by moving up) only by reducing the utility of Alice (moving left). This is true of all the points on this north-eastern boundary and all the points are, therefore, known as *Pareto optimal* distributions of utility.

Question	Do you think there are many Pareto improvements to be made in the economy? Do you think all Pareto improvements are desirable?

When interpersonal comparisons of utility are not thought to be possible, Pareto optimality plays a central role in social choice and public policy. If we are unwilling to make comparisons between people with respect to utility we can look only for improvements in which everyone is made better off. In conventional welfare economics, this remains an important belief. And improvements in which everyone is made better off do occur. For example, suppose that there are people who are unemployed and desperately want to work. Getting them into jobs not only makes them better off but also improves the welfare of the rest of society, who can now buy the extra goods produced by the previously unemployed people. Diagrammatically, this corresponds to point I in Figure 8.6. Alice and Ben can both be made better off by moving towards the frontier and point J. Although the idea might seem unobjectionable, there are two simple but significant problems.

First, many social choices and public-policy problems involve options in which there are winners and losers. Even simple traffic schemes, for example, affect pedestrians and vehicle users, taxpayers and even local residents in ways that set up complex patterns of winners and losers. Pareto improvements apply to those situations in which everyone is no worse off and some are better off than before. A second concern emerges if we consider what happens when one moves from point I to point K. The move is a Pareto improvement as Ben's utility is increased and Alice's stays the same, but the distributional consequences appear far from satisfactory. At point K, Ben is near his maximum level of utility, but Alice is still near her lowest utility level. Furthermore, all of the improvements have benefited Ben. So it seems that although Pareto improvements apply to only a limited set of distributions, even some of those might be undesirable (or unsustainable) by virtue of their distributive consequences. Nonetheless, if there were Pareto improvements, with acceptable distributional consequences, they would be worth seeking out. So a final question to ask is about what institutional mechanisms, if any, can be used to generate such distributions.

■ ■ ■ 8.3.4   Welfare economics: perfect competition and Pareto optimality

Notwithstanding some of the limits of Pareto optimality, it seems likely that there will be situations, such as the unemployment example, in which choices that satisfy Pareto optimality will be available. So a natural question to ask is whether we can find economic mechanisms or institutions that will deliver Pareto optimal outcomes. An economy made up of markets that satisfy all the assumptions of the model of perfect competition (Chapter 5, Section 5.2.1) would be a Pareto optimal economy. The argument supporting this statement is too complex to set out in detail here, but it is possible to gain an intuitive feel for why perfect competition produces a Pareto optimal outcome from the following argument. The optimality properties of perfect competition are the main reason for the influence of this model on economic policy.

Let us first consider a single market, and begin with consumers. As we saw in Section 8.3.3, consumers are assumed to gain utility from consumption, and to seek to maximize their utility from their incomes. It was argued that a consumer who maximizes his satisfaction (or utility) will alter his purchases at the margin until he gets the same amount of satisfaction (utility) from the last pound spent on each good. In other words, the *marginal* utility – the satisfaction from the last item – of each good bought is in a sense equal to the price. If the marginal utility from a good were less than the price, it would be worth too little to the consumer and the last item would not be bought. So price equals marginal utility.

Now consider the production side. Chapter 5, Section 5.2.3 established that under perfect competition the firm will produce the level of output at which $MC = P$. This is the main distinction drawn between perfect competition and the model of monopoly in Chapter 4. Because the firm is a price-taker it maximizes its profits when price equals marginal cost.

The implication is that, under perfect competition, the common price taken by firms and consumers becomes a mediator which ensures that the worth to the consumer of the last item of each good bought is equal to the marginal cost of producing it. Marginal utility equals price equals marginal cost: $MU = P = MC$.

Once the perfectly competitive market has settled at an equilibrium where these equalities hold, no further improvement is possible by expanding or contracting output. Since marginal costs are assumed to rise, and consumers' willingness to pay falls as output increases, a production increase will mean that consumers value the last unit below its marginal cost to society. And, conversely, lower output means marginal benefit above marginal cost, suggesting that the economy should produce more.

An example of a choice between two goods may help to show that a competitive equilibrium is Pareto optimal.

Question	Suppose that the equality of marginal utility with marginal costs does not hold. On the contrary, a consumer values the last meal at twice the last pair of socks, but the last meal costs three times as much to produce. Could production and consumption be rearranged to give more total benefit?

We could certainly extract more utility here. The consumer could sacrifice a meal and be compensated fully with two pairs of socks. But the resources released allow three pairs of socks to be produced. So either the consumer, or someone else, is better off to the tune of one pair of socks. Or the spare resources from one pair of socks can be used for some other beneficial purpose.

Hence, when the equivalence of marginal utility and marginal cost does not hold, there is scope for a Pareto improvement. In the above example the ratios of the marginal costs of socks and meals (the rate at which one could be replaced with the other at the margin) did not equal the ratios of the marginal utilities to the consumer. Thus rearrangement improved welfare. Once marginal costs are equated to marginal utility, there is no scope left for this kind of rearrangement.

In this way perfectly competitive markets lead to a Pareto optimal outcome. In equilibrium in a perfectly competitive market there are no benefits in further adjusting consumption/production, because the utility lost to the consumer if a good is not bought is exactly balanced by the marginal cost saved. In maximizing their own welfare, consumers and producers make choices at the margin which ensure that there is no better outcome for one participant except at a cost to another. Such a situation is Pareto optimal.

This intuitive explanation has referred to product markets and to two-good economies. It can, however, be extended to more complex economies as a whole, with markets for factors of production as well as goods and services. It can be shown quite generally that if all markets are perfectly competitive, then the equilibrium for the economy as a whole is Pareto optimal. Another way of saying this is that a perfectly competitive economy is **allocatively efficient**: resources could not be reallocated to improve anyone's welfare without reducing the welfare of another.

Allocative efficiency

Allocative efficiency occurs when resources are allocated among consumers and producers in such a way that no reallocation could improve anyone's welfare without reducing the welfare of someone else.

This efficiency property of perfect competition has constituted a powerful argument for free markets. But you should note how strong the conditions are. All producers and consumers in product and factor markets must be perfectly informed price-takers (Chapter 5, Section 5.2.1). The essence of allocative efficiency (or Pareto optimality) in perfect competition lies in the choices which producers and consumers make – between factors of production, in how much to produce and in the allocation of incomes between goods. Unless the prices of all products reflect marginal costs, consumers' choices will be based on misleading information – and analogous conditions apply to factor markets and production.

Hence to achieve allocative efficiency the entire economy must operate under conditions of perfect competition, a condition which is likely to be impracticable in real life. It requires only one monopolist or firm operating strategically in oligopoly to put price above marginal cost (which, as we have seen in Chapters 4 and 6, they will do to maximize their profits) for these efficiency characteristics in the rest of the economy to be lost. This dependence for allocative efficiency on universal applicability throughout the economy is a harsh blow to the practical use of perfectly competitive models as a basis for policy.

Perfect competition therefore achieves Pareto optimality (allocative efficiency) only under restrictive assumptions. Another such assumption is that there are no externalities. Network externalities were introduced in Chapter 3, and externalities will be discussed in more general terms in Chapter 9. The assumption is that any utility is derived from a person's own consumption activities, but we know this not to be true as externalities abound in real economies. Every person who buys a mobile phone, for example, serves to make everyone else's mobile phone a little bit more useful at no cost to everyone else (Chapter 3). Virtually all countries in the world are producing greenhouse gases likely to contribute to global warming and the destruction of wildlife habitats and coastal cities. Externalities may be positive or negative, but if they exist perfect competition cannot be relied on to generate Pareto optimal outcomes.

A further point is that there exists the possibility that other, non-market mechanisms for allocating goods and services can also be shown to be desirable, in the sense of satisfying Pareto optimality. Central planning is one alternative to setting prices, and although this prevails in only very few parts of the world as a dominant ideology, most governments around the world do allocate funds between regions (e.g. for health, education and transport). These formulae might be based on the number of people living in a region, say, and the rationale for their use is usually that they reflect need. As they allocate resources without reference to prices, they represent an alternative to the market.

Occasionally, economics uses concepts such as Pareto optimality that appear to be unobjectionable. But I want to suggest that only some Pareto optima are desirable. To see this, consider a game, called the ultimatum game, that illustrates the point. We have $100 to divide up between us. I get to propose a division, and if you accept my proposal, that determines what we get. If you reject my proposal, we both leave with nothing. What should I propose? And how should you react?

If I propose $99 for me and $1 for you, you should accept my generous offer, because $1 is better for you than nothing. Most people don't do this. If offered a very unequal division, most people respond by rejecting the proposal, even though it seems not be in their own personal interest. People thus reject Pareto improvements if they are very unequal. Furthermore, experimental studies show that very unequal distributions are rarely proposed, perhaps because they seem to be unfair, or perhaps because people know they are unlikely to be accepted (inequality is discussed in Chapter 9). This game is usually presented as evidence that people in competitive settings are not just interested in maximizing monetary income. But the point I want to stress is that only some Pareto optimal distributions tend to be proposed and accepted, namely those that are relatively equitable.

In my view, and notwithstanding some of the really important theoretical insights and results that the concept has generated, there are problems in trying to apply the concept of utility that have not had the attention they deserve. However, economists are now beginning to take more interest in the extent to which psychological evidence can inform the development of economic models. In the next section I want to look at well-being from a viewpoint in which empirical evidence plays an important role in generating theory.

8.4 Well-being

The assertion that well-being is important to many people should not surprise anyone. But what does it mean, and how does it relate to income and utility? In this section we will examine different aspects of well-being, a concept that has both subjective and objective aspects. We shall see that what one has is not the only thing that matters; what one is free to do (the opportunities people have) and the process by which decisions are made also determine well-being.

8.4.1 Happiness and its relation to income

One approach to welfare that is beginning to attract attention from economists, particularly those working on issues to do with labour markets, health and the macro economy, concerns the role of economic factors in explaining happiness. As we have seen, there is a tendency to supplement simple financial measures of economic welfare in a variety of ways, and one way of doing this is to ask people directly how they feel. Typically, people are given a question about their mental state (which might range from happy to depressed) and are asked to say how well they normally feel, on a five- or seven-point scale. Clearly, answers to such questions do need to be interpreted with care, but there are, nevertheless, some issues that we might address using this kind of data. First, we can ask what, if anything, is correlated with happiness. (The terms 'subjective well-being' and 'experienced utility' have also been used.) Does happiness vary with measures of economic well-being, or are other, non-economic, factors more important? Second, can we develop theories that explain behaviour? It has been noted that measures of well-being do not increase much over time, despite large increases in measures of national income such as GDP. Why is this? Third, and related to the previous questions, what can we say about self-reports relating to well-being and objective measures of economic welfare?

Veenhoven (1993) collated data from subjective well-being surveys over the period from 1946 to 1990 for 55 nations. His data have been analysed by a number of researchers, and perhaps the most significant finding is positive relationships between happiness or subjective well-being (SWB), economic welfare and a small number of other variables (Table 8.10). Links of this kind between statistical data are known as 'correlations'. The idea is that finding similarities between changes in two or more variables suggests that the changes in one variable are related in some way to changes in another. For example, if every increase in SWB were accompanied by an increase in GDP per head, and every decrease in SWB were accompanied by a decrease in GDP per head, it would seem unlikely that SWB and GDP per head are completely causally unrelated.

The measure of correlation is a number between 1 (an exact positive relation – whenever one variable rises, the other rises by the same amount) and −1 (an exact negative relation – whenever one variable rises, the other falls by the same amount). A zero correlation between two variables means that there is no empirical evidence of a relation between them.

Exactly what the relation between SWB and GDP per head might be is another story. At least, a strong correlation of this kind suggests an avenue to be explored. Perhaps GPD per head exerts a powerful influence on SWB – perhaps being rich does make you happy. Or does SWB influence GDP per head – if people are 'happy in their work', do they work more effectively and so produce more GDP? Table 8.10 lists four variables that are correlated with happiness (SWB). We may not be able to draw conclusions about the direction of causality but, referring to Table 8.10, we can link SWB and GDP per head more strongly than we can link, say, SWB and human rights. All of the correlations shown in Table 8.10 are sufficiently strong for it to be unlikely that they were generated just as a matter of chance.

Schyns' (1998) analysis identified four covariates of SWB, that is, variables that are correlated with SWB. GDP per head, the measure of economic welfare, is the most strongly correlated variable, but the third and fourth variables measuring gender inequality and the individualist or collective orientation of a country respectively are not far behind. Human

Table 8.10
Variables correlated with happiness for 55 countries

Measure	Correlation with SWB
GDP per head	0.64
Human rights	0.39
UN Gender Empowerment Measure	0.52
Triandis's Measure of Individualism/Collectivism	0.51

Source: Schyns, 1998, p.15

rights, referring to measures of political and civil rights, also turns out to be statistically significant. Schyns believes all three non-economic variables relate to freedom as an aspect of a country's culture.

However, as suggested above, correlation does not prove causation. It could be that happiness *is* caused by economic prosperity and freedom, but other causal explanations are possible. One possibility is that freedom causes happiness and economic prosperity, but separately. People are happy if their human rights are respected, and a nation is productive if people are free to make economic decisions for themselves. Support for such an interpretation might be taken from the fact that job satisfaction is only weakly related to job performance.

We have seen that, in dealing with welfare, economists have used objective measures such as income as well as subjective approaches such as utility. Recently, quality of life researchers have suggested that we need both objective and subjective perspectives to understand welfare properly. The difference between subjective and objective dimensions is nicely illustrated by events following the publication of the 1981 *Places Rated Almanac* (Boyer and Savageau, 1981), which judged, using objective measures, Lawrence, Massachusetts, the least desirable town in America in which to live. Objective measures are those that are independent of the views and feelings of the respondents and include criteria such as GDP per head, air quality, health status and traffic congestion. The media interviewed residents subsequently to see if they agreed, but found instead a group of people with a positive sense of community, who emphasized family and friends and shared a genuine attachment to their town. The subjective ratings of Lawrence's denizens gave quite a different picture from the external picture that emerged from the 'objective' assessment.

But how might we combine the objective and the subjective? Robert Cummins (2000) discusses the topic using an analogy with human anatomy. Human bodies have many mechanisms for controlling variables such as temperature or blood pressure, and Cummins suggests that our experience of well-being is similarly controlled. A large proportion of survey respondents report themselves as being at the top level of SWB, and it might be that people automatically adapt their subjective experience to changes in their objective situation. For example, many people find it easy to get used to increases in income and most people do adapt, if more slowly, to decreases in income. The process is not entirely symmetrical, however, because below certain levels of objective welfare, subjective well-being declines along with objective welfare. There are limits to people's adaptability.

If Cummins (2000) is correct, we might expect to see objective and subjective measures rise and fall together at very low levels of welfare. Once a threshold has been reached, objective welfare might increase without any observed impact on subjective welfare. As it happens, evidence from a number of studies in different countries is consistent with this idea.

▪▪▪ 8.4.2 Procedural utility

Sometimes people are concerned not just about outcomes, but also about processes. When a person is subjected to a miscarriage of justice these issues often stand or fall together. For example, a person might claim that they were unfairly imprisoned (an outcome) on the procedural grounds that some of the evidence produced by the prosecuting authorities had been manufactured. Conversely, when people are happy with an outcome they may be encouraged to view the process by which the outcome was produced as adequate. Procedures and our attitudes to them have been discussed and investigated extensively by psychologists and legal scholars, and there are some interesting studies in this field.

Table 8.11
Acceptability of
decision procedures

Procedure	Respondents finding this mechanism acceptable %
Negotiations	72
Referendums	39
Expert decision	34
Lottery	32
Willingness to accept compensation	20
Willingness to pay	4

Source: Oberholzer-Gee *et al.*, 1996

A study conducted by the Swiss economist Bruno Frey and his colleagues asked voters to indicate their attitudes to different procedures for locating a medium-level nuclear waste depository. The measures they sought to evaluate included willingness to pay and willingness to accept compensation, which are economic or market-based approaches. However, they also included other approaches, such as the consultation of experts and negotiations involving community representatives. The results of this study are summarized in Table 8.11.

The market-based approaches, willingness to pay to avoid the imposition of a waste repository and willingness to accept compensation for the imposition of one, are the least popular options. It is sometimes argued that where an indivisible good (or bad) has to be allocated between different individuals, the fair method to use is randomization via a lottery. This, at least, equalizes the probability of obtaining the good/bad, even if it cannot be divided equally between all the parties. Although this is acceptable to more people than the willingness to accept compensation or willingness to pay criteria, over two-thirds of the sample still do not find it acceptable. However, the lottery is only marginally less acceptable than expert decision, a method that has played a significant, albeit changing, role over the past 50 years. Most popular are the two forms of public consultation. Referendums are conducted frequently in Switzerland, and negotiation is acceptable to approximately three-quarters of the sample, possibly because it allows for a more open-ended dialogue between the parties involved (see also Frey and Stutzer, 2002). In reality, many social choices contain aspects of more than one of these approaches, but this survey work throws into stark relief people's attitudes to different aspects of decision-making processes.

▪ ▪ ▪ 8.4.3 Capabilities and well-being

Capabilities

Capabilities are abilities to do certain things, such as read, secure adequate nourishment and play a full part in the life of the community.

An approach attracting growing popularity among welfare economists, and one that draws together many of the strands in this chapter, has been developed by Amartya Sen, a Nobel laureate in economics (Sen, 1985). Instead of measuring economic development in terms of average money income, Sen argues that we should look at indicators of people's opportunities, as measured by indices such as literacy rates, nutrition and life expectancy. Such indicators are now widely used. They are also consistent with a different theoretical approach, the so-called 'basic needs' approach, which favours measuring and providing things that are fundamental to existence. As Sen has noted, however, the **capabilities** approach provides a rationale for monitoring political and civil liberties, which the 'basic needs' approach does not.

Table 8.12
Capabilities and achievements – results from a voter survey

	Capabilities	Achievements
Happiness	3rd	1st
Achievement	5th	7th
Health	2nd	3rd
Intellectual stimulation	4th	5th
Social relations	6th	4th
Environments	1st	2nd
Personal projects	7th	6th

Source: Anand and van Hees, 2001

In a number of important ways, Sen's approach is informed by and deals with the problems of earlier approaches to welfare, such as income or utility. It stresses the existence of subjective differences between people and suggests that money income measures only opulence, not well-being. But it is also consistent with the idea that there is an objective list of issues that are important to the happiness of nearly everyone. What really matters to people is the opportunity to make their own choices between valued options and that these opportunities are distributed equitably among people. People have rights to equal opportunities, and these may take precedence over maximizing utility.

We introduce you here to some empirical work that I conducted with Martin van Hees (Anand and van Hees, 2001), looking at well-being through the lens of Sen's capability–rights theory. Briefly, we noted that Sen's theory emphasizes two distinctions. The first is between *well-being*, which might include things such as health that have objective aspects, and *agency* goals, which concern things such as being a competent piano player that are more particular to an individual person. The second distinction Sen makes is between capabilities (i.e. what people are free to do) and their achievements (i.e. the outcomes of choosing between different capabilities).

Table 8.12 reports evidence from some of my own research using Sen's framework. Half the questions relate to people's opportunities and half to their corresponding achievements in seven areas of life. Respondents were asked, for instance, about the scope to seek happiness and to indicate their capacity on a seven-point scale (1 = very good, 7 = very poor). They were subsequently asked to indicate, again on a seven-point scale, the extent to which they agreed with statements about their achievements in various areas.

Happiness and health might be thought of as examples of areas related mainly to well-being, while achievement and personal projects are related more to agency. Intellectual stimulation, social relations and environments appear harder to classify, as they contribute substantially to both agency and well-being. The survey was given to a random sample of voters in England, and the analysis summarized in Table 8.12 is based on approximately 270 responses.

For our sample, the scope for being in pleasant environments was rated as most adequate, while the scope to develop personal projects was rated as least adequate. When it came to achievements, the respondents were in most agreement with the statement that their life was happy and least in agreement with a statement about satisfaction with what they were able to achieve. These findings are not necessarily what one would expect, although they appear to be consistent with related empirical research. Perhaps people are happy for reasons associated with the aspirations and adjustment argument put forward by Cummins (2000). Furthermore, when we investigated agreement with the statement

Table 8.13   Quality of life indicators for ten high-income countries

Country	Consumption (national income)[1]	Life expectancy[2]	Unemployment[3]	Suicide[4]	Education[5]	HDI rank
Canada	17 363 (8)	77.4	11.2	21	100	1
USA	20 170 (4)	76.0	7.3	20	95	2
Japan	18 918 (6)	79.5	2.2	22	77	3
Netherlands	15 693 (9)	77.4	6.8	14	88	4
Finland	19 364 (5)	75.7	13.0	45	96	5
Iceland	21 685 (2)	78.2	3.0	18	81	6
Norway	20 284 (3)	76.9	5.9	21	88	7
France	18 093 (7)	76.9	10.2	30	86	8
Spain	11 460 (10)	77.6	18.1	11	86	9
Sweden	23 389 (1)	78.2	4.8	22	78	10

[1] £ thousand per annum.

[2] Years from birth.

[3] Proportion of workforce unemployed.

[4] Annual numbers of male suicides per 0.1 million of population.

[5] Combined gross enrolment ratio.

Source: adapted from Quizilbash, 1997

'generally my life is happy', two capabilities were correlated, and of these the one with the stronger correlation was the judgement about the scope to develop personal projects. So there would seem to be some support for the idea that the achievement of happiness depends not just on the quantity of happy events in a person's life but also on their ability to develop and shape meaningful sequences of actions and events. This result seems to provide support for the emphasis on the relationship of personal projects to well-being found in the magnum opus of the philosopher Derek Parfit (1984).

A number of economists have explored the impacts of different measures of well-being. Mozaffar Quizilbash (1997), for example, has collected data that show clearly how the incorporation of different criteria changes, in some cases dramatically, how we rank countries with respect to the well-being of their populations.

The 'HDI' column in Table 8.13 requires a more extended explanation. The Human Development Index is constructed from data on a number of key indicators of well-being, including life expectancy at birth, health status, educational opportunities, employment and political rights. These indicators are expressed as an index number for each country, which makes it possible to rank countries in terms of human development.

Table 8.13 is valuable because it demonstrates how different conceptions of well-being give rise to different rankings. For example, if we measure well-being in terms of the amount spent on consumption, Sweden is ranked first and Spain last; using suicide as an indicator of well-being puts Spain first and relegates Sweden to joint last but one. It is worth noticing that HDI is a measure of well-being originally designed to aid policy makers in monitoring development in low-income countries. Most of the differences among the high-income countries in Table 8.13 are relatively small.

In short, we do have options for adopting measures of well-being that go beyond national income: the capabilities approach gives us a good indication of the kinds of things that really matter and deserve thoughtful measurement.

8.5 Conclusion

This chapter has looked at welfare from three perspectives.

The CF model focuses on money income and is the basis for three different ways of measuring national income. It provides a basis for a macroeconomic analysis. GDP per head is widely used as a measure of welfare despite its limitations.

People's preferences vary considerably, and so, reflecting this, economic theorists tend to base their analysis of individual welfare on utility, an idea that allows us to relate goods and services to their subjective value to individuals. The concept of utility has been used to characterize individual choice behaviour and, with Pareto optimality, to suggest the superiority of perfect competition.

However, welfare economics has a critical edge too. The welfare theorem establishing the desirability of perfect competition depends on a number of questionable assumptions.

The fact that environmental problems are now threatening extensive economic damage later this century provides an economic motivation for questioning the extent to which material goods and services are really what generate well-being. One theory, the capabilities approach, puts emphasis on the options people have and on what it is they achieve. If one looks around the world, or back in history, at the things people almost universally value – dignity, involvement, respect, happiness, social contact, meaning, achievement, joy, excitement and status, to name but a few – it is far from clear that these require, or are guaranteed by, the consumption of large amounts of material goods and services.

In their influential textbook, Samuelson and Nordhaus approvingly conclude their review of the limits of national income accounting by citing Arthur Okun (1970, p.124):

> It should be no surprise that national prosperity does not guarantee a happy society, any more than personal prosperity ensures a happy family . . . Still, prosperity . . . is a precondition for success in achieving many of our aspirations.
>
> *(Samuelson and Nordhaus, 1989)*

An alternative view is that an economic system has emerged from the private pursuit of goals and aspirations. This view implies that the causality runs in the opposite direction from that suggested by Okun (1970). For Okun, the provision of prosperity by the economy is a precondition of individual happiness, but the view underlying this chapter is that in pursuing happiness we create, almost inadvertently, an economic system. In that case, policy makers might ask, not what we should do for the economy, but what the economy can do for us.

Questions for review and discussion

Question 1 Figure 8.7 shows the circular flow of income model. Insert the labels below in their correct positions on the diagram:

Transfers exports, X savings, S imports, M investment expenditure, 1

Figure 8.7
Circular flow of
income model

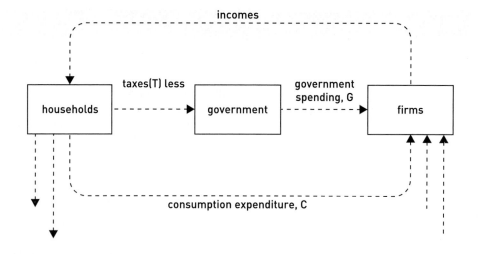

Question 2 The table shows values at GDP current prices and at constant 2000 prices for a hypothetical economy. Add the missing values in the spaces in the table.

	Year	
	2000	2001
GDP at current prices (€ million)	1500	
GDP at constant 2000 prices (€ million)	1500	1250
GDP deflator		200

Question 3 The following statements are about changes in total utility and marginal utility obtained as more of a good or service is consumed. Say which is the correct statement.

A ❑ If total utility is rising, marginal utility must be rising too.
B ❑ If total is remaining constant, marginal utility and total utility must be the same.
C ❑ If total utility is falling, marginal utility must be negative.

Question 4 Figure 8.8 shows a utility possibility frontier for Anna and Bjorn. Say which *three* statements below are correct.

Figure 8.8
Utility possibility
frontier for Anna
and Bjorn

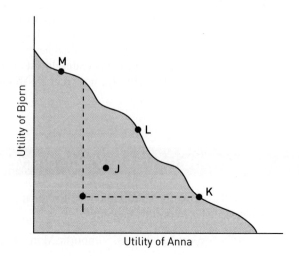

A ❑ Movement from I to J is a Pareto improvement.
B ❑ Movement from J to K is a Pareto improvement.
C ❑ L and K represent Pareto optimal distributions of utility but M does not.
D ❑ Movement from J to L is a Pareto improvement.
E ❑ Movement from I to K is not a Pareto improvement.
F ❑ K, L and M are all Pareto optimal distributions of utility.

Question 5 The table below presents data on GDP and changes in the price level for a country over a four-year period.

GDP and changes in the price level

	2000	2001	2002	2003
GDP at current prices (£ billion)	3.7	3.9	4.0	4.4
Price index	100	104	105	106

(a) Using the price index as a GDP deflator, calculate GDP at constant prices for each year.
(b) Draw a graph, plotting GDP at current prices and constant prices on the vertical axis and time along the horizontal axis.
(c) How would you describe the difference between the changes in GDP at current prices and the changes in GDP at constant prices shown in your graph?
(d) The Index of Sustainable Economic Welfare (ISEW) makes a number of adjustments to the consumption measure of income. Comment briefly on the nature of these adjustments and their rationale.

Question 6 Essay: To what extent does Sen's capabilities theory provide a persuasive account of well-being?

9

The economics of governance

Maureen Mackintosh

Objectives

After studying this chapter you should be able to:

- discuss the role of governance in promoting economic efficiency, equity and well-being
- explain concepts of market failure and discuss their policy implications
- analyse problems of collective action in governing shared resources and providing public goods
- understand measures of income inequality and use them to assess redistribution
- discuss how welfare states may influence both efficiency and equity
- outline economic explanations of government behaviour with respect to redistribution.

9.1 Markets, inequality and governance

It is a fundamental error to imagine that capitalist economics means an absence of government intervention.

(Barr, 1994, p.29)

The new economy is a place of hope and fear. The hope is that policy activism can cement in potential productivity gains; the fear is that government actions will not mitigate the seemingly ineluctable pressures towards social exclusion.

(Van Reenan, 2001, p.307)

Nicholas Barr is an economist specializing in the economics of the public services. He was writing in the early 1990s on the economic problems of the early stages of the transition in eastern Europe and the ex-Soviet countries from centrally planned economies to capitalism. In capitalist economies change is driven by private investment and market exchange. By 'capitalist economics' Barr means the economic theory of the operation of such economies: that is, the topic of this book. The transition economies initially faced rising unemployment and poverty, widening inequality, deteriorating 'social' provision such as health care, declining output and poorly functioning markets. Tackling those problems required the recognition that high-income capitalist economies both display and require high levels of government expenditure and regulation, to help markets work efficiently and to promote the access of all citizens to the economic benefits available.

The rate of technological change associated with the so-called 'new economy' at the turn of the last century, and the rising inequality and sense of insecurity this has brought with it within many high-income countries (Chapters 1 and 2), has led economists such as Van Reenan, concerned with industrial policy, to make similar arguments. Governments, particularly European governments of economies lagging behind the USA in productivity growth, need to intervene actively to promote effective innovation and import of leading-edge technologies, to support research and development, and above all to ensure that people have the skills to participate in the changing labour market (see the discussion of human capital in Chapter 7). The need is for 'smart' regulation (Van Reenan, 2001, p.331) encouraging innovation while fostering competitiveness, and at the same time for policies to avoid 'social exclusion' resulting from a lack of the capability to participate in markets.

These responses by two economists faced, several years apart, by two very different kinds of rapid economic change, illustrate a central theme of this chapter. Market-based – or capitalist – economies need governing *both* in order to promote market efficiency *and* to try to ensure the social inclusion of all citizens. Neither of these two authors sees those two broad objectives as necessarily in conflict, rather the contrary: achieving one will help support the other. And this approach reflects, I think, a real shift in economic policy debate at the beginning of the twenty-first century. While economists have long argued that greater efficiency may require the acceptance of greater inequality, there is today a more active search for policies that promote both equity and efficiency. As a result, there is a new acceptance of active government, after the political pressure of the 1980s and 1990s to restrict government activities. We seem to be leaving behind the late twentieth-century preoccupation with whether governments should be bigger or smaller, and turning instead to consider how governments can be *smarter* (Van Reenan, 2001).

Part of smarter government is a recognition that markets and economic activity are 'governed' not only by governments but also by voluntary collective action. People get together in a wide variety of associations, outside the framework of formal government, to influence aspects of our economic lives: for example, there are many charitable activities that help to support vulnerable people in capitalist economies. These associational forms of governance are sometimes summarized as 'civil society'.

By 'governance' in this chapter, we mean both government and such voluntary collective action. We begin the chapter by analysing some *efficiency* reasons why governments intervene in the economy: to make markets work better or supply goods and services markets cannot efficiently provide (Section 9.2). Section 9.3 then considers the scope for collective rather than government action to promote both efficiency and equity, using the example of local management of natural resources. In Sections 9.4 and 9.5 we turn to the 'welfare state'. To what extent does government provision of cash benefits and services such as health and education reduce inequality, and does this 'welfare' spending have costs in terms of economic efficiency? Finally, Section 9.6 considers democratic government itself, not as an independent economic agent, but as an agency to which we delegate actions too hard to achieve by voluntary collaboration. I analyse just one difficult case, where there is conflict between the interests of different voters: policies on redistribution.

9.2 Shaping market incentives and providing public goods

Markets organize the supply of many of the goods and services we consume, and our ability to buy them is therefore a key determinant of our well-being (Chapter 8). However, there are some goods and services that we wish to consume that cannot be efficiently supplied through markets. This section uses economic theory you have already learned to explore some reasons for such market failure, to see why voluntary collective action may not work either. It then develops a rationale for government intervention to improve market efficiency, both in the static sense of achieving a Pareto optimal allocation of resources (Chapter 8, Section 8.3) and in the dynamic sense of successful industrial innovation and competition (Chapters 2 and 3).

We explore the problem of market failure through an issue raised in Chapter 8, Section 8.2.4: the supply of environmental 'goods' such as clean air, or, to put the same point in another way, the supply of environmental protection from 'bads' such as pollution.

■ ■ ■ 9.2.1 Externalities and public goods

Public good

A public good is a good that is *not rival*, that is, my consuming it does not reduce the amount available for you; it is also *not excludable*, that is, if I am consuming it I cannot prevent you from consuming it too.

The first step to solving a problem is to admit that you have one. For Houston, years of living in denial about its polluted air have made things even worse. This conurbation, which each year pumps 200,000 tons of nitrogen oxide (a component of smog) into the air, has recently beaten Los Angeles for the title of America's smoggiest city.

(The Economist, *8 January 2000*)

The situation in Houston in Texas is an example of a worldwide problem of urban smog. Urban air pollution is generated by industrial emissions and by car exhausts. However, it can also be cleaned up: London had its last great smog in 1954. So what can economics tell us about why air pollution happens and the problems of stopping it?

We will start by analysing the problem from the point of view of the urban citizens.

> **Question** Suppose that residents of a polluted city such as Houston all want cleaner air. Could they buy that environmental improvement individually through the market? If not why not?

You may have thought of a number of problems. An obvious one is that air moves about and cannot be divided into packets above each house for private ownership and cleaning up. To clean up your own air is to clean up the air for everyone. Economists call goods like clean air **public goods**.

> **Question** Stop and think about that definition. Can you think of other examples of public goods, besides clean air?

The definition amounts to saying that a 'public good' is not divisible into separate bits for sale on a market. Rather, each person can use it as they choose without subtracting from the amount available for others and no one can be excluded from using it. Military forces ('defence'), street lighting and rural road networks: these goods and services, generally provided by governments, come reasonably close to the definition. Very few activities fit it precisely. As with many economic concepts, a 'public good' is an abstract idea which can be applied to explain aspects of the economic world. Street lighting, for example, benefits anyone walking down the street. Most rural and urban roads – until congested – are available for anyone who wishes to drive, cycle or walk along them. If the military deter armed aggression, everyone is defended.

Let us return to our polluted city, and consider further the problem facing citizens in search of clean air via market mechanisms.

Question Suppose I own a firm producing a well-tried gadget that greatly reduces pollution from industrial processes, such as petrochemicals production and oil refining in Texas, that are damaging city air. Why can't I sell my gadget to those who want to breathe clean air?

Put like that the question answers itself. I am trying to sell the gadget to the wrong people. It is no use to the consumers. The producers of the pollution are the industrial firms. So why not sell the gadget to them?

Well, why should they buy it? It is just another industrial cost (and the owners may well not live in the city). For the polluting firms, such as the petrochemical and oil refining industries of Texas, the damaging emissions are a by-product: a by-product of their activity that imposes costs on others (the citizens of Houston) for which the firms are not required to pay compensation (yet). In other words, the pollution is an **externality**.

Externality

An externality occurs when one person's action affects the welfare of another in ways that the first need not take into account. An externality therefore arises in a market when a producer's, seller's or buyer's actions influence the welfare of others in ways not reflected in market prices.

You have seen the concept of externalities before. Chapter 3, Section 3.4.2 explained 'network externalities' using an example of a telephone user whose benefits from their phone rise as more people acquire phones. You can think of externalities as 'spillover effects': effects of one person's or one firm's actions on the welfare of others that do not pass through the market mechanism. So pollution is an externality because firms do not have to pay for its costs to others.

So how about the consumers who want clean air paying the producers to use the clean-up gadget? Imagine you are one of the people who cannot breathe properly, and you want to do this. What is the snag? You probably cannot afford on your own to pay all the producers to use the gadget. You need all those who want clean air to get together to pay.

However, there is a problem with this kind of collective action. Each person will think, well, if I refuse, then others will pay, and I will have clean air for free. Once the air is cleaned up, anyone can breathe it. Having access in this way to a public good you have refused to finance is called *free-riding*: you are taking a free ride on the payments of others. If each person seeks to free-ride, then no one will pay for the clean up, and the air will stay polluted.

Question Think about free-riding. You have seen an economic problem of this form before. What is it?

The free-riding problem is an example of a prisoners' dilemma. There are lots of 'prisoners' (coughing citizens) in the polluted city, but you can model the basic problem by imagining a city of two people, as in Figure 9.1.

In this game, each citizen has a choice of paying to clean up the air, or not paying. If one agrees to pay and the other does not, then the one who pays must pay the full cost.

Figure 9.1
A prisoners'
dilemma facing
residents of a
polluted city

		Person 2	
		pay	do not pay
Person 1	pay	1, 1	−1, 2
	do not pay	2, −1	0, 0

If both agree to pay they split the costs. The pay-offs are the net benefits: the benefits of clean air less the cost of achieving it. Each citizen has the lowest pay-off from supporting the whole cost of cleaning up; in that situation the cost to a player far outweighs the benefits of clean air (pay-off −1). To that, each player prefers not to pay and to leave the air polluted (pay-off 0). Each, however, would rather pay half the cost of clean up and breathe clean air (pay-off 1). Finally, for each player, the highest pay-off comes from 'free-riding', breathing clean air while paying nothing (pay-off 2).

Question Work through this pay-off matrix carefully, assuming that each person makes their individual private decision. What is the dominant strategy for each person? What precisely is the dilemma?

The dominant strategy is 'do not pay'. Consider Person 1. If Person 2 does not pay, Person 1 will not pay (a pay-off of 0 is better than −1). If Person 2 pays, Person 1 will not pay (a pay-off of 2 is better than 1). So each player will decide not to pay, irrespective of the choice of the others. So the outcome is polluted air. Yet each person would prefer to pay half the cost and to clean up if only that could be organized. The dilemma is that individual decision-making results in an inferior result for each person. The attempt to free-ride is self-defeating. This two-person model can be applied to our example of a polluted city. If many players/citizens try to free-ride, then the air will remain polluted and citizens will continue to cough.

The example of environmental protection has some particular features explored further below. But the prisoners' dilemma model of free-riding applies generally to public goods. Voluntary payment for public goods provision tends to be undermined by free-riding.

■ ■ ■ 9.2.2 A rationale for government intervention

So how are public goods that citizens wish to consume to be produced? One method is government intervention. Suppose that a government – local, regional or national – wishes to intervene to 'produce' the public good of clean air. How might a government do that? Unlike some other public goods – such as street lighting – clean air cannot simply be produced and installed. Instead, a government needs to deal with the polluters.

To analyse the policy problem, let us start with externalities as a source of pollution and analyse their effects on the market for the products of a polluting industry such as petrochemicals. There is a cost of the air pollution that falls not on the firms in the industry but on local residents. It follows that the costs of production perceived by the firms are lower than the total costs of the production to society.

Figure 9.2
The divergence
between private and
social costs of a
polluting industry

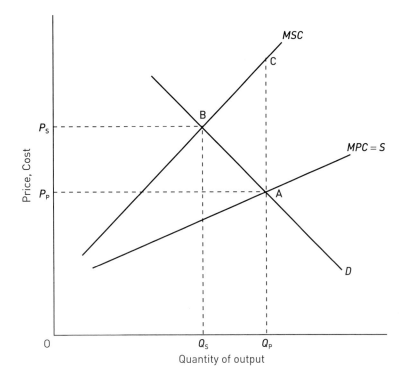

Figure 9.2 illustrates the effect of the externality on market efficiency. I assume that the polluting industry is perfectly competitive. The curve labelled $MPC = S$ is the supply curve for the industry, which is derived from the marginal cost curves of the individual firms (Chapter 5, Section 5.2). But this marginal cost curve only includes those costs which each firm actually has to pay. Hence it is the firm's marginal *private* cost (MPC) curve. The pollution is not the firms' problem (yet). So the marginal *social* costs (MSC), including the cost of pollution for residents, are higher than the marginal private costs as shown by the gap between the MSC and the MPC curves in Figure 9.2.

The private market equilibrium is at A, where firms equate their marginal private cost to marginal revenue with price P_p and output Q_p hence supply equals demand. But this is not an efficient market equilibrium.

Question Can you explain why not, using the diagram? Look back at Chapter 8 and remind yourself of the conditions for a Pareto optimal market outcome before reading on.

A market is at a Pareto optimum – that is, no one can be made better off without also making someone worse off – when $MC = P = MU$ throughout the market. This is not the case at point A. Individuals' marginal utility – expressed in their individual demand curves (look back at Chapter 8, Section 8.3 again if that statement puzzles you) – is equated to the price they pay. But the full marginal social cost when output is Q_p (point C) is above the market price P_p.

For an allocatively efficient market outcome, the sum consumers are willing to pay for the last unit of output (indicated by the demand curve) should be equal to the full marginal cost of generating that last unit. In Figure 9.2, this would be at point B with price P_s and output Q_s. At B the marginal benefit to consumers is equal to the full marginal social cost. Where there are externalities in production of the type described, Pareto optimality requires that price be equated to the marginal *social* cost:

$$MSC = P = MU$$

Market failure

A market in which competition does not bring about a Pareto optimal outcome is said to exhibit market failure.

Externalities therefore imply **market failure**.

A market failure identifies an opportunity for intervention to improve market outcomes. Note, however, an implication of Figure 9.2: consumers do not want pollution reduced to zero; rather the optimal outcome is less output and hence less pollution. We will consider the implications in two stages. First, we will look at how governments might achieve a market equilibrium at point B in Figure 9.2. Then we will consider what (smarter) policies might break this unappealing policy dilemma of less output or more pollution.

Governments have two basic methods open to them to force output and pollution down. They can impose a tax that *internalizes the externality*, that is, it increases firms' costs to include the full costs of their output including the social costs. This will cause them to make output decisions that move the market towards the social optimum. To see how that might work, we need first to analyse how taxes in general affect competitive markets (Figure 9.3).

Figure 9.3 shows a perfectly competitive market for an unspecified good. The market equilibrium without the tax is at A with price P and output Q. Imposing a tax *t* per unit of output shifts the supply curve upwards, because each firms' costs are increased by the tax. That is, before they take their profit on each unit, they must pay the tax, which they therefore experience as a cost.

Question   How large is the tax shown in Figure 9.3?

Figure 9.3
A tax on output in a competitive market

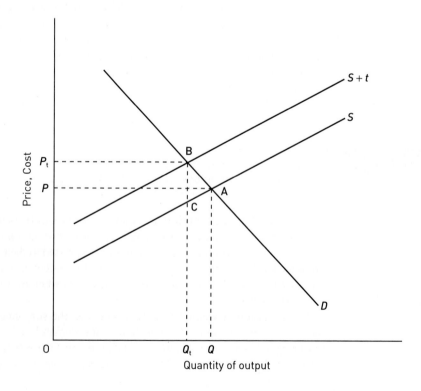

Figure 9.4
A specific tax on
polluting firms'
output

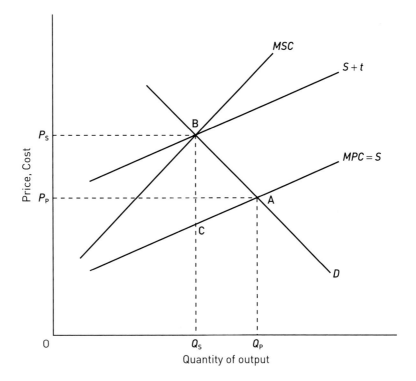

The tax t is measured by the vertical distance between S and $S + t$. This is equal to the distance BC on Figure 9.3. The market equilibrium with the tax is at point B, where the supply curve with the tax $S + t$ intersects the demand curve. Price has risen to P_t and output has fallen to Q_t.

Exercise 9.1

How will the supply curve including the tax $S + t$ change in shape if the tax is *ad valorem*, that is, if its value is a percentage of total revenue at each level of Q?

Now, armed with this diagrammatic analysis of taxes, we can return to the pollution problem. Figure 9.4 is based on Figure 9.2, and illustrates the use of a specific tax to force down output of the polluting industry to the optimum level.

The tax rate on Figure 9.4 is again the vertical distance between the supply curves S and $S + t$, equal to the distance BC. The market equilibrium without the tax is at A, with price P_P and output Q_P. The tax shifts the firm's supply curve to $S + t$, and the market equilibrium to B with price P_S and quantity Q_S. As the figure is drawn, the tax is at precisely the level to force output down to the market optimum level Q_S. Achieving that in practice would not be easy. Government officials would need to calculate what the market optimum should be, and the precise tax needed to achieve it. There is a great deal of room for error.

Even if you managed to pull this off, however, as Environment Minister, you might feel rather dissatisfied. All that effort, and yet the air is still (rather less) polluted.

Question	Why is that? What is it about the way the problem is set up that creates this outcome?

There are two key assumptions, I think. The first is that the right solution balances people's desire for output and for clean air, so we get a little less of one and more of the other – rather than completely clean air. There is no overriding priority on breathing properly; output matters too. Even more important, the analysis assumes that the technology used by firms is given. It doesn't allow for innovation, just for changes in output. Once there can be technological change and governments can support innovation, the dismal choice of less output and less pollution, or more of both, can be sidestepped.

▪▪▪ 9.2.3 Government intervention in market dynamics

Look back at Figure 9.4. How could the government, instead of accepting that the only options are less pollution plus less output or the status quo, create incentives for firms to find new technology and to clean up their emissions, that is, to innovate?

There are several ways in which the government can change the incentive structure facing firms. Let us start with the circumstances described above where a gadget already exists to clean up emissions. A government could use regulation to enforce its use: firms could be told that they must clean up to stay in business. This was a strategy used in Texas, where the state required cuts in industrial emissions of pollutants ahead of federal guidelines coming into force in 2007 (*The Economist*, 8 January 2000). Alternatively, firms might be taxed, not on output, but on measured pollution. Less pollution, less tax, hence an incentive to install the clean-up equipment.

Exercise 9.2

Consider a regulation that raises firms' average and marginal costs because they have to install new equipment and use a new process to clean up emissions. This reduces pollution to zero. Assume the industry is perfectly competitive.

1 Use diagrammatic analysis drawn from Chapters 3 and 5 to show what has happened to costs and supply at the firm level.
2 Show on a diagram how this change in firms' costs affects equilibrium price and output in the market.

So far, we have been analysing pollution policy using the model of perfect competition. However, suppose that we now pose the policy problem in terms of incentives for firms to innovate, for example by developing less-polluting production methods. We then need to move away from the perfectly competitive market model, and use more appropriate models of imperfect markets, in which technology can be changed by firms, and in which firms can have diverse capabilities. In such markets, there is the interesting possibility that low pollution might be a source of market advantage for innovative firms, allowing them to operate profitably in highly regulated environments and to sell on innovative solutions to lagging firms.

In those circumstances, governments can try to offer firms incentives and opportunities to innovate, with increased market power for the leaders as the 'carrot'. Policies can include support for product development: for example, the creation of better, cheaper equipment for reducing emissions. Different outputs that are less polluting are another route to innovating out of environmental crisis: new high-tech firms moving into Houston are unconnected with the petrochemical industry and are interested in a clean environment for plant and staff. Regulations that restrict or heavily tax pollution can give a firm that finds a less-polluting solution a first-mover market advantage (Chapter 6, Section 6.5).

The more governments can create incentives to break the dilemmas imposed by current technology, the more efficient the solutions can be. Encouragement of a nascent 'green' industry supplying environmentally friendly solutions can both generate new markets and new employment and improve the environment; regulations can help to generate markets for such nascent industries; and government support for relevant research and development can get them started. The general point is that policies that create incentives for innovative methods of compliance – that tell firms what to achieve but not how to do it, and benefit those that generate new ideas – are both easier to monitor and generate more net benefits. This kind of solution is an example of what in Section 9.1 we called 'smarter' government in a period of high industrial innovation and increasing environmental pressure.

It remains possible, however, that if governments impose restrictions, firms may move, to go and pollute someone else with a less interventionist government – that's capitalism!

9.3 Governing the commons: the scope for collective action

Section 9.2 argued that free-riding posed a problem for attempts to deal with externalities or provide public goods through voluntary payment. In this section, we look at circumstances in which collective action can overcome free-riding, using the example of the management of natural resources.

Clean air is a public good of a particular sort: a *global* free-access good, or part of the global 'commons'. The concept of the 'commons' comes from common ground: from land or water or forest resources held in some sense in common for free access by all. In the village I lived in as a child we would go to play 'on the common'. Historically, in high-income countries, and today in many lower-income countries, people rely on such common resources to supplement their incomes from gathering or fishing, to provide inputs to farming such as irrigation, and to provide some fall-back when private incomes fail. The loss of local commons can increase destitution and force people to work for less than a living wage.

As environmental awareness has grown (Chapter 8, Section 8.2.4), so has awareness that high-income communities depend on the 'commons' too. The global commons include sea that is alive and full of fish, and fairly stable global weather systems. All commons require co-operation to manage, and Section 9.2 explained the free-rider problem that undermines co-operation. The global free-access resources belong to all of us and to none of us, posing a huge international policy challenge that will be discussed further in Chapter 19.

Local commons, the subject of this section, are rather different. Local forests, rivers, grazing land and irrigation pools do 'belong' to an identifiable group such as a village or area, and sometimes those common ownership rights are legally binding. However, turning that collective ownership into effective management of a resource raises dilemmas and has met with solutions that may hold lessons for the larger scale.

▤ ▥ ▪ 9.3.1 The tragedy of the commons

Local common-pool resources can be accessed freely by a defined group. When used in non-damaging ways they are true public goods, in that one person can use them freely without reducing the resource available for another. Once overused, they become rival: more use by one person means less available to others. Free-riding can therefore cause them to deteriorate cumulatively. A much-cited article by Garett Hardin (1968) called 'The tragedy of the commons' is a classic statement of this problem. Hardin envisages a situation where local herdsmen are free to graze their herds on common land but its carrying capacity is limited. Each herdsman benefits from his own herd (in terms of the sale of cattle, meat and milk) and loses income when, beyond a certain number of animals on the land, overgrazing means each animal has less sustenance.

Hardin argues that, since each herder gains the whole benefit from his own herd, each wishes to increase it. However, once the point of overgrazing is past, each herder suffers only a small part of the losses from overgrazing which expansion of his own herd will cause. The rest of the losses fall on the other herdsmen, so they are *externalities*, this time in a non-market context. If all herders pursue their own interests, cumulative degradation of the land will occur. Hardin's conclusion – it reads more like a prediction – is infinitely gloomy: 'Each man is locked into a system which compels him to increase his herd without limit – in a world that is limited. Ruin is the destination towards which all men rush, each pursuing his own best interest in a society that believes in the freedom of the commons' (Hardin, 1968, p.1244). Hence the 'tragedy' of the commons.

Exercise 9.3

Hardin tells a story of a prisoners' dilemma and its consequences. Make up your own pay-off matrix to model this story. Start with two herders each of whom can follow one of two strategies: a moderate herd size, which, if chosen by both, will not cause overgrazing, or a very large herd size that will cause land degradation. Write in appropriate pay-offs and explain the herders' dilemma.

Hardin's conclusion from his prisoners' dilemma parable is similar to the conclusion from the analysis in Section 9.2: the government must prevent disaster through coercion to restrain overuse. In other words, people must voluntarily relinquish their rights over their local commons to a government which then exercises legitimate coercion to manage the commons in their collective interests. But is government really the only option? Or can communities break such prisoners' dilemmas and govern their own commons through forms of voluntary collective stewardship?

▤ ▥ ▪ 9.3.2 Governing the commons

Three widespread examples of the protection and management – and of failures of management – of local 'commons' are irrigation water, forests and woodlands, and local inshore fisheries. In recent years, all have been quite extensively studied for lessons for collaborative resource management. One conclusion that stands out is that such commons generally *are* managed in the sense of being run through understood procedures voluntarily adhered to, though these arrangements may and do break down. Free-riding and 'ruin' are not the universal experience.

So how do communities successfully break the prisoners' dilemma?

Question	Look back at Chapter 6, Section 6.2. Which of the methods discussed there of achieving a co-operative outcome in prisoners' dilemma games seem relevant to overcoming the tragedy of the commons?

Two ways of achieving co-operation to resolve the prisoners' dilemma are discussed. One is reliance on shared norms and practices. In this case, the pay-offs are not all that matters to players when they decide on strategy. The second way in which co-operation can be achieved is through repeated interaction. When a game is played repeatedly, individual players consider their cumulative pay-offs into the future, as well as current pay-offs, so individual strategies are forward-looking.

Each of these solutions appear relevant to the problem of protecting local commons from degradation. In Hardin's parable, people 'play' the prisoners' dilemma game repeatedly, with the same set of other people. Yet they learn nothing, and do not anticipate the future effects of their actions for themselves, nor the likely behaviour of their neighbours in response to their own actions. However, the herders would in practice be aware of these things, and each would take them into account in deciding their own actions. In repeated games, patterns of behaviour can emerge – such as not expanding a herd beyond the point which would be sustainable if everyone did the same – and be sustained so long as people know they will continue to interact into the indefinite future. People know that, cumulatively, such collaborative behaviour is in their own interests.

Economists try to explore these kinds of situations using simulated games (Chapter 6, Section 6.3): people play out a game, with stated pay-offs, in a 'laboratory' situation. These simulations (often called experiments) consistently show that people playing a repeated prisoners' dilemma game tend to seek the mutually beneficial collaborative solution unless they feel 'suckered' by others defecting to pursue their immediate self-interest. So individual strategies are observed to depend on experience of others' behaviour, but to favour co-operation if possible. The more people experience co-operative behaviour by others – and the more that it is clear that if people don't hang together they will hang separately – the more likely is continued co-operation for mutual benefit.

Furthermore, Hardin's herders care only about their own fate, not at all for the fate of others. When modelling the behaviour of firms, this may be a reasonable assumption; it is less appropriate perhaps for the behaviour of people in small communities. The more each herder cares about their neighbours, instead of considering only their own returns, the more likely it is that co-operation can be achieved, since each will value less highly the situation where they benefit at their neighbours' expense. A concern for others may be expressed in practice in local norms or shared understandings that set reasonable limits for individual use of commons. In the extreme, if each valued their neighbours' well-being as highly as their own, externalities would vanish, internalized in the decision-making process of each herder.

Exercise 9.4

Look back at the pay-off matrix in answer to Exercise 9.3. Can you use it to show how caring about their neighbours may resolve the prisoners' dilemma the herders face?

Finally, the herders might form an organization that has rules and can punish default. You can think of this as a formally constituted voluntary association (rather like a formal cartel, as described in Chapter 6, but for different purposes). This can help to achieve co-operation by reinforcing shared norms and practices through organized collective management.

This analysis, and the evidence from 'laboratory' experiments, together suggest that certain kinds of communities may find collaboration easier than others: notably small, socially homogeneous communities with strong mutual knowledge. However, field research on common-pool resource management suggests that this is too simple a conclusion. It is not just the basic characteristics of communities that matter to effective management of common-pool resources. Rather, societies successfully *build* effective collaborative institutions over time – or fail to do so. Communities may organize to impose rotational use rules, designate managers and forms of scrutiny, set use limits per household and so on.

Research on management of forests by communities that depend upon them shows that many such communities do find methods of allowing members access to the benefits of the forest resource while maintaining it intact; other communities let forests deteriorate. Crucial variables appear to include clarity about who are the users; about the boundary of the resource they hold in common; and about the right of the users to organize use of the resource. In countries as diverse as Japan and Papua New Guinea, communities have legally protected common rights to control forests and have continued to exercise them effectively in an increasingly commercial context (McKean, 2000).

Where local common-access forests continue to exist – whether or not based on legal rights – some communities manage better than others. In Nepal, a survey found that forest reserves that were improving were those that were actively managed (Varughese, 2000). Key determinants of success seemed to be the perceived fairness (not necessarily or even usually equality, but acceptability) of the rules for use, their clarity, and the ability to monitor and punish infringement. An Indian study (Agrawal, 1994) found that the best managed forests were those where both the rules for use and the monitoring process and fines for violation were accepted as legitimate by users.

Behind these findings lie the nature of the relationships on which management systems are built. Communities with high levels of inequality can manage common-pool forest resources, but this only functions well where access is truly available to the poor. In those circumstances, common forests can benefit the poor since the better off have a high opportunity cost of labour and may leave much of the forest products to the poor. Women's organizations have successfully promoted communal forestry in India and China (Agrawal, 1985). However, deep social divisions including differences of interest between men and women, and de facto control by one social group over the benefits of supposedly communal land, have frequently destroyed co-operative forest management (Agrawal, 1994; Agrawal, 1985).

This brings us back to concern for others. Organizations such as the *Chipko* movement against commercial forest exploitation in India are sustained by a mix of self-interest and care for the fate of others, and actively develop mutual understanding through organizing (Agrawal, 1985). To understand how common-access resources can be managed, we need a more complex view of people than a view that sees us as pursuing just our own – or even our family's – interests. People's objectives and strategies also emerge from involvement in wider social relationships. We can – though we may not – *learn* to manage collective resources despite social divisions.

9.4 Inequality and redistribution

redistribution . . . an unrequited transfer of resources from one person to another
(Boadway and Keen, 2000)

Section 9.3 ended on the theme of inequality and social division, suggesting that inequality within communities could block effective management of common-pool resources. We now turn to considering more explicitly the extent of inequality and the challenge it poses. The scale of inequality we live with in the world today – within and between countries – is enormous, and the scope for reducing inequality while sustaining or, better, increasing efficiency is a focus of the debate around 'smarter' government, as Section 9.1 explained. This section examines inequality within countries – Chapter 15 examines international inequality – and considers the extent to which governments effectively redistribute resources to the poor. Section 9.5 will look at some effects of redistribution on economic efficiency.

Question	Look back at Chapter 8, Section 8.3 and try to draw out of it some reasons why economists – and other human beings too – might want to reduce inequality.

The proposition that marginal utility diminishes as consumption rises has been used to argue for redistribution of income from rich to poor. If we are prepared to assume that all people have the *same* utility function, then redistribution will increase the utility of the poor more than it decreases the utility of the rich, thereby increasing the sum of human happiness (Chapter 8, Section 8.3). This argument assumes that we *can* compare utilities of different people, or at least are willing to make suppositions about similarity or difference.

Exercise 9.5

Can you think of counter arguments? Try to do so before reading on.

The capabilities framework (Chapter 8, Section 8.4) suggests another argument for reducing inequality by redistributing income to the poor: that people have a right to a 'fair chance' or equal opportunity. Public services such as education and health care, access to public goods such as a clean environment or common-pool resources, and cash benefits such as pensions: all these can help people to achieve valued capabilities such as health, participation in social relationships, and a measure of individual choice (or 'agency') concerning what they wish to do or be. To have this effect, they must be provided in such a way that resources are redistributed towards those who would not otherwise have access to them. This does not mean, however, that all those who approve of more equal opportunities see equality in itself as a good thing, or less inequality as necessarily better. Margaret Thatcher, before she became the UK Prime Minister, put her disagreement this way:

> Opportunity means nothing unless it includes the right to be unequal. Let our children grow tall and some grow taller than others if they have it in them to do so.
> *(Margaret Thatcher, 1975, quoted in Timmins, 1995, p.508)*

▪▪▪ 9.4.1 The welfare state and redistribution

Many government activities redistribute resources, and not always from rich to poor. The extent and nature of government activity therefore deeply influences the outcomes of the market system (as Nick Barr (1994) was arguing in the quotation in Section 9.1).

Figure 9.5
General government
expenditure as
per cent of GDP,
selected years
and countries

Source: based on
data in Tanzi and
Schuknecht, 2000,
pp.6–7

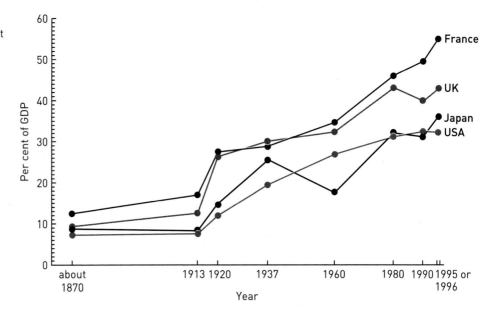

As capitalist economic development proceeds, the weight of government expenditure in the economy tends to rise, increasing this impact. Figure 9.5 shows this rise in expenditure in four countries over more than a century, starting earlier in the two European countries than the USA and Japan, with some levelling out after 1980, and a sharp drop in Japan in the aftermath of the Second World War.

Much government expenditure is *absorptive* (or *exhaustive*) *expenditure*, that is, expenditure on providing services such as health care, education and defence, that uses up (absorbs) resources such as labour and raw materials. The rest is *transfers*: shifts of spending power from one person to another, for example to provide old age pensions. Both types of expenditure may reduce inequality, or they may not. It is mainly high-income countries' governments that find the funds for transfer programmes.

Most governments in high-income countries – those in the Organization for Economic Co-operation and Development (OECD) – have an explicit commitment to the relief of poverty and to the provision of universal access to certain essential services such as health care and schooling. These services, and the cash transfers supposed to prevent destitution, are not without gaps – as the homeless sleeping on the streets of British cities testify – and the definitions of who is eligible can be narrowly drawn and discriminatory. However, only the United States among high-income countries lacks a principled governmental commitment to universalizing access to such services and benefits, known in shorthand as the **welfare state**.

There is no commonly accepted definition of the welfare state. Economics texts on the topic explicitly avoid defining it, and as the 'biographer' of the British welfare state puts it, 'Even the origin of the phrase is the subject of learned dispute' (Timmins, 1995). My working definition captures three important aspects: the mix of services and cash benefits; the mix of provision by government (i.e. the 'public sector') and ensuring provision and access by other means (e.g. contracting with private providers); and an *intention* to create a minimum level of welfare or well-being. It is not clear that a welfare state exists unless there is a real government intention to construct universal access and safety nets; hence the USA is sometimes described as the only high-income country without a welfare state, despite a high level of government spending on some relevant activities.

Welfare state

A set of
government
activities, notably
the provision
(or ensuring) of
universal access
to basic services
including health
care and
education, and
provision of cash
benefits, designed
(among other
objectives) to
ensure a minimum
level of well-being
for citizens of a
country.

▪ ▪ ▪ 9.4.2 Measuring inequality

To examine the redistributive impact of welfare spending we first need to be able to measure inequality of incomes. There are two preliminary decisions to be made. First, what is the best unit of measurement: the income of individuals or households? Some income is received and spent by individuals, other income is used for expenditure on goods and services that are shared with children, partners and other household members (not necessarily on an equal basis). We will use household income, while keeping in mind that this disguises intra-household inequality.

Second, should those incomes be adjusted to take account of the needs of the household? There is a good argument for doing so. A household consisting of one adult will have a higher standard of living than a household of two adults and four children on the same income. So, if one makes no adjustment, people in big households will seem better off than they actually are. Income distribution data are therefore generally adjusted by some 'equivalence scale' that scales down the income of large households and scales up the income of small ones. The UK Office for National Statistics (ONS), for example, treats a childless couple as equal to 1.00 (the reference household), and divides a given income by 0.61 for a single person household (increasing the income) and by 1.46 (reducing it) if a couple have two children between 8 and 10 (Goodman *et al.*, 1997, p.39). Income data in this chapter are adjusted in this way, though the precise equivalence scales used vary. In this sub-section the data are for 'disposable' income: income after income taxes are deducted and after the receipt of benefits such as pensions.

Now picture all the people in an economy lined up by 'equivalent' household income, starting with those in the poorest households and ending with the richest (Mackintosh and Mooney, 2000, p.89). Imagine yourself putting in a marker one-tenth of the way along – to mark off the 10 per cent of poorest people – then another marking off the 20 per cent poorest, and so on, until your ninth marker leaves just the 10 per cent of richest people above it. Each of these markers is at a *decile* – one-tenth of a population ranked by income.

This gives us one of the most graphic and widely used measures of income distribution: the ratio of the income at the ninth decile (P_{90}) to the income at the first decile (P_{10}), often referred to as the **decile ratio**.

The decile ratio is a good indicator of inequality because it measures the 'distance' across the income distribution between a high-income and a low-income person.

The same strategy of lining up people by order of equivalent household income gives us another couple of widely used income distribution measures: the Lorenz curve and the Gini coefficient. See the case study below on disposable income.

Decile ratio

The ratio of income at the ninth decile to income at the first decile of the income distribution (P_{90}/P_{10}).

Case study: Inequality measurement and the Lorenz curve

Column 1 of Table 9.1 ranks the population by deciles (tenths) from the poorest to the richest. Column 2 gives the percentage of total UK disposable income that goes to each tenth; the share gets larger of course as incomes rise. Columns 3 and 4 are the *cumulative* percentages of population and income. To construct cumulative income percentages, start with the percentage of income received by the poorest 10 per cent, that is, 2.9 per cent (column 2). Then add the proportion received by the next poorest 10 per cent (4.7 per cent in column 2) to give the share of the poorest 20 per cent (7.6 per cent in column 4).

Question

Check your understanding of Table 9.1 before moving on, especially the relation between columns 2 and 4.

Case study continued

Table 9.1
Data for Lorenz curve, UK disposable income, 1999/2000

(1) Deciles of population	(2) Share of disposable income %	(3) Cumulative percentage of population %	(4) Cumulative percentage of disposable income %
Lowest	2.9	10	2.9
2	4.7	20	7.6
3	5.4	30	13
4	7	40	20
5	7	50	27
6	9	60	36
7	10	70	46
8	12	80	58
9	15	90	73
Highest	27	100	100

Source: Department of Social Security, 2001, p.101, based on UK Family Resources Survey

Now look carefully at Figure 9.6. This shows a Lorenz curve constructed from the data in Table 9.1.

Along the vertical axis in Figure 9.6 we measure the cumulative percentage of total disposable in-come, and along the horizontal axis the cumulative percentage of the population, having ranked people according to their equivalized household income. The Lorenz curve plots the relationship between these two variables.

Figure 9.6
A Lorenz curve for UK disposable income, 1999/2000
Source: Department of Social Security, 2001, p.101, based on UK Family Resources Survey

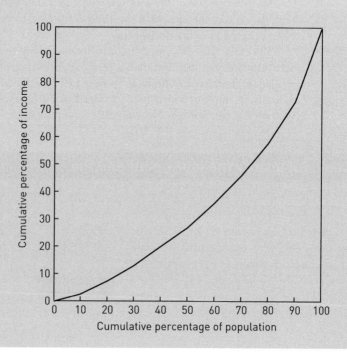

Question

Suppose that incomes were equally distributed, so each tenth of the population received a tenth of the income. What would be the shape of the Lorenz curve?

It would be a diagonal straight line. If that is not clear to you, write 10 in each row of column 2 of Table 9.1: each decile has 10 per cent of the income. Now calculate column 4 from your new column 2 and plot the curve on a figure like Figure 9.6.

Figure 9.7 adds this line of perfectly equal incomes to Figure 9.6.

Associated with the Lorenz curve is a measure of inequality known as the Gini coefficient (G). Look at Figure 9.7 again. The Gini coefficient is the ratio of the area between the diagonal and the Lorenz curve (the area marked A) to the area of the triangle beneath the diagonal (the area A + B). G varies between 0 in the case of perfect equality and 1 when all the income accrues to a single individual. The more the Lorenz curve is bowed away from the diagonal the more unequal is the distribution of income and the larger will be the value of G.

Figure 9.7
Lorenz curve and
diagonal line for
equal incomes

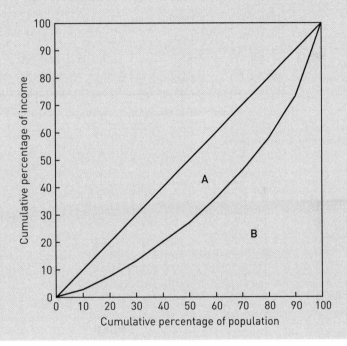

If you have understood the case study above, you should now be able to compare income distributions and to answer questions such as, to what extent are incomes in some countries more equal than in others? Here are some data for Gini coefficients and decile ratios for a number of higher income countries (Table 9.2). Figure 9.8 plots the two measures against each other, labelling the points by country. The figure shows that each measure gives similar answers to the question, which countries are the most unequal? On both measures, Mexico, Russia and the USA are the most unequal countries, having the highest Gini coefficients and decile ratios. However, the decile ratio picks up differences at the *ends* of the distribution; for example, if the rich are very rich relative to the rest this will be a large number. The Gini is a measure that particularly picks up differences in the middle income ranges. France and Canada, for example, have similar levels of inequality as measured by the Gini coefficient, but Canada has a larger decile ratio. Our choice of measure matters.

Table 9.2
Gini coefficients
and decile ratios
for a number of
high-income and
upper-middle
income countries,
mid 1990s

Year	Country	Gini coefficient	Decile ratio P_{90}/P_{10}
1994	Australia	0.311	4.33
1997	Canada	0.291	4.01
1996	Czech Republic	0.259	3.01
1994	France	0.288	3.54
1994	Germany	0.261	3.18
1995	Italy	0.342	4.77
1998	Mexico	0.494	11.55
1994	Netherlands	0.235	3.15
1995	Poland	0.318	4.04
1995	Russia	0.447	9.39
1995	Sweden	0.221	2.61
1995	Taiwan	0.277	3.38
1995	UK	0.344	4.57
1997	USA	0.372	5.57

Source: Luxembourg Income Study, http:\\lisweb.ceps.lu, 2 October 2001

Figure 9.8
Gini coefficients
compared with
decile ratios, by
country, mid 1990s

Source:
Luxembourg
Income Study,
http:\\lisweb.ceps.lu,
2 October 2001

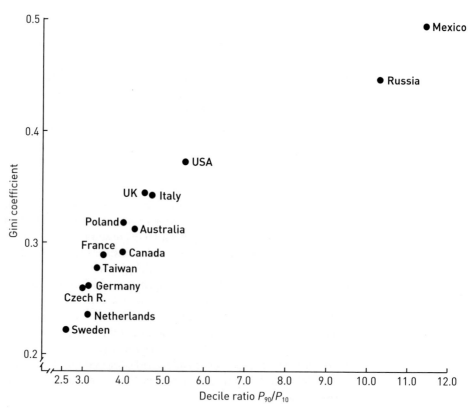

■ ■ ■ 9.4.3 Evaluating redistribution

All welfare states have emerged from a patchwork of earlier services, governmental and voluntary, and their institutional framework is very diverse. Let us judge them – in the language of our times – by their outcomes. Do they reduce inequality? Do they benefit the poorest people in high-income countries?

To answer these questions, we need to analyse the income distribution before and after government action on taxes, benefits and public service provision.

Question	Think about that last statement. Can you see a snag? Look back at Section 9.4.1 for a prompt.

Figure 9.5 showed that government spending, including both service provision and transfers, measured between 32 per cent (Japan) and 55 per cent (France) of GDP in the mid 1990s. This implies that economies cannot really be observed 'before' government activity. Individuals and markets would behave quite differently if the government and its economic activity suddenly disappeared or shrank dramatically. Indeed, some transition economies such as Russia suffered badly from this effect (Section 9.1). So we cannot strictly measure the income distribution 'before government'. Instead, economists measure the incomes of households from *market* activity (including wages paid by the government) and compare them to incomes including the effects of taxes, benefits and public services. Figure 9.9 shows how the UK Office for National Statistics explains the relation between various measures of income.

Primary (market, original) income distribution

The primary (or market or original) income distribution is the distribution of incomes produced by factor markets and asset ownership before taxes and transfers.

'Original', or market income, comes from wages and salaries, rent, interest payments on savings, private pensions and self-employment. The distribution of original income constitutes the **primary income distribution** that arises from the operation of the labour market and the market in financial assets and land. Private pensions, and other insurance payments, count as part of original income. As just suggested, we need to interpret the idea of 'original' income carefully: it does not represent the market outcomes we would experience were there no government.

The government, as part of its expenditure, pays out cash benefits such as state-provided pensions and assistance for those unable to earn an income, and deducts 'direct' taxes: taxes on income of people and firms. The result is 'disposable' income: the income data used in Section 9.4.2. We spend some of our incomes and the government levies 'indirect' taxes, such as value added tax (VAT), on those purchases: income after indirect taxes is 'post-tax' income. The government also supplies services free of charge, such as health care and education, and these 'benefits in kind' can be added to our incomes to give our 'final' income after all taxes and benefits. The distribution of final income constitutes a **secondary income distribution** which can be compared with the primary one.

Secondary (final) income distribution

The secondary (or final) income distribution is the distribution of income after taxes and benefits, including benefits in kind.

The *primary* income distribution in rich countries is very unequal, and would leave a great many people in poverty. Some people are unable to do paid work through age or disability, or because they are caring for children and do not find available options for childcare satisfactory. Some people who wish to get a job cannot find work. Figure 9.10 shows the effect of taxes and cash benefits on the UK income distribution. The data used for this are for fifths (quintiles) of the income distribution, and this time the horizontal axis shows cumulative percentages of *households* ranked by equivalized household income.

Figure 9.9
Redistribution by
government in the
UK: the relation
between different
measures of
income.

Source: based on
Lakin, 2001, p.37

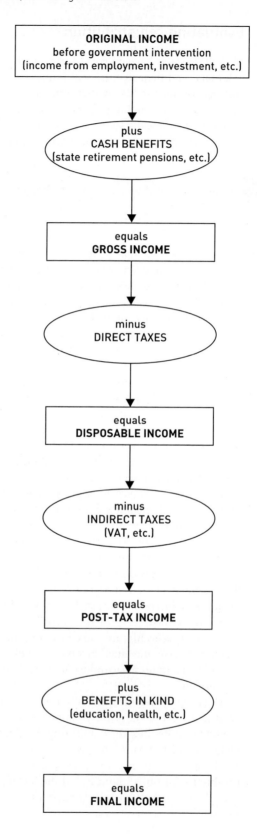

Figure 9.10
Lorenz curves for original and post-tax income for the UK, 1999/2000

Source: data in Lakin, 2001, p.66

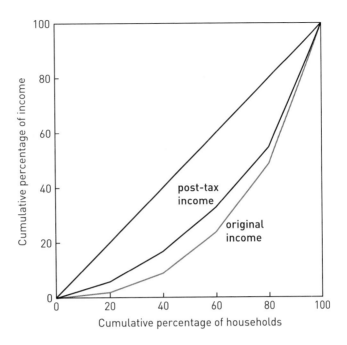

Question Describe the effects of taxes and benefits shown in Figure 9.10.

The Lorenz curve for post-tax income is closer to the diagonal than that for original income. So taxes and benefits reduce inequality between households.

Adding in benefits in kind to measure final income would have further reduced measured inequality, since government-provided health care and education are distributed more equally than cash incomes. The UK ONS calculates that benefits in kind more than double the post-tax income of the lowest decile, but add only 21 per cent to the post-tax income of the top decile (Lakin, 2001, p.53).

Welfare states in high-income countries generally reduce inequality. But what of our second question above: does the redistribution lift the poor out of poverty? Figure 9.10 raises some doubts: the poorest 20 per cent of households remain a very long way short of 20 per cent of income. To look more closely, we need to identify those in poverty. To do this, we need first to define a **poverty line**, that is, a level of income below which people are living in poverty.

There are two ways to define a poverty line. One is to calculate the income required to obtain a 'basket' of goods and services deemed essential. This method defines an 'absolute' poverty line that will only change as prices change. The second method is to define as 'poor' people living below some fraction of average or median incomes. (The 'median' income is the income at the fifth decile: the income of the person or household halfway along the distribution.) This method gives us a 'relative' poverty line, that is, a poverty line defined relative to incomes in the country that will rise as real incomes rise.

Poverty line

A measured level of income below which people are defined as living in poverty.

Question Suppose that you take a capabilities approach to well-being. Which poverty line might you prefer?

Table 9.3
Welfare state redistribution and poverty relief, mid 1990s

(1) Country	(2) Poverty rate before taxes and transfers %	(3) Poverty rate after taxes and transfers %	(4) Poverty rate relative reduction %
Australia, 1994	20.2	10.4	−49
France, 1994	22.3	8.5	−62
Germany, 1994	14.7	7.9	−46
Netherlands, 1994	19.5	9.1	−54
UK, 1995	26.2	9.8	−63
USA, 1994	21.6	18.2	−16

Source: Behrendt, 2000, p.6

Both may be relevant. You will want to ensure that the poverty line income allows access to the goods and services necessary to achieve essential capabilities. This suggests an absolute measure. But you may also recognize that essential capabilities such as participating in social relationships require different types of goods and services in different societies, so a relative measure may be useful too.

I will use a relative poverty line here. A very common one is to define as 'poor' people in households living on less than half of median income. If median incomes differ between countries, so will income at the poverty line.

Once we have defined a poverty line such as this we can calculate the proportion of the population living below it. This calculation gives the **poverty rate** for a particular country. On this basis, Table 9.3 compares the poverty-reduction effect of the welfare state in several high-income countries. In Table 9.3 the 'poverty rate' in columns 2 and 3 is the percentage of households headed by someone of 'prime age' (55 years and below) living at or below the poverty line just defined: it examines poverty relief for non-pensioner households only.

Poverty rate

The proportion of the population that is below a given poverty line.

Question | Explain what the table shows before reading on.

Table 9.3 columns 2 and 3 shows poverty rates, that is, the percentage of non-pensioner households with incomes below half of (equivalized) median disposable income in each country. The percentages are measured before taxes and transfers (i.e. original income) (column 2) and after transfers and direct taxes (i.e. disposable income) (column 3). Germany has the lowest poverty rate on the basis of original income; after taxes and transfers it is still the lowest, though the redistribution, measured as the percentage reduction in the poverty rate, is smaller than four other countries. At the other end of the scale, the table confirms that the US government redistributes very little to the poor, relative to the other countries, so ends up with by far the highest poverty rate after taxes and transfers.

One consequence of this brings us back to capabilities. Suppose that we are particularly concerned not with equality of income but of opportunity. We might then be particularly anxious that children get a fair start in life. Margaret Thatcher talked of all children growing tall. Research repeatedly shows that growing up in poverty has a negative effect on children's life chances.

Smeeding and Rainwater – two economists who specialize in income distribution issues – compared, across high-income countries, the real incomes of households with children.

Their comparison used a measure of income called 'purchasing power parity' that adjusts money incomes for differences in what money will buy in each country (e.g. housing is much cheaper in one country than another). They showed (Smeeding and Rainwater, 2001) that despite the much higher median incomes in the USA than in the other countries studied, the incomes of households with children at the lowest decile (P_{10}) in each country were *lower* in the USA than in all the other countries except the UK and Australia. Furthermore, poor children in the USA also had less access to benefits in kind than most of their peers in other high-income countries. The authors argue that:

> societies with wide income disparities across families with children have less support for public and social goods such as tax-financed health care, child care and education, because high income families can privately purchase above average levels of those goods with their higher incomes, rather than supporting high overall levels of tax-financed goods and sharing them with less well off children.
>
> *(Smeeding and Rainwater, 2001, p.24)*

We come back to this kind of political argument in Section 9.6.

9.5 The welfare state and economic efficiency

The welfare state does not only affect inequality; it also has a profound impact on the efficiency of the economy. In the 1980s and 1990s economists generally argued that the effects were negative. Policy makers saw themselves as faced with a 'trade-off': more equality meant less efficiency and policy had to choose. Now, as part of the search for 'smarter' government, economists are focusing on a search for synergy: for ways in which more equality and more efficiency might go hand in hand.

There are a number of reasons for this shift. One is the experience in Europe of the social, political and economic consequences of persistent unemployment from the mid 1970s onwards. Another is the rising perception of increased instability of employment in industries where jobs were previously expected to be long term (Chapter 1, Section 1.3.2). Economists are aware that many of the economic risks faced by individuals result from the operation of markets which – while 'imperfect' when compared with the perfect competition benchmark – have dynamic efficiency benefits such as innovation and growth. In these circumstances it is now widely argued that, if properly designed, the welfare state can help people to cope with the market risks effectively, and thereby increase the dynamic efficiency of the economy. This section aims to give you a flavour of these arguments and their critics, using the example of benefits for the unemployed.

9.5.1 Risk, market failure and social insurance

In market economies, we try to deal individually with risk by taking out insurance. We insure ourselves against burglary and car accidents. Many people in the UK pay into private pension schemes, seeking to insure themselves against destitution after retirement. 'Life' insurance is actually insurance against the consequences of our death for those who depend on us. In many countries – but few high-income countries – individual private health insurance is the only protection against the costs of treatment in illness.

The market for private insurance is, however, subject to market failure.

Suppose you are employed. Can you ring up an insurance company – say the one that insures your car – and buy insurance against losing your job? If not, why not?

In the UK at present you can do this to a limited extent. For example, if you have a mortgage on your house, you may be able to insure against being unable to pay the interest, perhaps for a year. And if you are in good health, you may be able to insure part of your income against losing your job because of severe illness. But apart from that you are on your own.

However, we do not want to find ourselves destitute if we lose our job. So why is the market not providing unemployment insurance? What is the source of this market failure?

Question Think about this. Suppose you have a job you dislike. How might unemployment insurance affect your behaviour?

Well, there are probably all kinds of ways of getting yourself sacked without the insurance company finding out that you have engineered it. The insurance company does not know the details of your individual situation; you have more information than the company. You can influence your own risk of unemployment, and the company cannot detect that – or not without major expense. The insurance policy furthermore has given you an incentive to change your behaviour – to engineer a paid break from work – to the detriment of the company's profits. This effect of insurance is called 'moral hazard'. It is a quite widespread problem in insurance markets, but particularly affects those markets where it is hard for companies to collect information about the insured.

Exercise 9.6

Think of some more examples of insurance markets affected by moral hazard.

In addition to moral hazard, companies providing private unemployment insurance also find it hard to assess the extent of individual risk because of poor information. So they cannot price their policies efficiently, by charging more for a higher risk. Worse still, companies are uncertain about the likely scale of unemployment in the future: if there is a sharp general rise in unemployment, insurance companies may fail. For all these reasons, private unemployment insurance is not generally available. Market failures have created a missing market: there is no supply of a service people would like to buy. There is thus a market efficiency problem: markets are not responding effectively to consumer needs.

So what can be done? What people want to ensure is income when unemployed. Provision of unemployment insurance in this sense has effectively been taken over by government in most high-income countries. There are two ways this can be done; they are complementary, and the mix varies between countries. Welfare state institutions are highly diverse, having grown in each country from a patchwork of local voluntary, mutual, government and private provision, but the economic *functions* those institutions fulfil are similar across countries.

Unemployment insurance can be provided through *social insurance*: compulsory contributions by all in work to a fund, to which employers also contribute and which governments may subsidize, that provides limited term benefits to those who involuntarily lose their jobs. 'Socializing' unemployment insurance in this way makes it viable, because the government has much more effective powers of investigation than a private company of reasons for leaving jobs. Furthermore, since the insurance is compulsory, it brings together those at high and low risk of unemployment, reducing the overall cost of insurance protection for those at high risk.

Social insurance of this kind is backed up, in most high-income countries, by *social assistance*: these are cash benefits which are paid on the basis of need, not on the basis of prior contributions. Social assistance is always surrounded by conditions such as evidence of actively seeking work for those able to do so, evidence of disability for those unable to, and evidence of a lack of other means to justify benefit payments. These often onerous conditions aim to reduce the effect of moral hazard on the costs of social assistance. Typically, the amount paid out in social assistance rises when long-term unemployment rises. The mix of social assistance and social insurance varies between countries, and the payments were all included in the category of cash benefits in Section 9.4. Together they respond to the missing market for unemployment insurance.

■ ■ ■ 9.5.2   Social insurance and economy-wide efficiency

Compensating for market failure in the sense of missing insurance markets is a positive efficiency effect of social insurance against unemployment. However, it has been widely argued that there are also economy-wide negative efficiency effects. The debate centres on the impact of the cash benefits on the labour market.

A central issue is the *amount* people should be paid when not in work, from a mix of social insurance and social assistance, relative to their earnings in work. This relationship is called the **replacement rate**.

Replacement rate

The ratio of income when unemployed to income (after taxes and transfers) when employed.

If replacement rates are high, people have incomes when out of work not much lower than when in work; if low, people experience a very large drop in income when they lose their jobs. 'The' replacement rate is not easy to measure. Rates differ for people with different levels of earning power, as well as varying with the structure and rules for benefits for different household members when out of work. Hence a replacement rate for a country will be an average of a number of different rates faced by people in different family and work circumstances.

Figure 9.11 shows one systematic estimate of how replacement rates changed over 40 years for a number of high-income countries. They vary enormously by country, the USA and Japan having persistently low rates. Most countries had stable or rising rates in the 1960s and 1970s. The 1980s saw rising unemployment throughout Europe, and this was accompanied by rising or stable replacement rates in most countries. The exceptions were the UK and, outside Europe, the USA.

By the 1990s, policy towards replacement rates had become contentious.

Question   Which of the two following arguments do you find most compelling and why?

1   High replacement rates increase unemployment, and reduce output, because they encourage people to remain unemployed.
2   High replacement rates improve labour market efficiency, and increase output, because they encourage people to take risks and to retrain.

This is a highly political debate and hard to resolve by the use of evidence. The fundamental problem is that the two arguments are rooted in different models of the labour market, including workers' behaviour.

Figure 9.11
Replacement rates,
1961–91, selected
OECD countries

Source: data from
OECD, 1994, p.226

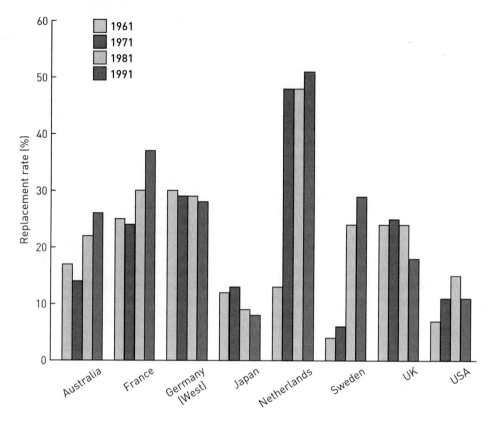

Argument 1, still the standard textbook argument, can be explained using a model of a perfectly competitive labour market (Figure 9.12). Suppose that there is a given level of benefit received by those not working, supported by a tax on employers for each worker they employ, as well as by workers' tax payments. Those benefits and the taxes that support them now fall relative to the going wage W_1. Two effects might occur in this model. Employers, paying a lower tax per worker, experience a lower total cost per worker, and labour demand shifts rightwards from L_{D1} to L_{D2}. Workers, receiving lower benefits, find that wages from employment are now higher relative to income if they stay at home. So more workers are willing to accept work at a given wage, so the labour supply shifts rightwards from L_{S1} to L_{S2}. Either effect will increase employment above L_1. The effect of the two shifts on the equilibrium wage may be to raise or lower it.

It is also argued that workers work harder if replacement rates are low because they fear the sack (Chapter 7, Section 7.5.1 similarly discussed the 'worker discipline' effect of increasing the gap between what workers could earn in, say, Ford and income they could earn elsewhere). These have been influential arguments. The OECD argued in 1994 that 'if unemployment is to be kept low, it is vital to limit entitlement to benefits' (OECD, 1994, p.213). In 1998 they complained of lack of 'progress' on this recommendation (OECD, 1998, p.15). During the 1990s, however, Germany, the Netherlands, France and the UK all reduced entitlements to benefits and/or restricted their duration.

Question   Can you think of criticisms of these arguments for lower replacement rates?

Figure 9.12
The effect of a
reduction in benefits
in a perfectly
competitive labour
market

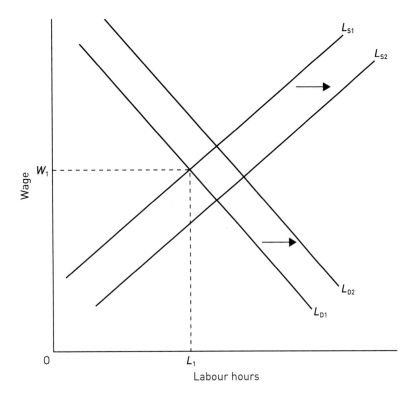

The model in Figure 9.12 assumes a unified labour market. However, in most countries the labour market is segmented. Workers in unionized 'primary sector' jobs have rights to unemployment benefit, while 'secondary sector' workers have few unemployment benefit rights. (Chapter 7, Section 7.4.2 examined labour market segmentation into primary and secondary sectors.) Social assistance benefits are generally lower than social insurance benefits, and require stringent evidence of seeking work. A reduction in replacement rates may be brought about (as in the UK) by heavily restricting unemployment benefits, forcing more people onto social assistance.

To see why this segmentation may provide support for Argument 2, consider a person's choice between taking a low-paid 'secondary' job, or waiting for a chance to get a primary sector job. If the conditions on benefit as well as its level are generous, a feasible choice might be to wait and retrain, increasing the chances of moving to a primary job.

> For the person laid off from Joe's Café it may be the best thing that happened to him if he is subsequently taken on by a firm of catering consultants.
>
> *(Atkinson, 1999, p.99)*

Chapter 7, Section 7.2.4 explained the concept of human capital and analysed training as an investment decision by people and firms. If a higher replacement rate encourages retraining and thereby raises the skill levels in the economy, and particularly if that in turn attracts investment from firms looking for skilled workers, the high replacement rate will benefit, not damage, the economy.

Finally, if primary sector employers require workers not just to do what they are told, but to use their energy and imagination in their work, the security offered by high replacement rates might encourage such productive behaviour. These are arguments about dynamic efficiency benefits, which assume imperfect and segmented markets for labour. Governments used these models in the late 1990s to try to redesign benefit systems to be more 'employment friendly', helping people to cope with the changing labour market while pushing them towards paid work: trying to combine poverty relief and unemployment reduction rather than being forced (as Argument 1 proposes) to choose between them. The Netherlands has been cited as a success story along these lines, having reduced its unemployment rate sharply while maintaining generous benefit levels (Purdy, 2001).

9.6 Why do governments do what they do?

> Freedom from Want cannot be forced on a democracy or given to a democracy, it must be won by them.
>
> *(Sir William Beveridge, 1942, quoted in Timmins, 1995)*

Sections 9.4 and 9.5 argued that government activity deeply affects the operation of market economies, and discussed what governments could and should do. Now we take the step of treating government decision-making as 'endogenous' to economic modelling, by asking to what extent economic analysis might be able to *explain* what governments do. This requires us to treat politicians, civil servants and those who work in government service as individuals responding to economic incentives, just as people do in markets, and just as people in communities do in the analysis of collective action (Section 9.3); for politicians, the incentives are created in large part by the preferences of the voters who elect them. This approach to understanding government is known (confusingly) as 'public choice' economics, since voters are treated as making choices much as consumers do in a market. To give you a flavour of public choice analysis, we look at just one question: why might a democratic government redistribute income to the less well off?

▪▪▪ 9.6.1 'Public choice' economics and redistribution

Question | Measured on the basis of disposable income the poor form a minority of the population in high-income countries. So why, in a democracy where everyone has a vote, should redistribution to the poor occur at all? Why should comfortable citizens vote to give away some of their primary income to the worst off?

We will consider answers to this question in two stages using a simplified model of how redistribution occurs. First, in a majority voting system, whose preferences expressed through voting actually 'count'? And second, what might influence those preferences?

Let us assume, initially, that in an election voters can be roughly lined up in terms of the amount of public goods and other public services they would like to see provided by government in kind and equally to all: from very few to a generous provision. And let us suppose that the distribution of voter preferences looks as in Figure 9.13: there are rather few extremists here. Most voters are moderate in their preferences, with the modal preference – the level commanding the greatest support – at the median, that is, halfway along the distribution.

Two candidates wish to be voted into office. Suppose their initial platforms are PG_S and PG_L. Now both politicians will spot an opportunity. Consider the politician proposing PG_L. Point A shows the number of voters who agree with him (measured on

Figure 9.13
Voters' preferences
and politicians'
proposals

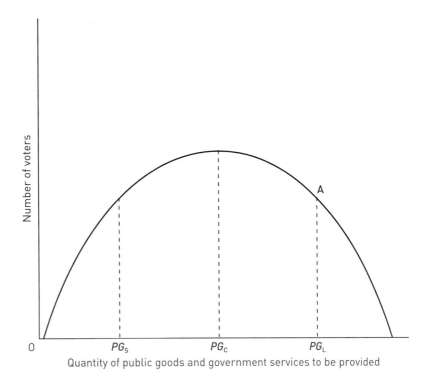

the vertical axis). If that politician moves towards the centre, offering rather fewer goods and services but still more than his opponent, he will gain more definite votes while not losing those voters who want a lot of provision: for them, he will still be the better of the two. The politician proposing PG_S, if smart, will spot the same idea and also move towards the centre. The politician who can dominate the centre – who can gain the vote of the median voter at PG_C – will take the election.

This conclusion is called the 'median voter theorem': the argument that the median voter swings an election. So, accepting this theorem for a moment, what determines the median voter's preferences? Suppose that those on lower incomes prefer more public goods and government services and those who are better off prefer fewer. This could be explained by self-interest: the well-off pay more in total in tax and feel less need for government provision, since for health and education they can supplement govern-ment services with private supply. Those on low incomes gain more from government provision relative to their market incomes (Section 9.4).

The preferences of the median voter may then depend on the shape of the income distribution. Figure 9.14 shows the UK income distribution (disposable income) for 2000 (*Social Trends*, 2001). It shows that the median individual has an equivalized household income well below average (mean) income even after cash benefits and direct taxes. One would therefore expect a majority for some redistributive policies.

However, self-interested voters may not see the choices quite like that. Consider a rather different story. Suppose that everyone pays taxes (as we do – even the poor pay indirect taxes) and those taxes are spent on, say, the education system. Now suppose that there are three distinct sets of preferences about this. The poor prefer to avoid the tax; their priority is income over education. The middle-income voters prefer more tax and more education provision. The high-income voters prefer to buy their education privately and pay less tax. Here the median voter may not rule; instead, the two extremes may out-vote the middle.

Figure 9.14
The UK income distribution of disposable income 2000

Note: there are also 2.6 million individuals with equivalized household incomes above £700 a week. They are not included because their inclusion would extend the distribution too far to the right to be displayed on the page.

Source: Department of Social Security, 2001, Figure 2.1, p.8

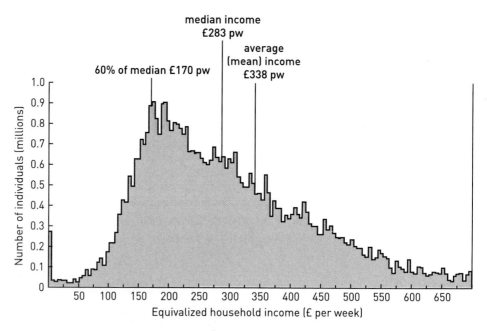

Something rather like this seems to have happened in Bristol, in the west of England, in February 2001. The local council held a referendum on council tax and education spending, and recommended more education and more tax. A majority of voters, on a 40 per cent turnout, rejected this, preferring a tax freeze and lower real education spending (*The Times Educational Supplement*, 23 February 2001). There is some evidence that the lowest- and highest-income voters tended to vote for the freeze option; one reason might be that (influencing the better off) about 20 per cent of Bristol's children were in private education in 2001, while (influencing the poorer voters) council taxes were already high by national standards.

■■■ 9.6.2 Political processes and endogenous preferences

The Bristol example suggests some general problems with 'public choice' analysis. First, voters are rarely given this kind of simplified choice over policies. Instead, in most democracies, voting seems to be as much a public expression of opinion, of allegiance to a party or even an individual, and of participation in governance processes as a citizen, as it is a process of choosing specific policies.

Furthermore, there is likely to be a strong influence of experience on preferences. People may have strong preferences about institutions as well as the precise distribution of benefits. For example, they may have a preference for free access to health care on the basis of need, and may be influenced in this preference by experience of systems that proclaim that objective. There is evidence for this in comparisons of voters' preferences in the USA and western European countries. The former appear to have a stronger tolerance of inequality in health care access than European voters who are used to both the costs and the consequences of European welfare states.

Experience is also influential in another sense. People are influenced by the existence of a welfare state. If they come to rely on it, it affects their work and spending choices. Changing the system therefore has large costs. Consider, for example, a well-off Swedish voter who has no private pension provision. He or she is unlikely to vote for a smaller welfare state. Middle-income voters may rely heavily on the insurance functions of the welfare state. Such voters may indeed see redistribution itself as having an insurance aspect. People's position in the income distribution is not fixed. For example, of adults in deciles three and four of the UK income distribution in 1991, nearly a quarter had fallen into the two lowest deciles in 1997 (*Social Trends*, 2000). The existence of a redistributive welfare state insures people against destitution when things go wrong in their lives.

Finally, the better off may vote for redistributive policies for reasons other than self-interest. They may believe it to be unacceptable on ethical grounds that a country with high average incomes should tolerate severe poverty. They may fear civil unrest if a part of society is excluded from the benefits most enjoy (another version of redistribution as insurance). And, in these views, they may have been influenced by politicians themselves. People may see the political process as delegating to selected politicians the task of thinking about important issues such as the level of spending on health services and cash benefits, and of taking a public lead in arguing for what they think should be done. One Bristol resident put that point rather forcefully: 'I voted for them to lead, and not abdicate responsibility for the most challenging decision of the year, namely setting the budget.' (Letters, *The Guardian*, 17 February 2001.)

So politicians may – perhaps should – devote some time to trying to change the shape of the distribution of voters' opinions, such as those shown in Figure 9.13, as well as to changing the income distribution itself. Government seems indeed to be 'endogenous' to a wider governance process, where voters and politicians interact in a public sphere that also includes the media and the existing institutions of social provision.

9.7 Conclusion: governance with endogenous economists

A.B. Atkinson, a well-known British economist writing about inequality and welfare who also has experience of government advising, argues that:

> Calls by economists for rolling back the welfare state are themselves part of the political process; we have not just endogenous politicians but also endogenous economists, whose behaviour has to be explained.
>
> *(Atkinson, 1999, p.187)*

What Atkinson is saying here is that economic analysis does influence policy, to some extent. Furthermore, economists analyse how the political process influences policy decisions. Yet economists are much less aware that we too are influenced in our choice of model by the politics of the day – and of the consequences that may have. Atkinson's book, from which the quote is taken, is 'endogenous' in this sense: he is trying to contest the assumption that the economic literature as it stands all supports 'rolling back the welfare state', showing that plausible models can generate alternative conclusions.

Economics is thus a highly political subject. I think that is one of its pleasures. This chapter has introduced you to some of the economic analysis of government and more broadly of governance, both in the sense of collective action and in the sense of voter–politician relationships. In the language introduced in Chapter 8, Section 8.1, we have considered both 'positive' and 'normative' approaches to governance: what will or can be done, and what 'should' be done. A particular theme has been the interrelation between equity – in the sense of both greater equality of incomes and more equality of opportunities – and efficiency in both a static and a dynamic sense. The next chapter applies some of the analysis in Chapters 8 and 9 to the economics of another highly political issue: health care.

Questions for review and discussion

Question 1 Figure 9.15 shows an industry in which there is a negative externality in supply. Insert each label below to match the appropriate explanatory phrase:

Curve 1   Curve 2   Curve 3 Q_1 Q_2 AC   BE   BD

(a) .... The difference between the allocatively efficient price and the free market equilibrium price.

(b) .... The allocatively efficient quantity of output.

(c) .... The industry supply curve.

(d) .... The amount of tax per unit of output required to achieve allocative efficiency.

(e) .... The industry demand curve.

(f) .... The difference between marginal social cost and marginal private cost at the free market equilibrium output.

(g) .... The marginal social cost curve.

Figure 9.15
Industry with negative externality in supply

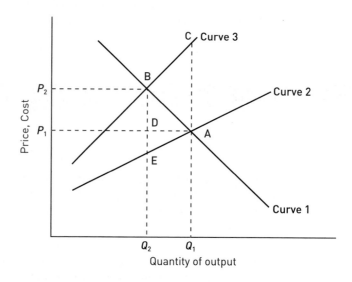

Question 2 Figure 9.16 shows two hypothetical Lorenz curves:

(a) Say which statement below is correct:

   A Lorenz curve L_1 shows that the bottom 5 deciles receive a higher proportion of total income than L_2 shows.

   B Lorenz curve L_2 shows that the bottom 5 deciles receive a lower proportion of total income than L_1 shows.

(b) Say which is the appropriate completion for the statement below:

The Gini coefficient corresponding to Lorenz curve L_1

   A is larger than that corresponding to Lorenz curve L_2.

   B is the same as that corresponding to Lorenz curve L_2.

   C is smaller than that corresponding to Lorenz curve L_2.

Figure 9.16
Lorenz curves

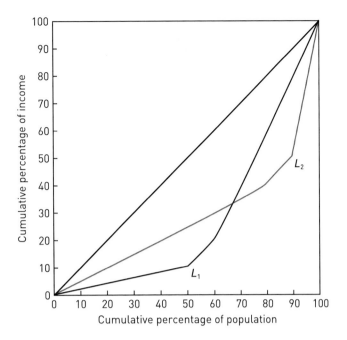

Question 3 Insert the correct word from the list to complete the following sentence:

Original   disposable   post-tax   final

Income from wages and salaries, rent, interest payments on savings, private pensions and self-employment *plus* cash benefits paid by the government *minus* direct taxes is known as . . . income.

Question 4 Figure 9.17 shows a perfectly competitive labour market. Suppose there is a rise in the level of benefit paid to those not working relative to the going wage. Suppose also that there is an increase in the taxes levied per employee, on employers that support these benefits. Draw a shift in the curve(s) as appropriate to show the likely impact on employment.

Figure 9.17
Perfectly
competitive
labour market

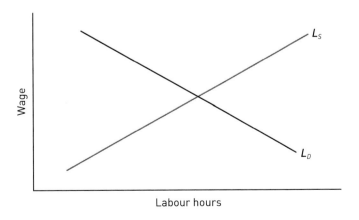

Question 5 Essay: In what ways, if any, can government policy both reduce income inequality and enhance economy-wide efficiency?

10

Health and health care: markets, ethics and inequality

Paul Anand and Martin Higginson

Concepts

- equity
- inequalities in health status and in access to health care
- social insurance
- private insurance
- adverse selection
- managed competition

Objectives

After studying this chapter you should be able to:

- appreciate the variety of health-care provision and finance in different countries
- apply microeconomic principles to the analysis of health care
- analyse market failure in health-care provision and finance
- understand the ethical issues raised by inequalities in health status and in access to health care.

10.1 Introduction

1 Don't be poor. If you are poor, try not to be poor for too long.
2 Don't live in a deprived area. If you do, move.
3 Don't be disabled or have a disabled child.
4 Don't work in a stressful low-paid manual job.
5 Don't live in damp, low quality housing or be homeless.
6 Be able to afford to pay for social activities and annual holidays.
7 Don't be a lone parent.
8 Claim all the benefits to which you are entitled.
9 Be able to afford to own a car.
10 Use education as an opportunity to improve your socio-economic position.

(Smith et al., 2001, p.xlviii)

These tips were put forward ironically in an academic text as alternatives to ten tips for better health offered by the UK government's Chief Medical Officer, and they reflect the strong relationship between health and economic status. The poor tend to be ill more

Table 10.1
Income per head
and mortality rates,
by country group

Country group	Population (1999) millions	Income per head (annual average) US$	Life expectancy at birth (years)	Under five mortality (deaths per 1000 live births)
Least-developed countries	643	296	51	159
Other low-income countries	1 777	538	59	120
Lower middle-income countries	2 094	1 200	70	39
Upper middle-income countries	573	4 900	71	35
High-income countries	891	25 730	78	6

Source: adapted from Commission on Macroeconomics and Health, 2001, p.2

often and to be more severely ill than the rich. On average, those on lower incomes live shorter lives (and have a lower life expectancy at birth) and are in poorer health while alive, that is, they have higher levels of morbidity. As Dr Gro Harlem Brundtland, Director General of the World Health Organization (WHO), argued in 1999:

First and foremost, there is a need to reduce greatly the burden of excess mortality and morbidity suffered by the poor.

(*World Health Organization, 1999*)

Table 10.1 shows just how dramatic is the association between poverty and mortality across the world.

The association between poverty, mortality and ill health also holds strongly *within* countries. Health policy observers look at how health varies according to occupational group, employment status, gender, area of residence and socio-economic category. Regardless of how social position is measured, those at the bottom of the social scale in the UK have higher death rates at every stage in life, from birth until well into old age. And the poor, and their children, typically experience higher morbidity rates: 'all the major killer diseases affect the poor more than the rich' (Whitehead, 1992). There is some evidence that those in poor health move down the social scale, as one might expect, but this explains only a small part of the disparity that exists. Lifestyle and material living conditions have a substantial influence on health status. Furthermore, as income inequalities have widened, so have health inequalities.

Rags or riches on the life line

The London health observatory says that a baby boy born in the east end borough of Newham, one of the capital's poorest areas, is now likely to die at 71, almost six years earlier than a boy born in the central borough of Westminster, one of the richest.

For baby boys born in the early 1990s, the life expectancy gap between the poorest and richest boroughs was only five years.

(*Carvel, 2001*)

Differences in infant mortality – that is, the proportion of children who die within a year of birth – are also increasing according to the report:

> Although the London average is similar to that for England and Wales as a whole, the capital has relatively high [infant mortality] figures in its inner areas.
>
> A boy born in Hackney, next to Newham, is more than twice as likely to die in the first year of life as a boy born in Bexley, in the south-east suburbs.
>
> The London observatory is one of eight regional organisations set up last year to monitor health inequalities. Although it is the first to report, it predicts that other regions will shortly announce a similar widening of the health gap between rich and poor in their areas.
>
> *(Carvel, 2001)*

Economists have looked closely at the association between income and health, and have concluded that poverty brings with it a whole raft of influences that cause poor health. But conversely, if good health care reaches the poor, it helps to relieve poverty.

There is considerable evidence that people are more concerned about inequalities in health than they are about inequalities in income. Equality of opportunity in the workplace is widely accepted, so it is reasonable to expect a similarly widespread belief that everyone should have an approximately equal chance of a long and healthy life. In view of the observed inequalities in health status, this belief is likely to be expressed in general support for a health-care system that is redistributive, enabling individuals on low incomes to obtain more health care than they could afford to buy in a competitive health-care market. In many rich countries there is something close to equitable access to health care, in the sense of equal access for equal need. Section 10.3 discusses some of the issues concerning health care and equity and examines how economists think about these issues. In looking at the ways in which health care is redistributive (Section 10.3.1), we shall be building on some of the concepts and techniques that were introduced in Chapter 9.

A commitment to redistribution through health-care provision implies a significant degree of economic activity by the government. In the UK this commitment has taken the form of the direct provision of health care by the public sector through the National Health Service (NHS). It is often said that public sector bodies and monopolies tend to be wasteful and inefficient because they are free from the competitive pressures that might otherwise force them to reduce costs. Section 10.4 examines an attempted reform of the NHS, which was prompted in part by worries of this sort.

Before we investigate these issues, it is important to appreciate the distinctive economic characteristics of health care. In Chapter 7 it was argued that, while the model of perfect competition can throw some light on labour market issues, the insights it provides are limited by the extent to which the assumptions of perfect competition fail to capture the particular characteristics of labour markets. This chapter follows a somewhat similar strategy: it introduces the distinctive features of health care by comparing markets in health care with the assumptions of the model of perfect competition (Section 10.2). However, while Chapter 7 saw the model of perfect competition as a partial explanation of labour market phenomena (e.g. wage differentials), this chapter invokes perfect competition in a different way. Given certain assumptions, the model of perfect competition may be used as a benchmark for allocating resources among people in a way that maximizes their welfare (Chapters 5 and 8). But the particular characteristics of markets in health care are significantly different from the assumptions about markets made in the model of perfect competition. This line of thought casts doubt on the suitability of a market relatively free from government intervention for the delivery and finance of health care.

It seems appropriate for the last chapter in this book to review some of the contents of the previous chapters. This chapter applies some concepts and techniques concerning equity and redistribution that were introduced in Chapters 8 and 9. It also focuses on the ways in which the analysis of monopoly and perfect competition in Chapters 4, 5 and 8 can illuminate health-care issues. In this way this final chapter of the book looks back over aspects of the economic analysis in earlier chapters and applies them to the topic of health care.

10.2 Market failure in health-care finance and delivery

Why is health care different from many other aspects of economic activity? Why is it not an appealing prospect to pay for health care in the way that we pay for, say, biscuits? Why do most people feel that it would be wrong to leave the delivery (or production or provision) of health care to Sainsbury's and its rival supermarkets? This section will address these questions.

The first step is to notice that, in the finance and delivery of health care, the diversity across countries suggests that there is no 'right answer'. This considerable diversity in the methods of health-care finance and provision is reported in Section 10.2.1. Section 10.2.2 examines the features of health-care delivery in hospitals, clinics and doctors' surgeries that distinguish it from the delivery of many other goods and services. Section 10.2.3 investigates the special problems surrounding the finance of health care. Why, even if it is agreed that some form of insurance is essential, does it seem unwise to leave people to insure their health on the commercial insurance market in the same way that they insure their houses or their cars?

■ ■ ■ 10.2.1 The diversity of health-care finance and delivery

In rich countries, people gain access to health care mainly through insurance or taxation. The need for health care is very hard to predict: in any year an individual may or may not fall ill; in a lifetime, some people need more care and treatment than others. Insurance, in principle, allows individuals to pay a predetermined amount and receive treatment if they need it. Paying taxes that support a public health-care system, such as those in the UK and Sweden, has the same effect: you pay a sum of money and receive treatment determined by clinical need, not by the amount you pay. Neither taxes nor insurance guarantees that you will receive all you need in practice. They do, however, allow people to receive expensive treatment – such as major surgery – that they could not afford if they had to pay for it at the time from their incomes.

Question	What is meant by 'social insurance'? Look back at Chapter 9, Section 9.5.1 to check your understanding.

Social insurance is insurance that is compulsory for all who can pay. The term generally refers to a system whereby employers as well as employees pay on a compulsory basis into insurance funds, and these funds provide access to a range of benefits, including health care.

Even in high-income countries, quite a lot of direct 'out of pocket' payments remain: for example, prescription charges in the UK, and 'co-payments' whereby a share of the

Table 10.2
Health-care
financing mix
in high-income
countries (as a
percentage of
total health-care
spending)

Country and year	Taxes %	Social insurance %	Private insurance %	Direct payments %
Denmark, 1987	84.7	0.0	1.5	13.8
France, 1989	0.0	73.6	6.3	20.1
Germany, 1989	17.7	65.0	7.1	10.2
Ireland, 1987	67.8	7.3	10.0	14.9
Netherlands, 1992	11.3	64.6	16.3	7.7
Spain, 1990	56.3	22.0	2.4	19.3
Sweden, 1990	71.9	17.8	0.0	10.3
Switzerland, 1992	28.7	6.9	40.5	23.9
UK, 1993	64.0	20.0	7.0	9.0
USA, 1987	35.5	13.3	29.2	22.1

Note: The totals for some countries may not sum to 100 due to rounding.
Source: Wagstaff *et al.*, 1999, Table 2, p.268

cost of treatment is paid by the patient in many social insurance systems. In many low-income countries, however, over half of the costs of health care are paid for 'out of pocket', by paying the fee demanded for each episode of treatment. This dependence on individual payment restricts access to health care in low- and middle-income countries.

Table 10.2 shows how health care is financed in some high-income countries. The table divides financing into four categories: taxation, social insurance, private insurance and direct 'out of pocket' payments. As you can see, the mix varies greatly. Only in the USA and Switzerland does more than half of health-care finance come from private insurance or direct payments. In Scandinavia, Ireland, Spain and the UK, taxes are the main source of finance. And in Germany, France and the Netherlands, social insurance provides most of the health care. The 'social insurance' element for the UK refers to National Insurance payments, some of which go to fund the NHS. Where efforts have been made to achieve universal access to health care, as in most of the countries in Table 10.2, cover for those who cannot pay is subsidized by the state. (The dates of the data sets reflect the time taken to compile comparable data sets from a wide range of sources.)

Tax-based financing of health care does not necessarily imply public sector provision. In the UK, the NHS was designed, at its inception in 1948, to use mainly tax-based finance to fund public sector provision. Internationally, however, countries vary considerably in their mix of providers, a mix determined by the history of the health services in each country, as well as by competition and political in-fighting. Tax funds can be and are used to buy health care from 'voluntary' (or non-profit) and private ('for-profit') facilities. Indeed, this is an issue arousing considerable political passion in the UK as we write, and we shall come back to it in Section 10.4. But first we shall look at how the variety of forms of health-care delivery and finance can be explained.

■ ■ ■ 10.2.2 Market failure in health-care delivery

There is such diversity in the ways in which health care is delivered because governments have, on the whole, been reluctant to leave the delivery of health care to the market. You have seen, in Chapters 5 and 8, that under conditions of perfect competition the market should deliver an efficient allocation of all goods. However, as this section will show, an unregulated market in health care is unlikely to fulfil the assumptions of perfect competition, and so would fail to be allocatively efficient.

Question	Look back at Chapter 5, Section 5.2.1. What assumptions underlie the model of perfect competition? What further condition necessary for perfect competition to yield a Pareto optimal outcome is explained in Chapter 8, Section 8.3.4?

The model of perfect competition is based on four assumptions. Perfect competition assumes that all firms and consumers are price-takers, that all firms and consumers are well informed, that the goods and services supplied are homogeneous, and that firms and consumers are free to enter and exit the market. The further condition is that, for perfect competition to be allocatively efficient, or yield a Pareto optimal outcome, there must be no externalities in the market. Economists have identified a number of reasons for believing that a free market in health-care delivery would fail to satisfy three of these conditions.

Informational asymmetry

It was explained in Chapter 5, Section 5.2.1, that a local fruit and vegetable market might approximate to the informational requirements of the model of perfect competition because consumers can easily discover the different prices and qualities available. For a market in health-care delivery, however, it is clear that most 'consumers' (i.e. patients) will not be experts in either the range of health-care services or the impact of these services on their own health. The need for diagnosis is a principal reason for seeking medical help. The fact that consumers do not know what is wrong with them, or what is needed to put it right, prevents them from shopping around in the way they might if buying a kilo of tomatoes. 'Informational asymmetry' is the term given to such a situation, in which one party to a market exchange – in this case, the health-care provider – has more information than the other – in this case, the patient as a consumer of health care.

Product variability

In the model of perfect competition, the products supplied by one firm are indistinguishable from those supplied by another. But health-care services resemble 'customized' rather than 'generic' or homogeneous products. You may have heard of Savile Row, a street in London in which tailors still make clothes to measure, by hand. Such tailoring is extremely expensive, and it illustrates an important feature of health-care services, which often have to be tailored to the needs of the patient. Not everyone needs to have the same tests done if they have a rash on their arm; not everyone needs the same amount of time to recuperate from an operation. If a free market were allowed to handle these transactions, it might be necessary for consumers to negotiate a separate price for every service delivered. Again, this means that it is difficult for patients to shop around and, therefore, difficult for competitive pressures to operate.

Externalities

Chapter 8 noted that externalities are an important source of market failure, and externalities play a role in the analysis of health care. For many treatments, the patient is the main beneficiary, so the external effects might be minimal. In fact health care is, in economic terms, largely a private rather than a public good (Chapter 9, Section 9.2.1). For example, hospital beds are rival goods, in that one patient's consumption reduces the number available for others, as waiting lists in the UK NHS testify. Most treatments are also excludable, in that providing health care for one patient does not benefit the others; your filling does not stop my toothache. Some public health interventions, however, do involve externalities. Vaccination against infectious disease, for example, benefits both the person treated and the many other people with whom that individual comes into contact. So vaccination produces positive externalities (Chapters 3, 8 and 9), in the form of a reduced risk of infection for people coming into contact with the vaccinated person. The benefits to society are greater than the benefits to the vaccinated person.

As Maureen Mackintosh explained in Chapter 9, Section 9.2, externalities can lead to a divergence between private and social costs. The analysis showed that in a perfectly competitive market, negative externalities generated in production, that is, externalities that impose costs on others, imply that equilibrium output in the market is too high, since output decisions take into account only private costs of production, and not full social costs.

Question	Can you think of an example of a production process that generates *positive* externalities for other producers?

A classic if homely example is beekeeping: the bees pollinate nearby apple orchards, creating 'external' benefits for apple producers, that is, a useful input for which they do not pay.

Vaccinations also generate positive externalities and these too can be analysed in a market framework. However, these externalities affect *demand* decisions and hence consumption, not the costs of production. If vaccinations are supplied in a market, people's demand for vaccinations depends only on the benefits for themselves, and they do not take account of the benefits for others. Hence total demand for vaccinations will be below the market optimum.

Figure 10.1 illustrates this point, on the assumption that vaccinations are sold on a perfectly competitive market. In the figure, the line labelled D_p is the private demand curve for vaccinations. The curve labelled *MSB* is the marginal social benefit curve: it traces the total benefits – for both the consumer of the vaccination and others – of the last vaccination purchased. The *MSB* curve lies to the right of the private demand curve because there are external benefits produced by each quantity of vaccinations purchased.

Exercise 10.1

1 Mark on Figure 10.1 the private market equilibrium price and quantity demanded. Then identify the social optimum output, and the market price that would have to be set to sell that output.
2 Comment briefly on the policies that might move the market to the social optimum quantity of vaccinations.

Figure 10.1
A positive consumption externality in a market for vaccinations

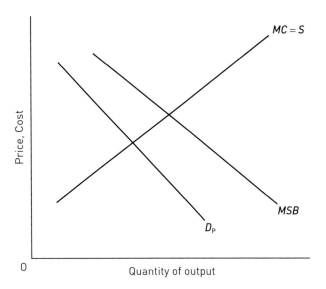

For these three reasons, a free market in health-care delivery would not be allocatively efficient.

▣ ▣ ■ 10.2.3 Market failure in health-care finance and insurance

But what about the financing of health care? Even if the market cannot deliver health care efficiently, a market solution might be an efficient way to pay for health care. Since the need for health care is uneven and unpredictable for individuals, people who have to finance their health care themselves often take out insurance rather than paying for health care as they need it. So the market for health-care finance involves considerations that are specific to insurance markets. Once again, we shall find that the assumptions of the model of perfect competition do not hold in the market for health insurance.

Insurance can help people to cope with the uncertainties of life. An individual's future health status is uncertain in that the health outcomes associated with future courses of action are not known. Will jogging in an urban area protect someone from coronary heart disease, provoke an asthma attack, cause irreparable damage to the knees or lead to serious injury in a traffic accident? What is the *risk* of each of the adverse outcomes? In a risky activity such as jogging on busy roads, the individual does not know the outcome with any certainty but can assess the probability of each possible outcome. This is the basis of insurance, and private insurance offers protection against many contingencies.

Arrow (1963), however, has argued that the market fails to offer individuals health-care insurance in many situations where it would clearly be desirable for such insurance to be available. This section analyses the strengths and limitations of private insurance.

Probability and private insurance

Insurance works on probabilities. Private insurance companies spend large sums of money trying to work out the probabilities of various calamities occurring to identifiable groups of people. The probabilities of particular occurrences can become rather stable and predictable for large groups of people. No individual knows whether they will fall ill and be unable to work next year, but it is possible to work out with reasonable precision what percentage of a large group of people, who are similar in age and general health, will become ill over the period.

So insurance works by identifying groups with predictable probabilities of incurring a given problem, and then charging them all a sum that allows the unlucky ones to receive compensation. Let us take the example of sickness benefit insurance payments, which are made if you fall ill while working. Suppose that a private insurance company knows that there is a 0.5 per cent chance of someone like you being off work in any month, and pays you £800 if you are off work. The premium that the insurance company will charge will be 0.5 per cent × £800 plus a mark-up to cover its administrative costs and profits.

Exercise 10.2

Suppose a group of people that includes you has a 1 in a 100 chance of being ill in any year, and that the average cost to the insurance company is £2500 per illness episode, plus £5 per person for administration and to make a profit. What annual premium will the insurance company charge?

Formally, if the probability of requiring a given compensation Z is p, and the administrative costs plus profit are A, the premium is:

$$pZ + A$$

You will pay if you can afford it and are sufficiently worried about the possibility. The insurance company will accept your premium if they think that, on average, they will make a profit. That is the principle of private insurance. To make it work, several conditions are essential.

First, enough people have to be insured to make the calculated probabilities reliable. This condition is called the 'law of large numbers'. In small groups of people, the proportion that will be ill at any time will vary greatly from year to year. But with very large groups, the average sickness rate becomes much more predictable. As a result, risks can be pooled efficiently.

Second, the probability that any one individual needs compensation has to be independent of the probability of the same problem for others. If your friend becomes ill it must not influence your state of health. Otherwise, the insurance company might have to pay out to a large number of people simultaneously, and so the amounts it will have to pay out will not be stable. Infectious diseases are obviously a problem here.

Third, the probability of the insured disaster must be less than one. If $p = 1$ the problem is certain to happen. If you are already sick or disabled, health insurance to cover the condition would cost at least as much as the treatment. This means the most vulnerable people in society can find it difficult to buy certain forms of insurance.

Fourth, people must not be able to influence the probability of the insured event occurring. Hence pregnancy is hard to insure against, and so is unemployment. You have seen this source of market failure before in Chapter 9, Section 9.5.1. It is called 'moral hazard'. The market fails to work efficiently in this case because the insurance company lacks good information on the actions of the insured person, which can influence the sums paid out.

Fifth, the insurer also needs good information about the risks attached to each individual. Otherwise, some high-risk people may represent themselves as low risks and so pay insufficient premiums. This in turn pushes up the costs for others. If the result is that truly low-risk individuals find average premiums rising to a point at which insuring themselves is no longer worth while, they will drop out, further raising the costs for others. This form of market failure is called 'adverse selection'.

| Question | What does this analysis suggest about the likely boundaries of private health-care insurance? |

The conditions for efficient private insurance are stringent. Taken together, they suggest that private health-care insurers are likely to avoid or charge very big premiums to high-risk individuals or individuals wanting insurance against new and unpredictable health risks.

The dynamics of the private insurance industry further undermine the prospects for allocative efficiency in private health-care insurance. Risk pooling means that there is substantial scope for insurance companies to benefit from economies of scale. Larger companies will, by pooling more risks, have more predictable outgoings. In principle, there is no limit to the benefits of pooling, and there are substantial economies of scale to be had in processing the collection of premiums and the payment of claims. It is likely, therefore, that an unregulated market for health-care insurance will become highly concentrated, creating monopoly power and hence another source of market failure.

The conditions for efficient private insurance also imply distributional problems. The highest premiums may be demanded of those on low incomes. Some people will be unable to acquire private health-care insurance however much they want or need it. If others in society want these people to be insured, some form of redistribution will be necessary.

Social insurance

So, private health-care insurance is problematic and is unlikely to be sufficient if society – however defined – wishes all its members to be insured to cover the costs of health care. Some people will be excluded by a lack of income, others by the nature of the risks themselves – given the market failures in private insurance – or by their own particular probability of succumbing to these risks.

Social insurance

Social insurance is compulsory and universal.

These problems can be used to explain the spread of social insurance in health care, as in other areas of concern (Chapter 9, Section 9.5.1). Have a careful look at the definitions of **social insurance** and **private insurance**. On these definitions, the state could in principle provide 'private' insurance. But social insurance would not be viable for a private insurer because it covers what are (privately) uninsurable risks.

So how can the state insure the uninsurable? The state has two major advantages over private insurers: its capacities for investigation and compulsion. By compelling universal coverage, the state can prevent low-risk people from refusing to enter a pooled system and hence reduce the costs of universal coverage.

Private insurance

Private insurance, in contrast, is not universal: access to it is based on actuarial calculations of risk and the acceptance of individual applications.

So, one explanation from economic theory for the rise and persistence of social insurance in health care is that it represents a response to insurance market failures. The boundaries between social and private insurance are contested in theory and are shifting in practice as the insurance industry develops. You should note, however, that social insurance schemes in practice combine risk pooling – true insurance – and redistribution from rich to poor. Risk pooling requires only that people make a common flat-rate payment, based on the average costs of the scheme. Social insurance payments, however, are often income-related, which implies that there is some redistribution between the better-off and the poorer in terms of the costs of access to the scheme, as well as redistribution towards those who fall ill (Section 10.3.1).

So the persistence of social insurance may be explained by its capacity to combine efficient insurance with rich-to-poor redistribution. It can be 'sold' as both an efficient safety net and an ethical system, and it has the additional advantage that, as contributors, people have rights to the benefits: there is none of the stigma attached to charity.

10.3 Ethics, rationing and redistribution

Section 10.2 suggested that health-care systems financed by social insurance are likely to be shaped by two principles: first, a commitment to redistribution and, second, the principle that everyone has a right to adequate health care. The aim of this section is to explore the implications of these two principles. First, we shall ask whether health care is in fact redistributive, in delivering to low-income people far more health care than they could buy from their incomes. Evidence from Europe and the USA strongly suggests that it is. Second, we shall discuss some of the issues arising out of the idea that people have rights to health care. Equity might be thought to require that these rights should be respected, but there are also reasons for believing that there may be limits to the rights that people have.

10.3.1 Is health care redistributive?

If poverty and ill health are associated, one way to weaken that link is to improve the health services that the poor receive. In the UK, as in many high-income countries, it is a widely accepted view that health care should be provided on the basis of *need* not income. Commitments of this kind are likely to be statements of principle rather than reality. In the UK, those with private medical insurance in addition to their right to publicly provided health care are the better-off, and articulate middle-class people may manage to extract more from the public system as well. However, if health-care systems in rich countries get anywhere close to distributing health care in response to need, then they are very redistributive indeed, in that they deliver to low-income people far more health care than they could ever buy from their incomes. This section looks briefly at whether this is the case.

There are two aspects to redistribution in health care: who pays for it and who gets it. In analysing both we can use the techniques you met in Chapter 9. Let us start with finance. Look at Figure 10.2.

This should look quite familiar to you. (Look back at Chapter 9 to check your understanding of Lorenz curves if necessary.) The gap between the curve labelled 'Lorenz curve for pre-tax income' and the diagonal line shows the inequality in pre-tax incomes. The new element is the line labelled 'health finance concentration curve'. This plots the cumulative proportion of total health-care financing (public and private) that is paid for by different cumulative proportions of the population, ranked by (equivalized) pre-tax income.

In interpreting Figure 10.2, take care not to think of the health finance concentration curve as indicating the distribution of *income*, as in the other Lorenz curves you have studied. Figure 10.2 is not comparing the distributions of original and post-tax incomes, as Figure 9.10 did. Instead Figure 10.2 shows the distribution of income and, with the health finance concentration curve, the distribution of the burden of payments for health care.

Figure 10.2
Analysing the progressiveness of health-care finance

Source: based on van Doorslaer and Wagstaff, 1993, Figures 3.5, 3.6

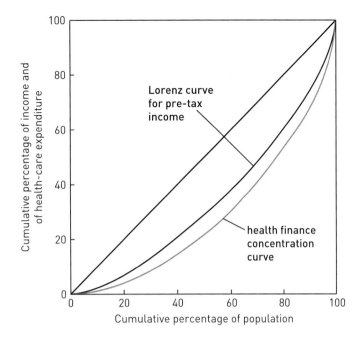

If the health finance concentration curve lies *outside* the Lorenz curve for pre-tax income, health-care finance is *progressive*: this means that lower-income groups pay a smaller proportion of their income for health care than do higher-income groups. If the health finance concentration curve lies *inside* the Lorenz curve for pre-tax income, health-care finance is *regressive*: this means that the burden falls more heavily on the poor in relative terms. If the two curves coincide, health finance is proportional: this means that the proportion of income used to pay for health care is the same for both lower- and higher-income groups.

Using this sort of analysis, researchers studied health-care financing in high-income countries in the early 1990s. They concluded (Wagstaff *et al.*, 1999) that the countries that rely most on private insurance – the USA and Switzerland – have *regressive* health-care financing systems overall, that is, health-care finance is more unequal than pre-tax incomes. It is easy to see why this is likely to be so. Private insurance payments depend on the extent of the insurance cover purchased, not on one's ability to pay. Those on low incomes purchase less, or no, medical insurance, but nevertheless tend to pay on average a higher proportion of their income for it.

The social insurance-based countries differ: in Germany and the Netherlands, the health finance system is also more unequal than pre-tax incomes, while in France it is *progressive*, that is, health-care finance is more equal than pre-tax incomes. Finally, in the largely tax-financed systems, health-care finance is either *proportional* – that is, distributed in a way similar to pre-tax incomes – or mildly progressive (more equal). The UK has progressive health-care finance, in part because private insurance is bought by the better-off but they are not permitted to opt out of tax payments.

That last point brings us to the provision of health care. Does health care go equally to rich and poor, or do those on lower incomes receive less care? To answer this question, we need to know how much care people *need*. As you would expect from the discussion in Section 10.1.1, poor people generally need more care than the better-off because they are ill more often and more severely. So health care is distributed *equally* only if those in equal need get equal care. But do they?

Figure 10.3
Concentration curves for actual and expected health-care utilization

Source: based on van Doorslaer *et al.*, 2000, p.556

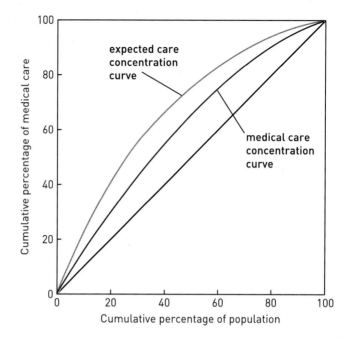

Economists have worked hard at analysing this question with reference to high-income countries. (The question is much less well explored for low-income countries.) In most cases the answer is no: that is, health care is distributed unequally in relation to need. Look at Figure 10.3. This is based on the Lorenz curve analysis but looks slightly different.

Look first at the curve labelled 'medical care concentration curve'. This shows the cumulative proportion of total medical care going to each cumulative proportion of the population, ranked by income (in this case, disposable income). Medical care is measured as the reported use of general practitioners (GPs), specialists and hospital care, valued on a comparable basis. As is typical in high-income countries, the poor use more health care. And so they should, they need more.

But is it enough? Are the poor getting their fair share? The curve labelled 'expected care concentration curve' is a measure of need. It is based on sample survey data that ask questions about self-reported levels of illness, including both general health and specific chronic conditions (which are particularly likely to be more prevalent among lower-income respondents). The answers are used to predict how much health care each individual needs, valued on the same basis as actual use.

Question	What does it mean if the concentration curve for expected health care lies above the concentration curve for actual care received, as is the case in Figure 10.3?

The implication is that those on lower incomes receive a lower proportion of the total care provided than they should do, were care provided on the basis of need. If the two curves coincide there is (estimated to be) equity in the distribution of health care in relation to need.

Estimates on this basis for high-income countries gave the following results. In all countries the lower-income groups received more care than the better-off: the medical care concentration curve was above the diagonal, as shown in Figure 10.3. The results differed, however, in terms of the type of care provided. If visits to a general practitioner

(GP) or primary doctor alone can be distinguished from specialist care (not all surveys distinguish the two, and not all countries have GPs), the distribution of primary (GP) care is close to the measure of need: that is, there is little evidence of inequity. (The countries surveyed included Denmark, Finland, Ireland, the Netherlands and the UK.) For a combination of GP and specialist care, however, half of the countries studied showed inequity in favour of the rich (the situation shown in Figure 10.3), including Finland, Sweden, the Netherlands and the USA. The greatest inequity was in the USA. Where specialist care could be separated from GP care, the provision was estimated to be biased towards the better-off in Denmark, Finland and the Netherlands, but not in the UK and Ireland.

These data have many limitations. For example, they assume that all care is of equal quality. If the quality of care for the more articulate and for those able to pay more is better, there is more inequity than is shown here; and this is likely to be particularly true where private medical insurance forms an important element of the financing.

Nevertheless, we can draw an important conclusion. The health-care systems of most of these countries, including the UK, are redistributive. To see this, consider financing and provision in the UK together. The financing is slightly progressive: that is, somewhat more equal than pre-tax income. The provision is also more equal than pre-tax income. Even when we allow for the ability of the better-off to buy more rapid or higher-quality care – not picked up here – those on low incomes are still receiving, on average, much more health care than they pay for. The association between poverty and ill health would be even stronger in the UK, and in many other rich countries, were it not for the health-care system. In the USA many millions of people lack insurance coverage, health finance is regressive and the indicators of care are inequitable in favour of the rich. But health-care systems that come close to including all citizens equitably, including those of most rich countries except the USA, strongly redistribute resources in the form of health care towards those on lower incomes.

▨ ◼ ◼ 10.3.2 The integration of claims

Resources are scarce, medical technology is developing all the time, life expectancy continues to rise, and in rich countries governments and voters could, if they chose to do so, spend more on health care through higher taxes and social insurance contributions. So should we allow public sector health systems to fund cosmetic plastic surgery – or is this a luxury that people should pay for out of their own pockets? Should we fund expensive heart operations that leave patients with low life expectancies?

Question	Before you read on, we would like you to imagine a situation in which there are two patients, Sita and Tim, who both need kidney transplants. However, there is only enough capacity to treat one of them, even though both will die quickly if untreated. You have to decide which patient is treated. What information would you ask for before making a decision about whom to treat?

One approach to allocating health care has been suggested by health economists working on non-market systems that try to allocate resources in response to need. It is based on making choices that result in the maximization of health across a population. To implement this approach, it is necessary to find out the benefits and costs of different treatments. A benefit–cost ratio can be constructed to express the benefits of a course of treatment as a percentage return on the costs of that treatment. Some treatments, such as hip replacements, might not cost very much and lead to a good quality of life for a long time (measured in quality-adjusted life years or QALYs). These treatments would have high benefit–cost ratios. Other treatments, such as heart operations, might lead to smaller increases in life expectancy and cost more, and so they would have lower benefit–cost ratios. To maximize the QALYs produced by the health-care system, we could try to rank all health-care treatments according to their benefit–cost ratios. One could then select the treatment with the highest benefit–cost ratio and work on down the list until the health-care budget runs out.

This idea has been much discussed in the context of European health-care systems, but it was the government of Oregon, a state in the USA, that was noted for implementing the QALY ranking procedure in the early 1990s. Government officials set priorities using information on QALYs and costs, and then consulted representatives of the citizens. They found that a few treatments needed to be moved up or down in the rankings, but the set of priorities that had emerged from the QALY maximization approach was accepted for the most part. This popular support is slightly surprising because the QALY has attracted much criticism from academics outside economics, especially medical experts and health philosophers (Anand and Wailoo, 2000). In what follows, we shall look at some of the objections that have been raised.

Rights and basic needs

We didn't tell you the ages of Sita or Tim. Is this relevant information? Suppose both are expected to live into their 70s if treated, but that Sita is 45 and Tim is 40. To whom would you give the transplant now? QALY maximization requires that the treatment goes to Tim, assuming that either patient would have a similar quality of life afterwards. But it is not clear that we *must* give Tim priority. You might think that Sita has a legitimate claim.

If you do not agree with the QALY approach in this case, it might be because you feel that basing the treatment decision on a five-year age difference for people who could have a life span of nearly 80 years seems somewhat arbitrary. In a sense, both Sita and Tim have something substantial to gain from the transplant – the rest of their lives; so some might say that both patients are equally entitled to the treatment. Many people have argued that everyone has a right to be as healthy as possible, and some economists have gone on to suggest that where these equal rights cannot be recognized because of resource constraints, people should be given equal *chances* of having their needs met.

For instance, one might flip a coin to determine who should be treated. In that case, they would be treated equally *ex ante* (a Latin phrase economists use to mean 'before the event'). Actually flipping a coin might be unacceptable, but other arbitrary rules could be, and have been, devised. One could set a budget each year and operate on all new cases until the funding runs out. This still leaves people untreated, but some might find it an acceptable if pragmatic approach, as it is based on the idea that people have the same rights to health care. But there are some arguments that suggest limits to the rights that people should have.

Responsibilities

With rights go responsibilities, or so we are told. People should be free to do certain things so long as they respect the rights of others. The sociologist Amitai Etzioni has been prominent in advocating this position through a social philosophy that came to be called 'communitarianism' (Etzioni, 1988). Communitarians believe that we should emphasize our duties to give to, and participate in, the local society. In North America at least, the push for rights has gone too far, they say, and Etzioni has proposed a ten-year moratorium on the creation of new rights. But what do responsibilities mean in health care? If a person's liver fails because of heavy drinking, have they fulfilled their responsibilities to themselves or others? The treatment of such patients might be given less priority.

The 'fair innings' argument

How would you feel if Sita were 25 and Tim were 70? If you felt that the claims were evenly balanced before, perhaps you now think Sita has a stronger claim. Tim has nearly matched the life expectancy of a man in a high-income country, while Sita may have over two-thirds of her life left. As the philosopher John Harris puts it, Tim has had a 'fair innings' but Sita has not. The transplant should be given to Sita so that she can have a fair innings too. The cost of the kidney transplant will be the same regardless of whom we treat, but Sita is expected to live much longer so the benefits are expected to be greater if she receives the treatment. This is how an advocate of QALY maximization would see things.

Contractual views

The idea that there might be a social contract between the governed and the rulers first came to prominence in the writings of the philosopher Jean Jacques Rousseau (1712–78) and was rejuvenated in 1972 with the publication of *A Theory of Justice* by the US philosopher John Rawls. To work out what a fair society would mean, Rawls invites us to consider a situation in which we negotiate with each other about what society will look like. But we do so from behind a *veil of ignorance*. We know what the lot of all the members of the society will be, but we don't know which particular slot any one individual will take up. So you would be invited to agree, for example, what the salaries or wages would be for all jobs, without knowing whether you would be the director of a multinational company or a waste removal operative. Rawls claims that one of the principles that would emerge from behind this veil of ignorance is the 'maximin' principle. This states that:

> Social and economic inequalities are to be arranged so that they are . . . to the greatest benefit of the least advantaged.
>
> *(Rawls, 1972, p.83)*

Rawls argues that people negotiating future social and economic arrangements would choose the 'maximin' principle because they would not know whether they would be among the most or the least advantaged members of the future society. Assuming that people are averse to risk, that is, that they want to 'play safe', they would be anxious, from behind the veil of ignorance, to ensure that the worst position in which they might find themselves would be as good as possible. Rawls interprets this idea of 'maximizing the minimum' condition of life in terms of primary goods, including health care and education, that no one would be willing to risk being without. In this view, health care goes to people because they need it, in that its provision is an essential component of an acceptable condition of life for the least advantaged members of society. It follows that, for Rawls, health care does *not* go to people because they will live longer and happier lives than others as a result, as is the case in the QALY approach.

Another strand of thought, related to but distinct from the contractual view, can be found in work that argues for the importance of public deliberation. As Chapter 8 noted, there is evidence of support for what some economists have called 'procedural utility', that is, the view that we derive intrinsic value from being involved in decision-making regardless of the outcome. In the UK, some health authorities have commissioned public consultations, although support for the idea is somewhat reduced by the fact that most lay people are not sufficiently informed about the options and issues. This is not to say that public consultation is not viable in the long run – the BBC has been doing it for years with some success – but doing it properly is an expensive process. More importantly, it leaves unanswered the question of what sort of views should be reflected in the determination of entitlements. There are clearly some views that we would not expect a national health service to listen to, which brings us full circle to the problem of what kinds of claims should count.

In this section we have seen that the health-care systems of most high-income countries are redistributive, redistributing resources in the form of health care towards lower-income groups. We have also examined several approaches to the issue of integrating competing claims on resources in public sector health-care systems. There is no simple answer to the question of which claims should count. In Section 10.4 we shall analyse a putative solution to another issue that has featured in debates about public sector health-care systems. This is the question of whether they are wasteful in their use of resources.

Case study: Managed competition in the NHS

This extended case study critically examines a specific attempt to reform a public sector health-care system. The reform discussed is one that took place in the UK National Health Service (NHS), but it is illustrative of the economic reforms that have sought to bring competition into previously monopolistic public sector social provision. Increasingly, the distinction between public and private sectors is blurring, largely because governments are looking for ways of bringing private sector incentives, mechanisms and funds into the provision of public services. This NHS reform was known as the 'internal market' but, as we shall see, its lessons may be relevant to other uses of market exchange in the NHS, including buying health care from overseas. This particular case study illustrates those lessons in the context of a major health-care reform. It also serves to show how you might apply and combine some of the general principles of microeconomic analysis you have been studying throughout this book.

Aneurin Bevan, Minister of Health in the 1946– 51 Labour Government, established the National Health Service (NHS) on 5 July 1948. Before that date hospitals in the UK were either voluntary, that is, funded by benefactors and fees, or managed by the local authority and financed in part by local taxes. By the 1930s over half the income of voluntary hospitals came from patients' fees, GPs charged fees and municipal hospitals raised a small part of their income from fees. The aim of the NHS was to ensure that equally good health-care services were available to everyone, including those who had previously been unable to pay. Central government brought under its control all the voluntary and local authority hospitals it needed for the NHS, to be financed out of general taxation. GPs became private contractors to the NHS. GP and hospital services were to be provided free at the point of delivery. When charges were introduced for spectacles and dentures, Bevan resigned in protest at this early departure from the principle of making health care available to the whole population free at the point of delivery.

The expectation was that demand for health-care services and hence expenditure on them would decline as the health of the population improved. The reality was rather different (Peden, 1985, pp.155–6, 190–1). Freed from expenditure constraints imposed by the limited resources of benefactors and political resistance to local tax increases, hospitals set out to achieve the best possible standards of care and to introduce new technologies (drugs, equipment and surgical procedures) when they had the resources to do so.

The expansion and improvement of health care under the NHS encountered two main difficulties. First, central government funding was necessarily limited and the financial constraints imposed on the NHS led to the appearance of waiting lists, even though expenditure on the NHS as a percentage of GPD rose in the 1960s (Peden, 1985, p.191). With no fees to raise to curtail demand, and with technological progress providing more and more expensive new treatments, hospitals used waiting lists to balance competing claims on their resources. Politicians and commentators who favoured free markets accused the NHS of inefficiency, as the monopoly provider of health care free at the point of delivery. Second, in the absence of any other information, the initial allocation of resources among the NHS hospitals and GPs was based on the resources each hospital and GP had been using before 1948 (a procedure sometimes known as 'grandfathering'). The effect was to perpetuate to some extent pre-NHS inequalities in the provision of health care among different regions and social groups (Peden, 1985, p.190).

Little could be done about these problems under the initial NHS management structure. Hospitals and GPs were administered separately and central government lacked the information necessary to reallocate resources more equally (Klein, 1983, Chapter 2). In 1974 the NHS was reorganized to allow greater centralization in the allocation of resources. The intention was to implement the original guiding principle of providing equally good health care everywhere, by allocating resources according to need. The RAWP (Resource Allocation Working Party) formula measured need in terms of the population served by a hospital or GP, with adjustments made for factors such as the proportion of children and old people and indicators of poverty, given the association between poverty and ill health

(Section 10.1). The perception remained among policy makers impressed by the efficiency gains provided by competition in free or lightly regulated markets that the NHS was wasteful of resources.

Let us now examine some of the issues surrounding the introduction of managed competition into the NHS in 1991.

What economists said about plans for managed competition

In the 1980s, Alan Enthoven, an American economist and long-time observer of the UK health scene, was invited to provide some ideas for what was to be one of the most radical and, in some ways, innovative economic reforms of the Thatcher era. His main proposal was that competition should be introduced into the NHS while leaving intact much of its public sector status. Enthoven's proposals were not for a free market, but to bring the essential benefits of competition into the public sector in a controlled manner by creating market-like relationships within the NHS (an 'internal market'). As he wrote:

> The markets for health insurance and health care are not naturally competitive like the markets for transportation, financial services, automobiles or jogging shoes. 'Deregulation' will not make them competitive. In a 'free market' made up of health plans on the supply side and individual consumers on the demand side, without carefully drawn rules and without active management by sponsors, the health plans would be free to pursue profits or survival by using numerous competitive strategies that would destroy efficiency and equity, and that individual consumers would be powerless to counteract.
>
> *(Enthoven, 1988, p.87)*

Enthoven discussed a number of issues that would be critical to the functioning of markets within the NHS. In particular, he noted that 'a competitive market will not automatically produce high quality care; especially to the extent the market is characterized

Case study continued

by poor information about quality' (Enthoven, 1988, p.108). He emphasized the importance of information about quality (of health care and outcomes), if quality was to be maintained. And he noted the importance of encouraging new entrants into health-care provision as a way of maintaining competitive behaviour. Well-informed, sophisticated buyers who could pool risks adequately and monitor quality would be central to the successful application of market principles to health.

Akehurst *et al.* (undated) provided a useful summary of some of the issues that economists raised prior to the implementation of the NHS internal market. We can divide them into two categories: efficiency and equity.

First, government-run organizations are frequently accused of failing to produce output at the lowest possible cost for a particular level of output. Competition between hospitals and other health-care providers should encourage both to drive costs down towards the minimum possible costs identified by the marginal and average cost curves (Chapter 4, Section 4.3.1 and Chapter 5, Section 5.3).

Second, it was felt that there could be improvements at the level of capacity planning. Because money would follow patients, providers would have an incentive to provide specialized services to patients outside their own geographical regions. It might then be possible to benefit from economies of scale. Furthermore, it was felt that a number of teaching hospitals had capacity that was under-utilized. Such hospitals would be able to generate extra revenue by using this surplus capacity.

On the question of equity, it was felt that the risks might outweigh the opportunities. A public health-care system in which access is free at the point of delivery is likely to produce results that are equitable, in the sense of not discriminating against those who are unwilling or unable to pay. But against this, there was a concern that specialization of service provision would mean that many patients would have to travel further for treatment. Those on low incomes might find the costs difficult to meet. Others argued that competition would also succeed in driving down wages in a sector of the economy in which wages were already perceived to be low.

The ability of patients or their doctors to choose health-care providers on their behalf was felt to offer an element of consumer choice that would favour patients and facilitate competition.

Implementation and results

Managed competition in the NHS, or the 'internal market', was an attempt to introduce competitive pressures into the NHS, while seeking to preserve its commitments to free health care at the point of delivery and to ensure the availability of equally good health care everywhere in the UK. A competitive market requires buyers and sellers, so an 'internal market' was created by dividing the institutions of the NHS into purchasers and providers. Health authorities as purchasers would use their allocation of funds from central government to buy services for their patients from hospitals, with the allocation of funds continuing to reflect the calculation of need. Incentives were put in place to encourage GPs to become budget holders, purchasing services for their patients directly from hospitals and seeking to secure the greatest amount of services with the budget at their disposal by 'shopping around'. Hospitals could opt to become 'hospital trusts', with incentives to generate extra income by winning new business by supplying services at a lower cost than their competitors.

Before the changes, there was much lobbying, particularly by the medical profession, to have the internal market dropped. For a while after the changes were implemented, very little happened. Health authorities and hospitals dealt with each other via block contracts – and these contracts were much like the old budgets, amounting to a single payment for all the services previously provided by the health-care provider. Health-care providers were supposed to make a surplus of 6 per cent (the word 'profit' was not used), which could then be ploughed back into the hospital's activities.

After the election of the Labour government in 1997, the experiment officially ended, just when some might say it was about to get going. Nonetheless, there are some very important general lessons about the operation of markets to be learnt, and a number of researchers in economics and other disciplines have evaluated aspects of the reforms. Appropriate data are not available to evaluate all the changes, but researchers at the King's Fund, a health-policy think-tank based in London, noted a number of outcomes (Le Grand *et al.*, 1998).

Equity

Two of the most important ethical issues raised by the NHS internal market are 'cream-skimming' and 'two-tierism'. Cream-skimming is the practice, evident in parts of the US health-care system that are in some ways similar to GP budget-holders, of discriminating against high-cost patients such as the elderly and the infirm in favour of low-cost patients. The internal market seemed to give GP budget-holders a financial incentive towards cream-skimming, which would help to avoid over-spending their budget. However, Goodwin (1998) found, after reviewing the research, that GP budget-holders 'have not undertaken cream-skimming despite the theoretical financial incentives to do so' (p.58). The explanation is threefold: budgets were generous, there was no personal financial penalty incurred by GPs who overspent and the government reimbursed GP budget-holders for the costs of treating an individual patient if they exceeded £5000 (Goodwin, 1998, p.58).

The term 'two-tierism' expresses the fear that the NHS internal market would create a two-tier system of GPs, with the patients of budget-holding GPs enjoying better access to health care than those of other GPs. Hospitals would favour patients from budget-holding GPs whose money they could spend on reducing waiting lists. Since it was expected that GPs serving disadvantaged urban areas would lack the administrative support that budget-holding required, this would reinforce existing inequalities in NHS health care. Goodwin (1998) found that 'most commentators accept that fundholding [budget-holding] has exacerbated two-tierism' (p.56). For example, patients of budget-holding GPs faced significantly shorter times for elective surgery. It is important to note that the two-tier issue 'arose not because of the intrinsic nature of an internal market,

but because this particular internal market had two kinds of purchaser [GP budget-holders and GP non-budget-holders]' (Le Grand *et al.*, 1998, p.124).

Efficiency

There is some evidence that cost per unit of activity (a measure of average cost) in the NHS fell more rapidly after 1991 than before and newly created hospital trusts had lower costs than other hospitals (Le Grand *et al.*, 1998, pp.120–1). Whether the superior cost performance of trusts can be attributed to the internal market is a controversial issue. Perhaps hospitals opting for trust status were able to do so in part because they already had lower unit costs. It is also possible that, insofar as falling costs reflected advances in medical technology, they would have been secured without the internal market.

A major issue in the public debate about the NHS reforms was the increase in management costs that the internal market was expected to cause. The decrease in cost per unit of activity implies that, if there was an increase in management costs that can be attributed to the internal market, it was outweighed by cost savings in other areas. It is not certain that management costs did rise, because there was some reclassification of senior nursing and health-care professional posts as managerial (Hamblin, 1998, p.105).

Market structure

On the supply side, between 25 per cent of hospitals and 38 per cent of patient episodes were conducted in situations in which there was some degree of monopoly power. So in terms of market structure there were reasons to suppose that competition would not be widespread. When it came to demand-side issues, the evidence was mixed. There was some evidence that providers and purchasers developed agreements lasting beyond a year to provide a secure market that could justify investment in new low-cost techniques, such as non-invasive ('keyhole') surgery. Contracts appeared to evolve and did not change radically every year. In part this cut down on negotiation costs, but it allowed providers some security of demand, on which they could plan investment.

Case study continued

An essential element for competition in practice is that customers can switch between suppliers with relative ease. There are a number of reasons why people do not change the brand of soap powder they use or the financial institution at which they bank. When GPs were asked about their willingness to refer patients to different hospitals, those who held their own budgets were much more willing to refer to hospitals that involved the patient travelling relatively long distances. In densely populated urban areas, and for relatively common ailments, travel probably played a relatively minor role in inhibiting competition. But one can see that competition in these markets depends on the willingness of patients to travel, as well as the referral behaviour of GPs, and that in rural areas, or for rarer conditions, both factors could serve to reduce the competitive pressures faced by hospitals.

Information

We have noted that information about service quality and outcomes is essential to the successful operation of markets, but there were serious problems with the information in the 'internal market'. The information systems were poor: there was a lack of data about current service provision and doubts about the accuracy of the data that was available; there was poor information about health needs and only crude information about costs and activity. The rise of information and communication technologies and pressures to reform have, in recent years, resulted in some improvements to these information systems.

However, these remarks apply to the large information systems operated by health regions and hospitals. GPs have access to more immediate before and after information about the health of their patients. For many conditions, GPs refer on a regular basis and so are well placed to monitor and evaluate service quality. But changes in the relationship between GPs and providers went beyond the flow of information. One anecdotal indicator, taken seriously nonetheless, was found in a reversal of the direction in which Christmas cards were sent. GPs had sent cards to consultants but, as the market turned the consultants into competitors looking for business, they began to send cards to GPs.

Questions

1 When introducing market mechanisms into a public service like the NHS, it is not always easy to predict what the impacts on efficiency are going to be: Do you agree or not agree? Why?

2 'Market mechanisms are likely to be produce unfair outcomes.' Does the case support this view? Discuss the evidence for your view.

Health service reform will remain on the political agenda for many years to come. This case study has highlighted the difficulty of achieving a balance between equity and efficiency, of preserving the distinctive values of the NHS while introducing competition into its operation. In the future it is likely that NHS reform will continue to pivot on dilemmas of this kind. However, it also seems likely that the infusion of competition will take a different form.

Redefining the National Health Service

The NHS will be decentralized with a plurality of providers operating within a framework of clear national standards regulated independently . . .

Changing it from a monolithic, centrally run, monopoly provider of services to a values-based system where health care providers – in the public, private and voluntary sectors – provide comprehensive services to NHS patients with a common ethos: free at the point of use, based on patient need and informed choice and not on their ability to pay . . .

NHS care does not have to be delivered exclusively by line-managed NHS organizations but by a range of organizations working with the national framework of standards and inspection.

(Alan Milburn, Secretary of State for Health, 2002)

Look back to Section 10.2.1.

Question

Look back to Section 10.2.1. How would you interpret Alan Milburn's 'redefinition' of the NHS in the light of our comments on health-care delivery in an international context?

There will be no change to the core values that have informed the NHS from its inception: the goal of health care free at the point of delivery or use and the goal of equally good health care for everyone everywhere. However, the much more recent introduction of market-based methods of delivering that

health care seems likely to remain in the forefront of NHS reform, although in a rather different form. The aim of NHS reform for the foreseeable future seems likely to lie in a more straightforward style of privatization than that exemplified by the *'internal market'*. Instead the emphasis will be placed upon *external* contracting, buying in health-care services from public, private and voluntary sector providers. In this way there seems to be a prospect of the UK losing some aspects of its distinctive system of health care and moving towards the mixed systems of health-care provision to be found in many other countries.

10.4 Conclusion

The economic analysis of health status and health care tells us something about a particular market, the generality and applicability of microeconomic principles, the normative nature of economics, and the extent to which economics can be enriched and tested by empirical applications. You might want to draw up a list of points that are reinforced or changed by some of the issues raised in this chapter, but let us conclude with a few notes of our own.

Perhaps the fundamental point is that health status is closely linked to economic status: the poor have a lower life expectancy and a greater likelihood of illness than the rich. In view of this link, it is important to remember that health care is often redistributive, in that it enables the poor to secure more health care than they would be able to purchase from their incomes. The fact that health care is redistributive reflects the extensive role of the state in most health-care systems, even though there is great diversity. This in turn is a response to the existence of market failures in both the delivery and the finance of health care. It is also a reflection of widespread views in society about equity, inequality and rights.

Health-care systems need to change, and the medical technologies with which the health professionals respond evolve on a continual basis. The managed competition experiment is just one example of the innovation and change that are features of health-care systems the world over. New drugs and equipment often embody the results of impressive scientific research, but their cost may leave those at the bottom end of the economic spectrum excluded from an ever-increasing set of opportunities. Balancing the hot pursuit of market opportunities against the protection of basic human rights and the promotion of human health is a dilemma that all modern economies now seem to face.

Questions for review and discussion

Question 1 Figure 10.4 shows the market for a particular vaccination. The industry is perfectly competitive but, in this market, there are positive externalities affecting consumption. Insert labels from the list below so as to label the diagram correctly.

Figure 10.4
Market for a
particular
vaccination

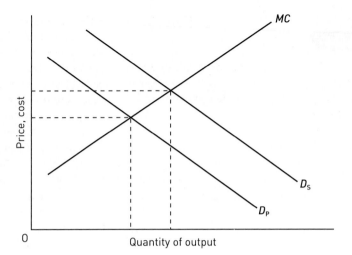

Q_P the free market equilibrium output
Q_S the allocatively efficient output
P_P the free market equilibrium price
P_S the allocatively efficient price
MC the marginal cost curve
D_P the free market demand curve
D_S the social demand curve

Question 2   Suppose that an insurance company quotes you a premium of £25 per month to insure you against loss of earnings if you are off work through sickness. The company will pay you £1000 per month if you are off work through sickness. This premium includes £5 for administration and profit mark-up. What is the insurance company's assessment of your probability of missing work through sickness in any month?

....

....

Question 3   Say which statement from the list below best explains what is meant by 'adverse selection' in an insurance market:

A ❑   The person insured has an incentive to change their behaviour so as to receive compensation to the detriment of the insurance company's profits.

B ❑   High- and low-risk people are both insured at an average premium. Low-risk people will feel this to be expensive and will drop out of the market.

C ❑   Asymmetric information leads people to be under-insured because they select unsuitable policies to cover their particular risks.

Question 4   Figure 10.5(a) shows the Lorenz curve for the pre-tax income and the health finance concentration curve for a hypothetical country called Erewhon.

Figure 10.5(b) shows the medical care concentration curve and the expected care concentration curve for Erewhon over the same period of time.

Say which statement correctly describes health care finance and provision in Erewhon.

Figure 10.5
(a) Lorenz curve for pre-tax income and health finance concentration curve for Erewhon
(b) Medical care concentration curve and expected care concentration curve for Erewhon over the same period

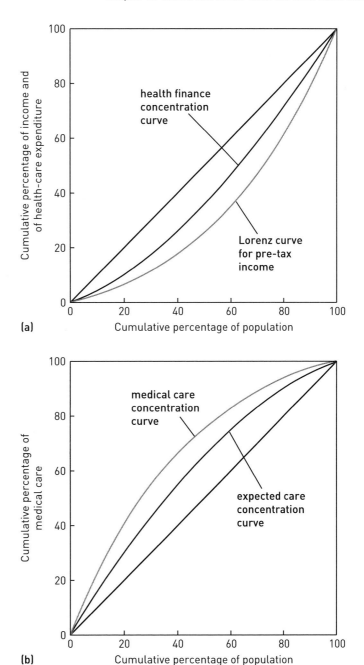

(a)

(b)

A ❑ Health-care finance is progressive; lower-income groups receive a higher proportion of total care than they would on the basis of need.

B ❑ Health-care finance is progressive; lower-income groups receive a lower proportion of total care than they would on the basis of need.

C ❑ Health-care finance is regressive; lower-income groups receive a lower proportion of total care than they would on the basis of need.

D ❑ Health-care finance is regressive; lower-income groups receive a higher proportion of total care than they would on the basis of need.

Macroeconomics

11

Macroeconomics and economic policy

Graham Dawson and Vivienne Brown

Concepts

- aggregate economy analysis
- Keynesian economics
- objectives, instruments and targets of policy
- economic liberalism
- monetarism
- discretionary policy and policy rules

Objectives

After studying this chapter you should be able to:

- appreciate the difference between Keynesian economics and economic liberalism
- understand the nature of the aggregate economy
- understand the relation between values and economic analysis
- appreciate the broad outline of recent trends in inflation, growth and unemployment in some of the main industrial economies.

11.1 Introduction

Chapters 12 to 20 are largely concerned with the performance of national economies and the scope for governments to improve that performance. This chapter will present the essential historical context to debates among economists about these issues as an introduction to the analysis of later chapters. For most national economies in the industrial world the last decade or so has been characterized by a relative stability of performance measured in terms of inflation, growth and unemployment. But to note this steadiness is not to imply that the performance of these economies has been entirely satisfactory. The persistence of weak economic performance at the national level is most clearly visible in the problem of unemployment among members of the European Union (EU). In the controversy surrounding policy responses to this problem we can detect the echoes of intellectual revolutions in economic theory over the past seventy years or so.

11.1.1 Macroeconomic stability?

The UK economy is currently experiencing its longest unbroken expansion since quarterly national accounts data began, with GDP now having grown for 50 consecutive quarters. With volatility in the UK economy at historically low levels and now the lowest in the G7, the domestic stability delivered by the Government's macroeconomic framework puts the UK in a strong position to respond to the global economic challenges of the next decade.

(HM Treasury, UK Budget Statement, *2005)*

It is certainly true that the UK economy as a whole, or the macroeconomy, has enjoyed a relatively long period of stability and few would argue with the claim that government policy has contributed to this satisfactory performance. In fact the UK's recent steadiness is not unique. Macroeconomic stability has been a salient feature of the industrialized world since the recovery from the recession of the early 1990s and policy in the USA, the UK and the Eurozone has contributed to this performance.

A recent study (Martin and Rowthorn, 2004) calculated the volatility of US GDP growth since the late nineteenth century and found that it had more than halved from 1973–83 to 1993–2003. Figure 11.1(a) puts this recent stability into historical context, while Figure 11.1(b) shows that the US performance is part of a wider trend among the major industrial economies.

As reported in *The Economist* ('A smoother ride', 18 March 2004), Martin and Rowthorn (2004) concluded that 'changes in monetary policy should take most of the credit for the reduction in macroeconomic volatility'. Monetary policy is the setting of interest rates and in the UK and the Eurozone governments have followed the US example and devolved interest rate decisions to independent central banks, such as the Bank of England in the UK. Chapters 12 and 13 explain the importance of money in the economy and how monetary policy works. It seems that central bankers have learned how to keep inflation under control and that this low-inflationary framework has contributed to the steadiness in the rate of output growth.

The stability of inflation and growth in recent years has been accompanied by another kind of stability, namely a period of relative intellectual calm in the debate about the role of government in the national economy. There is no credible challenge to the priority

Figure 11.1
Macroeconomic
stability

Source:
The Economist,
'A smoother ride',
18 March 2004

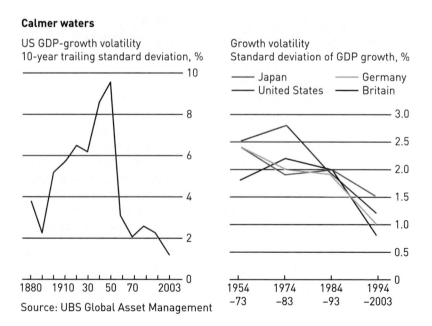

that policy makers and central bankers accord to the control of inflation. It is as though for the time being a settlement has been reached in the great and on occasion furious debate between the advocates of *laissez-faire* and the proponents of government intervention in the national economy. Those who believed in a policy of *laissez-faire* argued that the government should allow private individuals operating in markets to resolve the problem of unemployment, while those who made the case for intervention claimed that the government should itself engage in economic activity in an effort to provide more jobs.

In order to understand the current priority given to the control of inflation and the lack of a serious challenge to this policy stance, it is helpful to review the intellectual revolutions that have shaped contemporary economic thought about the role of government in the national economy. Two periods of upheaval stand out. In the 1930s the English economist John Maynard Keynes developed a radically novel way of analysing the national economy in order to provide a sound intellectual foundation for government intervention aimed at curing mass unemployment. In the 1970s neo-liberal thinkers such as Milton Friedman and Friedrich von Hayek seized upon the simultaneous occurrence of high inflation and high unemployment after years of Keynesian policies as evidence for the *laissez-faire* argument that only private individuals, freed from as much government regulation as possible, can create the conditions for full employment. They would both applaud the broad direction of current policies in most of the industrial world, with governments setting a low-inflation agenda and leaving the rest to markets.

However, it would be wrong to conclude from the current consensus on the importance of keeping inflation under control and the prevalence of low inflation outcomes that the problems of growth and unemployment have also been solved. Figure 11.1(b) shows that GDP growth in Germany and Japan has recently been less volatile than in previous decades but *The Economist* adds an important qualification: 'The snag is that in these countries output growth has settled around a much lower average rate.' The implications of low GDP growth for another aspect of the performance of national economies, unemployment, can be explored by considering the case of Germany, a core member of the European Union.

▨ ▨ ■ 11.1.2 Europe's unemployment problem

In the spring of 2005 the French and Dutch referendums on the proposed EU constitutional treaty returned No votes, precipitating the most serious crisis in the history of the EU. According to some commentators, many voters in France saw the proposed constitution as a vehicle for curtailing the scope for government intervention in the national economy and moving them in the direction of the 'free market'.

> In France, plagued by at least 10 per cent unemployment for 20 years, the easily inflammable fear was that 'social France', enjoying a generous welfare state, a deep commitment to public services and benign conditions of employment, would be replaced by a minimalist, hard-hearted 'anglo-saxon' approach to welfare in the name of economic efficiency.
>
> *(Will Hutton, 'My problem with Europe', The Observer, 5 June 2005)*

On the other hand there were politicians and commentators who saw the issue rather differently, identifying one source of voter dissatisfaction as the feeling that flexible labour market policies in the UK had proved more effective in getting unemployment down than the Eurozone members' more interventionist approach. Both sides agreed in seeing the central issue as that of determining the proper scope and limits of national governments in running their economies.

This issue had already surfaced in European political debate earlier in 2005, in connection with the German government's controversial reform of unemployment benefits. In January 2005 more than 5 million German people were unemployed, the most since 1932. The German government tightened the conditions for receiving unemployment benefit in an attempt to persuade long-term unemployed people back to work.

You have already seen how economists analyse this aspect of the problem of unemployment. In Chapter 9 Maureen Mackintosh distinguished two approaches to the analysis of replacement rates. The view that high replacement rates improve economic efficiency by encouraging people to retrain provides an economic argument in favour of the preference of many French voters for a generous welfare state. The alternative argument, that high replacement rates increase unemployment and reduce economic efficiency by encouraging people to remain unemployed, clearly informed the reform of unemployment benefits in Germany, taking the labour market a step closer to a 'hard-hearted, anglo-saxon' approach to welfare.

The main purpose of this chapter and of Chapters 12–14 is to introduce the analysis underlying the other main dimension of the debate on the EU unemployment problem. From the analysis of a particular market, the labour market, we move up to the analysis of the national economy as a whole, consisting of markets for goods and services and for money as well as for labour. This is macroeconomic analysis and it is concerned with how the national economy works and how much scope there is for government policy to influence national economic performance in terms of unemployment, inflation and growth.

Once again there are two alternative approaches and the issue that divides them is the desirability of government intervention to solve the unemployment problem. This time though it is a question of what governments can achieve in the short run by intervening, not in a particular market such as the labour market, but in the national (or EU) economy as a whole. On one side are the majority of policy makers, such as those who charged the European Central Bank (ECB), which sets interest rates throughout the Eurozone, with the objective of maintaining price stability, understood as an annual inflation rate below but close to 2 per cent. Similarly the UK government's 2005 Budget Statement asserts that the 'monetary policy framework seeks to ensure low and stable inflation'. On the other side are those, at present without influence on policy, who argue for a broadly Keynesian approach in which governments can make adjustments to the economy in the short run that will secure full employment. For example, the Euro Memorandum Group, a group of economists who advocate an alternative economic strategy to the one pursued by the ECB, call for 'an employment friendly macroeconomic framework' (Euro Memorandum Group, 2005, p.3).

These two opposing views are the contemporary manifestations of established positions in a long-running debate that has shaped the analysis of national economies and government policies for improving or at least maintaining their performance. The two sides of this debate will be introduced in the next two sections of this chapter. In Section 11.2 we examine Keynes's contribution to the theoretical understanding of unemployment. In Section 11.3, we consider an account of the resurgence of economic liberalism, and the ways in which this posed an effective challenge to what had become the Keynesian orthodoxy. A case study on German unemployment gives you an opportunity to compare the two approaches. Section 11.4 concludes the chapter.

11.2 The Keynesian revolution

▦ ▧ ■ 11.2.1 A new theoretical approach

The Great Depression of the 1930s saw unemployment in many countries at record levels. Those were the years of the hunger marches in the UK, when unemployed people marched on London to demonstrate their plight. Those were also the years that produced the great debate between the proponents of *laissez-faire*, who argued that the government should allow markets to resolve the problem of unemployment, and the proponents of intervention, who argued that the government should actively try to provide more jobs. It was during this period, too, that John Maynard Keynes published his book *The General Theory of Employment, Interest and Money* (1936), in which he developed a new kind of economic theory – macroeconomics – to back up the case for interventionist policies.

Before Keynes wrote *The General Theory*, unemployment was seen as the result of wages being too high. According to the supply and demand model of competitive markets, which you met in Chapter 5, more of a good can be sold only if there is a reduction in its price. By analogy, if a person's labour is thought of as a good to be bought and sold on the labour market, then more can be sold only if its price – the wage rate – is reduced. The implication for policy is that the government needs to do nothing at all, except ensure that trade unions are not so powerful that they try to buck the market and price their own members out of a job.

The view that workers simply had to accept lower wages in order to reduce unemployment was the reigning orthodoxy against which Keynes argued. An example of this orthodox 'classical' position is given by Professor Edwin Cannan's presidential address to the annual meeting of the Royal Economic Society, September 1932:

> But general unemployment is in reality to be explained almost in the same way as particular employment. In a particular employment, provided demand for its product is elastic, more persons can be employed if they will work for less remuneration. In all employments *taken together*, demand is indefinitely elastic, and consequently indefinite numbers can be employed if they do not ask for too high a remuneration. General unemployment appears when asking too much is a general phenomenon.
>
> *(Cannan, 1932, p.367, original emphasis)*

Cannan is arguing that particular and general unemployment both have the same cause and can be analysed in the same way using competitive supply and demand analysis.

Keynes protested against this way of thinking. Particular unemployment was not at all the same as general unemployment, he argued. If a single group of unemployed workers accept a reduction in their rate of wages, then more of them will be employed because they are now cheaper to employ compared with other workers. This is the case of particular unemployment. But if *all* workers accept a reduction in their rate of wages, this will have effects right through the economy and must be analysed at an economy-wide level.

For this reason, Keynes argued that it is inappropriate when analysing the entire economy to use only the analysis of supply and demand based on a particular commodity. This was the core of the theoretical innovation of *The General Theory*, in which Keynes introduced a new theoretical apparatus for analysing the economy as a whole, or the 'aggregate economy'. This branch of economics is now known as macroeconomics. In particular, Keynes focused on the role of 'aggregate demand' – the total demand in the

Keynesian economics

Keynesian economics, or Keynesianism, stresses the importance of the role of aggregate demand in determining the rate of unemployment.

aggregate economy – as a key determinant of the level of unemployment. (Aggregate demand is explained more fully in Chapter 13.)

Economists are still wrestling with the implications of Keynes's original argument. Keynes's theories have been the subject of an extensive debate among economists, who have not even agreed on what Keynes himself was trying to do with his new theoretical framework. That framework itself has been amended or criticized by many other economists who have formed themselves into distinct schools of thought. **Keynesian economics** tries to refine and improve on Keynes's work, while others criticize it as being fundamentally erroneous.

Later chapters will introduce you to macroeconomic theory. In the following sections of this chapter, there are overviews of some of the big policy debates that have shaped thinking about the aggregate economy, and we begin by focusing on the policy implications of Keynes's *General Theory*.

▨ ■ ■ 11.2.2   Do markets adjust automatically?

One of the main planks of pre-Keynesian thinking was that markets work automatically in a self-adjusting manner. As you learnt in Chapter 5, according to this way of thinking, the price mechanism works by allocating resources to where they are most needed. If a good is in short supply, then its price rises. When this happens, consumers become more sparing in their use of the good and producers are encouraged to produce more of it. Similarly, if a good is in oversupply, then its price falls. The fall in price encourages consumers to use more of it and at the same time producers have less of an incentive to supply it. Inevitably, it was acknowledged, this process does not work perfectly or immediately, but in the absence of large-scale interference by governments, trade unions and monopolies, it will tend to work in the way just described.

In the case of labour, if there is widespread unemployment, this must be the result of wage rates being too high. In time, a free labour market would see a reduction in wages to the full employment level. If this does not happen, it must be the result of interference in the labour market – either by trade unions in keeping up the level of wages, or through government legislation inhibiting the untrammelled operation of market adjustment. Keynes argued that this view was wrong and that markets, including the labour market, are not able to adjust automatically to eliminate unemployment.

Thus Keynes argued against the view that markets are somehow self-adjusting. This was how he characterized the two positions in a BBC radio broadcast in 1934:

> I have said that we fall into two main groups. What is it that makes the cleavage which thus divides us? On the one side are those who believe that the existing economic system is, in the long run, a self-adjusting system, though with creaks and groans and jerks, and interrupted by time lags, outside interference and mistakes . . . On the other side of the gulf are those who reject the idea that the existing economic system is, in any significant sense, self-adjusting. They believe that the failure of effective demand to reach the full potentialities of supply, in spite of human psychological demand being immensely far from satisfied for the vast majority of individuals, is due to much more fundamental causes . . . The gulf between these two schools of thought is deeper, I believe, than most of those on either side of it are aware of. On which side does the essential truth lie? That is the vital question for us to solve . . . I can scarcely begin here to give you the reasons for what I believe to be the right answer. But I can tell you on which side of the gulf I myself stand . . . Now *I* range myself with the heretics.
>
> *(Keynes, 1973, pp.486–9, original emphasis)*

Keynes argued that the fault with the *laissez-faire* argument was that it ignored the relationship between employment and the aggregate economy. A position of widespread unemployment can emerge because there is an imbalance at the level of the aggregate economy and it is this that prevents the labour market from adjusting. Keynes identified the main weakness of the economy at the aggregate level as being the lack of 'aggregate demand' for the output of the economy as a whole.

There are two main factors influencing the amount of employment that firms can offer: the wage rate (discussed in Chapter 7) and the demand for goods and services. If demand is high and the firm can readily sell its output, then it is more likely to take on new workers. Conversely, if aggregate demand for goods is low and the firm cannot sell its output, then it will not be able to carry on production and workers must lose their jobs. Keynes argued that aggregate demand was of overriding importance in determining the business environment in which firms made their hiring and firing decisions and that neglecting it had led earlier economists into erroneous conclusions.

Keynes's emphasis on the importance of aggregate demand highlighted the cumulative rather than the self-correcting nature of market disturbances. Once firms begin to lay off workers, this is likely to have cumulative effects. The increase in unemployment will reduce aggregate demand and therefore make it more likely that other firms will start losing orders and so have to make their workers redundant. In addition, business expectations about the future tend to a large degree to be reinforcing. Once a climate of pessimism sets in, firms are less likely to embark on new investment programmes, and this too depresses aggregate demand.

Keynes's analysis also posed a challenge to conventional notions of thrift and prudent behaviour. In a period of high unemployment, the prudent person would reduce expenditure in order to save more as a protection against future uncertainties. Similarly, firms taking a pessimistic view of the future would not embark on new investment. From the point of view of aggregate demand, these are the worst possible responses, as they put downward pressures on consumption expenditure and investment at a time when demand is already too low. It is far better for everyone to go out on a spending spree during a recession in order to boost aggregate demand and give employers an incentive to start hiring more workers.

11.2.3 The argument for government intervention

As individual workers and firms cannot decide to boost aggregate demand during recessions, is there any other economic agent that can? The Keynesian answer to this question is that governments can and should intervene to influence aggregate demand. In times of recession, when demand is low, the government should try to increase aggregate demand, and during booms, when the economy is in danger of overheating, it should try to damp it down. Thus the government should try to counteract the cumulative nature of movements in the aggregate economy by acting in a countercyclical manner to smooth out fluctuations and maintain a high and stable level of employment.

The Keynesian theory thus provides a clear theoretical rationale for government intervention. One way of understanding this is to see the aggregate economy in terms of a prisoners' dilemma game, such as the one presented in Chapter 6. There it was shown how individual decision-making in situations of interdependence can lead to inferior results for the players compared with the co-operative outcome. If the prisoners could agree on a co-operative approach, the pay-off for each of them would be higher than if each made the decision individually.

The prisoners' dilemma game shows how the presence of interdependence between decisions can crucially affect outcomes. Try to consider how different firms' expenditures and employment decisions might be interdependent.

The interdependence here comes from the fact that one firm's expenditure is another firm's income. If one firm employs more workers, then other firms experience this as an increase in demand for the consumer products that they make.

It follows from this that if there is a recession within a single country, and ignoring international influences for the moment, the best course of action is for firms to embark on a massive expenditure programme, generating jobs and incomes for workers which are then spent on their own products. If all firms do this, everyone benefits. This is the best option for society as it generates the greatest number of jobs. The trouble is that it is only worth it for any individual firm if it feels confident that other firms will do likewise. In other words, any one firm has to feel optimistic about the economy in general before it is prepared to expand. If it expects to be the only firm that expands, then its new expensive capacity will be redundant and profits will fall. But if all firms take this view, then no one expands, and the economy stays in recession. On the other hand, if a firm could let other firms start the process of generating activity, it could benefit from the increased employment and incomes available to spend on its output without having to be the first to take the risk of embarking on expensive investment. In this case, its profits would be even greater because it would benefit from the general increase in activity without having to incur the costs of investment at that stage.

This prisoners' dilemma game is shown in the pay-off matrix in Figure 11.2. In order to represent an aggregate economy in a 2×2 matrix, we have to imagine just two firms, each deciding in the recession whether to start straightaway on an expensive investment project, or whether to wait and see if the economy improves first. Firm A is shown in the cells on the lower left-hand side and Firm B is shown in the cells on the upper right-hand side. The pay-offs in the matrix denote the level of profits for each firm. It is to be understood in this game that a high level of profits would allow the firms to offer more employment. Remember that it is the structure of pay-offs that is significant in game theory; the actual numbers in the pay-off matrix are arbitrary and have been chosen to illustrate the internal structure of the prisoners' dilemma game. In this matrix you will find that it is in both firms' interest not to invest immediately but to wait and see. If they both do this, however, the outcome is the worst possible for the society overall as neither firm invests and total profits are only £40. In this case, because both firms wait and do nothing until the recovery occurs, the outcome is that the recovery does not happen. If both firms were to go ahead, however, and invest immediately, each firm would earn £100 and the recovery would be under way.

To understand this, consider the situation for Firm A. Should Firm A invest now or should it wait and see? Consider what it should do if it expects Firm B to invest now. If it expects Firm B to invest straightaway, then its pay-off is £100 if it also goes ahead and

Figure 11.2
The decision to invest during a recession represented as a prisoners' dilemma game

Firm A \ Firm B	invest now	wait and see
invest now	100 / 100	110 / 10
wait and see	10 / 110	20 / 20

invests now, or £110 if it waits. The pay-off is higher if it waits because it is not having to increase its own expenditure in order to benefit from the upturn in activity arising from Firm B's increased investment expenditure. If it expects Firm B to wait and see, Firm A's pay-off is £10 if it goes ahead and embarks on the new investment, and £20 if it also waits. Here again, the pay-off to Firm A is higher if it waits to see if there is going to be a general upturn before committing its own expenditure. If it invests now, its pay-off is only £10 because it has increased its expenditure, but as the other firm has not, its own investment was premature. Thus, whatever Firm A expects Firm B to do, it will be better off waiting to see whether there is an improvement before it commits itself to increased expenditure. The same line of reasoning applies to Firm B.

This example using the prisoners' dilemma may seem rather artificial as, to keep the matrix simple, I have had to present an entire economy as if it were composed of just two firms. The point it illustrates is nonetheless crucially important, as it shows the interdependence of expenditure decisions by economic agents. If all agents increase their expenditure, then aggregate demand is increased and the economy moves out of recession. If just a few economic agents increase expenditure, then the effect on aggregate demand is negligible and the economy remains stuck in a recession. This expenditure may take the form of consumption expenditure, investment expenditure, government expenditure or export expenditure. In the pay-off matrix, we concentrated on firms' investment expenditure, but the conclusion of the prisoners' dilemma game applies to all forms of expenditure: the best outcome for society as a whole occurs when firms (and other economic agents) increase their expenditure together in order to pull the economy out of recession; if expenditure decisions are taken individually, however, this best outcome is impossible and so the economy stays stuck in recession.

So the solution to the dilemma posed by the prisoners' dilemma game is co-operation. One way of securing this co-operation is to have a benevolent external agency which ensures the best solution. If an external agency can coax firms to increase their investment, for example by giving tax rebates or special investment grants, this gets over the paradox of the prisoners' dilemma. According to the Keynesian argument, the government admirably performs this role of a benevolent external agency which co-ordinates the actions of other agents.

Consider what would happen in the prisoners' dilemma game if the government were to offer a £20 investment grant to firms as an inducement to get on with their investment. The grant means that the pay-off to investing straightaway is increased by £20. What difference would this make to the outcome of the game?

Exercise 11.1

Enter the values in the pay-offs in the blank pay-off matrix in Figure 11.3 after the government offers firms a £20 investment grant. What will be the outcome of this version of the game?

Figure 11.3
Pay-off matrix showing the decision to invest during a recession when the government offers an investment grant of £20

Economic objectives

A government's economic objectives are the specific objectives of its economic policy programmes, normally expressed in terms of the rate of unemployment, rate of inflation and/ or rate of economic growth. Sometimes distributional objectives are included.

Policy instrument

Policy instruments are economic variables which are directly controlled by the government. For example, tax rates might be an instrument of policy.

Policy target

Policy targets are economic variables which are only indirectly and approximately subject to control by the government. For example, tax revenues might be a policy target; these are influenced by tax rates but also by other factors.

You should have worked out that the pay-off to investing now is increased by £20 for both firms. This means that the pay-off to investing now when the other firm also invests is raised to £120, and the pay-off to investing now when the other firm waits is raised to £30. The result is that both firms choose to invest now irrespective of what the other firm does. The reason is that the relative pay-off to investing now as opposed to waiting has been raised. Both firms invest, and so the recession is a thing of the past!

Keynes did not present his argument in the form of a prisoners' dilemma game, but as a new economic model for understanding the relationship between aggregate demand and the level of output and employment. The revolutionary policy implication of Keynes's theory, however, was that it provided a persuasive argument for government intervention in the economy.

This required the government to have a set of **economic objectives**. An ultimate economic objective might be some acceptable level of economic well-being, but expressed like this such an objective is hard to pin down. A more specific economic objective would be expressed in terms of some desirable rate of growth or an acceptable rate of unemployment or inflation. Sometimes a government has distributional objectives, such as greater equality in the distribution of incomes.

Different governments have different objectives, and these objectives may change in the course of time. During the 1950s and 1960s most Western governments attached a high value to the objective of low unemployment, but since the 1980s the prime economic objective has been the control of inflation.

The policy variables that are amenable to direct government control are sometimes called **policy instruments**. For example, the rate of income tax is a policy instrument as it is directly controlled by the government. A **policy target** is not under direct government control, but governments nonetheless try to influence it using the policy instruments at their disposal. For example, tax revenues may be a policy target which governments try to control using an instrument such as the tax rate, but they are influenced by other factors too.

The widespread acceptance of what came to be regarded as a Keynesian approach to **discretionary policy-making** embodied these basic distinctions between economic objectives, policy instruments and policy targets. Sometimes objectives shifted, and sometimes aspects of policy-making were moved from one category to another as priorities and constraints changed. But underlying the general approach to policy-making was the belief that governments would respond to changing economic circumstances by making discretionary changes in its economic policy.

▨ ▩ ■ 11.2.4 Income inequalities do matter

Discretionary policy-making

Discretionary economic policy requires the government to make policy changes on the basis of its judgement of current and future economic circumstances.

Once Keynesian economics had established an argument in favour of government intervention in the economy, boosting aggregate demand in times of recession and curbing it in times of boom, theorists also developed other functions for active state involvement. Keynes's emphasis on the need for increased aggregate demand during recessions highlighted the way in which inequalities in the distribution of income affect the level of aggregate demand. As Chapter 3 explained (in connection with a discussion of the incomes of consumers as an influence on market demand), the proportion of income that is spent rather than saved depends on the level of income. Those with a higher income spend a smaller proportion, whereas those on lower incomes tend to spend a higher proportion. It follows from this that a redistribution of income via taxes from the rich to the poor will increase aggregate demand and so will help to make the aggregate economy function more efficiently.

Such redistributive programmes are especially important for helping to counteract the effects of the economic cycle. During a recession, the high levels of unemployment mean a sharp reduction in purchasing power for those without a job, and so this reduces aggregate demand. Welfare programmes of payments for those without work thus serve not only the humanitarian purpose of giving support to those in greatest need, but also help to boost aggregate demand and hasten the time when jobs become available again. During the boom, less is paid out in welfare programmes as the numbers of unemployed fall, and tax revenues rise with the higher level of economic activity.

Thus, Keynesian macroeconomics came to have a predisposition towards a more egalitarian approach to the distribution of income. This follows partly from its concern with maintaining a high and stable level of aggregate demand and partly from its concern with unemployment, as it is the unemployed who have to bear the brunt of structural change and exogenous shocks impacting on the economy. But the links between Keynesian economics and redistributive policies run deeper than this. It is also associated with a more general commitment to the aspirations and ethos of the welfare state. Whether and to what extent the welfare state has contributed towards redistributing incomes is an issue that has been much debated and was discussed in Chapter 9. The point here is that William Beveridge's proposal for a social insurance model of welfare in the UK, encompassing all individuals in society, was based on the fundamental assumption that full employment could be maintained. It was this assumption of full employment that underwrote the insurance principle that everyone in society would be a paid-up member of the national insurance scheme and so would be entitled by right to social insurance protection when in need. The importance of this link is illustrated by its partial erosion during the 1980s and 1990s: with growing unemployment, the original connection between the welfare state and the insurance principle was subject to attack as critics of the welfare state tried to redefine and curtail its sphere of operations.

For these reasons Keynesian economics is connected with a more general political stance of attempting to reform what is seen as the worst ills of capitalism and was adopted by a broad swathe of social democratic thinking which attempted to save capitalism from its own worst evils. According to this position, relatively equal societies are not only more just; they are also more efficient in that everyone contributes productively, while everyone shares to some degree in the wealth so produced. It is therefore actively concerned to make capitalist economies work both more efficiently and more fairly, without fundamentally challenging the entrepreneurial ethos or the market allocation of resources. It values the political freedoms and the material advantages that are thought to accompany a relatively free system of markets in industrial capitalist societies, but it is also critical of what it sees as the shortcomings of an excessive reliance on market allocation. It therefore espouses a balance of the market mechanism and active state involvement to try to assure a less unequal distribution of the economic rewards and penalties associated with the inevitable process of structural change.

▨ ▥ ■ 11.2.5   A new concept of the aggregate economy

Another implication of Keynes's theory was that it provided a new notion of the 'aggregate economy' as the macroeconomy. We have seen this term a number of times so far in this chapter, but we should now pause for a moment to consider what it means.

The aggregate economy refers to the national economy as a structured set of economic relations between all economic agents. This implies a notion of the total economy as an aggregation (or adding up) of all the individual transactions within the economy and over all economic agents. As previous chapters have emphasized, there are many different kinds of agents. When we aggregate across the economy, however, we are abstracting from many of these differences and visualizing the economy as composed of a small number of different types of agents. There are *consumers*, who are the people who purchase the final output comprising goods and services. There are *workers* who sell their labour. There are *firms* which produce the final output. And there is the *government*.

Thinking of the aggregate economy in this way also implies a process of aggregating across markets. One such aggregated market is the markets for all goods and services. This market includes all the traded goods and services from motor vehicles, clothing and consumer goods to insurance services, meals out and shoe repairs. Another aggregated market is the labour market where all labour is traded. The other aggregated market is the money market, as you will discover in Chapter 12. Looking at the economy in the aggregate, therefore, it is composed of three main markets: the goods market, the labour market and the money market. The core of macroeconomics is concerned with trying to understand the various ways in which these three aggregated markets interact, and how employment and output are determined in a world of economic transactions denominated in money terms.

This aggregate economy also reinforces the notion of the national economy. Here the extent of the macroeconomy is determined by national boundaries. The government which intervenes to reduce unemployment is the national government, which has a particular responsibility for the performance of the national economy. Thus, Keynesian macroeconomics also helped to identify the national economy as being composed of a distinct set of economic relationships that are amenable to systematic analysis, and which is the particular concern of the national government. For this reason, Keynesianism carried with it a distinct political agenda which emphasized national priorities and a nationally bounded view of government intervention.

This section has argued that Keynesianism was based on a technical innovation in economic analysis, the aggregate economy, and the importance of aggregate demand in determining the level of output and employment. However, because of its challenge to *laissez-faire* ways of thinking, together with its arguments about the central importance of government policy in guiding the economy through the worst manifestations of capitalist instability, it was also embedded in a broader political and social agenda which set out to reform capitalism's own worst evils. It was associated with a concern to diffuse more widely the material benefits of industrialized economies, and to provide assistance to those who, through no fault of their own, were forced to bear the brunt of the massive dislocations to which the economy was periodically prone.

11.3 The resurgence of economic liberalism

11.3.1 Market adjustment

The inexorable increase in unemployment for most European countries in the 1970s and 1980s is shown in Figure 11.4 for the OECD area as a whole. The 1950s and 1960s are marked by relatively low and stable unemployment levels, although note how even here the level seems to peak about every four years. At the time these peaks caused considerable consternation, but they have been dwarfed by the increases that have taken place since.

Thus, half a century after the publication of one of the most influential books on unemployment and economic theory, some of the richest economies in the world were faced with an unemployment problem of similar, if not worse, dimensions than in the

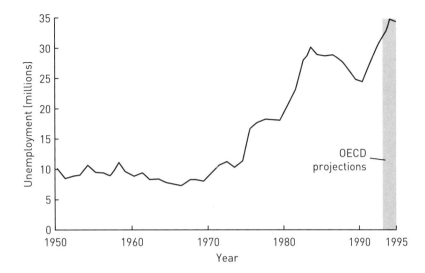

Figure 11.4
Unemployment in
the OECD area,
1950–95

Source: OECD
(1994) p.9

1930s. Why was this? Were Keynes's ideas misguided? How had changes in the world economy contributed towards this increase in unemployment and non-employment?

This view of the national economy and the role of government policy-making persisted as a new orthodoxy throughout the 1950s and 1960s. In the post-1945 era of economic reconstruction, both its economic analysis and its wider political assumptions were broadly acceptable to governments and electors alike in the industrialized countries. Looking back on those decades, they appear to have been economically successful in comparison with both earlier and later standards, and unemployment in the main industrialized countries was low during this period. Growth rates were also high by historical standards, as Chapter 19 demonstrates. Income disparities between these richer countries on the one hand and non-industrialized countries on the other were very large, but there was a general expectation that in the course of time these differentials would be reduced.

Some economists have seen this period as a kind of 'Golden Age', when macroeconomic performance achieved high and fairly stable levels of employment and growth by historical standards. It is a moot point as to whether this period of relative stability was achieved by the advance in economic thinking secured by the Keynesian revolution or whether it was simply the result of the unique circumstances of post-war reconstruction. Either way, the relative success of those years led to a widespread expectation that, in future, the path of economic expansion need not be fraught by the inexorable pattern of cyclical recessions and the harrowing experience of growing unemployment and the visible presence of poverty.

The pattern of cyclical activity, however, was only muted, not defeated, and at the time there was considerable concern that the progress of economic growth was still subjected to cyclical swings. If you look again at Figure 11.4, you will see that there was indeed a cyclical pattern in unemployment.

Question How would you describe the pattern of UK unemployment in the period from the late 1940s to early 1970s that is shown in Figure 11.5?

In Figure 11.5 the UK unemployment rate shows a cyclical pattern during the period from the late 1940s to the early 1970s, with peaks in 1947 (2.3 per cent), 1952 (1.7 per

Figure 11.5
UK unemployment
1920–92

Source: Crafts and
Woodward (1991)
updated using
Economic Trends

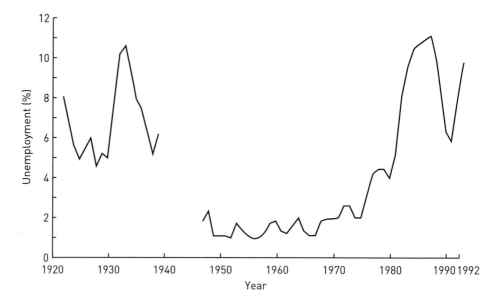

cent), 1958/59 (1.7/1.8 per cent) and 1963 (2.0 per cent). Unemployment then rose in 1967 to 1.8 per cent and carried on rising until the next peak in 1971/72 at 2.6 per cent.

Furthermore, the years of low unemployment seemed to coincide with years of rising inflation. Figure 11.6 reproduces the UK unemployment graph of Figure 11.5 for the post-1950 period, but it also includes a blue line showing the rate of inflation during these years.

Question	In Figure 11.6 what is the relationship between inflation and unemployment for the UK during the 1950s and 1960s? Which were the years of low unemployment and high inflation?

Figure 11.6 suggests that years of low unemployment are associated with high inflation. The years 1951, 1955/56, 1961 and 1965/66 were marked by relatively low unemployment

Figure 11.6
UK unemployment
and inflation,
1950–92

Source: Crafts and
Woodward (1991)
updated using
Economic Trends

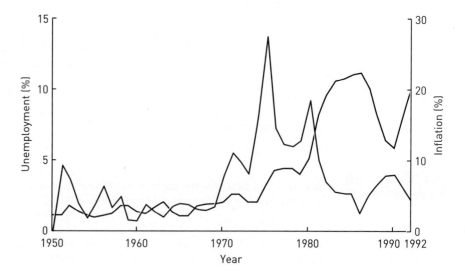

and high inflation. This inverse relationship between unemployment and inflation gave rise to the view that there was a 'trade-off' between unemployment and inflation: that reductions in unemployment could be secured only on the basis of increases in the rate of inflation. At a theoretical level this led to a re-examination of the links between the price level and aggregate demand. This in turn led to a more sceptical approach to the feasibility of conducting permanently expansionary policies in order to keep unemployment low. It also provided a fertile ground for more substantial theoretical criticisms of the Keynesian approach to take root.

Another disturbing trend was also in evidence during this period. Looking back to Figure 11.4, you will see that, excluding the peak in 1947, each cyclical peak in unemployment is higher than the previous one. Looking at the four peaks in 1952 (1.7 per cent), 1959 (1.8 per cent), 1963 (2.0 per cent) and 1971/72 (2.6 per cent), each has a higher rate of unemployment than the one before it. In 1967, Milton Friedman delivered an influential lecture to the American Economic Association in which he argued that the trade-off was itself a delusion, that inflation had to rise by increasing amounts in order to get the same reductions in the level of unemployment and that eventually there would be no trade-off at all: 'there is always a temporary trade-off between inflation and unemployment; there is no permanent trade-off. The temporary trade-off comes not from inflation *per se*, but from unanticipated inflation, which generally means, from a rising rate of inflation' (Friedman, 1968, p.11). There is more on this debate in Chapter 18.

During the 1970s the trade-off broke down in the UK as both inflation and unemployment were on a rising trend. In the OECD as a whole, inflation rose from 8.0 per cent average during 1970–74 to 13.5 per cent in 1980, and the unemployment rate rose from 3.5 per cent in 1974 to 5.7 per cent in 1980 (*OECD Economic Outlook*, June 1994). The old trade-off between unemployment and inflation seemed a thing of the past and Friedman's prediction seemed to be proved correct. Suddenly economists had to explain how rising unemployment and slow growth was compatible with rising inflation – **stagflation** as it was called.

Stagflation

The combination of *stag*nating growth and high in*flation* is known as stagflation.

On this issue there were two main answers. Some economists explained stagflation in terms of the inflationary effects of the Keynesian policies of the earlier period. Governments, they argued, had injected inflationary pressures into the system via government spending, so economic agents had come to expect inflation and anticipate its effects. But, by anticipating it, they were also nullifying its effectiveness in stimulating economic growth. Economists continued to argue over the causes, but governments responded to stagflation by trying to reduce government expenditure. In this recriminatory atmosphere, anti-Keynesian views began to develop and received a more sympathetic hearing.

During the period of the 1980s and 1990s, *laissez-faire* views became influential again at the policy level. The resurgence of economic liberalism during this period is associated with the economic and political writings of economists such as F.A. Hayek, as well as Milton Friedman, both of whom had always been sharp critics of Keynesianism and the growth of the state. Hayek and Friedman resuscitated the pre-Keynesian view that markets work more efficiently in co-ordinating economic activities than any other means yet discovered, and they also linked this to a statement of the overriding political importance of individual freedom. According to this view, the growth of state involvement in the economy entailed a reduction of individual freedoms as well as a throttling of the market mechanisms which secure an equilibrium between supply and demand. This emphasis on the fundamental importance of market price signals – including wage rates – in allocating resources to where they are most highly valued, led them to stress the dangers of government intervention and persistent inflation in distorting these price signals.

Three main aspects of this distortion were emphasized. First, it was argued that the extensive system of government taxes and subsidies had distorted relative prices. Goods and services receiving a subsidy were priced lower than warranted, while those that were taxed carried a price higher than the true cost. The high marginal rates of income tax discouraged effort and initiative, and high welfare payments to those out of work deterred them from accepting realistic wages and returning to work.

Second, they argued that unemployment was the result of wages being out of line with the requirements of demand. The main culprit here was the monopoly practice of trade unions in bargaining for wages that were too high and which distorted the necessary relativities between different trades and occupations.

Third, it was argued that these distortions were compounded by Keynesian policies of increasing aggregate demand, which had simply stoked up inflation, which in turn further distorted price information. In a situation of rising prices it can be difficult for economic agents to know when any particular price rise is due to the shortage of the good in question or to general inflationary pressure. For this reason, Friedman and Hayek argued that the control of inflation – not the reduction in unemployment – should be the prime policy objective. They argued that government attempts to reduce unemployment by increasing aggregate demand had been unsuccessful, as this had simply raised the rate of inflation, which would, in the long run, cause such a misallocation of resources that unemployment would eventually be that much greater:

> Full employment has come to mean that maximum of employment that can be brought about in the short run by monetary pressure. This may not be the original meaning of the theoretical concept, but it was inevitable that it should have come to mean this in practice. Once it was admitted that the momentary state of employment should form the main guide to monetary policy, it was inevitable that any degree of unemployment which might be removed by monetary pressure should be regarded as sufficient justification for applying such pressure. That in most situations employment can be temporarily increased by monetary expansion has long been known. If this possibility has not always been used, this was because it was thought that by such measures not only other dangers were created, but that long-term stability of employment itself might be endangered by them. What is new about present beliefs is that it is now widely held that so long as monetary expansion creates additional employment, it is innocuous or at least will cause more benefit than harm.
>
> *(Hayek, 1978, p.54)*

Monetarism

Monetarism is an economic theory which holds that inflation is a monetary phenomenon which has monetary causes. It argues that there is a close correlation between the money supply and the rate of inflation, and that the money supply can be used as an instrument of policy in order to control the rate of inflation, which is seen as the primary economic objective.

Hayek argued that government expenditure had an inbuilt tendency to go on rising. Reflationary measures thus outweighed contractionary measures, with a long-term upward movement in prices and eventually in unemployment itself. Hence Hayek and Friedman argued that the prime objective of economic policy should be a stable – ideally a zero – level of inflation. This would provide a stable monetary environment in which the price mechanism would succeed in allocating all resources – including labour – to those uses where they were most highly valued.

Hayek and Friedman emphasized the monetary causes of inflation and argued that a proper rein on the money supply would bring down the rate of inflation. These views came to be known as **monetarism** and were extremely influential at the policy level in the UK.

Given their opposition to the interventionist government policy of the Keynesian era, anti-Keynesian economists such as Hayek and Friedman were also opposed to discretionary policy. They argued that policy makers lacked the wisdom and the knowledge needed to

Policy rules

Economic policy is subject to rules when the government has no discretion in the implementation of policy but must adhere to fixed rules or strict policy guidelines.

exercise discretion in day-to-day policy-making. In addition, they argued that investing such enormous power in the hands of policy makers was inconsistent with a liberal defence of individual freedom. Accordingly, they recommended the use of **policy rules** rather than discretion, so that policy makers would have to adhere to agreed rules or guidelines in the conduct of policy.

Monetarism provided an ideal example of a rule-based policy in that it prescribes a constant rule in the form of a fixed annual increase in the money supply. The government's responsibility, it was argued, was to follow the monetary rule and not allow the money supply to increase at a faster rate than that prescribed. An additional advantage of this rule, it was argued, was that it was transparent for all to see, thus providing a visible yardstick according to which the success of government policy could be measured. A widely publicized adoption of this monetarist prescription was the Medium Term Financial Strategy introduced by Margaret Thatcher's government in the early 1980s.

Along with this argument that the government's first priority is to control inflation, monetarism also stressed that the attempt to control unemployment is futile. It rejected the Keynesian argument that the level of unemployment is related to the level of aggregate demand, and reiterated the pre-Keynesian argument that unemployment is caused simply by incorrect wage rates. According to this view, the only way to reduce unemployment is to reduce wage pressure by freeing labour markets, reducing union power, repealing legislation which protected workers' rights and reducing welfare payments. This resurgence of *laissez-faire* thinking and the development of monetarism thus emphasized a 'market-clearing' view of exchange transactions, according to which markets are essentially self-adjusting in the sense in which Keynes had earlier challenged. At the level of macroeconomic theory, this implied that, left to themselves, markets do adjust so that supply and demand, in the labour market as well as in the goods market, are always in equilibrium. Hence unemployment must be the result of wages being too high, and so should properly be regarded as voluntary unemployment in that it results from the optimizing choices made by individual workers.

Thus, just as the growth of Keynesianism was attached to a broader political stance, so was the resurgence of economic liberalism. In spite of the attachment to *laissez-faire* principles, monetarism implied that government policy was not so much in abeyance as taking another form – that of deflating the economy. Making the control of inflation into the prime economic objective while curtailing workers' rights and emphasizing free market outcomes imposed deflationary pressures on the economy which inevitably hit hardest those sections least able to defend their position. While providing economic opportunities for some, the emphasis on individual freedom and individual responsibility bore most heavily on those whose livelihood was jeopardized by the economic dislocations of that period and by the financial stringency following the implementation of monetarist policies.

■ ■ ■ 11.3.2 Government intervention at fault

We have seen the free market position argument that governments had been addressing the wrong issue using the wrong economic theory. But we have also seen that it went even further with the argument that the theoretical foundation which had supported the idea of active discretionary policy-making was unsustainable. It challenged the public interest view of the state that governments could operate as a benevolent external factor in ameliorating economic conditions. It challenged this notion by questioning the assumption that the government can function as an external agent which pursues the public interest. This criticism was noted in Chapter 9. Here we will draw out some of the implications of this debate for macroeconomic policy which will also provide another example of the power of different models in economic theory and policy-making. Previous chapters have shown how different models provide different ways of interpreting economic issues. Here at the macro level we find that the resurgence of economic liberalism provided a challenge to what had become the economic orthodoxy by providing a different set of interpretations which fundamentally changed current perceptions of the requirements of economic policy.

The first problem with the public interest view of the state, it was argued, relates to how the public interest is known in the first place. In democratic countries, electors vote for a broad programme of policies and it is not possible for governments to know how they should rank individual policies. Indeed, it is not always possible to derive any consistent overall ranking of aggregate policies from the individual preferences of the electorate, even if all those preferences were fully known to the government. This problem is known as Arrow's impossibility theorem, after the work of Kenneth Arrow in the area of social choice theory. It has proved a difficult conundrum for social choice theorists, and has made many economists much more sceptical of the ways in which elected governments can claim a mandate for their policies based on the preferences of those who voted them into power.

The second problem relates to the motivation of the government as an 'agent'. One rather cynical answer put forward by the free market position and 'public choice' school of economists is that governments are composed of individuals who pursue their own self-interest. The civil servants or bureaucrats employed in government departments seek their own self-interest by trying to enlarge their own departments because this is where their power and prestige are based. Government departments therefore have an inbuilt tendency to grow in size because this is the means by which government employees enhance their own careers.

Furthermore, in electoral democracies, politicians look after their careers by ensuring that they are re-elected. This can involve irresponsible expenditure programmes designed to buy electoral popularity, often in the run-up to an election, causing what is sometimes known as the 'electoral business cycle'. The outcome is a series of extremely short-term measures to manipulate a boom in time for an election, but with little attention to the long-term requirements of the economy. In addition, electoral popularity requires giving in to the organized special interest lobbies which spend considerable time and money trying to press their own case with the government. Far from being disinterested benevolent agents, politicians are 'captured' by the various powerful pressure groups which enrol government support for their own sectional interest. For these reasons, the free market position is extremely sceptical of political arguments which purport to be promoting the public interest and emphasize instead that governments pursue their own, and not the public, interest.

These arguments provided another criticism of discretionary policy, and suggested yet again that policy rules would offer better control of government actions. Far from government being a benevolent solution to the prisoners' dilemma game, it came to be seen as one of the players in a strategic game, seeking to maximize its own pay-off. Recasting government as a player in a game yields very different results and undermines the original Keynesian view that governments should take discretionary action. As Chapter 6 explained, an important aspect of game theory is its recognition of the interdependence of decisions. This means that, in making a decision, the players have to think ahead and consider the effects of their actions on the other players and take their expected reactions into account. This strategic approach therefore recognizes the central importance of agents' expectations. Earlier economic theories had assumed that agents' expectations about the future would be based pretty much on what had happened in the past. The new interest in expectations in the context of strategic decision-making showed that this was an unrealistic assumption to make (see Chapter 18).

The implications of taking agents' expectations into account within a strategic policy framework can be illustrated by thinking about a government's decision on whether to reflate the economy. According to the old way of thinking, a reflationary programme would reduce unemployment, although at the cost of some inflation. But taking strategic reactions into account shows that the actions of private agents anticipating the government's plans would undermine the reflationary programme, leaving inflation unchecked and with no improvement in employment.

Consider a game where the government has the choice of reflating or not reflating. The other player in this game is taken to be all other economic agents. Their choice is whether to act on the expectation that the government will reflate or the expectation that the government will not reflate. A crucial aspect of this game is that it takes on board the argument mentioned above that the effects of injections of demand on the level of unemployment and inflation depend on whether or not they are anticipated by agents. Thus, the trade-off between inflation and unemployment deteriorates every time that agents expect inflation to rise. (The details of this analysis are explained in Chapter 18.) This game is shown in Figure 11.7, where the pay-off (for both sets of players) is the rate of unemployment. Low levels of pay-off are therefore desirable.

Consider first the cases where agents expect the government *not* to reflate. If the government does not reflate, unemployment remains at 10 per cent, but if it does reflate, unemployment falls to 5 per cent. The reduction in unemployment is the result of taking agents by surprise as they do not expect a reflation to take place, and is an example of the trade-off between unemployment and unexpected inflation. Consider now what would happen if agents expect that the government will reflate. The expectation of inflation now results in a worse trade-off between unemployment and inflation, and so even a non-reflation will result in a worse unemployment rate of 20 per cent. However, if the government does reflate, this reduces unemployment to 15 per cent.

| Question | What would a rational government do in a situation represented by the matrix shown in Figure 11.7? |

Whatever the public expects, it is always rational for the government to reflate. This means that reflation is the dominant strategy as it is the preferred option for the government no matter what private economic agents expect. But, in this case, what are economic agents most likely to expect the government to do if they are also rational? The answer to this must be that agents will expect the government to reflate. This means

Figure 11.7
Matrix showing unemployment as the pay-off in different policy regimes

Other economic agents ⟍ Government	expect not reflate	expect reflate
not reflate	10	20
reflate	5	15

that the final outcome will be in the bottom right-hand cell at 15 per cent unemployment – not the best outcome.

The problem is that the government will achieve the best outcome if it can persuade other agents that it is going to stick with a low inflation policy, while actually reneging on that commitment. But as everyone knows that it can do better by secretly defaulting on its own policy statements, no one will believe those policy statements in the first place. The problem here is that **policy credibility** is lacking because other agents recognize that the government clearly has an incentive to renege on its own stated commitments.

Policy credibility

A policy has credibility if other economic agents believe that the government is totally committed to carrying out that policy.

In common with other strategic games, a solution to the impasse of policy credibility is provided by 'precommitting' the government to keeping to its declared policy statements as this would then make its policy credible. It has been suggested that one form of precommitment would be to impose 'rules' on government policy rather than allowing a degree of choice or 'discretion'. In this way the policy rules function as a form of precommitment because the government is unable to renege on them. For example, rules about the money supply (if they were believed) would function as a precommitment that the government will not renege in the fight against inflation. This thought influenced the UK government's decision in 1997 to give the Bank of England operational independence (i.e. control) over the setting of interest rates to maintain low inflation (Chapter 13). Pegging the domestic currency to another currency, as for example in the European Exchange Rate Mechanism (ERM), provides another example of a policy rule. The operation of the Gold Standard provides yet another example where individual currencies were tied to gold at a fixed rate.

The efficacy of policy rules depends on whether the government really is bound by the rules, and also on whether the rules are indeed appropriate for policy in all circumstances. The examples provided in the previous paragraph are a mixed bag in terms of both of these requirements.

Question	To what extent do you think these examples illustrate the efficacy of policy rules as opposed to policy discretion?

This consideration of the merits of rules versus discretion in the design of policy has had far-reaching effects in macroeconomic debates as it suggests that in some circumstances government policy may be more effective if it has less freedom of manoeuvre to respond to the immediate circumstances of the moment. It also highlights the importance of the institutional structure of policy-making in imposing political or other constraints on government freedom of action. Thus, it is sometimes argued that having an independent central bank in control of monetary policy reduces the area of discretion for the government, especially if the central bank is provided with mandatory instructions (Chapter 13). Either way, the debate is far removed from earlier Keynesian arguments which simply assumed that governments were sufficiently well motivated and well informed to pursue the public interest in macro policy-making.

▪ ▪ ▪ 11.3.3 Income inequalities are necessary

We have seen that the free market position is critical of the view that the state can act as a benevolent external agent and plan for the public interest. Additionally, it places considerable reliance on market forces in allocating resources at both micro and macro level. Consistent with these arguments, it criticizes the social democratic position that mature capitalist societies should, on political and social as well as economic grounds, try to avoid excessive inequalities in the distribution of income and wealth. Although not opposed to all aspects of the welfare state, the free market position is that the welfare state – the 'nanny state' – has become too large and is causing an erosion in the market incentives that are a necessary feature of capitalist societies. The activities of the welfare state should therefore be reduced, and the state should withdraw from as many areas of welfare provision as possible. It encourages the idea of private insurance and private, rather than state, provision of services such as health and education.

In the area of income distribution, it argues that inequalities are a vital part of the operation of the price mechanism. According to this kind of analysis, people should be paid according to the labour market's monetary evaluation of their abilities. People with higher skills and experience should, properly, receive the full monetary equivalent of their greater value. Furthermore, to tax the highly paid groups at a higher rate than low-paid groups is to interfere with this market process and distort market signals. This would eventually result in a lower rate of output from society as a whole as the higher-paid need to receive the full value of their higher earnings in order to be encouraged to work to full effect. Thus, allowing the distribution of income to derive from the operation of free markets would result in the greatest increase in income and output for the society as a whole. In the fullness of time, it is argued, the poor would benefit from this too, because when the effects of this increased wealth creation have 'trickled down', they would actually be better off than under a system of government redistribution to tax the rich and subsidize the poor. The Keynesian belief that redistributive policies can help to make the macroeconomy function more efficiently is seen as a myth based on a fundamental misunderstanding of the role of market signals. These ideas have influenced policy at many levels in a number of countries, including the UK, where tax reductions benefited top incomes the most.

Similarly, in the case of unemployment, it is inefficient to tamper with market evaluations. Unemployment, it is argued, is caused by wage rates being too high. The solution, therefore, is to let wages fall. To featherbed the unemployed by giving welfare payments for too long simply takes away the incentive to look for work, and makes the unemployed reluctant to accept the only jobs – the low-paid ones – that are available to them. The result of overgenerous welfare payments, together with wage rates that are too high relative to the skills offered, are the twin causes of persistent unemployment. Once again, it is argued, government schemes to help the unemployed turn out to have made the situation worse.

▫▪■ 11.3.4   Approaches to the aggregate economy

In view of these criticisms, it is not surprising that the re-emergence of economic liberalism was also associated with attacks on the Keynesian macro model of the economy and its emphasis on the central role of the level of aggregate demand. There were basically two kinds of criticism.

First, it was argued that the notion of the aggregate economy was misconceived unless it could be derived rigorously from the behaviour of the individual economic agents who comprise it. This criticism is akin to Margaret Thatcher's well-publicized argument that 'there is no such thing as society'. In each case, the fundamental element in the analysis is the individual person exercising choice and rationality in the various aspects of life, and so it makes no sense to try to look at society as a composite whole unless it can be understood as the summation of all the individual members. As a result of this criticism, there have been many attempts to ground the relations of the macroeconomy in the individual behaviour of the rational agents who comprise it. One area where this has taken place is in the field of expectations. As we have seen, once the expectations of private agents with respect to government policy are taken on board, this can overturn the results of previous economic theories.

Second, with Keynes's formulation of the aggregate economy and in stressing the role of aggregate demand, it overlooked the significance of aggregate supply. It is debatable as to whether this criticism should properly apply to Keynes's own economics rather than to a bowdlerized version that became popular in the period of Keynesian orthodoxy. The point itself, however, is now accepted among economists in the sense that, at the aggregate as well as the micro level, supply-side factors have to be analysed in conjunction with demand-side factors.

These criticisms of Keynesian arguments at both the theoretical level and the policy level resulted in a more market-oriented approach to policy in many countries during the 1980s and early 1990s. Different governments enacted different kinds of changes which reflect this reversal to a more *laissez-faire* approach but, in spite of this diversity, clear tendencies can be seen.

At the policy level, inflation came to be seen as a more pressing problem than unemployment, as the granting of a degree of independence to the Bank of England and to the European Central Bank shows. This resulted in a political toleration of high levels of unemployment that would have been regarded as unacceptable during the 1950s and 1960s. At the same time, government policy was not held to be accountable for these high levels of unemployment, which were viewed as the responsibility of individual workers who had held out for unrealistically high wages. This shift was accompanied by moves to reduce the power of trade unions at all levels in the UK, from national arenas for formulating policy right down to the factory floor. While unemployment has fallen in the UK, we have seen that it remains a problem in the Eurozone, particularly in Germany.

Government involvement in the economy was reduced in many different ways. Aggregate demand was no longer seen as a key policy variable for controlling the level of output and employment. Instead, inflation was to be controlled using monetary policy – sometimes using the money supply as an instrument (as in the Medium Term Financial Strategy in the UK) and more recently using the rate of interest as the main instrument. Government was to exercise greater financial rectitude, spending and borrowing less so that the government debt could be substantially reduced. In this way fiscal policy – that is, expenditure and tax policy – was used to control the level of government borrowing, a new policy target, thus indirectly supporting the fight against inflation. Individual initiative and enterprise were to be fostered by reducing direct personal taxation, encouraging the take-up of private pension and insurance schemes, and reducing the provisions of the welfare state.

In the face of this radical movement for economic change, Keynesianism seemed to have little new to offer. It was associated with a tired regime of endless government interference that seemed to have done more harm than good. The new economic era was to be based on low taxes and individual gain, initiative and enterprise. The new view was confident that the fruits of this programme would be increased economic efficiency and improved prospects of material gain for those who could satisfy the market with the right product at the right price. The revival of economic liberalism was therefore also associated with a wider political programme that made its economic recommendations appeal to a broad populist base. It stressed the advantages of economic freedom and the liberty of the individual – freedom from state restrictions and liberty for individuals to play the market for the biggest stakes. Its political appeal lay in a new notion of 'popular capitalism', a broadly based property-owning democracy with share shops on the high street, and bright new shopping malls at every turn.

Case study: Unemployment in Germany

Some economic numbers are as resonant as they are significant. One such figure was announced on Wednesday February 2nd by Germany's Federal Labour Agency. More than 5m Germans were unemployed last month, the agency revealed, the most since 1932, when the economic devastation of the Great Depression brought the Weimar Republic to an unhappy end.

The numbers are a little less resonant when adjusted for the season; the aftermath of Christmas never flatters the labour market. Taking this seasonal effect into account would reduce the jobless count to 4.71m, the statistics office said, an unemployment rate of 11.4 per cent. More importantly, the new year also brought a new policy. On January 1st, after parliamentary tussles and street protests, the government's controversial reform of unemployment benefits came into effect. This reform, driven forward by Gerhard Schröder, the chancellor, is supposed to prod the jobless back into work. But its first effect was to prod many who had dropped out of the labour market back onto the unemployment rolls.

Under the 'Hartz IV' reform, named after Peter Hartz, the man who proposed it, those who have been unemployed for over a year receive a flat-rate benefit, means-tested and paid only to those who seek work seriously. Previously, not everyone on long-term aid had to sign on at job agencies. Now they do. The labour office reckons that at least 222 000 people not counted as unemployed under the previous system are now registered as such.

Labour markets rarely function perfectly. But Germany's labour market is not really a market at all. It abjures free competition, which it likens to the law of the jungle. Firing is a last resort. Wages are negotiated collectively. These clubby, consensual arrangements served Germany well for several decades after the war, winning the country an enviable industrial peace. But now they have become, in effect, a conspiracy of insiders against outsiders. The 5m outsiders, who lack a job, might be pre-

pared to work for less than those who have a job. But employee protection and union rules insulate the insiders from any competitive threat the outsiders might offer. As a result, the insiders maintain wages above the level that would make it profitable for employers to hire those out of work.

They longer they remain out of work, the less the unemployed make their presence felt in the labour market. Writing about the Great Depression, Brad DeLong, an economic historian at the University of California, noted that the long-term unemployed become 'discouraged and distraught'. After a year without work, 'a job must arrive at his or her door, grab him or her by the scruff of the neck, and throw him or her back into the nine-to-five routine if he or she is to be employed again.'

In Germany, jobs are hardly knocking at the door. But thanks to the Hartz reforms, the long-term unemployed are having their collars felt a little. Employment agencies, which used to passively process their benefit cheques, are now supposed to take an active role in placing them in new jobs. They will employ as many as 600 000 of them in jobs that pay €1 per hour plus unemployment benefits. Those who turn down a job offer will have some or all of their benefits withheld.

(Adapted from 'Five million reasons to worry',
The Economist, *2 February 2005)*

Questions

1 Outline the ways in which the controversy surrounding the reform of unemployment benefits in Germany reflects the long-running debate between proponents of *laissez-faire* and government intervention.

2 Thinking back to Chapters 8 and 9 as well as Sections 2 and 3 of this chapter, to what extent can you detect the influence of values, as distinct from technical economic analysis, on the perception of unemployment benefit reform in Germany?

11.4 Conclusion

This chapter has introduced some of the themes covered in later chapters of this text by explaining the historical origins of aggregate economy analysis. Rather than posing a stark dichotomy between *laissez-faire* and interventionist policies, more recent debates have come to recognize that what is often at stake concerns the forms and mechanisms of policy measures, and not just the absolute size of the government sector. The debate over rules versus discretion, for example, concerns the appropriate mechanisms for securing particular targets or objectives. The debate over expectations and strategic games provides a model of the government as a player in a game, and these insights from game theory cannot be reduced to the simple dichotomy of intervention or abstention, as so much depends on the credibility of announced policy.

Running through many of these more recent debates is a keener awareness of the place of institutions in providing the context within which the big policy issues have to be debated. Thus, different institutional contexts in different countries contribute significantly to different standards of performance. For example, the reform of unemployment benefit in Germany is a reform of the social institutions in which the labour market operates. Institutions such as tax and welfare systems raise questions about incentives on the one hand and security of living standards on the other. The importance of institutions is discussed in Chapter 19.

One implication arising from this survey is that economic analysis and values are sometimes closely related. Technical economic analysis, views about the proper role for government and individual economic agency and the realm of ethical values are all so closely interlinked that the boundaries between analysis and values may become fuzzy at times. Discussions as to whether a sharp reduction in wages will reduce unemployment soon merge into the question of whether it is right, reasonable or even politically judicious for large sections of the population to be subjected to rapidly deteriorating standards of living. Discussions as to whether highly mobile international capital makes governments powerless to administer monetary policy within their own frontiers often slide into debate about whether governments ought to resist such attacks on their economic sovereignty.

Thus, economic controversies are based on unresolved value differences as well as unresolved issues of fact and analysis. In spite of the centrality of analytic and statistical techniques, economics as an academic discipline is nonetheless characterized by a kind of pluralism – a plurality of theories, views and values – that does not always sit comfortably with its own self-image of objective scientific endeavour. But that image too is also under reassessment, as the social sciences more generally take on board the implications of new approaches right across the academic spectrum which stress the open-ended and unresolved nature of much intellectual enquiry. Within this more sceptical environment, claims to truth and knowledge also need to be understood in terms of their own intellectual and political context. So too with this text, which is also conditioned by its time and place in reflecting current debates in economic policy.

Questions for review and discussion

Question 1 Discuss the differences between Keynesian and *laissez-faire* attitudes to income inequalities.

Question 2 Examine the differences and similarities between the 'Golden Age' of the 1950s and 1960s and the period of macroeconomic stability in the decade or so up to 2005.

Question 3 'Economics is thus a highly political subject' (Maureen Mackintosh, Chapter 9). Write a short dialogue between protagonists of Keynesian and *laissez-faire* theories in which they try to agree on a 'policy experiment' that would decide which is the superior theory.

12

The circular flow of income, national income and money

Malcolm Sawyer

Concepts	Objectives
■ circular flow of income ■ loans and money creation ■ money ■ base money ■ measures of money supply	After studying this chapter you should be able to: ■ appreciate the difference between an equality and an identity ■ understand the nature of the circular flow of income ■ appreciate the nature of financial flows between the various sectors of the economy ■ understand the role of money in a modern economy ■ understand the creation of money through the loan process, and the relationship between loans and deposits.

12.1 Introduction

US budget deficit to reach $427bn
The US budget deficit is set to reach a record $427bn (£229bn) in 2005, the White House has predicted.

(http://newsvote.bbc.co.uk/mpapps/pagetools/print/news.bbc.co.uk/1/business/4206,
accessed 30/06/05)

US trade deficit hits fresh high
The US trade deficit has widened to a new high as the world's largest economy consumed record imports . . .

(http://newsvote.bbc.co.uk/mpapps/pagetools/print/news.bbc.co.uk/1/business/4437,
accessed 30/06/05)

IMF Says Rise in US Debt Is Threat to World Economy

... the United States is running up foreign debt of such record-breaking proportions that it threatens the financial stability of the global economy, according to a report released Wednesday by the International Monetary Fund ...

(Becker, Elizabeth and Andrews, Edmund L., New York Times, *8 January, 2004)*

American private-sector borrowing is heading back into uncharted territory After share prices began to fall ... [f]irms slashed spending, but households continued to binge as though nothing had happened ... As net borrowers, American households can bring forward spending from the future. The snag is that by consuming ever more jam today, rather than saving and investing, America may be left with only dried bread tomorrow.

('America's economy', The Economist, *23 June 2005)*

The first two headlines refer to what are usually called the *thin deficits*. The US government is spending more money than it is receiving (in taxes) and is borrowing the difference, while the country as a whole is buying more goods from abroad than it is selling. To pay for the extra imports, it is apparently, as stated in the third extract, borrowing from the rest of the world on such a scale that it threatens the stability of the global economy. As if this was not enough, US consumers continue to 'binge' as though there is no tomorrow and, according to *The Economist* in the fourth quotation, the cost will be a tomorrow that is as bleak as today is sumptuous.

What exactly does it mean for a national economy such as that of the United Sates to be in debt to the rest of the world? Who precisely is doing the borrowing and how does an imbalance in the flow of goods into and out of a national economy lead to an imbalance in international flows of money? How, if at all, are the 'twin deficits', the budget and trade deficits, connected? And how, if at all, are they related to the indebtedness of American consumers? Finally, what is the connection between saving, itself the other side of the coin of consumer indebtedness, and investment? These are questions about how the different sectors of a national economy fit together and it is the purpose of this chapter to explain these interrelationships and interdependencies.

The economies in which we live are highly complex. Over the course of a day, a week or a year there are numerous economic interactions between people. As an individual you may buy goods and services from shops, from businesses and from other individuals. As you do this your expenditure provides income for those from whom you have bought the goods and services. You may sell your labour to an employer that provides your income which, in turn, enables you to buy goods and services you need from other producers, who may then employ other people. Such market exchange creates interdependence between the economic agents involved: one person's spending creates another person's income, and if one person does not spend another does not receive an income. Industrialized economies involve an immense amount of market exchange and interdependence between people. But some economies involve much less market exchange and interdependence. In subsistence economies where families produce much of their own food and clothing there will be only limited exchange of goods and services with others. However, in industrialized economies each of us produces little of what we need; we buy goods and services from a wide range of other people. What does this interdependence mean for the working of the economy as a whole? This chapter explores that question and finds that this interdependence is intimately connected to the level of national income at which the economy will settle in the short run.

Another feature of market exchange economies is the extensive use of money. Almost all transactions involve the use of money or the promise to make a payment in money at some future date. The interdependencies between people and the use of money are connected in that it is difficult to believe that interdependence in an economy could be so complex without the use of money. When we buy and sell we use money, and the more we buy and sell the more money we use. It is usually necessary to have money in order to be able to buy things. We also consider in this chapter what the role of money is and how money is created, notably by governments and the banking system. The banking system provides loans which are used to finance expenditure and, in the process, banks create money.

The plan of this chapter is that we start with a simple depiction of an economy using the device of the circular flow of income which we met earlier in Chapter 8. In order to simplify and explain the relationships between different agents we classify them into different sectors of the economy. A starting point is to think of households as principally comprising consumers who buy goods and services from firms. Finally, households also provide firms with financial resources in exchange for claims on firms' future profits.

What determines the level of income in such a simple economy? The answer is straightforward: since expenditure creates income, the sum of all the expenditures of all agents in such an economy (households and firms taken together) equals the sum of all incomes. When this point has been established, the model is gradually made more complex. First, more sectors are added, to encompass the activities of the government, and of foreigners who interact (as buyers and sellers) with domestic firms and households. Second, we consider the role of money and how it is created by government and by the banking system in the economy.

12.2 The circular flow of income

■ ■ ■ 12.2.1 The CF model: households and firms

The circular flow of income

The circular flow of income is the flow of income circulating around the economy as income and expenditure transactions between individuals, firms, the government and the rest of the world.

The general idea of **the circular flow of income** was introduced in Chapter 8. There Paul Anand showed that, for an individual firm, gross value added (the value of sales *minus* the value of raw materials, fuels and purchased intermediate goods) must be equal to the value of all incomes earned within the firm. Consider the example of a hairdressing salon. The value of sales in this case will be the total number of haircuts and other treatments multiplied by the corresponding price the salon changes for such services. It is equal to the total expenditure of the public at this particular firm. From this total the salon has to subtract the value of the consumable materials it buys in (shampoo, electricity, etc.). This is the total expenditure of this firm at other firms. The difference between these two amounts of money is gross value added. (This is *gross* rather than *net* value added because the salon has not yet subtracted any depreciation due to, say, wear and tear on the equipment used.) Gross value added is then distributed between those who work in the salon (as wages and salaries), those who own the premises (as rent) and those who own the business (as profits). Clearly, the total value of the public's expenditure at this salon (less the salon's expenditure at other firms) is equal to the total value of the incomes earned at this firm. Moreover, the total value of the *output* of the firm (quality produced times price charged) is also equal to gross value added. This equality between the value of the firm's output, the value of incomes earned and the total expenditure at the firm (less the firm's expenditure at other firms) can be exploited when we add up the corresponding values

Figure 12.1
The basic CF model
of income

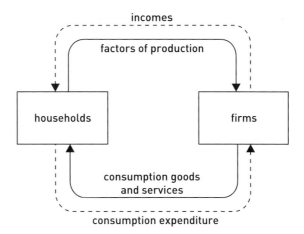

for all firms in the economy. Gross value added throughout the economy (also known as Gross Domestic Product) can be derived from *total expenditure* on the part of all households at all firms (purchases from other firms of intermediate goods and sales of intermediate goods to other firms are netted out). Gross value added also equals *total income* within the economy. Finally, it is equal to the value of *total output* in the economy. Because the income, output and expenditure measures of GDP are, in principle, the same (while differing in practice, due to measurement error) we can use the same symbol, Y, for all three.

This simple version of the economy (so far, we are excluding government and the foreign sector, and excluding any role for new investment) is depicted in Figure 12.1. The income flows from firms to households are shown as a dotted line in the upper part of the diagram while the corresponding transfer of factor services from households to firms is shown as a solid line. In the lower part of the diagram the flow of households' expenditures to firms is shown as a dotted line, while the corresponding flow of goods and services (which move from firms to households) is depicted by a solid line.

In Figure 12.1 households' consumption expenditure is the only source of income and households are shown as spending all their income. Thus

$Y = C$
where C is consumption expenditure

The next step is to include the possibility that firms are adding to the stock of capital by purchasing investment goods (I) from other firms. Such purchases are a form of expenditure that creates incomes just as consumption expenditure by households does. This means that gross value added will be greater and, on the expenditure side, we have

$Y = C + I$

Households are now receiving incomes that are, in aggregate, greater than the total value of their expenditure. This means that they must be *saving* part of their income. We can depict this by writing down the income side of the national accounts, and by drawing Figure 12.2.

$Y = C + S$

where S is aggregate saving. Clearly, in this case (where there is, as yet, no role for government or for the foreign sector), $I = S$.

Figure 12.2
The circular flow of
income with savings
and investment

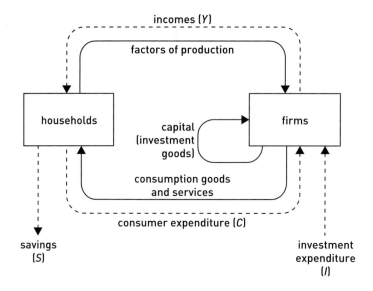

In Figure 12.2 dotted lines continue to represent flows of expenditure or income and solid lines continue to represent flows of goods and services. Both flows have to balance at each 'node'. Thus, if we consider the dotted lines entering the box marked 'firms' on the right of the diagram we have I plus C entering from below, with Y leaving from the top – and we know that $Y = C + I$. Similarly, on the left of Figure 12.2, we have S plus C leaving from the bottom of the box marked 'households' while Y enters this box from above, illustrating that $Y = C + S$.

Question   We have shown that $I = S$, but investment decisions and decisions to save are made by different decision makers (firms and households). How can this be?

To see how aggregate investment and aggregate saving are brought into equality in this model, consider what would happen if households, say, decided to save a smaller proportion of their income, but investment remained unchanged. In order to save less, households would have to raise their consumption expenditure (C would go up to, say, $C + \Delta$). This would raise income. Income would now be $Y + \Delta = C + \Delta + I$. Households would find that they were saving a smaller proportion of their new, higher incomes (as they wish to do), but aggregate saving (which is just $(Y + \Delta) - (C + \Delta)$) would be unchanged at I (= the previous value of S).

Exercise 12.1

Work out, in a similar way, what would happen if (a) households decided to save a larger proportion of their income, with unchanged aggregate investment and (b) firms decided to invest less, with households committed to saving the same proportion of their income as they did initially.

Before concluding this simple circular flow model, you should note a couple of things. First, what form do the savings of households take? The immediate form which savings take is the build up of the holding of money: more money is coming into the household in the form of income than is leaving in the form of expenditure. The next stage is often that the money is used to acquire financial assets; this may take the form of making deposits with financial institutions (e.g. banks), the purchase of new equity issued by firms or the purchase of assets from other households. Note that the sale of an existing asset (e.g. an equity or a house) by one household to another does not constitute higher net savings by households: one household is saving (acquiring an asset) but another is dissaving (selling an asset). Overall consumption, adding over both households, is unchanged and so overall saving too is unchanged. Financial institutions such as banks and building societies collect the savings of households, consolidate them and then lend the savings on to firms to help fund their physical investment. Financial institutions thus act as intermediaries between savings (by households) and investment (by firms).

Second, investment undertaken by firms means the acquisition of new capital assets, whether in the form of buildings, machinery, plant or equipment. An extensive discussion of the forms of investment and why firms undertake investment is to be found in Chapter 14. The point to note here is that in economic analysis 'investment' is given a rather specific meaning that differs considerably from everyday usage of the term. The depositing of household savings in the bank, while often called investment, is not the same as physical investment, which is the acquisition of directly productive assets. Economists would regard the latter as investment but not the former.

▨ ▩ ■ 12.2.2 Adding government

Until now we have assumed that households and firms are the only institutions in the economy. This leaves out a very important economic actor: the government. Governments tax households and firms and use this revenue to make transfers to households (e.g. social security payments) and to provide goods and services to households at zero or subsidized prices (e.g. education, health and transport services). In order to provide these goods and services, government purchases labour from households and intermediate goods and services from firms. It combines the labour of its own employees and purchased goods and services to produce a flow of goods and services to households which are, by convention, valued at cost. This means that there is no value added in government production and the total value of government output (G) is set equal to the value of the labour government purchases from households *plus* the value of the goods and services government purchases from firms.

Now, since G is a flow of expenditure just as C and I are, G adds to the incomes of those who produce government goods and services either directly (as government employees) or indirectly (as employees and owners of firms that sell intermediate output to the government). This means that the expenditure side of the national accounts must be modified to become

$$Y = C + I + G$$

At the same time, we must take into account the fact that households must pay taxes to government. (Households pay taxes directly, in the form of income tax, or indirectly, in the form of, say, value-added tax or corporation tax which are levied on firms but are, in effect, paid by households in their role as consumers or as owners of firms). Thus the income side of the national accounts is modified to become

$$Y = C + S + T$$

where T is aggregate taxation. Figure 12.3 shows the effect of including government spending and taxation in our basic circular flow model. (Note that the 'loop' showing

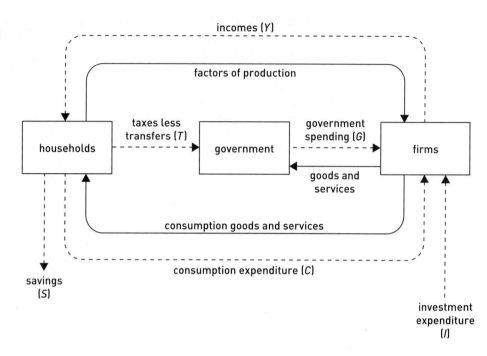

Figure 12.3
The circular flow of
income with the
government

factors of production provided by households to government and government spending
on those factors is omitted.) As before, the flows into or out of any of the boxes shown in
Figure 12.3 must balance. (You should check that this is so.) Also, we can conclude from
the fact that the expenditure and income measures of gross value added should give the
same answer that

$$C + I + G = C + S + T$$

or

$$I + G = S + T$$

■■■ 12.2.3 An open economy model

The final modification that is required is to incorporate the overseas sector into our
circular flow model. In an economy that trades with the rest of the world, some domestic output will be purchased by overseas residents. The income generated by such
purchases will add to gross value added in the economy and thus to domestic incomes.
But, at the same time, some expenditure by households on consumption goods, by firms
on new investment goods and by government will be on imported goods. Expenditure on
imported goods will not generate domestic incomes (though it will generate incomes
in the countries from which the imports come). Thus we must subtract expenditure on
imports (M) from $C + I + G + X$ to obtain the correct measure for gross value added and
hence for domestically generated income. Hence we have

$$Y = C + I + G + X - M = C + S + T$$

or

$$I + G + X = S + T + M$$

Figure 12.4
The circular flow
of income with the
government and the
rest of the world

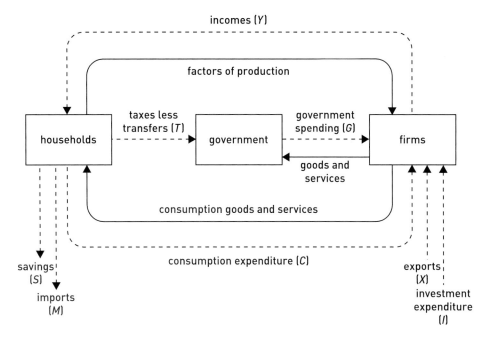

Figure 12.4 shows the final version of our circular flow model, incorporating both the government and overseas sectors.

It is now possible to apply the complete circular flow model to a real national economy. Table 12.1 reports the relative magnitudes of the four components of expenditure for the UK economy in 2003. It can readily be seen that consumer expenditure accounts for nearly two-thirds of total expenditure, with investment accounting for less than 20 per cent and government expenditure only slightly more. In 2003 imports exceeded exports (hence leading to a deficit on the balance of trade). Imports and exports each amounted to almost 30 per cent of gross domestic product, with a net balance of −3.0 per cent in that year.

Let us explore some of the interactions between domestic and foreign income flows in an economy with a government. The equation

$$I + G + X = S + T + M$$

Table 12.1
Composition of GDP
of the UK, 2003

Expenditure method	£m	%
Consumer expenditure	721 083	65.6
Gross investment	181 380	16.5
Government expenditure	229 892	20.9
Exports	277 539	25.2
Imports	310 212	28.2
Net exports	−32 673	−3.0
Statistical discrepancy	214	
GDP at market prices	1 099 896	

Note: figures do not necessarily sum to 100 due to rounding.

Source: *United Kingdom National Accounts (The Blue Book)*, 2004

can be rearranged by distinguishing between government expenditure on goods and services (Cg) and government expenditure on investment Ig, with $G = Cg + Ig$. Thus

$$S + (T - Cg) = I + Ig + (X - M)$$

The left-hand side is the sum of private savings plus government savings (excess of tax revenue over current government expenditure) and can be labelled total domestic savings. The right-hand side is the sum of investment plus the current account surplus which is equal to investment plus the capital account deficit (recall the current account surplus is equal to the capital account deficit). The right-hand side can then be seen as the sum of domestic investment plus (net) foreign investment (equal to the capital account deficit). The (net) foreign investment may be positive or negative. The equation can then be summarized by saying that total savings is equal to total investment, where investment includes that undertaken by government and savings includes taxation net of government expenditure.

As well as trading with the rest of the world, domestic residents may own overseas assets and overseas residents may own domestic assets. Owners of these assets will receive income from them in the form of interest and dividend payments. Inflows of such payments will add to (and outflows will subtract from) domestically generated incomes. Here it is useful to recall the distinction between Gross Domestic Product (GDP) and Gross National Income (GNY) introduced in Chapter 8. These interest and dividend payments form part of the GDP of the country where the incomes were generated but part of the GNY of the country where the owners reside. In the UK, at the end of 2004, net liabilities were over £141 billion; this means that foreigners own more in the UK than the UK owns abroad. However, the pattern of investment is unbalanced. UK investment overseas tends to be in the form of foreign direct investment (FDI). This means that the UK has significant net FDI assets but larger net financial liabilities. Since FDI tends to be riskier than, say, investment in a portfolio of foreign financial assets, the return on FDI is greater than the return on financial assets. This means that, despite its negative asset position, the UK actually receives more in investment income from abroad than it is required to pay out. This net investment income amounted to £24 billion in 2004 – equivalent to 2.1% of GDP.

Another complication is that some domestic residents may work overseas and receive wages and salaries for doing so while some overseas residents will be receiving wages and salaries for work performed here. These wages and salaries are counted as part of the Gross Domestic Product of the country in which the work is performed but as a part of the Gross National Income of the worker's country of residence. If we add together net property income from abroad and the net value of wages and salaries earned abroad and call the total R (net *factor* incomes from abroad), we can write

$$GNY = GDP + R$$

The uses of income relationship may now be written as

$$GNY = C + S + T$$

Thus

$$GNY = C + S + T = C + I + G + X - M + R$$

Rearranging, we obtain

$$(S - I) + (T - G) = (X - M + R) = 0$$

or

$$(S - I) + (T - G) + (M - X - R) = 0$$

In these equations $X - M$ is the *balance of trade* while $X - M + R$ is the *current account of the balance of payments*. Note that it is possible to have a balance of trade deficit $(X < M)$ while at the same time running a current account surplus $(X - M + R > 0)$ so long as net factor incomes from abroad (R) is sufficiently positive. Note also that if the UK is running a current account deficit this means that the overseas sector is in surplus.

In the previous equation the three terms in brackets correspond to the surplus or deficit position of the private sector $(S - I)$, the government $(T - G)$ and the overseas sector $(M - X - R)$, respectively. Moreover, this equation shows that a deficit in one sector (say, $I > S$) must be matched by a surplus elsewhere $(T > G$ or $M > X + R)$. This relationship between surplus and deficit sectors explains why, over time, we often observe the phenomenon of *twin deficits*: fiscal deficits and current account deficits (= overseas sector surplus) occurring at the same time. Thus, between 1998 and 2004 the UK fiscal position $(T - G)$ went from a surplus of 0.1 per cent of GDP to a deficit of 4.1 per cent of GDP. At the same time, the current account $(X - M + R)$ went from a deficit of 0.5 per cent of GDP to a deficit of 2.2 per cent of GDP. Over the same period in the USA the fiscal position deteriorated from a surplus of 0.4 per cent of GDP to a deficit of 4.1 per cent of GDP while the current account deficit grew from 2.4 per cent to 5.7 per cent of GDP.

However, twin deficits do not have to occur together: they only move in step if the private sector balance $(S - I)$ is not changing very much. A very dramatic counter-example occurred in the late 1980s in the UK. Between 1985 and 1989 the current account of the balance of payments went from a deficit of 0.2 per cent of GDP to a deficit of 5.1 per cent of GDP. But this was not associated with a growing fiscal deficit; on the contrary, the fiscal position improved from a deficit of 2.9 per cent to a surplus of 0.8 per cent of GDP. The explanation was a massive deterioration in the private sector's financial balance. During these five years household consumption grew by 24.5 per cent in real terms and investment grew by 36 per cent. GDP also grew (by 16.7 per cent) but since C and I grew much more than Y the private sector's financial position switched from a surplus of 3.5 per cent to a deficit of 5.9 per cent of GDP. The counterpart was a large deterioration in the current account as UK households and firms borrowed – ultimately from the overseas sector – to fund a consumption and investment boom. The implication is that a current account deficit may be the 'fault' of lax fiscal policy $(G > T)$ or an over-enthusiastic private sector $(I > S)$ – or possibly both.

▪▪▪ 12.2.4 Quantities and prices in the circular flow model

We have seen how expenditure by the same agents in the economy can create incomes for others. In the hairdressing salon example introduced in Section 12.2.1 it was easy to see that a decision on the part of a member of the public to have his or her hair cut on a particular day would create incomes in the salon. Expenditure, income and output (in this case, of haircuts) will all have risen as a result of this decision. However, until now we have implicitly assumed that all these increases are increases in *real terms*: we have said nothing about prices.

Often this will be a good approximation of what actually occurs. In the case of the hairdressing salon, prices are likely to be specified in advance and will not change just because an extra customer decides to have a haircut that day. If there is spare capacity in the salon large fluctuations in demand for hairdressing services may occur without a price change. However, in other sectors of the economy and in other circumstances, firms may respond to increased demand by raising prices. This means that increased expenditure will be translated into higher incomes (as before) but that the increase in output (in real terms) will not be as great as it would have been if prices had remained constant. Note that the circular flow model still applies in these circumstances and that the income, expenditure and output measures of gross value added (and, ultimately, of GDP) still coincide. But now we need to distinguish between nominal and real changes. Nominal changes correspond to changes in the *value* (price times quantity) of expenditure, income or output. Real changes correspond to changes which occur when we strip out the effect of price changes; that is the changes that would have occurred if prices had remained constant. For this reason, national accounts are always presented in both current price and constant price terms. For each component of the national accounts (investment, consumption and so on) there will be a price index (the deflator) linking the current price and constant price data series. It is also possible to define a deflator for the whole economy (the GDP deflator) which links nominal and real GDP. Deflators for different components of the national accounts will diverge if, for example, improvements in productivity in different sectors of the economy occur at different rates. However, in some circumstances prices throughout the economy will move together. This could be a consequence of a rapid growth in expenditure when many firms were capacity constrained or because wage rates have also risen. In such circumstances the circular flow model continues to describe the relationship between different sectors of the economy, but now we must be very careful to distinguish real from nominal changes.

■ ■ ■ 12.2.5 Financial flows and changes in assets

Within the private sector individuals and firms lend to and borrow from each other. When they do so, they exchange claims on future transfers of money in the opposite direction. For example, a homeowner who borrows from a bank may take out a mortgage which stipulates the repayments that must be made and the circumstances under which, if they are not made on time, the bank may take over ownership of the house. Or a firm may fund a new investment by borrowing from households and issuing equities which promise to pay the households a share of the future profits. Financial claims (mortgages, equities, corporate bonds) are often traded on secondary markets without these transactions affecting the original borrower.

If we aggregate households and firms into a single private sector we can net out all transactions within the sector and identify the net flow from the private sector to the rest of the economy. This corresponds to the excess of savings (by households and firms, S) over private investment (I). If $S > I$ in any period the personal sector must be accumulating financial claims on the rest of the economy. These claims constitute part of the personal sector's wealth. (The personal sector also owns other assets, such as land, houses and – very importantly – human capital.)

If the government sector is running a deficit ($G > T$) it must be borrowing from other sectors. It does this predominantly be selling (long-dated) bonds and (short-dated) bills to the private sector. But the government can also (via the central bank) print money. Bonds, bills and cash are all claims on the government that are held by the private sector and treated by the private sector as part of its wealth.

If the government is running a current account surplus ($X - M + R > 0$) domestic residents will be increasing their claims on foreigners. If the current account is in deficit ($X - M + R < 0$) domestic residents must be selling assets to foreigners (e.g. land or domestic businesses) or borrowing from foreigners by giving them promises (e.g. equities or bonds) to make repayments sometime in the future. This accumulation of assets by foreigners is acknowledgement of the resources they are providing – in the form of a capital inflow – to fund the current account deficit.

This three-sector model illustrates a more general point. Within the circular flow of income some are spending less than their income while others are spending more than their income. The former can be referred to as 'surplus units' and the latter as 'deficit units'. But it is an accounting identity that the sum of surpluses and deficits must be zero. What the circular flow then enables us to infer is that one sector's lending is another sector's borrowing. This is because, at the sectoral level, there is the requirement that the net lending or borrowing between sectors sum to zero.

It is also generally the case that any economic unit cannot be a 'deficit' unit forever. Each period's deficit adds to the debt of the individual or firm and the interest payments required to finance the debt increase. A continuing deficit would mean rising debt and more interest payments. The person concerned would find it increasingly difficult to meet the interest payments on their accumulating debt and to find others to borrow money from.

The national income accounts provide data which can be used to statistically illustrate the relationships among the surplus or deficit positions of the private sector (S – I), the government (T – G) and the overseas sector (M – X – R) that were identified in Section 12.2.3 above. Table 12.2(a) indicates the financial flows in terms of net lending or borrowing between sectors where the private sector has initially been further disaggregated into non-financial corporations, financial corporations and households. The net lending or borrowing of, say, the private sector does not completely correspond to the difference between savings and investment. There are, for example, transfers received by and paid out by the private sector that lead to a difference between savings and investment on the one hand and what the private sector borrows or lends on the other. The net lending or borrowing across the three main sectors add up to zero (apart from the statistical discrepancy). The flows involved appear to be large, amounting to several billions of

Table 12.2(a)
Financial flows between sectors for selected years, UK

Net lending/borrowing	1995 £m	1999 £m	2003 £m
Non-financial corporations	4 615	–12 910	14 604
Financial corporations	2 979	–16 904	8 362
Households	–42 001	9 384	–37 700
Private sector (total of above)	–34 407	–20 430	–14 734
General government	25 925	–3 213	–4 732
Rest of the world	8 432	23 643	19 187
Statistical discrepancy	–	–	279

Table 12.2(b)
Financial flows between sectors for selected years, UK

	1995 £m	1999 £m	2003 £m
Savings (S) – investment (I)	26 176	–36 926	10 896
Taxation (T) – Government expenditure (G)	9 015	24 416	–31 605
Current account deficit	–35 191	12 510	20 430
Statistical discrepancy			279

Source: calculated from *United Kingdom National Accounts* (*The Blue Book*), 2004

pounds, but they can be compared with the figure for GDP given in Table 12.1 to give some perspective. It can be seen that for the UK there were considerable swings in the net lending or borrowing by sectors, with the government budget position, for example, swinging from a surplus of nearly £26 billion in 1995 to a deficit of almost £5 billion in 2003. These figures illustrate that when one sector is in surplus at least one other sector must be in deficit and that the total surplus equals the total deficit (i.e. they sum to zero).

Question	Check these statements by examining the figures for any one year in Figure 12.2(a). For example, note the private sector deficit for 1995 and add the surpluses on the government and overseas sectors.

Rearranging the financial flows in terms of equation $(S - I) + (T - G) + (M - X - R) = 0$ leads to the figures in Table 12.2(b). Note, however, that I refers to private investment, while government investment is included in general government expenditure G. It can be seen that in 1999 UK private savings fell short of private investment to the extent of almost £37 billion, whereas there was a government budget surplus $(T - G)$ of over £24 billion. By 2003 there was a marked shift, with savings exceeding investment by nearly £11 billion, a budget deficit of over £31 billion and a current account deficit of £20 billion. These figures sum to zero, apart from the statistical discrepancy of £279 million. This statistical discrepancy arises from measurement errors, such as the difficulties of recording some types of income, etc. In effect, in 2003, the deficit of private savings (over private investment) was matched by government savings (excess of tax revenue over expenditure) and borrowing from overseas (the other side of the current account deficit). The net lending and borrowing figures for 1999 were relatively unusual in that it has been the norm for governments to run budget deficits and for the private sector to run surpluses (to some degree reflecting an excess of savings over investment). In the UK context, borrowing from the rest of the world, corresponding to a current account deficit, has been the more usual position.

Exercise 12.2

Fill in the blank cells for Table 12.3 which records the transactions of different sectors in a hypothetical economy. Assume that net income from overseas is zero.

Table 12.3

Variable	Amount
Savings (S)	20 000
Investment (I)	25 000
Savings (S) – Investment (I)	
Exports (X)	40 000
Imports (M)	45 000
Balance of trade	
Government expenditure (G)	50 000
Taxation (T)	
Budget deficit	

Let us now look at the net flow of each sector in some detail. The third term in equation $(S - I) + (T - G) + (M - X - R) = 0$, $(M - X)$, represents the economy's current account with the rest of the world. Since one country's imports are another country's exports, the worldwide level of exports and the level of imports are equal to one another. Similarly, one country's income inflow is another country's outflow. While some countries have a balance of trade (or current account) deficit, others must necessarily have a surplus.

The net payments $(X - M)$ are a monetary measure of the *balance of trade* on the international account. There is no particular need or reason why X and M should balance in any period, so there may be a trade surplus $(X > M)$ or a trade deficit $(X < M)$. The trade balance of $(X - M)$ in the circular flow model forms a major part of the current account (i.e. with the rest of the world). Another significant part of the current account is the net income received from abroad (i.e. the difference between income flowing in and income flowing out of the country). There is also a capital account which records the borrowing and lending activities of the economy with the rest of the world. Together with the current account it forms a country's overall *balance of payments* which is further discussed in Chapter 17.

A country with a current account deficit must finance that deficit in some way. One way would be that the reserves of foreign currency (held by the government or central bank) are used to finance the difference. There are some obvious limits to how far that can continue. The other, and dominant, way is that the deficit on the current account is matched by a surplus on the capital account. In other words, the country is borrowing from other countries. This borrowing can take a variety of forms: it would include foreign direct investment, the sale of existing assets to foreigners and the sale of government and other bonds to residents of other countries. When a country is running a trade surplus (so that exports exceed imports), it can either accumulate reserves of foreign currency and/or lend abroad.

The second term in the equation is $(T - G)$ and this is the excess of tax revenue over government expenditure. It is generally the case that this term is negative (i.e. the government runs a budget deficit), though that is not universally the case. The budget deficit can be financed in two ways, and usually by some combination of the two. First, the government can borrow from the public and pay interest on its borrowing. Much of that borrowing takes the form of the sale of government bonds to the public. These bonds will pay a fixed yield to the holders, which is set when the bond is sold. The bonds usually have a redemption date, that is, the date at which the government will repay the sum advanced. Borrowing by the government can take other forms, such as the sale of Treasury Bills (which are redeemed after 90 days) and directly from the public in the form of national savings. Second, the government, or more accurately the central bank on its behalf, can create money. Money created by the central bank (in the UK, the Bank of England) is called 'base money' and consists of notes and coins and deposits held by commercial banks at the central bank.

The final element to be considered from the equation is $(S - I)$, that is, the excess of private savings over private investment (sometimes called net private savings). It could be thought of as savings available to finance other sectors of the economy (the public sector and the foreign sector). Financial intermediaries such as banks, building societies and insurance companies play an important role in collecting these individual savings and making them available to deficit spenders in the economy, such as private sector firms, the government or economic agents in the rest of the world.

Case study: The US twin deficits

US trade deficit hits fresh high

Textile imports from China have soared this year

The US trade deficit has widened to a new high as the world's largest economy consumed record imports of consumer goods and industrial materials.

The US trade gap rose 4.3% to $61bn (£32bn) in February, data published on Tuesday showed, well above market forecasts of a $59bn shortfall.

The deficit – up from $58.5bn in January – continues to be swollen by America's appetite for imports.

These rose 1.6% to a record $161.5bn while exports rose 0.1% to $100.5bn . . .

The US thirst for imports shows no signs of abating, with a strong economy resulting in record imports of cars, consumer goods and industrial materials in February . . .

The US government has argued that the trade gap reflects strong consumer demand within the US.

http://news.bbc.co.uk

US budget deficit to reach $427bn

The twin budget deficits have caused market jitters

The US budget deficit is set to reach a record $427bn (£229bn) in 2005, the White House has predicted.

But officials said the administration would meet its pledge to cut the deficit in half over five years, partly by controlling public spending.

The forecast takes account of an extra $80bn the White House is seeking from Congress to fund military operations.

It comes as a non-partisan watchdog said the 2005 deficit, not including military costs, would be $368bn.

The Congressional Budget Office (CBO) had previously forecast a $348bn shortfall in the 2005 fiscal year.

The US budget deficit hit $412bn in the 12 months to 30 September 2004, after reaching $377bn in the previous fiscal year.

http://news.bbc.co.uk

IMF Says Rise in US Debts Is Threat to World's Economy

With its rising budget deficit and ballooning trade imbalance, the United States is running up a foreign debt of such record-breaking proportions that it threatens the financial stability of the global economy, according to a report released Wednesday by the International Monetary Fund. Prepared by a team of I.M.F. economists, the report sounded a loud alarm about the shaky fiscal foundation of the United States, questioning the wisdom of the Bush administration's tax cuts and warning that large budget deficits pose 'significant risks' not just for the United States but for the rest of the world.

The report warns that the United States' net financial obligations to the rest of the world could be equal to 40 per cent of its total economy within a few years – 'an unprecedented level of external debt for a large industrial country,' according to the fund, that could play havoc with the value of the dollar and international exchange rates. The danger, according to the report, is that the United States' voracious appetite for borrowing could push up global interest rates and thus slow global investment and economic growth. 'Higher borrowing costs abroad would mean that the adverse effects of U.S. fiscal deficits would spill over into global investment and output,' the report said.

White House officials dismissed the report as alarmist, saying that President Bush has already vowed to reduce the budget deficit by half over the next five years. The deficit reached $374 billion last year, a record in dollar terms but not as a share of the total economy, and it is expected to exceed $400 billion this year. But many international economists said they were pleased that the report raised the issue. 'The I.M.F. is right,' said C. Fred Bergsten, director of the Institute for International Economics in Washington. 'If those twin deficits – of the federal budget and the trade deficit – continue to grow you are increasing the risk of a day of reckoning when things can get pretty nasty.'

(E. Becker and E.L. Andrews, New York Times, *8 January 2004)*

Questions

What exactly does it mean for a national economy such as that of the United Sates to be in debt to the rest of the world?

Who precisely is doing the borrowing and how does an imbalance in the flow of goods into and out of a national economy lead to an imbalance in international flows of money?

How, if at all, are the 'twin deficits', the budget and trade deficits, connected? And how, if at all, are they related to the indebtedness of American consumers?

Finally, what is the connection between saving, itself the other side of the coin of consumer indebtedness, and investment?

Using information from the case study material and the equation $(S - I) + (T - G) + (M - X - R) = 0$, try to sketch out brief answers to these questions that were raised by the headlines and quotations that opened the chapter.

12.3 Money and the economy

What happens when there are plans to increase expenditure, for example when firms want to undertake investment or when the government plans to increase expenditures on health and education? Where do the resources required for these planned increases in expenditure come from? If these expenditures take place, then there will be changes in the circular flow of income which will give rise to increased incomes. But how can the planned increase in expenditures be initially financed, which it must be if the expenditures are to be undertaken?

12.3.1 Finance and money creation

If one individual wants to spend more than their income (so that expenditure exceeds income) they must be able to fund the difference. This individual would then become a 'deficit' unit since there is a deficit of income compared with expenditure, and would have to cover the deficit in some way, maybe through borrowing or through running down their wealth. But if one individual is running a deficit, the circular flow indicates that there must be another who is running a surplus (a 'surplus' unit), that is, someone whose income exceeds expenditure. In effect, the deficit units are (directly or indirectly) borrowing from the surplus units. Adding together all the 'deficit' units and 'surplus' units must lead to the outcome that overall there is a balance between income and expenditure.

This is also true at the global level. In particular, it means that one country's trade deficit (imports greater than exports) has to be balanced by another country's trade surplus (exports greater than imports). It is also the case that one country's imports must be another country's exports. You will study more about international finance in Chapter 17; here we concentrate on a single economy.

How are the individuals who are running deficits matched with the individuals who are running surpluses?

This could happen directly or indirectly. Let us consider the direct ways first. Some matching may be done through individual contact: you are running a surplus, your friend is running a deficit and you are willing to lend to your friend. In exchange you might acquire a financial asset, for example an equity share sold by a firm that needs funds for investment. A financial asset has been created and sold to you. The financial asset (an equity share) enables the 'deficit' unit (in this case the firm issuing the equity) to acquire finance from a 'surplus' unit. Similarly, the government may borrow from surplus units by the issue of bonds.

However, most of the matching between surplus and deficit unions happens indirectly through financial institutions such as banks, building societies and insurance companies. It is likely that if you are running a financial surplus you will be accumulating financial assets; for example, your bank balance will be increasing. The main way in which additional finance will be provided to deficit units is through loans from the banking system. When a bank provides a loan, it immediately adds to the borrower's bank balance and allows the borrower to draw cheques on this increased balance. The borrower (as a buyer) pays a seller for goods and services by writing cheques which instruct the bank to transfer funds to the seller's bank account. The seller, in turn, may decide to hold these deposits in the banking system or buy from yet another seller (in which case the deposit will be passed on again) or, possibly, to pay down a loan which the seller may have taken out previously.

Thus, financial intermediaries such as banks, building societies and insurance companies perform a very important function in industrialized economies. However, they can only perform this function due to the widespread use of money. The surplus income of households is held in *money* form, and firms receive *money* with which they buy plant and machinery. We now proceed to consider the nature of money and how money is defined and measured, before returning to elaborate on the ways in which banks are able to grant loans and create money.

▪▪▪ 12.3.2 What is money?

To appreciate the role of money we could try to envisage an economy without money; this is generally labelled a barter economy. In such an economy, people would be exchanging goods directly for other goods, and for exchange there would have to be the *double coincidence of wants*. What that means is clear from the following example. A person with apples who wanted pears would have to find another person who, at the same time, had pears but wanted apples in order to make the exchange (and they would have to agree on the rate of exchange between apples and pears). There are occasionally reports of some direct barter between companies, but these are relatively rare. We may ourselves be involved in some elements of direct barter – we may swap something we have with goods (or services) from our friends and neighbours.

However, the overwhelming majority of exchange transactions involve money. We sell something (such as our labour) for money, and then use that money to buy something else (such as food or clothes). All this was reflected in the circular flow of income with the two types of flows: of real goods and services in one direction (represented by solid lines in Figures 12.1–12.4) and of money in the other direction (represented by dotted lines).

In common parlance the word money is often used to denote wealth, in phrases such as 'he has lots of money' or 'she left all her money to her children'. Economists when they talk of money have a narrow concept in mind. They mean something which is widely used in the exchange of goods and services – a commodity or token which you will accept when you sell something. Throughout history there have been many examples where quantities of a particular commodity have served as money, with the best known examples being gold and silver. These commodities have an intrinsic value in themselves (e.g. in the manufacture of jewellery and in dentistry). Their use in coins involves a significant resource cost. For this reason, in most economies what serves as money has become either a physical object with little intrinsic value (e.g. coins, banknotes) or a bookkeeping entry with no physical existence (e.g. a bank deposit).

A banknote has no intrinsic value, but it is of value to an individual because someone else will be willing to exchange goods and services for it. And this second individual will do so because they expect a third person to accept the banknote in exchange for goods and services in the future. Interestingly, even paper money is becoming redundant: most transactions are now financed by the exchange of bank deposits. When you make a payment by cheque or debit card you authorize your bank to reduce your deposit by the specified amount and to increase the seller's bank deposit (which may be at another bank) by the same amount. This authorization is increasingly taking the form of electronic transfer.

Bank deposits are financial assets so far as the holder is concerned, but for the body that has issued the financial asset it represents a financial liability. Notes and coins have been issued by the central bank (on behalf of the government) and represent a liability on the government's part (they are part of the national debt). Bank deposits in a similar way are assets for the public but liabilities for the banks. A characteristic of money, then, is that it is a financial asset but that it also has the property of being easily transferable from one person to another and being universally accepted as a means of payment.

The historical evolution of **money** suggests that we need to define money in terms of its specific functions rather than by the physical characteristics that happen to apply to money as it exists today. Defining money in terms of its functions recognizes that the physical form money can take can vary. Thus the commonly accepted definition of money is that it is any commodity that performs the following functions in the economy:

Money

Money is a means of payment, store of value and unit of account.

- *Unit of account.* Prices, wages, rents and so on are measured in the units of money: pounds in the UK, euros in much of the European Union and dollars in the USA. Contracts will generally be specified in terms of this unit of account.

- *Means of payment.* When we wish to acquire some good or service the person selling the item will generally accept money and we will usually expect to offer money for the purchase of the item. There may be exceptions: we may, for example, directly exchange goods and services with our neighbours without any money being involved. Money facilitates exchange and it is often referred to as a *medium of exchange*. The wider term *means of payment* is used here as money is also used to settle debts (notably, tax obligations to the government) which do not arise from exchange.

- *Store of value.* This means that agents can hold money between the sale of one item and the purchase of another. To carry out this function at a minimum money should be able to retain its value between the time of receipt and the time of disbursement. As individuals, we may well receive our income in the form of money once a month and gradually spend the money during the course of the month. We would be unwilling to accept money if money was likely to lose a significant part of its purchasing power before the time came to purchase. During periods of very high inflation money loses value quickly (in terms of the goods and services it can buy) and hence it performs less well its function as a store of value; for example, an inflation rate of 100 per cent per year would mean that the value of money halved within a year.

▨ ▩ ■ 12.3.3 Measures of money

Money has been defined above in terms of three functions and one of those functions is that money is a generally accepted means of payment. Translating that definition of money into a measure of what actually constitutes money at a particular place and time faces some difficulties. For example, a cheque will not usually be accepted as payment for a bus fare, but trying to buy a house for cash is likely to raise suspicion. Small transactions and transactions where the participants do not wish to leave evidence (e.g. those that are illegal or of dubious legality) are likely to use cash, whereas large transactions are likely to use cheques, debit cards and electronic transfer.

> **Question**   Why might we be interested in wanting to measure the amount of money in the economy?

One of the reasons we are interested in measuring money is that, because of its role as a medium of exchange, the amount of money in circulation is also a measure of purchasing power in the economy. However, giving a precise statistical definition of money is fraught with difficulties. Partly this is because what we would include as money varies on whether we consider its function as a medium of exchange alone or also as a store of value. Accordingly there are five measures of money supply:

■ *M0* is the narrowest form of money and often referred to as the *monetary base* or *base money* is that issued by the central bank (in the UK, the Bank of England). It consists of notes and coins and deposits held by the commercial banks at the central bank. Since the central bank controls the issue of notes and coins and since it can also set the terms under which commercial banks can hold deposits with it, the central bank has effective control over the quantity of base money in the economy. Note, however, that this control has to be exercised with care. The deposits the commercial banks hold at the central bank are an important asset for them, particularly in times of financial crisis. If the public were to become suspicious about the solvency of a particular bank or, more seriously, about the banking system as a whole, the central bank would feel obliged to lend to the threatened bank(s) and this would increase the banks' deposits with it. By acting in this way as a 'lender of last resort' the central bank may be able to avert a financial crisis. However, acting in this way may not be consistent with maintaining control over the quantity of M0. While it remains true that the central bank *can* exercise effective control over M0 if it wishes, it may decide, in particular circumstances, that the cost of doing so is too high.

■ *M1* is a wider measure of the money stock which encompasses current account (demand) deposits within the commercial banking system plus notes and coins. Current account deposits may be readily transferred to others via the use of cheques or electronic transfers and are a generally accepted means of payment. But they are not a universally accepted means of payment, as you would find if you sought to pay your bus fare by cheque. As a consequence many small day-to-day transactions are paid in cash, while larger transactions will be paid through cheque or electronic transfer.

■ *M2* includes deposit accounts (time deposits) with banks, plus M1. A deposit account deposit cannot be immediately transferred to another person but it can be readily

Table 12.4
Stock of money in
the UK

Measure of money	Definition	Stock of money, December 2004 (seasonally adjusted) £m
M0	Notes and coins in circulation plus reserves held by banks with the central bank; sometimes called 'base money'	42 259
M1	M0 plus non-interest bearing bank deposits	675 224
M2	M1 plus other bank retail deposits	1 058 224
M3	M2 plus repurchase agreements, money market fund shares and paper	1 273 606
M4	Holdings by the private sector, other than monetary financial institutions, of sterling deposits including certificates of deposit, commercial paper, bonds, liabilities arising from repurchase agreements and sterling bank bills, notes and coins	840 523

Source: Bank of England, http://www.bankofengland.co.uk/mfsd/ms/020830/, accessed January 2005

moved to a current account deposit (held by the same person with the same bank) and then used as a means of payment. There may be some delay in being able to move money from one account to another (e.g., a period of notice has to be given) and/or some financial penalty involved.

■ *M3* is a broader measure still and includes M2 *plus* repurchase agreements and money market fund shares.

■ *M4* is the broadest measure and is made up of deposits with building societies *plus* the aggregates that constitute M3.

Table 12.4 gives figures for some of the widely used measures of money, along with their official definitions. It can be seen that for the UK, the narrow definition of money (M0) is around 8 per cent of M1. Recall that M1 is the measure of money supply that most closely corresponds to money as the main means of payment. In turn, M1 is less than half of the broader money measures such as M3 or M4. These broader moneys are financial assets with values fixed in terms of the unit of account; they can be readily and with little cost changed into M1.

It can be seen that most measures of the money supply include the value of bank deposits which are created by banks. As these financial intermediaries carry out their finance functions in modern economies through granting loans, they also create money. This is not, of course, intuitively obvious. The next section considers how this happens.

▪▪▪ 12.3.4 Banks, loans and money creation

In a Western industrialized economy the vast majority of transactions (measured in value terms) are financed by money as measured by M1. These transactions are by the transfer of bank deposits from one person to another. Although many transactions will be paid for by cash, those transactions will be small in value relative to the transactions which are paid for through the transfer of bank deposits. These may involve the writing of a cheque to transfer a deposit from one person's bank account to another person's. Or else the transfer may be accomplished by an instruction to the bank in the form of a standing order, a direct debit arrangement, a written instruction or an electronic instruction. Most of what is used as money is therefore held in the form of bank deposits.

A bank deposit represents an asset as far as the person holding it is concerned: it is part of their wealth. But a bank deposit is a liability so far as the bank is concerned: it has an obligation to pay (generally on demand) the depositor. A bank deposit is something of a liability to the bank in a more general sense; it may pay some interest on the deposit, although the interest rate is generally small (M2, M3) or zero (M1). In addition the bank incurs the costs associated with the transfer of deposits from one person to another.

Besides accepting and holding deposits, another major function carried out by banks is the provision of loans to the public. Banks, of course, charge interest on loans and it is a major way by which they make a profit. Loans are part of the assets of the banks since they yield interest to the banks and the loan holders are under an obligation to repay the loan. This relationship between loans and deposits illustrates a general feature of financial instruments: what is an asset for one agent (in this case, the bank) is a liability for another (the person who has taken out a loan from the bank). The commercial banks also hold deposits with the central bank and some notes and coins, and these are included in the term *reserves* in the consolidated balance sheet of the commercial banks.

A highly simplified version of the balance sheet of a bank is shown in Table 12.5. This balance sheet is simplified in two particular respects. First, the assets of the bank only include loans and reserves; the bank's ownership of other financial assets such as government bonds, buildings, land is ignored. Second, the two sides of the balance sheet are assumed to be equal, and hence the net worth of the bank is taken to be zero. These simplifying assumptions are made so that we can focus on the roles of loans and deposits.

The deposits which appear in the balance sheet of banks are generally seen as part of the stock of money. It can now be seen from this balance sheet of the banks that when loans increase then there must be some corresponding changes in reserves and in deposits. But, conversely, an increase in deposits (i.e. in the amount of money) would go along with some corresponding changes in loans and reserves. Since Table 12.5 represents a balance sheet, the expansion or contraction on one side must be accompanied by an expansion or contraction on the other side. In this context two particular questions arise. First, which side of the balance sheet tends to be the cause of the expansion: is it more likely to be deposits or loans? Second, since an expansion of the balance sheet may involve an expansion of reserves, can the availability of reserves limit any expansion? The reserves in the balance sheet of the banks are the reserves held with the central bank and holdings of notes and coins issued by the central bank; if the central bank restricts the availability of those reserves would that constrain the expansion of the balance sheet?

The way in which the banks expand their balance sheets and the consequences for the creation of money have been analysed in two rather different ways. From these analyses two rather different conclusions can be drawn. One view is that the expansion of the balance sheet comes from an expansion of the available reserves. For example, consider what would happen if the central bank expanded the amount of notes and coins in circulation. This could arise from the government financing some of its expenditure through the

Table 12.5
Simplified balance
sheet of a bank

Assets	Liabilities
Loans	Deposits
Reserves	

printing of notes and the minting of coins. Some of the individuals who receive the increased amount of notes and coins as payment for goods and services are likely to deposit some of it with the banks. The banks may hold some of those notes and coins as their reserves, and may place some of them with the central bank as reserves. But the banks would find that they have more reserves and more deposits than before, and are then in a position to extend more loans. The extension of loans requires that there are businesses and households who wish to take out loans (at the price being charged). The further extension of loans, and hence the expansion of the banks' balance sheets, also requires that the banks are willing to make the loans and can find credit-worthy borrowers to whom they wish to lend. But banks may feel that they should keep a particular 'safe' ratio between their reserves and the overall amount of deposits. Depositors may withdraw their money (in the form of notes and coins) from banks or demand that banks be in a position to meet those withdrawals at short notice. But others are depositing notes and coins with the banks. The banks keep some reserves to meet the possible differences between withdrawals and deposits, and those differences fluctuate from day to day, sometimes positive, sometimes negative.

How far the expansion of the banks' balance sheets can proceed can be illustrated as follows. To illustrate the mechanism consider the following example. The central bank prints some money, say 1000, which is received by individuals, and those individuals deposit 800 in their bank accounts and keep 200 in the form of cash. The banks receive the 800 deposits, and then decide to keep 10 per cent in the form of reserves (i.e. 80) and to lend out the rest (i.e. 720). In the next round, the loans are spent and received by others as money, and that money is kept (here by assumption) 20 per cent in the form of cash (144) and 80 per cent in the form of bank deposits (576). The bank deposits are further used by banks to make loans (to the extent of 90 per cent of deposits) and to keep reserves: in period 2 the additional loans amount to 518.40 and reserves of 57.60. This is shown in Table 12.6.

This process continues, with the 518.40 being spent and being received by others as money, which they keep in the form of cash (103.68) and as additional deposits (414.72). In each round the total money supply (cash *plus* deposits) increases, but at a slower rate. The cumulative process ceases eventually (though, strictly speaking, this needs an infinite number or cycles!) with the money supply having increased by $714.30 + 2857.00 = 3571.30$.

We can work out this increase in the following way, using B for the amount of base money (reserves R plus cash C). Let D be the level of deposits and M be the total stock of

Table 12.6

Period	Change in Cash	Change in Deposits	Change in Loans	Change in Reserves	Cumulative Change in Cash	Cumulative Change in Deposits	Cumulative Change in Loans	Cumulative Change in Reserves	Cumulative Change in Money
1	200.00	800.00	720.00	80.00	200.00	800.00	720.00	80.00	280.00
2	144.00	576.00	518.40	57.60	344.00	1376.00	1238.40	137.60	481.60
3	103.68	414.72	373.25	41.47	447.68	1790.72	1611.65	179.07	626.75
4	74.65	298.60	268.74	29.86	522.33	2089.32	1880.39	208.93	731.26
5	53.75	214.99	193.49	21.50	576.08	2304.31	2073.88	230.43	806.51
6	38.70	154.79	139.31	15.48	614.78	2459.10	2213.19	245.91	860.69
7	27.86	111.45	100.31	11.15	642.64	2570.55	2313.50	257.06	899.69
8	20.06	80.24	72.22	8.02	662.70	2650.80	2385.72	265.08	927.78
...	...	...	...	...	...	...	...	...	...
∞	0	0	0	0	714.30	2857.00	2572.00	285.70	3571.30

money (cash C plus deposits D). If we further assume that the banks wish to hold reserves which amount to a proportion r of total deposits, we can write:

$$R = rD$$

or

$$D = \frac{R}{r} = \frac{B - C}{r}$$

The stock of money M is held either in the form of notes and coins or in the form of bank deposits. We can write this as:

$$M = C + D$$

The extent to which the public wish to hold cash or to hold bank deposits would depend on payment practices that differ from economy to economy. For example, the ease of using cheques or electronic transfer to make payments would reduce the amount we wished to hold as cash. Let us call the proportion of money held as cash c, then:

$$C = cM$$

Substituting the values of C and D in $M = C + D$ from equation (4), we get the alternative expression for money supply (M):

$$M = cM + \frac{R}{r}$$

$$= cM + \frac{(B - C)}{r}$$

$$= cM + \frac{(B - cM)}{r}$$

This can be written as:

$$M(c + r - cr) = B$$

or

$$M = \frac{B}{(1 - (1 - c)(1 - r))}$$

The term $\dfrac{1}{(1 - (1 - c)(1 - r))}$ is often referred to as the money multiplier or the credit multiplier. Since the denominator is less than 1, it suggests that the stock of money is a multiple of the base money. This approach suggests that, although the amount of money is not under the control of the central bank, it is *indirectly* under its control, so long as the money multiplier is constant through time. This will be so if the banks' desired reserve ratio (r) and the public's desired cash-to-total-money ratio (c) remain constant. But is this likely?

Figure 12.5 shows the ratio of M4 to M0 (base money) in the UK between 1970 and 2004. This ratio has risen from about 6 to over 26: it is clearly *not* constant. A large part of the explanation of this change in the money multiplier lies in changes in payments technology over this period. But it is also notable that the most rapid change in the ratio occurred during the first half of the 1980s – the period during which the UK government put great effort into the attempt to control the growth of broad money.

Figure 12.5
Ratio of M4 to M0,
UK 1970–2004

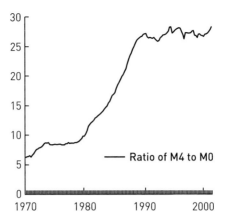

If the cash-to-money (c) ratio and the reserve ratio (r) are not constant but are influenced by economic conditions (or are 'endogenous', in the language of Chapter 13) control of the quantity of broad money by the central bank using the money multiplier mechanism will not be possible. In these circumstances the central bank's influence over the quantity of broad money will be only indirect via its influence over interest rates, inflationary expectations and the level of economic activity more generally.

Exercise 12.3

1 Look at Table 12.6 again. What measures correspond to the total quantity of base money (B) in the economy depicted there?
2 As a result of the central bank's action, by how much has base money increased? By how much has the money stock increased?
3 Using the fact that, in preparing the table, c was taken to be 0.2 and r was 0.1, confirm that the formula for the money multiplier gives the right answer for the increase in the stock of money.

The other view on the relationship between money and loans starts from an emphasis on the lending behaviour of banks. According to this view, the lending activities of banks are closely linked to the financing of expenditure. The expansion of loans outstanding (i.e. new loans being granted in excess of those being repaid) generates an increase in bank deposits and thereby in the stock of money. Immediately after a loan is arranged a deposit is created in the account of the person to whom the loan is extended. When this person draws on the loan to fund expenditure they transfer the deposit to the person to whom payment is made. In turn it can be expected that the person receiving the deposit (created by the loan) will spend it and pass it on to someone else. The newly created deposit thereby circulates through the economy. The stock of money has increased. (Note that the central bank has not played any role in this process.)

Someone receiving the deposit has a number of options. They can spend it on goods and services (in which case it will pass to someone else). They can decide to purchase an existing asset (in which case, again, it will pass to someone else). Another option would be to pay off part of an existing bank loan. With an overdraft this would happen automatically: as the deposit is paid in it would reduce the amount of the outstanding overdraft. In other words, loans can be extinguished and paid off as well as created. How much of the original loan remains in circulation (and thus how much the stock of money has increased) depends on how far individuals use deposits to pay off loans.

Clearly, according to this second view, the stock of money in an economy is the result of many decisions on the part of many different individuals and institutions – especially banks. The banks will meet the demand for loans provided that they think it will be profitable to do so. The profitability for banks of loans will depend on the interest rate which is charged for loans and on the risk of default on the loans. It is often observed that the rate of interest on loans is closely related to the rate of interest charged by the central bank, with the loan interest rate a mark-up over the central bank interest rate. The rate of interest charged by the central bank is the rate of interest which banks would have to pay the central bank if the banks sought to borrow reserves from the central bank.

The central bank acts as the *lender of last resort*, that is, the central bank will provide reserves to the bank system (at a price). The central bank stands ready to supply reserves when required. Thus, it is argued, banks can expand their balance sheets provided that the public wish to take out loans (at the price charged by the banks) and the public are prepared to hold the deposits which are generated. When this expansion requires more reserves, these will be augmented by the central bank.

Plans to undertake spending can only be made effective if they are backed by purchasing power: that is, we can only spend if we have the money. In many cases the money we spend in, say, a month has come to us as our income. If our expenditure is equal to our income then we may have some timing problems – we have to receive the money from income before we can spend it – but we can finance our own expenditure. If our expenditure exceeds our income then we have to find some way to bridge the gap between expenditure and income. We have to borrow from others to finance the difference. The particular importance of bank loans is that they permit an increase in expenditure over and above income and without drawing on the savings of others.

Figure 12.6 shows the relationship between lending by banks and building societies in the UK, and the stock of broad money (M4). The ratio of M4 to total lending is by no means constant, but the ratio does not vary as much as the money multiplier does in Figure 12.5. An insight into why this is so may be gained by extending the analysis of the simply economy we studied when we derived the money multiplier.

If L is the total value of loans extended by the banking system, we have (from the consolidated balance sheet of the banks in Table 12.5) $L + R = D$. Thus

$$L + rD = D$$
$$L = D(1 - r)$$
$$D = L/(1 - r)$$
$$M = C + D = C + L/(1 - r) = cM + L/(1 - r)$$

Figure 12.6
Total lending and
broad money (M4)
UK 1970–2004

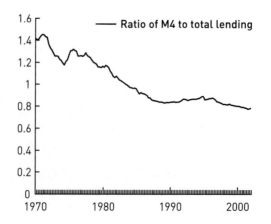

Thus

$$M(1 - c) = L/(1 - r)$$

and

$$M = L/[(1 - c)(1 - r)]$$

As with the money multiplier, this ratio will depend on c and r. As we have seen, c and r have changed dramatically over the decades, leading to large changes in the money multiplier. Here, though, the effect of changes in c and r is muted because, if c and r are both small relative to 1 (as they are), the ratio of M to L will be approximately 1 and will not depend very much on the actual values taken by c and r at a particular time.

Exercise 12.4

Consider a hypothetical economy, Xland, with several firms and households but only one bank. Households deposit 10 per cent of their incomes with the bank and the bank has a policy of keeping 10 per cent of its deposits as cash reserves, but lending out the remaining 90 per cent of deposits as loans to firms. The government of Xland has made currency notes and coins worth 1000 exes.

1 What is the total money supply in this economy?
2 Suppose Xland's neighbour Yland declares war on Xland and the government is forced to finance new military spending by printing additional currency of 500 exes. What will be the total money supply in the economy now?

▨ ▩ ■ 12.3.5 The demand for money by households

The demand for money by households and firms in the economy is closely related to the two main functions of money, namely as a means of payment and as a store of value. Any individual is continually receiving and paying out money, but the receipt of income and the payment on expenditure are not completely co-ordinated. If they were completely co-ordinated there would be little requirement to hold money. But, in reality, at any moment, an individual is likely to hold some money which is to some degree held in anticipation that the money will be spent in the relatively near future. The average amount of money held by an individual for use in the settlement of expected transactions is often referred to as that person's *transactions demand* for money. This demand is for holding money for the purpose of financing transactions: holding money between receiving it as income and making use of it to finance expenditure. We do not generally hold money because we like the pictures on the bank notes but rather because we anticipate spending it in the near future, though we may not have a precise plan as to what money will be spent on.

As an example, consider an individual who receives income on a monthly basis and usually spends all of their income evenly throughout the month. This person would have a holding of money as illustrated in Figure 12.7. On pay day, this person's holding of money would rise by the amount of the monthly income, and that holding would gradually run down over the month as expenditure takes place. In this example, the individual would have a transactions demand for money equal to half of their monthly income. This transactions demand would be the average amount of money held; for this individual the money held at the beginning of the month would be considerably more than the money held at the end of the month. As this individual spends money, others, of course, receive it, and their holding of money would also fluctuate.

Figure 12.7
The transactions
demand for money

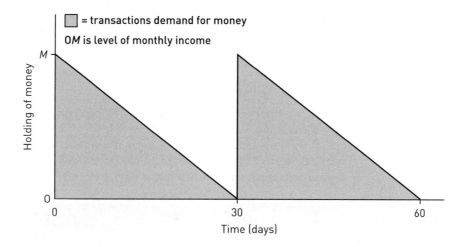

The average amount of money which an individual holds is likely to depend on a range of factors. One could be expected to be the frequency with which the individual is paid: a person paid weekly may hold less money, on average, than one who is paid monthly. If the holding of money by the person paid weekly follows a similar pattern to that in Figure 12.7, their average holding of money would approximate to half a week's pay. It could also be expected that the average holding of money depends on the alternatives available. If there are other financial assets available which yield a significant rate of interest and the costs of switching from money into that financial asset are low, it may be worthwhile, say for the person paid monthly, to switch, briefly, from money into that financial asset.

It could also be envisaged from Figure 12.7 that if an individual's income increased, the transactions demand for money (Md) would also increase, and in roughly the same proportion. The transactions demand for money may then be written as $Md = kY$ where Y is the level of (nominal) income. The factor k could be expected to depend on the interest rates on other financial assets for reasons indicated in the previous paragraph. It could also be expected to depend on matters such as the frequency with which a person is paid.

The transactions demand for money relates to money held to be subsequently used as a means of payment. If someone finds themselves holding money balances in excess of the amount needed to facilitate transactions they should, sensibly, reduce their money balances by purchasing assets which yield a return. These might be nominal assets (e.g. deposits in a savings account at a bank or building society, or National Savings Certificates) or government and corporate bonds and equities (the nominal values of which fluctuate) or real assets. Generally, the share of one's wealth that it is sensible to hold in the form of money is quite small. Nevertheless, some people – especially those on lower incomes – may hold a relatively large proportion of their wealth in the form of money. This may be because they are not aware of the existence of alternative assets or because they wish to avoid the transactions costs and record keeping associated with the ownership of non-monetary financial assets.

In some circumstances, however, it is sensible for even wealthy, sophisticated agents to hold money balances in excess of those they need for transactions purposes. This would be the case if the prices of alternative assets (government and corporate bonds, equities, property) were expected to *fall* in the near future. A relatively small fall in the value of such assets could swamp the yield (interest payments, dividends, rents) the assets provide. If asset prices generally are expected to fall, agents will respond by trying to protect the capital value of their wealth; holding a higher proportion of their wealth in the form of money is a way of doing this. This means there is an additional motive for holding money – variously known as the *portfolio*, *asset* or *speculative* demand for money. This motive will operate if asset prices are falling or are expected to fall in the near future – perhaps because they have *risen above* their usual levels in the recent past. The current situation in Japan illustrates this in a dramatic way. Following a speculative bubble in the late 1980s, asset prices in Japan have trended downwards. The Nikkei index of equity prices is now (June 2005) only 28 per cent of its peak value in December 1989, and the index has fallen in 120 of the 184 months since then. In addition, land prices have declined for thirteen consecutive years. It is understandable that Japanese households have preferred to hold money rather than hold these alternative assets. This preference for money has been exacerbated by the fact that consumer prices have also been falling, so the real value of money balances will tend to increase, even when no interest is paid on money holdings. Japanese households' increased demand for money is clear from the fact that the stock of broad money in Japan (M2 plus Certificates of Deposit) has gone from about 100 per cent of GDP in 1989 to nearly 140 per cent in 2004.

Agents hold money balances for both transactions and portfolio reasons. The first motive is likely to be influenced by changes in the transactions technology. The second motive is likely to be subject to macroeconomic conditions (including expectations about *future* economic circumstances) which may sometimes change very rapidly. This means that the demand for money tends to be quite unstable over time. ·

12.4 Conclusion

This chapter began by recalling the circular flow of income which you studied in Chapter 8. It developed the circular flow concept by adding new sectors: government and the overseas sector. It showed how some sectors can run financial surpluses while others run financial deficits. In the latter part of the chapter the role of money in the economy was explored. We distinguished three functions of money (unit of account, means of payment, store of value) and discussed various measures of money, especially in the UK context. We then introduced two views about how the stock of money is determined. The first attributed a key role to the central bank, through its ability to control the size of the monetary base and thus, through the money multiplier, broader measures of money. The second view placed more stress on the role of banks and especially bank lending. According to this second view the central bank may not be able to exercise effective control over the growth of broad monetary aggregates. We also saw that the demand for money on the part of households may be subject to both gradual changes (due to the transactions technology) and more sudden shifts (due to changing macroeconomic conditions and especially expectations about future conditions).

Questions for review and discussion

Question 1 Macroeconomic equilibrium requires equality between leakages and injections in the circular flow of income. Add appropriate letters to the boxes (from the five letters listed below) so that the macroeconomic equilibrium condition is shown.

$$S + \square + \square = \square + \square + \square$$

$$\boxed{G}\;\boxed{I}\;\boxed{M}\;\boxed{T}\;\boxed{X}$$

Question 2 Table 12.7 shows hypothetical data that might be included in the national accounts of an economy. Complete the table.

Table 12.7

Variable	Amount
Savings (S)	100 000
Investment (I)	75 000
Savings (S)–Investment (I)	
Exports (X)	250 000
Imports (M)	
Balance of trade	−10 000
Net income form overseas (R)	0
Government expenditure (G)	
Taxation (T)	300 000
Budget deficit	

Question 3 (a) Indicate whether the following statement about money is true or false:
M0, the monetary base, is a debt of the Bank of England.
(b) Indicate whether the following statement about money is true or false:
The broader measures of money include money created by banks other than the Bank of England.

Question 4 Which of the following changes would, other things being equal, lead to an increase in the value of the money (credit) multiplier?

A Banks decide to hold reserves which amount to a greater proportion of their deposits than before.
B The public decide to hold a smaller proportion of money than before as cash rather than as bank deposits.
C The Bank of England increases the amount of base money in existence.

Question 5 (a) Explain the three functions of money in a modern economy. Illustrate your answer with examples of how money is used in each of these functions.
(b) The Bank of Never-Never Land has the following balance sheet:

Loans	Deposits
800	1000
Reserves	
200	

(i) What is the current reserve ratio of this bank?
(ii) This bank management decides it is prudent to keep a reserve ratio of 5 per cent. What reserves would be needed to meet this ratio?
(iii) If this bank has 200 as reserves, and seeks to maintain a 5 per cent reserve ratio, what is the maximum amount of loans which it can extend?

(iv) There is now an increased demand for loans from the Bank of Never-Never Land and the management decides to grant these additional loans. Outline the process by which the expansion of loans can lead to an increase in the stock of money (bank deposits).

Question 6 (a) An open economy with a government sector is in an equilibrium position. Now imagine that the level of injections into the circular flow declines. Describe the process leading to a new equilibrium position, explaining what you would expect to happen to the level of income.

(b) Complete Table 12.8 using the following information about the economy of Utopia:

- the propensity to save (out of disposable income) = 0.2
- the propensity to import (out of total income) = 0.35
- the average tax rate = 0.35

(c) Would you regard the surpluses and deficits of the sectors involved in Table 12.8 to be sustainable over time?

Table 12.8
The economy of Utopia

Variable	Amount
Income	100 000
Disposable income	
Savings	
Investment	15 000
Savings – Investment	
Exports	40 000
Imports	
Balance of trade	
Government expenditure	
Taxation	
Budget deficit/surplus	

Question 7 What is money? How is it created in a contemporary industrialized economy?

Question 8 How can the money supply in an economy be measured? Explain how measures of the money supply can be related to the functions of money.

13

Aggregate demand

Giuseppe Fontana

<table>
<tr>
<td valign="top">

Concepts

- Say's law
- aggregate demand
- autonomous expenditure
- paradox of thrift
- transitory and permanent income
- multiplier

</td>
<td valign="top">

Objectives

After studying this chapter you should be able to:

- appreciate the difference between Say's law and Keynes's theory of aggregate demand
- explain the determinants of aggregate demand
- understand the multiplier process
- explain how national income and employment are determined
- understand the elements of macroeconomic policy.

</td>
</tr>
</table>

13.1 Introduction

In an article published in the *New York Times* (21 February 1998) it was claimed that Say's law had become American capitalism's guiding aphorism. The 'law' bears the name of Jean-Baptiste Say (1767–1832), a well-respected French businessman and scholar. Like the British economist Adam Smith (1723–1790), Say advocated the benefits of free markets. Say's most famous work is his *A Treatise on Political Economy* (1803) where he outlines his controversial 'law of markets', better known as 'Say's law'.

Say's law

Say's law is usually expressed as the idea that supply creates its own demand.

In summary form, **Say's law** states that aggregate demand, the total value of goods and services demanded in an economy, could neither exceed nor fall below aggregate supply, the total value of goods and services supplied in that economy. This later became encapsulated in the idea that 'supply creates its own demand' for the economy as a whole. In a famous passage from *A Treatise on Political Economy*, Say spells out his idea:

> When the producer has put the finishing hand to his product, he is most anxious to sell it immediately, lest its value should diminish in his hands. Nor is he less anxious to dispose of the money he may get for it; for the value of money is also perishable. But the only way of getting rid of money is in the purchase of some product or

other. Thus the mere circumstance of creation of one product immediately opens a vent for other products.

(Say, 1803, pp.138–9)

In effect, products can be sold because the people producing them want to spend the proceeds from what they sell, and their spending creates an equivalent amount of demand for other products. The implication of this 'law' is that any shortage of demand which causes workers to be laid off because products cannot be sold will always be balanced somewhere else by excess demand. So any fluctuations in the levels of output and employment in the economy should be only temporary and self-reversing. The economy is 'self-correcting' and any situation of unemployment should quickly revert to full employment.

Say's law and its economic implications were criticized by a well-known British economist, John Maynard Keynes (1883–1946), who revolutionized the economic profession with the publication of his book *The General Theory of Employment, Interest and Money* (1936). Great economists are all products of their times. Whereas Say and Smith were the spokesmen for the nascent capitalistic system, the work of Keynes was the product of the Great Depression. The Depression of the 1930s was one of the most disruptive economic crises in history. All the major Western countries experienced mass unemployment and greatly reduced levels of GDP. For instance, in 1933, one-quarter of the US labour force was unemployed and real GDP was less than 60 per cent of its 1929 level (Chapter 19). Economists appeared to be powerless in the face of this terrible reality. According to Say's law, the economy should have been self-righting, and yet the Depression continued year after year across all industrialized economies.

To explain why economists had little to offer against the problems of the widespread depression of the inter-war period we need to understand what, according to Say's law, should happen when there is unemployment; that is, when the supply of labour exceeds the demand for labour. In that situation the basic law of supply and demand (Chapter 5) suggests that the price of labour (wages) would decline until it reached a level at which the supply of labour services is just equal to the demand by firms for labour services. Thus, excess of supply in the labour market (unemployment) should force down wages and this reduction in the cost of labour services would encourage firms to produce more output and employ more labour.

But why should firms be able to sell this increased output? According to Say's law, workers would offer their services and employers would employ them because they both want to use the income they gain from the increased production to purchase other goods and services. This creates additional demand of a monetary value exactly equal to that of the increased output. In this way, the higher level of output should raise the level of aggregate demand just to the level needed for all the increased output to be sold; that is, up to the point where there would be full employment in the labour market. In short, taking Say's law and the law of supply and demand together, there is no reason for aggregate demand, and hence production, to fall short of the full employment level. In this framework then, unemployment can exist only as a transitory phenomenon. In equilibrium the economy would always be at full employment.

The persistently high levels of unemployment in the inter-war period led many economists to question the validity of Say's law. Keynes was thus stimulated to propose a new theoretical approach because the available economic tools of his time could not explain, let alone solve, one of the most dramatic problems of modern capitalism: the coexistence of mass unemployment and excess capacity with economies producing at a level of output well below what should have been possible.

Keynes presented a new way of analysing the economy, the theory of aggregate demand, which would allow for the possibility of underemployment equilibrium. In Keynes's vision there was no self-correcting property in the economy that would solve economic downturns. In his theory, the level of employment depends on the level of aggregate demand, which he claimed could settle at any level. As a result, the equilibrium level of employment in the economy could also be at any level between zero and full employment. As the dramatic events of the 1930s showed, there was no guarantee that a level of aggregate demand would prevail in which the economy's resources of labour and capital were fully utilized. In this way, Keynes concluded that full employment represents just one particular outcome of an economic system and that other levels of employment could also result and could coexist with unused productive capacity.

Aggregate demand

Aggregate demand is the sum total spending plans of the different sections of the economy.

In this chapter, we will develop the simple Keynesian model of **aggregate demand** for goods and services which underlies the determination of total income and employment in the economy. First, we will look at what determines two of the main components of planned aggregate demand, namely consumption and investment (Section 13.2). This will allow us to see why the level of income and the interest rate are key determinants of the level of aggregate demand in the economy. Section 13.3 explains the relationship between aggregate demand and national income through the 'multiplier', and extends the model of national income determination to include the government sector and the rest of the world. A consideration of the implications of the level of national income for labour demand allows us to determine whether there is full employment or unemployment.

Section 13.4 then extends this simple model to examine the scope for government intervention in the economy. Two main forms of intervention are considered: government spending and taxation (fiscal policy) and government control of interest rates and/or control of the money supply (monetary policy). In the simple model developed in Sections 13.2 and 13.3, we will assume that there is underutilized capacity and that prices do not change (or change only by a small amount) when the level of aggregate demand changes. This was a reasonable assumption in the context of the Great Depression when Keynes formulated the model. Later, in Chapter 18, this assumption is relaxed and the relationship between aggregate demand and price inflation is examined.

13.2 The determinants of aggregate demand in a closed economy with no government sector

In Chapter 12 we saw how the expenditure decisions of some agents in the economy determined the incomes received by others and how, at the aggregate level, GDP is determined by the sum of consumer expenditure, government expenditure, investment expenditure and expenditure on net exports by foreigners.

Question   Look again at Table 12.1. What is the main component of aggregate expenditure?

We can see from Table 12.1 that in 2003 some 66 per cent of aggregate expenditure consisted of spending by households on consumer goods and services such as clothes, food and cars; 16.5 per cent consisted of spending by firms for buying capital goods such as factories, machines and land; nearly 21 per cent was spent by the government in providing public services such as health, defence and education. Exports were equivalent to 25 per cent of GDP and imports 28 per cent leaving a net trade balance of –3 per cent of GDP.

While Table 12.1 can provide some useful insights into the size of the contributions of the different components of expenditure to national income, it does not tell us why the level of national income is what it is in each period. If we are interested in knowing why the economy has settled at a particular equilibrium level of income and employment we need to investigate the causal mechanism involved in arriving at that level of income. Since in equilibrium total income equals total planned expenditure, the level of income depends on expenditure plans. This means that we have to look at what determines the spending plans or intentions of households, firms and the government, and of foreigners. In this chapter we will do this in turn. Initially we will assume that the country we are discussing is a closed economy, meaning that it does not trade with the rest of the world. This allows us to ignore the demand for net exports and to concentrate on consumption expenditure and investment expenditure.

▦ ▨ ▪ 13.2.1 Consumption demand

We saw in Table 12.1 that consumer spending by households is the major component of total aggregate expenditure. Consumption demand consists of the expenditures that households plan to make on both durable and non-durable goods and on services. Durable goods are those commodities, such as cars and computers, that generate benefits for their owners over a substantial period of time. Non-durable goods are commodities, such as food and clothes, which are consumed or used over a relatively short time period. Individuals will generally purchase non-durable goods frequently, whereas they will generally purchase durable goods infrequently. Finally, services are those commodities, such as a haircut or a medical check-up, that have the characteristic of having to be consumed at the same time as they are produced.

Consumption demand and its fluctuations are an essential part of the explanation of economic booms and recessions. There are different theories to explain what determines the level of consumption demand by households. Keynes conjectured that planned consumption demand C depended mainly on Y_d, the level of current disposable income of households. Disposable income is simply income that households can spend; that is total income plus transfers less taxes. Since, for the moment, we are assuming a simple model with no government expenditures or taxation, disposable income is just the same as total income. This may seem like a rather obvious proposition – that our demand for consumption goods depends on how much income we receive – but it was in fact a very different way of thinking about demand from existing views in the 1930s.

To appreciate this, just stop and think for a moment about how it compares with the notion of market demand that you encountered in Chapter 3. Market demand in that microeconomic context was a function of both income and relative prices, while in the Keynesian model consumption demand is a function principally of current incomes. Why don't relative prices play a role here? The explanation is that we are focusing on *aggregate* consumption expenditure. This involves treating all consumption goods as if they were more or less the same, selling for a single price corresponding to the aggregate price level (captured by the Consumer Price Index). Nevertheless, viewed in a slightly different light, there *is* a role of a relative price effect here: the relative price of *future* to *current* consumption goods. If consumption goods are expected to be cheaper in the future relative to their price today, this provides a motive for delaying consumption; that is, for saving. There is evidence that expected inflation encourages consumers to bring purchases forward (and expected deflation provides a motive for delaying purchases). However, in most circumstances this inflation/deflation effect is not going to be very large and we will neglect it in the remainder of this section.

This idea that consumption depends on income can be summarized by equation (13.1) which gives the *consumption function*, presenting consumption as a function of disposable income:

$$C = C_0 + bY_d \qquad (13.1)$$

Here C_0 is 'autonomous consumption', that is expenditure which does not depend on households' income, so it is expenditure that households would undertake even if they had no income.

Writing the consumption function as in equation (13.1) makes the assumption that each additional increment to income has the same effect on consumption. In other words, households plan to spend a fixed proportion of each increment in income. This proportion b is known as the **marginal propensity to consume**. Its value is assumed to be positive but less than unity, on the grounds that people will spend some but not all of any increment in their income. So

Marginal propensity to consume

The marginal propensity to consume tells us the extent to which a marginal change in income is associated with a marginal change in consumption.

$$0 < b < 1$$

Note that the assumption that 'the marginal propensity to consume is constant whatever the level of disposable income' is a simplification we could dispense with. A more complicated version of equation (13.1) could involve a non-linear relationship between C and Y_d in which the marginal propensity to consume might be high (i.e. close to one) when income is low but might be substantially less than one for higher levels of income. For most purposes, however, the linear version of the consumption function given in equation (13.1) will do perfectly well.

Anything that the household does not spend is saved, and hence the consumption function in equation (13.1) also indicates that some part of any additional pound of income is saved. If S denotes the level of saving, then

$$S \equiv Y_d - C$$

So equation (13.1) implies that the saving function of the economy is

$$S = Y_d - (C_0 + bY_d) = -C_0 + (1 - b)Y_d \qquad (13.2)$$

Marginal propensity to save

The marginal propensity to save tells us the extent to which a marginal change in income is associated with a marginal change in savings.

The coefficient $(1 - b)$ is sometimes called the **marginal propensity to save** of the economy; it gives the proportion of each additional increment of income that is saved. It should also lie between 0 and 1 because some, but not all, of any additional income is saved.

A graphical illustration of the consumption function is shown in Figure 13.1. The marginal propensity to consume b is the slope of the consumption demand function: a consumption function with a higher marginal propensity to consume would be more steeply sloped than one with a lower marginal propensity to consume. The constant term C_0 is autonomous consumption and is represented by the intercept of the consumption function on the vertical axis.

The consumption function given in equation (13.1) above is clearly a rather simple one, and many have argued that it provides too simplistic a view of consumption behaviour. It claims that individuals immediately spend a proportion of any increase in current income. However, would you respond to a temporary rise in your income in the same way as you would to a permanent increase? When making decisions on what to spend and what to save, do you just pay regard to your present income or do you think more broadly about the longer-term prospects for your income? It is reasonable to suppose that the consumption plans of two people each receiving, say, £200 a week may be

Figure 13.1
The consumption
function

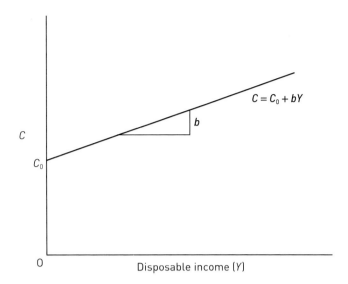

$$C = C_0 + bY$$

C

C_0

b

0

Disposable income (Y)

different depending on whether they think that £200 a week is the most they will ever earn or that their future income prospects are much better.

Keynes was aware that consumption was very likely to be influenced by expectations about the pattern of future income, by wealth and by interest rates, among other variables. Subsequently, the Nobel prize winning economist Franco Modigliani incorporated some of these variables into a more complex version of the consumption function. Modigliani started from the observation that income varies over a person's life and that people use saving and borrowing to smooth their consumption over their lifetimes. Thus, consumer demand should depend not only on current income but also on their future prospects for income and where in the life cycle they happen to be. This view forms the basis of Modigliani's *life-cycle hypothesis* that individuals will pay regard to their lifetime income prospects when making consumption and saving decisions. In those periods of their lives when their income is relatively high, people will save; in those periods when their current income is relatively low, people will dissave (and run down their past savings or borrow). In Modigliani's view, the main motive for saving is to fund consumption later in life and especially during retirement when income from employment is no longer being received.

Figure 13.2 illustrates an interesting implication of the life-cycle hypothesis. It shows a plausible pattern of income, wealth and consumption of an individual over their adult life. The amount of income (£) is represented on the vertical axis and time is measured on the horizontal axis. Modigliani argued that most people do not want a major decline in the standard of living when they retire. This means that during their working years this individual would save part of their income and accumulate wealth. After retirement they would use the income saved (dissaving) and wealth to keep enjoying their pattern of consumption. As drawn in Figure 13.2, the individual knows not only the pattern of income over their lifetime, but also the time of their demise. Their wealth falls to zero at exactly the time of death. Although this might be thought rather implausible, it is the case that individuals often purchase annuities with their pension wealth when they retire and that an annuity does cease to pay out when an individual dies. (The effect of purchasing an annuity is to shift the *risk* of living longer than the average person onto the company providing the annuity. Such companies are compensated by the profits they make from purchasers of annuities who die relatively early.)

Figure 13.2
The life-cycle
hypothesis

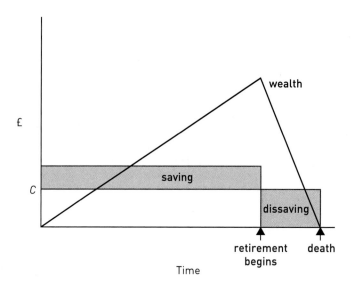

The life-cycle hypothesis suggests that people will, on average, save little over the full course of their lifetime, but that savings are used to shift consumption from periods when income is relatively high to periods when income is expected to be relatively low. If this is the case then the amount of net savings being undertaken in any economy would depend on the balance between relatively young people (assumed to be consuming current income or dissaving, that is, borrowing), middle-aged people (assumed to be saving) and relatively old people (assumed to be dissaving).

Another Nobel prize winning economist, Milton Friedman, proposed another theory of consumption which may be seen as complementing Modigliani's life-cycle hypothesis. Friedman suggested distinguishing between **'transitory' and 'permanent' income**, where the former is the part of income received in one period that is not expected to recur in the future, whereas permanent income is, as its name suggests, the part of income that is expected to go on year after year. He maintained that only permanent income should enter in the consumption function. Rational agents will prefer to smooth consumption and will use saving and borrowing to do this in the face of transitory changes to their incomes. Thus, transitory income (which may be positive or negative) would, Friedman argued, be ignored in the demand for consumption goods since the long-term prospects for permanent income are not changed. This is the core of his 'permanent-income' hypothesis.

These theories of consumption based on the life-cycle hypothesis and the permanent-income hypothesis suggest that consumption demand may be sensitive not only to current income but also to expected future income, to wealth and to interest rates. As such, they supplement the simple consumption function set out in equation (13.1).

'Transitory' and 'permanent' income

Transitory income is the part of income received in one period that is not expected to recur in the future. Permanent income is the part of income that is expected to recur in every period.

■■ ■ **13.2.2 Investment demand**

Investment consists of spending by firms and households to increase their capital. Firms make two types of investment spending: (a) fixed investment, when they buy capital inputs such as equipment and buildings to use in production, and (b) inventory investment, which consists of finished output in storage or work in progress that has not yet been sold. Household investment spending consists mainly of buying a home.

The demand for investment is the most volatile component of aggregate demand. This volatility derives from the fact that investment decisions are always forward-looking and

Figure 13.3
Rates of change
of components
of UK domestic
expenditure,
1970–2003

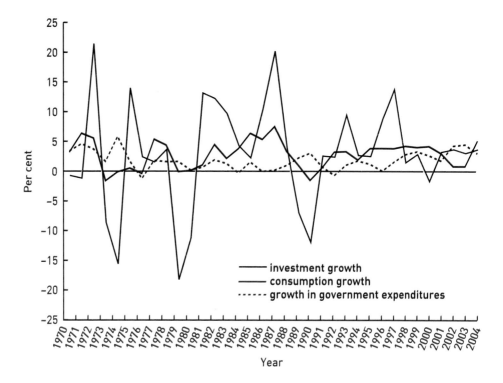

based on expectations. When firms make investment decisions they have to forecast the flow of future profits that a project is likely to generate. Whether based on guesses or careful calculations those expectations are inherently unstable and capable of sudden and sharp reversals. Thus, most of the changes in the level of income when a country experiences a boom or recession are thought to be due to a decline in, or a recovery of, investment demand.

Figure 13.3 plots the growth of the different components of UK expenditure over the period from 1970 to 2003. The graph shows quite clearly that investment expenditure is much more volatile than the other components of domestic expenditure. Thus, investment expenditure grew over 20 per cent per annum in 1972 and 1987, whereas it declined by over 15 per cent in 1974 and in 1979. This volatility alone makes investment demand difficult to predict in the aggregate. No two people would assess a risk in the same way, and one person would probably assess the implications of a risk differently at different times. What this means is that the level of investment depends heavily on the gut feelings and expectations of the managers of firms in the economy. Keynes wrote that in the main it was determined by entrepreneurs' 'animal spirits'. Since it is impossible to model such a factor, a simple response is to treat the level of aggregate investment at any moment as exogenous; that is, to set it at some given level, $I = \bar{I}$.

The next step is to try to incorporate some key determinants of investment into an investment function, analogous to the consumption function described above. What might these determinants be? Despite the large role of uncertainty there are two factors that firms are likely to consider when they plan investments. These are: (a) the cost of financing investment and (b) the expected returns on the projects they plan to invest in.

While firms can fund investment out of retained earnings, many firms have to borrow to pay for new investment goods. Some do so by issuing equities or selling corporate bonds to investors. Others (including almost all small firms) tend to rely on borrowing from the banking sector. For these firms, the interest rate on bank loans is the financial cost to firms of funding investment. Note that the relevant interest rate is the *real* interest rate: the nominal interest rate *minus* the expected inflation rate. This is because, in an inflationary environment, borrowers can repay loans after prices have risen, so the burden of debt is reduced. The link between investment demand and the real rate of interest r can be expressed as an investment function

$$I = I(r) \tag{13.3}$$

with the relationship between investment and the real interest rate being a negative one.

When firms decide to make an investment, such as buying a new machine or a new factory, they also take into account the additional profit that they may expect to earn from using the new machine or factory. They compare this additional profit with the interest that they would have to pay to borrow the money to finance that investment. If the real interest rate, or the cost of borrowing, is low relative to the returns they expect from the investment, firms will go ahead with the investment. If real interest rates rise, however, and the expected return from the investment stays the same, firms will be reluctant to proceed. For a given expected return, an increase in the real interest rate on loans raises the financing cost of investment and so lowers the demand for investment. How a firm decides whether an investment project is profitable will be explained in Chapter 14.

13.3 The basic model of income determination

In constructing a model of income determination, we distinguish between exogenous and endogenous variables. Exogenous variables are those variables that in the context of a particular model are considered fixed; that is, determined outside the model. By contrast, endogenous variables are those variables that are determined within that particular model. Variables are not intrinsically endogenous or exogenous; it is only in a particular model or theory that a variable is either endogenous or exogenous. In an economic model the exogenous variables determine the endogenous variables.

■ ■ ■ 13.3.1 Income determination in a closed economy with no government sector

We have studied the two main components of aggregate demand: consumption demand C and investment demand I. Assume, for simplicity, that we are considering a closed economy (there are no exports or imports), that there is no government (so that Y_d equals Y) and that investment demand is a function of the real interest rate alone. We can then write aggregate demand AD as a sum of its components:

$$AD = C + I$$

where, using equations (13.1) and (13.3)

$$C = C_0 + bY$$
$$I = I(r)$$

or

$$AD = C_0 + bY + I(r) \tag{13.4}$$

This equation states that the level of aggregate demand depends on a constant or exogenous term C_0 and the value of two other variables, namely the real interest rate r and the level of current income Y. This is an important result since it tells us which variables are directly capable of influencing the level of aggregate demand.

We can now use this information to find the equilibrium level of income in this simple closed economy. Note that I am assuming that there is plenty of unutilized capacity in the economy, so that whatever is demanded can be supplied without a significant rise in prices. The equilibrium position arises when the plans for aggregate demand are fulfilled, so that the level of output (and income) is equal to the level of aggregate demand, or

$$Y = AD$$
$$Y = C_0 + bY + I(r) \tag{13.5}$$

We can now ask how much income changes when a component of aggregate demand changes. To do this let us simplify equation (13.5) by neglecting the dependence of investment on the real interest rate and reverting to the simpler case in which investment is at some predetermined constant level $\bar{I}$. In other words, investment is now *exogenous* or *autonomous* in the sense that it is not determined inside the model. Collecting the terms with Y in them on the left-hand side, we get:

$$Y - bY = C_0 + \bar{I}$$

$$Y = \frac{(C_0 + \bar{I})}{(1 - b)} = \left(\frac{1}{1 - b}\right)(C_0 + \bar{I}) \tag{13.6}$$

This means that when either of the exogenous elements of expenditure, C_0 or $\bar{I}$, changes by a certain amount, income changes by $\dfrac{1}{1 - b}$ times that amount. Since b is less than one, $\dfrac{1}{1 - b}$ is going to be greater than one. This means that the change in income will be greater than the original change in exogenous expenditure. You can see this more easily when the simple model is shown diagrammatically as in Figure 13.4.

The lower line in Figure 13.4, $C + I$, is the sum of the consumption function, from Figure 13.1, and the predetermined level of investment $\bar{I}$. This line gives aggregate demand in the economy plotted against the level of income. Its slope is the same as that of the consumption function because investment does not vary with income but just adds a fixed amount to consumption demand. The equilibrium condition is to have equality between aggregate demand and aggregate supply (or total national income). In Figure 13.4, this is given by the diagonal 45° line through the origin.

Question	Why does the diagonal 45° line in Figure 13.4 show equality of income and aggregate demand?

Along the diagonal 45° line every point is the same distance from the X-axis as it is from the Y-axis. (Check this for yourself.) Here our X-axis variable income is total national income and the Y-axis indicates the levels of aggregate demand. So for every point on that line the equilibrium condition that income is equal to aggregate demand holds.

The equilibrium level of income in this simple model is Y_a where planned aggregate demand equals planned aggregate supply at point E_1. Check for yourself that at any point before Y_a and any point after Y_a the economy will be driven back to Y_a. If this is not clear read Chapter 12 (Section 12.2.2) again.

Figure 13.4
The determination
of national income
and the multiplier

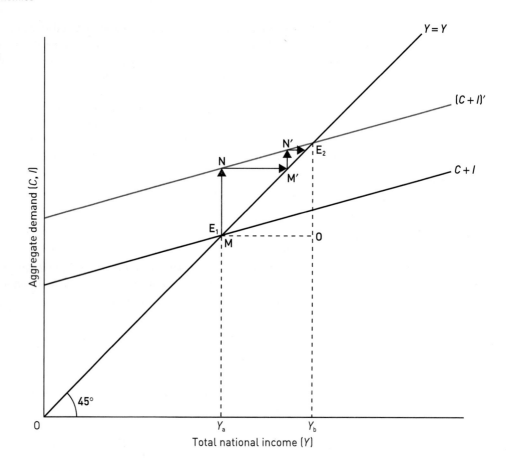

Now suppose that investment expenditure increases by MN. The aggregate demand schedule shifts upward by the extent of the increase in investment expenditure and is now represented by the upper line in Figure 13.4, labelled $(C + I)'$. The equilibrium level of income increases from Y_a to Y_b. The total increase in income is the distance MO (which is equal to $Y_b - Y_a$). Notice that MO > MN, which is what we would have expected; income has changed by *more* than the change in investment expenditure. The next section explains that the difference between MO and MN is the additional consumption expenditure induced by the initial increase in income via the multiplier process.

▨ ▨ ▪ 13.3.2 The multiplier process

Autonomous expenditure

Autonomous expenditure is expenditure on consumption, investment or by the government that happens independent of the level of national income.

The ratio MO/MN (the increase in income divided by the increase in investment expenditure) is referred to as the *Keynesian multiplier*. It measures by how much you have to multiply an increase in **autonomous expenditure** to work out the corresponding increase in income. In fact, the multiplier is $\dfrac{1}{1-b}$, the inverse of the marginal propensity to save.

Why is MO > MN? After the initial increase in investment demand, aggregate demand is greater than aggregate supply. Since there is unutilized capacity, income in the economy rises to NM' in the first instance (Figure 13.4). Due to this increase in incomes there will be an increase in consumption. From the consumption function we know that the increased consumption is a proportion b of the increase in income MN, where b is the marginal propensity to consume. This increased consumption adds to aggregate demand which is now higher by M′N′. So aggregate demand is now

$$MN + M'N' = MN + bMN$$

Since there is still unutilized capacity this increase in aggregate demand again creates new incomes for the suppliers of goods and services who will consume a proportion b of these increased incomes. Aggregate demand increases yet again, and so on. Since b is less than 1, each successive addition to aggregate demand is smaller than the first one. This process continues until we reach point E_2 in Figure 13.4 where the total increase in aggregate demand and incomes is $OE_2 = MO$. So MO is the total increase in aggregate demand in the economy:

$$MO = MN + bMN + b(bMN) + b(bbMN) + \ldots$$
$$MO = MN(1 + b + b^2 + b^3 + \ldots)$$

This means that the multiplier $\dfrac{MO}{MN}$ is $1 + b + b^2 + b^3 + \ldots$

We can work out how much this is by looking at it another way. At E_2, since the economy is back in equilibrium, MO is both the increase in income and the increase in aggregate demand. The increase in aggregate demand has two components. First, there is the increase in autonomous investment, MN, and, second, there is the increase in consumption bMO, as a result of the increase in the level of income, MO. So

$$
\begin{aligned}
MO &= \text{increase in income}\\
&= \text{increase in aggregate demand}\\
&= MN + bMO
\end{aligned}
$$

So

$$(1 - b)MO = MN$$

So the multiplier

$$\frac{MO}{MN} = \frac{1}{(1 - b)} \tag{13.7}$$

The multiplier thus tells us by how much the total amount of goods and services demanded changes after a change in some autonomous component of demand, here investment expenditure. (Precisely the same analysis could be used to explain the consequences of an increase in the autonomous component of consumption expenditure, C_0.) Firms are assumed to accommodate changes in demand through a corresponding change in output as there is unutilized capacity, and not to respond to the higher level of demand by raising prices. This means that the increase in the *value* of output and of income corresponds to an increase in *real* output and real income.

There is an important point to note about this conclusion. The multiplier is based on the assumption that all changes in aggregate demand are translated into corresponding changes in the level of output. In other words, the supply of output expands (or contracts) in response to changes in the level of aggregate demand. This may be a good assumption to make when there is underutilized labour and capital in the economy, but not when there is full employment of labour and capital.

Although you may have followed the algebra, and/or appreciated the diagrammatic exposition, a niggling thought may persist: how does it all happen? What is the economic process that underlies the multiplier result?

Consider, for example, what happens if Marks & Spencer decides to open a new shop. Investment expenditure in the UK economy rises by, say, £10 million. It wants to spend this money on the construction of a new shop, the hiring of more staff and the purchase of merchandise in order to accommodate this new demand. Building and merchandise companies may hire new workers or ask current employees to work longer hours. In any case, workers' incomes increase and so do the profits made by the companies involved. Note that this extra income (profits and wages) is equal to the monetary value of the initial spending. That initial £10 million becomes the wages of builders, shop assistants and workers in clothing factories and the profits of their employers. Therefore, £10 million extra income in the form of wages and profits now enters the economy. An expansion in investment spending of £10 million would therefore produce an initial increase in income of £10 million. This is the first-round effect of the new investment. But this is not the end of the story. Further increases in income occur when that £10 million is spent.

These workers and employers will now plan to spend some of their newly acquired income. They will not spend it all, as we know, because they will plan to save some of it. But assuming a marginal propensity to consume *b* equal to 0.6, the £10 million extra income leads to a rise in planned consumption and in real GDP of £6 million. This £6 million of new income is the second-round effect of the multiplier process. It represents the monetary value of the extra amount of goods and services demanded by the workers and the owners of building and merchandise companies when they plan to spend a portion (0.6) of their increased income. After this second round, aggregate demand has thus increased by £16 million: £10 million on the first round and £6 million on the second round. The cumulative change in real GDP and the changes in these two individual rounds in real GDP are shown in the first two rows of Table 13.1. However, the multiplier process does not stop after two rounds. Goods and services bought by these workers and employers are commodities produced by other firms. The workers and owners of those firms would now enjoy larger sales and higher income. As a result, their consumption spending would increase.

| **Question** | As a consequence of this third round of spending in the economy, total income increases by £3.6 million. Can you explain why? |

According to the basic aggregate demand model, consumption and income increases by *b* times the additional income, that is 0.6 times £6 million or £3.6 million. This £3.6 million increase in income is what economists call the third-round effect of the multiplier process. Taken together with the effects of previous rounds, the cumulative change in real GDP is now £19.6 million.

The process continues. Another £3.6 million consumption spending in goods and services means £3.6 million in income for workers and owners of companies who produce those commodities. The basic aggregate demand model tells us that consumption and income would again increase by *b* times this additional spending, that is 0.6 times £3.6 million. This £2.16 million increase in income is the fourth-round effect of the multiplier process. The cumulative change in real GDP is now £21.76 million. After additional rounds the cumulative change in real GDP gets closer and closer to the full impact of the multiplier of £25 million, as indicated in the last row of Table 13.1. In practice, the full impact of the multiplier is felt quite quickly, usually over the course of a year. Note that the size of the multiplier depends on the assumptions we made about the

Table 13.1
A numerical
illustration of the
multiplier CAP

Round	Change in real GDP £m	Cumulative change in real GDP £m
First round	10 000	10 000
Second round	6 000	16 000
Third round	3 600	19 600
Fourth round	2 160	21 760
Fifth round	1 296	23 056
. . .	. . .	. . .
. . .	. . .	. . .
After an indefinite number of rounds	0 000	25 000

marginal propensity to consume b which captures how consumers react to an increase in their income: how much of it they decide to spend and how much to save.

In this case the multiplier is

$$\frac{£25\ \text{million}}{£10\ \text{million}} = 2.5 = \frac{1}{0.4} = \frac{1}{(1-0.6)} = \frac{1}{(1-b)}$$

Exercise 13.1

1 What would be the effect on national income of a decrease in investment spending of £10 billion when the marginal propensity to consume b is 0.9?
2 How would your answer differ if the marginal propensity to consume were 0.4 instead of 0.9?

Multiplier

The multiplier measures the change in aggregate income (GDP) resulting from a change in an autonomous (exogenous) component of the aggregate demand (AD).

We are now in a position to define the multiplier more formally.

The **multiplier** is the ratio of the change in real GDP to the change in any autonomous or exogenous component of aggregate demand (e.g. investment demand or autonomous consumption expenditure):

$$\text{multiplier} = \frac{\text{change in real GDP}}{\text{change in autonomous component of } AD}$$

A component of aggregate demand is 'autonomous' if it is not influenced by the level of income; that is, it is an exogenous variable in the context of the economic model being used. Thus, in the model we have used above, consumption demand is influenced by the level of income, whereas investment expenditure is not influenced by income.

In the examples so far, we have considered only the expansionary effect of the multiplier since we have only considered increases in spending. Should autonomous spending decrease, the multiplier predicts a contraction effect on national income well below the initial contraction of expenditure. To illustrate this we have briefly to consider the paradox of thrift.

Question What will be the effect on aggregate demand of an increase in autonomous savings?

An increase in autonomous savings entails a fall in autonomous consumption. If people save more in preference to immediate spending, this will cause problems for firms who will not be able to sell some of their output. Faced with lower demand for their output and lower sales revenue, the likelihood is that firms will cut back on production. In so far as *any* increase in saving causes aggregate demand to fall, leading to lower output and lower employment, people saving a higher proportion of their income becomes a serious problem for the economy as a whole.

Paradox of thrift

The paradox of thrift refers to the negative effects of increased savings on aggregate demand and therefore national income.

Keynes puts this idea in terms of the **paradox of thrift**. The paradox is that though individuals may save more to enhance future consumption, collectively their actions may reduce future income and therefore consumption. An individual wanting to increase consumption in the future should save more now. Both the money saved and the interest gained as a result can be used to fund future expenditure. Higher saving at an individual level can also provide additional funds for investment. On the other hand, however, if everyone chooses to save more, the aggregate increase in saving, because it will come at the expense of aggregate consumption, will lead to a lower level of aggregate demand. This fall in aggregate demand will lead to lower levels of output and, in the context of falling sales, firms will be inclined to reduce investment and eventually shed workers.

The paradox of thrift is an example of the 'fallacy of composition' at work. The 'fallacy of composition' says that what holds at the individual level (the individual desire for increased savings as a means to achieve higher consumption) does not hold at the aggregate level (increased savings across the economy as a whole reduces aggregate demand and lowers output and employment). Actions which look sensible at the individual level can have profound negative implications at the aggregate level. Drawing on the discussion of the circular flow of income in Chapter 12, we can see that if households save more than firms plan to invest (i.e. if 'leakages' exceed 'injections') there will be a fall in the level of income, the extent of this fall in income being determined by the value of the multiplier. The fall in income will, in turn, result in lower levels of saving and investment.

> **Question** Say's law assumes that output is always equal to full employment output. If this assumption were to hold, what would be the effect on aggregate demand of an increase in savings?

An increased desire to save by households must come at the expense of a desire to consume: if more is to be saved then less has to be consumed (for a given level of household income). The consumption component of aggregate demand falls and the level of aggregate demand will then fall, unless investment expenditure rises to take the place of consumer expenditure. Supporters of Say's law would argue that a change in the rate of interest will bring about such a counterbalancing rise in investment expenditure. If the interest rate falls, investment is stimulated and (to some degree) savings inhibited. A sufficient fall in the rate of interest will bring about a sufficient rise in investment to compensate for the initial fall in consumption. The level of aggregate demand will be maintained though its composition will have changed; there will be more investment goods demanded and produced, and fewer consumption goods.

If Say's law holds it follows that a higher level of saving will allows firms to increase investment, with equality between savings and investment being brought about through adjustment in the rate of interest. Total income will remain constant, though now more income will be spent on investment and less will be spent on consumption. On this basis, supporters of Say's law argue that changes in aggregate demand (whether in the form of changes in consumption or investment) exert an entirely neutral effect on the overall level of income and output. They will, however, affect its composition, so that if people decide to save more, fewer consumer goods and more investment goods will be produced.

So as a consequence of the increased desire to save, economists who accept Say's law would predict that the rate of interest changes to bring about equilibrium in the market for loanable funds. Followers of the Keynesian argument, however, believe that it is the level of income that changes (contracts) to bring about a new equilibrium.

▪▪▪ 13.3.3 Extending the model: government spending

Government purchases are another important component of aggregate demand. The government pays for the building of roads, schools and hospitals, and for the services of teachers, doctors and other public sector employees. All those transactions make up government demand G. In most Western industrialized countries, government expenditure on goods and services represents around one-fifth of the total expenditure (Table 13.1). In the aggregate demand model presented here government demand is taken to be an exogenous policy variable; that is, the value of the variable is taken as a fixed value $\bar{G}$ determined, by policy makers, outside the economic model. So

$$G = \bar{G}$$

Governments finance these expenditures through the imposition of taxes, T. They may also print more money or borrow more from households in the economy. Taxes reduce the disposable incomes of households, but government spending adds to aggregate demand. If the level of taxes is exogenous, we can write $T = \bar{T}$. Note that this is not a very realistic assumption since the level of taxes in practice often depends on Y, the level of income, so that $T = T_0 + tY$ (with T_0 probably being negative).

If the government taxes households then consumption demand depends on disposable income, that is income minus taxes, and instead of equation (13.1) above we should write the consumption function as:

$$C = C_0 + b(Y - \bar{T}) \tag{13.8}$$

where $\bar{T}$ is taxes minus transfers, so that $Y - \bar{T}$ is disposable income.

Question Can you work out what the level of equilibrium income would be in this case?

Equilibrium in the economy now occurs when

$$Y = AD \equiv C + I + G$$

So

$$Y = C_0 + b(Y - \bar{T}) + \bar{I} + G$$
$$(1 - b)Y = C_0 - b\bar{T} + \bar{I} + \bar{G}$$
$$Y = \left(\frac{1}{1 - b}\right)(C_0 - b\bar{T} + \bar{I} + \bar{G}) \tag{13.9}$$

Question Compare the multiplier in equation (13.7) with that in equation (13.9). Is the multiplier larger or smaller? Why do you think this is the case?

The multiplier is the same, $\dfrac{1}{1-b}$, as it was for investment. An increase in government spending of ΔG (Δ meaning 'a small change in') increases national income by $\dfrac{\Delta G}{1-b}$. This is the same as the effect of an increase in autonomous investment. Again, because $\dfrac{1}{1-b} > 1$, an increase in government spending has an effect on national income greater than the original increase in spending. Taxation at the level $\bar{T}$ reduces national income by $\dfrac{b\bar{T}}{1-b}$.

An interesting feature of equation (13.9) is that when taxation is used to finance government spending completely (so that $\bar{T} = \bar{G}$) but both are increased by the same amount ($\Delta G = \Delta T$) the net result is an increase in national income. This is because $b < 1$ so that the reduction in national income due to the increased taxation $\dfrac{b\Delta T}{1-b}$ is less than the increase due to the government spending $\dfrac{\Delta G}{1-b}$. The reason is that all government spending is spent, while some of the income taxed to pay for it would have been saved if it had not been taxed. This phenomenon whereby national income may be increased without any change in the government's deficit is known as the *balanced budget multiplier*.

■■■ 13.3.4 Extending the model: the open economy

We can also extend the multiplier analysis further to the case of an open economy (with imports and exports) as additional influences on aggregate demand. Imports are taken to depend on the level of disposable income, so that $M = m(Y - T)$ where m is the marginal propensity to import, meaning that a certain proportion of a change in disposable income $Y - T$ is spent on imports M instead of being part spent on domestic output. (How much of their income people choose to spend on imports will also depend on the relative prices of imported and domestically produced goods – in other words, on the real exchange rate. But we will neglect this complication for the time being.) The level of exports, X, is treated as exogenous, as it depends not on domestic levels of income but on levels of income of foreigners (and on the real exchange rate). Aggregate demand is now:

$$AD = C_0 + b(Y - \bar{T}) + I + \bar{G} + \bar{X} - m(Y - \bar{T})$$

In equilibrium $Y = AD$:

$$Y = AD = C_0 + b(Y - \bar{T}) + I + \bar{G} + \bar{X} - m(Y - \bar{T})$$

or

$$Y(1 - (b - m)) = C_0 + I + \bar{G} + \bar{X} - (b - m)\bar{T}$$

or

$$Y = \left(\frac{1}{1 - (b - m)}\right)(C_0 + I + \bar{G} + \bar{X} - (b - m)\bar{T}) \tag{13.10}$$

Question Compare the multiplier in equation (13.10) with that in equation (13.9). Is the multiplier smaller or larger? Why do you think this is the case?

There is an extra leakage (imports) from the circular flow of income, so the multiplier is now $\dfrac{1}{1-(b-m)}$ which is smaller than in the case of the closed economy (since m is positive, the denominator of the multiplier formula is larger and the value of the multiplier is smaller). However, a stimulus to the circular flow of income could now arise from an increase in any of the components on the right-hand side of this equation. These are the autonomous components of aggregate demand, investment, government expenditure, exports and the autonomous component of consumption. A £1 million increase in exports would have the same impact as a £1 million increase in government expenditure or a £1 million increase in autonomous investment.

■ ■ ■ 13.3.5 Employment, unemployment and the real wage

The level of aggregate demand was seen above to determine the amount of goods and services that firms produce. Of course, firms have to use inputs to produce those commodities. As you know from Chapter 3, economists use the device of the production function to infer how much of an input is needed to produce a given level of output. Letting K and L represent the amount of capital and labour used to produce commodities, we can write:

$$Y = f(K,L)$$

Question   Recall the discussion of the production function in Chapter 3. How would the production function be modified if we were interested only in the short run?

The short run is the period of time for which the amount of at least one factor is fixed. Usually this is taken to be capital, in which case it is assumed that firms can vary only the amount of labour to change the level of output and to accommodate any variation in the aggregate demand. Thus, in the short run, the production function is written as:

$$Y = f(\bar{K},L) = g(L)$$

Firms in the economy will make hiring decisions according to this production function, assuming their capital stock is fixed. Once the quantity of goods and services is known, the production function will tell firms how much labour they should hire. In Chapter 7, you learnt that when the labour market is competitive firms demand labour up to the point where the marginal revenue product of labour is equal to the wage rate. Put differently, the marginal physical product (MPP) must equal the real wage rate $\dfrac{W}{P}$. So if firms already know how much labour they need they will also have a real wage rate in mind that will maximize the returns from employing that quantity of labour. Algebraically,

$$P.MPP = W$$

and

$$MPP = \frac{W}{P}$$

For a given state of technology and with a given capital stock, as more labour is employed its marginal physical product eventually starts to diminish so that firms will employ more units of labour only at a lower real wage rate. This equation, therefore, is the demand for labour by firms. The supply of labour, on the other hand, increases as the real wage increases.

From Chapter 7, what is the key variable that determines unemployment in the labour market?

According to the analysis in Chapter 7, the key variable in determining employment (and hence unemployment) in the labour market is the real wage rate. If the real wage rate moves freely then the labour market will clear so that labour demand is equal to labour supply. At the real wage corresponding to equilibrium in the labour market unemployed workers are all *voluntarily* unemployed in the sense that the wage they require in order to supply labour is above the equilibrium wage. When the only people who are unemployed are voluntarily unemployed the economy is at its maximum level of employment and output – what we might call *full employment*.

The analysis provided in this chapter has introduced a new factor which influences the level of employment. The demand for labour on the part of firms is a derived demand in the sense that it is derived from the demand for output. We have seen that the demand for output is not fixed at its full employment level but can fall below this level, depending on the determinants of aggregate demand. We therefore need a more general analysis of the relationship between the level of employment and the real wage to encompass the case in which output is less than full-employment output.

Keynes's own analysis of this link retained the standard demand-for-labour curve drawn in Figure 7.3 (as derived from the condition that the marginal physical product of labour equals the real wage). However, he dropped the assumption that the labour market would be at the point where this demand-for-labour curve cuts the labour supply curve. If the derived demand for labour (derived, that is, from the level of aggregate demand in the goods market) falls below the level corresponding to full employment, some workers will be *involuntarily unemployed*. The workers who *are* employed will have a relatively high marginal physical product. The firms that employ them will seek to price the output they produce as competitively as possible. This will lead these firms to cut the price of their output until the $MPP = W/P$ condition holds again. If the nominal wage does not change very much in response to a change in the level of aggregate demand (and Keynes assumed that it would not), lower output prices would translate into a higher real wage for those workers fortunate enough to have jobs. Workers who have jobs will receive a higher real wage than the wage at which they would be willing to supply labour. Some workers who do not have jobs would be very willing to work at this relatively high real wage; they are involuntarily unemployed.

It is important to note that, for Keynes, the real wage is high *because* there is unemployment. This contrasts with the pre-Keynesian view (which, of course, is often heard today, seven decades after Keynes wrote the *General Theory*) that there is unemployment *because* the real wage is too high. This raises an important question: is it possible to distinguish between the (Keynesian) case where unemployment is due to insufficient aggregate demand from the (anti-Keynesian) case where unemployment is due to too high a real wage? To investigate this, consider Figure 13.5.

Once the aggregate demand for commodities is known, the production function allows us to infer the derived demand for labour – based on the technology in use and the level of nominal wages – by firms in the economy. Corresponding to Y_a, the equilibrium level of income from equation (13.1), from the upper half of Figure 13.5 the production

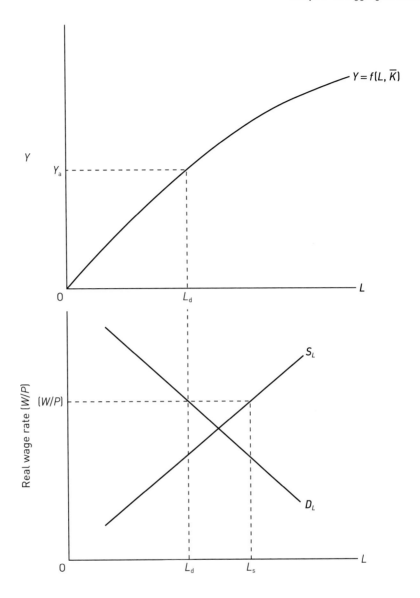

function allows us to read the corresponding level of demand for labour and therefore employment in the economy. This is L_d units of labour.

Question | **Is L_d units of labour the full employment level of labour demand?**

Full employment usually means the absence of involuntary unemployment; that is, the level of employment when all the labour supply offered is absorbed by firms that need labour to produce goods and services. This depends on the labour market and how much labour is supplied at the prevailing real wage rate. If all the labour that is supplied is absorbed by labour demand then we have no unemployment. If labour supplied is greater than the labour demanded then there would be unemployment. Returning to Figure 13.5, the lower half of the figure represents the labour market. L_s units of labour are supplied at the prevailing wage rate $\dfrac{W}{P}$. At this real wage L_s units of labour are supplied in the labour market, but only L_d units of labour are demanded by firms. So the distance from L_d to L_s represents units of unemployed labour.

Is this unemployment the outcome of too high a real wage or a deficiency of aggregate demand? First, an excessively high real wage would be responsible if the unemployment persisted even if an increase in aggregate demand were to increase the demand for labour to the notional equilibrium level at the intersection of D_L and S_L. If, following such an increase in the demand for labour, it was observed that the real wage fell and that, as a consequence, firms were willing to move down the labour demand curve D_L and workers down the labour supply curve S_L until the labour market cleared, it could be concluded that the initial unemployment was involuntary. On the other hand, if the increase in aggregate demand led to a refusal of workers in employment to accept the resulting fall in the real wage so that unemployment persisted at or near its original level, we could conclude that the original level of unemployment was due to too high a real wage.

13.4 The scope for government policy

A role for government intervention in the economy is suggested in this simple model to secure full employment because aggregate income and employment ultimately depend on the level of aggregate demand. Governments can intervene to increase or decrease aggregate demand directly by their spending actions, or indirectly by trying to influence interest rates in the economy. The taxation and spending activities of governments are their fiscal policies, while their interventions to influence interest rates (and therefore money supply) are their monetary policies. In this section we will briefly discuss these two chief instruments of macroeconomic policy available to policy makers.

■■■ 13.4.1 Fiscal policy

It is evident from equation (13.9) that government spending is a source of aggregate demand which has the effect of increasing national income and therefore employment. By raising the level of aggregate demand in the economy the government would in effect be increasing the demand for labour in the economy. As a consequence, employment and income in the economy can increase as a result of an expansion of government expenditure.

It would then appear that since government expenditure is policy determined, it can be used to stabilize the level of aggregate demand in the economy and to compensate for the volatility of investment. So in periods when investment expenditure is low, government spending can stimulate aggregate demand and restore employment. What are the limits on this? There are three which we will outline here. First, it takes time to decide on and implement changes in the level of public expenditure. The statistics on which the decision is based have to be collected and processed. Approval for changes in public expenditure may have to be secured through parliament. In sum, there may be considerable lags between, say, a downturn in investment expenditure and a response from government expenditure to offset that downturn.

Second, the funding of an increase in government expenditure would generally involve an increased budget deficit (or smaller surplus). Recall the formula from the previous chapter, $(S - I) + (M - X) + (T - G) \equiv 0$ which can be rewritten as $(G - T) \equiv (S - I) +$

$(M - X)$. In other words, the funding of a government deficit $(G - T)$ comes from a combination of net domestic savings $(S - I)$ and borrowing from overseas (recall that $M - X$ is the current account deficit equal to the capital account surplus). In so far as an increase in government expenditure leads to a higher level of income (through the multiplier process) then tax revenue also rises and the size of the budget deficit is not as large as the initial increase in government expenditure. The rise in income will also increase savings and imports; in effect the increase in private savings and in the capital account surplus fund the budget deficit. But the budget deficit does mean that the government is borrowing and is then committed to making future interest payments on its borrowing.

Third, the concern that an increase in government expenditure would stimulate demand to a level which exceeds the capacity of the economy to supply. When demand is high relative to capacity, there can be problems of inflation developing; this is further discussed in Chapter 18. Like any other increase in expenditure, an increase in government expenditure at a time when demand is in balance with capacity would be seen as inflationary.

Case study: Has government spending been used to counteract fluctuations in investment?

Figure 13.6 shows the annual percentage change in investment expenditure and in government expenditure in the UK economy between 1950 and 2003. Clearly, investment expenditure has been very volatile, with big increases in some years and sharp falls in others. The question is, did government expenditure tend to compensate for these fluctuations? From Figure 13.6 a countercyclical role for government expenditure is not very evident. Statistical analysis confirms this. During the 1950s there was some tendency for government expenditure to rise in years when private sector investment fell, but the negative correlation is very muted. During the 1960s and 1970s there was, in fact, a (very weak) *positive* correlation between these two components of aggregate demand, so that government expenditure exacerbated rather than damped fluctuations in aggregate demand arising from the volatility of investment. This is ironic, since these two decades are often viewed as the highpoint of the Keynesian consensus in UK policy-making. After 1980 the picture changes again, so that there is now a (weak) negative correction between investment and government expenditure which becomes slightly stronger the closer we get to the present. Again, there is an irony here, since 1980 is often cited as a turning

Figure 13.6
Changes in investment and government expenditure, UK 1950–2003, percentage per year

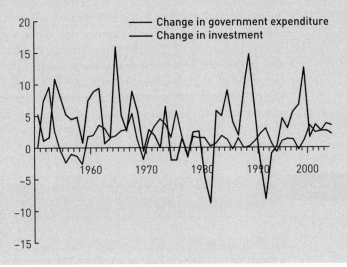

369

Case study continued

point in economic policy-making in the UK, marking a move away from the use of Keynesian counter-cyclical fiscal policy.

One explanation for the absence of evidence of an effective countercyclical fiscal policy in the earlier part of the post-war period is that policy makers were simply inept in using fiscal policy to stabilize the economy. Another is that they found other instruments (such as quantitative controls on consumer credit which were used extensively in the 1950s and 1960s) to be more effective. A third explanation is more subtle and speculative, but may be the correct one. In an interesting article published in 1968 called 'Why has Britain had full

employment since the War?', Robin Matthews noted that it was buoyant investment, not government expenditure, which had kept the UK economy at full employment during the post-war period. He suggested that entrepreneurs' confidence that the government *would* use fiscal and monetary policy to avert a slump encouraged them to invest vigorously. In doing so, they pushed the economy to full employment and reduced the need for fiscal fine-tuning. If this view is correct, the post-war boom in the UK economy was, in part, due to the explicit adoption of Keynesian policies, irrespective of the evidence presented in Figure 13.6.

■ ■ ■ 13.4.2   Monetary policy

Monetary policy, in the form of changing interest rates, can be used to influence the level of aggregate demand in the economy. It has been postulated above that investment expenditure is influenced by the rate of interest and other forms of expenditure (e.g. consumer expenditure) may also be sensitive to the rate of interest.

Banks usually set the price of providing finance, that is, the interest rate on loans r, as a mark-up m over the nominal short-term interest rate i set by the central bank. This is the interest rate that banks pay to each other for overnight loans of reserves held in the central bank. For banks, the nominal short-term interest rate is the cost of obtaining the necessary liquidity for their lending activity. Thus banks add a mark-up to cover their overheads and profits with respect to the short-term interest rate to arrive at the interest rate on loans r.

As the banker to the government and the banking system, the central bank oversees the circulation of money between the accounts of the government and banks and tries to smooth out any imbalance that may result. For instance, when the flow of money from banks to government is higher than the flow of money from government to banks, there can be a shortage of liquidity in the money market. This shortage of cash would be damaging to the level of economic transactions if there was not enough money to buy commodities, and this could have adverse effects on the level of income and employment. The central bank seeks to prevent such problems by supplying the extra cash – so-called monetary reserves – that the banking system needs to balance its accounts. But as the final provider of liquidity to the economic system the central bank can choose the nominal interest rate i at which the extra cash is provided.

Question

Why would the provision of extra reserves by the central bank increase liquidity in the economic system?

Recall from Chapter 12 that liquidity is the extent of money supply in the economy which is available for the purchase of goods and services. An increase in reserves increases the base money in the economy. It thus increases the ability of banks to create new money through loans. In turn, this expands the effective money supply in the economy.

In practice, the central bank does not directly control the nominal short-term interest rate i, which is determined by the supply and demand of reserves. The central bank can expand or contract the supply of monetary reserves in another way. This is by undertaking open market operations (OMO) which in turn determine the nominal short-term interest rate i. For instance, when the central bank wishes to lower the short-term interest rate it buys government assets such as Treasury securities from banks in exchange for cash. This purchase increases the quantity of monetary reserves in the money market and lowers the interest rate i.

Question If the central bank wishes to increase the interest rate should it sell or buy Treasury securities?

When a central bank wishes to increase the short-term interest rate i, it reduces the quantity of monetary reserves in the money market by selling government assets such as Treasury Bills to the banks. Thus, by choosing to supply the relevant amount of reserves to the banking system, the central bank can effectively keep the nominal short-term interest rate near its desired level.

The interest rate i corresponds to what in the USA is called the federal funds rate and in the UK the repo rate. The federal funds rate and the repo rate are set, according to the process described above, by the Federal Reserve System and the Bank of England, the central banks of the USA and the UK, respectively. In modern economies the nominal short-term interest rate i represents a tool central banks use to affect aggregate demand, and hence the level of output and employment.

The sequence of events through which a change in monetary policy eventually affects the level of income is called the monetary transmission mechanism. Figure 13.7 shows how the mechanism works. The operations of the central bank (the first box) in buying government assets and supplying bank reserves lead to a fall in the short-term rate of interest i which feeds through into a fall in the rate of interest on loans r (the second box). The fall in the rate of interest on loans tends to encourage investment demand (leading to the third box) and the additional investment demand adds to the level of aggregate demand which leads to a rise in GDP (fourth box).

The mechanism would also operate in reverse for a sale by central banks of government assets. When the central bank sells government assets, monetary reserves fall, the interest rate i and the interest rate on loans r rise. This means that, for a given expected return, the cost of investment is higher. Investment demand falls and, in that way, the level of real GDP and employment declines. Monetary policy is often used to target the rate of inflation. Hence, when the rate of inflation rises (or is expected to rise), interest rates are increased; this reduces the level of aggregate demand in the expectation that the lower level of aggregate demand will restrain inflation.

Figure 13.7
The monetary transmission mechanism

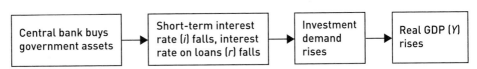

13.5 Conclusion

In this chapter we have developed the simple Keynesian model to explain the determination of aggregate income and employment in the economy. We have seen that aggregate demand determines the level of income in the economy through the multiplier process. The level of income in turn determines labour demand via the production function.

There are two main conclusions from the aggregate demand model presented here. First, the particular level of output and employment at which the economy would finally settle is determined by the complex interactions of individuals on the labour market, the money market and the commodity market. Second, and related to the first conclusion, the economy could potentially settle at any level between zero and full employment. The level of aggregate demand determines the final equilibrium level of output and employment, but that equilibrium is not necessarily a good one since expenditures and income may be lower than they could have been.

This model also suggests a role for government policy in stabilizing the level of aggregate demand in the economy, in order to maintain stability in national income generation and full employment. The government can intervene directly to raise aggregate demand in the economy through the use of fiscal policies. Alternatively it can use monetary policies to change interest rates and intervene indirectly to change aggregate demand.

Questions for review and discussion

Question 1   Complete the following text using appropriate words or phrases from the list below:
According to Say's law, ... creates its own ... An implication of Say's law is that equilibrium in the economy can occur. . . .

fiscal policy   monetary policy demand   supply equilibrium   excess capacity
at less than full employment   only at full employment

Question 2   This is a three-part question. Draw a diagram showing an AD curve and then move it as instructed below. In each case you should either change the slope of the AD curve or shift the position of the whole curve.

(i)   Move the AD curve as appropriate to show a reduction in the marginal propensity to save, other things being equal.

(ii)   Move the AD curve as appropriate to show a reduction in autonomous consumption demand for domestically produced goods and services, other things being equal.

(iii)   Move the AD curve as appropriate to show an increase in the marginal propensity to import, other things being equal.

Question 3   In a certain economy, the marginal propensity to consume is 0.8 and the marginal propensity to import is 0.2. Investment demand, government demand and export demand are exogenously determined. The multiplier is:

A 0.6
B 0.4
C 2.5
D 1.67
E 5.0

Question 4 Suppose that in a certain economy the initial equilibrium level of national income is €100bn. The marginal propensity to consume (*b*) is 0.75 and the marginal propensity to import (*m*) is 0.25. Investment demand, government demand and export demand are exogenously determined. Autonomous consumption now increases by €10bn and investment demand falls by €3bn. What is the new equilibrium level of national income, following the application of the multiplier process?

Question 5 Cabineria is a closed economy. The marginal propensity to consume is 0.75 and the autonomous component of consumption is 100.

(a) What is the marginal propensity to save?
(b) What is the consumption function corresponding to the figures given? Using graph paper, draw the consumption function.
(c) Calculate the level of consumption when income is (i) 1000, and (ii) 2000.
(d) Suppose investment is 500 and government expenditure is 600. What is the value of the multiplier and what is the equilibrium level of national income?
(e) Government expenditure increases to 800. What is the corresponding change in the equilibrium level of income?
(f) Briefly outline the limits on further expansions in the level of government expenditure.

Question 6 In a hypothetical closed economy with no government sector, the marginal propensity to consume is 0.6 and the autonomous component of consumption is £100.

(a) Write down the consumption function which corresponds to these figures, and calculate the level of consumption when income is (i) £1000, (ii) £2000.
(b) Define the marginal propensity to save and identify its value with the information given in (a) above. Write down the corresponding savings function.
(c) Investment is £300. A government sector is added to the economy and government expenditure and taxation are both £600. What is the equilibrium level of income?
(d) Due to a heavy investment on improving the transport infrastructure, government expenditure increases by £400. What is the new level of income in the economy?
(e) What is the numerical value of the multiplier in this economy?
(f) Outline briefly the possible limitations on continued expansion in the level of government expenditure.

Question 7 (a) How can money supply in an economy be measured? Explain how the measures of money supply can be related to the functions of money.
(b) Explain why monetary policy targets the setting of interest rates in the economy.

14

Investment and capital accumulation

David A. Spencer

14.1 Introduction

Who can seriously doubt that Britain has been chronically under-invested in for 20 years or that it harms not just our quality of life but our future prosperity. Every school we invest in helps our children earn more. Every extra nurse we employ in the NHS is a guarantee people won't be forced to go private to be treated when ill. Every penny spent on new track and trains . . . is a step towards the transport system that this country . . . needs. Yes, it takes time. It takes patience. But it takes, above all, investment. That is the choice we must make.

(Tony Blair, Speech, 22 November 2000)

Empirical studies show that levels of physical capital stock are closely correlated with productivity performance. The UK has long suffered from under-investment and is today significantly less capital intensive than its main competitors. The unexpected severity of the world economic slowdown will clearly impact on investment levels in the short term, although strong economic fundamentals are expected to give rise to an acceleration in investment as the global economic recovery gathers pace.

(H M Treasury, website accessed 5 April 2005)

These statements illustrate the importance often given to investment in economic policy. You may wonder, however, why there should be such a fuss about a component of aggregate demand that accounts for less than one-fifth of GDP.

Chapter 13 focused on the short-run implications of investment. It assumed that economic capacity and technology were unchanged, and so investment mainly played the role of creating demand. An important difference in the treatment of investment in this chapter is that it considers both the short-run and the long-run implications of investment. In the long term, investment enhances output creation and income growth in the economy by adding to the productive capacity of the economy. However, investment is quite volatile, being dependent on expectations and uncertainty, so it often takes place in fits and starts, giving rise to output cycles in the economy. Above all, it is this dual nature of investment, as capacity-creating in the long run as well as demand-enhancing in the short run, that makes it such a key variable in economic policy. On the one hand, fluctuations in investment provide a major source of instability in national incomes. On the other hand, investment, whether in the form of the acquisition of productive assets, the creation of new productive capacity or the development of human resources, is a catalyst for economic growth.

Not surprisingly, then, investment is the subject of keen interest at the policy level. Policy makers in the UK and elsewhere have seen the rate of investment and its stability as crucial to economic success, and the problem of under-investment has been singled out as a key reason for economic decline in the UK.

In this chapter we will consider why investment is important, what factors determine it and how it influences the tempo and rate of economic activity. The chapter begins by considering the nature of investment. Section 14.3 then examines the decision to invest and the various factors that influence that decision, ranging from the cost and availability of finance to profit expectations and the degree of uncertainty. Section 14.4 considers the short-term and, very briefly, the long-term aspects of investment, its impact on output stability and output growth. Section 14.5 looks at policy issues and explores the different options available to governments for raising investment levels in the economy.

14.2 Investment

We start by considering what we mean by investment and note the different measures of investment. We then look at the different forms that it can take, its links with productivity and how it is financed.

■■■ 14.2.1 What is investment?

When economists use the word investment, they refer to the acquisition of additional capital; that is, to the process of capital accumulation. The general notion of capital is that it is something that yields benefits now and into the future. The capital stock of the economy is built up period upon period through investment flows. Some of this investment merely replaces worn-out capital stock and some of it adds to the capital stock in the economy. In terms of the circular flow of income (Chapters 8 and 12), some income from the current period is kept aside as savings by households and made available to firms to expand production in successive periods. Investment is thus that part of current income that is not consumed but used to expand the productive capacity of the economy.

Gross investment

Gross investment measures total expenditure on capital goods during a given period of time.

How is investment measured? The total expenditure on capital goods is a broad measure of **gross investment** in the economy. However, plant and machinery do not last indefinitely and are liable to be less productive as time goes on. The contribution of physical assets to total output is diminished through wear and tear, and the term *depreciation* is used to measure the extent of the deterioration of the contribution of existing capital over time. Capital-replacing investment denotes the purchase of new physical capital to replace worn-out physical capital. Such investment ensures that the stock of capital available to firms remains at a constant level. With the ongoing development of superior physical capital and technology, existing capital and technology will become obsolete. So firms will need to update their stock of capital to maintain output and productivity levels in relation to industry *best practice*. Such replacement investment will also normally involve the upgrading of existing capital stock to enable increases in output and productivity (capital-enhancing investment). Gross investment consists of both replacement investment and capital-enhancing investment, and is undertaken to expand production capabilities through increasing the capital stock.

Net investment

Net investment is gross investment less replacement investment, and measures the net increase in the amount of capital available to firms.

A useful concept is therefore that of **net investment**. Net investment refers to capital-enhancing investment alone and is calculated as gross investment less replacement investment (depreciation). Most analytical discussion of investment is based around the accounting concept of net investment. When net investment in the economy is zero the economy just maintains its capital stock. The effect of positive net investment is to increase the amount of capital available to firms. Net additions to the quantity of total capital may give rise to increases in productivity.

Question	Recall the discussion of the production process in Chapter 3. Why would increases in net investment give rise to increased labour productivity?

There are three possible routes by which net investment can increase labour productivity:

1 Net investment may give rise to an increase in the scale of production and a consequent rise in productivity due to economies of scale.
2 There may be an increase in the capital intensity of production; that is, more capital is used for each worker. This should make each worker more productive.
3 Net investment is new investment, which may be technologically superior to the existing capital stock, thus giving rise to an overall increase in productivity.

Increased productivity in production is important because it allows the economy to realize a higher level of output with the same resources. It is this association of investment with higher productivity that explains why investment is given such a high priority at a policy level.

It is also useful to draw a distinction between **fixed investment**, which is also called 'fixed capital formation', and investment in stocks that results in increased 'inventories'. Investment in stocks is the accumulation of work-in-progress, raw materials and finished output (these are what are referred to as 'inventories'). Firms will choose to hold surpluses of raw materials in case of unforeseen contingencies, which might otherwise disrupt the flow of production. Finished output will also be held in stock in case of sudden increases in future demand. Stocks play an important role in granting firms flexibility in dealing with the unexpected. In circumstances where production takes time to be completed, at any one moment there will be output that is incomplete and thus some fraction of stocks will be held as work-in-progress. Accounting data usually classify changes in stocks separately, although they are included in total investment expenditure by firms (Chapter 12).

Fixed investment

Fixed investment is the purchase of fixed capital assets by firms for the purpose of creating additional output.

Table 14.1
Gross fixed capital formation (GFCF) at current producer prices by sector and by type of asset

	1995 £m	1999 £m	2003 £m
GFCF by sector			
Public non-financial corporations	3 990	3 046	3 184
Private non-financial corporations	64 444	93 756	96 659
Financial corporations	5 590	8 054	6 142
Central government	8 718	5 651	9 034
Local government	7 124	5 891	9 380
Households and NPISH[1]	27 582	38 249	54 517
Total GFCF	117 448	154 647	178 916
GFCF by type of asset			
Tangible fixed assets			
New dwellings, excluding land	21 664	25 700	40 485
Other buildings, and structures	31 843	41 680	52 036
Transport equipment	11 295	15 067	15 529
Other machinery and equipment and cultivated assets	45 012	59 766	52 995
Total tangible fixed assets	109 814	142 213	161 045
Intangible fixed assets	3 939	4 645	5 895
Costs associated with the transfer of ownership of non-produced assets	3 695	7 789	11 976

Notes: Components may not sum to totals due to rounding.

[1] NPISH stands for 'Non-profit institutions serving households' (e.g. housing associations)

Source: Tables 9.1 and 9.3 *United Kingdom National Accounts (Blue Book)*, 2004

Table 14.1 provides data on the composition of gross fixed investment across different sectors of the UK economy. Investment is measured by total expenditure on fixed (capital) assets and the cost of these assets is calculated at current prices. It can be seen from the data that gross fixed capital formation (GFCF) totalled nearly £179 billion in 2003; this represented roughly 16.5 per cent of total expenditure. In 2003, private non-financial corporations accounted for 54 per cent of total GFCF, by far the largest contribution of any of the individual sectors listed. Government accounted for a relatively small proportion of total gross investment; for example, expenditure on fixed capital by central and local government combined accounted only for just over 10 per cent of total fixed investment in 2003. Investment expenditure by households on fixed assets includes the purchase of new dwellings and the data shows that investment of this kind increased through the 1990s. Gross fixed capital investment as a whole was some 52 per cent higher in 2003 than in 1995 in money terms: allowing for inflation the increase in investment in real terms was 40 per cent.

Table 14.1 also gives figures on gross investment by type of asset purchased. In terms of tangible fixed assets, most gross investment falls into the category of 'other machinery and equipment and cultivated assets' ('cultivated assets' includes livestock and forestry). Total expenditure on tangible fixed assets has increased by some 62 per cent from 1995 to 2003. Investment in intangible fixed assets incorporates expenditure on such things as mineral exploration, computer software and entertainment, literary or artistic originals;

the purchase by a firm of computer software would be classified under this definition as investment in intangible fixed assets. These assets remain a very small fraction of total gross investment, and total expenditure on intangible fixed assets showed only a modest rise during the 1990s.

Forms of investment

The dominant image that springs to mind in the discussion of investment so far is that of huge factories and expenditures on machinery but this is by no means the only form that investment takes. Many different forms of expenditure constitute investment.

Question	Can you think of other examples that satisfy the attributes of investment that we have identified?

The chief attribute of investment is that it is expenditure undertaken at the present time that is capable of yielding a flow of benefits in the future. Expenditures on the building of roads and the construction of new railway lines, and on education and the training of labour, are all examples of investment. This investment in building roads and railroads has to be financed through loans or through taxation, both of which entail a sacrifice in current consumption for the economy as a whole. Similarly, training of labour enhances the productivity of labour and usually requires a sacrifice in current consumption by their households, whether directly or in terms of foregone earnings.

It is instructive to think about three broad forms of investment: investment in physical capital, investment in infrastructure and investment in human capital and training.

Physical investment is the purchase of productive assets (plant, machinery, buildings and vehicles) by producers in the economy and is by far the largest category of measured investment. These producers may be private firms or public sector corporations, but as we have seen in Table 14.1, private firms make much the largest contribution to physical investment. The important feature of investment in physical capital is that firms expect to more than cover the current costs of purchasing capital goods with enhanced future returns derived from the use of those goods in production. These returns will accrue from being able to cut costs and/or produce a higher output or from enhanced revenues through the production and sale of new products. These potential gains from investment motivate firms to increase their expenditure on capital goods; that is, to invest.

Investment in infrastructure (e.g. roads, railway lines, satellite lines or fibre optic cables) has some peculiar features as an investment good. First, it usually requires large *lumpy* investments, which take a long time to yield a return. This makes it somewhat unsuitable for private sector investment, which is perceived to be more short-term in its outlook than the public sector and therefore less willing to undertake investment that generates full returns only over many decades into the future. Second, it has a 'public good' nature, which means that private sector firms are likely to under-invest in it because they will not reap the full rewards from that investment. (Look back to Chapter 9 if you need to remind yourself of why public goods are likely to be under-provided by private firms.)

Governments provide an important source of such investment. In the UK, however, privatization of much of the former public sector has meant that the responsibility for investment in key parts of the infrastructure of the economy (e.g. railways, communication networks) has now shifted from government to the private sector. You can see this in Table 14.1 where the government sector share of investment declined between 1992 and 2000. However, there remains a strong rationale for public investment in infrastructure.

We look at the third form of investment – investment in human capital and training – in the next section.

▨ ▨ ■ 14.2.3 Investment and human capital

Human capital

Human capital denotes the knowledge and skills embodied in workers.

Firms are not just concerned with amassing fixed assets (whether tangible or intangible) but also retain an interest in improving intangible human assets. The development of human resources can be viewed as at least as important as the accumulation of physical capital in terms of improving output and productivity. The enhancement of education, skills and training is likely to aid the process of economic growth. Starting from the work of Gary Becker (Becker, 1962), considerable attention has been given to the effects of skill and knowledge on the productiveness of workers (see Chapter 7). Becker shifted the focus away from physical investment and towards investment in what he terms *human capital*. We refer to workers being endowed with **human capital**, with the latter acting as a proxy for the 'skilfulness' or 'knowledgeableness' of labour. Human capital impacts upon the quality of labour as measured by the output of each worker. Those workers who have accumulated more qualifications through schooling or attendance on relevant training courses may be expected to be better able to contribute to productive activity than those workers with fewer years of schooling and no formal training.

Human capital will vary among workers according to ability, educational attainment and skill acquisition. Becker claims that in view of this variation workers will be paid different wages and salaries, which will manifest itself in an uneven distribution of earnings. Workers will be motivated to make an investment in education and training to improve their human capital by the prospect of higher pay in high-productivity and high-skilled jobs. Higher monetary rewards in this case will cause workers to invest resources in acquiring qualifications via extended years of schooling and/or through participation on training courses. A student on an Open University course is investing in human capital to the extent that the objective of study is to enhance his or her work-related skills and productivity and hence future earnings.

Becker (1962) argued that individual workers will act like 'mini firms' in gaining human capital; that is, individual workers are assumed to undertake investment (in this case, investment of time and money) in education and training to accumulate superior human capital (here reflected in the acquisition of new skills and knowledge). Just as the individual firm undertakes investment in physical capital to enhance the opportunities for higher future profit, so the individual worker will invest in human capital in anticipation of higher future earnings. While there are obvious financial benefits from education, there are also costs. The most obvious cost is that of forgone income during the period of time workers spend in education. Thus, someone deciding to enter college will forgo some finite level of income by not taking up paid work on a full-time basis. According to the theory of human capital, they will do this only if the loss of current income is more than offset by the potential for higher earnings in the future (see Chapter 7, Figure 7.4). Investment in human capital in this case will be a matter of weighing up the current costs and future benefits of time spent in education or on training courses.

Firms will benefit from the investment made by workers in human capital. Firms will not only gain access to a larger pool of qualified applicants to fill outstanding vacancies, they also stand to benefit from higher productivity once workers begin work. Workers gain job-specific human capital through 'on-the-job' training, acquiring tacit skills through the experience of working on the same or similar tasks. These skills provide an additional source of productivity gain beyond the level of formal education and training. Workers may invest time in acquiring on-the-job training with a view to raising their bargaining power when it comes to negotiating for higher pay. Whether or not firms accede to demands for higher pay will depend, in part, on the extent to which workers' investment in human capital feeds through into higher productivity. In this case, there is the possibility for mutual gains from the investment made in human capital if not all the productivity gains have to be paid out in higher wages.

The discussion has so far been cast in terms of the investment in human capital being undertaken by workers themselves. While this is the norm in the case of education (e.g. a school leaver entering college), many firms are active in the development of human capital. They may seek to administer training courses with the aim of raising the individual and collective productivity of their workforce. The enhancement of human capital enables firms to get more output from their workforce and in turn provides a source of productivity gain beyond the physical limits imposed by the amount of available capital or the scale of production (where the latter is measured by available productive capacity).

There may well be a trade-off between investment in physical capital and investment in human capital. Faced with finite funds for investment, firms must prioritize their investment plans, and compromises may well have to be made in terms of pursuing investment in one direction rather than another. If firms opt to spend more on training their workforce, this expenditure may come at the expense of investment in physical capital.

Investment in certain capital inputs may require a particular type of skilled labour in order to be carried through successfully and the effectiveness of these capital inputs in yielding productivity gains may be held back by the skill levels of incumbent workers. If a firm is planning to invest in capital with a high-technology content, then it may be anticipated that the firm will need to undertake additional investment in equipping workers with the technical know-how required to use this capital in the most productive way possible. Investments in labour and capital are likely to be complementary aspects of production and hence firms undertake these forms of investment side by side. Indeed, the effective use of new capital equipment can require that existing workers be retrained.

Question	Until now we have treated investment in human capital and investment in physical capital similarly. In what ways do you think these forms of investment differ for a firm?

One crucial difference between investment in physical capital and investment in human capital is that the former involves the purchase of fixed assets, which may be sold off at a price once purchased, while the latter involves the development of knowledge and skills that are non-tradable (at least outside a society ruled by slavery). A decision to purchase fixed assets is often reversible, but a decision to acquire human capital cannot be reversed. The decision by a firm to invest in physical capital is reversible in the sense that, if the profits achieved through the use of purchased capital goods turn out to be below expectations, firms can liquidate (i.e. sell) some or all of those goods to others at a price. Once capital goods have been produced, they cannot (usually) be reconverted into other capital goods, and thus it would be inappropriate to refer to the reversibility of physical investment other than in terms of the resale value of purchased capital goods. Assuming the existence of a second-hand market for capital goods (a realistic assumption for vehicles, say, but not for highly specialized equipment designed for and installed in an oil refinery), firms will be able to recuperate some of the potential losses incurred through the pursuit of physical investment. The potential reversibility of physical investment means that firms will be willing to accept a lower chance of success (in the form of lower expected profits) from buying capital goods than might otherwise be expected if capital goods were non-tradable.

However, the decision to invest in human capital is irreversible. The costs of training include not only the direct costs of training provision but also the indirect costs of lost output while workers are trained – where the latter represent the opportunity cost of the time workers spend being trained. These costs cannot be simply recuperated by firms through the sale of trained workers on the open market. If firms endow their workforce with transferable skills, which could be used in other firms, there will be a risk that the offer of higher wages will entice newly trained workers away from their present jobs once their training is completed. In this case, while the firm undertaking the training incurs the full cost of training, it will receive none of the benefits. This need not be the case where firms equip their workers with job-specific skills that limit the options for workers to exit their jobs and which therefore offer firms greater scope to capture the productivity gains from training. In general, firms will have an incentive to pay for training only if they expect their present workforce to remain with them in the future. One way round the problem of firms covering the cost of equipping workers with transferable skills is to share these costs with the workers themselves. In this situation, firms can offer workers lower wages whilst the training is administered, with the inducement of higher wages in the future if the workers successfully complete their training and remain in their present jobs.

One criticism of the human capital approach is that it neglects to consider the non-economic benefits of undertaking education. In the human capital approach, the return to education has as its main motivation for investment the prospect of higher future earnings. It may well be the case that firms have economic motives in training their work-force but this same logic need not always apply to individual workers when they make the decision to enrol on a college course or to attend a training course. Learning involves important non-economic considerations, which may override the expected increases in labour productivity and future earnings that may result from education. Thus, for example, one may be motivated to pursue education by the pleasure derived from studying. In this case, the pursuit of economic interest will be of secondary importance in the decision to undertake education.

■ ■ ■ 14.2.4 Variable productivity and investment

Variable productivity

Variable productivity is the potential for output to vary for the same input of labour (where labour is measured either by total hours worked or by total employment).

One important point to take from the above discussion is the **variable productivity** of workers. Skills, in particular, will influence the quality and hence productivity of labour. However, there is also a wider issue here of the status of labour and its relationship to investment. Labour does not just involve hours worked, as a quantitative measure of total labour input used. It also encompasses the dimensions of effort and work intensity, which relate to the actual work done by workers. Economists have usually defined labour in *extensive* terms alone; that is, by the number of hours worked – given by the number of workers employed and the duration of work time. This is to be distinguished from the actual contribution made by labour to total output, which is defined in *intensive* terms by the total effort expended by workers.

This raises the question of how work-hours are converted into work effort. This depends on the organization of work and the use of technology. Investment in this case is not simply about adding more physical (capital) inputs to the production process via the acquisition of greater numbers of machines and additional plant. There is also an issue of getting more from existing labour inputs. Employers will seek to alter the organization of work and the use of technology in order to extract more effort from workers. The technical division of labour is a case in point. Subdividing tasks allows work to be done more efficiently, as Adam Smith noted in his famous example of pin manufacture (Chapter 2). Specialization of work tasks also enables firms to gain greater bargaining leverage over workers. Employers' enhanced control over workers can then be put to use in intensifying the pace of work. Technology that makes it easier for employers to monitor their workforce may be used to achieve the same outcome. The operation of an assembly line, for example, circumscribes workers' behaviour and reduces their ability to resist increases in the intensity of work. Firms can exploit this situation with a view to gaining more output from their workforce. One could also envisage the positive effects of an increase in the number of supervisors on work intensity. Under circumstances of tight supervision, there will be fewer opportunities for workers to evade the discipline of work, and the outcome is an intensification of work.

Employers' investment strategies for raising work intensity do not necessarily enhance skills. Some radical commentators have argued that employers will look to *reduce* the skill content of labour as part of a so-called 'divide and rule' strategy (Bowles, 1985). Firms may invest in training to enhance human capital by reaping the technical benefits of improved skills, where these benefits arise from workers' increased knowledge of ways of improving the flow of output. Yet, just as workers can learn how to enhance production, so they can learn how to impede production. Workers can draw individual and collective strength from the possession of specific skills. Employers may therefore pursue a policy of deskilling in order to enhance their control over production. Through this route, employers aim to reduce the potential for opposition from workers to any moves to increase the intensity of work.

Question — What does this discussion suggest to you about the influences on firms' decisions to invest?

The above discussion highlights the scope for investment decisions to be influenced by non-technical and social considerations. Firms will not be concerned just with the contribution made by physical assets and workers' skills to total output. They will also be interested in how physical capital and human capital affect the extraction of effort from their workers. Investment in capital may also be used to improve the amount of work done per hour. Employers may opt to invest in certain types of capital with the intention of reducing the amount of control exercised by workers over production, and investment of this sort may well come at the expense of investment in human capital.

Conventional measures of investment are in practice biased in favour of fixed investment and some types of infrastructure investment such as those undertaken by the government. The large category of expenditure on training is not usually included in measures of investment. We should, however, be mindful that increasingly economists consider these forms of investment as extremely important in explaining the long-term growth of incomes.

Exercise 14.1

Explain whether the following expenditures should be regarded as investment, and give reasons for your answers:

1 Research and development expenditures by firms.
2 Government spending on (a) refurbishing a school and (b) teachers' salaries.
3 Government spending on (a) building a new hospital for the NHS and (b) medical staff salaries.
4 Payments into pension funds by employers.

■ ■ ■ **14.2.5 The financing of investment**

We have seen that firms are the main agents undertaking physical investment plans in the economy. The question then arises of how firms finance their investment plans. Any source of finance involves costs so far as the firm is concerned. In this section we look at the principal internal and external sources of finance available to firms to carry out their investment plans. The source of finance a firm uses depends on its availability as well as the costs of using it.

Internal finance

Firms may rely on internal sources of finance to raise the funds required to finance investment. Internal finance takes the form of retained profits. The owner of a firm faces a choice about whether to use profit for consumption or investment. So there is an opportunity cost to be borne in devoting more profit to one type of expenditure as opposed to the other. The opportunity cost to the owner of a firm in using retained profits to fund investment is measured by the level of present consumption forgone.

To fund their investment programmes, firms may prefer to rely on retained profits; that is, profits not paid out as dividends to shareholders and the portion of the firm's revenue that has been allocated to cover depreciation. The reason is that these sources of internal finance involve no interest payment (although as indicated below it still involves an opportunity cost to the firm in terms of alternative revenues forgone). The use of external finance means a commitment to make future interest or dividend payments, which may create difficulties for the firm in the event of an economic downturn. Further, internal finance gives firms a degree of independence over the direction of investment, whereas external finance requires lenders (e.g. a bank or external shareholders) to be persuaded of the merits of the proposed investment.

Question | **Why might firms be limited in their access to internal finance?**

Internal finance depends on a firm having retained profits and accumulated depreciation funds. Access to retained profits will vary with the size and age of the firm. Internal finance will not be an option for newly formed firms. Smaller firms, which may face tight profit margins, may also face problems raising internal finance. Thus it may be expected that larger (profitable) firms will have greater scope to finance investment using retained profits. The level of retained profit will also fluctuate with the level of economic activity and there will be no guarantee that firms will have sufficient internal finance to fund investment at any particular point in time. In periods of economic slowdown, existing investment levels may come under severe pressure as profit levels are eroded. If recovery is gradual after a recession, then it may take time for profits to be replenished to the levels required to support previous levels of investment. This is a potentially serious problem given that recessions lead to erosions in the capital stock and losses in productive capacity.

However, it remains an open question as to whether investment should be seen as the cause or effect of retained profits. On the one hand, increases in retained profits provide the necessary stimulus for firms to undertake additional planned investment. Yet, on the other, it is possible that the desire for higher investment motivates firms to retain additional profits; in this case, the motive for investment precedes the growth in retained profit. While retained profits and investment may be observed to move in the same direction, it is not always clear what the direction of causation is between these two variables.

External finance

Faced with insufficient internal finance, firms will have to seek external finance to realize their investment plans. Two sources of external finance may be distinguished: the issue of securities and bank borrowing.

Securities take two forms: shares and debentures (equities and corporate bonds respectively in US terminology). Firms may issue shares or equities and use the funds raised in this way to finance planned investment. The sale of shares by a firm may appear at first sight to provide a way of raising finance at no cost (other than the transaction costs involved in the selling of the shares). However, those buying shares expect that there will be some future dividends payable on the shares, in addition to the prospect of a capital gain on their eventual sale. Dividends are payments made to shareholders out of profits. When a firm issues additional shares, future dividends will be shared among more people (i.e. both new and old shareholders). The dividends payable to existing shareholders will fall unless the increase in the number of shares is matched by an expansion in the firm's profits and hence in total dividends. There is also a question here of the relationship between dividends and profitability. Profits can be used to pay dividends but if they are retained they are a source of internal finance for investment. It can be argued that in the UK problems have arisen from the unresponsiveness of dividends to profits, so that high dividends have been maintained on occasions at the expense of higher investment, in spite of falling profits (Hutton, 1995). The trade-off between shareholder returns and investment in new capital (both physical and human) raises broader issues concerning the power of shareholders' interests.

Debentures (corporate bonds) entitle the purchaser to a fixed sum paid at some future date (usually referred to as the *redemption date*), plus a fixed interest payment up until the debenture becomes redeemable. Debentures therefore create a liability for the firm, which needs to be weighed against the expected proceeds gained from the investment. The advantage of debentures is that they offer firms a medium- to long-term source of finance at a guaranteed and predictable cost, so that firms are able to plan ahead their investment levels. Debentures are secured against the issuing firm's assets so that in the event of the firm going bankrupt debenture holders will be compensated with the revenue gained from selling those assets. Shareholders will only receive what, if anything, is left after paying all other parties with a claim on the firm. The scope for a firm to issue debentures may therefore be limited by the value of the fixed assets owned by the firm.

Bank borrowing is the second main source of external finance. This entails a firm entering into a loan agreement with a bank, which raises a number of issues. First, firms will be concerned with the cost of bank finance. The interest paid on bank borrowing will be a major influence on the decision to invest, with lower (higher) interest rates providing a positive (negative) stimulus to planned investment. Second, firms may be concerned with the length of time over which a loan is to be repaid if the length of the loan does not match the period during which the investment project yields profits. For example, a loan to be repaid over three years would mean that the firm not only has to make sufficient profits (on the project financed by the loan) to cover the interest charges, but also has to repay the full amount of the loan at the end of the three-year period. However, the project being financed may be one which yields steady profits over a longer period of time.

Third, firms may be concerned with the availability of finance as much as its cost. From the banks' perspective, there is always some risk that a loan will not be repaid if the investment project turns out to be unprofitable (as well as the risk that the borrower may default on the loan). Small firms, in particular, may be deemed as high risk owing to the greater probability of their demise and thus there may be greater reluctance for banks to lend to small firms compared with medium-sized and large firms. This greater reluctance may result in banks charging higher interest rates to those perceived to be at greater risk of defaulting on the debt or refusing loans altogether to those with poor credit ratings.

There is also the question of the flexibility of finance and whether firms have sufficient scope to adapt to changing economic circumstances in repaying outstanding debt. These issues are important for a firm's ability to continue investing on an ongoing basis. Where loans give firms little flexibility to cope with economic downturns by delaying repayment, investment plans (at least those with a medium- to long-term time horizon) may be severely circumscribed, perhaps to the point of being ruled out altogether. Think, for example, of loan finance taking the form of bank overdrafts secured against assets held by the owner(s) of a firm (for a small business, the owner's house may be security against debt default). In this case, it is highly doubtful whether planned investment will be able to survive downturns in economic activity. As pressure mounts on firms' finances owing to falling revenues, costs will need to be reduced in order to make repayments on the existing debt and stay within the limits of available overdraft facilities. The prospect of breaching these limits will cause firms to be more cautious in their investment behaviour and make them more reluctant to undertake investment on a long-term basis.

Under circumstances where the nature of loan finance is inflexible in relation to changes in the level of economic activity, risky investment projects, even those with a high expected return, might not be undertaken by firms concerned about limiting the possibilities for debt default. This may be a potentially serious problem with regard to raising productivity levels. High-risk investment projects are more likely to fail, but promise high returns in the form of increased productivity if successful. No one would undertake high-risk investment projects if the high risk was not compensated for by high potential returns. So the limits imposed by inflexible forms of loan finance on risk-taking behaviour may have adverse effects on the rate of investment. In many advanced economies, specialized venture capital funding has now emerged as an alternative to banks for such finance.

Case study: Financing investment in tourism

The following extract from the Partnerships UK website describes how the public sector is using private finance to invest in the UK tourism industry. After reading it, answer the questions below.

Forestry commission announces first PPP in the holiday sector

The Forestry Commission has invited the private sector to inject capital into modernising its thriving holiday business as it moves towards creating the first Public Private Partnership (PPP) in the UK's tourism sector.

Plans to raise £25 million private sector funding represents the next step in the Forestry Commission's timetable to develop its Forest Holidays business and, with it, the opportunity to join forces with a private sector partner to:

- Modernise the current touring caravan and campsite network
- Develop a new 100-cabin site
- Create permanent holiday let units on 300 pitches over five campsites.

Case study continued

Teresa Garnett, PPP Project Manager said: 'This offers the opportunity to transform Forest Holidays from a wholly Forestry Commission owned and controlled business to a PPP. The partnership would enable us to benefit from much needed capital, whilst we continue to meet the Forestry Commission's wider social and recreational objectives. We want to encourage people of all ages to enjoy the forests and woodlands of Great Britain.'

Forest Holidays is a unique brand and is ideally placed to maximise its recreational facilities including public woodlands and peace and tranquillity of its sites for the benefit of holidaymakers up and down the country.

This announcement comes against the backdrop of increased engagement between the UK public and private sectors across the whole range of public sector activity. This saw the Forestry Commission and Partnerships UK (PUK) enter into a Development Partnership Agreement in March 2003. PUK, itself a PPP, is playing a pivotal role in offering practical assistance at all stages to bring this PPP to fruition.

Michael Gerrard, Deputy Chief Executive of Partnerships UK said: 'PUK is delighted to make available assistance to the Forestry Commission on such a worthwhile project. This is an imaginative way of using public assets and extracting value from them and we are confident that we can help to develop a thriving holiday business which meets the aspirations of holidaymakers.'

Forest Holidays currently operates three self-catering log cabin sites and 21 campsites throughout Great Britain, providing 141 self-catering units and over 5000 touring pitches. The three cabin sites have recently been modernised – all cabins have been replaced by brand new units – funded by the Government's Capital Modernisation Fund and by the Scottish Executive. This however was a one-off support and PPP funding is now required to take the business forward.

Market conditions are very favourable for developing the holiday business. The short break market is buoyant and sustainable tourism and increased appreciation of the environment and conservation issues are growing trends. People are looking for self-improvement and development whilst on holiday and the natural forest environment addresses the aspirations of an increasingly health conscious public.

The Forestry Commission is confident that, not only will it retain its existing customers, but that its extra capacity created will draw new customers into its holiday business to take advantage of the new cabins, modernised touring caravan and camping facilities and create permanent new holiday let units at some sites.

(Adapted from Partnerships UK, 2005)

Questions

1 What reasons are there for categorizing the Forestry Commission project as investment?

2 The project involves injecting private capital into a public sector organization. To what extent is this public–private partnership reflected in the nature of the future benefits expected from the project?

14.3 Influences on investment

In this section we look at some of the factors that can influence a firm's decision to invest, including the cost and availability of finance, the rate of interest, the level of uncertainty and future expectations.

■ ■ ■ 14.3.1 Discounting and the present value criterion

Investment is undertaken at some cost now in the hope of benefits in the future. A firm building a new factory incurs the costs of construction in the present and hopes that the output to be produced in the new factory will be sold at a profit in the future. An individual may undertake training and acquire skills, which cost time and money in the present but offer the hope of enhanced earning power later on. In all these examples, there is an income flow in the future about which a decision has to be made today.

Question	Would a pound earned today have more or less value to you than a pound earned tomorrow?

For most individuals a pound earned today would be worth more than a pound earned tomorrow. This is because we are generally impatient, preferring consumption today to the same level of consumption tomorrow. We are also uncertain about what might happen tomorrow and so tend to underestimate the benefits of consumption in an uncertain tomorrow. Put differently, we will need to be paid something more to be persuaded to postpone our consumption to tomorrow. This is sometimes termed *positive time preference*, and is cited as the rationale for having a rate of interest on any saving.

In the presence of such positive time preference how might we measure the value of an income flow in the future? This is an important question for an investor who has to decide whether or not to invest today in the hope of obtaining returns in the future. The technique of **discounting** allows future benefits to be compared with money spent today. This section explains the technique and its use in decisions to invest.

Let us consider a simple example. Suppose you have £100 and you are undecided about whether to buy yourself a coat. Someone comes along and says that, if you would postpone your purchase until next year and instead lend them the money for this year, they would pay you interest in return for borrowing the money for a year. The rate of interest you would be willing to accept for making such a loan is the rate at which you are willing to discount benefits (in this case the use of a coat) when they are postponed for one year. You perceive consumption now as more valuable to you than consumption in a year's time. However, maybe £110 to spend in a year's time is the equivalent (in value to you) of £100 to spend today. In that case you will agree to lend your £100 at 10 per cent interest and therefore get £100 + £10 = £110 back in a year's time.

More generally, if £100(1 + r) in a year's time has the same value to you as £100 today, we say that you *discount the future* at a rate r. Another way to put this is that £100(1 + r) in a year's time has a present value of £100. In the example above, if you agreed to make the loan at 10 per cent interest it would be because the £110 you would get back in a year's time would have a present value of at least £100 – the £100 that you would forgo today to make the loan. With a 10 per cent interest rate, £100(1 + 0.1) = £110 has a present value of £100. Here, the discount rate r is expressed as a decimal rather than a percentage – in this numerical example, 0.1 for 10 per cent.

Discounting

Discounting offers a technique for converting future returns into an equivalent value in the present – the present value of that future benefit.

Questions	1 If you discount the future at a rate of 10 per cent, what is the present value of £100 in a year's time? 2 If you discount the future at a rate r, what is the present value of £100 in a year's time?

Let us return to the example. The present value of £100 to be received in one year's time is:

$$PV = \frac{£100}{1.1} = £90.91$$

What is the present value of £100 to be received in two years' time? It is:

$$PV = \frac{£90.91}{1.1} = \frac{£100}{(1.1)^2} = £82.64$$

Present value (PV)

The present value, PV, of a future benefit, FB, in t years' time is given by the formula:

$$PV = \frac{FB}{(1 + r)^t}$$

In general, the **present value (PV)**, of a future benefit, FB, is given by the formula:

$$PV = \frac{FB}{(1 + r)^t}$$

where r is the discount rate and t stands for the number of years which elapse before the benefit becomes available.

Let us apply the discounting formula to an investment decision made by a firm. Take as an example a firm deciding whether to purchase a new machine which is expected to produce £3000 per annum. The machine is to be scrapped after five years. The machine costs £10 000, so the firm can either invest £10 000 in this machine or keep the £10 000 in a bank and earn a rate of interest on it.

In order to decide whether or not to invest in the machine, the firm needs to compare the present value of the future benefits (in this case, £3000 each year for five years) with the cost of the machine. If the present value of the future benefits is greater than the cost of the machine, then the firm is better off making the investment in the cost of the machine rather than holding the money in a bank. If the present value is less than the cost of the machine, then obviously the firm is better off holding its profits in a bank.

Question	What is the rate of discount the firm should use in working out the present value of the future benefits?

The rate of discount the firm should use is the rate of return on holding money as a bank deposit, because this is the alternative use of its money. The present value of £3000 a year for 5 years, assuming banks pay an interest rate of 10 per cent on deposits, is calculated as follows (rounded to the nearest pound):

(i) The present value of the return in the first year ($t = 1$) is given by:

$$PV = \frac{£3000}{1 + 0.1} = \frac{£3000}{1.1} = £2727$$

This implies that £3000 in a year's time is worth £2727 today. Another way to put this is that £2727 deposited in the bank today at an interest rate of 10 per cent would realize £3000 in a year's time.

(ii) Following the same procedure as above, the return in the second year (£3000 in two years' time) has a present value given by:

$$PV = \frac{£3000}{(1 + 0.1)^2} = \frac{£3000}{(1.1)^2} = £2479$$

(iii) The total present value of the investment to the firm is the sum of the present values of its returns in each of the next five years:

$$PV = \frac{£3000}{1.1} + \frac{£3000}{(1.1)^2} + \frac{£3000}{(1.1)^3} + \frac{£3000}{(1.1)^4} + \frac{£3000}{(1.1)^5}$$

$$PV = £2727 + £2479 + £2254 + £2049 + 1863 = £11\ 372$$

Net present value (NPV)

The net present value of an investment is the present value of its returns net of (i.e. minus) the cost of the investment.

This figure of £11 372 is an estimate of the present value of all future returns arising from this investment. It is not as much as the total returns of $5 \times £3000 = £15\ 000$ because these are not all available today and so have to be discounted in calculating their present value. In this case, the firm will invest in the new machine because the present value of future benefits (£11 372) exceeds the cost of the new machine (£10 000). The **net present value (NPV)** of an investment is the present value of its returns net of (i.e. minus) the cost of the investment. In this case, the net present value of the investment is £11 372 − £10 000 = £1372. Because the investment's NPV is positive, using a 10 per cent rate of discount, the firm should make the investment.

Deciding on this basis is called using the net present value criterion. If the cost of the machine exceeded the present value of the expected returns from the investment, then its NPV would be negative. In this case, the firm will gain more by depositing the money in the bank and earning interest on it.

▪▪▪ 14.3.2   The rate of interest and the rate of discounting

We can use discounting and the net present value criterion to illustrate more clearly the impact of changes in the rate of interest and the rate of discounting upon investment decisions. You have already seen this intuitively in Chapter 13, but discounting shows clearly how and why lowering the rate of interest can work to increase the volume of investment.

Consider the example in Section 14.3.1 again. Suppose a firm does not have £10 000 to spend but would have to borrow from a bank to finance that investment project. The firm would need to apply the rate of interest that the bank charges on loans as its rate of discount in evaluating its investment projects. The rate of interest that the bank charges on borrowing is 10 per cent. We saw that at this rate of discount, the NPV of the investment would be £1372.

Question How would the NPV of the investment change if the bank were to charge a higher rate of interest of 20 per cent on its loan?

The present value of returns to the investment in the first year would now be:

$$PV = \frac{£3000}{1.2} = £2500$$

and the present value of the investment over all five years would be:

$$PV = \frac{£3000}{1.2} + \frac{£3000}{(1.2)^2} + \frac{£3000}{(1.2)^3} + \frac{£3000}{(1.2)^4} + \frac{£3000}{(1.2)^5} = £8972$$

This means that the NPV of the investment is £8972 − £10 000 = −£1028, which is negative. So at this higher rate of interest, the investment is no longer profitable as the present value of the returns it will yield to the firm will be less than it costs the firm to pay for the machine. Note that this conclusion would hold even if the firm were not borrowing the money. Why? Because the firm could earn more by lending out its money than it would by investing in this project (assuming it would receive the same rate of interest). Since all producers in the economy are likely to behave in this way, we can conclude that the higher the cost of borrowing (i.e. the higher the rate of interest), the lower the volume of investment, since fewer investment projects will be undertaken.

Exercise 14.2

Use a calculator to work out the NPV of this investment if the interest rate is 15 per cent. Would the project be undertaken in this case?

Thus far, we have been using the rate of interest charged for loans as the rate of discount. This is reasonable when we think of a firm deciding whether to hold money in the bank or to invest in plant and machinery, if it feels quite secure about the returns it would get in either case. The financial asset (leaving the money as a bank deposit) and the investment project are 'substitutes' (using the term in the sense explained in Chapter 3). But this may not always be the case: one or other option may be perceived as particularly risky. Sometimes bank deposits may not inspire confidence and people may not want to hold them. Alternatively, people may believe that investment is the riskier option. In times of market instability, for example, firms may not be sure they will be able to sell their products in the future and reap the planned returns on their investment. How would firms then evaluate their investment projects? In these cases the rate of discount applied would include a subjective element that depends on perceptions as to relative risks. In risky times people are likely to see present income as more secure than promises of future income; they may therefore apply a rate of discount that is higher than the rate of interest charged for loans.

Again, the higher the rate at which the future is discounted, the lower the present value of future income. So, the higher the rate of discount, the smaller the number of projects whose anticipated present value exceeds the initial costs; that is, that have a positive net present value. There is always a negative relationship between the volume of investment and the rate of discount.

The central bank of a country may have some control over the rate of interest, but in so far as producers use subjective rates of discount to value their investment projects, it is their expectations with respect to risk that matters. These expectations may be influenced by any manner of guesses about the future and they usually come into play in circumstances of financial instability. These expectations are also out of the control of any policy-making body.

■ ■ ■ 14.3.3 Expectations and uncertainty

We saw in the last section how expectations could affect the valuation of a future stream of investment through influencing the rate of discount. Following Keynes, economists have stressed the importance of expectations about the future (especially of demand and profitability) on the decision to invest. Firms will hold vague expectations about the future course of economic activity and there will be a tendency for firms to revise their expectations in a sporadic and sometimes volatile manner. Keynes (1936) referred to the 'animal spirits' of investors, which sums up the volatile and precarious nature of business confidence. This section briefly explores the role of expectations and uncertainty, using once again the technique of discounting.

First, let us consider the case when expectations change dramatically. Imagine you are an airline company, thinking about buying a new aeroplane for £7000 in the expectation of selling summer holidays with water sports activities in the Hawaiian Islands. Lending rates are 6 per cent and market surveys lead you to have buoyant expectations. You expect to earn revenues of £2000 in the first year, followed by £4000 in the second and third years and £6000 in the fourth year. Should you make the investment? You calculate the present value:

$$PV = \frac{£2000}{1.06} + \frac{£4000}{(1.06)^2} + \frac{£4000}{(1.06)^3} + \frac{£6000}{(1.06)^4} + = £13\ 557.82$$

You find that this is well over the cost of the new aeroplane and so you decide to invest in it. While you are in the midst of negotiating a deal on the new plane, the events of 11 September 2001 happen. Market surveys now tell you that airline travel to the US is at an all time low. You have to revise your demand expectations. Now the revenues predicted are £700 in the first year, £900 in the next two years and £1000 in the fourth year. Would you still go ahead with your purchase? No, because your present value calculations now tell you that the investment is only worth £3009.125, less than half of what you would spend on the plane. Notice that interest rates have not changed at all, but pessimistic expectations of market demand have made your valuation of the same investment different within the space of a few months.

Exercise 14.3

The government senses a fall in investor expectations and lowers the interest rate to 4 per cent. Would you now invest in the additional aeroplane?

▨ ▦ ■ 14.3.4   A change in income levels

If growth is strong in the present period, firms will be able to use the higher profits gained from increased sales to finance a higher level of investment. Moreover, strong current growth in sales may also cause firms to increase investment for another (indirect) reason. Firms may choose to take the current growth of output as a guide to future demand and profitability. Firms may form the expectation that the growth of output is going to continue into the future, and their optimistic expectations about the future will motivate them to pursue a higher level of investment. In this case, firms' optimism about the future may lead to investment that goes beyond the limits of retained profit and requires borrowing. Sudden rapid increases in demand also put pressure on firms' existing capital and force revisions in investment plans. In these circumstances, firms are encouraged not only to replace existing capital as it wears out but also to invest in new physical capital to meet the increase in demand. The idea that there exists a relationship between (demand-induced) changes in output and net investment forms the basis of the accelerator model.

The need for net investment arises from the fact that firms need more capital to be able to produce more output. Firms have some idea of what capital stock they want in light of what they expect to produce and sell, and make decisions on investment in order to reach this desired capital stock. A theory of investment must then include a model of the planned level of capital stock and how firms realize these plans through their investment activities. Remember the capital stock at the end of period t is simply the capital stock at the end of period $t-1$ plus the net investment in period t. Investment is simply the means by which the actual capital stock K is adjusted towards the desired stock K^*. When $K = K^*$, net investment will cease and the only gross investment will be replacement investment to keep the capital stock at K^*. So the rate of growth of K will be zero since firms would have fully realized all their investment plans.

A very simple model of investment, known as the 'accelerator model', assumes that there is a fixed **capital–output ratio**, that is, that the amount of capital used per unit of output does not vary. If firms then use the level of demand (output) in the economy to form their views of the desired capital stock:

$$K^* = vY$$

where v is the capital–output ratio.

The second assumption of the accelerator model is that firms take just a single period to make whatever investment is necessary to realize their desired capital stock. So, at any moment, actual capital stock K equals desired capital stock K^*. This means that net investment in each period is simply a result of changes in output:

$$I_t = K_t - K_{t-1} = K_t^* - K_{t-1}^* = v(Y_t - Y_{t-1})$$

This model is known as the 'accelerator' because an increase in output leads to greater investment, augmenting the capital stock and thus accelerating the growth in output. The reason that the increase in investment is greater than the increase in output is that, for most businesses (and for the economy as a whole), the capital–output ratio is substantially greater than one.

Capital–output ratio

A measure of the amount of capital required for production.

14.4 Investment and output cycles

A disputed question in the theory of investment and capital accumulation is whether the adjustment to K^* happens instantaneously or over time. This question pertains only to the medium or long term as in the short term capacity is fixed. In the medium term additions to capacity are realized slowly and desired capital stock may be quite different from the actual capital stock. This might mean that in some circumstances the investment plans are out of step with aggregate demand and short-term equilibrium (Chapter 13). Section 14.4.1 will show that this can give rise to output cycles.

In the medium term, the accelerator operates in conjunction with the 'multiplier', which you met in Chapter 13. The notion of the multiplier expresses the idea that an increase in aggregate demand will bring about a more than proportionate increase in output and income. This is because the initial increase in aggregate demand will have important knock-on effects on the employment, income and consumption of workers throughout the economy. If a firm decides to increase investment in new plant and machinery, this will lead to employment gains in the sector producing capital goods.

The additional workers employed in this sector will spend their new income on goods and services. Extra workers will then be employed to produce these goods and services. These workers will, in turn, spend their new income on goods and services and so on. In this case, the initial increase in expenditure on investment will have a multiplied effect on total output and income. The initial increase in aggregate demand expands the total income of an economy through the effects of the multiplier by more than the initial increase in demand.

This expansion of total income in turn gives rise to greater investment. With increases in aggregate demand, firms' desired capital stock will be higher. This requires new investment spending above that needed for replacement purposes. This additional investment spending also has a multiplier effect and thus generates a further increase in aggregate demand. So the desired capital stock that firms would like also rises and further new investment is required. And so the process continues.

In the boom phase of the cycle, these two mechanisms, the accelerator and the multiplier, reinforce each other to generate increases in output and investment. The boom will persist as long as output continues to grow. However, with no increase in output, investment will fall to the level consistent with the replacement of existing capital and this fall will feed through the multiplier to lower aggregate demand and lower output – a downturn in economic activity. In the downturn phase of the investment cycle, reductions in output and investment reinforce each other in the opposite direction. Each reduction in output generates a reduction in investment (through the accelerator) that, in turn, generates a reduction in output (through the multiplier).

Unless some external limit is reached, booms and recessions would continue in this manner unabated. From the interaction between the accelerator and the multiplier, we also gain some insight into the cyclical pattern of economic activity as captured by the notion of the business cycle. To produce a cycle some exogenous factor(s) must stop booms and recessions. In an upturn such an exogenous factor could be reaching full employment or a bottleneck in some part of the economy. The movement out of recession could be caused by a surge in export demand or in government spending, or by more favourable business expectations increasing investment spending.

Exercise 14.4

In Table 14.2, an economy that has a capital–output ratio of 2 begins in period 1 with a constant output (= income) of 100 units and a capital stock of 200. In the absence of an external shock, the economy will reproduce itself indefinitely as in period 1. There is now a shock to the economy and output rises to 110 in period 2.

Table 14.2
The multiplier and the accelerator

Period	Output	Change in output	Total capital	Net investment	Change in investment
1	100	0	200	0	–
2	110	10			
3					
4					
5					
6					
7					

1 If we assume the multiplier is 1.5, what will be the effects on net investment of an increase of 10 units of output in period 2? Fill in the rest of the table for period 2.
2 Complete the table for the remaining periods. What will happen to output in period 8?
3 What does the above table tell you about the operation of the accelerator?

The interaction of the accelerator and multiplier provides one view of the causes of fluctuations in the level of economic activity over the course of the business cycle. But some have argued that the accelerator does not operate for all of the business cycle:

> It is well known that large reserve capacities exist, at least throughout a considerable part of the cycle, and that output may therefore increase without an actual increase in existing capacities.
>
> *(Kalecki, 1954, p.285)*

That is, firms will tend to retain large reserves of capacity because this gives them the flexibility to respond to sudden changes in demand. The accelerator will be much more relevant in periods where economic activity is growing rapidly and firms encounter capital shortages in meeting the demand for their output.

14.5 Investment and policy

Given the centrality of investment to economic growth and the different influences upon investment, what can governments do to encourage investment? Governments confront many different policy options for raising investment levels. The policy chosen will depend in part on the government's views on the barriers to higher investment.

One approach, which has been applied in the UK and elsewhere, is to offer various tax incentives. For example, lower taxes on profits may be pursued as a positive spur to investment. The problem with this approach, however, is that there is no guarantee that the higher after-tax profits gained by firms will feed through into higher investment. Higher after-tax profits may simply go to pay shareholders higher dividends or the tax reductions may be appropriated in the form of higher salaries.

Measures to reduce taxes on profits may therefore have a negligible impact on investment. A more targeted strategy at the fiscal level is to introduce capital allowances, either for all investment or for particular types of investment (e.g. investment in new technology). These allowances offer firms tax exemptions if they increase the capital-intensity of production. However, even these may not work:

> Academic consensus is that tax and subsidy measures generally only affect the timing of investment, rather than its quantity.
>
> *(Driver, 1998, p.195)*

From this perspective, there would seem to be more important obstacles to raising investment levels.

Governments could also manipulate interest rates in order to stimulate investment. Changes in interest rates alter the cost of investment and can provide both positive and negative stimuli to investment. However, aside from the question of how responsive investment is to changes in interest rates, governments may no longer have the power to manipulate interest rates to target investment. Over recent years, most governments have handed over responsibility for the setting of interest rates to independent central banks, and the priority of interest rate policy is usually the achievement of low and stable inflation. The manipulation of investment, in this case, comes about only as a by-product of moves to control inflation, and raising the level of investment is never the direct focus of interest rate policy.

The present (2005) New Labour government in the UK has sought to increase investment by creating a more stable environment for businesses to make investment decisions. It argues that past macroeconomic instability, particularly a high and volatile inflation rate, depressed investment levels in the UK. In part, this explains the investment gap between the UK and other countries. Historically, UK businesses have tended to invest less in new and replacement capital than most competitor nations:

> The capital stock per worker in the UK business sector is estimated to be around 20 per cent lower than in the US and Germany. This is a reflection of past low levels of business investment and is a major factor in the UK's relatively low level of labour productivity.
>
> *(Budget Report, 2000)*

Though there are some signs that this gap narrowed during the late 1990s, there remains a significant capital deficit in the UK. The New Labour government has sought to close the gap by setting clear rules for the conduct of fiscal and monetary policy. The creation of a more predictable policy environment, one which allows firms to plan ahead with greater certainty, is seen as desirable in underpinning moves to raise investment levels in the economy.

> 'In a global marketplace with its increased insecurities and indeed often volatility and instability', the chancellor, Gordon Brown, argued, 'national economic stability is at a premium . . . and no nation can secure the high levels of sustainable investment it needs without both monetary and fiscal stability together.'
>
> *(Brown, 2000)*

Whether or not stability alone is sufficient to reverse the problem of under-investment in the UK remains an open question. Firms invest in order to make profits, but there may be other less expensive routes to higher profitability. One such route involves labour intensification by which firms extract greater effort from their existing workforce – in the extreme case, workers may be expected to work harder for no extra pay. Unlike a policy of higher investment, this route cannot lead to sustained increases in output in the longer run. Where incentives exist for firms to increase profitability, incentives that can be fulfilled through increases in the intensity of work, firms may well forgo increased investment in preference to gaining more output from their existing labour input. The labour intensification option, the 'low route' to greater profitability, may offer greater short-term gains and also involves less immediate financial expense than the investment option, the 'high route' to greater profitability. Firms will face least resistance in terms of pursuing the 'low route' where the workers' bargaining position is weak.

So, we cannot just expect firms to respond to lower interest rates or lower taxes by raising investment; we also need to consider the incentives created for non-investment routes to higher profitability. Where firms can exploit the vulnerable position of workers (e.g. because of diminished trade union power), there may well exist significant obstacles to increased investment even with favourable changes in interest rates and taxes. Certainly, evidence for the UK economy indicates that productivity gains were achieved through higher work intensity during the 1980s – a period in which the strength of unionized labour was greatly diminished (Chapter 7; Green, 2001). This indicates the need for a broader discussion on the barriers to investment and on the policies needed to overcome these barriers.

14.6 Conclusion

This chapter has focused on the nature and determinants of investment. It has been established that investment is vital for achieving and sustaining economic growth. Investment adds to the productive potential of the economy by creating new physical and human assets. The use of these assets within production in turn provides the basis for growth in output and productivity. However, investment requires finance and firms will be reluctant to undertake much investment if they expect only moderate growth in future sales. The problem for firms is to balance the costs of investment against the potential gains as measured by higher revenues. Governments can create incentives for firms to invest though, as suggested above, policy towards investment is far from straightforward. The volatile and precarious nature of investment behaviour means that the problem of sustaining a high level of investment remains a key concern for policy makers in the UK and elsewhere.

Questions for review and discussion

Question 1 Table 14.3 gives information on the incomes that can be earned (spread over eight years) upon completion of a training programme that costs £2000 per annum for three years. Table 14.4 gives the present value of these incomes at different rates of discount. Use the information contained in the tables to advise the government on the appropriate rate of interest to ensure the take-up of training loans.

Table 14.3

Year after training completed	Additional earnings £
1	700
2	800
3	900
4	1000
5	1000
6	1000
7	1000
8	1000

Table 14.4

Rate of discount %	Present value of earnings £
3	251.293
4	−67.241
5	−358.541
6	−625.121

Question 2 Explain how government policy can influence the level of investment.

Question 3 Why does the level of investment tend to be volatile and prone to surprise policy makers? Why does the level of investment matter to them?

15

International trade and production

Anthony Venables

Objectives

After studying this chapter you should be able to:

- understand the role of comparative advantage in determining the pattern of trade
- understand how the terms of trade help to explain the distribution of the gains from trade
- appreciate the importance of market structures in determining the pattern of trade
- discuss the significance of foreign direct investment as an alternative to trade.

15.1 Introduction

Globalization is one of the most hotly debated features of today's world economy. Its basis is increased cross-border interaction: primarily in the form of increased flows of trade in goods and services, but also through increased flows of international capital. The UK's international trade in 1999 amounted to around 26 per cent of GDP; that is, imports per head and exports per head both averaged approximately £4300. Nearly one-half of these imports and exports were with partner countries in the EU, a further third with other high-income countries and the remainder with middle- and low-income countries.

These international flows affect all of us as consumers, and most of us as 'producers'. The prices of the goods we are able to purchase as consumers and the variety available are determined, directly or indirectly, by international trade. Some productive activities are not directly involved in international trade (the standard example is haircuts) – but most of them are. In many sectors of the economy the market conditions faced by firms are determined by competition in world markets. These world market conditions also affect firms' employment levels, and hence wages and incomes throughout an economy.

It is not only individuals in high-income countries who are affected by the flows of trade and investment. Trade creates new opportunities for economic development that have been successfully taken up by some low-income countries. The combined exports of many of the economies of East Asia have increased ten-fold in real terms over the last 25 years. Other low-income countries have been less successful in responding to the opportunities created by trade, and some have even come to see trade as more of a threat than an opportunity.

The objective of this chapter is to lay out the basic economics of international trade and foreign direct investment. In Section 15.2 we will outline the facts concerning trade. How large are trade flows, and how and why have they increased? We will also look briefly at the institutional structures in which trade takes place, in particular the World Trade Organization (WTO).

International trade poses several questions for the economist. First, what determines trade flows? Part of the answer to this question can be found in the differences between countries. Some goods are produced more cheaply in some countries than in others, and these differences create profitable opportunities for trade. Differences of this type are referred to as a *comparative advantage* and they will be explored in Sections 15.3 and 15.4. But it is not only differences between countries that generate trade. We also observe high volumes of trade between similar countries – within the EU, for example. This trade is the natural outcome of competition between firms located in different countries, and it often takes the form of 'intra-industry' trade. We will examine this phenomenon in Section 15.6.

Firms also penetrate foreign markets and access foreign sources of supply by becoming multinational; that is, by undertaking production in more than one country. These long-term investments in factories or service operations are referred to as *foreign direct investment* (FDI) and will be the subject matter of Section 15.7.

The second set of questions looks at the effects of trade on the economy. In particular, they ask about who gains and who loses from trade, and whether trade is beneficial for the economy as a whole. The existence of *gains from trade*, under a wide range of circumstances, is one of the most important conclusions from international trade theory. We will examine these gains in Section 15.3. Even if society as a whole gains from trade there may well be individual gainers and losers, so we will also investigate the way in which trade can redistribute income within an economy.

The third set of questions concerns trade policy. What are the effects of deploying trade policy instruments such as *import tariffs*? Should countries follow a policy of free trade, or should they take a more protectionist stance? If trade restrictions are employed, who gains and who loses from such restrictions? These questions form the subject matter of Section 15.5.

The method we use to answer these questions is the usual one of building models. The topic is potentially enormous, so it is essential that we focus on the key questions and exclude other issues from the analysis. At the outset two such exclusions should be noted. This chapter will not deal with the balance of payments or exchange rate determination (both of which are discussed in Chapter 16). This is not as strange as it may seem. A balance of payments deficit occurs if, collectively, the citizens of a country consume more than they produce. It can be financed only by running down previously held assets or by borrowing from the citizens of other countries, and neither of these activities can continue indefinitely – people will lend only if they expect to be repaid. What this means is that, on average over time, a country's balance of payments must be in balance: a deficit and borrowing today must be associated with a surplus and a paying back at some other date. This chapter is concerned with long-run fundamentals rather than short-run fluctuations, so it is proper for us to concentrate on situations in which the balance of trade is in balance. The same goes for exchange rate determination; we are concerned with the underlying competitiveness of different sectors of the economy, and to investigate this we do not need to study short-run exchange rate movements or inflation rates. Indeed, we will simply discuss relative prices, without specifying whether they are denominated in dollars or euros.

15.2 World trade

'Globalization' hit the headlines after many years in which world trade increased substantially faster than world income. The ratio of exports to national income over time for countries grouped by per capita income is shown in Figure 15.1. There have been modest increases in the ratio for high- and middle-income countries, and a much larger increase for low-income countries. It has been argued that the picture painted by Figure 15.1 may even understate the importance of the growth of trade, as rich countries devote an ever-higher share of income and expenditure to service activities that are largely non-traded – health care, for example. If we exclude this aspect and simply look at the ratio of trade to merchandise GDP (the value added in the production of physical goods), we see much sharper increases – the ratio for high-income countries jumped from around 40 per cent in the early 1980s to 60 per cent in 2000.

It is interesting to put these changes into historical perspective. The period from the nineteenth century to the start of the First World War also saw a growth in trade to income ratios. The inter-war period saw a collapse in world trade, followed by a steady recovery from 1950 onwards. In the UK, the 1913 level of the trade to income ratio is only now being overtaken.

What has driven these dramatic changes in trade volumes? One factor is transport and communication technologies: estimates of the real costs of ocean shipping show rates falling by nearly two-thirds between 1830 and 1910, and then halving again by 1960. Some more recent experience is given in Figure 15.2. Ocean and air freight charges fell substantially in the post-war period but bottomed out from 1960 for ocean freight and

Figure 15.1
Export to income ratios
Source: World Development Indicators, World Bank, various years

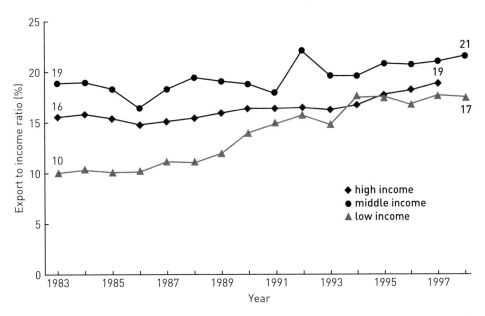

Figure 15.2
Transport and communication costs

Source: Baldwin and Martin, 1999, p.13

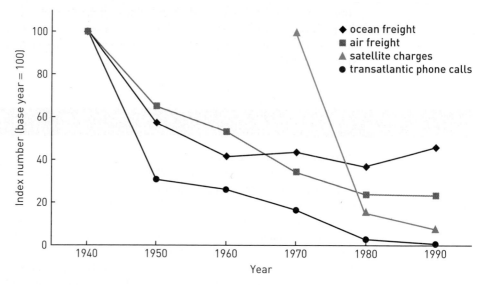

the early 1980s for air freight. New information and communication technologies have also had an impact on trade volumes. Furthermore, the combination of better telecommunications, air freight and faster ocean transport has led to substantial time savings in international transactions, which have facilitated trade growth.

In addition to the steady decline in transport and communication costs, there has been the much less steady pattern of trade policy. The historical record is shown in Figure 15.3. The vertical axis is a measure of import tariffs (i.e. the percentage tax rates on imports) for a sample of 35 countries. Nineteenth-century tariff rates were low, and Britain had completely free trade. The average was rising somewhat, however, as the USA and some European countries sought to industrialize behind tariff barriers. The inter-war period saw a dramatic lurch into protectionism by all the major countries. The notorious

Figure 15.3
World average tariff rates, 35 countries (unweighted percentage)

Note: The gaps mark the dates of the First and Second World Wars.

Source: Clemens and Williamson, 2001, p.32

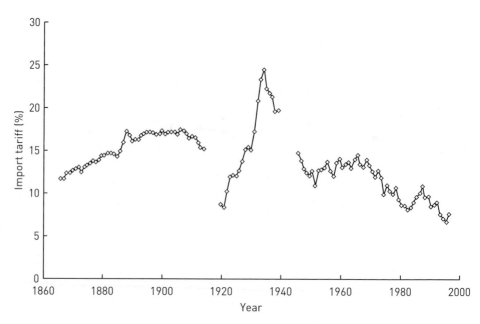

Smoot–Hawley Act of 1930 raised average US tariff rates to over 60 per cent, and by 1933 the exports of the main industrial nations had fallen to 25 per cent of their 1929 levels.

After the Second World War responsibility for liberalizing world trade was taken up by the General Agreement on Tariffs and Trade (GATT). This was set up by the allied powers as part of the post-war settlement, along with the International Monetary Fund (IMF) and the International Bank for Reconstruction and Development (IBRD, more commonly known as the World Bank). GATT initiated negotiations to liberalize trade, and deep tariff cuts were made in the late 1940s and early 1950s. These cuts were followed up by the Kennedy Round of trade negotiations in the 1960s, the Tokyo Round of the 1970s, the Uruguay Round of the 1980s and 1990s, and the recent Doha Round. The success of these negotiations has been impressive and they have brought about a steady decline in tariff rates. In developed countries the import tariffs on manufactures now average less than 4 per cent, although agricultural protection remains high: in 1999 agricultural import tariffs averaged 17 per cent in the EU and 11 per cent in the USA.

Two other developments are noteworthy. GATT became the World Trade Organization (WTO) in 1995 and extended its role in several ways. One was to start promoting the liberalization of trade in services (under the General Agreement on Trade in Services (GATS)) and the removal of barriers to inwards investment (under the Trade Related Investment Measures (TRIMs) agreement). The members also agreed to accept a dispute settlement procedure, under which trade disputes go to a WTO panel with binding powers.

The other development has been the formation of numerous regional integration agreements alongside the 'multilateral' trade liberalizations of the GATT/WTO system, in which countries have agreed to liberalize internal trade between member states. The most successful of these agreements, sometimes known as 'free trade areas' or 'customs unions', has been the EU. Other major agreements include the North American Free Trade Agreement (NAFTA; comprising Canada, the USA and Mexico) and Mercosur (comprising Argentina, Brazil, Uruguay and Paraguay). NAFTA, Mercosur and other countries in the Americas are also currently holding discussions with a view to forming a Free Trade Area of the Americas. In the middle of 2000 some 114 regional integration agreements were in effect and more than one-third of world trade took place within such agreements.

The growth of world trade outlined in this section has occurred only because individual producers and consumers perceived a benefit from trading with foreign countries, despite the inevitable trade and transport costs that international trade incurs. What are the sources of these benefits?

15.3   Comparative advantage and the gains from trade

The basic framework for analysing the determinants of trade flows and the effects of trade on the economy is the idea of comparative advantage. We will follow tradition by developing the idea in terms that go back to David Ricardo, writing in 1817.

■ ■ ■ 15.3.1   Comparative advantage

The simplest model is one with only two countries (which we will call Home and Foreign) and two goods (bicycles and coats). Each country can produce both goods, and consumers in each country want to consume both goods. If there is no trade, the

Figure 15.4
Production
possibility frontiers
and the gains from
trade

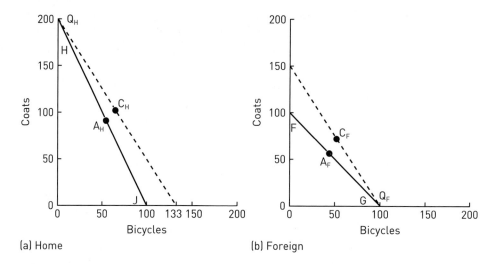

(a) Home

(b) Foreign

consumers must be supplied by local production. What happens when there is trade? The country that is, relatively speaking, more productive in terms of producing bicycles expands the output of bicycles and exports them; the country that is relatively more productive in the coat industry expands the production of coats and exports coats.

This apparently obvious statement has some hidden depths. To bring them out we must first study the productive potential of each economy in more detail. We can do this using the concept of a *production possibility frontier*, which describes how much of the two goods each country can produce. Figure 15.4 illustrates the production possibility frontiers (from now on abbreviated to ppf) for the two countries, Home and Foreign. The vertical axis is the number of coats produced and the horizontal axis is the number of bicycles produced. Concentrate for the moment on the bold line H–J on Figure 15.4(a). This is Home's ppf, and the points on the line indicate the output levels that Home can achieve. Thus if Home produces no bicycles it can produce 200 coats; if it produces no coats it can produce 100 bicycles. A number of combinations are possible, so the output mixture 100 coats and 50 bicycles also lies on the ppf line.

The ppf is a rather general concept. It certainly need not be a *straight* line, as in Figure 15.4, and it can be generalized into more dimensions to handle more than two goods, in which case it can no longer be represented by a line at all. For our purposes here we want to keep the shape of the ppf simple and investigate what underlies the ppf in each country. We can do this by developing a somewhat detailed numerical example. Suppose that Home has 100 workers and that each worker can produce either two coats or one bicycle. The Home ppf is constructed by observing that if all the workers are employed in the coat industry, Home can produce 200 coats; if all the workers are employed in the bicycle industry, Home can produce 100 bicycles. Employing some workers in each industry means that a number of different combinations of bicycles and coats are possible, and these combinations are given by the ppf.

The Foreign ppf is given by the line F–G on Figure 15.4(b). It is constructed in a similar way but using different numbers. Let us assume that Foreign has 200 workers, each of whom can produce either 0.5 coats or 0.5 bicycles. If all workers are employed in the coat industry, the output is 100 coats and zero bicycles, and so on.

If there is no trade between Home and Foreign, a situation known as *autarky*, the level of production in each country is determined by consumer demand at, say, point A_H in Home and A_F in Foreign.

| Question | Suppose that the Home economy wants to consume one more bicycle. What is the cost to the Home economy of this extra bicycle? |

Although we usually measure the cost of something in terms of money, a more fundamental measure is what has to be given up in order to attain the thing. This is referred to as the *opportunity cost*. Thus, the opportunity cost of a bigger house is the holiday you forgo; the opportunity cost of working another hour is the leisure you miss. In our example, the opportunity cost of one extra bicycle in the Home economy is two coats. This is because one worker has to be reallocated from the coat industry to the bicycle industry to produce the extra bicycle, causing coat production to fall by two units. If we do the same thought experiment in Foreign, we can see that to produce one more bicycle here means reallocating two workers, thereby cutting the output of coats by one unit. The opportunity cost of one bicycle in Foreign is therefore one coat.

Now allow for trade, and suppose that the relative prices on the world market (in which our two countries are the only traders) are such that 1 bicycle costs 1.5 coats. We can think of this in terms of the price of a bicycle being \$300 and the price of a coat being \$200, although it is not necessary to specify these prices exactly. It is only the ratio that matters – that is, 1.5:1. How does this ratio affect production and consumption in each economy? In Home, the production of each bicycle has an opportunity cost of 2 coats, but importing a bicycle costs 1.5 coats. Home therefore closes its bicycle industry and specializes in the production of coats at point Q_H on Figure 15.4(a). It can purchase bicycles on the world market, and the combinations of bicycles and coats it can attain by producing coats at Q_H and trading are shown by the dashed line.

| Question | Why does the dashed line in Figure 15.4 strike the horizontal axis of Home bicycle production at 133 bicycles? |

If all Home's coat production were exported it could afford to import 133 units of bicycles (200 coats at a price of \$200 can fund the purchase of 133 bicycles at a price of \$300). But consumers want to consume both goods, so Home's consumption will not go this far but will stop at a point such as C_H.

In Foreign we have the converse situation. Each bicycle produced has an opportunity cost of 1 coat and exporting a bicycle finances the purchase of 1.5 coats. The bicycle industry expands, and the Foreign economy ends up at point Q_F on Figure 15.4(b), that is, specializing in bicycles (100 bicycles).

| Question | If Foreign exports all its bicycle production, how many coats can it buy? |

If Foreign exported all of its bicycle production (100 units) it could afford to import 150 coats (100 × \$300/\$200), but the domestic demand for bicycles will mean that some are consumed at Home. So consumption will end up at a point such as C_F.

Note that the pattern of trade we have outlined is consistent, in so far as each good is exported by one country and imported by the other. It must also be the case that the exact quantity exported by each country equals the quantity imported by the other (i.e. supply equals demand in world markets). The world prices of the two goods will adjust so that this is true.

Comparative advantage

A country has a comparative advantage in the production of good X if the opportunity cost of producing a unit of X, in terms of other goods forgone, is lower in that country than it is abroad.

Absolute advantage

A country has an absolute advantage in the production of good X if it costs less in terms of resources to produce a unit of X in that country than it does abroad.

We have looked at this example in detail as it allows us to draw some important conclusions. First, trade is determined by a comparison of the opportunity costs of producing each good in each country. Bicycles are exported by the economy with the lower opportunity cost of producing bicycles (Foreign) and imported by the economy with the higher opportunity cost of producing bicycles (Home). Because it is cheaper (in terms of opportunity cost) to produce bicycles relative to coats in Foreign than it is in Home, we say that Foreign has a **comparative advantage** in bicycles. In the same way, Home has a comparative advantage in coats. It is comparative advantage that determines the pattern of trade.

Note that our example has been constructed with Home having an **absolute advantage** in the production of both goods – it is assumed that Home's workers are more productive than Foreign's workers in the production of both bicycles and coats. But this does not mean that Home exports both goods. This is obviously impossible, as Home would be importing nothing in return and Foreign would not have the export revenue to finance its imports. Instead, each country specializes in the good in which it is *relatively* productive (i.e. it has comparative advantage) and exports that good. This leads us to a further observation. Every country has a comparative advantage in something. A country may be unproductive in every activity, but compared with other countries it will be relatively less unproductive in some activities than others – and these are the activities in which it has a comparative advantage.

Superficially, there is a paradox here. How can a country that is unproductive in all activities compete in world markets? The paradox is resolved by observing that wages differ from country to country. To apply our example again, recall that the price of a coat is $200. Each worker in Home works in the coat industry and produces two coats; so if the markets are perfectly competitive the worker earns $400. At this wage the cost of producing a unit of output just equals the price it will fetch (assuming for the sake of simplicity that there are no other factors of production that must be paid). In Foreign all the workers are employed in the bicycle industry; each produces 0.5 of a unit of output, which sells for $300, giving the workers a wage of $150. Absolute efficiency differences have therefore created wage differences between the two countries.

Table 15.1 pursues this line of reasoning and summarizes the model. The first block of the table gives the labour inputs required to produce a bicycle and a coat in each country. If the wages are as shown in the second block, the unit costs of production of each good in each country are as described in the third block. If we compare these costs with world prices (which, with free trade, are also the internal prices in each country) it is clear that the pattern of production and trade must be as predicted by comparative advantage. Home's firms can just break even by producing coats, but any firm attempting to produce bicycles would make a loss. Similarly, Foreign's firms break even producing bicycles, but any Foreign firm producing coats would make a loss.

Table 15.1
Wages, costs and prices in a simple trade model

	Labour units to produce 1 unit		Wages $	Unit cost of production		World price	
	bikes	coats		bikes $	coats $	bikes $	coats $
Home	1.0	0.5	400	400	200	300	200
Foreign	2.0	2.0	150	300	300	300	200

■ ■ ■ 15.3.2   Aggregate gains and the terms of trade

The argument so far shows why trade will occur and what the pattern of trade will be. Another important conclusion that follows from the principle of comparative advantage is that each country *gains from trade*. Consider Figure 15.4 again. If there is no trade, Home consumption has to lie somewhere along the line H–J; that is, without trade you can consume only what you produce. Similarly, Foreign's consumption has to lie along the line F–G. Trade increases the size of each economy's consumption set, in the sense that each economy can now afford to consume more than it could in the absence of trade. Thus the points C_H and C_F have a higher consumption (of both goods) than do the points A_H and A_F. There are two reasons for this welfare gain. First, trade allows countries to specialize according to comparative advantage, thus bringing about an efficient world allocation of production. Second, countries are no longer constrained to consume what they produce; they can exchange goods through world trade and hence consume along the dashed lines in Figure 15.4.

There may also be individual winners and losers within countries, and trade liberalization often encounters fierce opposition from potential losers. We shall see further examples of this later in the chapter. However, the theory tells us that each country as a whole gains from trade, in the sense that total gains exceed total losses; each country could therefore afford to compensate the losers and still come out with net gains.

Although both countries gain from trade, it does not follow that both countries gain equally. The theory says simply that both countries are better off with trade than they are without trade. To analyse the distribution of the gains between countries we need to look more closely at the prices at which trade takes place. In the example so far, world prices are such that 1 bicycle costs 1.5 coats. What would happen if the price of bicycles fell, so that 1 bicycle could be purchased for 1.25 coats (or, in dollars, if the price of a bicycle falls to $250 while the price of coats stays at $200)? The effect of this would be to flatten the dashed lines on Figure 15.4 (the world price ratio). Home's entire output of 200 coats (point Q_H) now generates enough revenue to purchase 160 bicycles instead of 133 bicycles, but Foreign's entire output of 100 bicycles (point Q_F) will buy only 125 coats not 150 coats. The effect on the consumption points is clear. Home will be made better off by the price change, as C_H can move up and to the right; but Foreign will be made worse off, as the original point C_F can no longer be afforded.

Terms of trade

A country's terms of trade are the ratio of its export prices to its import prices.

$$\text{Terms of trade} = \frac{\text{index of export prices}}{\text{index of import prices}} \cdot 100$$

The change in the price of bicycles we have just described is referred to as a change in the *terms of trade*. For Home, exporting coats, the fall in the price of bicycles is a terms of trade improvement, and it is made better off as a consequence. For Foreign, exporting bicycles, it is a terms of trade deterioration, and it is made worse off as a consequence.

This shows that it is the terms of trade that determine the distribution of the gains from trade between countries, and that changes in the terms of trade cause one country to gain and the other to lose. Thus falling primary commodity prices in the world economy have caused real income losses for many low-income countries. But they are still better off trading than not trading. Our analysis of the gains from trade still applies, but a country that has experienced a terms of trade deterioration is getting a smaller share of the gains.

Terms of trade changes can be an important mechanism for spreading the benefits of economic growth in one country to other countries. For example, suppose that rapid technical progress increases labour productivity in the manufacture of computers, and suppose also that the UK has no computer manufacturing industry. The UK has no workers in the computer industry, so it does not gain directly from the productivity increase. But as productivity increases, the price of computers falls. This will show up as a terms of trade improvement for countries importing computers, such as the UK, which are thereby able to share the benefits of the technical progress.

The concepts of comparative advantage and the gains from trade outlined in this section are sometimes regarded as the most important results in the whole of economics. They apply at the national level and at the individual level. It may be that a doctor is better than a farmer both at practising medicine and at growing potatoes. It does not follow that the doctor should both practise medicine and grow potatoes. If each specializes in the activity in which they have a *comparative* advantage, and then engages in trade, they are *both* better off than they would be if each tried to be self-sufficient.

One of the first economics Nobel laureates, Paul Samuelson, was once challenged by a distinguished mathematician to name one proposition in the social sciences that was both true and not trivial. He found it difficult, or so the story goes. But some time afterwards he realized what he should have said – comparative advantage and the gains from trade. To quote from Samuelson,

> that it is logically true need not be argued before a mathematician; that it is not trivial is attested by the thousands of important and intelligent men who have never been able to grasp the doctrine for themselves or believe it after it was explained to them.
>
> *(Samuelson, 1969)*

15.4 Sources of comparative advantage

We have examined the argument that comparative advantage determines the pattern of trade, but we have not examined why a country might have a comparative advantage in a particular product or set of products. In the previous section we took the easy, but unsatisfactory, expedient of simply assuming that some economies were relatively more productive in some goods (as measured by the productivity of the workers in each industry). In this section we will look a little deeper into the determinants of comparative advantage.

Question What do you think are the likely determinants of national comparative advantage?

The two main sources of comparative advantage are cross-country differences in technology and in endowments; that is, the stocks of labour, capital and other resources in a country. We saw some of the implications of cross-country differences in technology in Section 15.3. These differences arise because of different intensities of research and development (R&D) activity, and different speeds of absorption of new technologies in different countries. The study of this takes us well beyond the scope of this chapter, but there are two issues that should be noted. First, in so far as technology is itself internationally tradable, this does not provide a basis for comparative advantage. It is only by being able to keep continually ahead that technology gives a country a comparative advantage. Second, to say that technological leadership is a possible source of comparative advantage is not much use unless we know what determines technological leadership. We must therefore push further back to see what gives a country a comparative advantage in R&D.

This suggests that we should also focus our attention on the second source of comparative advantage referred to above – international differences in endowments. Each economy contains within it quantities of natural resources, land of different types, labour of different skill levels and physical capital of different sorts (machines, roads, houses and so on). We can refer to each of these human and physical resources as a separate *factor of production*. And we can refer to the collective stock of factors of production as the *endowment* of the economy. Endowments may change over time – as saving leads to the accumulation of more capital, or education raises the skill level of the labour force. But at any given moment the endowment determines the productive potential of the economy, the relative productivity of the economy in each good and hence the comparative advantage of the economy.

The relationship between an economy's endowment and its comparative advantage is the subject matter of the Heckscher–Ohlin theory of trade. (Eli Heckscher and Bertil Ohlin were Swedish economists writing in the first half of the twentieth century.) Their theory is based on two observations. First, that economies differ in the relative quantities of their different factors of production. India is relatively abundantly endowed with unskilled labour, the USA with skilled labour and Germany with physical capital (e.g. machinery). Second, that the production of different goods requires the usage of factors of production in different proportions: aircraft production is quite skilled labour intensive; the assembly of electronics is rather unskilled labour intensive. Putting these observations together, the theory predicts that countries will have a comparative advantage in goods that are relatively intensive users of the factor of production with which they are relatively well endowed. Thus, the USA has a comparative advantage in aircraft production.

The theory accords well with common sense, although it has not been easy to find empirical support for it. In the first attempt to test the theory (published by Wassily Leontief in 1953) it was found that, contrary to expectations, US imports were more capital intensive than its exports. This perverse finding was probably due to the fact that Leontief failed to distinguish between skilled and unskilled workers, and hence failed to capture the skilled labour (or human capital) intensity of US exports. More recent studies have disaggregated countries' factor endowments – for example, a study by Bowen *et al.* (1987) looked at seven types of labour, three types of land and physical capital, but still found only weak support for the theory.

The Heckscher–Ohlin theory has more to offer than the observation that countries have a comparative advantage in (and hence will export) the goods intensive in factors with which they are relatively well endowed. It also provides a structure within which we can investigate the effects of trade on the prices of different factors of production; that is, on the wages of skilled and unskilled labour, land rents and the return on capital. Suppose that Foreign is well endowed with unskilled labour and Home is relatively poorly endowed with unskilled labour. One would then expect the wages of unskilled labour to be relatively low in Foreign (there is a lot of it) and high in Home (where it is relatively scarce). Now allow for trade. Foreign will export goods intensive in unskilled labour, which will have the effect of raising the demand for unskilled labour and hence will raise the wage. Home will import goods intensive in unskilled labour, so reducing the demand for Home's unskilled labour and reducing the wage. This argument suggests two things. First, that we can identify the gainers and losers within each economy from trade. And second, that trade will tend to bring about the convergence of factor prices across countries.

The identification of gainers, and possible losers, is straightforward. Relatively abundant factors in a country will gain from trade, and relatively scarce factors may lose. For example, consider the enlargement in 1994 of the North American Free Trade Agreement (NAFTA) to include Mexico.

Question	Decide which of the following are likely, in principle, to be in favour of the extension of NAFTA to include Mexico:

- skilled labour in the USA
- unskilled labour in the USA
- unskilled labour in Mexico
- owners of capital in the USA.

It is to be expected that the owners of capital and skilled labour in the USA would have been in favour of the treaty, as capital and skilled labour are the factors that the USA is abundantly endowed with, relative to Mexico. At the same time, it is to be expected that unskilled labour in the USA would have been opposed to the treaty, as their position of relative scarcity would have been removed once there was free trade with Mexico. This was true in the run up to signing the treaty, just as it is now the case that some US labour unions are among the most vocal opponents of globalization. Furthermore, recent decades have seen a large increase in wage inequality in the USA, with the wages of high-skill workers rising much more rapidly than those of unskilled workers. Some of this is probably attributable to trade, although the consensus among people who have researched this issue is that the development of new technologies has been much more important than trade (e.g. the replacement of unskilled workers by automated production processes).

The prediction that trade will bring about an international convergence of factor prices has important implications, although it is controversial. Evidently, factor prices are not the same in all countries, and the theory predicts that any barriers to trade or any international differences in technology will limit factor price convergence. (As we saw in Section 15.3, international differences in technology lead to differences in wages.) Despite these reservations, the idea that trade may lead to an international convergence of factor prices is clearly of great importance in a number of contexts. For example, it suggests that openness to trade is a good policy for a less developed country seeking to raise the wages of unskilled workers. A less developed country is likely to have a comparative advantage in products that require intensive unskilled labour; by exporting these products the country will raise the demand for unskilled labour and bid up their wages.

Another example concerns East–West trade. There are currently enormous differences between wages in Eastern and Western Europe, and the EU is concerned about the possible flows of migrants from Eastern Europe that this might cause. Trade theory suggests that this concern should lead the EU to have a liberal trade policy, permitting Eastern Europe to export labour-intensive products to the West. This will raise the demand for labour in the East, and contribute to narrowing the East–West wage gap. This argument can be put in starker terms. Existing East–West wage differentials are probably unsustainable; they can be narrowed either by Eastern workers moving west to take jobs (migration), or by the development of labour-intensive industry in the East that sells its products to the West (trade). The latter is probably politically preferable. A similar analysis can be applied in other contexts. For example, if NAFTA narrows the gap in wages between unskilled labour in Mexico and unskilled labour in the USA, this may reduce Mexican immigration pressures on the USA in the long run.

Each of these arguments illustrates how trade can change the distribution of income in a country, but we must remember that the gains from trade results still hold. There may be gainers and losers, but the economy gains in aggregate from trade liberalization, so the gainers could afford to compensate the losers (in principle if not in practice).

15.5 Trade policy

Tariff

Tariffs are taxes imposed on imports of goods or services.

So far we have concentrated on two rather extreme situations – no trade and free trade. However, historically at least, free trade has been rather rare. Governments have employed a variety of trade policy measures both to restrict trade volumes and, by taxing trade, to raise government revenue. The main instruments of these interventions have been import tariffs and quotas. A **tariff** is a tax imposed on imported goods, in addition to the usual domestic taxes. A **quota** is a quantity limit on import volumes, typically administered by making importers obtain a licence and ensuring that a fixed supply of licences is available. Other instruments of trade policy have been used at times, for example the creation of trade or shipping monopolies. Trade policy can be used on exports as well as on imports, for example many oil exporters set an export tax on oil.

▪▪▪ 15.5.1 The effects of trade policy

Quotas

Quotas are quantitative limits placed on the volume of imports of specific goods or services over a specified period.

How does trade policy affect the economy? In order to study this problem we will concentrate on a single good that is both imported and produced domestically, and consider the implications of putting a tariff on the good. We will conduct the analysis by looking at supply and demand for the single good. But first we must note a few of the implications of the tariff for the wider economy.

A tariff will cut the volume of imports to the economy. In Section 15.1 we argued that an economy's trade must be in balance in the long run. If a tariff cuts imports it must, in the long run, also cut exports. The mechanism through which this is brought about is a change in relative prices, which we can think of as a change in the exchange rate. A lower volume of imports will improve the balance of trade, which will lead the exchange rate to be higher than it would have been otherwise, which in turn will reduce exports. This negative effect of import policy on exports is sometimes overlooked, with dire consequences. Many less developed countries have followed policies involving tight import controls, causing their currencies to be overvalued and frustrating attempts to develop export industries.

A partial equilibrium analysis of a tariff is given in Figure 15.5. The horizontal axis measures the production and consumption of the good under study; the vertical axis measures the price of the good. The home economy's supply (S) and demand (D) curves are illustrated. If there is no trade the price would have to be P_a; that is, the price at which home supply equals home demand. Suppose now that the price of the good on the world markets is P_w (expressed in domestic currency units). If there is free trade this is also the price inside the home economy. At this lower price, consumption is C_f and production is Q_f. The difference between domestic consumption and production, $(C_f - Q_f)$, is met by imports.

Figure 15.5
The welfare effects
of a tariff

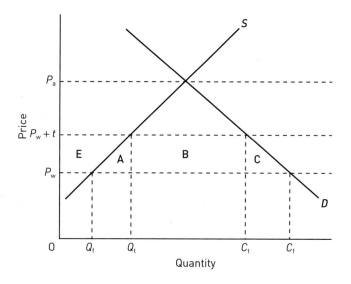

Exercise 15.1

Explain what would happen if P_w were above P_a in Figure 15.5. Illustrate your answer with a diagram.

Now consider the effects of a tariff at a per unit rate of t. This is added to the world price, giving a price (in the home economy) of $P_w + t$, and a consumption and production of C_t and Q_t respectively. As would be expected, imports fall.

Question   Who are the gainers and losers from the tariff?

Note first that the government collects the tariff revenue; the value of this is the volume of imports $(C_t - Q_t)$ times the tariff rate, t, so it is given by the area B. Consumers lose, as the price they pay for the good has increased by t per unit; the cost is the price increase multiplied by the consumption level C_t, giving the area E + A + B, plus the cost associated with the tariff-induced reduction in consumption (area C), giving a total cost to consumers of area E + A + B + C. Home producers receive a higher price. Their gain is the area E, measuring the higher price on the quantity they produce (E + A), minus the increased marginal cost of supply, A. Aggregating these items we have a net *loss*:

$$B - (E + A + B + C) + E = -(A + C)$$

The tariff has therefore reduced welfare in the economy as a whole.

In intuitive terms, this loss comes from two sources. Recall that the home supply curve also gives the home marginal cost of production as a function of quantity produced. As production expands from Q_f to Q_t, so the economy is producing at a marginal cost greater than P_w, the price at which the good could be imported. Evidently, this is inefficient, and it costs the economy A. It is similar on the demand side. The demand curve measures the marginal benefit of consuming each quantity. Cutting consumption from C_f to C_t means that consumers forgo consuming units of the good for which the marginal benefit (the height of the demand curve) exceeds the cost of supply (P_w), generating a loss C.

A number of remarks need to be made about the observation that a tariff causes a welfare loss. First, the result is obviously intimately related to our earlier discussion of the gains from trade. You can see how welfare levels change (how the size of the area A + C changes) as the level of the tariff, t, is varied from zero (free trade) to the prohibitive level at which trade goes to zero ($P_w + t = P_a$).

Second, the analysis makes clear the gainers and losers from a tariff. Government gains revenue from the tariff. In societies with poorly developed tax systems this makes trade an attractive tax base for the government, and goes some way to explain the historical importance of tariffs. Consumers lose from the tariff. Producers in the protected sector are better off. It is worth reflecting for a moment on who these 'producers' are. The beneficiaries will usually be the owners of factors of production used intensively in the protected sector. To take an example, a tariff (or other means of protection) on imports of agricultural produce will usually raise the price of land (a factor used intensively in agricultural production) and thereby benefit landowners. Of course, these landowners are also consumers, but not all consumers are landowners. Thus it is usually the case that consumer losses are widely spread across the population and may be small for each consumer, while producer benefits affect fewer people but are relatively large for each individual affected. It is often argued that this makes it easier to organize effective producer lobbies than it is to organize consumer lobbies, which may result in a protectionist bias to government policy. This is so even though the analysis tells us that the combined gains and losses (to government, consumers and 'producers') are negative, producing a net loss for the society as a whole.

Case study: Trade liberalization and agricultural tariffs

Progress at last

After months of deadlock, the Doha round of global trade talks has taken a big step forward, thanks largely to an abstruse but important deal over agricultural tariffs

Just as it seemed time to declare the Doha round[1] of world trade talks dead, the negotiations have seen an infusion of energy. Thanks to a new face, a new partnership and an important technical breakthrough in the crucial talks on farm trade, this week's gathering of trade ministers in Paris marked a big step forward.

The new face is Rob Portman, a Republican congressman from Ohio, who was formally confirmed

by the Senate as America's trade representative on April 29th. Three days later in Paris, Mr Portman had his first official meeting with Peter Mandelson, the European Union's trade commissioner and a man who had a notably strained relationship with Bob Zoellick, Mr Portman's predecessor. Messrs Portman and Mandelson, in contrast, were all smiles and both were pointedly focused on getting Doha going again. Writing in the *Financial Times* on May 3rd, Mr Mandelson said the time for 'bickering' was over. By July, he argued, there needs to be a 'rough approximation of what a Doha undertaking might look like'. Mr Portman, too, made clear in Paris that the trade round was a big prize: 'Doha . . . will boost jobs and prosperity and can help lift literally millions out of poverty if we do the right thing.'

To underscore that determination, the two trade supremos helped push a breakthrough on the calculation of agricultural tariffs, dispute over which had held up the farm-trade talks for months. On May 4th, negotiators from America, the European Union, Brazil, India and Australia hammered out a

[1] The historical context of the Doha round was explained in Section 15.2.

formula for converting specific tariffs on agricultural goods, such as 10 cents per pound in weight, into percentage (or so-called *ad valorem*) tariffs.

Measuring all tariffs as a percentage of the goods' value is a prerequisite for further progress in talks about reducing trade barriers for agricultural goods. Under the broad outline for the farm-trade talks agreed last summer, countries pledged to divide their tariff barriers into different tiers. Higher tariffs will be cut more than lower ones. Not surprisingly, those countries that protect their farmers most wanted a conversion formula that translated specific tariffs into lower percentages, as that would imply smaller cuts down the road. In the end, the deal was based on a compromise proposal made by the European Union.

Last-minute breakthroughs after seemingly interminable deadlock are a hallmark of all trade talks. Nonetheless, the ministers gathered in Paris this week gave the Doha talks exactly what they needed: a concerted political shove. But there is still much to be done by the time the full crowd of World Trade Organisation (WTO) member states meet for their 'ministerial' in Hong Kong in December. It is conventional wisdom that Doha can only succeed if the big political bargains are struck in Hong Kong. That is because George Bush's fast-track negotiating authority – which limits the ability of America's Congress to unravel

any trade agreement – runs out in July 2007. Mr Bush barely won initial congressional approval for fast-track. Given rising protectionist sentiments among America's lawmakers, another renewal two years from now looks extremely unlikely. That suggests any Doha deal will need to be formally signed by early 2007. Since it takes trade negotiators around a year to wrap up a deal once the big political breakthroughs are made, Hong Kong is widely viewed as a crucial deadline.

And there is still a huge amount of negotiating to do. In farm trade, this week's breakthrough on the technicalities of tariff conversion merely opens the door to the real haggling over how to structure tariff cuts for farm goods. And in the other areas of farm trade – such as export subsidies and domestic support – the horse-trading has barely started.

(The Economist, *'Global Agenda'*, 5 May 2005)

Questions

1 What is the economic argument in favour of the claim that 'Doha . . . will boost jobs and prosperity and can help lift literally millions out of poverty if we do the right thing'?

2 How can economic analysis help to explain why international trade talks tend to entail 'seemingly interminable deadlock' and 'a huge amount of negotiating'?

■ ■ ■ 15.5.2 The optimal tariff

In the preceding subsection we argued that protection reduced welfare. Are there circumstances in which this result can be overturned? The answer is affirmative in two quite distinct sets of circumstances. These circumstances go under the labels 'the optimal tariff argument' and 'second best tariffs'. We will explore these circumstances in this and the following section.

In our analysis of tariffs we assumed that the world price of the product under study was constant and unchanged by the tariff policy. But this may not be the case, as the effect of a tariff is to reduce demand for the product, which may have an effect on the world price. In general, a fall in demand will tend to reduce the world price, and this is a terms of trade improvement from the point of view of the importing country. It will bring a gain in welfare which could offset the losses identified so far, and it may even bring a net gain to the economy. The optimal tariff is the tariff rate that maximizes this net gain.

Figure 15.6
Optimal tariffs and welfare

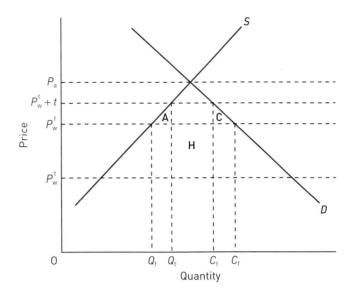

Exercise 15.2

Explain in your own words how a tariff on imports can reduce the world price for a good.

Figure 15.6 illustrates this point. The free trade position is P_w^f with production Q_f and consumption C_f, as before. What happens when a tariff of size t is imposed? The world price now falls. We will discuss the determinants of how much it falls later on, but for now just suppose that it falls to P_w^f. However, the domestic price, inclusive of the tariff, rises to $P_w^t + t$.

How does this change our welfare assessment? Changes in the welfare of consumers, the welfare of producers and government revenue can be found in the same manner as before. Doing this, the net effect of the tariff is seen to be a loss A + C, as before, plus a new element, a gain H. The interpretation of H is straightforward. The economy is now importing $C_t - Q_t$. The tariff has caused the world price of its imports to go down by an amount equal to $P_w^f - P_w^t$. The value of this reduction in the price of imports (a terms of trade gain) is the quantity imported times the price reduction; that is, area H. By reducing the world price of imports the tariff has improved the terms of trade of the home economy, and the value of this is area H. It is certainly possible that area H is greater than the area A + C, which means that it is possible that welfare can be increased by a tariff. The value of the tariff that maximizes the gain is called the 'optimal tariff'.

Does this provide a practical case for trade policy intervention? Answering this question requires us to consider two points. First, whether countries can influence their terms of trade. This depends on the elasticity of the supply curve that each country faces for its imports. The foreign supply curve is not shown on Figure 15.6 (which is complicated enough), but we can work through the implications of a number of different cases. If it is infinitely elastic (horizontal) the world price is fixed, the country is unable to improve its terms of trade and the optimal tariff is zero. A less elastic (steeper) supply curve means that reductions in import demand lower the world price and hence support larger optimal tariff rates. The slope of the curve is an empirical matter, which turns on how much of world demand (or supply) of a product a country controls. It is unlikely that

Mauritius, for example, can affect the world price of oil by anything it does. But it is likely that if the US were to raise the domestic price of oil significantly (e.g. by a tax or tariff) it would reduce demand by enough to cause a reduction in the world price, thereby improving the terms of trade of oil-importing countries.

Second, the effect of these policies on other countries. One country's terms of trade improvement is, necessarily, another country's terms of trade loss. A tariff that improves the terms of trade is therefore a 'beggar thy neighbour' policy. If one country employs the tactic it may gain, but only at the expense of others. If all countries employ the tactic, they are all worse off. This is a standard prisoners' dilemma (see Chapter 6). The message is, of course, that international co-ordination of behaviour is needed precisely to avoid mutually damaging trade wars. This is a major function of the World Trade Organization.

So far in this section we have talked about imports, but an exactly analogous argument holds for exports. The optimal import tariff argument is that a country may be able to drive down the price of its imports by importing less. Analogously, a country may be able to drive up the price of its exports by exporting less. This argument is familiar at the firm level from monopoly theory – a firm raises price by restricting sales. At the country level it asserts that a country may be able to exploit monopoly power over the rest of the world by cutting exports, raising prices and thereby improving its terms of trade. At first, it seems a little surprising that a country might want to cut its exports, but OPEC's example makes the point. By restricting oil exports OPEC was, in the 1970s and early 1980s, able to increase the world price of oil dramatically, and turn the terms of trade in favour of OPEC (and other oil-exporting countries) and against oil-importing countries. Many other groups of primary commodity producing countries have tried to emulate OPEC's initial success by forming export cartels to restrict exports and thereby raise prices. However, single countries have not usually had sufficient monopoly power to be able to control world prices effectively, and cartels formed of a number of countries have frequently failed to agree on export limits and so have had very limited success.

▪▪▪ 15.5.3   Second best tariffs

A perfectly competitive economy leads to an efficient allocation of resources (see Chapter 8); that is, price signals work to equate the marginal social benefits and marginal social costs of different activities in the economy. However, the presence of 'imperfections' in the economy – externalities, monopoly power and so on – means that price signals are no longer accurate measures of social marginal costs and benefits. When this happens there is a possibility that policy intervention can be employed to bring gains to the economy. The question we address in this section is: in the presence of such imperfections in the economy, what is the role of trade policy?

The answer is that trade policy may have a *second best* policy role. The idea is simple. Imperfections call for a policy response, and we define the *first best* policy to be that policy which is targeted directly at the imperfection. For example, if there is domestic monopoly, the first best policy is to regulate so that the firm is forced to set price equal to marginal cost (see Chapters 4 and 5). However, if the first best policy cannot be implemented (for whatever reason) there *may* be a welfare gain from using some less well targeted policy instrument, this being referred to as a second best policy response. Trade policy may be such an instrument. But for imperfections in the home economy, international trade policy is *never* first best.

The idea of policy targeting and the distinction between first best and second best policy are important because trade policy is sometimes advocated as an instrument for just about everything from curing unemployment to preserving national culture. The theory of policy targeting provides a systematic way of appraising these proposals. It says that given a policy proposal, one should first identify the problem and subject it to careful diagnosis. On the basis of this a hierarchy of policies can be formulated in which the first best is a policy targeted directly at the problem that has been identified, the second best is less well targeted, so may have some undesirable side-effects of its own, the third best is even less focused and so on.

The general theory of microeconomic policy formulation is well beyond the scope of this chapter. However, we can get a flavour of these arguments using the example of the famous infant industry argument for protection. The infant industry argument is that a new industry – which may be perfectly efficient and profitable in the long run – may need initial assistance to get started, and that this assistance can be provided by offering protection (an import tariff) in the early stages of development. In view of the theory of policy targeting, how should this argument for protection be assessed?

The starting point is the observation that (if there are no imperfections) the economy only wants the industry if it is profitable, in the sense that the present value of future profits is greater than present losses. But in this case, forward-looking entrepreneurs should be able to anticipate the future profits, and investment in the industry would go ahead, even without protection. This just says that in order to make the case for policy intervention, we need to identify the imperfections that might prevent entrepreneurs from undertaking the investment. What might these imperfections be?

Clearly, the particular imperfections depend on the industry and country under study. One sort of problem identified in the literature is associated with *short termism*. This arises if there is a shortage of entrepreneurs, or if there are problems in the capital market that make it difficult to raise capital to finance current losses on the basis of expected future profits. In this situation there is a case for policy intervention – without it the economy might forgo profitable long-run projects. But first best policy is evidently the capital market; markets for venture capital must be established to finance long-term projects. If this is impossible, however, protection could be used to create incentives strong enough to attract even short-term investors. This ensures that the investment is undertaken. But as the policy is not properly targeted, it will have undesirable side-effects. For example, the tariff reduces consumer welfare (the loss of area C in Figure 15.5, Section 15.5.2). The policy is therefore second best, and there is ambiguity about its overall desirability.

A second sort of imperfection is relevant to the infant industry argument as applied in the context of low-income countries. In many low-income countries urban industrial wages are many times higher than wages in agriculture, which leads to massive urban unemployment and the creation of large 'informal' urban sectors. Relatively high urban wages discourage investment from coming in and soaking up this unemployment. The first best policy response is to subsidize modern sector urban employment, in order to make the wage paid by employers closer to the real supply price of labour in the economy. However, such a policy is probably infeasible – revenue for an employment subsidy is simply not available. An alternative policy is to set an import tariff and protect the industry. Such a policy has been widely followed in many low-income countries, and has had some initial success in expanding industrial employment. But the policy is certainly second best, and its costs are now widely recognized. Countries that followed these *import substituting* policies typically ended up with an industrial structure out of line with their comparative advantage. In particular, their industrial structure was relatively capital intensive, and so failed to employ labour to the extent required. Tariffs and import substitution also – as we have seen – damaged export industries, in some countries hitting agriculture in particular. And because the new industries were not in line with comparative advantage, hopes that tariffs could be removed after the industries had 'grown up' proved to be false.

These examples confirm our theoretical expectations about the role of trade policy in acting as second best policy to offset imperfections elsewhere in the economy. Second best tariffs have benefits, for example they may well enable a country to meet some objective, such as increasing employment in an 'infant' industry. But they also have costs, precisely because they are second best instruments and are not targeted exactly on the distortion in the economy. Some of these costs can be easily anticipated, for example the consumer welfare loss discussed in Figure 15.5. Other costs (e.g. the damage that import tariffs cause to export industries) are often not fully anticipated when the policy is introduced. The message is that second best policy will have implications throughout the economy that may be difficult to quantify, which policy makers can overlook, and that the costs of these might outweigh the intended benefits of the policy.

15.6 Trade and market structure

The careful reader will have noted that throughout the discussion so far we have maintained two very strong assumptions. First, that if a country imports a product, it does not also export products of the same industry; that is, we have assumed that all trade is *inter*-industry. However, in reality a very high proportion of trade, particularly between similar countries, such as trade within Europe, is *intra*-industry trade; that is, trade which involves a country both exporting and importing products of the same industry. Second, that markets are perfectly competitive; we have so far largely ignored issues to do with market structure or firms' market power.

It turns out that these two assumptions are closely related, and in this section we will relax them both. We will allow for market structures that are less than perfectly competitive, and investigate the way in which this may generate intra-industry as well as inter-industry trade. As will become apparent, relaxing these two assumptions requires the extension, but not the replacement, of the analytical framework and results discussed thus far.

■ ■ ■ 15.6.1 The pattern of trade

Why should a country both import and export products of the same industry? There are two very natural explanations. The first is based on variety. Within most industries output consists of the production of differentiated goods; different firms produce different varieties of product, designed to appeal to different sections of the market. If each variety on offer appeals to some consumers in each country we expect to see intra-industry trade, with home varieties being exported and foreign varieties being imported.

The second is based on the behaviour of firms in markets that are less than perfectly competitive. If markets are imperfectly competitive, even putting issues of product differentiation to one side, firms located in the home country will have an incentive to try to export to the foreign market. Foreign firms have the same incentive, so that the natural process of competition between firms will generate intra-industry trade. It is worth exploring this point in slightly greater detail.

Suppose that conditions are such that the price of the product under study is equal in the two countries, home and foreign. If there is perfect competition then each firm chooses the level of output at which marginal cost equals price, and the firms do not care where their output is sold. Under these circumstances we would not observe two-way intra-industry trade in the same product. But if there is imperfect competition the firms will have separate marginal revenue schedules in the two markets. Even though price may be equal in both markets, marginal revenue may not be, and this generates incentives to sell in both markets. Putting the same point differently, firms will form separate sales strategies in each market and this will generate international trade. The precise form of the sales strategies – and hence the marginal revenue curves and volumes of trade – will depend on the form of the competitive interaction between firms (Chapters 4 and 6).

How does the existence of large volumes of intra-industry trade fit in with our previous discussion (in Sections 15.3 and 15.4) of the determinants of the pattern of trade? To combine these ideas we have to distinguish between gross and net trade flows. *Gross trade flows* are the total volumes of imports and exports in an industry, and *net trade flows* are the difference between them; so the UK has large gross imports and exports of motor vehicles but is a net importer of vehicles. We now have two complementary theories of international trade. Gross trade flows are determined by product differentiation and the interaction of firms in imperfectly competitive markets. Net trade flows depend on which country has most of the industry's production in relative terms, and this is determined by comparative advantage – the technological and factor endowment differences discussed in Section 15.4.

■ ■ ■ 15.6.2   Gains from intra-industry trade

The gains from trade that we have identified so far come from allowing production to locate according to comparative advantage. To this we now add two further potential sources of gain. First, the *product variety effect* of trade: trade presents consumers with an increased range of varieties. Although this effect is difficult to quantify, few of us would deny that we would be impoverished if imported varieties of goods ceased to be available.

Second, the *pro-competitive effect* of trade. To see this point, consider a monopolistically competitive industry in an initial position with no international trade. Production in the industry is subject to increasing returns to scale and the number of firms is determined by the condition that there are, in the long run, no abnormal profits. The equilibrium of a single firm in the industry is illustrated in Figure 15.7. Marginal costs are represented by the line MC, and increasing returns to scale mean that average costs, AC, are falling

Figure 15.7
Equilibrium of a firm in monopolistic competition before and after trade

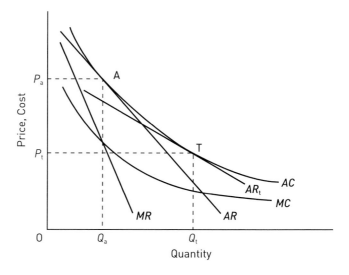

with output (these can be thought of as long-run average costs). The marginal revenue, MR, and average revenue, AR, curves are downward sloping, and the equilibrium is at point A with output Q_a and price P_a. At this point the firm chooses output to maximize profits (production is where $MR = MC$), and the number of firms in the industry has adjusted to give zero profits ($AR = AC$). The key point to note about the diagram is that AR is below AC everywhere except at point A, where it is tangential to it; in other words, the best that the firm can do is make zero (abnormal) profits.

What is the effect of trade on such an industry? The simplest thought experiment is to suppose that there are two identical economies, each containing the same number of firms in the industry. Reducing trade barriers between the economies causes intra-industry trade to occur, as each firm now exports as well as supplying its home market. Each market is now supplied by twice as many firms (both home and foreign). This increase in competition in each market will usually squeeze price–cost margins and hence force some firms out of business – through bankruptcy or merger. The remaining firms become larger and, if there are increasing returns to scale, will have lower average costs. This is illustrated in Figure 15.7. Increased competition means that the AR curve facing each firm becomes flatter – if one firm increases price it now leads to a larger loss of sales to rivals. The new AR schedule is illustrated by the line AR_t and equilibrium is at point T, where AC is tangential to AR_t. The number of firms in the industry may have changed, and it must certainly be the case that each remaining firm's scale has increased, from Q_a to Q_t. There are increasing returns to scale, so average cost and price are now lower, with price falling from P_a to P_t. The lower price, lower average cost and increased exploitation of economies of scale provide an additional source of gains from trade. To summarize, the effects of trade are more firms supplying each market, and hence there is more intense competition, and fewer firms producing in each country, with the remaining firms larger and operating at lower average cost. This reduction in average cost is a source of efficiency gain in addition to the comparative advantage gains and variety effects.

Several further points need to be made about what we have labelled the pro-competitive effects of trade. First, the example above has the gains from increased competition driving firms down their average cost curves. It may also be the case that an increased intensity of competition forces firms to improve their internal organization, thus reducing costs further. Such effects have been found by econometric studies of corporate performance (e.g. Nickell, 1996).

Second, it is possible that the potential pro-competitive effects of trade can be frustrated by what may appear to be rather small trade barriers. Part of the motivation for the Single Market Programme of the EU in 1992 was the observation that, despite several decades of free trade between member states, national borders were still acting to restrain competition between firms. Obstacles to trade, such as frontier formalities, differing national product standards and a pro-domestic bias in government procurement policies, seemed to be allowing firms to retain dominant positions in their home markets. The European Single Market sought to remove these barriers and thereby increase the intensity of cross-border competition and release the pro-competitive gains of trade outlined above.

Third, the qualification that – unlike gains from comparative advantage – it is not *necessarily* the case that all countries are gainers. This point is best made by modifying the previous example. In Figure 15.7 it was assumed that there were a large number of firms in the industry, so entry and exit reduced abnormal profits to zero. Now consider an industry that has extreme increasing returns to scale, for example very high product development costs, such as in the aircraft industry. Suppose that these returns to scale are large enough that, when trade barriers are high and there is no trade, each country has just a single firm which acts as a monopolist. This situation is illustrated in Figure 15.8(a),

Figure 15.8
Monopoly and trade:
(a) monopoly before
trade; (b) duopoly
with trade; and (c)
monopoly at a world
level

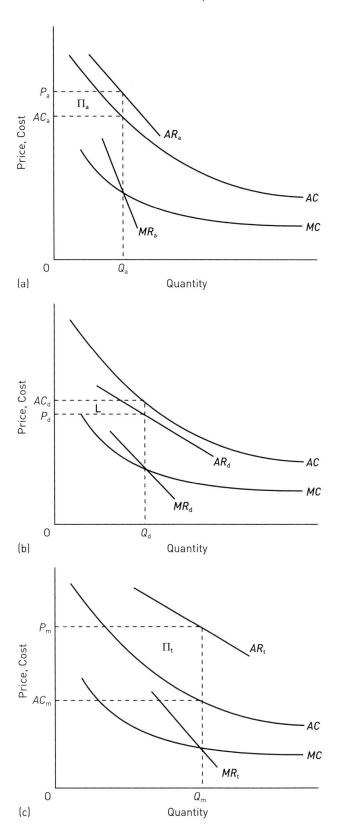

(a)

(b)

(c)

in which MC and AC curves are drawn, and the curves AR_a and MR_a are the average and marginal revenue curves faced by the firm. The firm produces at Q_a and charges price P_a. Average cost at this level of output is AC_a. Since P_a exceeds AC_a the firm makes abnormal profits, given by area Π_a. But these profits are not large enough to encourage the entry of a second firm.

What happens if trade is liberalized? The firms now compete, thus squeezing their profit margins. Figure 15.8(b) has the same cost curves as Figure 15.8(a), but the average and marginal revenue curves correspond to those that would be faced by the firm if it were a duopolist; that is, a domestic monopolist competing in world markets with a single foreign firm. These curves are labelled AR_d and MR_d; as discussed previously, increased competition makes the average revenue curve flatter (compare Figure 15.8(b) with Figure 15.8(a)). The example is constructed with AR_d below AC everywhere, illustrating that, with duopoly, the firms are bound to make losses. The minimum attainable loss is area L. This means that one firm must exit the industry.

Figure 15.8(c) is drawn following the exit of one of the firms, so the remaining firm is a monopolist at the world level and has the average and marginal revenue curves AR_t and MR_t. This world monopolist sets price P_m, and makes profits given by area Π_t.

In this example then, trade causes one firm to disappear and the other to become a world monopolist. Who are the gainers and losers from this? As before, increasing returns to scale means that average costs fall, so the world as a whole is getting the product more efficiently. But the country that is now importing the product has to pay the monopoly price, P_m in Figure 15.8(c), whereas before it was paying the average cost of production, AC_a in Figure 15.8(a). This makes the importing economy as a whole worse off – the real cost per unit has gone up from AC_a to P_m. The loss comes from the disappearance of the profits Π_a in Figure 15.8(a) in the importing economy. This is often called the *profit shifting* effects of trade. The remaining firm, of course, now makes larger profits: the area Π_t in Figure 15.8(c) rather than Π_a in Figure 15.8(a).

The points raised here suggest that, if we add some consideration of intra-industry trade and market structure, it is likely that the gains from trade will be many times larger than is suggested by comparative advantage alone. However, once we add these considerations a far richer range of possibilities arises. Large gains are likely, but it is certainly possible to construct examples where one economy loses from opening up to trade.

15.7 Foreign direct investment and the multinational firm

Firms' international operations do not take place solely – or even primarily – through international trade. Firms also become multinational by purchasing or constructing production or service facilities in other countries. This activity is known as *foreign direct investment* (FDI). The word 'direct' refers to the fact that the firms hold a controlling interest in their foreign subsidiaries, and is used to distinguish this sort of investment from foreign portfolio investment. Portfolio investment arises when firms or individuals buy shares in foreign companies (or purchase other financial assets such as foreign government bonds) but do not acquire a controlling interest.

In recent years FDI has increased even more rapidly than has trade. Most FDI takes place between rich countries, particularly within the EU and across the North Atlantic, although there has been an upsurge of firms investing in production facilities in many East Asian countries, especially China. The importance of FDI is perhaps best gauged by looking at the sales of foreign affiliates compared with exports. In manufacturing sectors in the EU, the affiliates of US multinationals have sales that are more than three times larger than the EU's manufacturing imports from the USA. Broadly similar figures hold for the sales of EU-owned firms producing in the USA compared with US imports from the EU. And for services, which generally require local supply rather than international trade, the ratio is many times higher. What these figures suggest is that firms' international activities, at least between high-income countries, take place more through investments than through trade.

The economic analysis of the reasons why FDI occurs has two main elements. One is to explain the advantage obtained by splitting production between countries, and the other is to explain why this should be done inside the firm (or its subsidiaries) rather than simply by trade (e.g. by importing component parts made by a foreign firm rather than parts from a subsidiary).

The second of these questions is answered by noting that FDI often involves firms that have a good deal of 'knowledge capital'. This knowledge capital might take the form of particular technical knowledge, or it could be more general skills in the organization of production or marketing, or the reputation of a brand name. These are all assets that are hard to protect, so there is a danger that they may be stolen or abused in a contractual relationship with another firm. For example, a firm may be willing to purchase some of its inputs from other firms, but it may want to keep a particularly specialized component, in which it has invested R&D and which involves high-level production skills, inside the company, rather than license it out to independent suppliers.

Given that the firm wants to keep some of its activities internal to the organization, what is the advantage of producing in many countries, particularly since this is bound to involve co-ordination and management costs? One answer derives from the fact that there may be barriers to importing the product, so gaining access to a market requires local production. This sort of FDI is called *market oriented* or *horizontal*; horizontal because it involves duplicating the same stage of production in many plants in different countries. The barriers to importing may arise because of artificial barriers (e.g. import tariffs) or they may just be due to technical difficulties in importing. Goods that are expensive or slow to ship may be better assembled in the final marketplace than imported. Of course, this is necessary for services too – Starbucks has to brew its coffee in London, not import it from Seattle.

The other possible advantage from producing in many countries is that different stages of production have different input requirements, and it is thus a cost-saving measure to move the production of each stage to where inputs are cheapest. Thus, the design of a computer chip may take place in Silicon Valley, the fabrication in Taiwan and the assembly in Malaysia, before final sale in the USA. These stages correspond to Silicon Valley's comparative advantage in computer scientists, Taiwan's in production engineers and Malaysia's in low-skilled labour. This sort of FDI is called *cost oriented* or *vertical*; vertical because the vertical production process is being broken up between different stages. Unlike horizontal FDI, it does not involve doing the same thing (e.g. final assembly) in different places, but involves doing each stage of production in the location with the lowest cost for that stage.

The two sorts of FDI have different motives, and suggest quite different predictions for the sorts of countries in which FDI takes place and the effect of FDI on trade. Horizontal FDI typically goes to where markets are large, and it is a substitute for trade. Thus, most of the FDI within Europe and between Europe and the USA is horizontal, for example General Motors has car-assembly plants in the USA and in Europe, and the markets are served largely from these plants rather than from trans-Atlantic trade. By contrast, vertical FDI seeks out low-cost locations, and it is a complement to trade. Increased levels of vertical FDI will increase trade flows, as some of the components of the product may cross borders many times – first as components, and then embodied in progressively more advanced stages of the final product.

The fact that vertical FDI is so trade intensive suggests that it will occur as trade barriers and transport costs become very low, and this is consistent with the evidence. Researchers who have sought to distinguish between vertical and horizontal FDI demonstrate that, until recently, most FDI was horizontal in nature (e.g. US investments in Europe). However, the recent surge of investments into middle- and low-income countries is increasingly vertical, representing the development of global production networks.

15.8 Conclusion

It is likely that international trade will come to play an ever larger role in economic activity. This is partly because of the success of the WTO in reducing trade barriers; partly because of the development of regional trading arrangements such as the EU and NAFTA; partly because many less-developed countries are now pursuing more outward looking economic policies; and partly because technical change continues to reduce the cost of making international transactions. In this chapter we have explored the causes and effects of international trade. Undoubtedly, trade poses many challenges, necessitating adjustment to new economic circumstances and, in the course of this adjustment, creating gainers and losers. However, the main message of the chapter is that there are great gains from participation in the trading system. Trade allows countries to consume at points outside their ppf; it permits the specialization of production according to comparative advantage; it makes new varieties of product available; and it increases the intensity of competition and enables firms to expand and exploit economies of scale.

Questions for review and discussion

Question 1 Assume there are just two countries, Bestovia and Potamia, each of which has 100 units of labour for use in production. Labour is the only factor of production and there are just two goods, widgets and gadgets, which are produced according to the resource requirements in Table 15.2:

Table 15.2
Bestovian and Potamian resource requirements

	Bestovia labour requirement per unit of production	Potamia labour requirement per unit of production
Widgets	0.25	2
Gadgets	0.5	1

(a) Draw the production possibility frontier for the two countries.
(b) Assuming there is no trade, what is the price of widgets (relative to gadgets) in Bestovia? What is it in Potamia?
(c) Does either country have an absolute advantage in the production of widgets or gadgets? If so, which country? Explain your answer.

(d) Does either country have a comparative advantage in the production of widgets or gadgets? If so, which country? Explain your answer.

(e) Now assume Bestovia and Potamia enter into trade with one another. What will happen to the quantities produced of widgets and gadgets in the two countries? What could you say about the direction of movement in the world price ratio of widgets to gadgets?

Question 2   Assume there are two countries, A and B, and labour is the only factor of production. Two goods, opals and orchids, are produced according to the resource requirements in Table 15.3:

Table 15.3
A and B resource
requirements

	Unit labour required (hours per unit of output)	
	A	**B**
Opals	60	120
Orchids	30	40

(a) Calculate how many orchids would be traded for opals in each country. What is this ratio called?

(b) Does either country have an absolute advantage in the production of opals or orchids? If so, which? Explain your answer.

(c) Does either country have a comparative advantage in the production of opals or orchids? If so, which? Explain your answer.

(d) Suppose there is no trade. Each of the two countries has 300 workers who work 40 hours per week. Assume each of the countries employs half of its resources in producing each of the two goods.

Complete the Table 15.4:

Table 15.4
A and B goods
production

	Output of opals and orchids with *no* trade		
	A	**B**	**Total 'world' output**
Opals			
Orchids			

(e) Now assume A and B enter into trade with one another. What will happen to the quantities produced of opals and orchids in the two countries?

Question 3   Figure 15.9 shows the domestic demand for (D) and supply of (S) chocolate bars with and without the imposition of a tariff, *t*, per unit. The world price is OA.

(a) Make a copy of Figure 15.9. Identify the domestic price, and the quantity imported, in a situation of free trade.

(b) Now imagine that a tariff of size *t* is imposed on imports of chocolate bars. On the same diagram, identify the domestic price in the new situation, and the quantity imported.

(c) By how much does domestic production of chocolate bars change as a result of imposition of the tariff?

Figure 15.9
The demand for and
supply of chocolate
bars

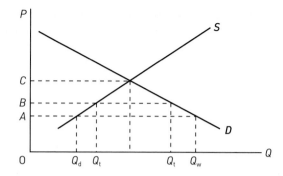

(d) Indicate on your diagram the area representing the extra consumer payments for the quantity purchased.
(e) How much of this accrues to the government as tariff revenue, and how much to domestic producers?

Question 4 (a) Use the data in Table 15.5 to answer (i) to (iii).

Table 15.5
Vladimar and
Latvin resource
requirements

	Units of resources to produce 1 unit of output		Total resources available
	One digital camera (Digicam)	Bottle of wine	
VLADIMAR	0.4	0.3	300
LATVIN	0.8	0.5	200

(i) Graph the production possibility curves for Vladimar and Latvin (on one diagram) and comment briefly on the distribution of *absolute* advantage shown by these data.
(ii) What are the pre-trade opportunity costs for both digital cameras and wine within Latvin, and within Vladimar? Explain how you obtained your answers.
(iii) Which products will be exported and imported by each country according to the theory of comparative advantage? Briefly explain your answer.
(b) Explain why comparative advantage may provide only a partial account of international trade flows, and suggest alternative explanations for the trade flows recorded in Table 15.6.

Table 15.6
US–Canadian
Trade, 2004

US exports to Canada	US$bn	US imports from Canada	US$bn	US$bn net* [US–Can]
Cars	10.8	Cars	36.2	−25.4
Motor vehicle parts	17.6	Motor vehicle parts	11.2	+6.4
Lorries	6.2	Lorries	8.8	−2.6
Motor vehicle engines	5.6	Motor vehicle engines	4.1	+1.5
Tractors	2.0	Tractors	1.2	+0.8
Other vehicle related	2.5	Other vehicle related	1.8	0.7

Note: * minus (+) denotes that the US is a net importer (exporter) from (to) Canada

Source: International Trade Administration, National Trade Data, http://www.ita.doc.gov/

Question 5 How does the concept of comparative advantage help to explain the pattern of international trade?

Question 6 To what extent does economic theory support the global trend towards the liberalization of international trade through the removal or reduction of tariffs?

16

Globalization, inequality and economic growth

Suma Athreye

Concept

- the multinational firm

Objectives

After studying this chapter you should be able to:

- appreciate the extent of the gains from international trade and production

- understand the relationship between globalization and increasing inequality

- understand the relationship between international trade and production and economic growth.

16.1 Introduction

Your study of the gains from trade in Chapter 15 may have persuaded you that international trade is a good thing and that more of it should make most economies better off. You have also learnt that trade may sometimes be profitably replaced by international production, which brings in efficient global firms and raises investment and possibly productivity and growth in the economies to which it goes. These arguments suggest that greater international trade and production will lead to more prosperity throughout the world. Indeed, the world over, a number of economists have successfully made this case to their governments with the result that the late 1980s and the 1990s saw an unprecedented liberalization of trade and financial flows in the world economy. Tariffs were brought down and domestic markets opened up to international trade in many economies of the world.

The late 1980s and the 1990s were special in other ways as well. You already know that many analysts regard it as the period of the 'new economy', aspects of which were discussed in Chapters 1 and 2. Transportation costs fell generally and the rise and spread of Internet technologies collapsed distance altogether for many products. E-commerce became a reality and many goods and services (books, music, financial services, software) could be bought and sold over the Internet. At the same time the fall of the Berlin Wall meant that new markets opened up in Eastern Europe offering opportunities for trade and foreign investment in those economies. The economic boom of the 1990s also created labour shortages in particular areas, such as software programming, which led to a considerable migration of skilled labour from low-income to high-income countries. In the popular press all of these happenings were collectively described under the umbrella term 'globalization' and many people expected it to make all the economies of the world better off.

However, the emotive protests against globalization that took place in several nations in 2001 suggest that increased globalization may have produced some bitter 'losers'. Many of these protests have taken place in low-income countries with a strong anti-West flavour, but the most vocal of the protests have taken place in the USA and Europe (Seattle, Quebec, Geneva, London) – in countries whose peoples we may think have benefited from the whole process of globalization. At the same time multilateral organizations such as the World Trade Organization, the International Monetary Fund, the United Nations and the World Bank are increasingly faced with mediating conflict between the interests of their member states. All of this evidence about strife suggests that the arguments about increased prosperity for all through greater globalization were perhaps misplaced and the actual story of gains from globalization is more complex.

This chapter will argue that though international trade and production benefit economies by integrating them with each other, such integration in international trade and production has been limited to a few economies, many of which are high-income Western economies, with some countries gaining more from integration than others. Even in Western countries where we expect to see gains from specialization and global integration, not all groups or countries have gained uniformly. So, while globalization can increase economic growth, it also creates inequality. Thus, the protests against globalization may actually be protests about its unequal impact across the world economy and sections of society rather than about the phenomenon of globalization itself.

16.2 What is globalization?

Dollar and Collier (2001) defined globalization as the growing integration of economies and societies around the world as a result of flows of goods and services, capital, people and ideas. Though the term 'globalization' is of fairly recent origin, a process of integration of the world's economies, which is what is meant by globalization, has been under way for most of human history. In this section we look first at that historical background and then at how the current process of globalization relates to the world economy.

16.2.1 A historical perspective on globalization

Over many years of human history globalization has been taking place through travel and trade, through the migration of peoples from one part of the world to another and through the travel of ideas (including scientific, political and religious ideas) from one region to another. Before the Renaissance, the direction of globalization was from East to West, as Arab traders carried important ideas and scarce goods from China and India into Greece and thus to Europe.

In his book, *The Wealth and Poverty of Nations*, the historian David Landes (1998) points out that a thousand years ago China and the Arab world were at the forefront of technological developments just as the Western world is today. The Western world borrowed heavily from these civilizations. This position is reversed today and the reversal

Figure 16.1
Anti-globalization
protesters
Source: © Sarah
Herman, 2002

happened through a mixture of effective competition, adoption of technologies in the Western world and the development of institutions of global economic power to perpetuate such growth and development. Since the middle of the nineteenth century globalization has tended to centre more on the West and the movement of goods, services and technology from Western nations to the eastern and southern regions of the world.

The current debate about globalization has its intellectual origins in the early nineteenth century. David Ricardo, writing in England in 1817, clearly saw the advantages of free trade and developed the theory of comparative advantage, which we still learn about in our textbooks today (see Chapter 15). Free trade was an important component of the ideology of *laissez-faire* that dominated British policies from the middle of the nineteenth century. Britain saw a cheapening of food prices in her own economy after liberalizing trade, and this helped to keep wages down in the economy. The economic historians Lindert and Williamson (2001) argue that liberalization of trade by Britain was quite egalitarian in its impact. It saw gains for everyone except the land-owning aristocracy in England, whose main source of income, rent from land, fell as cheaper food imports flooded the country. Food exporters in the New World and some Scandinavian countries prospered, as did English labourers and English factory owners. The historian Eric Hobsbawm (1982) has pointed out that the popularity of *laissez-faire* policies in Britain occurred at a time when it was the first industrial nation with an unrivalled competitive advantage in manufacturing.

The world looked very different from Germany, which was trying to catch up with Britain who led in the race to industrialize. Not surprisingly the first and most important treatise on the need for protection came from Germany. Soon after David Ricardo wrote about comparative advantage and the gains from trade, Fredric List penned his piece on the benefits of protection for infant industries. He argued that Germany needed to shield its infant industries from foreign competition in order to give them a chance to learn and grow. In time this protection would allow high-cost domestic industry to learn and thereby lower the costs of production (Chapters 3 and 14). Many of the industries that Germany wanted to protect, such as steel and chemicals, were in fact increasing-returns industries. Thus, in the nineteenth century, Germany wanted the right to protect its infant industries while Britain wanted free trade.

Lindert and Williamson (2001) tell us that there is at least one other period of history that saw a similar process of globalization to the contemporary one – the period between 1870 and 1914. For about 45 years following 1870, falling transport costs led to sharp increases in world trade relative to world income. The traded commodities were mainly primary products and global integration took place around this trade. The stock of foreign capital in the then low-income countries, including in 1870 the USA and Australia, rose from 9 per cent of their income in 1870 to 32 per cent in 1914. About 60 million individuals migrated from Europe to the New World. North–south migrations were a small trickle as people from the poorer periphery were kept out of the new labour markets by restrictive immigration policies, much as they are now. Worldwide inequality rose, much of the increase being accounted for by within-country inequality, which was related to the degree of protection afforded to land rents. Then, as now, there were exceptions. In Britain inequality fell, as did the fortunes of much of the aristocracy. There was a limited decrease in between-country inequality as the USA, Australia and the rest of Europe caught up with Britain and France. This was also a period of growing divergence between the incomes of colonies and those of the imperial powers.

After the long boom of 1870 to 1914 came a series of retreats from globalization to nationalism that lasted until 1950. The first retreat was on the checks put on emigration that had helped so many poor from Europe flee to better lives in the New World. The second came with the Great Depression, which persuaded some countries, led by the USA, to impose protectionist tariffs. The third retreat came in the form of retaliatory tariffs by other countries. It is a sobering thought that the world took so long to recover from the consequences of the end of the rapid globalization of 1870–1914.

Thus, throughout history globalization has divided governments and nations all over the world and today one can hear many modern echoes of this old debate. For example, the recent opposition to the liberalization of trade in services and disagreements concerning the scope of intellectual property laws have divided high-income countries, almost crippling the World Trade Organization in the process. Against this background, the question to be explored in this chapter is: why do we find protests against increased globalization when most of what we have learnt so far suggests that more international trade and production is good for all economies? For most of the chapter we consider the recent period of globalization beginning in the late 1980s.

16.2.2 Globalization and the contemporary world economy

In this chapter we think about globalization as the increased integration of the world economy through international trade and international flows of capital, which together expand the international production of world output. There are, however, broader aspects of globalization as a process, involving as it does the movement of peoples and of ideas. While the jury is still out on the role and influence of these upon growth, it may well turn out that they are the two most important catalysts in the process of growth and change. Here, we adopt the more restrictive definition that excludes a discussion of the migration of people and ideas for two reasons. First, the study of migration and in particular the migration of ideas and its impact on economic growth is only now being systematically developed. Second and more importantly, the theoretical concepts you

Table 16.1(a)
The pace of globalization (1980–95): annual average rates of growth for selected indicators

	1980–85 %	1986–90 %	1991–95 %
Exports of goods and non-factor services	−0.1	14.6	8.9
Royalties and fee receipts	−0.7	21.9	12.4
Foreign direct investment inflows	–	23.6	20.1
Foreign direct investment outflows	0.8	27.1	15.1
Sales of foreign affiliates	1.3	16.3	13.4
Total assets of foreign affiliates	–	18.3	24.4

Source: UNCTAD, *World Investment Report*, various volumes

Table 16.1(b)
Importance of globalization for world production: shares of international investment in world GDP

	1980 %	1985 %	1990 %	1996 %
Inward FDI stock as a proportion of GDP				
World	4.6	6.5	8.0	10.6
High-income economies	3.8	4.9	6.6	7.6
Low-income economies, excluding China	4.9	9.1	8.9	14.4
China	–	1.5	4.8	24.7
Outward FDI stock as a proportion of GDP				
World	5.0	5.9	7.8	10.8
High-income economies	5.2	5.9	7.8	10.1
Low-income economies, excluding China	0.7	1.3	1.9	5.2
China	–	–	0.6	2.6

Source: UNCTAD, 1998

learnt in Chapter 15 will help you in understanding the debates about globalization as international trade and production.

The late 1980s and the 1990s saw a remarkable acceleration of international economic flows as measured by increased international trade and flows of capital. This is clear from Tables 16.1(a) and 16.1(b). Table 16.1(a) reports the average annual rate of growth of some indicators of international trade, investment and production for three sub-periods. We look at the annual rates of increase of these indicators to get an idea of the pace at which the world economy is expanding the international content of its production and trade. The rate of growth of these indicators is an indication of the pace of globalization.

Question	What can you conclude about globalization from Table 16.1(a)?

Table 16.1(a) shows, first, that the pace of globalization was fastest in the late 1980s and slowed down somewhat in the early 1990s. Even though all the indicators grew more slowly in the 1990s, their rate of growth was still much higher than that observed between 1980 and 1985. Second, Table 16.1(a) shows that the growth in foreign investment and production was much higher than the growth in international trade. (An exception to this is the growth of trade in technological services; however, the export of technological services is likely to have a big intra-firm component.)

A more useful measure of globalization may be one that measures how *important* international trade, investment and production are in the world economy. This is rather different from measuring how fast they have grown, in that they might have been growing rapidly but from a very small base. One way to assess that importance is to ask how much GDP comes from such international activity. This is what we report in Table 16.1(b).

Question	What conclusions about the importance of globalization can you draw from Table 16.1(b)?

You can see that, whether we look at inward or outward foreign direct investment (FDI) as a proportion of GDP, international investment is equivalent to about 10 per cent of world GDP. Inward international investment is significantly more important for low-income countries than it is for high-income countries and it is exceptionally important for China.

At the heart of the increases reported in Tables 16.1(a) and (b) is the growing economic integration and interdependence of the world's economies through trade and even more through international production. We can see and feel its effect in the production of many everyday goods. The following case study draws upon Abrams and Astill (2001) to illustrate this point.

Case study: Global production of Lee Cooper LC10 jeans

Consider an ordinary pair of Lee Cooper LC10 jeans, which in 2002 could be bought for under £20 in any one of Cromwell's Madhouse outlets in the UK, and think for a moment about where the different parts of this pair of jeans originated. You may be surprised to learn that the cotton denim used to make the jeans is grown in Benin in Africa while the cotton for the pockets comes from Pakistan. The denim is woven in Italy and stonewashed with pumice in Turkey and dyed indigo blue with dyes made in Germany. The stitching of the jeans is done in Tunisia, where wages are considerably lower than in the UK, and finally the jeans are shipped to the UK where they are sold.

Figure 16.2 shows the origin of all the parts of a pair of LC10 jeans, including ones we have not discussed, such as rivets, zips and the distinctive yellow-dyed thread. It also neatly illustrates the high degree of integration among different nations of the world through international trade and international production. A consequence of such integration is that producers in different economies, some of them in very poor areas, become economically interdependent in production. This interdependence has co-operative and competitive consequences.

The co-operative elements are easy to see. All the producers involved in the making of the Lee Cooper jeans gain from the demand for those jeans in the UK. For each of these individual producers, such as the German dyers, the cotton growers of Benin and the women who do the stitching in Tunisia, the existence of a demand from Lee Cooper for their products is a source of sales and revenue. Their interdependence also means that if the demand for Lee Cooper jeans increases, they will all benefit from the increased sales, at least in the short run. Similarly, advances in technology that make threads stronger, zips more easy to use, rivets more elegant, etc., will all add to the quality of jeans and maybe eventually to the revenue from the sale of jeans that incorporate these innovations.

Such co-operative interdependence, however, coexists with increased competition between different manufacturers in any single part of the production chain. Consider, for example, the production chain in the making of jeans. While cotton is not grown in the UK, zips are manufactured in England and so is polyester thread. The English producers of these products compete with each other and the producers of zip teeth in Japan and polyester thread

Case study continued

Figure 16.2
Global
production of
Lee Cooper
LC10 jeans
Source: © Sarah
Herman, 2002

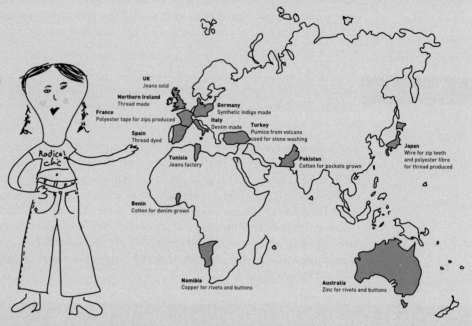

UK
Jeans sold

Northern Ireland
Thread made

France
Polyester tape for zips produced

Germany
Synthetic indigo made

Italy
Denim made

Turkey
Pumice from volcano used for stone washing

Spain
Thread dyed

Japan
Wire for zip teeth and polyester fibre for thread produced

Tunisia
Jeans factory

Pakistan
Cotton for pockets grown

Benin
Cotton for denim grown

Namibia
Copper for rivets and buttons

Australia
Zinc for rivets and buttons

Radical chic

producers from Northern Ireland despite being in different regions. An unemployed worker in the UK might like to have the chance to operate the machines that do the stitching of the pair of jeans and in an uncharitable moment may even feel that the Tunisian worker stole his or her job with Lee Cooper.

The increased competition among producers from different regions is also a consequence of increased integration of nations and the fact that with globalization many markets in different countries actually start behaving as if they were one market. This increased competition is of course good for the manufacturers of jeans as they can buy their thread and zips at the best possible prices, but we cannot say the same for the English zip and thread manufacturers. Some of these firms probably lose their profits to the increased competition from producers in Japan and Northern Ireland.

Even from this single example of globalization we can see that the sources of gain and loss to the UK economy from the international production of Lee Cooper jeans are different. Furthermore these gains and losses are likely to involve different groups of people. The same is true for the other countries that are involved, such as Benin,

Germany, Turkey and Tunisia. In all these countries those parts of the economy that are involved in international production and trade will often gain but other parts of the economy may be worse off. For example, Tunisian producers of wheat may find they have to pay higher wages to their female workers at harvest time as many of them can now work more profitably for Lee Cooper.

Question

Can you think of other examples of globalization, similar to that of the Lee Cooper production of jeans?

The making of Lee Cooper jeans is clearly not the only example of globalization. The international production of cars by Ford or Toyota, or of computers by IBM or Compaq, are some other examples of globalization, involving both international production and trade. If you were to trace a map of the different countries from which materials and components are sourced by these firms it would show a similar web of integration to the production of Lee Cooper jeans, but involving other countries.

16.3 How much of a gain?

Should all the countries involved in the making of Lee Cooper jeans support increasing international trade and production? We might expect the policy makers of countries involved in the international production of Lee Cooper jeans to evaluate the sources and the extent of gains and losses in order to estimate the net benefits of their participation. In this section we will take a closer look at the extent of gains from international trade and production and argue that both in theory and in fact some economies may gain more than others through globalization.

16.3.1 The extent of gains from international trade

Chapter 15 introduced you to the notions of comparative advantage and gains from trade. It also showed that the actual gains from trade between any two countries are indeterminate, because they depend crucially on the terms of trade (i.e. the price earned by a country's exports as a ratio of the price paid out for its imports).

There are two principles about the terms of trade that help us to understand the distribution of the gains from trade. First, that typically the terms of trade will lie between the price ratios that would obtain in the two countries under autarky with no trade. Why? Let us reconsider the example of comparative advantage explained in Chapter 15, Section 15.3.1. Initially the ratio of world prices is such that importing a bicycle from Foreign costs Home 1.5 coats rather than the 2 coats that would have to be sacrificed for an extra bicycle in the absence of trade. So Home gains from trade if the ratio of world prices is more favourable than the opportunity costs underlying its domestic production possibility frontier. Second, we also saw that, if the world price of bicycles fell so that 1 bicycle could be purchased for 1.25 coats, Home could buy more bicycles (160 instead of 133) by exporting all of its output of coats (200). Home has experienced a favourable movement in its terms of trade. The most favourable outcome of all for Home would take its terms of trade as close as possible to 1 bicycle for 1 coat, which is the opportunity cost underlying Foreign's domestic production possibility frontier.

> **Question** Why is the qualification 'as close as possible' necessary? What is stopping Home's terms of trade from actually reaching 1:1, so that it could import 200 bicycles in exchange for its 200 coats?

In the two-country world, Home's terms of trade gain is Foreign's terms of trade loss. If the ratio of world prices of coats and bicycles were ever to reach 1:1, Foreign's terms of trade would be no more favourable than its domestic opportunity costs in the absence of trade and Foreign would therefore have no incentive to trade.

This example illustrates the two principles about the terms of trade that inform our understanding of the distribution of the gains from trade. First, it is clear that the terms of trade must lie between the trading nations' domestic opportunity cost ratios under autarky, because there would otherwise be no incentive for both to trade. Second, the further the terms of trade are from a country's own domestic opportunity cost ratio, the more it gains from trade. This is because it benefits more from the different technology of its trading partner and its own comparative advantage. The trading partner (such as Foreign in our example) benefits more in the opposite situation for the same reasons.

This being the case, it follows that, although both countries gain something from trade when compared to their no-trade positions, they do not gain equally. It also follows that the extent to which any one country (or group of similar countries) gains is dependent upon the extent to which their trading partner(s) do not gain. You also saw in Chapter 15 that several instruments are available to governments to influence the terms of trade they face, among the most common being the use of tariffs and quotas (Chapter 15, Section 15.5). Institutions like GATT and the WTO exist to mediate international trade conflicts and prevent the misuse of these instruments. These institutions ensure that, in the desire to compete, countries do not engage in mutually destructive retaliatory tariff wars, which would force the world's economies to settle back to their no-trade positions, where everyone is worse off.

Question	Ignoring the presence of such institutions, what economic factors might ultimately determine the prices of exports and imports?

The discussion of markets and prices in Chapters 3, 4 and 5 strongly suggests one factor: the extent of market imperfection. Markets that are more imperfect will have higher prices than competitive markets for the same good. However, market structure is ultimately specific to particular goods. In general, markets for agricultural commodities tend to be more competitive than markets for most manufactured goods and so a country that primarily exports agricultural commodities and primarily imports manufactures may face an adverse terms of trade. In other words, for such a country the price of its exports may rise more slowly than the price of its imports.

Market structure is not the only factor that influences the terms of trade. First, transport costs are important, and a fall in transport costs can cheapen both export and import prices quite dramatically. Second, productivity increases in a particular sector can affect the terms of trade. For example, we saw in Chapter 15, Section 15.3.2 that productivity increases in computer manufacturing can lead to falling computer prices, which show up as a terms of trade improvement for computer importing countries such as the UK. Third, a low elasticity of demand for exports can improve the terms of trade for the exporting country if demand rises. In fact, in the period before 1870, primary producers in the New World saw an increase in their terms of trade as food prices increased in the world economy due to a surge in demand for food as urbanization grew in Europe.

The modelling of gains from trade in Chapter 15 was based upon a trading model where factors of production such as labour and capital were immobile, while goods could be traded freely across international boundaries. In such a situation only the terms of trade, and the elasticities of supply and demand of exports and imports, determine the extent of gains from trade. The question to ask now is: will adding in international production change any of these conclusions? By including international investment, as firms establish centres of production in other countries, we relax the assumption that capital is immobile, and assume instead that along with goods it too can move across international boundaries seeking the highest rate of return.

Multinational firms

A multinational firm is one that owns and controls centres of production in more than one country.

Multinational firms (also known as multinational corporations or MNCs) are likely to invest in the economies where they believe that their activities will be most profitable. Empirical research on multinational investment suggests that multinational firms largely exploit existing sources of comparative advantage to locate their production activities and thus minimize overall production costs. If this is true, international investment and hence production will reinforce the original comparative advantage of nations in international trade. Growing international production also means that intra-firm trade will account for a larger and larger portion of the trade between nations. Does this affect the gains from trade?

The answer is yes for three reasons. First, the possibility of having a firm that is headquartered in the USA exporting from the UK implies that the gains from trade are not all national gains that accrue to the UK economy alone. Indeed the profits of the firm will be repatriated to the USA. (The repatriation of profits is one reason for the divergence between UK GDP and UK GNP (Chapter 8, Section 8.2)). Governments seek to control the proportion of profits that can be repatriated. However, while the profits of a domestic exporter of goods are likely to be reinvested in the domestic economy, with multinational firms we cannot be sure.

Second, intra-firm trade is subject to different constraints from those on trade between independent firms located in different countries. For example, assuming profit maximization, an independent firm will aim to maximize its own profits. In intra-firm trade, multinational firms will try to maximize the joint profitability of all of their different production arms. If necessary, the profitability – and perhaps the jobs – of one of its overseas factories may be sacrificed to this overall aim.

Third, multinational firms have complete control over the prices that different arms charge each other and it is these prices (also called transfer prices) that determine how much each country gains, rather than the world price for the commodities traded. Transfer prices are often manipulated by multinational firms to transfer pre-tax profits from one country to another with the aim of maximizing post-tax profits for the company. Thus, the MNC subsidiary in the UK may pay out less as dividends but more as royalty payments to the parent firm in the USA if they wish to shift profits from the host economy (the UK) to the home economy (the USA). Apart from making it difficult to assess the true national gains from trade, transfer pricing also worries governments, who may find their efforts on taxation or on the control of foreign currency expenditures frustrated by multinational firms.

A consideration of the role of multinational firms takes us back to the issue of market structure. Multinational firms mostly operate in imperfect market environments for final goods. There are several signs of imperfect competition – brands, heavy advertising and, in high-tech products, heavy expenditure on research and development (Chapter 4). The effect of market imperfections is to increase price–cost margins and to make supernormal profits for the firms. Thus, Lee Cooper is able to sell its jeans at £19.95 even though the ex-factory price of the pair of jeans in Tunisia is about £5. Even factoring in the 10p per pair price of transportation, the manufacturer is able to make a huge profit, especially compared with what the Tunisian economy might gain from the same activity. This is just the price paid by Lee Cooper to the Tunisian women who stitch the jeans – roughly 58p per hour worked (Abrams and Astill, 2001) – multiplied by the total hours required to stitch a pair of jeans.

Question Should the Tunisian government stop participating in international trade and production because the profits that its firms make are a fraction of the profits made by the multinational firm?

This will depend upon two types of factor: what is the opportunity cost of not participating for the Tunisian firms, and what are the macroeconomic impacts of participation in international trade and production for the economy? For many poor countries like Tunisia, with high levels of unemployment and low levels of domestic industrialization, such opportunities for employment as those provided by the Lee Cooper trade are often very welcome. However, if women working for Lee Cooper suddenly found a great demand for their labour in local boutiques, they would not want to work at the less lucrative Lee Cooper wages, and there may be very little the Tunisian government can do to affect this.

From the point of view of the government the more important question may be what proportions of total employment and income come (directly and indirectly) from such exporting activities. Remember that exports add to aggregate demand, which in turn encourages investment and (in turn) the growth of incomes and employment. It also brings in foreign exchange that can be used to buy imports. If the proportion of exports to GDP is not initially very large, the country may be less affected by not participating in such trade. But even then the Tunisian government might want to encourage such production and trade because it brings in foreign currency through exports that can be used to import machinery or medicines. If, however, a large percentage of income and employment does come from such export trade then not participating in international trade could certainly cause a decline in aggregate demand and hence a recession.

Sadiq and Bolbol (2001) report that in 1998 the textile sector in Tunisia that has attracted much international investment accounted for 47 per cent of the country's exports and 6.5 per cent of its GDP and employed over half the workforce of the manufacturing sector. Further, in 1997, exports from foreign affiliates (such as the Lee Cooper jean factory) accounted for 30 per cent of all Tunisian exports. In the UK on the other hand, the textile sector is a fading one, despite the higher profits being made by UK firms relative to Tunisian firms. However, the Tunisian government may still wish to press for more such investment and actively engage in trade in textiles. This is on account of both comparative advantage and the sector being more important in proportionate terms for national income and employment.

Exercise 16.1

Use the foreign trade multiplier you learnt about in Chapter 12, Section 12.2.3 to analyse the relative impact of Tunisian textile exports worth €30 000 to the UK.

1 What would be the impact of this export on Tunisia's national income if the Tunisian consumers have a marginal propensity to consume of 0.6 and there are no imports?
2 If UK consumers reduce their spending on domestically produced goods by the same amount, what would be the impact of imports of textiles worth €30 000 from Tunisia on the UK's national income? Assume that UK consumers have a marginal propensity to consume of 0.6 and a marginal propensity to import of 0.2.

So far we have discussed the gains from trade, while recognizing that in recent years the involvement of multinational firms has meant that a larger proportion of trade is now intra-firm trade. Estimates for the USA by Feenstra (1999) suggest that about a third of US exports and 43 per cent of US imports in 1992 consisted of intra-MNC trade, handled between a US or foreign MNC and its affiliates. We have also noted that such trade carried within it the scope for the repatriation of profits through transfer pricing, with adverse implications for the tax revenues of host country governments. In Section 16.3.2 the focus will shift to a discussion of the gains from international production itself.

16.3.2 The extent of gains from international production

Two aspects of the foreign investment that international production entails have always worried policy makers. The first is the impossibility of completely controlling the activities

Table 16.2
Seller concentration
and foreign shares
in sales

Sector	Country (year)	Share of sales obtained by:	
		the 4 largest firms %	foreign-owned firms %
Food	France (1972)	8	16
	Germany (1977)	6	11
	Italy (1977)	25	21
	UK (1972)	39	12
Chemicals	France (1976)	35	27
	Germany (1976)	32	23
	UK (1976)	28	23
Agricultural engineering	France (1976)	65	52
	Germany (1972)	37	23
	UK (1973)	79	83
Electrical appliances	France (1976)	38	18
	Germany (1973)	5	73
	Italy (1973)	15	62
	UK (1975)	41	54
Electronic appliances	France (1976)	34	37
	Germany (1973)	8	51
	UK (1975)	20	77
Tyres	France (1974)	88	26
	Germany (1974)	72	50
	Italy (1974)	94	48
	UK (1975)	89	46
Textiles	France (1976)	8	6
	Germany (1976)	5	7
	UK (1976)	31	5

Source: author's compilations based upon Tables 2.3, 2.4, 2.6, 2.7, 2.9 and 2.10 in Fishwick, 1982

of multinational firms, precisely because of their spread over two or more nations. The second is that foreign investment and concentration are positively correlated. This has been reported in different studies for the UK economy, but it also seems to be true of other parts of the world, such as France, Germany, Guatemala, Brazil, Mexico, Australia, Canada and New Zealand. In Table 16.2 we report the results from such a study, conducted by Fishwick (1982), which shows seller concentration in a market and foreign investment in the corresponding industrial sector.

Exercise 16.2

1 Plot the data on seller concentration and foreign shares in Table 16.2 as a scatterplot.
2 The correlation coefficient is calculated in Tutorial 11 on the website. How would you interpret the scatterplot and the correlation coefficient?

Does the positive correlation between seller concentration in a market and the extent of foreign investment in it mean that foreign investment causes the sector to be more monopolistic than it would otherwise have been? The answer to this question is much debated but is still imperfectly understood. On the one hand your study in Chapter 15 of why multinational firms emerge at all should alert you to the fact that they tend to appear in markets that are already imperfectly competitive and often characterized by market failures. So, in some sense, imperfect markets attract foreign investment because profits tend to be higher where market imperfections limit competitive pressures. On the other hand, there are several examples where foreign investment successfully competed against domestic firms to displace the competition from them. Think here about the UK car industry or the UK computer industry. This discussion also underlines an important principle of empirical analysis: that correlation between two variables cannot tell us very much about the direction of causation between them.

Despite the hostility and scepticism with which foreign investment has been viewed in the past, we saw that the most recent period of the 1990s has actually seen an acceleration of international foreign investment flows. Many countries, including prominently the UK, have pursued policies of actively attracting foreign investment into their economies. What are the gains that they expect from such investment?

The productivity gains from foreign investment are in fact variable across economies. What factors account for this variability? Blomstrom and Kokko (1998) review studies that have attempted to explain the observed variability and suggest we need to distinguish between demonstration effects of foreign investment and the competitive effects that flow from it. Demonstration effects are one-off effects whereby domestic firms learn to imitate the better organizational practices of the foreign firms. The first reason why many economies want to attract foreign investment is therefore that they expect it to introduce superior technology, which will then spread in the host countries' economies through imitation and learning by local firms. Put differently, foreign firms are seen as vehicles through which technology transfer can take place, which in turn can lift long-run rates of growth in the economies into which they flow.

Competitive effects depend upon the ability of domestic firms to compete with foreign firms to win back domestic market shares. In doing so, domestic firms may compete on the basis of pricing strategies or of more innovative and productive technological practices. When this happens the economy as a whole benefits from a virtuous cycle of competition, innovation, increased productivity and more competition. This suggests a second reason for the warm welcome accorded to foreign investment, in that multinational firms are seen to have an important role to play in breaking domestic (often public sector) monopolies. To some extent, and in some countries, they have succeeded. A good example here is the car industry in India, which until the late 1970s manufactured only two models of cars. Foreign investment into the sector began in the form of a joint venture with Toyota of Japan in the 1980s, and after 1991 the sector was fully opened up to foreign investment. The result has been a proliferation of car varieties, domestic and foreign, and a dramatic reduction in car prices. Such stories of the success of foreign firms in catalysing dynamic growth of sectors coexist with other examples of foreign firms displacing domestic firms, as happened with IBM's entry into the UK computer industry.

But it is also easy to imagine situations in which domestic firms just surrender their market shares to entering multinationals and are unable to win them back. In such situations governments can come under enormous political pressure to restore the market shares of domestic firms in other ways. Most frequently this happens with some active discrimination against the foreign firm in the form of higher taxes on their goods or inputs, restrictions on their ability to expand production or strict rules about how much profit they can repatriate. All of these measures effectively reduce the actual profitability of the foreign firm and give the less competitive domestic firms a chance to compete again.

Case study: Globalization and unemployment in developing countries

New Year shock: millions set to lose garment jobs

One of the most sweeping acts of global liberalisation is about to be unleashed on some of the world's poorest workers, with devastating consequences for the millions, mostly women, who are expected to lose their jobs.

At midnight on 31 December 2004, the World Trade Organisation will scrap the quota system that governs the global clothing and textile trade, ending at a stroke 30 years of protection for one of the developing world's staple industries.

From New Year's Day 2005, the Multi Fibre Agreement (MFA) will go and the new rule will then be – survival of the fittest. A recent World Trade Organisation (WTO) study stated that 27 million workers world-wide could lose their jobs.

In a hard hitting new report, *Rags to riches to rags*, Christian Aid warns that unless urgent action is taken, millions of garment workers will lose their jobs – plunging them yet further into poverty and debt.

With few employment alternatives, there are growing fears that the sacked garment workers will end up in far worse jobs, with some ending up in the sex trade. There will also be increasing pressure to lower labour standards for those factories that do survive.

'The losers in this new trade landscape will be some of the most vulnerable workers in countries such as Bangladesh, Cambodia, Sri Lanka and Nepal. They will be hard-pressed to cope when garment industries there lose their protection,' said Andrew Pendleton, Christian Aid's Head of Trade Policy.

'We are deeply concerned that the new year will spell misery for huge numbers of garment workers. In Bangladesh alone, it is predicted a million jobs will go. Most of these are women, who have used the work to help haul themselves out of poverty,' he added.

'The scrapping of the MFA was undertaken without proper weight being given to the impact on those people most likely to be affected. Changes in global trade policies, especially those as seismic as the MFA phase-out, should put the interests of poor people first – rather than simply aiming to liberalise markets at any cost,' said Pendleton.

'The MFA was by no means perfect, but it did provide the opportunity for countries like Bangladesh to get onto the first rung of industrial development.'

Advocates of scrapping the MFA suggest it will lead to greater efficiencies, lower costs to Western consumers and more jobs in China and India.

But the Christian Aid report, that focuses on the plight of Bangladeshi women garment workers, argues that the cost of this liberalisation is too high and must be halted.

'International trade must not be governed by a "race to the bottom" that pitches one set of poor people against another,' said Mr Pendleton. 'Furthermore, the cost of the expected savings on the price of a shirt or trousers here is likely to be minimal, while the impact in places such as Bangladesh will be huge.'

Christian Aid hopes that while Western consumers do their Christmas shopping they will give some thought to the workers from poor countries who made them, said Mr Pendleton.

'Rich retailers especially have a real obligation to ensure they look after their workforces. They must not succumb to the lure of a quick profit by cutting and running from countries such as Bangladesh. They make large profits from the efforts of these workers, especially at Christmas, and they must live up to their social responsibilities.'

(http://www.christian-aid.org/news/media/ pressrel/0401217p.htm, 17 December 2004)

Questions

How has the ending of the Multi-Fibre Agreement affected the well-being of (a) Western consumers and (b) garment workers in Bangladesh?

To what extent is the continuing liberalization of global trade likely to enhance human welfare, well-being or happiness?

16.4 Globalization and growing inequality: are they related?

The integration of economies through globalization has been an extremely uneven process. Some countries and regions have gained much more from it than others, an outcome that has increased inequality *among* economies. At the same time, globalization has increased inequality *within* successfully integrated economies, favouring some groups above others. In this section we will deal with the evidence on each of these issues in turn.

■■■ 16.4.1 The unequal international impact of global integration

In Section 16.2 we drew attention to the increasing shares of international trade and production in the late 1980s and the 1990s as indicative of the growing importance of economic globalization. Tables 16.3(a)–(c) report further data on the distribution of world trade and foreign investment across the economies.

Question | Examine the data in Tables 16.3(a)–(c). Do they suggest that all countries have experienced increases in international trade and investment or have such increases been concentrated in a few economies of the world?

What is quite remarkable from Tables 16.3(a)–(c) is that only a few countries account for the larger portion of the increases in world trade and international investment. The data suggest that, far from being a general process that has affected economies the world over, economic globalization has in fact been important in integrating only a few countries in the world economy. Consider for example the disproportionate role of China among low-income economies in attracting inward investment stocks (Table 16.3(b)) and inward FDI flows (Table 16.3(c)).

Other data support this general point. The World Bank estimates that exports of manufactured goods rose from 25 per cent of poor country exports in 1980 to 80 per cent in 1998. This integration was concentrated in 24 low-income countries (including China,

Table 16.3(a)
Distribution of world trade: percentage of total exports

	1970 %	1980 %	1991 %
High-income market economies	72.1	63.7	73.2
North America	19.9	15.2	16.3
Europe	45.6	41.7	47.5
Japan	6.5	6.8	9.3
Low-income market economies	17.0	29.7	23.7
Oil exporting	5.8	15.6	4.9
Non-oil exporting	11.1	14.1	18.8
Eastern Europe and Soviet Union	10.9	6.6	3.1
Eastern Europe	6.6	3.6	1.7
Soviet Union	4.3	3.0	1.4

Note: figures may not sum exactly to totals because of rounding.

Source: *Economic Survey of Europe*, 1993, calculated from Appendix Table C.1, p.279

Table 16.3(b)
Distribution of
foreign investment
stocks, 1980–2000

	1980	1985	1990	1995	2000
Total inward stock ($bn)	481.9	734.9	1716.9	2657.9	6314.3
High-income economies share (%)	77.5	73.2	80.1	73.9	66.7
Of which, US share (%)	22.2	34.3	28.8	29.2	29.4
Low-income economies share (%)	22.5	26.8	19.9	26.1	31.3
Of which, Chinese share (%)	0.0	1.7	4.1	18.6	17.5
Total outward stock ($bn)	513.7	685.6	1684.1	2730.2	5976.2
High-income economies share (%)	98.8	96.9	95.9	92.1	87.8
Of which, US share (%)	43.4	37.8	27.0	28.1	23.7
Low-income economies share (%)	1.2	3.1	4.1	7.9	11.9
Of which, Chinese share (%)	0.0	0.6	3.6	8.1	3.8

Note: percentages may not sum exactly to 100% because of rounding.

Source: Feenstra, 1999, p.333; UNCTAD, 2001, for the 2000 figures

Table 16.3(c)
Distribution of FDI
flows, 1983–2000

	1983–88	1991	1993	1995	1997	2000
Total inward flows ($bn)	91.6	157.8	207.9	314.9	477.9	1270.8
High income economies share (%)	78.4	73.8	64.8	68.4	56.8	79.1
Of which, US share (%)	47.9	19.3	31.8	29.7	38.1	28.0
Low income economies share (%)	21.6	26.2	35.2	31.6	39.2	18.9
Of which, Chinese share (%)	9.2	10.6	37.6	37.6	23.6	17.0
Total outward flows ($bn)	93.7	210.8	225.5	317.9	466.0	1149.9
High income economies share (%)	94.2	95.8	85.4	85.2	85.2	91.0
Of which, US share (%)	16.1	16.6	35.9	35.3	24.1	13.3
Low income economies share (%)	5.8	4.2	14.6	14.8	14.1	8.7
Of which, Chinese share (%)	8.5	10.3	13.3	7.4	3.9	2.3

Note: percentages may not sum exactly to 100% because of rounding.

Source: Feenstra, 1999, p.334; UNCTAD, 2001, for 1997 and 2000 figures

India and Mexico) which were home to 3 billion people. These countries doubled the ratio of trade to national income and their per capita incomes rose by 5 per cent per annum. Yet for another 2 billion of population in low-income countries, including much of Africa, the ratio of trade to national output fell and income per head shrank in the same period. Similarly more than half of the foreign investment inflows to low-income economies are concentrated in just five countries.

Has this uneven distribution of international trade and production contributed to a widening of income differentials between countries in the late 1980s and the 1990s? Table 16.4 reports on some standard measures of inequality, some of which you encountered in Chapter 9.

Question   What conclusion can you draw about the changing distribution of world income from the data in Table 16.4?

Table 16.4
More unequal:
world income
distribution
(1988–93)

Inequality measure	1988	1993	Percentage change
Gini coefficient of world incomes	63.10%	66.90%	6.0%
Poorest decile's share of world income	0.88%	0.64%	−27.3%
Richest decile's share of world income	48.00%	52.00%	8.3%
Median income as share of poorest decile	327.00%	359.00%	9.8%
Richest decile as share of median income	728.00%	898.00%	23.4%

Source: Wade, 2001, Table 3

The data in Table 16.4 point to a widening of world inequalities in income over the 1980s and early 1990s. For example, the Gini coefficient of world incomes increased by 6 per cent from 1988 to 1993. Even more striking is the decline in the percentage of world income available to the poorest decile of the world's population. The richest decile has benefited from a dramatic increase in their incomes expressed as a percentage of median world income.

We may think of global inequality in incomes as being made up of two parts, the inequality of incomes between countries and the inequality of incomes within a country. It has been found that for OECD countries between 1980 and 1985, a greater proportion of the inequality of incomes came from within-country inequality and that within-country inequality increased during this period. Similarly, for the category of more globalized countries (those countries that show a high share of trade to GDP), within-country inequality increased over the period 1980–95.

Rising inequality is always potentially a political issue. But globalization is not the only factor responsible for these widening income differentials. As you will learn in Chapter 18, technological improvements and their diffusion, investment in human capital and the maintenance of a high rate of investment in some economies are also important explanatory factors in explaining growth and divergence of incomes between rich and poor countries.

Nevertheless, globalization is an important factor in that a disproportionate amount of international trade and production originates and integrates economies in the West, and the world is roughly divided between the prosperous West together with a handful of very low-income countries and a large group of low- to middle-income countries. This fact alone goes some way towards explaining why anti-globalization protests often take the form of anti-West protests, despite the fact that many of the low-income countries want to emulate the economic achievements of the West.

The evidence on world income inequality in Table 16.4 does not explain why many of the anti-globalization protests have in fact happened in Western countries. Very often they have included vocal sections that were protesting on behalf of the poorer non-Western countries, but this is not true of all the protestors. Could it be possible that in Western countries too there have been large numbers of losers due to increased international integration? It is to this question that we now turn our attention.

▪ ▪ ▪ 16.4.2 Trade and income inequality within economies

In order to identify the losers from trade we need to look more closely at what happens to economies as they start specializing according to their comparative advantage. In recent decades the UK has discovered that it has a comparative advantage in services and following on this the share of services in UK national income and employment has grown. The other side of the coin, however, is that UK producers find that manufacturing of many products is best left to the Chinese or the Taiwanese. These are the UK's sectors of comparative disadvantage, in which production will begin to decrease. At first, people working in a range of manufacturing industries may find that it is harder to find new work and that prices in these industries are higher than elsewhere. As comparative advantage and specialization progress, the share of such manufacturing in national income and employment will fall and the share of services in income and employment will expand. Thus, the structure of production and employment in the economy will have changed.

It is argued that the UK economy went through a period of restructuring in the mid- and late 1980s. The UK's comparative disadvantage in manufacturing eroded the manufacturing basis of national production while its comparative advantage in services (financial and business) boosted the share of the services sector in national income. A consequence of this was that several older industries such as steel and coal that depended upon the manufacturing sector for demand had to shut down, causing huge unemployment in those sectors. This led to a great contraction of jobs in these industries and arguably contributed to the growing inequality between the south-east and the rest of the UK economy.

Such restructuring of the economy is the consequence of trade when there is comparative advantage. While the difference in no-trade price ratios gives the scope for gains from trade, when trade actually takes place each economy ends up facing the same (world) price ratio and producing more of the good in which it has a comparative advantage. In simple models of trade, as one price ratio obtains in both the countries, the wage rates of people working in the sector of comparative disadvantage fall to the levels of the country that has the comparative advantage. This is called *factor–price equalization* and is an implication of the Hecksher–Ohlin factor endowment model of the sources of comparative advantage (Chapter 15, Section 15.4). Under some very restrictive assumptions, including the assumptions of the model of perfect competition, the model shows that factor–price equalization is a consequence of free trade. The rather strong result implied by factor–price equalization is this: even if factors of production (labour, capital) were fully immobile across countries, free trade in goods would substitute for the trade in factors and have the same effect on relative wages across trading countries. For example, the implication of factor–price equalization for the UK would be that eventually wages for low-skilled work in manufacturing would fall towards the wages earned for such work in low-income economies that are abundantly endowed with low-skilled labour. Low wages give such economies a comparative advantage in manufacturing and specialization and trade will increase their demand for low-skilled labour, causing wages to rise until equality of wages for the same type of labour is achieved across different boundaries.

A lively debate started in the USA in the mid-1980s concerning the claim that increased trade was contributing to worsening income inequality in the US economy. Figure 16.3 depicts the main trends in within-country income inequality for selected high-income countries for the period 1977–97. It plots the Gini coefficient of incomes (which you learnt about in Chapter 9) for selected OECD countries on the Y-axis, against time on the X-axis.

Question What does Figure 16.3 tell us about within-country income inequality in the high-income countries selected over the period 1977–97?

Figure 16.3
Changes in income
inequality within
selected high
income countries
1977–97

Source: Atkinson,
1999, p.4

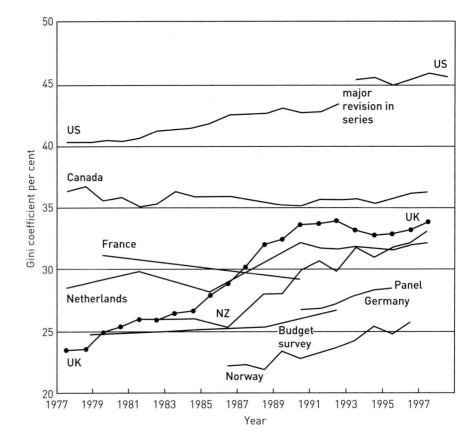

For many high-income economies the 1980s and 1990s were a period of worsening income distribution within their economies. Figure 16.3 shows clearly that in several countries inequality in incomes rose in the late 1980s and the 1990s. The rise was particularly sharp in the UK, but was also observed for New Zealand, Germany, Norway and the USA. It is tempting to conclude that the growth in international trade and production was entirely responsible for these trends and that these worsening inequalities merely represent some kind of factor–price equalization. In the same period, however, Canada showed no great change in its income inequality and France showed decreased inequality. There is no evidence at all that they were participating less vigorously in the globalization of their economies. So could this be another example of wrongly inferring causation from observed association?

Some economists, such as Atkinson (1999), argue that the growing inequality in the OECD countries cannot be attributed to trade alone. Many more important and signific-ant changes took place in the 1980s and 1990s. In the UK, perhaps the most significant of all the changes of the 1980s was the loss of trade union bargaining power after the failure of some famous strikes in the Thatcher era. The same was true in several other European countries as well, and in the USA, although there are fewer trade unions there. In con-trast, French truckers and farmers still regularly exercise their rights to strike and demand pay increases, as many of us remember from unfortunate ferry crossing experiences. In many cases this change in the strength of unions affected the wages at the lower end, and you may recall that the coal pit workers and miners were not the highest income earners even in the old technology days and neither were their products directly traded. The emergence of new technologies in the 1980s and 1990s also rewarded technological skills and training, widening the wage differential between skilled and unskilled labour. A relative scarcity of such trained workers meant that some of them could earn very high incomes and negotiate very high salaries for their skills.

Both of these different pressures on the higher and lower end of incomes together may have widened income inequality. Indeed, there is some evidence suggesting that upward pressure on skilled incomes contributed more to the growth in UK income inequality than downward pressure on the unskilled wage component. Is such a worsening of income distribution inevitable? As you have learnt, governments have many means at their disposal to improve income inequality and the consequences of such inequality. A major tool is redistributive taxation. However, here again the 1980s and 1990s were remarkable in the UK and the USA. Tax rates fell drastically in both economies and public investment correspondingly decreased in real terms.

The picture regarding within-country inequality is if anything worse for low-income countries, even the so-called globalizers who have benefited from huge increases in per capita incomes over the period 1980–97. Prominent examples in this group are India and China. Even as growth rose and poverty fell, inequality increased. Systematic investigation into the influence of trade on inequality has shown that while on average across all countries there was no relationship between participation in trade and within-country inequality, in low-income countries trade was *always* associated with greater within-country inequality.

Foreign investment may also play a role in contributing to income inequalities. While foreign firms are famous for shifting their production to lower cost locations in search of profits and have questionable practices in their treatment of legal and environmental regimes in these countries, foreign firms almost always raise wages in the economies and sectors that they enter. This is a well-established empirical fact, noted by Jenkins (1983) and confirmed in most studies on foreign investment and wage rates.

Question	Why should the entry of foreign firms raise incomes in the sector in which they enter?

It is easy to understand why foreign firms have a favourable impact on wages in the sectors they enter. They simply add to the labour demand for the same supply of labour, raising wages in the sector and thus increase wage dispersion. Just as an example of how potent that effect can be, it is interesting to note that software engineers working in India earn about 20 times the national average income for manufacturing. Much of this increase happened in the early 1990s when foreign multinationals set up software subsidiaries in India, offering salaries that were 20 per cent higher than those offered by domestic firms.

Foreign investment in low-income countries also happens in selected regions, called free trade zones or specialized export zones where better infrastructure conditions prevail and where the investment is often subject to different tax and labour laws from the rest of the country. So the benefits of greater integration are often confined to these regions, increasing the disparity between regions of the entire economy. Thus, in China the inequality between the prosperous south-east coast and the rest of mainland China has increased. In India too, the south and west of the country have prospered with the software boom while the rest of the country has not benefited in this way, contributing to inter-regional inequalities.

16.5 Globalization and economic growth: are they related?

In this section we will turn to the macroeconomic impact of globalization and examine the question of whether increased trade and investment raise the growth of national incomes over time.

Do trade and foreign investment affect the rate of growth and, if so, how and why? As you will learn in more detail in Chapter 18, the rate of growth of national income is ultimately determined by three factors: the rate at which the economy as a whole saves and is able to free resources from current consumption for investment in the economy, the rate at which investment is actually undertaken and the productivity of investment. International trade affects the opportunities that an economy has for profitable investment and so is capable of influencing growth. Foreign investment is in principle capable of affecting all three factors that influence growth. This is true for both inward and outward foreign investment.

Sections 16.5.1 and 16.5.2 discuss a variety of evidence on trade, foreign investment and growth. The issue of openness to international trade and production and its effect on growth is a very contentious one on empirical grounds. For one thing, there is the old problem of inferring causation from observed correlations. Can we really tell the difference between growth causing improvements in productivity and therefore greater exports, and exports causing increased productivity and growth? Put differently, is growth a cause or consequence of openness to international trade and production?

There is a second and subtler point. Detailed studies of export-led growth suggest that the success of one country is due in part to policies and failures of all other countries in that time frame. South Korea and Taiwan were the first countries to break out of the mould of growing through expanding domestic production to replace imports by finding some industries where they saw a potential to grow through exporting. They were lucky in being able to seize the opportunity when there was no competition from other countries with similar skills. Mexico also opened up to investment and collaboration with US firms at about the same time. It is useful to think about this as a race between countries for opportunities to better their growth. Some countries are selected as winners. But their victory is as much due to their own abilities as due to what others in the race did not do. In this sense their history is unique and unrealizable in any other way.

■ ■ ■ 16.5.1 Trade and growth

International trade increases the potential market available for the supply of raw materials and demand for products when compared with a less open environment. This has a powerful impact on both investment and the productivity of investment. To understand why this is so, conduct the following thought experiment. If resources were available for investment, how might entrepreneurs go about deciding to invest? First, they may decide how many investments are already there and whether they should step in additionally. Compared with a closed economy an open economy is likely to have many more investment opportunities simply because the demand facing the economy is larger. Second, they might want to rank investment projects according to the return they will get on them. If they were restricted to investment in the domestic economy, the most productive projects may already be taken and they may have to be content with a lower rate of return. But in an open economy there is a greater variety of projects and rates of return. For both these reasons international trade affects investment and the productivity of that investment.

Theoretical possibilities aside, have countries that participated more in international trade grown more? In this subsection we will try to assess the empirical evidence on this issue. As was noted in the introduction to this chapter, several low-income countries opened up their economies to trade by adopting a more liberalized policy regime towards trade. Table 16.5 below lists 32 low-income economies and when they adopted liberal policies. In the third column of the table we report a figure on the change in growth. This measures the difference between the average rate of growth three years post-liberalization

Table 16.5
Trade liberalization and growth in low-income countries (post-1985)

Country	Year of liberalization	Change in rates of growth of national income
Mali	1986	0.1018
Philippines	1986	0.1004
Chile	1985	0.0855
Uganda	1987	0.0807
Malaysia	1988	0.0740
Tanzania	1986	0.0495
Nigeria	1986	0.0364
Malawi	1988	0.0341
Costa Rica	1985	0.0334
Argentina	1989	0.0320
Colombia	1985	0.0314
Venezuela	1989	0.0226
Senegal	1986	0.0226
Madagascar	1987	0.0195
Côte d'Ivoire	1985	0.0184
Vietnam	1986	0.0177
Bangladesh	1991	0.0039
Mexico	1985	0.0018
Indonesia	1986	−0.0006
Korea	1987	−0.0009
Thailand	1989	−0.0014
Sri Lanka	1987	−0.0101
Pakistan	1988	−0.0160
Ghana	1987	−0.0182
Kenya	1988	−0.0233
Cameroon	1989	−0.0292
India	1991	−0.0297
South Africa	1990	−0.0370
Peru	1989	−0.0435
China	1988	−0.0531
Brazil	1987	−0.0776
Zaire	1990	−0.0932
Mean change in rate of growth		0.0104
Standard deviation		0.0476

Source: adapted from Greenaway *et al.*, 1997, Tables 1 and 2, pp.1887–8

and the average rate of growth observed three years before liberalization. A positive value for this figure means that the average rate of growth of the economy increased after liberalization, a negative value that it decreased.

What can you conclude from Table 16.5 about the effects of liberalization on growth for low-income countries?

Surprisingly we cannot draw any very firm conclusions. Of these 32 countries that liberalized, 14 saw negative effects on the rate of growth of national income. Across the group the average increase in GDP growth rates was 1.04 per cent and the dispersion of this increase in both directions was wide, as indicated by the large standard deviation of 4.76 per cent. However, the before-and-after picture of the impact on growth rates of opening up the economy, as illustrated in Table 16.5, can be a misleading one. For one thing, we know that low-income countries often liberalized in response to specific balance of payments crises. Second, the benefits associated with increased trade that we have outlined require a long period of integration through trading relations with other economies for their effects to be apparent. So it may be that a better test of the economic impact of liberalization would look for a range of indicators over a long period of time. Dollar and Kray (2001) do just this and their results are reported in Table 16.6.

Table 16.6
Characteristics of globalizing and non-globalizing low-income economies: population-weighted averages

	24 globalizers	49 non-globalizers
Population, 1997	2.9 billion	1.1 billion
Per capita GDP, 1980	$1488	$1947
Per capita GDP, 1997	$2485	$2133
Inflation, 1980	16%	17%
Inflation, 1997	6%	9%
Rule of law index (world average = 0)	−0.04	−0.48
Average years		
Primary schooling, 1980	2.4	2.5
Primary schooling, 1997	3.8	3.1
Average years		
Secondary schooling, 1980	0.8	0.7
Secondary schooling, 1997	1.3	1.9
Average years		
Tertiary schooling, 1980	0.08	0.09
Tertiary schooling, 1997	0.18	0.22

Note: globalizing countries are the top third of the low-income countries when ranked according to their trade to GDP ratio. The 24 countries in this group are: Argentina, Bangladesh, Brazil, China, Colombia, Costa Rica, Côte d'Ivoire, the Dominican Republic, Haiti, Hungary, India, Jamaica, Jordan, Malaysia, Mali, Mexico, Nepal, Nicaragua, Paraguay, Philippines, Rwanda, Thailand, Uruguay and Zimbabwe. China accounts for a third of the total population of this group of countries. The group of non-globalizers includes all the remaining low-income countries for which data are available.

Source: Dollar and Kray, 2001, p.15

Do you think that Table 16.6 reveals any significant differences between the globalizing and the non-globalizing low-income countries?

Table 16.6 classifies economies into 24 globalizers and 49 non-globalizers based upon the trade to GDP ratio. The average import tariff for non-globalizers fell by 11 percentage points while that for the globalizers fell by 34 percentage points. Some interesting differences emerge. The 24 globalizers were poorer than the 49 non-globalizers in 1980 yet by the end of 1997 they were richer. They had lower inflation and better educational attainments at primary level compared with their 1980 levels and the non-globalizing countries.

Figure 16.4 plots the rates of growth of national income over the period 1960–90 on the X-axis and the rate of growth of the volume of international trade (exports + imports) between 1960 and 1990 on the Y-axis. Perhaps because of the jeans factories, Tunisia's GDP grew at an annual rate of 5.8 per cent between 1960 and 1990 while its volume of international trade grew at 7 per cent.

What is the broad relationship between the annual average growth rate of GDP and the average annual growth rate of trade shown by Figure 16.4?

Notice that the scatterplot has a broadly upward drift. This indicates that generally countries that have experienced higher growth in the volume of international trade have also experienced higher rates of growth of GDP. We could try to fit a line to this scatterplot, which would allow us to estimate the effect on the rate of growth of GDP of a 1 per cent increase in the growth of international trade but again, we cannot be sure which is cause and which is effect.

Figure 16.4
Growth in trade and GDP 1960–90

Source: Jones, 2001; data provided by Jones, personal communication, 2002

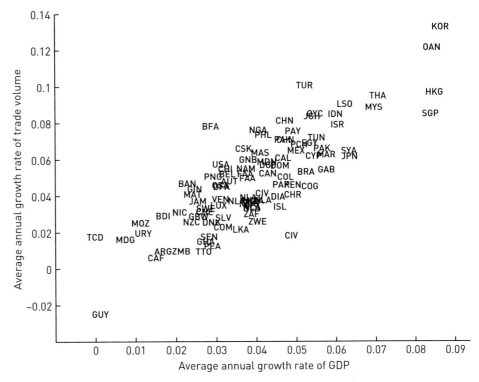

■ ■ ■ 16.5.2   Foreign investment and growth

Over a long period, foreign investment contributes to growth in two ways: raising productivity in the host economy and raising the rate of savings because of the higher profitability of foreign firms.

Both of these effects depend, however, on what foreign investment does to the quantity and productivity of domestic investment. In other words, it depends upon whether the relationship between the level and productivity of foreign investment is complementary or substitutive to the level and productivity of domestic investment. If the relationship between foreign and domestic investment is complementary, so that a rise in foreign investment increases the quantity and productivity of domestic investment, the long-term impact of foreign investment on growth should be beneficial. If, however, foreign investment largely wipes out domestic investment, the long-term effect of foreign investment on growth is not beneficial to the host economy. These arguments do not change when we use more sophisticated growth models, or more recent endogenous growth models (Chapter 18).

The impact of foreign investment on growth is not straightforward, because it affects a range of other macroeconomic aggregates such as domestic savings, domestic investment and the balance of payments (see Chapter 16). Casual empiricism too suggests that this is so. China has experienced large foreign capital inflows and high growth in recent years, while South Korea grew rapidly in the 1980s without significant levels of foreign capital inflow. Many Latin American countries have experienced low growth despite openness to foreign capital while much of sub-Saharan Africa has experienced low growth and poor investment flows.

The most careful study of the relationship between FDI, domestic investment and the balance of payments in host countries was undertaken by Fry (1995) for a sample of 16 large low-income countries. He found that, in general, inflows of foreign investment seem to have a negative effect on domestic investment, after correcting for a host of other factors. Besides, foreign investment also tends to reduce domestic savings by more than the reduction in domestic investment, so that the impact on the current account (the balance of exports and imports) is often negative. Thus, Fry finds that foreign capital inflows often have a perverse impact on the host economy's balance of payments position. In the longer term, however, foreign capital inflows have a more beneficial impact on investment, savings and growth. Fry finds that, lagged five years, foreign capital inflows are positively related to domestic savings, investment and growth.

Fry also discovers that the impact of foreign investment differs among countries in his sample. Thus, for a sub-sample of Pacific Basin countries, foreign investment raised total investment by the full extent of the FDI inflow, with generally benign effects on growth. Outside the Pacific Basin, foreign investment served as a substitute for other kinds of flows; here lower investment, savings and growth accompanied larger inflows of foreign investment.

16.6   Conclusion

The period of the late 1980s and the 1990s saw an acceleration in world flows of international trade and investment, and in international and national debates this began to be referred to as globalization. Participation in international trade and production has the potential for several economic gains. Globalization pulls economies of the world together in production and potentially gives the benefits associated with large single markets. However, the extent of gains from globalization depends on several factors that are likely to vary from country to country. One crucial factor is the terms of trade between countries.

This chapter has shown how the effect of recent globalization has been limited to a few countries, and has on balance been associated with a more unequal world. Even as some countries appear to catch up with the Western world, there is increasing inequality within both high-income and low-income countries. Whether globalization has been the main factor creating these increases in inequality is a moot point. For the high-income countries this link is unclear, while for the low-income countries the link between globalization and inequality is stronger.

The current ire about globalization should be understood at least partially in terms of doubtful economic outcomes, which, when they do happen, also appear to be polarizing the world. Inequality always creates the potential for political conflicts.

Questions for review and discussion

Question 1

(a) Explain how increased trade can cause inequality between and within countries in the world economy.

(b) Figure 16.5 is a scatterplot of data on the Gini coefficient of income distribution in different countries against the proportion of their GDP that is traded internationally. Discuss whether the scatterplot of the data is consistent with the hypothesis that trade increases income inequality, using examples from the dataset.

(c) What other factors may explain the observed trends in growing income inequality in the OECD countries in the 1980s and 1990s (shown in Figure 16.3)?

Figure 16.5
Inequality and trade, 1985

Source: Based on data in Appendix II of Chakrabarti, A (2000) vol.25, no.2, pp.1–21.

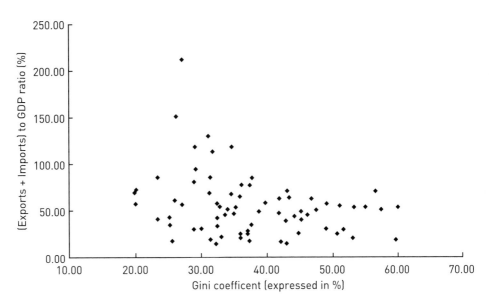

Question 2

The bitter truth about European sugar

We in the West continue to take with one hand what we give with the other. The European Union's donations to the tsunami appeal out-stripped those of any other state or region. Yet its agricultural policies continue to undermine the efforts of farmers in the developing world to earn a living, condemning them to poverty and dependence on aid.

A case in point is sugar, of which Europe is a very high cost producer. To keep them in business, European farmers are supported by artificially high prices and generous subsidies. Oxfam estimates that six European processing companies received more than $1bn (£254m) in EU subsidies in 2003. An inevitable consequence of these sweeteners is that Europeans grow too much sugar. The surplus – some 5m tons a year – is dumped on world markets. One effect of this is to undermine farmers in Africa and elsewhere who cannot compete with their highly subsidised counterparts.

The Union also supports its producers by blocking the entry of developing country imports into its market with tariffs of more than 300 per cent. Oxfam estimated that Malawi could have significantly increased exports to the Union in 2004 but that market restrictions deprived it of a potential $32m in foreign exchange earnings, equivalent to around half its public health spending . . .

Several member states whose producers profit from the grossly market-distorting mechanisms in place are threatening to block even the most modest reform proposals currently on the table . . .

Negotiations are under way over a possible reform of EU sugar policies. Ministers from a British government committed to seeing development prioritised this year need to win the argument with their partners. This will not be easy. No government likes to take on powerful economic interests and it is far easier to provide one-off aid cheques . . . than to undertake meaningful reforms that impose domestic costs.

(Financial Times, *25 February 2005, written by Anand Menon, Director of the European Research Institute, University of Birmingham)*

Referring to the article above, assess the arguments for and against the use of tariffs to restrict sugar imports into the European Union.

National currencies and international money markets

Andrew Stevenson

Concepts

- balance of payments
- current and capital accounts of the balance of payments
- bilateral and effective exchange rates
- nominal and real exchange rates
- fixed and flexible exchange rate regimes
- monetary union

Objectives

After studying this chapter you should be able to:

- understand the main principles of the balance of payments accounts and their macroeconomic significance
- understand a model of exchange rate determination
- discuss the arguments for and against fixed and flexible exchange rate regimes
- understand the benefits and costs of European monetary union
- discuss the arguments for and against UK participation in the euro.

17.1   Introduction

For the first two decades after the Second World War, the UK, along with the other market economies in the world, operated a fixed exchange rate regime, under the so-called Bretton Woods system. Only under exceptional circumstances, such as in 1967, did the pound alter its exchange rate with respect to its trading partners. The Bretton Woods system broke down in the early 1970s and, since then, the British economy has, for the most part, tried to operate with a flexible exchange rate; that is, the exchange rate is free to fluctuate day to day in line with market pressures. Occasionally, the British government has experimented with running the economy with a fixed exchange rate. Nigel Lawson was instrumental in attempting to peg sterling's exchange rate to the Deutschmark in the late 1980s and, more significantly, the UK joined the Exchange Rate Mechanism (ERM; a forerunner of the euro) and fixed the exchange rate with respect to our EU partners in 1990–92. The politically calamitous departure from the ERM signalled the end of UK experimentation with fixed exchange rates, and sterling has floated on world foreign exchanges ever since. In the meantime, 12 EU countries went ahead with the creation of the euro and the establishment of the ultimate in fixed exchange rate regimes (known as 'euroland' or 'the Eurozone'). The issue of what to do about the exchange rate has not gone away, and the central question remains of whether and when sterling should be replaced by the euro and the UK should join the European fixed exchange rate club and the European Monetary Union (EMU).

This choice between alternative exchange rate regimes lies at the heart of this chapter. However, to confront the relevant issues we need first to outline the main features of the balance of payments and the determinants of exchange rates. We then go on to analyse how domestic macroeconomic policies are affected by the choice of exchange rate regime, before finally discussing the operation and performance of the Eurozone and considering the UK's potential entry into it.

An open economy is one where there are economic and financial transactions with the rest of the world. We saw in Chapters 15 and 16 that the overall degree of openness of the world economy is increasing steadily as part of the process of globalization. Openness was measured in terms of increasing trade flows and increasing levels of foreign investment and production. International trade and production of goods and services is only one aspect of openness. Even more spectacular has been the growth of international capital transactions. Capital transactions are international purchase and sale of financial assets (i.e. international lending and borrowing). Residents of one country can lend to another country by purchasing financial assets from that country, and vice versa. This can take any number of different forms. Residents may buy stocks and shares from a company or a government of another country. This would channel funds to the foreign country and is regarded as a *capital outflow*. By the same token, domestic stocks and shares bought by an overseas resident would be a *capital inflow*. Alternatively, capital movements might simply involve switching a bank account from one country and currency to another. The growth in international capital movements in the second half of the twentieth century was spectacular, and capital is now regarded as highly mobile, since national barriers to international capital movements were dismantled. For example, the UK finally abolished all capital controls in 1979, and European capital markets were further liberalized with the introduction of the Single European Market in 1992. At the same time, domestic capital and financial markets have been significantly deregulated in the past thirty years.

Accompanying these legal and institutional changes, the IT revolution and the associated development of global communications have improved market information and enabled international lending and borrowing transactions to be effected much more cheaply and efficiently than before. As we shall see, capital movements are likely to respond to interest rate differentials. These factors have combined to make capital movements much more sensitive to financial conditions in different countries as international investors are now able to respond to market changes more efficiently, with important implications for the operation of both domestic monetary policy and fiscal policy. It is clear from Table 17.1 that the scale of international capital movements has increased dramatically over the past 50 years, and their importance in foreign exchange transactions dwarfs the scale of foreign trade. In April 2004, average *daily* transactions in world foreign exchange markets were 1900 billion dollars (compared with 18 billion dollars in the early 1970s). This is more than 100 times the value of daily international trade in goods and services.

It is therefore clear that economies are much more open than they were in the middle of the twentieth century. The main theme of this chapter is to explore the implications of this openness for macroeconomic policy and to assess the issues involved in the decision as to whether to join the euro. Before we embark on this discussion, however, we need to examine in a little more detail the nature and determinants of international economic transactions as a prelude to setting out our explanation of what determines exchange rates.

Table 17.1
Cross-border
transactions in
bonds and equities[1]
as a percentage of
GDP

	1970 %	1975 %	1980 %	1985 %	1990 %	1998 %
Canada	5.7	3.3	9.6	26.7	63.8	331.0
France	–	–	8.42[2]	21.4	53.3	415.0
Germany	3.3	5.1	7.5	33.9	57.5	334.0
Italy	–	0.9	1.1	4.0	26.7	640.0
Japan	–	1.5	7.0	60.5	118.6	91.0
UK	–	–	–	367.5	690.1	–
USA	2.8	4.2	9.3	36.4	92.5	230.0

Notes:
[1] Gross purchases and sales of securities between residents and non-residents.
[2] 1982.
– not available.

Source: Bank of International Settlements, *Annual Report*, various issues

17.2 The balance of payments

Open economies engage in a wide range of different kinds of transactions with the rest of the world. The annual account of these transactions is set out in the *balance of payments*. A discussion of these accounts will serve as a useful preparation for the remainder of the chapter. The 2004 balance of payments accounts for the UK are set out in Table 17.2.

The balance of payments records the total annual value of all transactions between a given economy and the rest of the world under different headings, or *accounts*. The main accounts are the *current account*, the *capital account* and the *financial account*.

17.2.1 The current account

The most important element in the current account is exports and imports of goods and services. *Trade in goods* (sometimes called *visible trade*) refers to imports and exports of physical goods such as wine, cars, washing machines and oil, with imports being recorded as a debit item (money is flowing out of the country to pay for these imports) and exports are a credit item (foreign expenditure is flowing into the country). If imports exceed exports, the economy is running a *visible trade deficit*, and if exports exceed imports, the country is running a *visible trade surplus*. The UK has run a visible trade deficit every year since 1982 (the surpluses before that date being attributable to North Sea oil), and in 2004 the visible trade deficit was £57 944 million. This deficit is partly offset by *trade in services* such as transport and financial services, where exports have consistently outstripped imports. In 2004, the surplus on services was £19 118 million.

The current account also includes two other items – *Income* and *Current transfers*. Under *Income* is recorded profits, interest and dividend income accruing from investments held abroad (and outflows arising out of foreign ownership of UK stocks and shares) and earnings by UK residents by working overseas (also with corresponding outflows). The former is much more important than the latter and is responsible for the income account moving into substantial surplus in the UK in recent years (to £24 004 million in 2004), largely due to the expanding overseas business of the financial sector.

Table 17.2
UK balance of
payments 2004

	£m
Trade in goods and services	
Goods	−57 944
Services	19 118
Total trade	−38 826
Income	
Compensation of employees	79
Investment income	23 925
Current transfers	−10 860
Current Balance	**−25 682**
Capital Balance	**2 073**
Financial Account	
Direct investment	7 105
Portfolio investment in UK	−55 709
Other investment	75 825
Reserve assets	−193
Net Financial Transactions	**27 028**
Net Errors and Omissions	**−3 419**

Source: *UK Balance of Payments* (*The Pink Book*)

Current transfers records money flows which are not in exchange for goods or services, loans or income flows. It includes items such as payments to and receipts from the EU (and other international organizations such as NATO), and emigrants' remittances (e.g. money sent by workers in one country to family members in another country). In 2004, current transfers showed a deficit of £10 860 million.

If we sum all these elements then we arrive at the current account balance, which in 2004 was a deficit of £25 682.

Question	What are the main macroeconomic factors which you think will affect the current account of the balance of payments?

If we simplify the current account to comprise only net exports, we can see that the state of the current account will reflect developments in domestic income, income in the rest of the world and the domestic economy's competitiveness in world markets. Other things remaining equal, increases in domestic income will be associated with increases in domestic expenditure and therefore increases in imports. Thus, domestic income growth, unless it is accompanied by export growth, will tend to increase imports relative to exports and move the current account towards deficit. Income growth in the rest of the world, on the other hand, tends to increase demand for exports and therefore tends to move the current account towards surplus. Competitiveness is most familiarly concerned with relative prices. If domestic exports are relatively cheap in world markets this increased competitiveness will feed through into increased exports. Price competitiveness depends on prices at home and abroad, and on the exchange rate. It can be measured by *the real exchange rate* (Section 17.3).

How can a current account deficit be financed? If an individual household spends more than its income in a given period, it has to find the excess from somewhere, most probably by borrowing or running down its financial reserves, if it has any. It is the same for a country. It must finance a current account deficit either by borrowing from abroad or by running down its foreign exchange reserves, and these transactions are also recorded in the balance of payments, in the capital account and the financial account.

■ ■ ■ 17.2.2   The capital and financial accounts

The *capital account* is relatively unimportant, recording what is known as capital transfers – where capital assets change ownership without any payment being made (e.g. debt cancellation). Much more important is the *financial account*, which records the purchase and sale of financial assets (i.e. international lending and borrowing). It is important to remember that lending money abroad means that domestic residents are acquiring foreign assets. Purchasing a bond from the French government, for example, means lending to the French government. Since funds are going abroad, this would be a capital outflow. Capital movements take a wide range of forms. *Direct investment* is where firms (often multinational companies) expand their business interests in other countries, either by taking over other companies or expanding companies which they already own. *Portfolio investment* is the purchase of stocks and shares in another country. It is sometimes useful to distinguish between short-term and long-term capital movements, since short-term capital movements are held to be potentially more unstable and prone to bursts of speculative activity. This may take the form of individuals or companies buying (selling) stocks and shares from (to) residents of other countries. It could even take the form of simply adding to an existing bank account in another country.

Question	What factors might motivate international capital flows?

Direct investment is likely to be in response to perceived profit opportunities in another economy (e.g. direct investment flows into the USA in the 1990s). Portfolio investment is more likely to be affected by differential interest rates between countries and, especially in the case of short-term capital movement, expectations about the future course of the exchange rate. Capital flows might also be directly related to foreign trade, for example an importer may borrow from abroad in order to purchase imports. In this case, the imports (a debit item on the current account) are exactly matched by a capital inflow (a credit item on the financial account). This last example is important in making a more general point. A deficit/surplus on the current account must be matched by offsetting surplus/deficit items elsewhere in the balance of payments. For example, a current account surplus means that the economy is accumulating foreign assets, which means there is a capital outflow. Similarly, a current account deficit means that our trading partners are acquiring UK assets (i.e. we are borrowing to finance the deficit), which means there is a capital inflow.

Take the example of a current account surplus and a resulting net inflow of foreign currency into the economy. Suppose domestic residents do not wish to hold foreign currency or any other foreign asset. They will then sell foreign currency on the foreign exchange market (or at least their bank will). What happens next depends on the government and the central bank. If the government does nothing, these net sales of foreign currency will cause sterling's exchange rate to rise, with further consequences for the balance of payments. Alternatively, if the government does not wish to see sterling's exchange rate rise, they may buy the foreign exchange and sell sterling. In this case, the Bank of England would accumulate additional foreign exchange reserves. This kind of *intervention* in the foreign exchange market would be required if the government was running a *fixed exchange rate* regime (Section 17.3).

Because current account deficits/surpluses have financial consequences which necessarily show up in the financial account as either capital movements or changes in official foreign exchange reserves, the balance of payments accounts as a whole must sum to zero. Thus, the current account surplus/deficit plus the capital account surplus/deficit must equal the increase/decrease in foreign exchange reserves. In reality, because of problems in data collection and measurement, it does not sum exactly and it requires an additional *Errors and Omissions* item to complete the accounts.

Thus, in 2004, the current account deficit of £25 682 million was accompanied by a total surplus on the capital account and financial account (excluding changes in foreign exchange reserves) of £29 294 million, with errors and omissions of −£3419 million, and an increase in foreign exchange reserves of £1559 million. Put at its very simplest, in 2004, the economy's borrowing from abroad exceeded the current account deficit, and the excess was bought (in exchange for sterling) by the Bank of England. (Note that increases in foreign exchange reserves are a negative item in the accounts.)

An open economy engages in a wide range of transactions with the rest of the world, with a wide range of different factors affecting them. Trade flows are likely to be influenced by factors such as international competitiveness and world and domestic income levels, and capital movements, while partly a reflection of trade flows, will also be affected by considerations such as profit opportunities abroad, interest rate differentials and market expectations about the future course of exchange rates. Note also that almost all the transactions recorded in the balance of payments require domestic currency to be either bought or sold on the foreign exchange market. Any surplus item in the balance of payments will therefore tend to increase demand for sterling and vice versa. If the current account plus the capital account and financial account (excluding changes in foreign exchange reserves) is in overall surplus, this will generate increased demand for sterling in the foreign exchange market. If the Bank of England does not intervene in the market, selling sterling, the exchange rate will rise.

Exercise 17.1

Would the following transactions appear as a credit or debit item, and on the current account or on the capital/financial accounts of the UK balance of payments? Explain the reason for your answer in one sentence.

1 Imports of shoes worth £10 000 from Italy by a clothes superstore in the UK.
2 Dividends of £5000 paid to US shareholders by a UK plc.
3 A UK resident buying shares worth US$20 000 in Telecom Inc., USA.
4 A UK student receiving an EU grant worth £6000 for study in England.

17.3 Exchange rates and factors influencing their determination

All balance of payments transactions are recorded at the prevailing exchange rate of a currency. The exchange rate of a currency is its price in terms of other currencies. In this section we will look into the question of what factors determine exchange rates in the international economy.

▪ ▪ ▪ 17.3.1   Exchange rates: definitions and measurement

Economies engage in a wide range of international transactions with the rest of the world. All of these transactions require domestic currency to be exchanged for foreign currency, or vice versa. Thus, when we buy imports from abroad, we need to obtain foreign currency with which to pay for these imports, unless the foreign exporter is prepared to accept sterling. Either the importer has to buy the currency of the exporting country (and sell sterling) or buy a currency which the exporter will accept (perhaps US dollars). On the other side of the coin, when we sell exports abroad, the foreign importer will have to buy sterling (or some acceptable currency) to pay for our exports. The same applies to international capital movements. Domestic residents purchasing foreign assets must first purchase foreign exchange, while capital inflows require foreign residents to purchase domestic currency. Thus, the financing requirements of balance of payments flows mean that currencies are being exchanged for each other on the foreign exchange market. Purchases or sales of dollars dominate foreign exchange market activity, accounting for 88 per cent of transactions in 2004.

Bilateral exchange rate

The bilateral exchange rate is the number of units of foreign currency that exchange for one unit of the home currency.

The exchange rate is the rate at which one currency is exchanged for another. It can therefore be regarded as the price of a unit of one currency in terms of another. In the UK, it is customary to express the exchange rate as the number of units of foreign currency required to buy one unit of domestic currency, for example £1 = \$1.75. If the exchange rate is expressed in this way, a fall in the exchange rate is a *depreciation* of the domestic currency, while a rise in the exchange rate is an *appreciation*.

The **bilateral exchange rate** is the one with which readers will be most familiar – the rate of exchange between two currencies (e.g. the sterling/dollar rate, the yen/euro rate). Bilateral exchange rates show only the relative price of one currency in terms of one other currency. However, if we are interested in the overall strength or weakness of a currency, we need a measure of that country's average exchange rate against all other relevant currencies (i.e. currencies of the countries with which that country trades). In this case, we need to compute the **effective exchange rate**. This is a weighted average of a country's exchange rate against all its trading partners, where each bilateral exchange rate is weighted according to its share of the domestic country's foreign trade. The effective exchange rate is expressed as an index.

Effective exchange rate

The effective exchange rate is the value of the home currency expressed in terms of a basket of foreign currencies, each weighted by its share of trade with the home country.

Both bilateral and effective exchange rates are measures of *nominal exchange rates*. That is, they are concerned with measuring the relative price of the currency in terms of another currency or currencies. This is to be contrasted with the *real exchange rate*. Instead of measuring the relative price of the two currencies, the **bilateral real exchange rate** measures the relative price of the goods produced by the two economies. The bilateral real exchange rate is the ratio of the two countries' price levels, converted into a common currency by the nominal exchange rate. Thus we have

Bilateral real exchange rate

The bilateral real exchange rate is the nominal bilateral exchange rate multiplied by an index of domestic prices and divided by an index of prices in the foreign country.

$$e' = e \cdot \frac{P}{P^{\mathrm{f}}}$$

where e' is the real exchange rate and e is the nominal exchange rate. P is the domestic price level (expressed in domestic currency terms) and P^{f} is the price level in the foreign country (expressed in foreign currency terms). The real exchange rate can be seen as the ratio of domestic prices (converted into foreign currency) to foreign prices. This must be expressed as an index and is a measure of changing competitiveness between the two

459

Figure 17.1
Real and nominal
effective exchange
rates, £ sterling,
1975–2002

Source: *International
Financial Statistics
Yearbook*, various
issues.

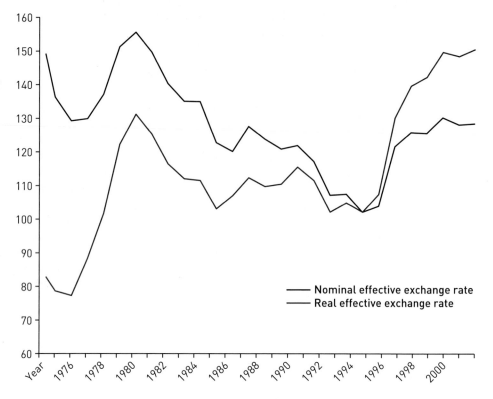

**Effective real
exchange rate**

The effective real
exchange rate is
the effective
exchange rate
multiplied by an
index of domestic
prices and divided
by a weighted
average of price
indices across
foreign countries.

countries. Thus, competitiveness is measured by the real exchange rate and not the nominal exchange rate. For example, competitiveness is increased by P falling relative to P^f and/or by the nominal exchange rate falling. It is quite possible for a change in the nominal exchange rate to be offset by a change in domestic prices, leaving the real exchange rate and competitiveness unchanged. For example, a 5 per cent depreciation in the nominal exchange rate will not affect the real exchange rate if it is accompanied by a 5 per cent increase in domestic prices relative to world prices.

It is also possible to construct an **effective real exchange rate**, which would provide a measure of the country's competitiveness vis-à-vis the rest of the world. This would be a trade-weighted average of the relevant bilateral real exchange rates.

In Figure 17.1 we set out the real and nominal effective exchange rate indices for sterling. The two series are different, though they do occasionally move together (reflecting the fact that nominal exchange rates might change more quickly than price levels).

Exercise 17.2

1   You will see on Figure 17.1 that the real exchange rate appreciated by more than the nominal exchange rate in the period from 1979 to 1981. What does this imply about UK inflation compared with the rest of the world?
2   What would be happening to UK inflation compared with the rest of the world if the nominal exchange rate appreciated and the real exchange rate depreciated at the same time?

Figure 17.2
A simple model of
the exchange rate

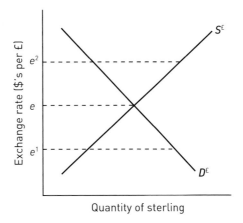

Quantity of sterling

■■■ 17.3.2   A simple model of the exchange rate

Exchange rates are determined in the foreign exchange market, which exists because of the foreign currency needs of individuals and institutions involved in international trade and international capital transactions. In what follows, we take as an example the bilateral nominal exchange rate between sterling and the dollar, expressing the exchange rate as the number of dollars to the pound. The exchange rate is the price of one currency in terms of another and in the foreign exchange market, as in all other markets, the price is determined by conditions of supply and demand. A simple model of the exchange rate is set out in Figure 17.2.

In this model, we can see that the demand for sterling (purchases of sterling and sales of dollars) increases as the exchange rate falls, and the supply of sterling (sales of sterling and purchases of dollars) rises as the exchange rate rises. As in any other market, equilibrium is attained at the price (the exchange rate) at which the supply and demand curves intersect (demand equals supply). To understand more clearly what determines exchange rate behaviour, however, we need to understand why the supply and demand curves in Figure 17.2 are sloped this way, and what might make them shift. Both the supply and demand curves are affected by current account transactions and capital account transactions, and we consider these in turn.

■■■ 17.3.3   Current account factors

Why should the demand for sterling increase as the exchange rate falls? The simplest explanation relates to competitiveness and the demand for domestic exports. At given foreign and domestic prices, a fall in the nominal exchange rate represents a fall in the real exchange rate and therefore an increase in competitiveness. Other things remaining equal, this will lead to increased foreign demand for domestic exports. For example, suppose a UK manufacturer produces a car which sells for £20 000 in the UK when the exchange rate is £1 = $1.50. This car would then sell for $30 000 in the USA. Suppose the exchange rate now falls to £1 = $1.25. With the sterling price of the car unchanged, the price in US markets would fall to $25 000, increasing the attractiveness of the car to US consumers. More cars would then be sold, US importers would increase their purchases of UK cars and would therefore need to need to purchase more sterling with which to pay for these cars. The same argument would apply to other UK exports and so the market demand for sterling would increase. The more price elastic the demand for UK exports, the greater will be the demand for sterling.

Similarly, the supply of sterling on the foreign exchange market reflects domestic demand for dollars, since, in order to buy dollars, sterling holders need to sell sterling. A rise in the exchange rate, for given dollar prices, will lead to reduced import prices in sterling terms. This will tend to increase the demand for imports and therefore the demand for dollars (increase the supply of sterling) with which to pay for these imports. By this argument, the supply of sterling will be an upward-sloping function of the exchange rate.

We now have an initial explanation of the supply and demand curves in Figure 17.2 – both curves reflect how trade flows respond to changing exchange rates and therefore competitiveness. In Figure 17.2 we can see that at an exchange rate such as e^1 demand for sterling is greater than the supply. If we ignore capital movements for the moment, this can be taken to mean that exports exceed imports. In the foreign exchange market, the exchange rate is bid up; that is, the exchange rate *appreciates*. As this happens, export demand (and therefore the demand for sterling) begins to fall while the demand for imports (and therefore the supply of sterling) starts to rise. This continues until the exchange rate reaches it equilibrium value at e. An analogous story applies to an exchange rate such as e^2, where imports exceed exports and the exchange rate *depreciates*.

Of course, there are other factors besides the exchange rate which affect imports and exports and if any of these factors change the curves in Figure 17.2 will shift, causing the exchange rate to change. The exchange rate is important because it affects competitiveness, but of course it is the real, not the nominal, exchange rate which determines competitiveness. Thus, at a given nominal exchange rate, competitiveness may increase if domestic prices fall relative to foreign prices (i.e. if domestic inflation is lower than inflation abroad). In this case, exports will rise at a given *nominal* exchange rate, shifting the demand for sterling curve to the right in Figure 17.2, and imports will fall, shifting the supply of sterling curve to the left, leading to an appreciation in the exchange rate.

Question How do you think the exchange rate might be affected by changes in domestic and foreign GDP?

Domestic and foreign income levels are likely to be important in determining trade flows. Increasing incomes abroad will tend to increase demand for exports, and therefore the exchange rate, while increasing domestic incomes will tend to increase imports, causing the exchange rate to fall. Thus, other things remaining equal, anything which causes exports to rise or imports to fall will cause the exchange rate to rise, and vice versa.

A major limitation of this analysis so far is that, in the absence of capital movements, the adjustment of the exchange rate to equilibrium would require actual trade flows to adjust. At the very least, this is unlikely to occur in the short run as it takes time for trade flows to adjust. As we will see, short-run adjustments in exchange rates are more likely to involve capital movements than trade adjustments. Before we turn to these, however, there are additional issues regarding exchange rate and trade flows to be considered.

Trade flows and elasticities

It is important to note that these supply and demand curves in Figure 17.2 reflect the *values* (in domestic currency) rather than simply the *volumes* of exports and imports, and this raises potential complications. The domestic currency value of exports is measured by their sterling price multiplied by their quantity. Suppose the exchange rate falls.

Assuming exporters continue to charge the same price in domestic currency, the price in dollars (say) will fall, increasing demand for exports to a degree dependent on the price elasticity of demand facing exporters in foreign markets. Demand increases at a given sterling price, increasing the sterling value of exports, and the greater the elasticity of demand, the more it will increase.

The position with imports is slightly different. Again assume a fall in the exchange rate. If the foreign exporter keeps prices constant in dollar terms, the price of imports will rise in sterling terms, reducing demand for imports. If demand is elastic, the value of imports will fall (as the fall in demand will be proportionately greater than the rise in price), but if demand is price inelastic, the fall in the exchange rate will actually increase the value of imports and therefore *increase* the supply of sterling, raising awkward questions about the stability of the market. More specifically, for trade flows to work in the way implied in Figure 17.2, a fall in the exchange rate must increase demand for sterling relative to the supply of sterling; that is, increase the value of net exports. Clearly, this is more likely, the greater the price elasticity of both imports and exports. If elasticities are low, then it is possible for a fall in the exchange rate to reduce the value of net exports. This conclusion is embodied more formally in the Marshall–Lerner conditions, which state that for a fall in the exchange rate to increase the value of net exports (and a rise to reduce it), the price elasticities of demand for imports and for exports must sum to greater than unity (in absolute terms).

Empirical evidence suggests that the Marshall–Lerner conditions are likely to be met, with import and export demand elasticities summing to between 1.5 and 2, but over a two- or three-year period, when demand patterns have time to adjust. Over the shorter term, it is probable that demand elasticities are much lower. One reason for this may simply be that it takes time for consumers to switch allegiance from the brand of one country's producer to that of another country. An additional reason may lie in the existence of contracts and the lag before these can be renegotiated. These lags imply that, following a fall in the exchange rate, 'things can get worse before they get better', as illustrated in the *J-curve*, as in Figure 17.3.

Measuring time along the horizontal axis and the value of exports on the vertical axis, we assume the fall in the exchange rate occurs at time period t^1. The value of net exports initially falls, as the volume of imports and exports fails initially to respond to the change in relative prices. However, once demand patterns begin to adjust to the new exchange rate at t^2, the value of net exports begins to rise. The time period $t^1 - t^2$ may be around 9 months or even longer.

Figure 17.3
The J-curve

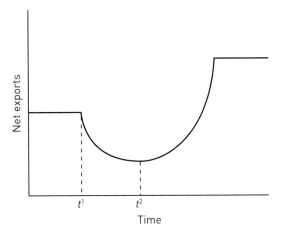

Exchange rate changes and pricing strategies

There are other reasons why trade volumes may respond sluggishly to exchange rate changes. Oligopolistic firms may be reluctant to change prices in line with exchange rate changes. In addition, exporters, having incurred the sunk costs of gaining a foothold in a foreign market, may be reluctant to retreat from a market because of an unfavourable change in the exchange rate in the short run, since re-entering the market will incur the same entry costs all over again. Thus, trade flows are unlikely to respond much to small changes in the exchange rate, especially if they are expected to be temporary. This is known as the beach-head effect (see Krugman and Obstfeld, 2003).

Real and nominal exchange rate adjustment

For a decline in the nominal exchange rate to be effective in increasing net exports, it must be translated into a real fall; that is, it must not be accompanied by an offsetting increase in domestic prices. However, there is a real danger of precisely this happening. Following a fall in the exchange rate, which initially increases competitiveness, exporters may incur diminishing returns in increasing their output to meet increased export demand, leading to higher prices. Moreover, the fall in the exchange rate will increase the domestic currency price of imported raw materials and consumer goods, the former increasing producers' costs directly, and the latter possibly leading to increased wages, as workers attempt to protect the real spending power of their wages. Thus, the short-run increase in competitiveness and net exports brought about by a fall in the nominal exchange rate can be eroded and ultimately removed by its inflationary consequences. The corollary of the above argument is that exchange rate increases can be a potentially effective anti-inflation weapon. Thus, a higher exchange rate reduces import prices, reducing both input costs and some consumer prices, reducing inflationary pressures in the economy.

In conclusion, it would seem that a model of exchange rates based on trade flows alone is likely to be deficient, at least in the short run, given the slow and uncertain response of trade flows to exchange rate changes, and, as we noted earlier, trade-related transactions are only about 1 per cent of total activity on the foreign exchange market each day. It is to capital movements we must turn to complete our analysis of exchange rate determination.

Exercise 17.3

1 What do you think are the likely consequences for a country's exchange rate if its income growth is consistently above that of its trading partners?
2 How do you reconcile your answer with the experience of rapidly growing countries with customarily strong currencies, such as Germany in the 1970s and 1980s?

■ ■ ■ 17.3.4 Exchange rates and the capital account

Capital transactions are concerned with international lending and borrowing, which generally take the form of the international sale and purchase of financial assets. As noted earlier, there are many different kinds of capital movements, but we might usefully divide such transactions into short- and long-term capital movements. Long-term capital movements include direct investment (most importantly the financing of investment projects by multinational companies) and certain portfolio investment (principally the purchase and sale of long-term bonds and equity). These capital movements may be affected by the perceived availability of profit opportunities in an economy. For example, the investment boom in the USA in the late 1990s attracted a substantial direct capital inflow which had the effect of bidding up the dollar's exchange rate, with serious consequences for the current account. However, short-term capital movements can be much more volatile. Short-term capital movements refer to transactions in short-term assets, frequently bank accounts. It is generally this kind of transaction which is involved when we refer to highly mobile international capital.

In analysing capital movements, it is useful to think of a world where there is a large number of portfolio holders (such as international fund managers) seeking to maximize the rate of return on their portfolios by allocating their funds between assets denominated in different currencies, taking into account the expected rates of return of these assets and their perceived degree of risk. There are two principal factors which taken together measure the relative rate of return of assets denominated in different currencies – relative interest rates and expected exchange rate changes.

Interest rates will have a more significant effect on capital flows the closer domestic and foreign assets are substitutes. For example, if UK and German assets were very close substitutes, and assuming that the exchange rate was not expected to change, an increase in German interest rates would bid funds away from the UK into Germany. This would bid up UK rates and bid down German rates. The closer the two sets of assets are substitutes the nearer their interest rates will be bid to equality.

In the limiting case where assets are perfect substitutes, domestic and foreign interest rates would have to be equal (at least in the absence of exchange rate expectations). This is sometimes referred to as *perfect capital mobility*. It is certainly the case that the development of international capital markets, associated with financial deregulation and advances in information technology, has increased the degree of capital mobility quite remarkably. However, so long as some assets are regarded as riskier than others and other factors, such as taxation treatment, differ between countries, financial assets will not be perfect substitutes between countries. Under these circumstances, the riskier assets, for example, will have to yield higher interest (the *risk premium*) to compensate portfolio holders.

Interest rates are not the only factor motivating short-term capital movements. Portfolio holders will also take into account *expected future changes* in exchange rates in assessing the relative rates of return of alternative assets. As an example, consider a UK investor deciding between holding a UK (sterling denominated) asset bearing 6 per cent, and a US (dollar denominated) asset bearing 8 per cent. In the absence of exchange rate expectations, the US asset is bearing a risk premium of 2 per cent.

Question	Suppose now that the market forms the expectation that the dollar is going to depreciate with respect to sterling by 5 per cent in the coming year. How will this affect investors' calculations?

First, the actual interest payment (assuming it is paid at the end of the year) will be worth 5 per cent less in sterling terms. This is, however, a minor adjustment, on its own reducing the effective rate of interest from 8 per cent to 7.6 per cent (i.e. 95 per cent of 8 per cent). Much more significant is the fact that the capital invested will be worth 5 per cent less in sterling terms, if the expected dollar depreciation comes about. It is this expected capital loss which dramatically reduces the rate of return on the dollar asset compared with the sterling asset, more than offsetting the nominal interest differential between the two countries. In this example, £100 invested in the UK at 6 per cent is worth £106 (£100 × 1.06) at the end of the year. By contrast, the same £100 invested in the US asset, and then converted back into sterling at the end of the year is worth only £102.60 (£100 × 1.08 × 0.95). In other words, the expected rate of return on the dollar asset is reduced by (approximately) the expected depreciation of the dollar over the year, and investors would be likely to switch their funds out of dollars and into sterling.

The relationship between exchange rate expectations and interest rates under perfect capital mobility is highlighted in the concept of the uncovered interest parity (UIP) condition. It is important to note that this condition assumes that domestic and foreign assets are perfect substitutes. In that limiting case, in the absence of any expected change in exchange rates, we would expect domestic and foreign interest rates to be equal. That is,

$$r = r_F$$

where r is the domestic (or, in the above example, the UK) interest rate, and r_F is the 'world' (or the US) interest rate.

Now suppose that markets form the view that the sterling exchange rate is going to change in the coming year; where that expected change is denoted by Δe. If Δe is positive, then markets are expecting a sterling appreciation. This would generate a capital inflow, increasing the demand for sterling in the foreign exchange market. This would serve to bring about the uncovered parity condition that

$$r = r_F - \Delta e$$

or alternatively, that

$$r = r_F - \Delta e$$

What this condition states is that if the domestic currency is expected to appreciate, then the domestic interest rate should be below the world interest rate by an amount equal to the expected appreciation.

This condition can be amended to take into account less than perfect capital mobility, by adding a term to denote the risk premium. Thus, where domestic and foreign assets are imperfect substitutes, we have

$$r = r_F - \Delta e + x$$

where x is the risk premium. If x is positive, domestic assets are deemed to be riskier than foreign assets.

Note the implication of UIP for the effects of an increase in domestic interest rates. Suppose the Bank of England increases UK interest rates. This will attract a capital inflow, bidding up the exchange rate. What happens next? The exchange rate will rise until it is sufficiently high that the market expectation is that it will fall back in the future. Once the expected future fall in the exchange rate matches the interest rate differential, the capital inflow will cease and the market will be in equilibrium. The increase in interest rates has generated an appreciation, and the expectation of a future depreciation. This is sometimes called *overshooting*.

Short-term capital movements can be crucially important in explaining day-to-day changes in exchange rates. Consider once more the behaviour of international asset-holders and let us assume that the assets in their portfolios are imperfect, but close, substitutes. The demand for any given asset will be a positive function of its expected rate of return and a negative function of the rate of return on alternative assets. This means that an increase in domestic interest rates or the expectation of a future appreciation will increase the exchange rate today. Let us examine each of these in turn.

Suppose the Bank of England increases domestic interest rates. This will induce a capital inflow bidding up the exchange rate. For equilibrium to be re-established in the foreign exchange market, the increase in the exchange rate must stem the capital inflow. This implies that the demand for sterling on the capital account is a negative function of the exchange rate.

Question	If domestic interest rates are higher than foreign interest rates, why should an increase in the exchange rate discourage the resultant capital inflow?

This can be explained in two alternative ways. If domestic and foreign assets are not perfect substitutes, the rise in the exchange rate increases the relative price of sterling assets and therefore reduces demand for them. Alternatively, using the notion of UIP, we can argue that exchange rate rises increase the expectation of a fall in the exchange rate in the future, reducing the demand for sterling assets today. Either way, in our example, the rise in sterling offsets the effects of the domestic interest rate and the exchange rate is at a new equilibrium value. In terms of Figure 17.2, we are noting (i) that the demand for sterling will shift to the right as domestic interest rates are increased and (ii) that the slope of the sterling demand curve is determined not only by trade flows but also by the effect of the exchange rate on capital movements.

Similarly, an expected future change in the exchange rate must affect the current exchange rate. If portfolio holders expect a currency to depreciate in the future, this will reduce demand for that currency, shifting the demand curve to the left in Figure 17.2, reducing the exchange rate today. It is now customary to analyse the exchange rate as an asset price, and the current price of any asset may embody all the information currently available which could affect its future price. Any new information (which we might call *news*) must therefore lead to a change in the current price of that asset. Therefore, it is not only current policy changes which affect the exchange rate, but also *expected* policy changes. Indeed, if policy changes were anticipated, by the time they are carried out, their effects may already be factored into the exchange rate. An obvious source of relevant news is credible announcements by the authorities about the future course of policy. It is arguable that the appreciation of sterling in 1979–81, evident in Figure 17.1, was partly attributable to a *Thatcher effect* whereby markets anticipated restrictive monetary policy and higher interest rates, and this caused the exchange rate to rise in advance of such measures being adopted. (This is not the only explanation of this episode. North Sea oil similarly generated expectations of a sterling appreciation at that time.)

Thus, interest rates and expectations of future capital movements are important determinants of capital flows, and therefore exchange rates, and are likely to be much more important in explaining short-term exchange rate movements (and at times instability). This, in turn, may have serious consequences for the current account and the real economy. If capital inflows bid up the exchange rate, this may reduce competitiveness and export demand.

■ ■ ■ 17.3.5 A fixed exchange rate system

Up to now, we have assumed that the authorities (the government and the central bank) are happy to see the exchange rate floating and responding freely to market conditions.

Figure 17.4
Intervention in the
foreign exchange
market

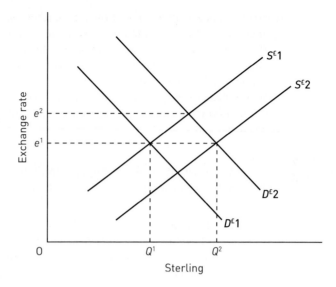

However, it may be that the authorities prefer to see the exchange rate fixed. The arguments for fixed as opposed to flexible exchange rates are central to the discussion about
the advantages and disadvantages of adopting the euro as the UK currency, and we review
these arguments later. Here, we simply outline how the authorities would seek to fix the
exchange rate and its implications for domestic monetary policy.

Consider Figure 17.4 where the initial equilibrium exchange rate is e^1. Suppose now
that the demand for sterling increases (perhaps reflecting a change of view in the market
that sterling is likely to appreciate in the future). As explained above, this will induce
international investors to increase their holdings of sterling assets now, so as to enjoy the
expected future capital gain which the expected appreciation would yield. This generates
a capital inflow and increased demand for sterling, shifting the demand for sterling curve
from $D^{£}1$ to $D^{£}2$. Under a regime of flexible exchange rates, this would lead sterling to
appreciate to e^2. Suppose, now, that the authorities wish the exchange rate to remain at
e^1. To secure this, the authorities must *intervene* in the foreign exchange market, selling
sterling and buying foreign exchange. (In this example, this would be recorded as an
increase in foreign exchange reserves in the balance of payments accounts). In Figure 17.4,
this would increase the supply of sterling and shift the supply curve to the right. In effect,
the central bank is standing prepared to sell as much sterling as the market wishes to buy
at the exchange rate e^1, and the supply curve has shifted to the right to the same extent as
the demand curve shift, *pegging* the exchange rate at e^1. Another way of describing this is
to say that the domestic country is running a balance of payments surplus (caused by the
capital inflow) of the amount $Q^1 - Q^2$, and is accumulating foreign exchange reserves at
the rate of $Q^1 - Q^2$ per period. (Note that, if the exchange rate were floating, there would
be no foreign exchange intervention, foreign exchange reserves would not change and
there would be neither a balance of payments surplus nor a deficit.)

Alternatively, consider a balance of payments deficit. Suppose, again starting from
equilibrium, there is a fall in domestic exports (perhaps reflecting falling world incomes).
In this case, the demand for sterling would fall, shifting the demand for sterling curve to
the left and putting downward pressure on the exchange rate. In this case, pegging the
exchange rate would require the authorities to sell foreign exchange and buy sterling, to
offset the excess supply of sterling on the foreign exchange market. This would mean that

foreign exchange reserves were being depleted. Of course, the domestic country could not persist with this policy ad infinitum as it does not possess an infinite stock of foreign exchange reserves. In the long run, the authorities would need to implement other policies to remove the balance of payments deficit and ease the downward pressure on sterling.

Operating a regime of fixed exchange rates by foreign exchange market intervention raises a number of important issues for the domestic authorities. First, it has implications for domestic monetary conditions. Assume a balance of payments surplus, so that pegging the exchange rate requires the authorities to sell sterling. Although this enables the central bank to accumulate foreign exchange reserves, it also increases the amount of sterling in circulation; that is, it increases the domestic money supply. This will tend to put downward pressure on domestic interest rates. Alternatively, when the balance of payments is in deficit, and the central bank is pegging the exchange rate by buying sterling (and running down its stock of foreign exchange reserves), the domestic money supply is being reduced, placing upward pressure on domestic interest rates.

Are the monetary consequences of exchange rate intervention avoidable? To some extent they are, if the domestic authorities undertake offsetting action. Such policies are referred to as *sterilization policies*. Take the case of a balance of payments surplus where excess demand for sterling is putting upward pressure on the exchange rate and the authorities are buying foreign exchange. As noted above, this increases the domestic money supply. However, the authorities might sell government bonds domestically to mop up the domestic monetary consequences of the foreign exchange intervention, using open market operations as described in Chapter 12. However, domestic residents need to be induced to buy these bonds, which may require increased interest rates. Similarly, in the case of a deficit and the authorities buying sterling, sterilization policies would require the authorities to buy bonds domestically, putting downward pressure on interest rates.

Sterilization policies are almost impossible in a world where international capital is highly mobile. If the authorities in a surplus country attempt to sterilize by selling bonds domestically, the consequent increase in domestic interest rates will induce a capital inflow, regenerating the initial balance of payments surplus, requiring further open market bond sales and higher interest rates, and so the cycle continues. Under conditions of highly mobile international capital, sterilization policies are impracticable and balance of payments surpluses and deficits must be reflected in changes in the domestic money supply. In short, if a country wishes to operate a fixed exchange rate regime under conditions of capital mobility, it must surrender control of its domestic money supply. Economists sometimes refer to fixed exchange rates, independent monetary policy and free capital movements as *the impossible trilogy*. It is impossible to have all three.

The above analysis also gives a clue about how inflation can spread internationally under fixed exchange rates. A high-inflation country is likely to be running a balance of payments deficit with respect to a low-inflation trading partner for reasons of competitiveness discussed earlier. Under fixed exchange rates, not only will the price of imports into the low-inflation country be rising, but that country will also be running a balance of payments surplus due to its increased competitiveness. In the absence of successful sterilization policies, its money stock will be increasing as a counterpart to this surplus, and this will be inflationary. Many economists attributed the upsurge in world inflation in the late 1960s and early 1970s to the US balance of payments deficit (arising partly out of the Vietnam War) and the increase in the world money supply which this generated.

The development of international capital markets has made it very difficult for one country's authorities to effectively peg the exchange rate by means of intervention policies alone. The potential scale of capital movements is now so large relative to the foreign exchange reserves of most individual countries that they do not have the financial muscle to out-buy or out-sell the market. For example, suppose the authorities attempt to set the exchange rate at a level which the market believes to be too high (or alternatively sets interest rates at a level which is too low for that exchange rate). There will be a large-scale capital outflow. To maintain the exchange rate by means of intervention, the authorities would have to purchase all the sterling being sold as the counterpart of the capital outflow and, even if they had sufficient reserves to do this, the monetary contraction caused by the purchases of sterling would imply unacceptably high interest rates. This is not to say that the authorities cannot determine their exchange rate, but that, in order to do so, they must implement domestic monetary policies consistent with their exchange rate target so that the market accepts the exchange rate as *credible*. It is to a discussion of the interrelationships between exchange rates and domestic macroeconomic policies that we turn in the next section.

Exercise 17.4

Starting from a balance of payments equilibrium, what form of intervention would be required to peg the exchange rate if:

1 there was a sudden switch in tastes away from domestic exports?
2 world inflation surged ahead of domestic inflation?

17.4 Monetary and fiscal policies in an open economy

The aim of this section is to compare the effectiveness of monetary and fiscal policies under fixed and freely floating exchange rate regimes, assuming a high degree of capital mobility. We have just seen that the authorities cannot hope to peg the exchange rate by means of intervention in the foreign exchange market unless they are following a domestic monetary policy which is believed by agents in that market to be consistent with their exchange rate target. The implication is that the authorities can control monetary policy (setting the money supply or interest rates) or the exchange rate, but not both. In an open economy with international capital mobility, the authorities can control domestic monetary policy, provided they permit the exchange rate to respond freely to market forces, or they can fix the exchange rate, provided they implement whatever monetary policy is necessary to win credibility on the foreign exchange market.

■ ■ ■ 17.4.1 Monetary and fiscal policies under fixed exchange rates

Let us consider how monetary policy is affected by adoption of a fixed exchange rate regime. Suppose first that aggregate demand has been increased by means of expansionary monetary policy with fiscal policy kept neutral (i.e. fiscal policy is neither expansionary nor contractionary). Let us think of expansionary monetary policy as open market bond purchases by the central bank, having the effect both of increasing the money supply and reducing interest rates. Given international capital mobility, lower interest rates are difficult to sustain, as this leads to a substantial capital outflow, putting downward pressure on the exchange rate. In the face of this, the authorities cannot peg the exchange rate by sterilized intervention. If the exchange rate is to be defended, the interest rate must be raised back towards its original level. Another way of telling the same story is that the expansionary monetary policy has provoked a massive capital outflow, reducing the money supply back towards its original level. The greater the degree of capital mobility, the greater will be the capital outflow, and the greater will be the offsetting fall in the domestic money stock. Under perfect capital mobility, monetary policy is completely ineffective. Thus, under fixed exchange rates, the authorities lose control of the money supply and interest rates to an extent dependent upon the degree of capital mobility.

By contrast, the effectiveness of fiscal policy accompanied by a neutral monetary policy may be enhanced under fixed exchange rates, at least in the short run. If it was unaccompanied by any increase in the money stock, then a fiscal expansion will place upward pressure on domestic interest rates (as the government increases borrowing to finance the fiscal expansion). In a closed economy, this increase in interest rates would tend to dampen the effects of the fiscal expansion but, in an open economy, it will generate a capital inflow with results which are the opposite of the monetary policy case. The capital inflow increases the domestic money stock and reduces interest rates back towards world levels. Thus, fiscal policy is likely to be more effective than monetary policy under fixed exchange rates.

The notion of fiscal expansion generating a balance of payments surplus, even in the short run, may seem counter-intuitive. Certainly, the expansion will cause the current account of the balance of payments to move towards deficit as increased domestic spending sucks in imports. The point is that this is more than offset by a short-run capital account surplus reflecting the higher domestic interest rates associated with the fiscal expansion. However, unless there is perfect capital mobility (i.e. a perfectly elastic supply of world capital funds available to be borrowed by the domestic country), it is unlikely that the domestic economy will be able to borrow indefinitely to finance its current account deficit at a given interest rate. In the long run, it will come under pressure to take measures to correct the current account deficit, and the exchange rate will similarly come under pressure.

Question	Do current account deficits always tend to weaken the exchange rate?

A distinction is sometimes drawn between *good* current account deficits and *bad* current account deficits. An example of the former might be a deficit which is the counterpart of a domestic investment boom sucking in imports and the economy borrowing from abroad to finance more rapid economic growth. A country with a *good* current account would find it easy to attract international capital (in the same way as a successful rapidly growing firm would find it easy to obtain funding on the stock market), and the capital inflow will keep the exchange rate relatively strong. Certain South-east Asian economies (at least before the crisis of 1997–98) and the USA in the second half of the 1990s are examples of this. By contrast, a *bad* current account deficit might be one which is caused by a domestic consumption boom, perhaps encouraged by imprudent fiscal policies, which are viewed by markets as unsustainable. An extreme example of this might be the Mexican economic crisis of the early 1990s, when there was capital flight and a collapse of the peso. This is also an example of domestic economic policies rendering the level of the exchange rate non-credible.

■ ■ ■ 17.4.2 Monetary and fiscal policies under flexible exchange rates

How are these results altered by operating under flexible exchange rates? Again, let us start with the example of expansionary monetary policy, in the form of open-market bond purchases by the government increasing the money supply and reducing interest rates. Again, this will induce investors to sell sterling and buy foreign assets, but, under flexible exchange rates, this will lead not to a balance of payments deficit, as under fixed exchange rates, but rather to a fall in the exchange rate. What happens to domestic interest rates and to the domestic economy? The fall in the exchange rate permits the domestic interest rate to fall relative to foreign interest rates because of uncovered interest parity. The exchange rate falls enough to lead foreign investors to expect a rise in the exchange rate in the future. This expected appreciation is then consistent with a lower domestic interest rate. At the same time, the lower exchange rate increases export competitiveness, further enhancing the effectiveness of the monetary expansion. In summary, then, a flexible exchange rate regime affords greater sovereignty to domestic monetary policy and enhances its effectiveness.

Contrast this with the case of expansionary fiscal policy. As noted earlier, fiscal expansion places upward pressure on domestic interest rates, inducing investors to switch from foreign to domestic assets. This generates excess demand for sterling in the foreign exchange market and a rise in the exchange rate. This leads to a fall in competitiveness and net exports, reducing the effectiveness of the fiscal expansion. Again, however, this result needs to be accepted with care, as it depends on the argument that fiscal expansion generates an exchange rate appreciation. Given that fiscal expansion is likely to be associated with a weakening current account position, it may be that the exchange rate appreciation does not survive in the long run. In addition, both the fixed and flexible exchange rate outcomes for fiscal policy depend on the assumption that fiscal expansion leads to increased interest rates, which may not be the case if, for example, the fiscal expansion is financed by borrowing from the central bank (i.e. by increasing the money supply).

In conclusion, it is clear that monetary policy is strengthened by a regime of flexible exchange rates. Indeed, the response of the exchange rate to monetary policy actions becomes a key element in the transmission mechanism of monetary policy. This conclusion is particularly important for anti-inflation policy. Suppose the Bank of England increases interest rates in an attempt to reduce the inflation rate. Under flexible exchange rates, the resultant appreciation validates the higher domestic interest rate, which has effects on domestic demand. In addition, however, the appreciation has two further important effects on inflation. Not only does the appreciation reduce net exports and therefore demand pressures in the economy, it also reduces import costs (as the sterling price of imports falls). The conclusions for fiscal policy are slightly less clear. If fiscal expansion generates a capital inflow, then fiscal policy becomes more effective under fixed exchange rates and less effective under flexible exchange rates. However, these results depend partly on how markets react to the likely current account deficit arising from fiscal expansion, especially in the long run.

17.5 The euro

■ ■ ■ 17.5.1 The movement towards a single european currency – the ERM

The proposal for a European Monetary Union was first set out in the Werner Plan in 1970, which envisaged the gradual harmonization of exchange rate policies in the EU. These plans were derailed by the breakdown of the Bretton Woods system and the widespread adoption of floating exchange rates, but the setting-up of the European Monetary System (EMS) in 1979 gave fresh impetus to the process. The key element in the EMS was the introduction of the Exchange Rate Mechanism (ERM), whereby six member countries (France, West Germany, Belgium, Denmark, the Netherlands and Ireland) undertook to keep their bilateral exchange rates stabilized with respect to each other within bands of the agreed central bilateral rates (these bands were fixed at 2.25 per cent until 1993). Once bilateral rates reached these bands, the two central banks concerned were to intervene in the market to push the exchange rate back towards its central rate. The central points of the bilateral rates were agreed at the outset, but these could be changed by negotiated agreement. Such realignments were quite common in the first half of the 1980s, but became much less frequent as the system bedded down. Thus, between 1979 and 1983 there were seven realignments, while between February 1987 and September 1992 there were none. Over time, other countries joined the ERM. The UK joined in October 1990, but only stayed until September 1992. In the course of the summer of 1992, the system effectively broke down under successive waves of speculation against individual currencies. The lira, sterling, the peseta, the escudo and the punt were all devalued. The UK suspended its membership of the ERM in October 1992 and the remaining members widened parity bands to ±15 per cent. As a dummy run for the euro, the ERM seemed to have failed. (For a full analysis of the ERM episode, see Artis and Lewis, 1993).

The immediate cause of the collapse of the ERM was the *asymmetric shock* to the European economy provided by German reunification. This was essentially an inflationary shock which impinged on Germany but not directly on the rest of Europe. Germany's preferred response to this shock would have been a Deutschmark revaluation, but other members (particularly France) resisted this, partly on the grounds of maintaining the credibility of the system. In the absence of such a realignment, Germany increased domestic interest rates, placing other ERM countries under pressure to follow in order to keep their exchange rates within the ERM parity bands. This meant, particularly in the case of the UK, that domestic monetary policy was constrained from pursuing domestic objectives. German rates were rising just at the time when the UK authorities were attempting to reduce rates in order to encourage a recovery from domestic recession. In a sense, the collapse of the ERM exemplified the impossible trilogy mentioned earlier (Section 17.3.5), and the commitment to a fixed exchange rate was abandoned by the UK.

17.5.2 The Maastricht Treaty and the introduction of the euro

Even before the ERM crisis of 1992, the Maastricht Treaty (which translated the European Community (EC) into the European Union (EU)) was signed, committing Europe to the introduction of a common currency and European Monetary Union. (For a full account, see Zestos, 2006.) On 1 January 1999 exchange rates between members of the Eurozone were irrevocably fixed, expressed in terms of the euro. Euros could be used for various transactions (including foreign exchange transactions) and held as private bank accounts, and on 1 January 2002 the euro physically came into being with the replacement of national currencies by euro notes and coins. However, during the 1990s much macroeconomic groundwork had to be laid as preparation for the introduction of the new currency.

Most importantly, the prospective members of the Eurozone had to comply with certain key macroeconomic conditions to demonstrate that their economies had successfully *converged*. These conditions were known as the five Maastricht criteria. They can be summarized as follows:

- Inflation rate no more than 1.5 percentage points above the average inflation rate of the three countries with the lowest rate of inflation.

- Long-term interest rate no more than 2 percentage points higher than the average of the lowest three inflation countries.
- Budget deficit of no more than 3 per cent of GDP.
- Government debt-to-GDP ratio of no more than 60 per cent.
- Exchange rates within the parities of the ERM.

Once the common currency was in place, the European Central Bank (ECB) would implement a common monetary policy for the entire Eurozone and the convergence criteria were designed to ensure that the member countries' economic cycles, interest rates, exchange rates and inflation rates would be reasonably synchronized. In addition, each potential member country was required to enact legislation conferring an appropriate degree of independence on their national central bank, in line with the envisaged independence of the ECB, of which national central banks would essentially become branches.

During the 1990s, candidate countries' performance in achieving the Maastricht criteria were carefully monitored, and in 1998, 11 countries were admitted to the Eurozone (Austria, Belgium, Germany, Finland, France, Italy, Ireland, Luxemburg, the Netherlands, Portugal and Spain) and these were later joined by Greece. However, the criteria with respect to fiscal deficits and, more significantly, government debt were not strictly applied. In 1998, Greece ran a fiscal deficit of 4 per cent of GDP and the debt-to-GDP ratios of Austria, Belgium, Germany, Greece, Ireland, Italy, the Netherlands, Portugal and Spain all exceeded the Maastricht limit of 60 per cent. Moreover, in some cases the fiscal deficit reductions were achieved either by some creative accountancy or by one-off measures which had only temporary impact.

The euro was traded on foreign exchange markets from the beginning of 1999. Over the first two years, it depreciated by around 20 per cent, but thereafter recovered much of its value. This pattern is largely, but not entirely, a reflection of the performance of the dollar over the same period, as private capital flowed into the USA. It is possible that some of the initial weakness of the euro also reflected the substantial compromises in the application of the Maastricht criteria.

▪▪▪ 17.5.3 The economic case for fixed exchange rates

To a large extent, the arguments in favour of a common currency are the same as those for an individual country pegging its exchange rate (see Krugman, 1989). These arguments are briefly set out below.

Reduction in exchange rate uncertainty and risk

Unstable exchange rates increase risks and uncertainties, and therefore costs of international trade. These risks can be insured against by operating in the forward exchange market (i.e. agreeing to buy or sell currency at a future date, but at an exchange rate determined today). However, this is costly and forward markets are thin beyond 6 months. This case is stronger the more trade is concentrated with the country (or countries) with which the exchange rate is fixed. Note that some less-developed countries which peg their exchange rate to the dollar can suffer from the dollar's exchange rate fluctuations. A good example here is Argentina, whose currency board arrangements were pegged to the dollar, but whose trade was not particularly concentrated with the USA.

The anti-inflation discipline argument

Governments face the temptation to run fiscal deficits and to finance these deficits by printing money (i.e. borrowing from the central bank). Under fixed exchange rates, this would lead to balance of payments difficulties and exchange rate pressures which would require the government to implement deflationary policies. Under flexible exchange rates, this discipline would be removed. More particularly, under fixed exchange rates high-inflation countries hope to benefit from the domestic monetary policy of the low-inflation partner. If the low-inflation partner's central bank enjoys greater credibility than the domestic central bank, this will make anti-inflation policy more efficient. This was largely the argument in favour of the UK shadowing the Deutschmark in the 1980s and joining the ERM in the 1990s. It is essentially an extension of the argument that under fixed exchange rates, the economy is not insulated from world inflation shocks, but in this case, the world inflation shocks are favourable. The counter-argument, as we shall see, is that this amounts to a loss of monetary sovereignty, which may be costly in the event of an asymmetric shock. Moreover, the argument relies on the assumption that the fixed exchange rate partner is, indeed, a low-inflation economy with a central bank blessed with a high reputation.

A more stable exchange rate environment

The argument here is that flexible exchange rates will be more unstable than fixed exchange rates and that this instability has macroeconomic costs (as well as costs to traders). While this may appear self-evident, there are a number of points to be borne in mind. First, it is the instability of real exchange rates which is relevant, and fixing nominal exchange rates may simply make real exchange rates unstable if countries are subject to asymmetric inflationary shocks. Second, it is not necessarily the case that flexible exchange rates are unstable. Proponents of floating rates argue that flexibility does not mean volatility, on the grounds that the actions of speculators should ensure that exchange rates are always at, or at least adjusting towards, their equilibrium value. Speculators, on this view, buy when the price is *too low* and sell when the price is *too high*. Speculators who consistently make mistakes will go out of business.

Question | **Does this mean that speculators always make exchange rates more, rather than less, stable?**

Not necessarily. Frequently asset markets are driven by the herd instinct, where speculative surges in the market can feed upon themselves and market expectations become self-fulfilling. A closely related notion is that of a *speculative bubble* where even rational speculators know that the exchange rate is, for example, rising progressively away from equilibrium, but their belief that the bubble is not quite ready to burst means that they perceive the prospect of a further capital gain which is just enough to compensate them for the risk of the bubble bursting prematurely. In any case, speculators may also be rational, but act on false information. *News* may trigger a change in exchange rates, but when this news transpires to be false, the exchange rate adjusts back, adding to instability. Finally, it can be demonstrated that a small number of irrational or ill-informed speculators can exert a disproportionate degree of instability on markets before they eventually go out of business.

■ ■ ■ 17.5.4   A common currency: some further issues

The issues raised by the adoption of a common currency are essentially an extension of those for fixed exchange rates set out in Section 17.5.3, but with the following important additions. (For a full account see De Grauwe, 2003.)

One currency

Under a common currency, not only are there gains to be made through the elimination of exchange risk, but there are also gains from the fact that prices are quoted in a single currency. Currencies no longer need to be exchanged, reducing transaction costs (estimated to be around 1 per cent of GDP), while price comparisons between countries are now transparent, increasing the degree of competition and therefore a spur to efficiency.

One monetary policy

Although it is implicit in the analysis of fixed exchange rates with capital mobility that individual countries lose their domestic monetary sovereignty, this is much more explicit in the case of a common currency area. In the Eurozone, monetary policy is conducted by the European Central Bank. To maximize the anti-inflation credentials of the ECB, its constitution (substantially modelled on that of the Bundesbank) ensures its independence and sets out *price stability* as its primary objective, setting a ceiling of 2 per cent in the inflation rate. The key point is, of course, that within the Eurozone, whatever short-term interest rate is set by the ECB applies in all the member countries. This has come to be known as the *one size fits all* monetary policy, and this is the loss of monetary sovereignty of the individual countries. The key question is, of course, whether one size will indeed fit all, or whether the interest rate policy of the ECB will be inappropriate for individual countries.

The potential problem of asymmetric shocks

The loss of monetary sovereignty and the possibility of inappropriate monetary policies for individual countries is an important potential cost of a common currency area. It is usually argued that a greater degree of real economic integration within the area will lower these costs. This is because the more integrated the economies are, the less susceptible they will be to asymmetric shocks. An *asymmetric shock* is a macroeconomic disturbance which affects one economy differently from others within the economic union. Asymmetric shocks may arise from a number of sources. An individual economy may have a particular structure of extra-zone trade, making it differentially vulnerable to specific disturbances. Italy, for example, competes to a greater degree than other EU countries with South-east Asian economies in traditional sectors such as textiles. This meant that the exchange rate consequences of the Asian crisis of 1997–98 had particular effects on Italy. Alternatively, it may be that certain economies are more inflation prone. For example, it is sometimes argued that countries with more centralized wage bargaining structures are better able to absorb supply-side inflation shocks than those with more decentralized systems.

Let us suppose Germany experiences a fall in aggregate demand relative to the rest of the Eurozone and enters recession. To the extent that the German shock impacts on the Eurozone as a whole the ECB might cut interest rates, but not by as much as Germany would require to alleviate the recession. The situation could be resolved in a number of ways within the euro framework. First, Germany could implement fiscal expansion. However, this could be constrained by the Stability and Growth Pact (see below). Alternatively, fiscal transfers could be made within the EU budget, but the scope for this is limited. The centralized EU budget is less than 1.5 per cent of GDP. Second, wage and price flexibility, especially in Germany in this example, where the unemployment caused by the fall in aggregate demand could place downward pressure on wages and prices, and increase the profitability and competitiveness of German firms, offsetting the initial negative demand shock. This is the classical adjustment mechanism where the exchange rate cannot be changed. But many believe that such an adjustment would be painful. (A similar adjustment would be required if an economy exhibited a higher inflation rate within the Eurozone.) The alternative adjustment would be through migration, with labour moving from Germany to the rest of Europe, but this assumes greater regional mobility of labour than perhaps exists.

Doubt about the efficacy of these mechanisms implies that the absence of independent monetary policy is a correspondingly important cost for a common currency area. In the above example, flexible exchange rates would enable Germany to cut interest rates, resulting in a German deprecation which would offset the asymmetric shock. But this assumes that exchange rate changes work. As we noted earlier, it is adjustments in the real exchange rate which are required and, if German workers adjust their wages in line with increased import costs, the nominal depreciation of the exchange rate will not translate into to a real depreciation.

It is usually argued that the more integrated economies are, the lower the costs of loss of monetary sovereignty. (It is sometimes also argued that joining a common currency might encourage economic integration.) First, greater integration would increase the effect of a depreciation on import costs and domestic prices, making it more difficult to effect a real depreciation. Second, a greater degree of integration might imply a lower likelihood of asymmetric shocks (European Commission, 1990). The argument here is that greater integration brings with it more intra-industry trade, so that changes in demand or cost conditions are likely to be spread more evenly across all countries. (Note that this view has been questioned in Krugman (1991) who argues that economies of scale might lead to more, rather than less, regional concentration of production, citing the US car industry as an example.)

Fiscal policy in a common currency: the Stability and Growth Pact

The implication of the above discussion is that, following an asymmetric shock, it would fall to fiscal policy to stabilize the economy. Sticking to our original example, the effects of the fall in aggregate demand in Germany could be offset by fiscal expansion in that country. For this to work, the German authorities would need to have enough independence in setting domestic government expenditure and tax rates. However, within the Eurozone, this independence is curtailed by the Stability and Growth Pact (SGP).

Essentially, the SGP is the continuation of some of the Maastricht convergence criteria. The essence of the Pact is that budgets should be balanced in the long run, but during recessions deficits of up to 3 per cent of GDP are permitted (or more, if the recession has reduced GDP by 2 per cent in a given year). In addition, debt-to-GDP ratios are to be held at 60 per cent. In 2004, Greece (110 per cent), Italy (105 per cent), Belgium (95 per cent), Germany (66 per cent), France (65 per cent), Austria (65 per cent) and Portugal (62 per cent) were in violation. Given the absence of any significant centralized fiscal policy in the EU, the SGP can be seen as a compromise between two sets of considerations – stabilization policy and fiscal discipline. On the one hand, autonomous national fiscal policies may be required to manage asymmetric shocks, so that countries should be able to run deficits during recessions. Whether this would reflect discretionary fiscal policy or simply the operation of automatic stabilizers would depend on the severity of the recession and the underlying fiscal stance of the country. However, the Pact places greater emphasis on the need for fiscal discipline. If national governments do not exert fiscal discipline, there is the danger that active use of fiscal policy may generate excessive deficits (some economists worry about the problem of *fiscal deficit bias*), which in turn could threaten either the inflation target of the ECB or financial stability. Large fiscal deficits can generate an unsustainable debt/deficit position, when governments cannot levy sufficient taxes to pay interest on outstanding debt and therefore borrow more, increasing the interest burden and generating a spiral of increasing indebtedness. Under flexible exchange rates (i.e. with monetary sovereignty), an obvious option is to resort to financing the deficit by increasing the money supply, which generates inflation and reduces the real value of the outstanding debt. This option does not exist within a monetary union and so the outcome of excessive fiscal deficits would be increasing interest rates, partly in the form of an increase in the risk premium of the country in question, but possibly also some increase in interest rates in the Eurozone as a whole. The latter effect would increase the debt financing costs of the other countries. In extreme cases, this could threaten financial stability in the Eurozone, and might even persuade the ECB to relent on its inflation target and co-operate in the monetizing of the debt.

Either way, this is not an attractive proposition, and it was principally to remove this prospect that the SGP was devised. The other side of the coin is, of course, that the possible role for fiscal policy in confronting asymmetric shocks is reduced. With economies aiming for fiscal balance in the medium term, during recessions the fiscal deficit may be increased to 3 per cent of GDP. Is this enough flexibility? Evidence from the early 1990s suggests that even with a less than 2 per cent fall in GDP, deficits increased by more than 3 per cent. More recently, in the past few years, economic slowdown has resulted in deficits greater than 3 per cent of GDP in France, Germany, Greece, Portugal and the Netherlands. Crucially, the EU has not employed the sanctions available to it for those countries breaking the Pact, and the future of the SGP in its current form has been thrown into considerable doubt.

Question	What would happen if an economy suffered a recession such that automatic stabilizers generated a deficit in excess of 3 per cent, but GDP had not fallen by 2 per cent?

In such a case, to abide within the SGP the unfortunate economy would have to either increase tax rates or cut government expenditure. This would, of course, make the recession worse and destabilize the cycle. Reform of the SGP is very much on the EU agenda.

Case study: The UK and the euro

As we all know, the UK has opted not to join the European Monetary Union (EMU) and adopt the euro, at least for the time being. There are a number of reasons for this observed reluctance. The UK economy is, economically, not one of the core members of the Eurozone (Germany, France, Italy, Austria and the Benelux countries). Although UK trade with the EU has grown substantially from around one-third of UK trade in 1970 to more than half now, this is still a smaller proportion than the UK's European partners. Similarly, over the last 10 years UK inflation has been higher more often than lower than the euro-average, implying a potentially painful adjustment. (Note the trend of the real exchange rate relative to the nominal exchange rate in Figure 17.1.) At the same time, estimates of the appropriate entry rate for sterling into the Eurozone tended to indicate that sterling was over-valued. For example, Wren-Lewis (2003) estimated an appropriate entry rate of £1 = 1.37 euros – somewhat higher than previous estimates, but still lower than the then current rate of around £1 = 1.45 euros. This means that an appropriate entry rate would require a devaluation of sterling with associated inflationary pressures. There are also fears that there is an in-built asymmetry in the UK economy attributable to the importance of the housing market. The importance of mortgage rates and house prices in affecting household expenditure, and the greater importance of short-term variable rate mortgages, mean that interest rates may have a stronger effect on consumption expenditure in the UK than elsewhere in Europe. So, even if there was a symmetric shock, the ECB's interest rate response could have asymmetric effects on the UK.

Monetary and fiscal policy considerations also play their part in a certain reluctance to join. The anti-inflation credibility argument which was so important in the 1980s and early 1990s does not seem so persuasive now. The Bank of England was given interest-rate-setting independence as soon as Gordon Brown became Chancellor of the Exchequer in the 1997 Labour government, and most commentators see the move as successful, with inflation being consistently lower (Chapter 13). The argument for handing over this task to the ECB, with the consequent loss of monetary sovereignty, is correspondingly weaker. Some observers also argue that the Bank of England's inflation targeting rule (where under-shooting the target is just as unacceptable in theory as overshooting the target) avoids the deflationary bias which, it is alleged, is implicit in the ECB's target, which is in the form of a ceiling.

For fiscal policy, Britain has its own version of the Stability and Growth Pact: Gordon Brown's *golden rule* (whereby the current budget has to be balanced over the economic cycle, but government investment can be financed by borrowing at any time) and the *sustainable investment rule* (which aims to keep the debt to GDP ratio below 40 per cent). The perceived advantages of the UK framework over the SGP are:

- Balancing the budget over the cycle allows automatic stabilizers to work. Recall that the SGP makes no formal reference to cyclical influences on the budget.
- Financing investment expenditure by borrowing means that future generations partly pay for projects from which they will derive benefit. It also means that public investment is, to some extent, ring-fenced from fiscal policy. Recall that the SGP makes no distinction between current and capital expenditure.

More generally, the domestic political costs of sterling's dramatic exit from the ERM have not been forgotten by UK politicians. At the same time, it is more difficult to persuade domestic voters of the case for joining at a time when, in terms of economic growth and unemployment, the UK is performing relatively well outside the Eurozone.

Question

Look back at the economic case for a single currency set out in Section 17.5.3. What long-term benefits might membership of the single currency bring to the UK economy?

It is the government's view that there are long-term benefits to be derived from EMU membership (HM Treasury, 2003). In particular, the reduction of transactions costs and exchange rate risk afforded by a common currency would encourage a significant growth in UK–Eurozone trade of up to 50 per cent over a 30-year period, boosting GDP by up to 9 per cent over the same period. In addition, it is possible that euro membership will encourage inward direct investment into the UK, as a base in Europe. However, to inform the final decision, the government devised five economic tests to determine whether the government could recommend membership before putting the matter to a referendum (HM Treasury, 2003.) The five economic tests are:

- Has the UK economy converged sufficiently to accept the ECB-determined interest rate?
- Is the economy sufficiently flexible to cope with an asymmetric shock?
- Would EMU membership encourage and foster increased long-term investment in the UK (through lower long-term interest rates in Europe and increased foreign direct investment)?
- Would EMU membership benefit the competitive position of the UK financial sector?
- Would EMU membership benefit economic growth, stability and employment?

After widespread consultation and research, the government announced in 2003 that the first two tests had not been passed, although it should be noted that UK labour and product markets are quite flexible by European standards. The euro-decision was put on hold, and in the 2005 Budget speech Gordon Brown stated, 'In this Budget, the Treasury does not propose to initiate a further euro assessment.' It would seem that, whatever benefits might accrue to the UK economy in the long run, early entry into the EMU and replacement of the pound by the euro in UK shops is not likely.

17.6 Conclusion

A great deal of this chapter has been about understanding foreign exchange markets and the implications of trading currencies for determining exchange rates in both short and long run. We also discussed the macroeconomic variables that could be affected by the exchange rate, such as the price level, interest rates and ultimately aggregate demand in the economy. The nature of the exchange rate regime emerged as a decisive factor in the ability of governments to control these macroeconomic variables.

Under fixed exchange rates the authorities lose control over domestic liquidity. They must therefore choose between a monetary target and an exchange rate target. This result depends crucially on the assumption that capital is internationally mobile; in fact, the world economy has moved in this direction. The consequence is not only that monetary and exchange rate targets are incompatible but also that fixed exchange rate systems, however appealing their perceived benefits, are hard to sustain. Under flexible exchange rates, the inflation of the domestic economy relative to those of its international competitors and the interest rate differential between domestic and foreign currencies become the most important determinants of the exchange rate. Unless a new worldwide exchange rate system emerges to replace Bretton Woods the choice facing European policy makers (including those in the UK) is, therefore, between a single currency, such as the euro, or floating exchange rates.

Questions for review and discussion

Question 1 (a) The bilateral exchange rate between US dollars (US$) and Canadian dollars (C$) is given by C$/US$ (the amount of Canadian dollars required to purchase one US dollar). Draw supply and demand schedules for US dollars in terms of C$/US$ and determine the equilibrium exchange rate. Illustrate the effect on the equilibrium exchange of (i) a deterioration in the US trade balance with Canada and (ii) a rise in US interest rates relative to Canadian interest rates. Explain briefly your answers.

(b) Using the data in columns 1–5 of Table 17.3, discuss how both short-term and long-term influences on the foreign exchange market can help explain the exchange rate movements depicted in column (6).

Table 17.3
US–Canadian exchange rate movements

Year	US–Canadian trade balance[1] US$bn (1)	Inflation rate % US (2)	Canada (3)	Interest rates[2] % US (4)	Canada (5)	Exchange rate[3] C$/US$ (6)
1997	−17.9	2.3	1.6	5.62	3.53	1.39
1998	−20.7	1.6	1.0	5.47	5.04	1.48
1999	−34.4	1.9	1.8	5.33	4.89	1.49
2000	−52.8	3.7	2.6	6.46	5.78	1.49
2001	−53.2	2.8	3.5	3.69	3.98	1.55
2002	−49.8	1.6	1.2	1.73	2.62	1.57
2003	−54.7	2.3	2.8	1.15	2.97	1.40
2004	−66.8	2.9	1.5	1.56	2.31	1.30

Notes:
[1] Minus sign denotes US trading deficit with Canada (www.ita.doc.gov)
[2] Interest rates based on three-month short-term rates
[3] Exchange rate expressed as the amount of Canadian dollars (CAD) to purchase one US dollar ($)
Source: OECD *Main Economic Indicators*, various issues (www.oecd.org)

Question 2 (a) Imagine there is an unexpected increase in aggregate demand in the UK, brought about by expansionary monetary policy under a system of freely floating exchange rates. Outline the impact of this increase in aggregate demand on the UK exchange rate, explaining clearly the direction of movement of the long-term exchange rate. How would your answer differ if the monetary expansion had been anticipated?

(b) Table 17.4 gives the sterling exchange rate against the yen and the interest rates in Japan and UK for the period 1993–2000.
  (i)   Plot these data as a line chart.
  (ii) Has the pound appreciated or depreciated against the yen since 1993?
  (iii) To what extent do the data in Table 17.4 help you to explain the movement of the exchange rate between the pound and the yen? What other factors might be relevant?

Table 17.4
UK and Japanese
exchange rates and
interest rates
1993–2000

Year	Exchange rate (£1 = ? yen)	Interest rate in UK	Interest rate in Japan
1993	166.73	3.97	2.14
1994	156.40	3.66	1.70
1995	148.37	4.11	0.90
1996	170.00	3.05	0.30
1997	198.12	3.63	0.30
1998	216.75	4.48	0.27
1999	183.94	–	0.12
2000	163.27	–	0.07

Question 3 (a) Briefly outline the factors that determine the exchange rate, distinguishing between short-run and long-run factors.

(b) Imagine there is a recession in the USA and a widespread expectation that interest rates will remain low or fall further. How will these expectations affect the exchange rate for the dollar? Give reasons for your answer.

(c) Consider the exchange rate of the pound against a basket of foreign currencies shown in Figure 17.1. To what extent do the data confirm what you have learnt about the influences on the exchange rate?

18

Unemployment and inflation

Graham Dawson

Concepts

- unemployment
- inflation
- the Phillips curve
- adaptive and rational expectations
- the long-run vertical Phillips curve
- monetary policy rule
- the aggregate demand/inflation curve

Objectives

After studying this chapter you should be able to:

- discuss different estimates of the costs of unemployment and inflation
- understand different interpretations of the relationship between unemployment and inflation
- understand changes in the policy response to unemployment and inflation.

18.1 Introduction

In the late 1970s and early 1980s, policy makers throughout the large OECD economies abandoned the goal of full employment that had guided macroeconomic policy throughout the 1950s and 1960s and made their first priority the elimination of inflation. They did so because they believed that inflation does more damage to the economy than unemployment, in part because they became convinced that inflation itself caused unemployment. This change in macroeconomic policy was taken a step further in the 1990s as first the EU and then the UK government delegated the control of interest rates, the crucial weapon in 'the battle against inflation', to their respective central banks. Thirty years earlier, UK finance ministers and their economic advisers had made short-run adjustments in interest rates (and other macroeconomic policy instruments affecting aggregate demand) with the aim of reducing unemployment by allowing inflation to rise or curbing inflation at the cost of higher unemployment. Today, finance ministers throughout the EU set a strategic objective of price stability (in practice, an inflation rate very close to zero) and leave it to their central banks to decide on the level of interest rates that will achieve it. The aim of this chapter is to examine the reasons for this change in policy regime.

Section 18.2 examines the underlying principle of much macroeconomic policy-making in the 1950s and 1960s: that there was an inverse relationship between unemployment and inflation. The issue for policy makers was to achieve an appropriate balance between them, for example by trading off higher inflation for lower unemployment. In these circumstances it is important to decide which is the more serious problem – inflation or unemployment? Why does getting inflation down matter? What price is paid for getting inflation down when unemployment increases – and who pays it? Section 18.3 assesses the costs of unemployment and inflation. The outcome of this inquiry is that the costs of high rates of inflation are substantial. Section 18.4 examines theoretical developments that have influenced macroeconomic policy from the 1970s onwards, based on the argument that there is a risk that moderate inflation will accelerate into high inflation. The policy implications are discussed in Section 18.5, using current UK macroeconomic policy as a case study. In this way the chapter seeks to explain why, in 1997, the UK government granted the central bank a greater degree of independence in operating monetary policy and why the focus of policies for economic stabilization has shifted from the management of aggregate demand to the reform of the supply side.

18.2 The trade-off between inflation and unemployment

Unemployment

An unemployed person is someone who is actively seeking work but unable to find it. The total of those working and seeking work constitutes the labour force. The unemployment rate expresses the number of unemployed people as a percentage of the labour force.

The fundamental dilemma confronting economic policy makers is to decide whether government intervention in the economy will improve its performance or make things worse. Whatever the area of economic policy under consideration, there is no escape from the disturbing thought that any policy intervention itself might do more harm than good. The idea of a trade-off between unemployment and inflation is directly relevant to this dilemma in the macroeconomic field. This trade-off, expressed in the Phillips curve analysis outlined below, was developed in the 1960s into a guide for policy makers whose main objective was full employment:

one could achieve and maintain a permanently low level of unemployment merely by tolerating a permanently high level of inflation.

(Mankiw, 1990, p.1647)

The aim of this section is to examine the relationship between **unemployment** and **inflation** that informed macroeconomic policy-making in many countries during the 1960s.

■ ■ ■ 18.2.1 The Phillips curve

Inflation

Inflation is a rise in the general level of prices. The rate of inflation measures the annual percentage increase in the general level of prices.

The first step in answering the question of whether there is a trade-off between unemployment and inflation is to inspect the annual rates of inflation and unemployment over a reasonably long period of time and see if unemployment comes down when inflation goes up and vice versa. This is almost what Phillips (1958) did for the British economy, initially for the period 1861–1913. It is not *exactly* what he did, because, while we think of inflation as a rise in the general level of *prices*, Phillips plotted the rate of *wage* inflation (i.e. the rate of increase of the general level of wages) against the unemployment rate. The result of fitting a curve through these data points was an initially steep curve becoming

Figure 18.1
The original Phillips curve for the British economy 1861–1913
Source: Phillips, 1958

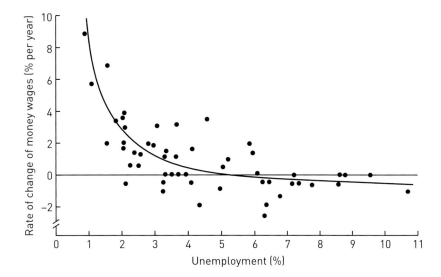

The Phillips curve
The Phillips curve is a graph showing a trade-off between unemployment and inflation: the lower the rate of unemployment, the higher the rate of inflation.

gradually flatter – **the Phillips curve** (Figure 18.1). The same curve fitted the data for the years 1948–57 almost as well, suggesting that there was indeed a trade-off between unemployment and inflation over the previous hundred years.

The next question is: what does this empirical relationship mean? How is it to be explained? The interpretation offered by Phillips is an application of supply and demand analysis to the labour market. Suppose initially that wages are stable (the rate of wage inflation is zero) and the labour market is in equilibrium. If the demand for labour falls, unemployment above equilibrium in the form of an excess supply of labour driving down its market price or, in other words, leading to a fall in the general level of wages, the rate of wage inflation is negative. If, instead, the demand for labour rises, excess labour demand bringing unemployment below its equilibrium level and initiating wage rises, the rate of wage inflation is positive.

Phillips (1958) stimulated further research into the relationship between unemployment and inflation. Price inflation as distinct from wage inflation was also found to be negatively correlated with unemployment and it became customary to think of the Phillips trade-off in these terms. This was more useful for policy makers because unemployment and (price) inflation were in the 1960s, as in the 2000s, two of the central macroeconomic problems they faced. The Phillips curve now presented policy makers with a range of options from which to choose the optimal, or least undesirable, combination of inflation and unemployment. For example, the inflation rate that would have to be tolerated to achieve full employment could simply be read off a Phillips curve diagram such as the one shown in Figure 18.2. The popularity the Phillips curve quickly won with policy makers is shrewdly commented on by Humphrey (1986):

> the Phillips curve appealed to policy makers because it provided a convincing rationale for their failure to achieve full employment with price stability – twin goals that were thought to be mutually compatible before Phillips' analysis. When criticized for failing to achieve both goals simultaneously, the authorities could point to the Phillips curve as showing that such an outcome was impossible and that the best one could hope for was either arbitrarily low unemployment or price stability but not both.

> *(Humphrey, 1986, p.15)*

Figure 18.2
An expansionary
movement along
the Phillips curve

Source: *OECD
Economic Outlook*
(various years)

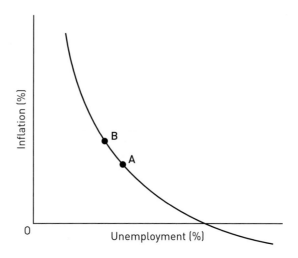

■■■ 18.2.2 Demand-pull and cost-push inflation

This section will introduce two theories of inflation, demand pull and cost push, using the Phillips curve analysis to distinguish them. Let us start by considering the case of a government which wants to reduce unemployment and is prepared to live with an increase in inflation to do so. A set of expansionary monetary and/or fiscal policy measures is therefore introduced and the economy duly moves along its Phillips curve in a north-westerly direction – from A to B in Figure 18.2. Inflation has indeed risen and unemployment fallen. When inflation is caused in this way, by an expansion of aggregate demand, it is known as *demand-pull* inflation.

The aggregate demand expansion is reflected in a rise in prices which, if money wages are fixed by contractual agreements, leads to a fall in real wages. Firms therefore hire more labour and use it to increase output. So an expansion of aggregate demand raises the price level and output and reduces unemployment. The Phillips curve relates inflation (the rate at which the price level is changing) and unemployment.

Not much more than a decade after Phillips had reported his discovery of a trade-off between unemployment and inflation going back almost a century, it appeared to break down. Plotting the time path of inflation against unemployment for the UK economy in the 1970s reveals a relationship that cannot be depicted by the downward-sloping Phillips curve and cannot readily be explained in terms of demand pull (Figure 18.3).

Question	Did the Phillips curve simply cease to exist in the 1970s or do traces of it continue to be observable?

The first and second oil price shocks of the 1970s are quite clearly visible in the almost vertical movements of the curve in Figure 18.3 for 1973–74 and 1979–80. The increase in inflation in 1973–75 and 1978–80 was not associated with a fall in unemployment.

The empirical relationship between unemployment and inflation had become more complex than that observed by Phillips for the British economy for 1861–1913. The Phillips curve analysis could easily be modified to reflect the more complex unemployment–inflation relationship now observed throughout the industrial world. Basic supply and demand analysis has shown you that curves shift if there is a change in the conditions we

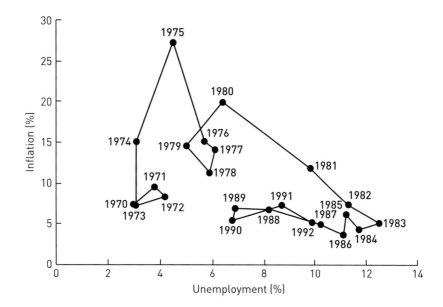

Figure 18.3
Inflation and unemployment in the UK, 1970–92

Source: *OECD Economic Outlook* (various years)

hold constant in drawing the original curve. Perhaps all that had happened was that the Phillips curve had shifted outwards or to the right? For example, the oil price rise of 1979 could be seen as shifting the UK Phillips curve in this direction; higher oil prices fed through into higher prices in general, so that any given unemployment rate was associated with a higher inflation rate. An increase in oil prices raises transport costs throughout the economy. Producers will attempt to pass on some of the cost increases to consumers in the form of higher prices and in this way the oil price increase leads to an economy-wide increase in the costs of production. When inflation occurs in this way, it is classified as *cost-push* inflation.

However, there are two segments of the time path plotted in Figure 18.3 that slope downwards like a Phillips curve, one only briefly in 1975–77, the other over the years 1980–83. These Phillips curve remnants may reflect the response of policy makers to the cost-push inflationary episodes which shifted the Phillips curve outwards.

Question	What policy measures might have initiated these south-easterly movements on Figure 18.3?

It seems that policy makers wished to reverse the inflationary consequences of the increases in oil prices. Certainly, the south-easterly movements are consistent with their using monetary and/or fiscal policies to reduce aggregate demand (Chapter 13, Section 13.4.2). The reduction in aggregate demand would cause inflation to fall and unemployment to rise. The following exercise asks you to consider what will happen if policy makers are more concerned with unemployment than inflation.

Exercise 18.1

Explain how the UK Phillips curve shown in Figure 18.3 might have looked if policy makers had sought to reduce unemployment a little following the oil price rise in 1979.

18.3   The costs of unemployment versus the costs of inflation

One possible reason for policy makers prioritizing the defeat of inflation over the achievement of full employment is that the costs, or adverse effects, of inflation are much greater than those of unemployment. This section surveys theoretical arguments and empirical research on the costs of unemployment and inflation, with the intention of discovering whether inflation is more damaging to economic activity than unemployment.

■ ■ ■ 18.3.1   The costs of unemployment

> I received ten minutes notice on being made redundant.
> I felt better – money in the bank – less tired – plenty of fresh air – an opportunity to do things with my life without the frustrations and claustrophobia of factory life . . . [a couple of years later] depressed and insecure, no success in finding even part-time work to supplement savings.
> Whenever I get a sufficient amount or come into money I spend it fast, mostly on drink. I seem to panic when I have money to spend.
> To survive this unwanted gap in one's life one has to be drunk or half-crazy most of the time it seems.
> I feel like an autistic child in relation to other working folk.
>
> *(Dawson, 1992)*

For many people, those words, spoken by interviewees taking part in a research project, may be enough to convince them that full employment is the only objective of macroeconomic policy worth pursuing. Would policy makers not do better to listen to unemployed people talking about their experiences rather than just analyse tables of economic statistics?

The human cost of unemployment

The costs of unemployment are incurred mainly by the unemployed people themselves and concern health, current income and future income and employment. It is clear that many unemployed people and their families experience a deterioration in their psychological well-being, ranging from anxiety and boredom to severe depression and despair. Even if the majority of unemployed people are still able to get a lot out of life, this may mean not that unemployment is only a trivial setback but that considerable moral strength has been invested in coming to terms with the major crisis. There is a greater incidence of physical ill health among unemployed people, although the degree to which this reflects a previous record of poor health continues to be a matter of academic dispute.

It is not easy to generalize about the degree of financial hardship imposed on unemployed people and their families, because national benefit systems vary both in their conditions of eligibility and in the *replacement ratio*, which expresses unemployment benefit as a percentage of previous earnings (Chapter 9, Section 9.5). In the USA during the high unemployment of the early 1980s, for example, married couples where the previously employed partner was paid close to average US earnings were likely to face a replacement ratio somewhere between 45 per cent and 66 per cent. For the UK during that same period of high unemployment, most unemployed people – single or married couples with no children – were looking at replacement ratios of less than 60 per cent unless earnings when last in work had been very low. The only group likely to be 'better off on dole' comprised married couples who have four or more children and were previously on less than half average male manual earnings (about four per cent of unemployed people came into this category). A replacement ratio as high as 80 per cent still means the loss of a fifth of income from work, typically from an already low income. So unemployment has a severely regressive effect on the distribution of income.

There is, however, much more to the impact of unemployment on the people who are unemployed than the effect it has on current income. Unemployment inflicts

> a longer-term 'scar' through the increased future incidence of unemployment and lower subsequent earnings in employment.
>
> *(Arulampalam* et al., *2001, p.F577)*

Unemployment scarring captures the idea that the worst effects of unemployment are concentrated on the unemployed people themselves in two ways: the first period of unemployment tends to bring further periods of unemployment and re-engagement tends to be associated with a lower earnings profile.

Arulampalam *et al.* (2001) offer two explanations of why unemployment scarring occurs, which can be understood in terms of labour market concepts introduced in Chapter 7. Leaving a job has been found to lead to a permanent loss of human capital that is specific to the firm but the effects of unemployment on human capital are wider (human capital was explained in Chapter 7, Section 7.2). At the very least, for the duration of unemployment, the unemployed person is denied opportunities to gain further work experience, develop existing skills and acquire new ones. The effects are likely to be more far-reaching, particularly for long-term unemployment, in that skills may deteriorate or even be lost. The concept of efficiency wages, also introduced in Chapter 7, sheds further light on unemployment scarring. The assumption underlying efficiency wage theory is that the worker's productivity is unobservable. Prospective employers may interpret periods of unemployment as an indication of a worker's low productivity and either refuse job offers or link job offers to lower wages.

In a symposium on unemployment scarring, the *Economic Journal (EJ)* in 2001 published three papers attempting to estimate its importance for unemployed men in Britain. The focus on unemployed *men* is explained by the different unemployment experience of men and women in the early 1980s. A large number of skilled and less-skilled manual jobs that had traditionally been occupied by men were lost in manufacturing and mining, while the number of women entering the labour market to take (often part-time) jobs in service industries increased. Unemployment scarring in the 1980s and 1990s was in this sense a largely male phenomenon. The papers in the *EJ* symposium sought to address a weakness in the methodology of early studies of unemployment scarring, which failed to include information on workers who kept their jobs during the years of high unemployment. The consequence was that there was no *control group* against which to compare the experience of unemployed people. Suppose for example that men lost their jobs in a declining industry and were subsequently re-employed in the same industry at lower real wages. This does not necessarily amount to unemployment scarring because real wage cuts might have been experienced by workers retained in employment in the declining industry. The possible effect of industry decline on real wages can only be taken into account by comparing the real wage profiles of unemployed individuals with those of people who remained in work throughout the period.

All three *EJ* papers use very large data sets, covering the labour market experience of large numbers of men during the 1980s and 1990s and enabling comparisons to be made between

> workers with unemployment histories as well as those with no interruptions to the employment experience.
>
> *(Arulampalam et al., 2001, p.F578)*

The results confirm the importance of unemployment scarring as a consequence of the mass male unemployment of the 1980s in Britain. According to Arulampalam, a

> spell of unemployment is found to carry a wage penalty of about 6 per cent on re-entry in Britain, and after three years, they are earning 14 per cent less compared to what they would have received in the absence of unemployment.
>
> *(Arulampalam, 2001, p.F585)*

Gregory and Jukes (2001) reach a broadly similar conclusion once allowance is made for an important distinction. This is the distinction between the effect on *re-engagement* wages of the incidence of unemployment; that is, its occurrence among the individuals being studied and the duration of unemployment. Incidence, or the fact that someone has experienced a spell of unemployment, is found to have only a temporary impact – 'an average earnings setback of 10 per cent on initial re-engagement largely eroding over two years' (Gregory and Jukes, 2001, p.F607). By contrast, the effect of unemployment duration is permanent, 'a one-year spell adding a further penalty of 10 percentage points' (ibid.). Combining these two elements brings the results of the two studies broadly into line. The fact that Arulampalam (2001) did not find any effect from duration is in part explained by differences in the data that reflect changes in the administration of unemployment benefits. Gregory and Jukes (2001) covered the 1980s (as well as the 1990s) when long-term unemployment was high, while Arulampalam (2001) focuses on the 1990s when many long-term unemployed men had been transferred onto sickness benefits.

The third paper in the *EJ* symposium examines the further effects of unemployment scarring on inequality and poverty. Gregg (2001) undertakes a long-term analysis to try to discover whether there is a correlation between *cumulated* experience of unemployment (adding up separate spells of unemployment) in the 16–23 age range and that in the 28–33 age range. The result is that there is such a correlation, implying that unemployment is concentrated on a minority of the workforce. This minority is characterized by low educational attainment, financial deprivation and childhood behavioural problems. There are clear policy implications:

> attacking low educational achievement, and preventing the build-up of substantial periods in unemployment as youths, may reduce the extent to which a minority of men spend a large part of their working lives unemployed.
>
> *(Gregg, 2001, p.F626)*

The output cost of unemployment

The principal cost which unemployment imposes on society as a whole is the loss of output that would have been produced if resources, including labour, had been fully employed. The simplest approach to measuring this output loss is to assume that everyone who is out of work would, if found a job, produce as much as the average person already in employment. But unemployed people tend to be less skilled than the labour force as a whole so that, other things being equal, the average product method may exaggerate the scale of output loss.

On the other hand, there are reasons why the average product method might under-estimate the output loss. When recorded unemployment rises, other symptoms of spare capacity emerge. Part-time work falls (without adding to the officially recorded unem-ployment figures) and so too does overtime working. There is usually a decline in the participation rate (i.e. the percentage of the population of working age who declare them-selves to be part of the labour force by seeking work) because the poor prospects of finding a job discourage some people from trying. An increase in hidden unemployment occurs when firms 'hoard' labour, even though there is nothing for the workers con-cerned to do, with the aim of retaining skilled workers who might be difficult to replace when demand picks up.

A more promising approach is therefore to extrapolate the trend rate of output growth under full employment through the years of unemployment, and to measure the *output gap*, the amount by which actual output during the years of high unemployment falls short of full employment output. Using an output gap method, Okun (1970, p.140) con-cluded that 'a reduction in unemployment . . . has a much larger than proportionate effect on output'. Okun's method takes into account the hidden spare capacity associated with recorded unemployment. The estimate of the output loss using this method is sensitive to the level of unemployment chosen as an approximation to feasible full employment.

Empirical estimates applying Okun's methodology to periods of historically high unemployment suggest that the output costs of unemployment are substantial. For example, in 1983 the output of the German economy was estimated to be up to a fifth lower than it would have been if the economy had been running at full capacity (Junankar, 1985). For the German, UK, Italian and French economies in 1983, the out-put gap was more than 10 per cent; in other words, each economy produced 10 per cent less output than it was capable of producing at full employment. Nevertheless, you might feel that the loss of goods that might have been produced but were not and never will be is a somewhat intangible, hypothetical deprivation. But this loss of potential output has serious effects on people's well-being. In the circular flow model of the economy, output equals income (Chapters 8 and 12). So everyone bears some of the output costs of unem-ployment in the form of a reduction in income. People's incomes are lower on average than they would be if there was full employment.

The *incidence* of output loss, or the impact of unemployment on the distribution of income, falls disproportionately on unemployed people, because of the limited extent to which social security benefits compensate unemployed people for the loss of earned income (see 'The human cost of unemployment', p.488). The fiscal cost of unemployment represents that part of the incidence of output loss that is in principle placed on taxpayers as public spending on unemployment benefits rises and income tax revenues fall. For most OECD economies, each one per cent increase in unemployment raises unemployment benefits paid out by 0.2 or 0.3 per cent of GDP (OECD, 1993, p.39). Then there is the loss of income tax revenue when people lose their jobs. The rise in unemployment in the early 1990s did in fact lead to a deterioration in the public finances of many OECD countries.

There is no doubt that unemployment seriously damages the health of the economy and the well-being of unemployed people. But governments in many industrial nations seem to believe that inflation carries an even more alarming health warning. What are the economic arguments for this position?

▨ ▨ ■ 18.3.2 The costs of inflation

After twenty years of variable, if moderate, inflation, *The Economist* proclaimed that

> the best inflation rate . . . means zero because anything higher interferes with the fundamental function of prices – their ability to provide information about relative scarcities.
>
> (The Economist, *22 February 1992*)

The elimination of inflation or the lasting achievement of price stability has been, and in many economies remains, the principal objective of macroeconomic policy. During the past ten years central banks throughout the world have adopted long-run price stability as their primary goal (Temple, 2000). Does inflation inhibit output growth? Are there other costs that inflation imposes on people?

The costs of anticipated inflation

Inflation may be anticipated by economic agents if their expectations about the future rate of inflation are correct and they are free to adjust their economic activity in the light of those expectations. There are two reasons for believing that even perfectly anticipated inflation might impose welfare costs on society: 'shoe leather' (or monetary) costs and menu costs.

1 **'Shoe leather' costs:** One way of anticipating, or guarding against, inflation is for people to economize on cash balances and demand deposits in favour of time deposits (Chapter 11, Section 11.3.3) so that the interest earned will protect the purchasing power of their income. The 'shoe leather' used up in making frequent trips to the bank is a metaphor for all the productive resources consumed in this way, including fuel and lost output as workers leave their jobs to queue at banks. Shoe leather costs probably contributed to economic collapse under hyperinflation in Germany during 1922–23. Empirical studies on the shoe leather costs of moderate inflation are highly sensitive to the assumptions made in the theoretical models underlying them. In a survey of theoretical models of shoe leather costs, Orphanides and Solow (1990) found a variety of outcomes, depending mainly on the interest elasticity of the demand for cash and on the definition of money, given that cash (or *narrow money*) is a relatively small proportion of the broader money supply.

2 **Menu costs:** The menu costs of inflation are the sum of the costs of changing prices and adjusting wages. Resources are used up in revising not only menus but catalogues, price tags, vending machines and so on. Adjusting nominal wage rates may involve a potentially lengthy process of negotiation and hence the costs of the management time devoted to it.

During inflation the price of a good may rise either as part of the inflationary process or as the consequence of a change in market conditions (in this case an increase in demand or a decrease in supply). So menu costs include the costs of gathering information about market conditions. Assuming that firms operate in imperfectly competitive markets and are therefore price makers, they may choose to delay a price rise in response to an acceleration in inflation. Firms may be assumed to change nominal prices only at regular intervals or only when actual prices diverge too far from their optimal level

(Blanchard, 1983; Ball and Mankiw, 1994). The costs of changing prices – the menu costs – deter firms from constant monitoring and immediate revision. The irregularities of price changes during inflation may disturb the pattern of relative prices. So relative price variability may be the outcome of the inflationary process itself, even when the inflation is perfectly anticipated (Briault, 1995, p.36). If so, menu costs reinforce the *inflationary noise* argument that inflation leads to inefficiency and low growth (see below).

The costs of unanticipated inflation

The most serious costs of inflation are experienced when inflation is unanticipated. Unanticipated inflation is thought to impose costs on society in two main ways: through the unplanned redistribution of income and wealth and through the reduction in economic growth.

Estimating the redistributive effects of inflation is complicated because there are many different routes along which the inflationary process might affect income distribution, making some individuals or groups better off while making others worse off. In class terms, inflation has sometimes been seen as redistributing income away from the capitalist class towards the working class. If rising wage awards are driving inflation, then inflation is associated with an increase in the share of wages in national income at the expense of profits. Inflation also erodes the value of non-indexed financial assets that are disproportionately held by the upper middle class. So inflation can have a progressive impact on income distribution. On the other hand, inflation can undermine the living standards of low-income groups relying on state benefits. In many economies, social security benefits such as unemployment benefits and old age pensions are indexed to rise with inflation by earnings. However, if such benefits are tied to the consumer price index when average wages are rising more rapidly, pensioners and other recipients will experience a decline in their standard of living relative to that of the employed population. The redistributive effects of a period of inflation reflect not only inflation itself but also the bargaining power of different social groups. In general it has proved difficult to disentangle the redistributive impact of inflation from the forces of supply and demand, such as changes in the pattern of demand for goods and services and hence changes in the derived demand for different kinds of labour.

The difficulty of making general statements about the redistributive effects of inflation, such as that they always benefit a particular group or are always progressive, does not imply that they are unimportant. Far from it – it is precisely the unpredictability of the redistributive effects of inflation that are sometimes claimed to be responsible not only for its unpopularity but also for much of the real damage that it causes. Baumol and Blinder exemplify this view:

> Why then is the redistribution caused by inflation so widely condemned? Because its victims are selected capriciously . . . The gainers do not earn their spoils, and the losers do not deserve their fate. This is the fundamental indictment of inflation.
> *(Baumol and Blinder, 1988, p.104)*

The *inflationary noise* argument states that without price stability markets cannot allocate resources efficiently. Inflation distorts the transmission of price signals so it is said to resemble the *noise* or background interference that distorts the transmission of radio signals. If you think back to Chapter 5 on perfect competition, you will recall that changes in the conditions of supply and demand – changes in the relative scarcity of resources and in the relative popularity of products – cause price changes that act as signals to consumers and producers. Friedman (1977, p.466) argued that as the inflation rate rises so does its volatility, with the consequence that 'an additional element of uncertainty is, as it were, added to every market transaction'. Economic agents might confuse a price rise that is merely part of the general inflationary background with a price rise that signals a real change in relative scarcity. For example, suppose that a firm buying copper as an input to a production process observes a price rise in a highly inflationary environment. If the price rise genuinely signals a change in relative scarcity but the firm dismisses it as *noisy*, it will waste this newly scarce material. If, on the other hand, the price rise is purely inflationary or noisy but the firm misinterprets it as a scarcity signal, it will incur extra costs in needlessly economizing on copper, perhaps by searching for a substitute or a possible alternative supply.

The implication is that high inflation will slow down economic growth. Hence we can evaluate the inflationary noise argument by asking an apparently straightforward factual question: is inflation positively associated with low economic growth? A substantial amount of empirical research on the possible links between inflation and growth has been carried out in recent years. The methodologies used in this research vary considerably. For example, there are different models of economic growth, some of which assume technological change to be endogenous while others take it as given. Again, some models use time series analysis to test for a correlation between inflation and growth for a single country over many years; others employ cross-country analysis to test for a correlation between inflation and growth at a given point in time.

Two main results emerge from this large and diverse body of empirical work. First, as Friedman (1977) predicted, the variability (or volatility) of relative prices increases as inflation accelerates (Fischer and Modigliani, 1978; Clare and Thomas, 1993). Does this correlation lead to the further link between inflation and growth? The answer is a significantly qualified 'yes'. The result of most studies is that there is a significant negative correlation between inflation and growth at higher rates of inflation. For example, Temple (2001, p.419) concludes from an exhaustive survey of empirical studies that there is 'general agreement that high inflation, say above 100 per cent a year, inhibits growth'. Note the qualification: it is 'high' inflation that damages growth. There is no unambiguous evidence that moderate inflation inhibits growth and it has proved 'extremely difficult to quantify the output gains of moving from, say, 5 per cent inflation to price stability' (Temple, 2001, p.419).

A further qualification must be made to the broad trend of empirical research results. The correlation between high inflation and low growth does not imply that high inflation causes low growth. As noted in Chapter 8, correlation does not establish a causal relationship and certainly does not indicate the direction of causation. Does high inflation cause low growth or does low growth cause high inflation? Or are inflation and (low) growth both the effects of other factors? This interpretation of the evidence is in fact offered by Briault, who concludes that

> the available evidence supports the view that well-run economies with strong and efficient productive structures tend to exhibit both low inflation and high growth.
>
> *(Briault, 1995, p.33)*

The evidence does not therefore vindicate the choice of price stability as the objective that guides the central banks of the EU and the UK. However, another possible justification for eliminating inflation emerges from statistical work on inflation and growth, one

J.M. Keynes on inflation and unemployment

Cartoon by BIF from Peter Pugh and Chris Garratt, *Introducing Keynesian Economics*, Icon Books Limited, 2000

that receives support from some theoretical work. This is that policy makers should aim to keep the inflation rate below about 40 per cent a year, on the grounds that there is a risk that it will accelerate rapidly beyond that rate (Bruno and Easterly, 1998; Bruno, 1995). The case against 'learning to live with moderate inflation' ultimately rests upon the fear that it might accelerate into high inflation, reducing the rate of economic growth. The policy implication is that the only safe inflation target is price stability, because moderate inflation may accelerate out of control. Section 18.4 examines the theoretical arguments for this view.

18.4 Inflation, unemployment and expectations

Some people think we can choose between inflation and unemployment. Let inflation rise a bit they say to get unemployment down. But it doesn't work like that. The two go together. Higher inflation means higher unemployment. It's like an addictive drug, the more you get the more you need and the more damage it does to you.

(Geoffrey Howe, Budget broadcast, 10 March 1981)

Since the late 1970s economic policy in industrial countries has been dominated by the belief that policy intervention based on the assumption of a trade-off between unemployment and inflation will only make things worse – adding to inflation without bringing unemployment down because 'the two go together'.

■ ■ ■ 18.4.1 The expectations-augmented Phillips curve

Section 18.3 showed that the unemployment/inflation trade-off appeared to break down after 1970. This was not in itself fatally wounding to the Phillips curve analysis because it was possible to interpret the combination of rising inflation and unchanged or even rising unemployment as a series of short-run Phillips curves shifting outwards. However, some economists had always been sceptical of the Phillips trade-off on theoretical grounds and they seized upon its empirical difficulties as confirmation of their misgivings.

The theoretical deficiency of the Phillips curve analysis, according to Friedman (1968) and Phelps (1967), concerned its microeconomic foundations, in particular the assumptions it incorporated about the behaviour of economic agents in the labour market. Friedman argued from two main premises. First, he assumed that the supply and demand of labour were functions not of the nominal wage rate but of the real wage rate, that is, nominal wages divided by prices, W/P. Second, he proposed that, in bargaining over wage rates, workers use their experience of past inflation to predict future price rises and aim to anticipate these in wage settlements. Friedman's conclusion was that, while there is a trade-off between unemployment and inflation in the short run, a permanently lower level of unemployment cannot be secured by accepting a higher rate of inflation.

Friedman's analysis of the labour market exemplifies the perfectly competitive approach or model (see Chapter 5 and Chapter 7, Section 7.2). Accordingly, he assumed that workers and unemployed people are rational individual economic agents no less than the profit-maximizing firms they deal with. In other words, the analysis abstracts from considerations of social norms and the psychological pressures of unemployment and from wage bargaining institutions. It presents decisions to accept or reject job offers, to remain in or give up a job, as matters of individually weighing up the disutility of working against its financial rewards. This approach implies that unemployment may occur, not simply because people are actively seeking work but cannot find a job, but also because people are actively seeking work but cannot find a job that provides adequate compensation for giving up leisure or adequate rewards for skills. The concept of frictional unemployment captures the idea that unemployment may occur because of the time it takes to find appropriate work; it underlies the natural rate of unemployment (see below). Friedman believed that government intervention to try to trade off higher inflation for permanently lower unemployment would change agents' expectations and their behaviour in a way that would only make matters worse.

Let us remind ourselves of how a demand expansion works in the absence of inflationary expectations (i.e. expectations are for zero inflation and remain unchanged). Policy makers might suppose that a moderate increase in inflation would reduce unemployment. A monetary expansion increases the demand for goods, causing a general rise in prices. Nominal wage rates are slow to respond, so real wage rates fall, persuading employers to move down their labour demand curves and recruit the extra workers they need to increase output. Unemployed people do not incorporate past inflation into their expectations, assuming prices will be stable in the next year. They are willing to work at the unchanged nominal wage rates on offer and unemployment falls. This combination of rising inflation and falling unemployment is shown by a movement north-west from A to B along the short-run Phillips curve PC_1 in Figure 18.4.

Once we stop and think about this from the perspective of the model of a perfectly competitive labour market, it seems implausible. If people are calculating their prospective rewards from employment – and in the perfectly competitive labour market people are modelled as rational agents who do exactly that – it is common sense to adjust the money wages on offer for inflation. A rational agent would fail to do so only if there had

Figure 18.4
The expectations-augmented Phillips curve

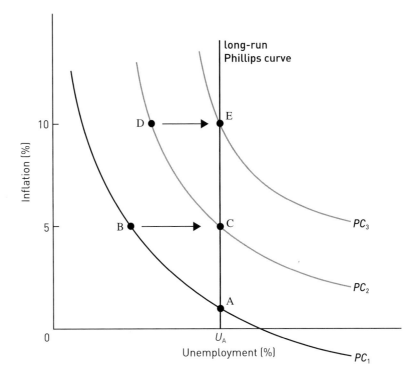

been so little inflation that the adjustment was not worth the effort. Once we have decided to model people's decisions in the labour market as those of rational agents, we are more or less committed to incorporating expectations of inflation into their behaviour.

That is just what Friedman did. He argued that the process of trading off higher inflation for lower unemployment worked only on the assumption that people did not bother to form expectations about future inflation or that their expectations were mistaken. Once the newly recruited workers incorporate last year's inflation into their expectations of inflation in the next year, they either decide it is not worth working and leave their jobs or negotiate higher nominal wage rates. Either way, unemployment returns to its original level but at the new rate of inflation. This is how the short-run Phillips curve PC_1 shifts outwards to PC_2 as the economy moves from B to C on Figure 18.4.

Policy makers, the story continues, interpret their failure to secure a permanent drop in the unemployment rate as a sign that their choice of expansionary monetary medicine was correct but the dosage was too low. The course of treatment is therefore repeated and the economy moves along PC_2 from C to D while workers are surprised by the new, higher rate of inflation. But once again, as soon as this inflation rate is used as the basis of expectations, the prospect of low real wages reverses the fall in unemployment and the short-run Phillips curve shifts to PC_3 as the economy moves from D to E. The outcome is the original unemployment rate combined with a higher inflation rate, showing that in the long run there is no trade-off between unemployment and inflation. The long-run Phillips curve is vertical, joining the points the economy returns to after each expansionary phase – A, C and E.

Friedman called the rate of unemployment at A, C and E, to which the economy returns after each episode of expansionary monetary policy, the **natural rate of unemployment**. This is defined as the rate at which the labour market clears; that is, when labour supply and demand are in equilibrium (Chapter 7). Friedman noted that it reflected some institutional characteristics of the labour market, such as

Natural rate of unemployment

The natural rate of unemployment is the rate at which the labour market clears.

the cost of gathering information about job vacancies and labour-availabilities, the costs of mobility and so on.

(Friedman, 1968, p.8)

Of the other institutional factors mentioned by Friedman, attention has tended to focus on social security benefits. The level of unemployment benefit influences people's individual labour supply curves. If the level of benefit is increased, the urgency of finding work might be diminished, increasing the number of people out of work when the labour market is in equilibrium (i.e. the natural rate of unemployment).

In the short run, expansionary monetary or fiscal policies can lower the actual rate of unemployment below this long-run equilibrium, or natural, rate even on competitive assumptions. It follows that the natural rate will prevail only in the absence of expansionary policies. The *natural rate hypothesis*, as this first result of Friedman's analysis is called, states that there is no permanent trade-off between unemployment and inflation because in the long run unemployment returns to its natural rate. The vertical long-run Phillips curve is the diagrammatic representation of the natural rate hypothesis. If expected inflation is the same as last year's inflation, then in the absence of expansionary policies pushing the economy along a short-run Phillips curve actual inflation this year will be the same as last year and hence the same as expected inflation, and the economy is in equilibrium at the natural rate of unemployment. Table 18.1 shows how Figure 18.4 could be interpreted in the light of this model.

Table 18.1
Expected and actual inflation and changes in unemployment

Expected inflation %	Actual inflation %	Change in unemployment
1	5	falls A to B on PC_1
5	5	rises B to C, PC_1 to PC_2
5	10	falls C to D on PC_2
10	10	rises D to E, PC_2 to PC_3

Question On this model, how could policy makers maintain unemployment below its natural rate in the long run?

This can be done only by continually expanding aggregate demand, so that the rate of inflation is always accelerating. Workers are therefore constantly surprised by inflation, always, if you like, being a year behind in their expectations. This leads to the *accelerationist hypothesis*, the second of Friedman's results. It states that unemployment can be maintained below its natural rate only by constantly accelerating inflation (Figure 18.5). As people's expectations chase after actual inflation, inflation must accelerate to keep ahead of those expectations. Attempts to peg unemployment below its natural rate will eventually provoke hyperinflation.

The natural rate and accelerationist hypotheses both depend on Friedman's assumption that expected inflation is precisely equal to last year's inflation. However, while it came to be widely believed in the early 1970s that inflationary expectations were the main cause of the outward shift of the observed Phillips curve, the analysis of those expectations underwent a major revolution.

Figure 18.5
The accelerationist
hypothesis

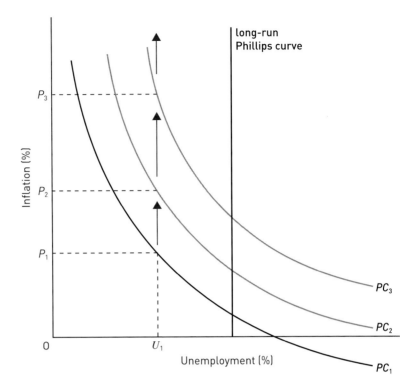

The main problem with Friedman's assumption about expectations, known as adaptive expectations, was that it committed economic agents to making easily avoidable errors in forecasting inflation. Under adaptive expectations, in forming expectations about the future course of an economic variable, agents rely solely on past values of that variable. They might calculate a weighted average of inflation over the past few years, the greatest weight being attached to last year's inflation and so on. Or they might learn by their mistakes, incorporating an error-learning mechanism to adjust forecasts by some fraction of the discrepancy between last year's expected inflation and last year's actual inflation – hence the term adaptive expectations. For example, if expected inflation is 6 per cent and the outcome is actually 10 per cent, then the expected inflation rate for next year will be revised upwards.

This procedure works reasonably well if the rate of inflation is stable or changes only slowly but during variable inflation it locks agents into systematic errors, such as constantly being surprised by ever-accelerating inflation. In any case, it is intuitively implausible to suppose that people would focus solely on past inflation to the exclusion of obviously relevant 'background' information, such as the election of a government committed to fighting years of high inflation or the move from national currencies to a single (e.g. European) currency. Surely, it came to be thought, the rational agents who inhabit economic models can do better than adaptive expectations.

■ ■ ■ 18.4.2 Rational expectations

The rational expectations hypothesis was advanced by Muth (1961), although its significance for macroeconomic theory and modelling was not fully exploited until the 1970s. Muth's basic premise was that 'information is scarce, and the economic system generally does not waste it' (p.316). This probably does not seem particularly remarkable but Muth went on to argue that the information relevant to the formation of inflationary expectations included knowledge of the structure of the model of the economy being used by policy makers. Carter and Maddock explain the significance of this step:

> The innovation introduced by Muth was to consider the expected price as endogenous to the model, and generated by the model itself . . . The agents in the market are assumed to know the structure of the model . . . and to use this information in order to form their expectations.
>
> *(Carter and Maddock, 1984, p.30)*

So now 'agents in the market', such as workers negotiating wage claims and unemployed people deciding on job offers, are assumed to know the precise structure – expressible in a series of equations for forecasting the future course of output, inflation and so on – of the economic model used by policy makers. Since economists are notoriously prone to error in making such forecasts, however, it seems implausible to assume that people with no professional interest in them routinely do better.

However, proponents of rational expectations insist that there is no suggestion that all or most individual people in the real world actually form their expectations of inflation in any systematic way. According to Minford and Peel (1983, p.4), all that is being claimed is that the *typical individual* 'utilizes efficiently the information available to him in forming expectations about future outcomes'. Since this is a belief about the 'typical individual', it 'cannot be falsified by examples of behaviour by any actual individual' (p.5). As long as enough real people who 'contribute a dominant proportion of the variability in aggregate behaviour' make the efficient use of all the available information, 'this would be sufficient to generate aggregate behaviour that exhibited rationality' (p.5). What this amounts to is the claim that irrational ways of forming expectations, being randomly distributed across a large sample of the population, cancel out, so that the aggregate outcome is *as if* all agents were rational. The implication is that workers and job-seekers will not make systematic errors, such as those arising from relying solely on past inflation, in forming their expectations of inflation. For example, agents will perceive an expansionary monetary policy aimed at reducing unemployment as a sign of higher inflation, revise their expectations of inflation upwards and act accordingly.

> **Question** If agents form their price expectations rationally, it seems that they cannot be surprised by a change of macroeconomic policy. Looking back to Figures 18.4 and 18.5, how would this affect the outcome of the strategy of repeated expansions of aggregate demand to peg unemployment below its natural rate?

Under adaptive expectations, the policy reduced unemployment below its natural rate only temporarily, until agents adjusted to the new inflation rate. But, if they form their price expectations rationally, they can never be surprised by policy decisions. So their expectations of inflation will always be accurate and unemployment will not fall below its natural rate even temporarily. The policy will be entirely ineffective. For example, in connection with expansionary monetary policy, Minford and Peel (1983, p.19) argue that if the government changes the money supply rule which they are following, output (and hence unemployment) will not be affected because the new monetary stance is 'incorporated into people's expectations . . . and cannot cause any surprises'.

This result requires one more assumption in addition to the rational expectations hypothesis: that all markets, including the labour market, clear continuously and immediately in response to shocks, or unexpected changes in the conditions of supply and demand. This is a corollary of the model of perfect competition. The rational expectations hypothesis plus the market-clearing assumption have an important implication for policy: that disinflation (i.e. the reduction of the inflation rate) can be achieved without any cost in higher unemployment and lost output.

Rational expectations theory asserts that agents can never be surprised by systematic macroeconomic policy. They incorporate policy rules not only into their forecasts of future inflation but also into their behaviour. So, for example, they react to a contractionary monetary policy by anticipating its downward effect on the rate of inflation, thereby bringing about that effect as they negotiate contracts of various kinds on the assumption of lower inflation. Agents' reactions to policy make the policy work. Price inflation falls but no wage gap opens up and so there is no change in the level of unemployment. If policy makers are convinced that they can rely on agents reacting to policy in this way, they will be much more inclined to tackle inflation without worrying about their policies' effects on unemployment.

Exercise 18.2

To check that you have understood the discussion so far, try completing Figure 18.6. The quadrants of the matrix identify the outcomes of the government's inflationary and disinflationary policies, given the reaction of the other economic agents in the economy. The left-hand quadrants show what happens to unemployment and inflation if agents allow themselves to be surprised. The right-hand quadrants show the outcomes if agents rationally anticipate policy effects. The top left-hand quadrant has been completed as an example. Fill in the others.

The implication of the exercise, which you should complete before reading on, is that an expansionary monetary policy to reflate the economy and reduce unemployment is successful if agents fail to react by anticipating upward price level effects, but that under rational expectations (and one further condition explained below) agents anticipate an acceleration in the rate of inflation, thereby bringing it about and leaving the level of unemployment unchanged. A contractionary monetary policy to eliminate inflation works painlessly, without adding to unemployment, provided agents anticipate the downward pressure on prices, but in the absence of this reaction unemployment will rise, at least in the short run.

The effect of introducing adaptive expectations into the analysis of the trade-off between unemployment and inflation was to limit it to the short run. It seems that the

Figure 18.6
Matrix for predicting the effects of inflationary and disinflationary policies on unemployment and inflation

		Agents' expectations	
		do not change	fully anticipate policy
Government policy	expansionary	unemployment falls, inflation rises	
	contractionary		

impact of introducing rational expectations and market clearing into the analysis is more dramatic: there is no trade-off at all because macroeconomic policy has no effect on output and unemployment.

▪ ▪ ▪ 18.4.3   The costs of reducing inflation

> Rising unemployment and the recession have been the price we have had to pay in order to get inflation down – but that is a price well worth paying.
> *(Norman Lamont, Chancellor of the Exchequer, House of Commons, 16 May 1991)*

Section 18.4.1 discussed the grounds for believing that attempts to exploit the inflation–unemployment trade-off depicted by the short-run Phillips curve will shift the curve outwards, returning unemployment to its natural rate but at ever higher inflation rates. So there is a case for reducing inflation, providing the costs of doing so are acceptable. The view discussed in Section 18.4.2 and based on rational expectations and market-clearing is that disinflation is 'painless'; that is, achievable without any cost in higher unemployment and lost output. However, as the quotation above admits, getting inflation down *has* caused unemployment to rise. This section surveys empirical research on the costs of reducing inflation and discusses some of the theoretical issues it raises.

This account of the costs of reducing inflation draws on Dawson (2002). The costs of reducing inflation are the costs of the higher unemployment brought about by disinflationary policy measures. The standard approach to measuring the costs of reducing inflation, the sacrifice ratio, focuses on the output costs of unemployment, abstracting from the other costs discussed in Section 18.3.1. The sacrifice ratio is the ratio of the cumulative percentage loss of GDP incurred by the policy for each one percentage point reduction in the inflation rate thereby achieved (Ball, 1993). Considerable uncertainty surrounds empirical estimates of the sacrifice ratio. Reviewing the historical evidence, Ball (1993) estimated average sacrifice ratios for a number of economies; they ranged from 2.92 for Germany and 2.39 for the USA to 0.79 for the UK and 0.75 for France. Sacrifice ratios for disinflationary episodes are dispersed around these averages. The different theoretical perspectives on the Phillips curve examined in Sections 18.2, 18.4.1 and 18.4.2 underlie conflicting empirical estimates of the probable magnitude of the output loss. There are five main influences on the sacrifice ratio.

The initial inflation rate

The standard shape of the short-run Phillips curve shown in Figure 18.1, which is flatter at lower rates of inflation, implies that the output cost of reducing the inflation rate by one percentage point is lower if the inflation rate at the outset is higher. So the cost of each successive percentage point of disinflation increases the more closely price stability is approached.

Expectations

Adaptive expectations imply that after a lag economic agents adjust to a new inflation rate, in which case reducing inflation incurs costs only during the lag while unemployment is above the natural rate. The length of this lag and hence the duration of the costs of reducing inflation depends on the speed with which agents' expectations that influence the wage and price-setting process adapt to the new inflation rate.

The pace of adjustment

This is the dilemma between gradualism and 'cold turkey'. Policy makers will phase in a disinflationary policy gradually if they believe that people take time to adjust their expectations of inflation, while others believe that a 'shock effect' might precipitate a rapid adjustment of expectations. Cold turkey may be the appropriate policy response to hyperinflation, because the costs associated with a very high inflation rate are likely to be greater than the costs of a sharp disinflation (Briault, 1995).

Policy credibility

Policy makers have credibility to the extent that economic agents believe their announcements of policy rules. In addition to the government's commitment to a systematic disinflationary policy being unequivocal, disinflation can be achieved at low cost to the extent that there is a consensus in favour of the policy (Sargent, 1986).

Imperfectly competitive markets

If all markets cleared instantaneously and approximated to the model of perfect competition, there would be a minimum of delay in adjusting to a new policy stance. But labour markets are imperfectly competitive, with wage bargaining between employers and trade unions being informed by assumptions about a 'fair wage' (Chapter 7, Section 7.4; Chapter 13, Section 13.2.4). Wage bargaining typically involves annual inflation adjustment. Goods markets are imperfectly competitive, giving firms some discretion in the timing and extent of price changes. Menu costs

> include the time taken to inform customers, the customer annoyance caused by price changes and the effort required even to think about a price change.
>
> *(Mankiw, 1990, p.1657)*

While menu costs seem small at the aggregate level (Section 18.2.2), they may be sufficiently large for individual firms to make them reluctant, in monopolistically competitive markets, to lower their prices when the demand for their goods declines as a consequence of disinflationary policies.

The importance of expectations and credibility is widely appreciated among economists and policy makers but few believe that markets clear rapidly, so the general view is that reducing inflation incurs significant costs at least in the short run. Policy credibility and expectations also influence the scale of those costs. Using a model developed by the IMF, Chadha *et al.* (1992) found that the sacrifice ratio is lower if the policy is phased in gradually, if the policy stance is credible and if expectations of future inflation play a large part in determining wage and price setting. Perfectly informed policy makers would weigh these costs against the costs of inflation and might conclude that 'there are advantages in achieving and maintaining price stability' (Briault, 1995, p.42).

18.5 UK macroeconomic policy

This section will trace the policy implications of the theoretical developments expounded in Section 18.4, using current UK monetary and growth policies as an illustration. One lesson that policy makers seem to have taken from macroeconomic theory and performance since the 1970s is the importance of keeping inflation low to prevent the damage to output and employment that occurs when it accelerates towards an annual rate of 40 per cent. Another lesson is that if the rate of inflation has to be reduced, costs in terms of lost output and employment will be incurred, mainly because economic agents operate in imperfectly competitive markets. And, finally, it is clear that if policy design and implementation take into account the importance of policy credibility and inflationary expectations, the costs of getting inflation down and keeping it low can be reduced. It follows from these considerations that the role of macroeconomic policy is to manage aggregate demand with the objective of maintaining low inflation. This strategy raises two questions, which this section will address. First, what are the implications for the conduct of monetary policy within such a framework? Second, if policy towards aggregate demand is so constrained, what can the government do about unemployment and the growth of output?

18.5.1 Aggregate demand and inflation

In many industrialized economies the central bank has been assigned the task of meeting an inflation objective, and to do so through changes in nominal short-term interest rates. This degree of central bank independence is thought to enhance the credibility of a low-inflation strategy because central bank officials will not be deflected by considerations of political unpopularity. The central bank seeks to do so by raising interest rates when inflation rises, on the view that such an increase in interest rates will reduce aggregate demand and hence inflation. In acting in this way central banks are following a monetary policy rule (Chapter 13, Section 13.3.2). The monetary authorities could target a single economic variable, such as inflation, or a combination of variables, such as output, employment and inflation. The simplest monetary policy rule is to change the interest rate in response to variations of inflation. It is the mandatory policy rule of the Bank of England to use the rate of interest to reach a target rate of inflation.

The Bank of England ('the Bank') is the central bank of the United Kingdom. It was founded as a private bank in 1694 but soon became the banker of the government. It was nationalized in 1946 and gained operational independence in 1997. The Bank is responsible for ensuring the effectiveness and the stability of the UK financial system and also for operating monetary policy. If the UK government sets the objective of low inflation (in 2002 this meant inflation in the range 1.5 to 3.5 per cent per annum) the Bank has the duty of staying within these limits through its conduct of monetary policy; that is, through variations in the rate of interest.

The Bank sets an interest rate for its own dealings with the market and that rate then affects the whole pattern of rates set by the commercial banks for their savers and borrowers. This in turn affects spending and output in the economy, and eventually costs and prices. Broadly speaking, interest rates are set at a level to ensure demand in the economy is in line with the productive capacity of the economy. If interest rates are set too low, [aggregate] demand may exceed [aggregate] supply and lead to the emergence of inflationary pressures so that inflation is accelerating; if they are set too high, output is likely to be unnecessarily low and inflation is likely to be decelerating.

(Bank of England, Notes on Monetary Policy, *www.bankofengland.co.uk)*

Interest rate decisions are taken by the Monetary Policy Committee (MPC) of the Bank. The MPC is made up of the Governor, the two Deputy Governors, two executive directors and four external members appointed directly by the Chancellor of the Exchequer, and meets monthly to make decisions on interest rates. When the inflation rate is forecast to exceed the target range, the Bank of England raises the short-term interest rate in order to reduce the level of aggregate demand. Conversely, if the inflation rate is forecast to fall below the lower limit of the target range, the Bank of England drops the short-term interest rate in order to increase the level of aggregate demand.

The sequence of events through which the central bank affects the level of national income and the inflation rate is known as the transmission mechanism (Chapter 12, Section 12.3.2). Figure 18.7(a) shows the monetary policy rule line. When the forecast rate of inflation increases from π_0 to π_1, the central bank raises the short-term nominal interest rate from $i(\pi_0)$ to $i(\pi_1)$. As a result of this change, the cost of liquidity for commercial banks is now higher. Banks consider the interest rate i as the direct cost of liquidity over which they mark up their profit margin:

$$r = (1 + m)i$$

where r is the price of loans to firms (i.e. the interest rate on loans) and m is the percentage mark-up (i.e. overhead and profit) which the banks apply. It is assumed here that, in general, banks maintain a constant mark-up. Therefore, when central banks change the interest rate i, banks increase their lending rates r by the same proportion. For a given expected return, this means that the investment demand falls. As the investment curve in Figure 18.7(b) illustrates, the increase in lending rates from $r(\pi_0)$ to $r(\pi_1)$ leads to a decrease of the level of investment from I_0 to I_1. Investment demand is a component of the aggregate demand and so, other things being equal, the level of aggregate demand decreases.

Figure 18.7(c) shows the aggregate demand/inflation curve, which summarizes the relationship between the level of output and the rate of inflation when the monetary policy rule is to change the interest rate in response to changes in the inflation rate: the higher the rate of inflation, the lower the level of output. The monetary policy rule of setting interest rates to maintain low inflation or price stability together with the investment demand explains the negative relationship between the rate of inflation and the level of output.

The aggregate demand/inflation curve is a relationship between two economic variables: the level of output Y (equal to the level of income), and the inflation rate π that measures the rate of change of the general level of prices. The rate of inflation is measured on the vertical axis and the level of output on the horizontal axis. The aggregate demand/inflation curve then tells us the total demand of commodities by households, firms, government and foreigners at any given inflation rate, which is translated into a corresponding level of output. The aggregate demand/inflation curve is downward sloping, showing that, other things being equal, a fall in the inflation rate would raise the demand for goods and services.

Figure 18.7
The aggregate
demand/inflation
curve

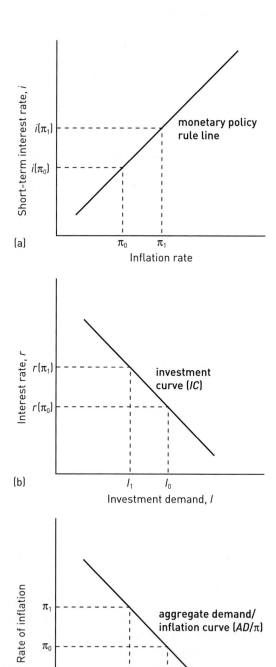

The Bank of England's monetary policy rule, and the UK government's anti-inflation stance in the years preceding the Bank's operational independence, have important implications for the shape of the short-run Phillips curve.

Case study: The UK Phillips curve 1991–2001

Question

What does Figure 18.8 tell you about the relationship between unemployment and inflation in the UK in the 1990s?

The UK Phillips curve in the 1990s resembles the almost flat segment of the original UK Phillips curve (Figure 18.1). Over the period 1991–93 the inflation rate fell while the unemployment rate rose, suggesting a trade-off between unemployment and inflation. Since then the curve has been virtually flat, as unemployment has fallen while inflation has been held steady. This can be explained as the outcome of UK policy makers' recognition that the long-run Phillips curve is vertical and their successful use of a monetary policy rule to maintain low inflation. Why has unemployment fallen in such circumstances? One answer is that rising productivity, in part associated with new information technology, has fuelled output growth and increased employment.

Haldane and Quah (1999), for example, argue that current UK policy makers' behaviour 'gives rise to the horizontal Phillips curve, with inflation anchored at target by monetary policy and output driven by productivity shocks'.

Does this mean that policy makers have discovered how to control inflation but have had to acknowledge that output and employment, 'driven by productivity shocks', are beyond their control? Not necessarily, for two reasons. First, the aggregate demand/inflation curve showed that inflation and output are negatively related, other things being equal, lower inflation being associated with higher output (Figure 18.7). The explanation is that while inflation is low, the Bank's monetary policy rule implies that interest rates are also low, leading to higher investment and hence higher output. Second, there are other economic policies that governments can deploy to influence productivity and output growth. These can be explained in terms of a shift in the aggregate demand/inflation curve.

Figure 18.8
The UK Phillips curve 1991–2001

Source: Office for National Statistics, 2002

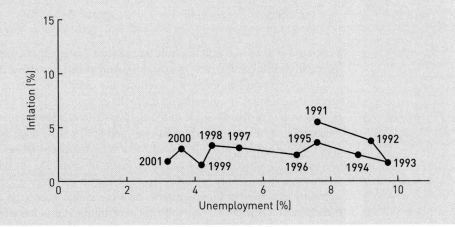

▪▪▪ 18.5.2 Output expansion and the supply side

Policy makers can seek to influence output growth in two ways. Getting inflation down would move the economy along the aggregate demand/inflation curve to a new combination of lower inflation and higher output (Figure 18.7). Increasing the level of output

Figure 18.9
A shift in the
aggregate
demand/inflation
curve

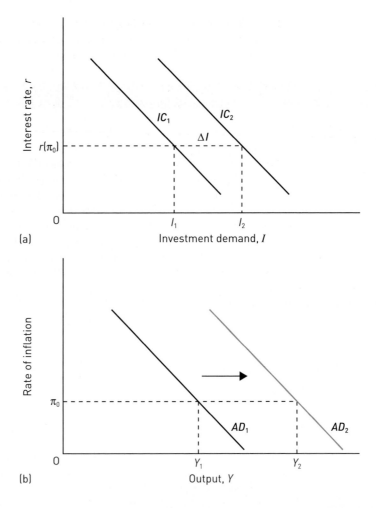

(a)

(b)

associated with a given inflation rate would shift the aggregate demand/inflation curve to the right, as shown in Figure 18.9(b). How might this be achieved?

The interest rate on loans, representing the cost of borrowing money from banks, is one of the main factors affecting investment demand and hence aggregate demand. This relationship explains the slope of the aggregate demand/inflation curve. However, when the expected returns on investment rise (perhaps because firms become more confident about the prospects for future growth), the demand for investment also rises. Figure 18.9 illustrates this situation in which, for a given interest rate, an increase in the expected returns on investment produces an increase in investment demand and hence in aggregate demand. In Figure 18.9(a), any event that raises the expected returns from investment increases the profitability of investment and so increases investment demand for a given interest rate. The investment demand curve therefore shifts outwards. Figure 18.9(b) shows the positive effect of this change on the aggregate demand/inflation curve. For any rate of inflation, an increase in the expected returns from investment shifts the aggregate demand/inflation curve to the right.

Among the events that might increase the expected returns on investment is a positive *productivity shock*, perhaps caused by the introduction of new technology (Chapters 2 and 3). This would offer the prospect of a greater than proportionate increase in output and hence potentially greater profits from investment in additional inputs of labour and capital. A range of 'supply side' policies can be used to increase the productive capacity of the economy (i.e. its potential for supplying goods and services) by increasing productivity. Competition policy seeks to encourage innovation, with potential productivity gains as well as greater efficiency from more intense competition (Chapters 4 and 5). The Chancellor of the Exchequer (UK finance minister) has recognized the possible macroeconomic benefits of competition policy.

As one commentator put it,

> Thanks to the Chancellor, we are witnessing a recognition of the fact that competition policy has an important role to play in achieving the macroeconomic goal of sustained non-inflationary economic growth.
>
> *(Selzer, 2001, p.101)*

Labour market policy measures to encourage the development of human capital held out the prospect of improved labour productivity (Chapter 7). Governments can reduce frictional unemployment by providing counselling and information services to employees, and recruitment services to employers.

The final step in explaining the theoretical foundations of current macroeconomic policy is to relate the increase in output for a given inflation rate, shown by an outwards shift in the aggregate demand/inflation curve, to the long-run Phillips curve. The monetary policy rule has established a nearly horizontal short-run Phillips curve, which represented maintaining low inflation and leaving output to productivity shocks. The implication is that, in the absence of such shocks, unemployment will remain at its natural rate. The falling unemployment rate depicted by the horizontal short-run Phillips curve in Figure 18.8 is therefore likely to be at least in part the result of a series of positive productivity shocks. Technological progress increases the demand for skilled labour and policy measures to improve training and reduce frictional unemployment allow this to be met without increasing inflation through higher wages and hence production costs. Technological innovation and supply-side policies may have combined to reduce the natural rate of unemployment, shifting the long-run vertical Phillips curve from U_{n1} to U_{n2} in Figure 18.10. This shows that for a given inflation rate the natural rate of unemployment is lower following a positive productivity shock.

Figure 18.10
The effect of a positive productivity shock on the natural rate of unemployment

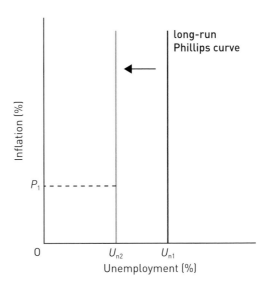

18.6 Conclusion

Unemployment and inflation are the headline issues of macroeconomic policy-making, reported by the media month by month and year on year. This chapter has focused on these issues, which used to be thought of as the concerns of short-run macroeconomic policy but which are now much more influenced by considerations of the long-run growth prospects of the economy. In the 1960s and early 1970s macroeconomic theorists generally advised policy makers to tolerate moderate rates of inflation in an effort to achieve full employment. Since then there has been a shift towards the view that price stability is either a necessary condition of long-run growth and high, if not full, employment or at least a sign of a competently, even prudently, managed economy (see Chapter 19). There is general agreement that an appreciation of the importance of expectations and policy credibility has the potential to improve macroeconomic management, provided that policy is also guided by an understanding of the way in which imperfectly competitive markets work.

Questions for review and discussion

Question 1   This is a four-part question, (a) to (d). In each part, you are asked whether a given statement is true or false. The diagrams illustrate different phases of the expectations-augmented Phillips curve analysis.

(a) The movement from A to B in Figure 18.11 represents the short-run effect of a reduction in aggregate demand on inflation and unemployment.
  ❏ True
  ❏ False

Figure 18.11
Expectations-augmented Phillips curve analysis

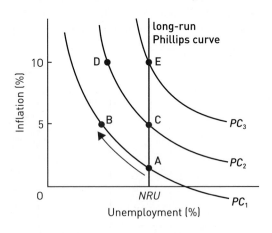

(b) The movement from B to C in Figure 18.12 occurs when workers incorporate past inflation into their expectations of future inflation.
  ❏ True
  ❏ False

Figure 18.12
Expections-
augmented Phillips
curve analysis

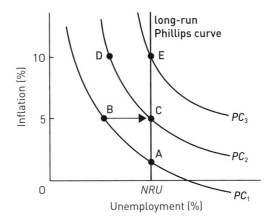

(c) On the hypothesis of adaptive expectations, the economy would move from C
directly to E (Figure 18.13) as a result of expansionary monetary or fiscal policy.
❑ True
❑ False

Figure 18.13
Expections-
augmented Phillips
curve analysis

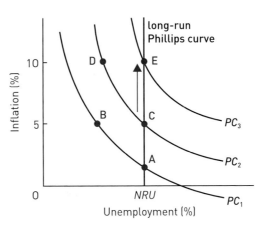

(d) Rational expectations theory allows for rising inflation with no fall in
unemployment but not for falling inflation with no rise in unemployment.
❑ True
❑ False

Question 2 Complete the sentences below by choosing the correct phrase from the list below for
each gap.

The main welfare costs imposed on society by anticipated inflation are . . . and . . .
The main welfare costs imposed on society by unanticipated inflation are . . . and . . .

reduced economic growth   *menu costs*   *'capricious' income redistribution*
'shoe leather' costs

Question 3 Figure 18.14 shows an aggregate demand/inflation curve. Select the correct statement
from those given below.

Figure 18.14
Aggregate
demand/inflation
curve

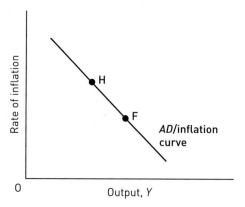

A Following a monetary policy rule would lead the monetary authorities to raise
   interest rates if inflation rose, leading to a fall in AD and hence output, as shown by
   the movement from F to H.
B A movement from F to H illustrates that a fall in the demand for goods and services
   would reduce output and hence raise the rate of inflation.
C If investment demand were to become more responsive to changes in interest rates,
   the slope of the AD/inflation curve would become steeper, other things being equal.
D An increase in interest rates would shift the AD/inflation curve to the left.
E Increasing the magnitude of the interest rate adjustment made in response to a given
   change in the inflation rate would shift the AD/inflation curve.

Question 4 Discuss the inflation and unemployment experience of the EU-11 economies during the
period from 1970 to 1997, as it is represented in Figure 18.15.

Figure 18.15
Phillips curves
for the EU-11
aggregate, 1970–97.
Note: EU-11
aggregate data are
the average
of inflation and
unemployment
figures for the
eleven economies
that have belonged
to the EU (and its
predecessors)
during the period
1970–97

Source: Bertola,
2001

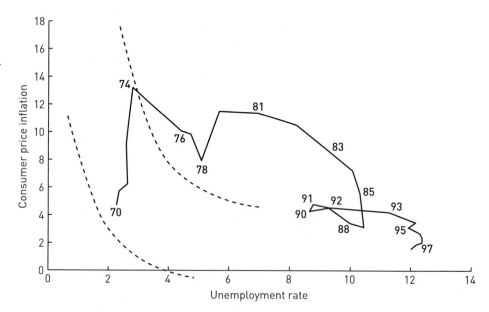

Question 5 (a) Briefly explain why higher inflation rates may be associated with lower growth rates.
(b) To what extent would you say that the data on inflation and GDP growth for
   the UK economy between 1965 and 2001 (see table) support the hypothesis that

higher inflation rates may be associated with lower growth rates? Explain your answer.

The data you will need for Question 5 are located on the Economics and Economic Change website/CD. A copy of the data appears in the Table 18.2.

Table 18.2
Inflation and GDP growth for the UK economy, 1965–2001

	Inflation %	GDP growth %
1965	4.8	2.5
1966	3.9	2.0
1967	2.5	2.3
1968	4.7	4.1
1969	5.4	2.0
1970	6.4	2.4
1971	9.4	2.0
1972	7.1	3.6
1973	9.2	7.3
1974	16.0	−1.7
1975	24.2	−0.7
1976	16.6	2.8
1977	15.8	2.4
1978	8.3	3.4
1979	13.4	2.7
1980	18.0	−2.2
1981	11.9	−1.3
1982	8.6	1.8
1983	4.6	3.7
1984	5.0	2.4
1985	6.1	3.8
1986	3.4	4.2
1987	4.2	4.4
1988	4.9	5.2
1989	7.8	2.1
1990	9.5	0.7
1991	5.9	−1.5
1992	3.7	0.1
1993	1.6	2.3
1994	2.4	4.4
1995	3.5	2.8
1996	2.4	2.6
1997	3.1	3.5
1998	3.4	2.6
1999	1.5	2.1
2000	3.0	3.0
2001	1.8	2.2

Figure 18.16
Unemployment and
inflation in UK,
1965–2001

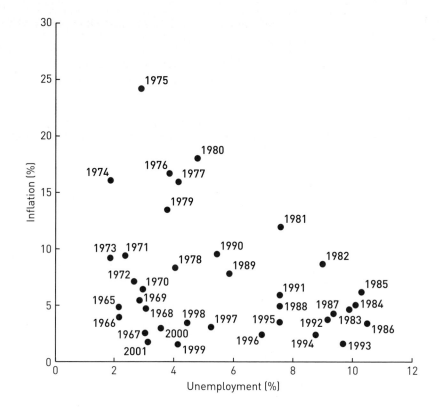

Question 6 Explain how expectations can influence the outcome of a government's anti-inflationary policy. Illustrate your answer with examples drawn from the history of UK macroeconomic policy towards inflation.

Question 7 Figure 18.16 is a scatterplot showing UK inflation and unemployment 1965–2001. Each point is labelled by year. In addition, you are given the following information:

Regression equation: Inflation = 10.5 − 0.6 unemployment
R Squared = 0.1

Using the scatterplot, the data above and economic theory explain the possible relationships between unemployment and inflation in the short run and in the long run.

19

Macroeconomic performance and stabilization

Nicholas Crafts

Concepts

- GDP per head
- inflation
- unemployment
- real GDP
- NAIRU (non-accelerating inflation rate of unemployment)
- shadow economy
- Taylor rules
- hyperinflation
- economic growth

Objectives

After studying this chapter you should be able to:

- appreciate the importance of historical data in assessing macroeconomic performance and the limitations of standard measures of macroeconomic performance
- understand the perennial problems faced by macroeconomic stabilization policy makers
- understand the interactions between the forces influencing long-run economic growth and the effects of short-run stabilization policies.

19.1 Introduction

The approach taken in this chapter is relatively uncommon in macroeconomic textbooks. It provides you with the opportunity to:

(a) explore a wide range of historical experience using basic macroeconomic concepts without needing lots of prior knowledge;

(b) consider the long-run consequences of policy decisions aimed at dealing with short-run problems; and

(c) examine the difficulties for short-run policy-making of changes in long-run economic trends.

The first question to answer is, of course, 'what happened?' Economic history offers a wide range of outcomes, including mass unemployment, hyperinflation, full employment, severe deflation and strong growth with price stability. Awareness of this diversity of experience is one key ingredient in addressing a second question, 'how good is a country's present performance?', although this knowledge clearly needs to be supplemented by an assessment of the conditions under which it would be feasible to emulate the best results from the past.

Probably the most common reason for (generally spurious) comparisons of economic performance is to score party political points about the effectiveness of economic policy – as in the rough and tumble of Prime Minister's Question Time in the British House of Commons. This prompts two further closely related issues worth exploring in some detail and with some care: 'how far is economic policy responsible for short- or long-term outcomes such as recessions or differences in growth rates?' and 'what explains failures in the design of economic policy for stabilization?'

▦ ▪ ■ 19.1.1 Macroeconomic performance: an historical overview

Research by economic historians has produced a wealth of data from which this section draws some edited highlights. Inevitably we must consider a good deal of quantitative information. In doing so, the objective will be to extract key points rather than to drown in a sea of minute detail. The account that follows concentrates on the standard measures of macroeconomic performance: growth, inflation, unemployment and volatility. In Section 19.1.2 the value and reliability of these indicators are considered, but our first task is to see what the data say.

> **Question** Consider Tables 19.1 and 19.2, which contain a summary description of levels of real GDP per head and of economic growth in industrial countries since 1870. What surprises you most in the tables? How would you describe the relative performance of the UK?

Assessment of relative growth performance is a topic which is fully developed in Section 19.4. For the moment, however, it seems appropriate to notice that the long-run experience of the UK has been one of continuing relative economic decline, although in absolute terms incomes have risen steadily. Table 19.1 shows that the UK has fallen from second highest GDP per head in 1870 to seventeenth in 1999. This implies that over the long term UK economic growth has been less rapid than in other countries, which is confirmed in Table 19.2. The UK is below the median growth rate in each period. As to the biggest surprise, there could well be many different answers, but the most popular might be to pick out the exceptionally rapid growth of the 'Golden Age' (1950–73). Explanations for that unusual episode and the marked slowdown that followed it in the last quarter of the twentieth century will be reviewed in Section 19.4.

In a typical year OECD countries experience economic growth, but these long-period averages conceal substantial short-run fluctuations. Table 19.3, which is divided into periods that will be convenient for subsequent discussion, reports a sizeable standard deviation of the growth rate especially prior to the Second World War. Put differently, all economies go through years of recession when real output contracts rather than increases; for example, in the post-war period the UK has experienced decreases in real GDP per head in eight years (1952, 1958, 1974, 1975, 1980, 1981, 1991 and 1992). In fact, in most of these cases the declines were small (2 per cent or less). In really bad times, falls in GDP have been much more severe. The worst experiences in the West came in the Depression of the early 1930s when for the advanced countries the average decline in real GDP between 1929 and 1933 was 17 per cent and in the USA it was 25 per cent (Maddison, 1983). By comparison, the turbulence of the recent past pales into

	1870	$	1913	$	1950	$	1973	$	1999	$
1	Australia	3645	Australia	5715	USA	9561	Switzerland	18 204	USA	27 975
2	UK	3191	USA	5301	Switzerland	9064	USA	16 689	Norway	23 717
3	Netherlands	2753	New Zealand	5152	New Zealand	8453	Canada	13 838	Singapore	23 582
4	New Zealand	2704	UK	4921	Australia	7493	Denmark	13 945	Denmark	22 389
5	Belgium	2697	Canada	4447	Canada	7437	Sweden	13 493	Switzerland	21 609
6	USA	2445	Switzerland	4266	Denmark	6946	Germany	11 966	Canada	21 331
7	Switzerland	2202	Belgium	4220	UK	6907	France	13 123	Australia	21 045
8	Denmark	2003	Netherlands	4049	Sweden	6738	Netherlands	13 082	Netherlands	20 805
9	Germany	1913	Denmark	3912	Netherlands	5996	Australia	12 759	Japan	20 431
10	France	1876	Germany	3833	Norway	5463	New Zealand	12 513	Germany	20 415
11	Austria	1863	France	3485	Belgium	5462	Belgium	12 170	Hong Kong	20 352
12	Ireland	1775	Austria	3465	France	5270	UK	12 022	France	20 054
13	Canada	1695	Sweden	3096	Germany	4281	Japan	11 439	Belgium	19 892
14	Sweden	1664	Ireland	2736	Finland	4253	Norway	11 246	Ireland	19 756
15	Italy	1499	Italy	2564	Austria	3706	Austria	11 235	Sweden	19 380
16	Norway	1432	Norway	2501	Italy	3502	Finland	11 085	Austria	19 264
17	Spain	1376	Spain	2255	Ireland	3466	Italy	10 643	UK	19 030
18	Finland	1140	Finland	2111	Spain	2397	Spain	8 739	Finland	19 012
19	Portugal	997	Greece	1592	Singapore	2219	Greece	7 655	Italy	17 994
20	Greece	913	Japan	1385	Hong Kong	2218	Portugal	7 343	Taiwan	15 720
21	Japan	737	Singapore	1279	Portugal	2069	Hong Kong	7 104	New Zealand	15 335
22			Portugal	1244	Japan	1926	Ireland	6 867	Spain	14 746
23			South Korea	893	Greece	1915	Singapore	5 977	South Korea	13 317
24			Taiwan	747	Taiwan	936	Taiwan	4 117	Portugal	13 289
25					South Korea	770	South Korea	2 841	Greece	11 620

Source: derived from Maddison, 2001, updated to 1999 using World Bank, 2001. Estimates for Germany refer to the area of West Germany prior to unification throughout from Maddison, 1995; the 1999 figure is extrapolated from 1994 using growth rate of unified Germany

Table 19.1 Levels of real GDP per head for benchmark years, 1870–1999 (US$, 1990 international)

insignificance, although the oil shocks of the 1970s marked the end of a long post-war boom characterized by exceptional stability.

Table 19.3 also introduces a summary of inflation performance. Here it is apparent that average inflation in the G7 countries has varied substantially over time – much more so than the rate of economic growth. Prior to the Second World War, peacetime inflation rates were generally close to zero. Indeed, prices were generally falling between the mid-1870s and mid-1890s and in the inter-war period policy makers worried about price deflation rather than inflation. The period after the breakdown of the Bretton Woods international monetary system stands out as one of high inflation.

In Table 19.4's more detailed account of inflation in the UK, the 1970s stand out as an aberration. In 1975, the peak year, inflation reached the record level of 27.2 per cent, over four times the rate experienced in West Germany. By contrast, in the early 1920s when prices fell by over 30 per cent in three years in the UK, Germany experienced hyperinflation. This highlights the point that, while there can be common inflationary threats such as oil price shocks, domestic policy and circumstances tend to matter much more, at least in episodes of very rapid inflation.

Table 19.2
Rates of growth of real GDP per head for selected periods, 1870–1999 (percentage per year)

1870–1913	%	1913–50	%	1950–73	%	1973–99	%
Australia	1.0	Australia	0.7	USA	2.4	Switzerland	0.7
UK	1.0	USA	1.6	Switzerland	3.1	USA	2.0
Netherlands	0.9	New Zealand	1.4	New Zealand	1.7	Canada	1.7
New Zealand	1.5	UK	0.9	Australia	2.3	Denmark	1.8
Belgium	1.0	Canada	1.4	Canada	2.7	Sweden	1.4
USA	1.8	Switzerland	2.1	Denmark	3.1	Germany	1.7
Switzerland	1.6	Belgium	0.7	UK	2.4	France	1.7
Denmark	1.6	Netherlands	1.1	Sweden	3.1	Netherlands	1.8
Germany	1.6	Denmark	1.6	Netherlands	3.4	Australia	1.9
France	1.4	Germany	0.3	Norway	3.2	New Zealand	0.8
Austria	1.4	France	1.1	Belgium	3.6	Belgium	1.9
Ireland	1.0	Austria	0.2	France	4.0	UK	1.8
Canada	2.3	Sweden	2.1	Germany	5.0	Japan	2.3
Sweden	1.5	Ireland	0.7	Finland	4.2	Norway	2.9
Italy	1.3	Italy	0.8	Austria	4.9	Austria	2.1
Norway	1.3	Norway	2.1	Italy	5.0	Finland	2.1
Spain	1.2	Spain	0.2	Ireland	3.0	Italy	2.0
Finland	1.4	Finland	1.9	Spain	5.8	Spain	2.0
Portugal	0.5	Greece	0.5	Singapore	4.4	Greece	1.6
Greece	1.3	Japan	0.9	Hong Kong	5.2	Portugal	2.3
Japan	1.5	Singapore	1.5	Portugal	5.7	Hong Kong	4.1
		Portugal	1.4	Japan	8.0	Ireland	4.1
		South Korea	−0.4	Greece	6.2	Singapore	5.4
		Taiwan	0.6	Taiwan	6.6	Taiwan	5.3
				South Korea	5.8	South Korea	6.1

Source: derived from Table 19.1

Table 19.3
G7 macroeconomic indicators (percentage per year)

	Inflation		Real GDP growth	
	Mean %	Standard deviation %	Mean %	Standard deviation %
Gold Standard (1880–1913)	1.0	3.4	1.5	3.7
Inter-war (1919–39)	−1.1	7.7	1.2	6.8
Bretton Woods (1945–71)	3.6	4.6	4.2	2.7
The OPEC years (1974–89)	7.2	3.3	2.2	2.3
1990–99	2.2	1.1	1.8	0.8

Source: Bordo, 1993; IMF, 2000

Table 19.4 also displays information on estimates of the rate of UK unemployment over time, based on the OECD definition, 'persons without work, available for work and seeking employment for pay or profit'. The number of people unemployed is estimated from a survey of a sample of the population, unlike the official UK figures which are derived

Table 19.4
UK inflation and unemployment rates

	Inflation %	Unemployment %
1870s	−1.0	4.3
1880s	−0.6	5.9
1890s	0.6	5.2
1900s	0.6	6.6
1920s	−3.1	*7.7*
1930s	0.3	11.1
1950s	4.2	2.0
1960s	3.6	2.7
1970s	14.1	4.4
1980s	6.1	10.6
1990s	3.3	8.8

Source: inflation is measured by the GDP deflator, Feinstein, 1972; *Economic Trends*, 2001; unemployment relative to civilian work force pre-First World War, Boyer and Hatton, 2002; inter-war, Feinstein, 1972; post-war, Layard *et al.*, 1994; OECD, 2001

from counting the number of people claiming unemployment benefit (Chapter 18). These estimates are constructed so as to be broadly comparable, which is in fact quite difficult given the varying sources of information that have to be used. The difference between periods is pronounced. Whereas the inter-war years and the late twentieth century were times when many of those looking for work were unsuccessful, the 1950s and 1960s stand out as an age of exceptionally low unemployment. Moreover, in the 1980s, even with over 10 per cent unemployed, inflation averaged about 6 per cent. This compares with inflation around 4 per cent while unemployment was under 3 per cent in the early post-war decades.

Table 19.5 reports unemployment rates on the standardized (OECD) definition which sometimes differs from the headline rate most commonly reported in individual countries. The OECD definition can be applied consistently across countries and so enables international comparisons to be made. The inter-war data are not as accurate as those for the recent past but the broad picture is informative. There are clearly some common features across countries. Thus, 1933, at the worst of the Great Depression, was a year of relatively high unemployment in every country, while the universal experience in 1973, at the end of the post-war Golden Age, was the opposite. The late twentieth century, however, saw some interesting differences in unemployment trends; it is instructive to compare France and Italy with Ireland and the Netherlands.

Question | Compare Tables 19.1 and 19.5. What relation across countries is there between the level of unemployment and the level of GDP per person at the end of the twentieth century?

Unemployment tends to be lower in countries with relatively high income and productivity levels (the rank correlation coefficient is −0.61). This is an interesting observation because it goes against a widely held belief that adopting better technology and improving labour productivity inevitably lead to higher unemployment. The same inference can be

Table 19.5
Standardized
unemployment
rates

	1929 %	1933 %	1937 %	1973 %	1983 %	2000 %
Australia	8.2	17.4	8.1	2.3	9.9	6.6
Austria	5.5	16.3	13.7	0.9	3.7	3.7
Belgium	0.8	10.6	7.2	2.7	12.1	7.0
Canada	2.9	19.3	9.4	5.5	11.8	6.8
Denmark	8.0	14.5	11.0	1.0	10.4	4.7
Finland	2.8	6.2	2.6	2.3	5.4	9.8
France	n/a	n/a	n/a	2.7	8.3	9.5
Germany	5.9	14.8	2.7	0.8	8.0	8.1
Ireland	n/a	n/a	n/a	5.7	14.0	4.2
Italy	1.7	5.9	5.0	4.4	7.0	10.7
Japan	n/a	n/a	n/a	1.3	2.6	4.7
Netherlands	1.7	9.7	10.5	2.9	12.0	2.8
Norway	5.4	9.7	6.0	1.5	3.4	3.5
Spain	n/a	n/a	n/a	2.5	17.2	14.1
Sweden	2.4	7.3	5.1	2.0	2.9	5.9
Switzerland	0.4	3.5	3.6	0.0	2.4	2.6
UK	7.2	13.9	7.7	3.1	12.5	5.5
USA	3.1	24.7	14.2	4.8	9.5	4.0

Source: inter-war from Maddison, 1991; post-war from Layard *et al.*, 1994, updated using OECD, 2001

drawn by looking at what has happened to unemployment over time. Clearly, by 1973, labour productivity was much higher than in the inter-war years, yet unemployment rates were much lower. Similarly, the USA, which experienced a late-twentieth-century boom based on massive investment in information and communication technology (ICT), had lower unemployment in 2000 than in either 1973 or 1983.

The message is that a theory of unemployment based on job losses caused by new technology would not be valid. Unemployment depends on economic and social factors. Broadly speaking, there are two aspects to bear in mind. The first deals with institutional arrangements in the labour market with regard to industrial relations, training and the terms on which unemployment benefits are made available (see Chapters 7 and 9). These are fundamental to the true 'tightness' of the labour market associated with any recorded level of unemployment and thus to the unemployment rate that is consistent with stable prices – the **non-accelerating inflation rate of unemployment (NAIRU)**. These arrangements affect how quickly unemployed people can find appropriate work and hence the rate of frictional unemployment, which underlies the natural rate of unemployment (NRU) (Chapter 18, Section 18.4.1). The NRU is the rate of unemployment to which the economy returns after each episode of expansionary monetary policy and accelerating inflation, for example after the movement from B to C in Figure 18.4. So the NRU is reached after a period of rising unemployment at a stable, or non-accelerating, inflation rate and is therefore related to the NAIRU. The term 'NAIRU' does not imply that unemployment is the outcome of voluntary choices by unemployed people waiting for a more appropriate job offer. Instead, it reflects the mutual consistency between wages and prices for both firms and workers. For firms, the prices they are setting for their products give an adequate mark-up over the wages they pay. For workers, the wages agreed are

Non-accelerating inflation rate of unemployment (NAIRU)

The non-accelerating inflation rate of unemployment is the level of unemployment at which the inflation rate is constant.

satisfactory, given the prices they face. This mutual consistency prevents any upward or downward pressure on prices and hence underlies a stable, non-accelerating inflation rate.

Institutional arrangements in the labour market influence both the NRU and the NAIRU. Industrial relations, training provision and the level and eligibility conditions of unemployment benefit affect the NRU. Social norms concerning the adequacy of mark-ups (and hence profits) for firms and real wages for workers influence the NAIRU. Since both sets of institutional arrangements have varied over time and across countries so have the NRU and the NAIRU.

The second factor to consider is demand. In order to sustain employment at the NAIRU, the output which is produced must be purchased: supply and demand must balance. In fact, demand fluctuates unpredictably from year to year, sometimes by large amounts as in times of adverse macroeconomic shocks such as in the Great Depression of the early 1930s or the OPEC oil price rises of the 1970s. Keynesian theories of unemployment claim that depressed demand is a key factor (Chapter 13). This is perhaps most plausible as an explanation of short-term fluctuations in the labour market but these can leave long-term 'echoes' if they lead to changes in the skill base of the labour force. Persistently high unemployment brings long-term unemployment with attrition of the skills and morale of unemployed people, which permanently reduces sustainable output.

▨ ▪ ▪ 19.1.2 How good are standard measures of macroeconomic performance?

This question can be broken down into three parts:

1 Are the statistics that are commonly used measured accurately?
2 Are the right aspects of performance being measured?
3 What relative importance should be given to different aspects of performance?

Each of these deserves serious consideration.

From time to time there are debates about the accuracy of economic statistics. One reason for this is that politicians devise new ways of presenting data which are more favourable to the assessment of their policies, for example the many changes to the official claimant count of UK unemployment in the 1980s. This is not, however, the central issue and in any case the scope for such activity is heavily constrained by international agreements to collect statistics, such as GDP and labour market measures, on a common definition. The data presented in Tables 19.1–19.5 have not been contaminated by political manipulation.

On the other hand, conventional methods of compiling the statistics may sometimes lead to misleading results. The best-known, and perhaps the most important, recent example of this kind of problem was highlighted by the report of the Boskin Commission in the USA (Boskin et al., 1996). The report examined the procedures used to calculate changes in the cost of living and concluded that in the mid-1990s inflation was being overestimated by about 1.1 percentage points per year. Some of the commission's concerns related simply to the sampling procedures in the collection of prices against a background of rapid changes in retailing. Other problems concerned the methods used to aggregate price changes for individual items into an overall index. Finally, and most importantly, the commission found that there was a failure to allow adequately for improvements in quality and to introduce new products into the index quickly enough (see Chapter 2).

The problems to which the Boskin Commission drew attention are not, of course, unique to the USA nor do they affect only the measurement of inflation. In fact, when inflation is wrongly measured so too is the growth of real GDP. The output of the economy is measured in terms of the sum of value added in the economy each year measured in current prices. To work out how much of the increase since the previous year is accounted for by greater volume of production and how much by higher prices, the figure in current prices is deflated by a price index and the result expressed as GDP in the prices of the base year (Chapter 8). A tendency to overestimate the rate of inflation therefore implies that the rate of economic growth will be underestimated by a similar amount.

Why should we measure macroeconomic performance at all? Presumably we care because it says something about economic welfare or well-being, and a very common use of the national income accounts is to compare standards of living either over time or across countries (Chapter 8). If this is the case, then there are genuine reasons for concern as to the accuracy of GDP measurement. The concept of GDP was originally devised as a way to measure changes in production, which would be useful for attempts to stabilize the level of economic activity and to assess the pressure of demand on productive resources in the market economy.

Even as a measure of production, GDP is inadequate in important respects. First, there is the existence of the *shadow economy*; that is, production of goods and services which could be bought and sold quite legally but which are hidden from the statistical agencies typically to avoid either taxation or regulation. Some estimates of this component of economic activity are shown in Table 19.6. By its very nature, the shadow economy is, of course, very difficult to quantify. The estimates in Table 19.6 are derived from the proposition that in general such transactions rely disproportionately on the use of cash and are based on inferences from changes in the demand for currency. They should be used with caution, as their authors frankly admit.

Question	What are the implications of the estimates in Table 19.6 for the use of Tables 19.1 and 19.2?

The main feature of Table 19.6 is the general increase in the relative importance of the shadow economy in the last decades of the twentieth century. This implies that growth rates of real GDP are underestimated by conventional national income accounting and that the slowdown after the European Golden Age was not quite as bad as official estimates suggest. However, since most countries are affected to a similar extent (about 0.4 to 0.5 percentage points per year), relative growth performance across countries is not seriously distorted by failing to take the shadow economy into account. Discrepancies in the relative size of the shadow economy between countries do change the rank order of the level of GDP per head; in 1999, for example, Belgium moves above Switzerland if these adjustments are applied. This underlines a general point: economic statistics are typically measured with error, but how much this matters depends on the question that is to be answered.

Further, GDP does not include production such as housework and care of relatives that would contribute to value added if it were performed in the context of a market transaction (Chapter 8, Section 8.2). These activities are substantial relative to GDP; for example in 1995, valued at industrial equivalent pay rates in a pioneering attempt at measurement, they comprised output equivalent to 56 per cent of the national accounts total (Murgatroyd and Neuburger, 1997). If, as more married women have participated in market work, household production activities have declined over time, growth as estimated by the national accounts concept is overstated.

Table 19.6
Shadow economy as
a percentage of GDP

	1960 %	1970 %	1980 %	1998 %
Australia				14.1
Austria	0.4	1.8	3.0	9.1
Belgium		10.4	16.4	22.6
Canada			10.6	15.0
Denmark	4.3	6.4	8.6	18.4
France		3.9	6.9	14.9
Germany	2.0	2.8	10.8	14.7
Greece				29.0
Hong Kong				13.0
Ireland		4.3	8.0	16.3
Italy		10.7	16.7	27.8
Japan				11.3
Netherlands		4.8	9.1	13.5
Norway	1.5	6.5	10.6	19.7
Singapore				13.0
South Korea				38.0
Spain		10.3	17.2	23.4
Sweden	1.6	7.3	12.2	20.0
Switzerland	1.2	4.1	6.5	8.0
Taiwan				16.5
UK		2.0	8.4	13.0
USA	3.1	3.6	5.0	8.9

Source: Schneider, 2000; for Hong Kong, Singapore, South Korea and Taiwan (estimates for 1990), and Japan (estimate for 1997) from Schneider and Enste, 2000; in some cases estimates are mid-point of a range

National income, as famously defined by Hicks (1939), is the maximum amount that can be consumed while leaving the capital stock intact. This essentially sees matters in terms of sustainability and raises a series of issues taken up elsewhere in this book. Nevertheless, it reminds us that it is consumption rather than production that contributes to well-being and that GDP overstates potential consumption because it includes investment expenditures to make good depreciation.

This suggests that, in principle, it would be preferable to measure national income in terms of utility (i.e. its value to consumers) rather than production, and just such an approach has been suggested by Nordhaus (2000) (see Chapter 8). This would have several important implications. First, it would imply that some aspects of GDP are 'bads' rather than 'goods', for example, reflecting the costs of commuting or making good environmental damage, as explained in Chapter 8, Section 8.2. Second, it would imply that we should explicitly recognize that the same GDP per head produced with fewer hours worked or with lower mortality risks represents superior outcomes. It would then be natural in looking at changes of living standards over time to ask how much extra consumption of final goods included in GDP would be needed to compensate people for giving up gains in leisure and/or life expectancy. Given that in the UK hours worked per year in full-time employment have nearly halved and life expectancy at birth has nearly doubled since 1870, it is plausible that growth of real GDP per person significantly under-states gains in living standards over that period (Crafts, 1997).

Which is better: a fast growth economy with high unemployment or a low growth economy with low unemployment?

Presumably everyone would agree that a fast growth economy with low unemployment is to be preferred to either of these eventualities but each of the options on offer are better on one indicator but worse on the other. The answer that people give to the question will depend on how big the differences are in each aspect of performance and how much they value each outcome; in other words, what trade-off they would make between unemployment and growth if that is the choice with which they are confronted. Politicians are likely to view such a trade-off in terms of votes won and lost and at least in Britain their implied assessment seems to have varied over time; for example, in the Thatcher period growth was accorded relatively more weight compared with unemploy-ment than had been the case previously (Crafts, 2002).

Is it possible to devise a weighting scheme based on empirical grounds as opposed to value judgements or political considerations? Probably not, but there is some evidence to hand in the form of responses to opinion polls which ask questions about happiness. Analysis of these data by Blanchflower and Oswald (2001) results in an estimate that to compensate an unemployed American man for lack of work would require on average a payment of US$60 000 per year. This suggests that, when there is a trade-off at the margin, policies designed to make labour markets work better should be a higher priority for policy makers than those aimed at improving productivity growth of those already in work.

One further important point to note is that over the long run economic growth has not been associated with increasing happiness in OECD countries; on the contrary, lev-els of happiness reported to the opinion pollsters have tended to decline slightly since the 1970s. The best interpretation of this seems to be that aspirations tend to increase with income (Easterlin, 2001). This means that threatened with a reduction to past income levels people would see that as making them worse off and regard the prospect of future growth as making them better off. But it is better to travel hopefully than to arrive.

19.2 Macroeconomic management: some perennial problems

In an ideal world what would macroeconomic management achieve? The answer might be to maintain price stability at the NAIRU with the level of output consistent with these objectives. The requirement for this would be to smooth out fluctuations in demand that push economic activity away from this equilibrium level. In the short run, excessive demand causes output to rise above and unemployment to fall below the optimum and is associated with rising inflation, while the opposite is true for inadequate demand. In the long run, if demand growth, fuelled perhaps by excessive creation of money, is per-sistently above the growth of production there will be persistent inflation which becomes generally anticipated and the economy will return to the NAIRU. Thus the long-run macroeconomic management task would be to ensure that the growth of purchasing power matches the growth of productive potential in the economy.

▨ ▧ ▪ 19.2.1   Taylor rules

The government can influence the pressure of demand in the economy through a number of policy instruments including both monetary and fiscal policy. In situations where demand needs to be restrained, the options are to raise interest rates and/or tax rates and/or reduce government expenditure. If demand needs to be raised, the menu of policy options comprises the reverse of these actions. In the so-called Keynesian era of the 1950s and 1960s, there was widespread belief in governments' ability to undertake 'fine-tuning' of demand and achieve good outcomes both in terms of low inflation and low unemployment. The experience of the 1970s and 1980s made this earlier faith seem illusory. In the 1990s, however, when, across the OECD, monetary policy was increasingly delegated to central banks with 'constrained discretion', successful macroeconomic management once again seemed within the realms of possibility.

The 'constrained discretion' that central banks exercise in conducting monetary policy usually means in practice that they follow a monetary policy rule linking interest rates to macroeconomic variables such as the inflation rate and the level of aggregate demand (Chapter 18, Section 18.5.1). These are sometimes known as Taylor rules, after the US economist John B. Taylor who proposed a rule for the US central bank (Taylor, 1994).

Question	Recalling the discussions of monetary policy in Chapters 12 (Section 12.4.2) and 13 (Section 13.5.1), when do you think the central bank is likely to raise interest rates and when is it likely to reduce them?

The central bank is likely to raise interest rates if the inflation rate is forecast to rise above an upper limit usually set by the government, because higher interest rates will reduce investment, aggregate demand and inflation. The central bank is likely to reduce interest rates if the level of aggregate demand is forecast to fall below that which is required to keep the economy operating reasonably close to full employment (or the NAIRU), because lower interest rates will increase investment, aggregate demand and reduce unemployment. A Taylor rule for the nominal interest rate on loans, r, that embodied these two principles might look like this:

$$r = \pi + 1.5(\pi - \pi^*) + 0.5(Y - Y^*)$$

Since it is the real interest rate that influences investment decisions, the nominal interest rate, r, must first respond to the inflation rate, π. It must also respond to any deviation of inflation, π, above its target rate, π^*; the coefficient on that deviation is greater than 1 to ensure that, if inflation picks up, real interest rates increase. The final part of the equation can be read as saying that for each percentage point that output Y falls below the level associated with the NAIRU, Y^*, interest rates fall by half a per cent.

Although demand management can play a key role in stabilizing prices and reducing the severity of economic fluctuations, these days supply-side policy instruments are rightly regarded as the key to achieving a lower NAIRU and a higher rate of long-term economic growth. With regard to the former, microeconomic labour market policies relating to training, welfare programmes and industrial relations are at the heart of the matter; with the latter, policies that influence the incentives to invest and/or to innovate (e.g. competition policy and addressing market failures in research and development) are central. Having said that, it does seem to be the case that macroeconomic instability in the form of pronounced business-cycle fluctuations does have an adverse effect on long-term growth through adverse effects on the rate of investment (Oulton, 1995) and severe recessions can provoke policy responses which are damaging to the supply side so that good macroeconomic management may have a bonus in terms of raising medium-term productive potential.

Question	Why has demand management not delivered better results (see Tables 19.3 and 19.4)?

Successful demand management depends on a great deal of accurate information and the ability to act quickly if need be. The latter tends to be much more possible if interest rates are the main policy instrument rather than adjustments to tax and government spending. The most obvious reason is that the policy makers are blown off course by unpredictable macroeconomic shocks.

If these are big and unpleasant enough, there may be no way to achieve a satisfactory outcome quickly. Broadly speaking, this is true of the exceptional situation facing OECD countries in the 1970s when oil prices quadrupled in the first OPEC shock and then doubled in the second. The impacts of these events were *stagflationary* in that they pushed inflation up while also reducing domestic demand. In the short term, the choice was how much extra inflation and/or unemployment to accept; attempting to stop prices rising through reducing demand would push unemployment up still further.

Referring to the Taylor rule as set out above, a more pervasive problem is to know how big the output gap is given that the underlying rate of productivity growth may vary over time and the NAIRU itself will respond to changes in labour market arrangements. In retrospect, this was a major aspect of the 1970s inflation both in the UK and the USA. Towards the end of the Golden Age in the UK, productivity growth slowed down, wage bargaining became less centralized and benefits more generous. At the time, economic policy makers failed to appreciate the implications of these developments and so allowed excessive demand growth; econometric analysis suggests that this may have been responsible for as much as half of UK inflation in the 1970s (Nelson and Nikolov, 2001). But the pleasant surprises of the 1990s have also posed problems with regard to the output gap, especially in the USA in the context of the so-called new economy in which the ICT revolution stimulated productivity growth but also created great uncertainty about how big its medium-term impact would be. This is discussed further in Section 19.5.2.

▪▪▪ 19.2.2 Inflationary bias

If there are 'cock-up' reasons for poor macroeconomic management, are there also 'conspiracy' aspects? There is indeed a serious problem in that encouraging policy makers to use discretionary intervention creates the opportunity for misuse of policy for short-term political ends. In general, the problem is one of *inflationary bias*. This is the conclusion of the influential Barro–Gordon model (Barro and Gordon, 1983). The Barro–Gordon argument is captured in simplified form in the pay-off matrix of Figure 19.1. (You might want to refer to the discussion of the pay-off matrix in Chapter 6.) The public is assumed to be worse off if inflation deviates from its expected rate. The government gains by raising demand to create surprise inflation which lowers unemployment as workers temporarily believe that real wages have risen. Conversely, creating lower than expected inflation hurts the government because it raises unemployment. The government loses from higher than anticipated inflation which annoys voters with no compensating output gain because real wages are predicted correctly.

Figure 19.1
The Barro–Gordon
model

		Public	
		zero expected inflation	high expected inflation
Government	zero actual inflation	0, 0	−2, −1
	high actual inflation	1, −1	−1, 0

Exercise 19.1

With reference to the Barro–Gordon model and Figure 19.1 answer the following questions.

1 Given the pay-offs, explain why it is better for the government to have inflation.
2 Would you believe a promise by the government not to create inflation?
3 Which cell of the matrix shows the outcome if the public have rational expectations?

The example is of a situation where the government has a dominant strategy: high inflation is better for it whatever the public expects (compare the government pay-offs under either zero or high expected inflation). The implication of the example is that governments will break promises not to create inflation. We should expect that the government's optimal strategy will be anticipated by the public and will thus lead to inflation without raising output – ending up in the bottom right-hand cell. If the government can make binding commitments about inflation through a rule that cannot be broken, the problem would be avoided. This is because there would be no possibility of imagining that surprise inflation could benefit the government; hence rules are better than discretionary demand management according to this line of argument (see Chapter 14).

What are the downside risks of committing yourself to a policy rule? The most obvious is that it is no longer possible to respond to adverse demand shocks. In other words, there may be a trade-off between the welfare losses from inflation if discretion exists for the government and from possible unemployment if there are rules that bind the government. Even more worrying is the possibility that, if the 'wrong sort of shock' occurs, the policy rule may exacerbate its effects. A graphic example of these problems, discussed in Section 19.3.2 and in Chapter 17, can be found in the consequences of remaining on the Gold Standard in the Great Depression.

Fixed exchange rates are one way to eliminate discretion and thus to address the issue of inflationary bias (Chapter 17). In a world of capital mobility, maintaining a fixed exchange rate implies that independent monetary policy is not possible since arbitrage will force interest rates at home and abroad to be the same. Since the end of the Bretton Woods era in 1971, a world of generally floating exchange rates has permitted independent monetary policy to coexist with international capital mobility. The conduct of that monetary policy has increasingly been delegated to central banks, who are given an inflation target rather than strict instructions as to how to achieve it and are not seeking votes for re-election. Their lack of immediate democratic accountability is an antidote to inflationary bias and constitutes a form of pre-commitment by the government.

Such arrangements are still vulnerable to adverse external shocks such as those of the 1970s, however. Given a serious oil price increase, an attempt to stick rigidly to a pre-existing inflation target would imply an episode of high unemployment. This might lead to calls for the return of discretionary policy since delegation to the central bank is not an irrevocable act. Alternatively, there has to be some mechanism for temporarily adjusting or suspending the inflation target.

■ ■ ■ 19.2.3 Common problems

In sum, macroeconomic policy is formulated by economists whose understanding is limited by an inability to perform controlled laboratory experiments and by governments who wish to get re-elected. All this makes policy errors only too likely. More specifically, the key problem areas which lead to departures from the equilibrium position are:

- the exercise of discretion by short-termist politicians
- unwelcome shocks from abroad
- relying on an *ex post* unfortunate policy rule
- incomplete information and forecasting errors.

Damaging consequences ensue because the economy has rigidities that prevent markets clearing immediately (Chapter 17).

19.3 Case studies of stabilization failure

This section reviews some episodes of macroeconomic crisis. The historical notes provided are, of course, no more than thumbnail sketches and are written so as to illuminate and extend key ideas introduced above. References are given to more comprehensive accounts.

Case study: German hyperinflation, 1918–23

The inflation in early 1920s Germany is deservedly famous. By the end of November 1923 a one-kilo loaf of rye bread cost 428 billion marks. At the end of the war in 1918, currency in circulation was 33 billion marks; this had grown to 608 million trillion marks by December 1923. (The most useful academic study for macroeconomists remains that of Webb, 1989.) Table 19.7 displays some details of the inflationary experience and several of its features should be noted:

- the inflation stopped, restarted and then accelerated spectacularly
- during the inflation the government ran huge budget deficits, yet the real value of its outstanding debt was almost completely wiped out

- although we know the nominal money supply had soared, prices had risen much more so that the real money supply fell dramatically.

In a proximate sense the inflation resulted from the massive rise in the money supply and the excess demand for goods that this provoked. As inflationary expectations took hold, people tried to avoid holding money. This added further to the inflationary pressure and is reflected in the falling value of M0 (the narrowest form of money consisting of notes and coins and reserves held by the banks with the central bank) as the price level rose even faster than the money supply (Chapter 12, Section 12.3.3). Webb rightly points to more deep-seated causes:

Table 19.7
Hyperinflation in
Weimar Germany

	Wholesale prices (1913 = 1)	Real M0 (1913 = 1)	Real government debt (1913 billion marks)	Real budget deficit (1913 billion marks)
1919/I	2.74	2.63	54.10	1.50
1919/II	3.08	2.49	50.00	3.39
1919/III	4.93	1.59	32.10	1.98
1919/IV	8.03	1.18	17.30	0.78
1920/I	17.09	0.65	10.90	0.35
1920/II	13.82	0.93	14.20	1.19
1920/III	14.98	0.91	14.80	1.65
1920/IV	14.40	1.03	16.00	0.74
1921/I	13.38	1.07	17.50	0.20
1921/II	13.66	1.12	18.40	1.82
1921/III	20.67	0.82	12.40	1.23
1921/IV	34.87	0.65	8.70	0.92
1922/I	54.33	0.47	5.62	0.50
1922/II	70.20	0.45	4.15	0.30
1922/III	287	0.22	1.20	0.58
1922/IV	1475	0.17	0.95	0.83
1923/I	4888	0.23	1.30	1.05
1923/II	19 385	0.22	0.68	1.09
1923/III	23 900 000	0.26	0.47	2.64
1923/IV	1 261 600 000 000	0.09	0.21	1.93

Source: Holtfrerich, 1983; Webb, 1986, 1989

The inflation did not happen because the Reichsbank's printing press had a faulty tachometer. It happened because the German government faced irreconcilable demands from labour, industry, and the Allies. The German government chose the policies that led to inflation because they appeared to offer lesser evils in the short run.

(Webb, 1989, p.v)

As might be expected, the policy regime in place during the hyperinflation did not contain rules to discipline politicians. There was a floating exchange rate and, unlike the post-Second World War Bundesbank, the Reichsbank was not independent and freely purchased government debt, thereby translating the government deficit into the monetary base of the economy. The public recognized that this created inflation and rational expectations of

inflation increased when additional public expenditure unmatched by new taxes was announced.

Early Weimar governments were coalitions of centrist parties threatened by extremists on both the left and the right. Raising additional taxation was extremely difficult politically. Nevertheless, by 1920 sufficient had been done to persuade the financial markets that the public finances and thus monetary growth were basically under control. In May 1921 the Allies demanded reparations (compensation for the costs of the First World War) amounting to an initial flow of about 10 per cent of national income. When it became clear that taxes were not to be further increased, monetary growth and inflationary expectations were revived. Stabilization was delayed because there was something akin to the war of attrition now familiar to the political economy literature (Rodrik, 1996) over who should bear the costs. Failure fully to meet

Case study continued

reparations payments then provoked, in 1923, the French invasion of the Ruhr and the final acceleration of inflation with excess demand now exacerbated by falling production.

Question

Stabilization was achieved and hyperinflation ceased at the end of 1923. Reviewing the above and the ideas of Section 19.2, what would have been required to bring this about?

The basic ingredient had to be a credible commitment by government to curtail its borrowing and the monetization of its debt. In turn, this had to seem less painful politically than the alternative of continuing to slide further into economic collapse. The stabilization was achieved by a return to the fixed exchange rate Gold Standard system, by the introduction of strict limits on purchases of government debt by the Reichsbank, and, conditional on this, by the 1924 Dawes Plan which reduced reparations and provided a large international loan.

Case study: The Great Depression of the early 1930s

The Wall Street Crash of October 1929 and the slump which followed it are legendary. Naturally such momentous events raise a huge range of issues in the historical literature. Here the focus is narrowed to three related questions which illuminate the abstract arguments of Section 19.2:

1 Why did output decline so dramatically in the USA?

2 What were the implications of the US slump for other countries?

3 Why did Britain escape so lightly by comparison?

Among major countries, the slump in the USA was the most severe and that in the UK the least severe of the 1930s. Table 19.8 shows that US prices and output both fell abruptly during 1929–33. The contraction in the money supply and investment were both pronounced and most famous of all was the collapse of stock market prices. (A useful textbook treatment can be found in Hall and Ferguson, 1998.)

It is generally accepted that the Great Depression resulted primarily from demand shocks and that errors in monetary policy played a major role in precipitating the crisis. It is clear, however, that output fell by more than can be explained simply by a money supply shock by itself (Bernanke, 1983). Precise attribution of the relative importance of the various components of the demand shock is still highly controversial. Factors which undoubtedly mattered included uncertainty linked with the volatile behaviour of stock prices which, together with rising real debts, hit consumer spending; in addition house-building investment was drastically curtailed as earlier overbuilding was corrected.

The USA also experienced a major financial crisis culminating in 1933 when over 3000 banks failed. This engendered a 'scramble for liquidity' as the public sought to convert bank deposits into cash and further contracted the money supply. M3 (a broad measure of money defined in Chapter 12, Section 12.3.3) fell rather than M0. The supply of loans was curtailed as banks were forced to hold higher reserves and collateral dried up (Calomiris and Wilson, 1998). The problems of a fragile banking system were a strong testimony to the weakness of bank regulation in the USA as the Roosevelt Administration's subsequent legislation underlined.

Initially very restrictive monetary policy sought to restrain the stock market boom of the late 1920s. When recession set in policy was slow to respond but in any event was effectively precluded by membership of the Gold Standard, especially from autumn 1931 to spring 1933. Recovery came after leaving gold and was stimulated by the subsequent vigorous monetary expansion (Romer, 1992) which stands out in Table 19.8.

What stood in the way of better policy-making? To an extent problems resulted from lack of appropriate data and experience. More fundamentally, the decentralized decision-making structure of the Federal Reserve System (central bank) made

Table 19.8
The UK and the
USA in the Great
Depression

	GDP	Exports	Consumption	Investment	Price level	M0	M3	Equity prices
UK								
1929	4216	986	3765	461	100	558	2542	113
1930	4210	849	3822	463	99.6	565	2549	91
1931	3980	684	3863	454	97.2	555	2523	71
1932	4008	669	3839	396	93.7	560	2571	68
1933	4046	678	3937	409	92.5	613	2782	84
1934	4334	704	4051	498	91.7	627	2721	102
1935	4496	794	4163	518	92.6	626	2874	113
1936	4633	771	4285	565	93.1	658	3080	131
1937	4834	810	4357	584	96.6	699	3205	122
USA								
1929	104.4	5.2	79.0	16.2	100	7.1	46.2	260.2
1930	95.1	4.0	74.7	10.5	96	6.9	45.2	210.3
1931	89.5	2.9	72.2	6.8	85	7.3	41.7	136.6
1932	76.4	2.1	66.0	0.8	77	7.8	34.8	69.3
1933	74.2	2.2	64.6	0.3	75	8.2	30.8	89.6
1934	80.8	2.7	68.0	1.8	80	9.1	33.3	98.4
1935	91.4	2.8	72.3	8.8	79	10.7	38.4	106.0
1936	100.9	3.0	79.7	9.3	82	12.2	42.9	154.7
1937	109.1	4.0	82.6	14.6	83	13.4	45.0	154.1

Note: components of aggregate demand in £, 1938 million (UK) and in $, 1929 billion (USA); money supply measures in £ million (UK) and $ billion (USA); equity prices 1938 = 100 (UK) and 1941/43 = 100 (USA)
Source: Mitchell, 1988; US Bureau of the Census, 1960; Capie and Collins, 1983; Temin, 1976

decisive and rapid countercyclical monetary policy very difficult and commitment to a strict policy rule in the form of the fixed exchange rate severely limited freedom of action (Eichengreen, 1992).

How did all this affect other countries? Most obviously it cut back demand for other countries' exports and curtailed US foreign lending, thus undermining balance of payments positions abroad. More subtly, but more importantly, impacts came through the Gold Standard system of fixed exchange rates based on convertibility of currencies into gold, as the excellent introductory analysis by Newell and Symons (1988) reveals.

Deflation in the large US economy led to the prices of internationally traded goods falling generally by about 25 per cent between 1929 and 1932. Restrictive US monetary policy had to be matched by other countries to protect convertibility and the fixed exchange rate and exposed other fragile banking systems to bank failures (Grossman, 1994). Unilateral expansionary initiatives, whether monetary or fiscal, threatened the exchange rate via their implications for the balance of payments and were thus precluded by the Gold Standard. Restoration of internal balance and international competitiveness needed large falls in both prices and wages but wage adjustments were far too sluggish to play this role (Bernanke and Carey, 1996).

In these circumstances, in the absence of co-ordinated international monetary expansion, leaving the Gold Standard and allowing the currency to depreciate made a lot of sense. This restored policy makers' discretion to use stabilization policy, permitted unilateral monetary expansion and interest rate cuts, and removed the need for further falls in prices and wages. Figure 19.2 shows clearly the

Case study continued

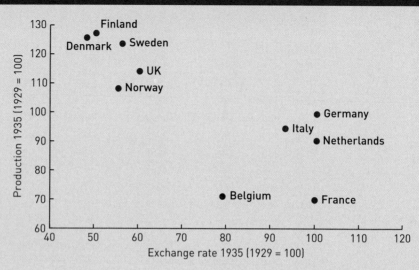

Figure 19.2
Changes in
exchange rates
and industrial
production,
1929–35

Source:
Eichengreen and
Sachs, 1985

different outcomes for countries that left the Gold Standard, such as Sweden, whose exchange rate fell and whose economy recovered, and for countries that persevered with the Gold Standard, such as France, that remained mired in depression with an unchanged exchange rate. In 1925, returning to the Gold Standard had looked highly desirable as a rule that would prevent inflation; thinking of the German experience of hyperinflation, the Governor of the Bank of England called it 'knave proof'. By 1931, adherence to this policy rule in the face of the shock of the world depression inflicted deep wounds, and discretion in economic policy seemed much more desirable.

The UK experienced a relatively early recovery. This is despite the apparent downward inflexibility of money wages much remarked by contemporaries. Moreover, Keynesian demand stimulus through fiscal policy was not pursued in the early 1930s. Compared with the USA, the favourable circumstances were rather to be found in being forced out of the Gold Standard in September 1931, in the absence of bank failures and in much more buoyant investment opportunities in house building. Accordingly, Table 19.8 shows that M3 fell only very slightly in 1930–31 and rose appreciably in 1932–33, while prices fell much less than in the USA.

Changes in economic policy included imposition of a general tariff on manufactures and encourage-ment to firms to collude to raise prices and restore profitability. After 1935, rearmament provided a significant fiscal stimulus. Unfortunately, the general implication of these policy moves was to reduce the competitive pressures on British firms to make productivity improvements (Broadberry and Crafts, 1992). This is quite a good example of how recessionary shocks can impact via induced policy responses on future trend growth (Section 19.4).

Question

Why was the aftermath of the 1987 stock market crash so different from that in 1929?

The Wall Street Crash is often talked of as the reason for the Great Depression. Clearly, this is too simplistic given the different experience 60 years later when there was no subsequent decline in economic activity. This section suggests some reasons why the late 1980s did not see a repeat of the early 1930s. Most obviously, the policy response was very different. Mindful of the lessons of the earlier experience, monetary authorities around the world co-ordinated an immediate easing of monetary policy in response. Equally important, the world was not locked into the Gold Standard. Finally, it is very doubtful that in the absence of restrictive monetary policy the 1929 Crash would have had devastating consequences for the US economy.

Case study: The Asian crisis of 1997–98

The so-called Asian tigers were the most spectacular growth success stories of the last quarter of the twentieth century (see Tables 19.1 and 19.2). The 'developmental state' approach taken by countries such as South Korea, Singapore and Taiwan was much praised for its blend of market economics supplemented by government intervention to address capital market failures and to mobilize high levels of investment; it was heralded by the World Bank (1993) as *The East Asian Miracle*. Against this background, the crisis of 1997–98, which was marked both by large falls in real GDP and massive currency depreciations, was a tremendous shock to most observers. The shock was compounded by the absence of the usual warning signs of macroeconomic distress in the form of fiscal deficits, soaring inflation or balance of payments problems. Yet, as we shall see, the crisis was not an aberration or an indicator of the capriciousness of financial markets but had its roots in badly designed economic policies.

The policy mix that had prevailed in the region during the early 1990s was based on exchange rates pegged to the dollar together with financial liberalization that saw large foreign capital inflows and the build up of a great deal of short-term foreign debt denominated in dollars. The period was one of investment boom which, at least in retrospect, was characterized by excessive risk taking and in which tendencies to overheating could not easily be dealt with by macroeconomic stabilization measures, since the fixed exchange rate removed the option to

use monetary policy and a big fiscal squeeze was out of the question. A clear description of this episode and its implications is in Corbett and Vines (1999). Why did output decline so much in 1998? The proximate reasons were a very sharp outflow of foreign capital, a severe contraction of credit availability, and with it investment, and a large fall in wealth combined with a loss of consumer confidence that deterred consumer spending (Berg, 1999).

Question

Consider the data presented in Table 19.9. What macroeconomic or financial variables seem to be most closely correlated with slump of output and collapse of the exchange rate?

Signs of fragility of the banking system in the form of loans that could not be serviced and weak regulation are the key to vulnerability in East Asian countries in 1997–98. This problem was not by any means universal – it did not apply to Hong Kong, Singapore or Taiwan – but it was of huge significance in South Korea and Thailand. The implication for these countries was that financial liberalization entailed substantial risks and this should not be particularly surprising given that, across the world, financial liberalization is frequently a leading indicator of financial crisis (Goldstein *et al.*, 2000).

The impetus to financial liberalization and, in particular, a prominent role for foreign capital came from a shift away from a heavy state involvement in

Table 19.9(a)
Aspects of the Asian crisis: Growth rates (per year)

	1996 %	1997 %	1998 %	1999 %	1997–98 exchange rate fall %
Hong Kong	4.5	5.0	−5.3	3.0	0
Indonesia	8.0	4.5	−13.1	0.8	77
Malaysia	10.0	7.3	−7.4	6.1	35
Philippines	5.8	5.2	−0.6	3.4	32
Singapore	7.7	8.5	0.1	5.9	12
South Korea	6.8	5.0	−6.7	10.9	34
Taiwan	6.1	6.7	4.6	5.4	13
Thailand	5.9	−1.4	−10.8	4.2	36

Case study continued

Table 19.9(b)
Aspects of the
Asian crisis:
Pre-crisis
danger signs

	Fiscal surplus (GDP) %	Current account (GDP) %	Real exchange rate (1990 = 100)	Non-performing loans %	Banking regulation rank
Hong Kong	1.9	−1.2	145	4	2
Indonesia	1.4	−2.8	108	17	6
Malaysia	3.6	−7.6	112	16	3=
Philippines	−0.9	−4.6	122	14	3=
Singapore	2.4	16.3	122	4	1
South Korea	0.1	−2.7	98	16	5
Taiwan	0.3	3.2	95	4	n/a
Thailand	1.0	−7.2	112	19	7

Source (both tables): Burnside *et al.*, 1999; Caprio, 1998; IMF, 2000

industrial finance towards greater reliance on the market as development moved beyond the early stages. Handled well, this promised a better allocation of resources and access to more funds without having to sacrifice domestic consumption. But the banking system is notoriously prone to market failure from problems of incomplete and asymmetric information which can give rise to excessive risk taking because no one has sufficient incentive to monitor bank lending behaviour, especially if deposits are guaranteed (implicitly or explicitly) by the government. To address such problems typically requires strict regulation that insists on capital adequacy, transparent accounting and risk management. This was noticeably absent in the countries which experienced financial crises (Mishkin, 1999).

What precipitated the events of 1997–98? The answer seems to be an increasing realization that the balance sheets of the financial institutions were becoming stretched, combined with a fear that governments either might not be able to honour the guarantees that underpinned the banking system or were facing massive fiscal deficits if they did. Either was sufficient to trigger capital flight and a currency crisis (Burnside *et al.*, 1999). A big devaluation would, however, only make matters worse in the financial system since it raised the value of all the foreign claims in terms of home currency.

In some ways this story is reminiscent of the experience of the USA in the early 1930s. Badly designed macroeconomic policy combined with a poorly regulated financial system was in each case a lethal mixture in economies which had a strong growth potential. There are differences, however. In the US case there were no guarantees to depositors and the country was a net exporter of capital and devaluation was an unmitigated blessing.

▨ ▦ ■ 19.3.1   A perspective on the case studies

The three examples above comprise a set of examples of desperate failure of macroeconomic stabilization policies. They are, of course, exceptional episodes and do not represent anything like the average experience. A marked contrast will be found in the happy experience of the Golden Age (1950–73), which is reviewed in Section 19.5.1. These examples do, however, illustrate the scope for things to go very badly wrong. As such, they put into perspective the much smaller failings that have damaged the reputation of British governments, for example in the mid-1970s or early 1990s.

In sum, two themes stand out:

- there is a crucial recurrent question of the choice of an appropriate policy framework to limit policy makers' freedom of action; both complete discretion and badly chosen rules can do great damage
- adverse shocks can reveal the flaws in financial systems with devastating consequences for macroeconomic stability as they overwhelm the ability of policy makers to respond; a high standard of financial regulation is crucial to complement conventional monetary and fiscal policy instruments.

19.4 Interactions between trend growth and stabilization policy

Long-run growth in output per worker results from capital accumulation and technological progress. Decisions to invest and/or to innovate depend on expected rates of return and are thus influenced by the economic environment. Important aspects of this include the supply of complementary factor inputs, such as human capital and infrastructure, and the stability of the economy as well as more immediate business concerns such as taxes and subsidies, the structure of industrial relations and the availability of finance. In firms where managers are not well controlled by their shareholders, pressure of competition is likely to be important in keeping management on its toes in terms of rapid implementation of cost-reducing innovations.

At the same time, understanding how fast growth in labour productivity will be over the medium term is central to assessing the output gap and thus to implementing Taylor rules for demand management (Section 19.2). Labour productivity growth also determines how much wages can increase without leading to price inflation and/or reduced profits for employers. In periods when labour productivity growth is low relative to real wage aspirations, the level of unemployment required to keep wages consistent with normal profits (the NAIRU) is increased. Conversely, when labour productivity growth is high relative to real wage aspirations, the level of unemployment required to keep wages consistent with normal profits is reduced.

Accordingly, there are several important potential interactions between stabilization policy and trend growth. For example, a badly designed policy that creates uncertainty and volatility is likely to reduce investment and growth (Ramey and Ramey, 1995). Severe recessions and financial crises have in the past led to protectionist and regulationist policy responses that have reduced the degree of competition and supply of finance. Conversely, the achievement of a credible agreement between workers and employers that delivers wage moderation in return for high investment might be expected to promote both a low NAIRU and faster growth (Eichengreen, 1996). As was noted earlier, the surprise of the productivity slowdown in the 1970s was important in derailing stabilization policy at that time.

This section looks at the historical record in the light of these points. In order to do so, it is necessary first to build up some basic ideas about both the proximate sources and also the underlying determinants of long-run economic growth. This will also enable us to consider comparative growth performance both over time and across countries and will prepare the way for case studies of the Golden Age of European growth and the new economy of the 1990s in the following section.

▦ ▦ ■ 19.4.1 The proximate sources of growth

Growth in real income and output per person requires increases in labour productivity. In turn, these result from the use of extra capital per person and from additions to *total factor productivity* (TFP) which accrues from greater efficiency in the use of factors of production (obtained through better technology, improved organization of production and so on). Increases in the amount of capital available come from net investment which should be thought of in a broad sense to include investment not only in plant, equipment, etc., but also in the skills and expertise of the labour force; that is, in human capital.

Technological progress is the main driving force for long-run growth in labour productivity. This has both an embodied and a disembodied component. The former arrives in new varieties of capital goods (such as steam engines in the eighteenth century and computers in the twentieth century) while the latter can be thought of as making possible additional output from existing factors of production (such as occurred with the reorganization of factories that electrification made possible) which leads to growth of TFP.

These proximate sources of growth explain how growth comes about but not why. More fundamental reasons for why growth rates differ relate to the determinants of international differences in capital accumulation strategies and in real cost reduction. These are to be found in incentive structures, institutions and political decision-making which are discussed in Section 19.4.2.

Growth accounting techniques provide a systematic framework to quantify the proximate sources of growth and some results are displayed in Table 19.10. Growth accounting seeks to assess the contributions of capital and labour to output growth, and then it attributes the remaining growth to TFP growth. TFP growth comes from greater efficiency of factor use. The theory behind growth accounting is set out formally below.

The increase in output due to increased capital equals the change in the amount of capital employed, ΔK, multiplied by its marginal product, $\dfrac{\Delta Y}{\Delta K}$, and the increase in output due to using more labour equals the change in the amount of labour employed, ΔL, multiplied by its marginal product, $\dfrac{\Delta Y}{\Delta L}$. So the total increase in output due to changes of both kinds is:

$$\Delta Y = \left(\frac{\Delta Y}{\Delta K}\right)\Delta K + \left(\frac{\Delta Y}{\Delta L}\right)\Delta L \tag{19.1}$$

Dividing through by the level of output, the rate of growth of output, $\dfrac{\Delta Y}{Y}$, is given by:

$$\frac{\Delta Y}{Y} = \left(\frac{\Delta Y}{\Delta K}\right)\left(\frac{K}{Y}\right)\left(\frac{\Delta K}{K}\right) + \left(\frac{\Delta Y}{\Delta L}\right)\left(\frac{L}{Y}\right)\left(\frac{\Delta L}{L}\right) \tag{19.2}$$

where the first term on the right-hand side has been multiplied top and bottom by K (leaving it unchanged) and the second term top and bottom by L (leaving it unchanged). If factors receive their marginal products as they would if all markets conformed to the model of perfect competition, then

$$\frac{\Delta Y}{\Delta K} = \text{the rate of return on capital}$$

So

$$\left(\frac{\Delta Y}{\Delta K}\right)\left(\frac{K}{Y}\right) = \text{the share of profits in national income}$$

Similarly

$$\left(\frac{\Delta Y}{\Delta L}\right)\left(\frac{L}{Y}\right) = \text{the share of wages in national income}$$

Equation (2) shows that the rate of growth of output, $\frac{\Delta Y}{Y}$, is a weighted sum of $\frac{\Delta K}{K}$, the rate of growth of capital, and $\frac{\Delta L}{L}$, the rate of growth of labour, where the weights or 'coefficients' are given by the respective shares of capital and labour in national income. So the share of profits in national income, $\left(\frac{\Delta Y}{\Delta K}\right)\left(\frac{K}{Y}\right)$, gives the coefficient on the growth rate of capital, and the share of wages in national income, $\left(\frac{\Delta Y}{\Delta L}\right)\left(\frac{L}{Y}\right)$, gives the coefficient on the growth rate of labour. These coefficients can be interpreted as the percentage growth in national income that a 1 per cent growth in capital (or labour) would produce. That these coefficients equal the respective shares of capital and labour in national income has been found to be a reasonable approximation in empirical work which for the recent past has found a coefficient of 0.3 on $\frac{\Delta K}{K}$ and of 0.7 on $\frac{\Delta L}{L}$. The TFP growth is then calculated as a residual, the excess of actual growth over that predicted by filling in the values of the right-hand side of equation (2).

The formula to account for growth of labour productivity is:

$$\Delta y = \alpha \Delta k + \text{TFP growth}$$

where the lower case symbols represent output per labour input (y) and capital per labour input (k) and α is the share of profits in national income. The first term on the right-hand side is known as the contribution of capital-deepening.

A number of problems with this approach have been much discussed. The most serious is the treatment of human capital. In principle, this can be incorporated into growth of the labour input and when this is done the usual method is to adjust for years of schooling and the extra wages that workers gain from education. Any improvements in labour quality not measured by adjustments to the quantity of the labour input will end up in residual TFP growth, as in the estimates of Table 19.10.

Question Consider the estimates reported in Table 19.10. How do the growth accounts for 1950–73 compare with those for other periods?

The period 1950–73 is commonly referred to as the 'Golden Age' of European growth and this is reflected in West Germany's productivity growth in these years. This resulted from a relatively strong contribution from capital accumulation but especially from extraordinary TFP growth. More detailed investigation suggests that this owed a good deal to reconstruction which put the capital stock (most of which survived the Second World War intact) back to work as, for example, the transport system was rehabilitated. On top of this, Germany gained from improved efficiency as the economy was opened up

Table 19.10
Accounting for
labour productivity
growth (per cent per
year)

	UK %	Germany %	USA %
1871–1911			
Labour productivity growth	0.80	1.40	1.60
Capital deepening	*0.45*	*0.55*	*1.35*
Total factor productivity	*0.35*	*0.85*	*0.25*
1911–37			
Labour productivity growth	0.90	1.10	1.10
Capital deepening	*0.20*	*0.10*	*0.30*
Total factor productivity	*0.70*	*1.00*	*0.80*
1950–73			
Labour productivity growth	2.99	5.18	2.34
Capital deepening	*1.69*	*1.20*	*0.68*
Total factor productivity	*1.30*	*3.98*	*1.66*
1973–99			
Labour productivity growth	2.13	2.29	1.08
Capital deepening	*0.90*	*0.65*	*0.65*
Total factor productivity	*1.23*	*1.64*	*0.43*

Note: for 1871–1937 analysis is based on output per worker but for 1950–99 on output per hour worked. Changes in the quality of labour from human capital formation are not explicitly accounted for and will contribute to residual TFP growth. Estimates pre-1937 rounded to nearest 0.05
Source: 1871–1937 derived worksheets underlying Broadberry, 1998; 1950–99 from Crafts and O'Mahony, 2001.

to freer trade and agriculture contracted, and from the emulation of US technology. The key feature of these years was the reduction of a large US productivity lead that had built up in the first half of the twentieth century. The post-war period saw a much more rapid and complete transfer of US technology to Europe than had been achieved before as unique US advantages from a large market and cheap natural resources diminished, multinationals flourished and Europe raised its technological capabilities (Nelson and Wright, 1992).

Question | What does Figure 19.3 suggest about the importance of catch-up in the periods 1950–73 and 1973–99?

Figure 19.3 shows a strong inverse relationship between initial GDP level and subsequent growth for 1950–73 but not for the later period, at least among the more developed economies. (Note the difference in the scale along the horizontal axis in the two parts of the figure.) The earlier period is indeed one where growth performance was dominated by catch-up. This suggests that some of Germany's superiority in TFP growth relative to the UK in those years is explained by its initially larger productivity gap and greater scope for catch-up. It is very important to normalize for these differences in evaluating growth performance. Having said that, there also seems to be evidence of under-performance

Figure 19.3
Growth
performance and
'catch-up'
(a) Real GDP per
head, 1950, and
growth rate of real
GDP per head,
1950–73, Western
European countries

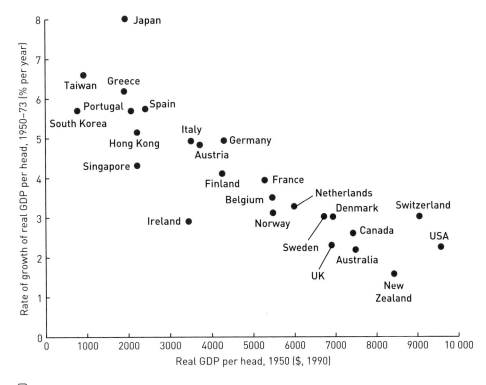

(b) Real GDP per
head, 1973, and
growth rate of real
GDP per head,
1973–99, Western
European countries

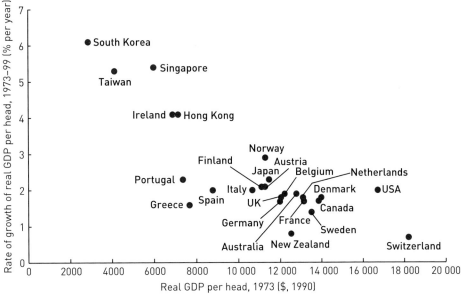

by the UK in that its growth was appreciably slower than that of many countries with similar initial income levels. This was confirmed formally by a regression of growth rates across European regions which took account of initial income levels and employment structures and found that, controlling for these factors, UK growth was about 0.5 percentage points lower than elsewhere in Europe (Crafts, 1995). Rapid catch-up growth was transitory and had greatly diminished by the 1980s when the productivity gap had become much lower.

Nevertheless, throughout the post-Second World War period labour productivity growth in both the UK and Germany has exceeded that of earlier years. This has reflected both more investment and faster technological change in societies which were devoting far more resources to education and research and development than they had in the nineteenth and early twentieth centuries. The decline in TFP growth in 1973–99 in all three countries in Table 19.10 is probably exaggerated by the increasingly problematic measurement of real GDP growth which was discussed in Section 19.1.2.

■■■ 19.4.2 Incentive structures and growth

Two aspects of incentive structures matter for long-run growth performance. The first and more obvious aspect relates to the impact on investment and innovation decisions by the private sector. The second aspect concerns the actions of government and the possible conflict between seeking votes and enhancing productivity performance.

An analysis of the key factors influencing firms' decisions to invest and to innovate highlights issues relating to the ability to appropriate returns and to *agency problems* within firms. The pay-off to an investment may in some circumstances be appropriated by another party. For example, the results of R&D may be copied, the training of skilled workers can accrue to those who poach them, returns may be taxed away or even expropriated by government. Where investment involves substantial outlays on sunk costs, fears that appropriation of returns may not be possible are likely to discourage investment.

The notion of agency problems in this context relates to the difficulty that shareholders (the principals) may have in aligning the actions of managers (the agents) with their interests. In particular, reducing costs and adopting new technology as soon as it is cost-effective to do so requires considerable effort and perhaps even pain on the part of management. If it is hard for shareholders to know whether managers are working optimally on their behalf, managers may be less than diligent in pursuing improved productivity provided profits are 'adequate'. The situation is compounded if no shareholder is big and powerful enough to find it worthwhile to devote substantial resources to monitoring management.

Competition potentially plays an important role in mitigating these agency problems. This is partly because it quickly reveals to shareholders (through market share and profits) that managers could do better, and partly because it offers greater possibility of giving managers an incentive by performance-related rewards. In the typical British case where shareholding is diffuse, there is clear evidence that greater competition has a strongly positive impact on productivity growth (Nickell *et al.*, 1997). The evidence for the UK also suggests that lower market power is associated with greater innovative activity except where the market is very close to perfect competition, when its impact is more than offset by worries about appropriation (Aghion *et al.*, 2002). This underlines how damaging was the retreat from competition during the macroeconomic crisis of the 1930s which left about three-quarters of British manufacturing operating under the auspices of cartels (Broadberry and Crafts, 2001).

| Question | What predictions about the productivity performance of state-owned enterprises follow from the above analysis? |

In general, there was little or no competition for British nationalized industries. The key issue is whether anyone had a strong incentive effectively to monitor and whether it was possible to establish credible rewards and punishments based on verifiable performance targets. The general experience, in the UK at least, is that establishing a satisfactory framework proved impossible and that productivity performance was indeed disappointing (Vickers and Yarrow, 1988). This has an important implication for stabilization policy in that it suggests the immediate post-war Labour government's strategy of attempting demand management through controlling the commanding heights of the economy and exercising direct control over investment had a big downside in its implications for productivity and is not a good blueprint for economic management (Broadberry and Crafts, 1996).

Why might governments find that votes are lost by policies that promote economic efficiency and productivity improvement? A classic case, familiar to students of international trade, reveals an important reason. Protectionism (in the form of tariffs or subsidies), a policy that cushions inefficient domestic firms, heavily rewards relatively small but well-organized and easily identified groups of producers at the expense of a large but disparate group of consumers and taxpayers for whom it is too expensive to organize a protest but whose less identifiable losses far outweigh the gains for the few. A more acute version of this problem arises in the context of technological change where productivity growth involves processes of creative destruction. New types of jobs appear, others disappear; for example, entry and exit of establishments accounted for about half of all labour productivity growth in UK manufacturing in 1980–92 (Disney *et al.*, 2000). The pain is obvious and immediate and entails unemployment while the benefits, though real, are in the future and probably not recognized by the gainers. The temptation for short-termist politicians is to intervene.

Fear that unemployment loses votes means that macroeconomic management has been a major influence on supply-side policy in the UK in the past. In particular, this has been true whenever governments have attempted to reduce the NAIRU through negotiating deals with the trade union movement aimed at wage restraint. These typically involved understandings that, for example, industrial relations or the structure of taxation or state ownership of industry were not to be reformed and that lame ducks would survive (Bean and Crafts, 1996).

19.4.3 Main themes

Three main points have emerged in this section:

- TFP growth is fundamental to long-run growth performance but varies both across countries and over time
- policies designed with short-term macroeconomic objectives in mind can have effects on long-run growth outcomes because they influence incentives to invest and to innovate
- short-term macroeconomic considerations can undermine supply-side reform as politicians (implicitly) trade off long-run growth against unemployment.

19.5 How growth and stabilization interact: case studies

This section considers two historical episodes with a view to illuminating ideas discussed in the previous section. As in Section 19.3, there is no attempt to offer a comprehensive account but references are provided for those who wish to probe more deeply.

Case study: The Golden Age

In Sections 19.1 and 19.4 we saw that the years between the early 1950s and early 1970s were a time of rapid growth, low inflation and low unemployment for Western European countries. How did this happy state of affairs, the so-called Golden Age of European growth, come about and why did it not last? Should well-designed policy take credit for this economic success?

We have already seen that this was a time when productivity growth was very rapid in a period of transitory catch-up growth. The results of a cross-section econometric analysis of European growth reported by Temin (2002) confirm that this was the context of the Golden Age. Temin found that in the early years growth outcomes were dominated by reconstruction and the contraction of agriculture as economic liberalization took hold, and in the later years were explained by the remaining productivity gap with the USA. In addition, as Table 19.11 shows, there was a sharp rise in investment as a share of GDP compared with the inter-war period. All these factors might explain why there was an interval of very rapid growth then a slowdown as the once-and-for-all sources of catch-up became exhausted and investment ran into diminishing returns.

Question

Table 19.11 shows a marked rise in investment in the Golden Age compared with the inter-war period. What do you think might explain this?

The context of an unusually strong catch-up growth is surely part of the explanation, since this provided an economic environment in which returns could be high. Nevertheless, the opportunity still needed to be grasped and this draws attention to the role of economic policy. Macroeconomic management played a part, though not, as was once thought, through active attempts to smooth out fluctuations via Keynesian-inspired fiscal policy. Rather the situation was characterized by the acceptance of the discipline of fixed exchange rates under the Bretton Woods agreement but with restrictions on capital mobility that allowed a degree of independence in monetary policy in a world of much more tightly regulated banking systems. There was no repeat of the egregious monetary policy errors in the world's leading economy that had been so damaging in the early 1930s. In sum, macroeconomic stability reinforced the confidence of investors (Boltho, 1982).

Another key feature of post-war Europe that underpinned both low unemployment and fast growth was the prevalence of post-war settlements that entailed a rapprochement between capital and labour after the conflicts of earlier decades. This involved deals brokered by the state to ensure wage moderation in return for high investment that achieved effective monitoring and commitment and was most successful under the auspices of centralized wage bargaining (Eichengreen, 1996). Wage restraint on the part of powerful trade unions, which meant unemployment was less important in reducing wage demands, was a key to lowering the NAIRU in this period, even in countries such as the UK where collective bargaining was more decentralized (Broadberry, 1994). In addition, the rapid productivity growth of the period was a pleasant surprise to wage bargainers and, in the most successful

Table 19.11 Gross non-residential investment in the 1930s and 1960s (percentage of GDP)	1929–38 %	1960–73 %
France	12.1	17.0
Germany	9.8	17.6
Japan	13.6	26.6
Netherlands	14.0	19.8
UK	6.0	14.2

Source: van de Klundert and van Schaik, 1996

countries, such as Germany, easily exceeded wage aspirations in the early post-war period (Giersch *et al.*, 1992).

By the early 1970s, all these favourable factors looked much weaker and were bringing the Golden Age to an end even before the stagflationary oil price shocks. In particular:

- the balance of productivity growth and after-tax wage aspirations was less conducive to low unemployment once catch-up growth weakened and taxes to finance welfare state social transfers rose
- the discipline of the fixed exchange rate system collapsed, destroyed by a combination of US monetary indiscipline at the end of the 1960s and the needs for realignment consequent on 20 years of rapid catch-up growth.

Policy makers were badly caught out and reacted much less strongly to incipient inflation in the early 1970s than the Taylor rules would suggest, in retrospect, that they should have.

During the Golden Age, the UK experienced rapid relative economic decline which should be seen as a failure to make as much of the opportunity for catch-up growth as other countries did. It is quite easy to point to aspects of supply-side policy that were unfortunate from the point of view of investment and productivity improvement. These included the failure to reform industrial relations, serious tax distortions and the low priority given to promoting product market competition. Further, the overriding desire for low inflation and low unemployment constituted a crucial obstacle to reform, given the need to placate organized labour or, put differently, the relative difficulty of achieving a social contract.

Case study: The new economy in 1990s USA

The 1990s was a period of exceptionally good macroeconomic performance in the USA in terms of inflation, unemployment and economic growth. At the heart of economic resurgence seemed to be the spread of new ICT, including computers and the Internet, which was dubbed the new economy, and seemed to many the onset of a new industrial revolution (see Chapter 2). However, there was considerable uncertainty about the size of the output gap and how far the trend rate of productivity growth had increased in the 1990s. Accordingly, policy makers faced difficult decisions and non-trivial risks both of allowing the economy to overheat and of severe recession if they misread the situation.

Question

Consider Table 19.12. What important information does it contain for the Chairman of the Federal Reserve System? What else might he have wished to know?

Table 19.12 uses the tools of growth accounting that were set out in Section 19.4.1. The version used

captures the embodiment of ICT in new varieties of capital. It explicitly identifies a contribution from labour quality growth that was subsumed in TFP growth in the format of Table 19.10. The striking feature of the table is the surge in labour productivity growth after 1995. In turn, this seems to owe a substantial amount to an increased impact from ICT both in terms of capital-deepening and TFP growth in the manufacture of ICT. There is also a strong increase in TFP growth in the rest of the economy. If these developments are taken at face value as a change in the trend rate of productivity growth, then at any point in the late 1990s the output gap was greater than would previously have been thought and so the stance of monetary policy could be more relaxed.

This raises a number of questions, however. First, in so far as there was an increased impact of ICT, for how long would it be sustained? The key driver of these developments was the phenomenal rate of increase of the power of computer chips, which was driving down the price of ICT and stimulating ICT capital-deepening besides underwriting a massive rate of TFP growth in ICT

Case study continued

Table 19.12
Contributions
to US labour
productivity
growth, 1974–99
(percentage per
year)

	1974–90 %	1991–95 %	1996–99 %
Capital deepening	0.81	0.62	1.10
ICT capital	*0.44*	*0.51*	*0.96*
Other	*0.37*	*0.11*	*0.14*
Total factor productivity	0.33	0.48	1.16
ICT manufacture	*0.17*	*0.23*	*0.49*
Other	*0.16*	*0.25*	*0.67*
Labour quality	0.22	0.44	0.31
Labour productivity growth	1.37	1.53	2.57
Memorandum items			
ICT capital income share	3.3	5.3	6.3
ICT manufacture output share	1.4	1.9	2.5

Source: Oliner and Sichel, 2000; estimates refer to non-farm business sector

manufacture. If this were to cease to operate, future growth prospects would be undermined. Second, how should the behaviour of TFP growth in the rest of the economy be understood? An optimistic interpretation would be that the upturn reflected spillovers from ICT; that is, disembodied technological progress as the private sector gradually learnt about the possibilities that it opened up rather like the redesign of factories in the 1920s (Brynjolfsson and Hitt, 2000). A pessimistic interpretation would be that it was merely cyclical and denoted more intensive utilization of capital and labour inputs that the official data had not picked up (Gordon, 2000). In the late 1990s it was too soon to tell.

The public enthusiasm for the new economy, reflected in sky-high prices for technology stocks in the late 1990s, suggests that both firms and households were more inclined to a miracle rather than a mirage view. If so, then expectations of very rapid growth in future would underpin both consumption and investment expenditure. If, however, these expectations were suddenly perceived to have been incorrect (a mirage after all), then the correction of this error by both households and firms would entail a severe cutback of demand and the possibility of a deep recession (IMF, 2000). The subsequent

collapse of technology stock prices suggests that this risk was non-trivial.

In these circumstances, how should monetary policy be conducted? It seems that the normal reliance on a Taylor rule is hazardous because estimates of the output gap become extremely difficult. If so, more weight may have to be given to the inflation term and perhaps other indicators of economic performance. In fact, the Federal Reserve Bank appears to have acted as if it followed academic economists in trying to update its estimates of the NAIRU in the context of the changing balance between wage aspirations and productivity growth and relaxing policy accordingly, rather than amending the rule that it used (Ball and Tchaidze, 2002). In any event, it was much more alert to the possibility of misreading the output gap than policy makers had been in the 1970s.

After the boom subsided and, as always, too late for those operating in real time, academic research appeared to suggest that the optimistic interpretation was nearer to the truth at least for the late 1990s. Basu *et al.* (2001) investigated the issue of capacity utilization and concluded that, if anything, the underlying improvement in technological progress was greater than indicated by the growth accounting estimates.

▨ ▨ ■ 19.5.3   A perspective on the case studies

These episodes were basically pleasant surprises quite unlike the cases discussed in Section 19.3. Neither the Golden Age nor the new economy was really foreseen. In the aftermath of the Second World War, the general expectation was that, far from being on the threshold of the longest ever boom, there was a widespread fear of a return to the mass unemployment of the inter-war period. In the late 1980s, the USA seemed to be mired in a productivity slowdown, notwithstanding the rapid diffusion of computers, and the US economy was widely perceived as in relative decline, about to be overtaken by Japan.

Three important points can be taken from these examples. First, it is important not to exaggerate the role of policy makers in delivering strong growth: changes in the underlying rate of TFP ultimately depend on the rate of technological progress and are outside their control. Second, poor policy, including sacrificing supply-side reform to macroeconomic short-termism, can, however, get in the way of exploiting technological opportunities when they come along, as is shown by the instructive example of Britain in the Golden Age. Third, changes in productivity trends make the design of monetary policy difficult, even when, as in the 1990s, the surprises are pleasant, because at first it is difficult to be sure what is happening.

19.6   Conclusion

In the introduction we considered two key questions. These were 'how far is economic policy responsible for macroeconomic outcomes?' and 'what explains failures in the design of stabilization policy?' It is now time to pull together what has been learnt about these issues, offering some reflections on some of the main themes in the material that has been covered. Please regard these as claims whose validity you may wish to debate rather than definitive conclusions.

First, it is clear that technological change has a profound impact on the rate of economic growth, but technological change is not controlled by economic policy makers. Likewise, shocks to the price of oil. In this context, the best that can be done is to respond well to the new situation. However, poor policy design can make a significant difference to outcomes; for example, the UK coped much less well with the stagflation of the 1970s and took less than full advantage of the growth opportunities of the Golden Age than did West Germany.

Second, incomplete information, exogenous shocks and inadequate economic models are important reasons for macroeconomic policy failure but not the whole story. When policy is in the hands of politicians we can expect inflationary bias at best and egregious failures rooted in inability to impose fiscal and monetary discipline at worst. This suggests that it is better to delegate monetary policy to the central bank and accept that, in this area, there are limits to democratic accountability.

Third, on balance, macroeconomic policy-making has improved. Inflation targeting on the basis of the Taylor rules is likely to deliver better results than, say, a return to the Gold Standard. Nevertheless, it is important to recognize that in the face of adverse shocks not only might it be impossible to deliver a good outcome but that the institutional arrangements themselves might not survive, since a return to unconstrained discretion could seem very attractive when in great difficulties.

Fourth, it does seem right to regard the achievement of a low rate of unemployment as a top policy priority. Nevertheless, it should be recognized that if this goal is pursued without regard to the consequences for incentive structures, the cost in terms of forgone productivity growth can be substantial.

Questions for review and discussion

Question 1   Figure 19.4 shows the Barro–Gordon model. Which of the following statements correctly expresses the significance of the numbers shown in the matrix?

A The numbers –2 in the top right cell and –1 in the bottom right cell show that, when expected inflation is high, the government will lose an estimated twice as much in tax revenue by holding inflation at zero as it will be creating high inflation.

B The numbers –1 in the bottom left cell and 0 in the bottom right cell stand for percentage changes in the rate of employment of labour.

C The two zeros in the top left cell show that actual inflation and expected inflation are running at zero (the price level is neither rising nor is expected to rise).

D The numbers in all cells are used only to indicate benefits or costs. They do not refer to any specific economic variables such as tax revenue or rate of employment.

Figure 19.4
The Barro–Gondon model

		Public	
		zero expected inflation	high expected inflation
Government	zero actual inflation	0, 0	–2, –1
	high actual inflation	1, –1	–1, 0

Question 2   Using Figure 19.4, is the following statement true or false?
The government has no dominant strategy as it is bound to be worse off if the public expects high inflation.
❑ True
❑ False

Question 3   Refer to Figure 19.3 on page 539, which shows a strong inverse relationship between initial GDP level and subsequent growth for the period 1950–73 but not for the later period 1973–99.

(a) Briefly explain why initial levels of GDP might influence subsequent economic growth.

(b) Comment on the statistical association between the initial GDP level and subsequent growth for both periods.

The data for this question are drawn from Chapter 19, Tables 19.1 and 19.2. A copy of the data appears in Table 19.13.

Table 19.13
Levels of real GDP per head and rates of growth of real GDP per head for selected periods

Country	Real GDP per head, 1950 $	Real GDP per head, 1973 $	Rate of growth of real GDP per head, 1950–73 %	Rate of growth of real GDP per head, 1973–99 %
1 Australia	7493	12 759	2.3	1.9
2 Austria	3706	11 235	4.9	2.1
3 Belgium	5462	12 170	3.6	1.9
4 Canada	7437	13 838	2.7	1.7
5 Denmark	6946	13 945	3.1	1.8
6 Finland	4253	11 085	4.2	2.1
7 France	5270	13 123	4.0	1.7
8 Germany	4281	11 966	5.0	1.7
9 Greece	1915	7 655	6.2	1.6
10 Hong Kong	2218	7 104	5.2	4.1
11 Ireland	3446	6 867	3.0	4.1
12 Italy	3502	10 643	5.0	2.0
13 Japan	1926	11 439	8.0	2.3
14 Netherlands	5996	13 082	3.4	1.8
15 New Zealand	8453	12 513	1.7	0.8
16 Norway	5463	11 246	3.2	2.9
17 Portugal	2069	7 343	5.7	2.3
18 Singapore	2219	5 977	4.4	5.4
19 South Korea	770	2 841	5.8	6.1
20 Spain	2397	8 739	5.8	2.0
21 Sweden	6738	13 493	3.1	1.4
22 Switzerland	9064	18 204	3.1	0.7
23 Taiwan	936	4 117	6.6	5.3
24 UK	6907	12 022	2.4	1.8
25 USA	9561	16 689	2.4	2.0

20

Environmental sustainability

Graham Dawson

Concepts

- ecological economics
- sustainable development
- intergenerational justice
- the land ethic
- emissions trading

Objectives

After studying this chapter you should be able to:

- discuss some of the ethical arguments about the environmental impact of economic growth
- understand the argument from ecological economics that there are physical limits to growth
- appreciate the strength and weaknesses of carbon trading as a policy response to climate change.

20.1 Introduction

On 23 March 2001 debris from the Mir space station, most of which had burnt up on re-entry to the Earth's atmosphere, crashed into the South Pacific (Figure 20.1). To those watching from the island of Fiji, it looked like a shower of shooting stars, beautiful but potentially dangerous if it had come much closer. To the Russian technicians at mission control outside Moscow, the splashdown, at the right time and place, was the final success in a triumphant era of space exploration. To one economist it evoked thoughts of comets and shooting stars as portents of hard times or even disaster. Was this man-made comet a metaphor for environmental catastrophe?

Shortly before the Industrial Revolution, the English philosopher John Locke propounded a theory of property that reflected the emerging capitalist system. This theory has often been interpreted as supposing that we, the human race, live on a frontier with the natural world, looking across to plentiful resources and untameable wilderness. In the 1960s, Kenneth Boulding, an economist from Liverpool who worked mainly in the USA, caught the mood of environmental anxiety by labelling this approach 'the cowboy economy'. He contrasted it with the idea of Spaceship Earth, its astronauts, the human race, depending for our lives on the fragile atmosphere and depleted resources of a tiny planet spinning through an indifferent universe. Will Spaceship Earth land on a new frontier or

Figure 20.1
The end of an era:
the remains of the
Mir space station
light up the sky over
the Pacific Ocean

crash burning into the ocean? There are those who predict disaster, seeing the human race as Icarus, the young man in Classical Greek mythology whose ambition outstripped the technology available to him. He flew using wings made for him by his father, Daedalus, but the wax holding the wings together melted when he approached too close to the sun. (In Figure 20.2, Bruegel's *Landscape with the Fall of Icarus*, you can just see Icarus's legs sticking out of the water in the bottom right-hand corner of the painting.)

The aim of this chapter is to explore some of the ways in which economists think about environmental sustainability using as a case study potentially the most serious

Figure 20.2
*Landscape with the
Fall of Icarus*, by
Pieter Bruegel the
Elder (c.1558)

environmental problem of all: climate change or global warming. The first question is whether there are physical limits to economic growth (Section 20.2). According to ecological economists, much economic activity and theory overlooks the brute fact of physical limits to growth, forever frustrating technological attempts to overcome them. They believe that it is important to locate the economy in the physical world, in ecology. For example, one of the things that are illustrated by global warming is the concept of *carrying capacity*. The Earth's atmosphere can absorb only so much carbon dioxide without climatic stress, and economic activity should be informed by an appreciation of these physical limits to growth.

What are the prospects for a consensus? Are enough people ever going to share a belief in putting environmental concerns first? This raises the question of values (Section 20.3). As markets are the institutions that define market or capitalist economies, we must consider how values are treated in markets and in the economic analysis of markets. Can markets reflect a social consensus that may evolve, or are they irretrievably dominated by the forces of self-interest and hedonism to the detriment of ethical principles? Are there ethical or social limits to economic growth?

Policy interventions to try to achieve an environmentally sustainable economy see markets both as the cause of the problem and as part of the solution. The state regulates the markets that cause environmental damage and uses market-based instruments, such as pollution taxes, to modify market incentives (Chapter 9, Section 9.2). The state may even create markets where they did not previously exist, setting objectives and then using markets as a means of achieving them efficiently (Section 20.4). Climate change negotiations, which try to get international agreement to reduce global warming by reducing greenhouse gas emissions, often envisage the use of markets in this way. At Kyoto in 1997 the negotiating states agreed to try to reduce greenhouse gas emissions and decided to set up a market in emissions permits as one way of achieving their aims. And a 'carbon market' already exists, despite the collapse of the Kyoto negotiations.

20.2 Physical limits to growth

Climate change negotiations in a series of international summits, from Rio to Kyoto via Montreal and Berlin, have put the prospect of global warming, its consequences and the question of how to reduce vehicle and industrial emissions firmly onto the political agenda. It is widely known that many scientists believe that greenhouse gas emissions must be reduced and that many politicians of different political persuasions accept their claims. The aims of this section are to place the problem of climate change in the context of the physical limits to economic growth and to examine the idea of sustainable development as a response to the identification of such limits.

▪▪▪ 20.2.1 Climate change

The term 'global warming' refers to an increase in the mean global temperature as a result of the 'greenhouse effect'. The greenhouse effect is a natural process. Energy from the sun passes through the atmosphere. Some of the heat that is radiated back from the Earth is blocked by atmospheric gases, usually called 'greenhouse gases' (GHGs) because they cause the atmosphere to warm. These gases include carbon dioxide, ozone, water vapour, chlorofluorocarbons (CFCs), methane and nitrous oxide. Carbon dioxide (CO_2), the most important GHG, is mainly the result of the burning of fossil fuels such as oil and coal to meet our energy needs. At the moment these emissions occur predominately in the industrialized North. The atmosphere can assimilate (absorb and process) some but not all of the GHGs, and some human activities 'use up' the Earth's capacity to absorb CO_2 and other GHGs. Deforestation intensifies the greenhouse effect by contributing some 15 to 20 per cent of the GHGs in the atmosphere. At a meeting in Shanghai in February 2001, the Intergovernmental Panel on Climate Change (IPCC) estimated that the global mean temperature would rise by 2.5 °C to 10.4 °C over the next 100 years.

Three main effects of the resulting climate change are expected. First, sea levels will rise as global warming causes the water in the oceans to expand (Houghton, 1997, p.109). Sea levels may rise by 3 to 10 centimetres a decade if no action is taken to prevent climate change, and low-lying land by the sea may be inundated. Second, agriculture in many areas will be more vulnerable to disruption by drought. A reduction in the levels of soil moisture and the risk of summer drought may be accompanied by changes in regional rainfall, which could make arid zones even more arid. Third, there may be an increased risk of extreme weather events, such as floods, heat waves, storms, cyclones and typhoons. All of these effects will tend to have a bigger impact on low-income countries than on the industrial world that caused the climate change. For example, coastal defences against a rise in sea levels are feasible for the Netherlands but well beyond the financial reach of most low-income countries. Also, agriculture constitutes a greater percentage of the economic activity in low-income countries, which tend to have a large subsistence sector with poor farmers who are unable to afford insurance.

There are, however, many scientific uncertainties in this field. There is evidence that the climate has changed since the Industrial Revolution, but this slight warming is consistent with natural variations in the climate. The uncertainty surrounding the predicted rate of warming leaves plenty of scope for fierce debate concerning the gravity of the effects that may (or may not) take place. In fact, some scientists have reasoned that global warming is a myth, or at least is so uncertain that we are under no obligation to take remedial action. Nevertheless, it is clear that in the last 200 years human activity has increased the amount of CO_2 in the atmosphere by 30 per cent. It is difficult to see how this increase could fail to have some impact on the world's climate. Moreover, there is already some evidence, from the insurance industry for example, that extreme weather events have become more frequent over the last 30 years. It may be too late to avert entirely the adverse consequences of global warming, including the possible creation of millions of environmental refugees.

▨ ▨ ■ 20.2.2 Ecological economics and physical limits to growth

Climate change can probably best be understood in economic terms as an example of the physical limits to economic growth that ecological economists, and others, have warned of since the 1970s.

Until the 1970s economists had generally assumed that the physical world did not impose any limits on growth. This was not an oversight, but an implication of the way in which most economists had traditionally looked at the economy. The intuition behind this approach was that, if one natural resource ran out, it would always be possible to replace it with another that would maintain the rate of economic growth. It is important to recall here the definition of economic growth that these economists relied upon.

All goods or services that are exchanged for money count towards the value of the national income (Chapter 8). This assumes that there is nothing unique and irreplaceable about any particular component of economic growth, or about any particular resource used in producing goods and services. Using the concepts of capital and the production function, this section seeks to clarify the assumption that economic growth is free from physical limits.

Capital – defined broadly – provides a stream of benefits over time. Thus capital provides a return, and current and future generations are believed to derive well-being from this return. Chapter 3 set out the production function, which specifies the way in which inputs such as manufactured capital are transformed into outputs through production processes:

$$Q = f(F_1, F_2, \ldots, F_n)$$

This time Q is human well-being and the Fs are forms of environmental and manufactured capital. The basic idea is that if we have less of one particular capital component then, other things being equal, we would expect to be able to generate less well-being. A simple rule for economic growth to continue is that capital should be left intact; that is, productive capacity should not be eroded. This might be achieved via capital bequests; the current generation must pass on a capital stock that is at least as large as the one it inherited in terms of its productive capacity.

Does this mean that the composition of the capital stock must remain unchanged? Must we have as much of each F, or can the Fs be substituted for each other? The example in Chapter 3 suggested that, in general, each of the inputs can be combined in many different ways with each of the other inputs. For example, consider the way in which a restaurant combines inputs to produce meals: it is clear that employing skilled chefs would make it possible to use fewer raw materials because of the reduction in waste. Let us turn this example around and suppose that there is a long-term shortage of raw materials. It would be possible, in principle, to maintain the output of meals by recruiting skilled chefs to make the reduced quantity of raw materials 'go further'. What has happened here is that the restaurant has substituted one input, the skill and knowledge of chefs, for another, raw materials. Economists tend to assume that inputs or productive resources – the Fs – can be substituted easily one for another. It is not unusual for a firm to substitute new technology for unskilled or low-skilled labour. However, it may in practice be very hard to replace the loss of environmental capital (raw materials) with human capital (skill and knowledge) and manufactured capital (machinery). The extent to which human and manufactured capital can be substituted for environmental capital over time is a highly contentious issue.

For ecological economists, the economy must be situated in or be seen as embedded in the physical world (Lutz, 1999, pp.226–35). In Figure 20.3 energy is drawn from the environment, from the physical world, to be used in production and consumption and returned to the environment as waste.

The significance of this way of thinking about the economy is its demonstration that the foundation of ecological economics lies in the natural sciences, and ultimately in physics. In this view, economics is based on the second law of thermodynamics and the concept of entropy.

Physics tells us that matter and energy are governed by the laws of thermodynamics, or the *science of energy*. The first law of thermodynamics states that matter and energy can neither be created nor destroyed. The second law of thermodynamics, also known as the *law of entropy*, goes on to state that entropy always increases. In a thermodynamic system the unchanging quantity of energy undergoes a qualitative change from available, concentrated or low-entropy energy to unavailable, dissipated or high-entropy energy. For example, oil is found in the Earth's crust in a state of low entropy, turned into fuel and emits CO_2, which is dissipated throughout the atmosphere in a state of high entropy. It is beyond the scope of this chapter to explore the epistemological status of the entropy law,

Figure 20.3
A model of the economy embedded in the environment

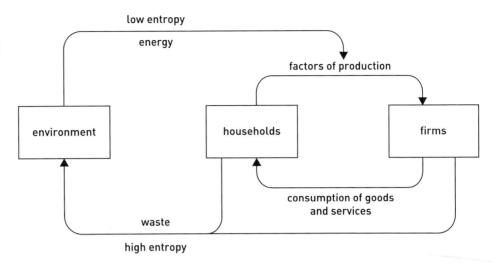

so we will simply note that it stands on solid experimental ground; that is, it has withstood experiments designed to falsify it.

The application of the entropy law to economics is contentious. Georgescu-Roegen (1971) introduced the concept of entropy into economics, claiming that economic processes are entropic; that is, they transform low-entropy energy into high-entropy energy, or available energy into unavailable or waste energy. Since low entropy is a necessary condition of usefulness, the entropy law is essential to understanding the concept of scarcity. This line of thought is therefore the theoretical foundation for the central principles of **ecological economics**, which are that economic processes must be understood as part of the physical world and that there are physical limits to economic growth. It is possible to draw out the implications of these principles by considering the irreversibility of time.

The theoretical basis of irreversibility as a source of environmental problems is that energy flows in one direction and cannot be recycled. When the energy from the raw materials that the environment provides has been used up, economic activity comes to an end. Natural resources are used in the manufacture of goods and eventually transformed into pollution, thus depleting the available energy. So, for the ecological economist, the terrestrial stock of these natural resources represents a physical limit to economic activity. Climate change is another example of the effects of resource depletion. The atmosphere's capacity for absorbing waste GHGs is a natural resource, and it is the exhaustion of this capacity that is the main cause of climate change. In the longest of long runs, the only sustainable economy is one that leaves the stock of energy-bearing natural resources undepleted. This is a stringent condition to impose on economic activity, and Georgescu-Roegen (1971) concluded that the future for humanity is reversion to a 'berry-picking species'. The more that energy use can be curtailed, and the more efficient energy use can be made, the longer it will take us to reach this situation.

Ecological economics

Ecological economics holds that there are physical limits to growth because economic processes are part of the physical world and hence subject to the law of entropy.

Question

Please read the following extract from James Greyson's (1996) article for *Renew*. Greyson uses the term 'quality' to mean the opposite of 'entropy', and the shift from low to high entropy is described here as a movement from high to low quality. Can you detect any grounds for a less pessimistic forecast for the future of humanity than Georgescu-Roegen's?

Quality
The scientists described our dependence on nature in terms of quality, defined as the concentration and structuring of matter. Quality is the material value of a resource; higher quality means it's more useful. Pure water is more useful than polluted water. Concentrated iron is more valuable than ore, whilst iron structured into, say, a girder is yet more valuable. Nature structures concentrated materials using genetic information whilst we do it using human designs. The important thing about quality is that there's no free lunch. Absolutely the only way to produce quality is to consume more quality from somewhere else. In material terms, the real price of production in any economy is the inevitable consumption of quality elsewhere. This loss of quality is evident as waste; dispersed matter with lost concentration and structure. Fortunately nature continuously produces quality by reconcentrating and restructuring waste into valuable resources. This production is done by the green cells in plants which can use energy arriving free-of-charge from the sun. This quality cycle has run smoothly throughout history, until our recent linear economy started consuming quality faster than it could be reproduced in nature. The resulting loss of quality is our debt to nature, evident as mounting wastes and diminishing resources.

Throughout evolution the Earth has experienced a continual increase in quality. The surface has become steadily cleaner and capable of supporting more complex forms of life. Humanity is now experiencing evolution-in-reverse. Each day this goes on diminishes everyone's prospects for prosperity, health and, sooner or later, survival. We know we must urgently re-establish a global economy which pays its debts as it goes. We will know when we are successful because wastes of all kinds will no longer accumulate.

(Greyson, 1996)

There seem to be grounds for a moderate optimism in the processes by which 'nature continuously produces quality by reconcentrating and restructuring waste into valuable resources'. The implication is that the physical limits to growth are not so much a buffer at the end of the line as more of a speed limit. The problem is that 'our recent linear economy started consuming quality faster than it could be reproduced in nature'.

What then are the implications for the question of economic growth of taking an ecological approach to economics? Ecological economics insists on placing the economic system in the context of physical limits to growth. This is particularly relevant to the question of the 'new economy' (Chapter 2). An early statement of the ecological point of view put it in these words:

But we can be fairly certain that no new technology will abolish absolute Scarcity because the laws of thermodynamics apply to all possible technologies.

(Daly, 1973)

Some proponents of the absolute newness of the new economy have contradicted this claim, however, arguing that overthrowing the physical limits to growth is exactly what it does.

Gone is the view of a thermodynamic world economy, dominated by 'natural resources' being turned to waste and entropy by human extraction and use . . . The key fact of knowledge is that it is anti-entropic: it accumulates and compounds as it is used . . . Conquering the microcosm, mind transcends every entropic trap and overthrows matter itself.

(Gilder, 1989)

The ecological economist would reply that it is still necessary to use materials in making PCs and other physical manifestations of the new economy and to use energy in manufacturing them and shipping them all over the world (Lutz, 1999, p.231).

What light does this understanding of the physical limits to growth shed on the specific issue of climate change? Global warming is likely to be irreversible in practice, because of the pressures of growing populations and economic growth. Population growth increases the pressure on natural resources, while economic growth may increase resource requirements per head of the population. Both result in increased energy use and, as more fossil fuels are burnt, an increase in the emissions of GHGs. Even if countries were to commit themselves to reducing emissions of GHGs, the concentrations of these gases in the atmosphere would still increase for some time to come (although this will vary with the extent of the reduction). So future warming of global temperatures is already inevitable, even if action were to be taken now. Global warming might also be irreversible in practice simply because current generations find the adjustments required unpalatable. Given the uncertainty associated with alleged environmental change, they may well prefer to carry on 'business as usual'.

This issue will be taken up in Section 20.3, but part of the groundwork for thinking about it is the idea of environmental sustainability. The feasibility of sustainable development depends in part upon the view that is taken of the physical limits to growth.

▨ ▨ ■ 20.2.3   The idea of sustainable development

Sustainable development

Sustainable development can be defined as an increase in human well-being for the current generation without compromising the well-being of future generations.

The most commonly cited public definition of **sustainable development** came from the 1987 World Commission on Environment and Development (WCED, or the *Brundtland Commission*). Sustainable development is development that

> meets the needs of the present without compromising the ability of future generations to meet their own needs.
>
> *(WCED, 1987, p.8)*

So, sustainable development is development that generates current human well-being without imposing extra costs on the future. For the Brundtland Commission, significant costs means the inability to meet future development needs. For Pearce and Warford (1993), sustainable development is development that secures an increase in the well-being of the current generation without decreasing the well-being of future generations. This effectively takes the same form as the Brundtland definition but substitutes 'welfare' for 'needs'. What it implies is that we should not acquire well-being now at the expense of well-being in the future.

If it is accepted as a worthwhile social goal, sustainable development implies that development should be distributed evenly across the generations. This does not mean that economic progress is sacrificed so that each generation is guaranteed equal levels of well-being. What it means is that progress today must not be reversed at a future date. The way in which the current generation is using the environment may entail large costs being passed on to the future. In this sense, we may be buying our development at the expense of our descendants. The suggestion that this is not an acceptable trade-off raises philosophical issues concerning fairness or justice which are not easy to resolve.

Sustainable development is therefore based on a concept of 'intergenerational' justice that refers to its distribution across generations. This is distinct from distribution within a generation, or 'intragenerational' justice (Chapter 9). It is worth noting that environmental problems also impose significant costs on the present generation and raise their own questions of intragenerational justice. For example, pollutants emitted from power stations, such as sulphur dioxide (SO_2), generate significant current costs in terms of their adverse effects on human health.

How could the current generation secure sustainable development, assuming for the moment that it wants to do so? The current generation holds a stock of capital that can be used to derive well-being now and into the future. Sustainable development is connected to the notion that the current generation should aim to bequeath to the future at least as much capital as it inherited. However, using up this capital by degrading the environment erodes the opportunities of future generations. Is it feasible to compensate them for this loss?

Two schools of thought can be identified, which are related to the rival viewpoints on the physical limits to growth. One school believes that it does not matter what form this bequest takes, while the other believes that particular components of environmental capital must form part of the bequest. The first school is that of the *technological optimists*, who believe that improved technology will always look after the interests of future generations. They regard the concept of sustainable development as irrelevant, because technological progress ensures that it is always the current generation that is the poorest. The assumption behind the second school, associated with *ecological economics* (Section 20.2.2), is that these resources are unique and their contribution to development cannot be equalled by substitutes. We will explore this debate a little further by examining the possibility of technological progress.

Technological progress expands the opportunities open to the future, enhancing the production and consumption possibilities of an economy by raising the productivity of capital. One way to think of this is that greater output can be obtained for the same level of inputs. This reduces the onus on the current generation to pass on to the future as much capital as it inherited. It also raises another possibility. Environmental capital, which ecological economists and others suggest is a unique provider of certain benefits, may not be seen in this way in the future because of the development of substitute goods or substitute processes made possible by technological breakthroughs. The technological optimists would argue that history is full of such instances.

Technological optimists are convinced of the pervasiveness of improved technologies in overcoming constraints on development, but surprisingly little is known about how such change actually comes about. According to the *theory of induced innovation*, the development of new technologies represents a response to pressing problems. For example, a number of technical solutions to global warming have been put forward. One suggestion is the emission of dust particles into the atmosphere, which would have a cooling effect on the climate by reflecting the sun's rays. Similarly, sulphur dioxide from the burning of fossil fuels may help to mitigate the global warming process by reflecting radiation from the sun. Sulphur dioxide is transformed in the atmosphere by chemical reactions to form sulphate aerosols, which reflect radiation in the same way as dust particles but are probably more powerful coolants. However, sulphur dioxide is a pollutant, both in its own right and as a precursor of acid rain, which is a significant source of damage to human health, buildings, materials and ecosystems. In addition, sulphate aerosols contribute to visibility loss. Many scientists regard attempts to control the global climate with suspicion. Induced innovation is more likely to contribute to the gradual abatement of climate change through, say, the development of fuel cells.

Question	Please read the following extract. What do you think is the significance of fuel cell technology for the debate between technological optimists such as George Gilder and ecological economists such as Herman Daly?

Figure 20.4
HydroGen1, a
fuel cell car

Get ready, because life is about to change forever. In the next 20 years global warming will subside, the Los Angeles smog will disappear, people will head for downtown Tokyo in search of a breath of fresh air and who knows, nightingales may yet sing in Berkeley Square.

Sounds crazy, perhaps. But life could be like that if fuel cell technology takes off, as many people expect it to. While car makers focus on powering future cars and other vehicles, fuel cells are already being tested to generate electricity for houses and factories all over the world.

Fuel cells may well prove to be the energy source for the 21st century, but they have actually been around for some time. Welsh judge and amateur scientist, Sir William Grove, first had the idea in 1839 when he reckoned it should be possible to reverse the process of electrolysis, where hydrogen is extracted from water using electricity.

He was right, and fuel cells now consume hydrogen and oxygen to produce electricity, with only water as a waste product. They are shaping up to be a vital source of power to mankind because unlike fossil fuels – petroleum, oil, gas and coal – hydrogen is not only a renewable form of energy but also the most abundant element in the universe . . .

Vauxhall's parent company, General Motors, is at the forefront of fuel cell development and has just demonstrated its fuel cell car for the first time. Based on a Vauxhall-Opel Zafira, the fuel cell car is called HydroGen1 [see Figure 20.4]. . . [and it] has a stack containing 200 cells . . .

Manufacturers will face new challenges: were GM to produce one million cars a year, it would need to produce over half a million individual fuel cells per day . . . Think about it. No fossil fuels burnt by cars, power stations or heating systems would . . . reduce emissions of the greenhouse gas CO_2 enormously.

By using pure hydrogen, they would eradicate it altogether, providing a solution to one of the biggest problems yet faced by mankind.

(adapted from Crosse, 2000, pp.22–4)

There is no doubt that fuel cell technology could reduce significantly CO_2 emissions and make a major contribution to the abatement of climate change. To that extent it provides a way of alleviating a physical limit to growth. But there are grounds for doubting whether fuel cell technology vindicates the technological optimists' claims that knowledge, such as that embodied in fuel cells, can overcome entropy. The manufacture of cars and fuel cells – perhaps half a million a day from one car manufacturer – clearly entails a continuing drain on environmental resources. What matters is the rate at which the environment is degraded. Fuel cell technology will help to bring GHG emissions below the rate at which the atmosphere can absorb them without climate change. But that amounts to changing economic activity in the light of knowledge about the physical limits to growth, rather than surmounting those limits.

Can the distinction between technological optimists and pessimists be applied more generally to climate change? The main difference seems to be between engaging in less carbon-emitting activity, which is implicit in the pessimistic view, and reducing the carbon emissions associated with an unchanged level of such activity, as the optimists suggest. In practice, it is likely that a workable and effective response to climate change must draw on both approaches. The Case study below indicates how much carbon emission can be saved by scaling down various everyday activities and turning to more carbon-efficient methods of engaging in others. The problem is devising a structure of incentives or constraints that would be adequate to the task of achieving such changes in behaviour.

Case study: Cutting down on carbon

- Low flow showerheads reduce hot water use by 10 to 15 per cent and can save up to 300 lb of CO_2 emissions per year.
- Lowering your thermostat by 2 °F (approx. 1.5 °C) can eliminate 500 lb of CO_2 emissions per year.
- Insulating your water tank can save 1000 lb of CO_2 emissions per year.
- Replacing three regular light bulbs with compact fluorescent bulbs can eliminate 750 lb of CO_2 emissions per year.
- Insulating your home can save 1000 lb of CO_2 emissions per year.
- The average car in the USA emits approximately 1 lb of carbon per mile, which can be halved by switching to a more fuel-efficient vehicle.
- Every mile on a train is responsible for 0.5 lb of CO_2 emissions.

- Recycling all your newspapers every week can reduce CO_2 emissions by 250 lb per year.
- Recycling six glass bottles every week can reduce CO_2 emissions by 250 lb per year.

Question

Examine the list of carbon-saving measures above. In what ways are you a carbon-saver? The list is not complete, and you may be saving carbon in ways that are not mentioned here. What do you think would be the most effective way of persuading you to save more carbon? Think, for example, of fuel taxes and utility prices, of laws and regulations, and of campaigns to raise awareness of the importance of saving carbon.

What, if anything, would make the consumers and voters of industrial countries – past, present and future – change their behaviour in these ways? If political resistance by voters in some countries has obstructed measures to alleviate climate change, political pressure from environmentally concerned voters has pushed governments elsewhere towards an early implementation. Moreover, markets in renewable energy and energy-saving technology have evolved alongside increasing public awareness of environmental degradation. What have economists had to say about the ethical values, principles and beliefs that inform the choices of voters and consumers? How can economists address the role of the ethical and social norms that constitute part of the institutional structure of the societies in which markets are embedded?

20.3 Ethics and the social limits to growth

Chapters 4 and 5 highlighted the advantages of competition: perfect competition reduces costs and the competitive process speeds innovation. There is, however, another perspective on competition, put forward by Fred Hirsch in *The Social Limits to Growth* (1976), which draws attention to its disadvantages. Hirsch argued that competition can be socially destructive. In clarifying this argument, he introduced the concept of positional competition to denote competition among consumers for finite resources when the acquisition of those resources involves denying them to others. For example, people moving out of the city to be closer to the tranquillity of nature cause more houses and roads to be built, thereby denying that finite and fragile resource to others. For Hirsch, the root of the problem was self-interest, which economists generally assume to be the most powerful motive driving competition among producers and consumers alike. The solution Hirsch recommended was 'moral re-entry', so that economic agents believe themselves to be obliged to co-operate, on the basis of traditional social norms, religious beliefs and a sense of civic duty. In order to appreciate Hirsch's position, it is necessary to consider some aspects of ethics and, in particular, the role of reason in ethical decision-making.

20.3.1 Subjective preferences and ethical principles

In economics, values are generally treated as subjective tastes or preferences. In explaining shifts in the demand curve, Chapter 3 mentioned changes in tastes or in fashion as a possible cause. If the demand in question is for, say, ice cream, then it seems reasonable to think of the value consumers place on different flavours in this way. Perhaps consumers become bored with vanilla and strawberry and so ice-cream parlours try to renew their enthusiasm for the product by introducing pistachio, caramel fudge and tequila sunrise. But something seems to be left out if the same approach is taken to the demand for solar panels, electricity from renewable sources or low-emission vehicles.

What seems to be left out of the standard economic approach to values is reason. The distinction between positive statements and normative judgements is characteristic of a certain interpretation of reason and the scope for rational thought. Positive statements are objective or scientific explanations of the way the economy works. Normative judgements are recommendations, reflecting subjective or personal feelings or preferences. This distinction underlies the 'instrumental' conception of reason, according to which subjective or personal feelings provide us with wants, needs or desires, while reason gives us the means to achieve those wants, needs or desires. The eighteenth-century Scottish philosopher David Hume, a friend of Adam Smith's, put it rather memorably:

> Reason is, and ought only to be, the slave of the passions, and can never pretend to any other office than to serve and obey them.
>
> *(Hume, 1906, pp.414–15)*

The 'passions' dictate to us what we want, and reason tells us how to get it. For example, your passions, inflamed no doubt by advertising, might tell you that you must have the new fragrance from Karl Lagerfeld or a grooming product for men from Aramis. Reason, according to Hume, does not come into wanting such things. What rational thinking does is to show you how to get what you want in the world as it is. Reason, in the shape of scientific investigation, helps us to understand how things really or objectively are – the way the economy works, for example – whether we like them that way or not. If economists remain within the bounds of the positive, their advice deserves to be treated as expert knowledge – and the conduct of monetary policy will be no less scientific an endeavour than the generation and control of electricity. But if their judgements are wholly personal or subjective, as positive economics insists that all value judgements are, economic debate will be constructed upon highly subjective foundations, which are not themselves amenable to rational debate.

This interpretation of reason does not do justice to the situations of moral conflict, reflection and uncertainty familiar to most people. It fails to distinguish between sub-jective tastes, such as a liking for toffee fudge ice cream, and moral principles, such as loyalty, responsibility, sympathy or a sense of duty. Every motive or desire, every spring of action, is regarded as a 'passion', a subjective feeling. This seems to me to be an exces-sive restriction of the role of reasoned argument and critical reflection in human affairs, for we *do* revise our normative judgements, and even our feelings about moral matters, in the light of experience.

An interpretation of our moral experience that can accommodate reflection and affords a more positive role for reason is provided in a tradition of moral philosophy that goes back to Aristotle. The philosophy and economics of Karl Marx have their roots in an Aristotelian account of human nature and human flourishing, and the medieval philosopher and theologian St Thomas Aquinas developed a system of thought from Aristotelian foundations which continues to be influential today in Catholic social teach-ing. This very brief statement of broadly Aristotelian views draws on Yuengert (2001).

For Aristotle, human happiness or flourishing comes only through virtue. A virtuous person is one who is disposed to perform good actions, which requires three conditions to be met. First, they must have a worthy goal in mind, rather than a merely subjective preference. Second, they must be able to identify the best action in a particular set of circumstances. This second capacity Aristotle thought of as 'practical wisdom', and it is clearly very close to the instrumental rationality of the typical economic account. Third, the virtuous person must perform the action identified as good. This means that

> he must not be ruled by his passions, which often militate against reasoned
> deliberation and moral action.
>
> *(Yuengert, 2001, p.6)*

It is an approach that offers some scope for a more active role for reason than that found in Hume and in the instrumental rationality of much economics. This more active role is mainly concerned with rational reflection on the goals of action, which are understood to include upholding principles and embodying virtues as well as expressing preferences. The wisdom of following a particular principle or being guided by a particular virtue is a matter for rational reflection on experience. The implication is that, as economists, we should not be satisfied with an account of environmental values that presents them as just another set of subjective preferences.

As the Aristotelian approach suggests, it seems that ethical principles have something in common with economic theories: both are susceptible to revision after we confront them with data, evidence or experience. In other words, the passions are subject to guidance and direction by reason. That is not to say that we should put our economic theories to the test of experience in the same way that we revise our moral principles in the light of experience, but that the relation between economic theories and values is too subtle and complicated to be captured by a simple dichotomy between subservient reason and the active passions. Our ethical principles, and even our feelings about moral issues, are subject to critical reflection as a kind of 'testing' – unlike our subjective tastes, which we tend to take as 'given'.

Amartya Sen has argued for the importance of a 'careful assessment of aims, objectives, allegiances, etc., and of the conception of the good' (Sen, 1987, p.42). In order to illustrate the 'careful assessment' characteristic of moral reasoning, let us consider a hypothetical example based on Sen (1976). Suppose that you are a geologist and that you have spent your career exploring for oil reserves. Soon after you arrive in an area that is vulnerable to sea level rise for your latest assignment, you decide that you must confront the growing disquiet you have felt for some time about the role of fossil fuels in causing climate change. You consider the options that seem to be open to you: returning home to early (and financially comfortable) retirement; continuing to direct the oil exploration project; joining an environmental pressure group to campaign for a GHG emissions reduction programme; or setting up your own renewable energy supply firm.

You might try to calculate what is in your own self-interest and rank the options as shown in column A of Table 20.1. But should self-interest be your guiding principle? You might try another ranking, based on your conception of what would be the 'most moral' thing to do (column B). But can you live up to such a rigorous moral code? Do you have the personal qualities required of an environmental campaigner or an entrepreneur? A careful assessment of your past behaviour, the likely consequences of the different courses of action and your capacity for political lobbying and business leadership leaves you in little doubt that your actual decision will reflect the ranking shown in column C. Nevertheless, you are aware that a person of greater moral courage would take the risks involved in campaigning or in business enterprise. This suggests that moral choices prompt us into a process of critical reasoning and self-examination. You might also rank the rankings themselves, perhaps in the order B, C, A.

Table 20.1
Ranking moral choices

A 'Self-interest'	B 'Most moral'	C 'Actual'
Drill for oil	Environmental campaign	Early retirement
Early retirement	Renewable energy entrepreneur	Drill for oil
Environmental campaign	Early retirement	Environmental campaign
Renewable energy entrepreneur	Drill for oil	Renewable energy entrepreneur

Case study: Opportunities for ethical investment

Consider a list of investment opportunities that you can avoid on ethical grounds: say, environmental degradation, armaments, tobacco, alcohol and gambling.

■ Is there something more than a chance set of tastes or feelings linking the list of ethically blocked investments, or some of the items in it?

Case study continued

- Are the different prohibitions applications of, or derivations from, a general moral principle or set of core values?
- What role in selecting ethical investment options might be played by a consideration of the consequences of the prohibited activities?
- Suppose that you came to the list with a disapproval of one item on it but no strong views on the other investment categories. Would seeing the activities listed together put you under an obligation to try to take a consistent or coherent line on all of them?
- What difference would it make to your deliberations if you were informed that some categories of ethical investment are substantially less profitable than investment unconstrained by

ethical considerations? Should it make any difference at all?

Question

Try constructing a table ranking the moral choices for the ethical investment opportunities in this Case study. You may choose your own descriptions of the preferences for the top of the columns. One possible set of descriptions might be something like this: profit-maximizing investment free of ethical constraints; environmentally sensitive investment; investment avoiding gambling, tobacco and alcohol; investment avoiding armaments; and 'across the board' ethical investment avoiding all the other categories.

This approach does not confine reason to the discovery of reliable means to ends determined solely by subjective feelings. It argues that reason is also concerned with bringing our beliefs, experiences, feelings and values into some sort of harmony or coherence. In that case, we can begin to work out a role for values or normative judgements in economics without compromising its claim to be a systematic and rational form of inquiry. The next section applies this approach to ethics by considering Hirsch's ideal of 'moral re-entry' in the context of climate change.

20.3.2 Markets, self-interest and environmental values

Hirsch's ideal of moral re-entry can be illustrated using two ethical principles of particular relevance to the issue of climate change. If political resistance to a GHG emissions reduction programme is to be overcome, many environmentalists and ecologists advocate two departures from the self-interest that Hirsch deplores. These altruistic principles are a sense of justice for future generations and a perception of the intrinsic worth of the non-human environment.

A sense of justice for future generations

Chapter 8 explained the concept of Pareto efficiency or the Pareto principle. The Pareto principle states that society is better off if a change in the allocation of the inputs or outputs of economic activity leaves at least one person better off without making anyone else worse off. This gain is known as a Pareto improvement and, when all such gains have been exhausted, Pareto efficiency is achieved. When the Pareto principle is used to analyse the efficiency with which resources are allocated between current and future generations, it can generate implications that are somewhat similar to those of sustainable development. If environmental resources are being used up, such as the capacity of the atmosphere to absorb CO_2 without climate change, this particular environmental endowment will decrease. Consequently, there is less to be passed on to future generations, which decreases the economic opportunities open to future generations to meet their development goals. This violates the requirement for sustainability laid out in the Brundtland Report. It also contradicts the Pareto principle if it is extended to consider future generations. A gain in current well-being at the expense of future well-being is not an improvement by the Pareto criterion.

Intergenerational justice

Intergenerational justice is the obligation to ensure a fair distribution of resources between the current generation and future generations.

The concept of **intergenerational justice** underpins the argument for sustainable development and hence the arguments for climate change abatement policies. This concept has been debated at length by philosophers, political scientists, economists and environmentalists. The basic problem, as the economist and philosopher John Broome (1992) points out, is how to weigh up goods and bads that occur at different times. This is particularly relevant to global warming, as global climate change would continue for 70 years, as a consequence of past emissions, even if CO_2 emission ceased today. Climate change abatement is therefore inescapably altruistic, and intended to benefit people who do not yet exist.

Some commentators have raised the issue of uncertainty and set it against the equal consideration of future welfare. We, the current generation, do not know what future generations will want, so discounting future benefits may be a reasonable response to this uncertainty. Discounting is a technique for comparing the worth of goods and bads that occur at different times by expressing future benefits and costs in terms of an estimate of their present value (Chapter 14, Section 14.3). Uncertainty about what future generations will want could be a reason for preferring current benefits over future benefits that are, at the time they occur, of the same magnitude.

The problem is that such discounting favours the present generation over future generations and therefore seems to involve an unacceptable concession to self-interest. We may feel instead that, morally, the well-being of future generations should be given equal consideration to that of the current generation. We might derive such a principle from a concept of fairness, perhaps understood as impartiality between individuals. We could extend this impartiality across time in arguing that the well-being of each generation should be equally valued.

The land ethic

A sense of the intrinsic value or moral worth of non-human nature expresses a very different attitude to nature from the perception of it as a repository of resources for production. The idea of *use value* captures the economic attitude to nature as something to be appropriated and exploited. By contrast, the concept of *existence value* captures the valuing of something in and of itself rather than for its uses. People clearly value the existence of species such as elephants, mountain gorillas or humpback whales, and they value whole ecosystems such as rain forests. Donations to environmental groups represent one mechanism by which existence values are revealed in people's behaviour.

The land ethic

The land ethic expresses a sense of the intrinsic value of non-human nature.

A classic statement of one aspect of existence values is **the land ethic** propounded by the American environmentalist, Aldo Leopold, in his *A Sand County Almanac* (Leopold, 1970). Much of the book is devoted to celebrating the virtues of the non-human world: the grace of a plover, the valour of a chickadee, the harmony of a river ecosystem, the accumulated wisdom of a stand of pine trees – a natural wisdom which silences the people who walk below.

(Leopold, 1970, p.37)

The main principle of the land ethic is the aspiration towards 'a more positive, sustainable position of respectful dwelling in nature'. This entails a rejection of the assumption that use values are the only way of valuing nature: 'We abuse land because we regard it as a commodity belonging to us' (p.94). The alternative view hopes that when 'we see land as a community to which we belong, we may begin to use it with love and respect' (p.92). The implication for economic activity is that the 'destruction, overuse or excessive appropriation of nature is morally wrong' (Cafaro, 2001). In Leopold's own words,

A thing is right when it tends to preserve the integrity, stability, and beauty of the biotic community. It is wrong when it tends otherwise.

(Leopold, 1970, pp.158–9)

Climate change threatens to disturb, and arguably has already disturbed, the integrity and stability of many biotic communities across the world. This aspect of the effects of climate change did not figure prominently in the negotiations leading up to the Kyoto Protocol.

Moral re-entry and markets

A concern for the well-being of future generations and a sense of the intrinsic value of the non-human world are both excluded from consideration in the market process, where the competitive process operates to induce innovations that in many cases cause environmental degradation. Clearly, future generations cannot themselves be market agents because they do not yet exist. Any part of the non-human environment that is not someone's property – for example, the atmosphere – is vulnerable to environmental damage. If it is not owned by anyone, using it does not entail having to pay, and so it may easily become an apparently free receptor of waste products or pollution. Can values such as a concern for future generations and a sense of the intrinsic worth of non-human nature be accommodated by markets along with everyday consumer preferences? Can they be found a place in economic analysis among the norms and values that surround and shape market activity? The following discussion may help to clarify some of the issues involved.

Read the following brief extract from the transcript of the BBC Radio 4 programme 'What austerity does for you', first broadcast on 11 January 2001 as part of the series *Analysis*. Those taking part are:

- Frances Cairncross, BBC presenter and economics journalist and writer
- George Monbiot, environmentalist
- Daniel Bell, Emeritus Professor of Sociology, Harvard University
- Dr Zaki Badawi, President of the Muslim College and Chairman of the Islam Mosque Council.

Cairncross: What might persuade the spoilt and wealthy children of the early 21st century to make communal sacrifices? The environment perhaps?

Monbiot: There are certain activities which are so environmentally costly that we should not be pursuing them or not pursuing them in the way we do today.

Cairncross: Do you think that people care enough about the environment to impose the necessary restraint upon themselves?

Monbiot: It's not simply going to happen through people's free will. We need regulation to say there are certain environmental toxins that we should not be pouring into the environment. Regulation creates the commercial environment in which companies operate and in which consumption operates. With the right kind of regulation you can ensure that people's quality of life remains just as high – or hopefully very much higher – while preventing the most damaging environmental effects.

Cairncross: But the austerity that environmentalists seek would need to be lasting with the benefits fairly distributed not just within a nation but across the globe. Daniel Bell, do you think that capitalist society is capable of such a response?

Bell: To the extent that capitalism depends upon the stimulation of demand and this is a response to various forms of display and hedonism, intrinsically no. But at the same time there's still an awareness of the excesses of the market or the fact that markets often fail. So there's a need for certain kinds of redress and certain kinds of restraint.

Cairncross: So capitalism, with its intrinsic hedonism, is quite incapable of inspiring austerity in a society for any length of time. The intervention of government is needed. What about the clerics? How does Zaki Badawi think he can hold at bay the forces of consumerism?

Badawi: By preaching. There's very little else, I'm afraid. But we are helpless really because the people who are producing the consumer goods are the people who control the media and they want people to consume more because they make more profit.

Monbiot: The only way to persuade of the virtues of austerity is to show that in some respects it leads to an enrichment of the quality of life, perhaps to a slowing down of life, which allows you to ponder, to wonder what it's all about.

(http://news.bbc.co.uk/hi/english/s . . . analysis/transcript/austerity.txt)

Questions	Now answer the following questions:

1 What do you think are the main implications of the views expressed in the extract for Hirsch's idea that there is a need for moral re-entry in contemporary society?

2 Drawing on your own values, as well as on the economic understanding you have gained from the course, comment on the views expressed in the extract. With which of the points made do find yourself most strongly in agreement, and which do you find least convincing?

In response to Question 1, the discussants seem to be in agreement with Hirsch's critique of the centrality of self-interest in contemporary society. They believe that markets are imbued with the prevailing values of capitalist society, which are hedonistic and self-interested. Bell refers to a hedonism on which capitalism depends and to the excesses of markets, while Badawi believes that the prevailing values of society are those that increase profits. For both discussants it seems that capitalist values arise from complicity between consumers and producers, with each group pursuing its own self-interest. And there seems to be a general pessimism about the prospects for change in the direction of Hirsch's moral re-entry. In their different ways both Badawi and Monbiot believe that preaching is the only source of alternative values, with Badawi advocating it in a specifically religious context and Monbiot urging the attractions of a more austere and hence less pressured way of life. Neither, however, holds out much prospect of a shift towards the values they seek to promote. For Monbiot, action from consumers or private citizens for a more environmentally sustainable economy seems to be out of the question, and Badawi believes that the power of commercial interests is overwhelming.

There is no single 'right' answer to Question 2 because it asks for personal judgements. You might have thought of some of the following points. Monbiot's claim that government regulation 'creates the commercial environment' within which firms and consumers operate in markets accords with a view in which markets are shaped by the institutional frameworks in which they are embedded. In view of the political resistance to climate change regulation, not only in the USA, it is important that government intervention should reflect a consensus. Perhaps Monbiot's suggestion that the virtues of austerity enrich the quality of life expresses an awareness of this point. Building a consensus involves preaching, by political as well as religious leaders, and by environmentalists, entrepreneurs and scientists, too.

Second, we should not be convinced by the pessimistic view of values in markets that seems to be shared by the discussants. It seems to be true that economic activity in contemporary market economies is overwhelmingly driven by values that it is reasonable to think of as self-interested, hedonistic and concerned with display, as Bell claims. The discussants' view that this is a cause for concern rather than celebration is also reasonable. However, their dismissal of the markets as beyond redemption or retrieval is not reasonable.

Question	Please read the following extract from Greyson's (1996) article for *Renew*. Do you think that it offers support for a less pessimistic view of markets and environmentally sensitive values than that expressed by the discussants in the radio programme?

Dr Robèrt started The Natural Step organization so the consensus process could include everyone who was willing to participate. These days 19 networks of ten thousand professionals (scientists, engineers, doctors, business executives, etc.) are working with The Natural Step. Some of these people have extended the initial consensus towards 'what can be agreed' in their fields. Others put the concepts into practice, leading the market-place and providing examples of what can be achieved. The largest companies working with The Natural Step have formed a 'Challenge' group to co-ordinate their planning and investments. The Swedish Rail company, SJ, is collaborating with Bilspedition (one of Europe's largest freight companies), IKEA and Electrolux to drastically reduce road haulage. One of the country's largest oil companies, OK Petroleum, is investing in bio-fuels and lobbying for increased taxes on fossil fuels. The Challenge group's chief executives met with the Prime Minister of Sweden in March 1995 to tell him the goal of economic growth was illusory and that the time is ripe for the shift to a cyclic economy. He agreed. These examples are important for The Natural Step since it only works with consensus information. It doesn't prescribe to people what changes they should make since everyone knows their own business best. Instead The Natural Step asks people's advice about how this consensus might apply in their area and then supports exemplary practice.

(Greyson, 1996)

The significance of this extract is that markets can, it seems, in principle, reflect values other than hedonistic and self-interested ones. It is possible for economic agents in markets to co-operate as well as compete, on the basis of traditional social norms, religious beliefs and a sense of civic duty, aspects to which Hirsch (1977) drew attention.

One reason it is not always easy to see this is that economics tends to explain the motivation of consumers and producers, of buyers and sellers in markets, in ways that lend credence to the depiction of them as hedonistic and irretrievably self-interested.

From the standpoint taken by most economists it is difficult to understand how ethical principles, environmental values, a sense of civic duty and so on can get a foothold in market transactions. They must do so if economic activity is to be redirected towards less environmentally damaging products and, in particular, towards low-carbon or no-carbon technologies.

What policies might be used to guide economic behaviour in a more environmentally sustainable direction? One way of redirecting economic activity is for the state to intervene in markets where there is market failure, shaping market incentives through taxes and regulation (Chapter 9, Section 9.2). The next section examines a rather different market-based policy instrument: emissions trading.

20.4 Beyond Kyoto: making a carbon market?

In Chapter 9, Maureen Mackintosh introduced the idea of 'smart government' – for example, designing regulations that both encourage competitiveness in markets and tackle social exclusion. It seems reasonable to develop the idea of smart government to encompass the use of markets as instruments for achieving objectives set outside the markets through the political process. The climate change negotiations that culminated in the Kyoto Protocol envisaged a major role for market mechanisms, notably emissions trading, in reducing GHG emissions in accordance with agreed targets or aspirations. Once permits to emit agreed quantities of CO_2 and other GHGs have been issued, they can be traded. Participants able to emit less than their permits allow can sell the surplus permits to participants who find it costly to bring their emissions down to the agreed level. In principle, the market in permits to emit GHGs could both enhance competitiveness and innovation and help to avert the adverse consequences of climate change. However, the fact that markets are inevitably embedded in society opens them up to other social and political pressures and constraints. These might or might not be conducive to the sort of technological progress that is required in response to climate change.

20.4.1 The climate change negotiations

The UN Framework Convention on Climate Change (UNFCCC) set the overall objective of stabilizing the concentration of GHGs to prevent dangerous climate change, while ensuring that food production was not threatened and sustainable economic development could proceed. The story of the Kyoto negotiations is that collective agreements to that end were modified to add 'flexibility', through international transfer mechanisms such as emissions trading. This reflects the key clash between the EU's desire for a co-ordinated approach based on flat-rate emission reductions and the anti-interventionist stance of the USA, which was sensitive to its citizens' and industries' attachment to cheap fuel. The EU sought a flat-rate GHG emissions reduction target for all Annex I countries (the industrial polluters) of 10 to 15 per cent, while the USA and Japan aimed for an average 0 to 5 per cent decrease with differentials and flexibility.

The outcome of the Kyoto negotiations was a set of reduction targets averaging out as a 5.2 per cent cut on 1990 levels of GHG emissions by 2008–12. There are different national targets around this average, ranging from the EU's 8 per cent reduction on 1990 levels of GHG emissions by 2008–12, through 7 per cent for the USA, 6 per cent for Japan and 0 per cent for Russia and Ukraine, to increases of 8 per cent for Australia and 10 per cent for Iceland. It was not possible to sustain the commitment to flat-rate targets proposed by the EU after the EU departed from its own principle, arguing for differential targets across EU countries, averaging to 8 per cent. The 5.2 per cent GHG emissions-reduction programme agreed for the period 2008–12 should be assessed in the light of the IPCC judgement that a 60 per cent cut in GHG emissions is needed in order to stabilize atmospheric concentrations by 2050. Friends of the Earth described the outcome of the negotiations as 'pitifully inadequate'. Furthermore, there is little prospect that even these reductions will be achieved.

Most industrial countries are falling short of their Kyoto aspirations. Japan's weak economic performance during the 1990s has slowed the rise in emissions there, but not enough to put Japan on track to meet its 6 per cent Kyoto target. In the EU only Germany, because of economic collapse in the former East Germany, and the UK, after the 'dash for gas' (the fossil fuel with the lightest GHG emissions) associated with utility privatization, are likely to comply with their targets under Kyoto. In the USA, emissions had risen 12 per cent above 1990 levels by 1999 and were predicted to rise another 10 per cent by 2008. Achieving the Kyoto target for the USA of a 7 per cent reduction from 1990 levels would now require a 25 per cent decline from 'business as usual'. According to Victor (2001, p.2), US citizens are unlikely to accept the high costs of compliance with Kyoto. For example, half of US electricity is supplied by coal, the fossil fuel that emits most GHGs. The US Congress refused 95–0 to ratify the Kyoto Protocol, and in March 2001 President Bush abandoned it. Other countries, notably the EU member states, remain committed to the objectives of the climate change negotiations.

The significance of creating markets as a policy response to climate change is associated with the role of competition in reducing costs and hence making compliance with Kyoto more politically acceptable. In the USA, for example,

> full-blown trading could lower the annual costs [of compliance with the Kyoto target] by a factor of ten – to a more palatable $100 per American household.
>
> *(Victor, 2001, p.3)*

Emissions trading

An emissions-trading regime applies when countries are given permits to produce maximum levels of GHG emissions that they are then allowed to trade.

By 'full-blown trading', Victor means the combination of three international transfer mechanisms that were negotiated at Kyoto: joint implementation agreements, the clean development mechanism and emissions trading. Under the joint implementation (JI) agreements, two industrial countries can each earn credits towards their emission reduction targets by jointly investing in a project that cuts emissions. The clean development mechanism (CDM) allows an industrial country to earn credits towards its emission reduction target by investing in an emission-reducing project in a low-income country. The idea behind **emissions trading** is that an industrial country can increase the maximum level of GHG emissions it is allowed during a set period by buying unused allowances from another industrial country.

■ ■ ■ 20.4.2 Emissions trading

The governments of the countries participating in the Kyoto negotiations stipulated a quantitative target for the reduction of GHG emissions and decided to make use of market processes to achieve that target. Permits to emit GHGs were issued up to an agreed maximum for each country. Countries could then buy and sell their permits. A country that needed to reduce emissions might choose to buy other countries' permits if it was cheaper than reducing their own emissions. A country facing relatively low costs for investment in energy-efficient technologies to reduce GHG emissions would sell the permits it no longer required to one facing higher costs. In this way, the costs of reducing GHG emissions could be minimized.

In the case of climate change, the world's biggest polluter, the USA, is reluctant to incur the costs of reducing its GHG emissions in accordance with the Kyoto Protocol. It is not only that those costs could be as high as $1000 per US household (without emissions trading); there is also the fear that the sacrifice will be futile if emissions from low-income countries, in particular China and India, increase on a 'business as usual' basis. This is where economists can help. You will recall that markets can reduce costs and speed innovation. In applying this general insight to the case of carbon emissions, the following extract explains the potential benefits of emissions trading, or carbon trading.

What are the key benefits of carbon trading?

The key benefit is flexibility and, therefore, cost-effectiveness. Because the cost of reducing greenhouse gasses varies enormously from company to company and from country to country and because the global environment benefits regardless of where emissions are reduced, it makes sense for reductions to take place initially where it is least costly. For example, rather than investing in costly emission reduction technologies within its own plant, a company can decide to make a less costly investment in reductions elsewhere and obtain credits which can then be applied towards its own net greenhouse reductions.

Trading also encourages the development of new environmentally advanced plants and processes. It allows flexibility to innovate and experiment and encourages the adaptation and financing of new technologies in developing countries. Inevitably, it will mobilize large amounts of resources towards poorer nations leading to greater engagement by the developing world in global efforts to reduce emissions.

(http://www.carbonmarket.com/FAQs.htm#top.Anchor)

Emissions trading might therefore make a post-Kyoto GHG emissions-reduction programme more politically acceptable to US voters and facilitate a much less carbon-intensive development trajectory for China and India.

A serious problem with carbon trading is that government intervention is required to define property rights (i.e. to set the targets for GHG emission reductions for each country) and hence the number of permits that can be issued. Without property rights there is nothing to be exchanged. You cannot be a seller unless you actually own what you want to sell. There is also the need for an authority to monitor and enforce the contracts that are made, explicitly or implicitly, whenever goods change hands in a market. These pre-conditions of market processes are particularly important in the case of climate change. Since it is a global problem being addressed through intergovernmental negotiations, a 'world government' seems to be required. In the absence of such an organization, the difficulties of defining property rights in CO_2 emissions have so far proved insuperable. As Victor (2001, p.14) puts it, 'international law has no central authority that can compel countries to remain part of a treaty'.

Emissions trading in the Kyoto Protocol

The difficulties of creating a system of emissions trading under the Kyoto Protocol demonstrate the importance of clearly assigned property rights and adequate monitoring and enforcement procedures to the functioning of markets. The history of the Kyoto negotiations also shows that the effectiveness of a market in emissions permits depends crucially upon the political and social pressures in which market processes, including the creation of the new market itself, are embedded. The capacity of an emerging market in emissions permits to reduce costs and induce innovation may therefore be compromised by the political pressures that have shaped it. To understand emissions trading in the Kyoto Protocol, we must look at its origins. Who proposed it? What might they have stood to gain from it? To what extent has this presumed pursuit of self-interest impeded the functioning of the market in emissions trading?

It was representatives of the fossil fuel industries who lobbied most strenuously in favour of a flexible approach to emissions-reduction targets, including emissions trading. The fossil fuel lobby includes the coal, oil and automotive industries and states whose economies are energy intensive or dependent on the export or use of fossil fuels. The Global Climate Coalition (GCC) is a pressure group for predominantly US fossil fuel interests (i.e. the coal and oil industries), but also the chemical and car industries. GCC ran mass-media campaigns seeking to discredit the scientific evidence for climate change, lobbied energetically at Kyoto and formed an alliance with the OPEC countries. It is estimated that US industry 'threw probably up to $100 million into fighting the whole process' of climate change regulation (Grubb *et al.*, 1999, p.112).

It is clear that the appeal of emissions trading to the fossil fuel lobby was that it held out the prospect of allowing leading emitters to avoid taking serious domestic action. The USA faced high costs for reducing GHG emissions in the form of political resistance from the powerful fossil fuel lobby and from voters. The USA 'got virtually everything it wanted in terms of flexibility for Annex I (industrial countries) commitments' (Grubb *et al.*, 1999, p.93). Russia and Ukraine were in the best position to sell surplus permits as they have zero abatement costs (the costs of reducing GHG emissions). In Russia and Ukraine, emissions fell as a consequence of economic collapse, and

> over successive months teams of US officials went to the East to explain the windfall that could be waiting.
>
> (*Grubb* et al., *1999, p.93*)

As Victor (2001, p.10) concludes, the accidental nature of the surplus means that the US scheme 'buys paper compliance but no reduction in global warming'. The emissions reductions in Russia and Ukraine were 'free' in that they came about as the unintended side-effects of economic collapse. Rather than 'ring fence' this zero cost contribution to climate change abatement, the US proposal would have allowed it to be dissipated in higher US emissions.

As the negotiations at Kyoto continued it became clear that Japan and other industrial countries wanted to take part in emissions trading with Russia and Ukraine. However, the difficulties of establishing property rights in emissions permits, and in devising workable monitoring and enforcement procedures, proved to be insuperable. Negotiations over emissions trading among participating countries were therefore deadlocked when President Bush announced the US abandonment of the Kyoto Protocol. Is this the end of the road for attempts to create a 'carbon market' as a way of curbing GHG emissions? Or are the potential advantages of such a market sufficient to make a resumption of attempts to create it probable or even inevitable?

The justification of the original US plan to buy all, or almost all, of the surplus emissions permits from Russia and Ukraine appealed to the standard arguments concerning the advantages of markets. Markets not only reduce costs and allocate resources efficiently, but they also encourage innovation.

Questions	1 Can you think of any reasons for doubting whether the case for the advantages of markets applies to a market in emissions permits?
	2 If so, is there anything that Russia and Ukraine could do with the proceeds of the sale of emissions permits that might lead you revise that judgement?
	You might find it helpful to consult the discussion of perfect competition in Chapter 5 in connection with the first question, and the account of monopoly in Chapter 4 with respect to the second.

There seems to be two reasons for being sceptical about the benefits of markets. First, the argument for markets reducing costs and achieving allocative efficiency is based on the model of a perfectly competitive market. Among the conditions a market must satisfy, if it is properly to be described as perfectly competitive, is the presence of large numbers of buyers and sellers. Only if there are many transactions among numerous buyers and sellers can a prevailing market price emerge to convey the information they need to make the decisions that yield cost reductions and hence an efficient allocation of resources (Rosenbaum, 2000, pp.477–8). The possibility of useful price signals in a market consisting of one buyer and two sellers seems remote. Second, there is the nature of the costs to be reduced. You might feel that the political rather than the economic nature of the USA's costs of abatement undermines its case. Japan, for example, has high abatement costs because it is already highly energy efficient. Reducing its GHG emissions would therefore require a difficult choice between engaging in substantially less carbon-emitting activity and improving still further the efficiency of an unchanged level of such activity (Section 20.2.3). In the USA there is still considerable scope for relatively low-cost improvements in energy efficiency.

On the other hand, it could be argued that political resistance in the USA to a GHG emissions reduction programme is the most serious obstacle to climate change abatement. The economic case for emissions trading rests in part on the reduction of the costs of abatement precisely because lower costs would make an agreement on a GHG emissions-reduction programme more politically acceptable.

Turning to the second question, you might have wondered whether Russia and Ukraine could use the money from the sale of surplus emission permits to modernize and restructure their industries, with the aim of making them more energy efficient. Indeed, the US delegation to Kyoto argued that emissions trading would enable the USA to finance investment in carbon-saving technology in Russia and Ukraine. The US position is that it does not matter *where* GHG emissions reductions are achieved as long as they are achieved. In this way, emissions trading could, in principle, exemplify the capacity of the competitive process in monopolistic markets to encourage innovation.

Two comments seem appropriate here. First, Russia and Ukraine could use the proceeds of surplus emissions permits in many other ways, and their investment in carbon-saving technology would need to be monitored and, if necessary, enforced. This is an example of the dependency of markets on state institutions. Second, the US case applies to the purchase of surplus emissions permits by any country, not just the USA.

. . . And afterwards

An extraordinary thing is happening across the world today. Firms and other organizations are buying and selling CO_2 emissions permits and trading in the carbon market even though the governments of the world have not yet set the rules for such a market. There is no international agreement governing property rights in CO_2 emissions or procedures for monitoring and enforcing contracts. Yet a carbon market exists.

How is it possible to set up a carbon market in advance of internationally agreed rules for trading carbon? There are a number of specific trades taking place, not only in CO_2 but also in other GHGs (see *Environmental Finance*, 2001). Consider the UK Government's Emissions Trading Scheme (ETS) (see Rosewell, 2001). The UK government believes that, sooner or later, there will be an internationally ratified agreement to reduce GHG emissions and consequently it has put policies in place, such as the Climate Change Levy – a tax on energy use by businesses. So it is worth establishing the ETS if it promises lower abatement costs and more advantages than other measures. The first step in setting up a market is to establish property rights, so that economic agents, firms in this case, have something they can sell. Firms can enter the ETS through an auction, bidding for permits to emit no more than a specified quantity of particular GHGs, perhaps at specified sites, for a year. If they meet their targets (i.e. emit less than the specified amount of GHGs) they can collect an incentive payment from the government or they can sell the surplus permits to any firm that is willing to buy them. The UK government has set aside £215 million to fund the incentive payments over the first five years of the ETS. By the end of that period, emissions trading should be working sufficiently well to make further incentive payments unnecessary.

Questions	Please read the following extract from a carbon-trading website and answer the following questions. You might find it helpful to consult the account of 'high-tech' industries in Chapter 2.

1 Why are firms trading in the carbon market in the absence of the normal and apparently indispensable legal framework?
2 What makes it worth incurring the risk of trading partners reneging on contracts or being unable to enforce their putative property rights?

Specific carbon trades

Suncor, the Canadian energy company, has purchased 100,000 metric tonnes of CO_2 from US-based Niagara Mohawk Power Corp. This deal was one of the world's first international emission trades. Carbon emissions reductions will occur as Niagara Mohawk switches from coal to natural gas, undertakes renewable energy projects and promotes the efficient use of energy by customers. Reductions will be measured and verified by the Environmental Resources Trust, an independent third-party organisation, to ensure they have a true net benefit to the atmosphere. Suncor also has an option to purchase an additional 10 million tonnes of greenhouse gas reductions from Niagara Mohawk after the year 2000.

Tesco, the UK supermarket chain, is buying carbon from the Carbon Storage Trust to absorb the CO_2 emissions caused by a particular fuel's consumption. This fuel is then being marketed as having no net carbon emissions.

Toyota has created an $800,000 model forest which is being monitored with emissions measuring equipment to calculate CO_2 absorbed. They are also working with botanists to develop genetically engineered trees that absorb CO_2 faster.

BP has initiated an internal carbon trading system, involving 10 business units around the world. The scheme will see trading amongst the business units as well as trading between the units and outside parties. One of the first external trades has been between BP's Kwinana refinery in Western Australia and the state forestry organisation.

Pacific Power, one of Australia's largest electricity generators, has purchased the carbon credits from a newly planted 1000 hectare forest plantation on the north coast of New South Wales (NSW) from the NSW State Forests organisation. The trade covers a ten year period during which the plantation is expected to sequester 250,000 tonnes of CO_2.

(http://www.carbonmarket.com/FAQs.htm#top.Anchor)

The answers to both questions are based on the idea of 'first-mover advantage' (Chapter 6). Firms believe that, despite the failure of the Kyoto negotiations to establish the rules for carbon trading, a carbon market is inevitable in the near future. There are advantages in being among the first participants in such a market. These include 'learning by doing'; that is, learning about the successful tactics and pitfalls of the process of trading carbon by actually doing it and so preparing the culture and systems of the firm for the day when the carbon market is fully established. There may also be public relations advantages to a firm gaining a high profile in efforts to control climate change. Firms engaged in carbon trading before the establishment of property rights and arrangements for monitoring and enforcing contracts will be consulted by governments drawing up the legal framework that will eventually regulate such matters. The opportunity will be there to influence the design of these institutions to the firms' advantage.

There seem to be three conclusions to be drawn from this review of the scope and limits of emissions trading in reducing GHG emissions. First, the emerging carbon market has considerable potential to enhance the political acceptability of a GHG emissions reduction programme by reducing the costs of compliance and accelerating innovations in carbon-saving technology. Second, there is a risk that the industrial countries responsible for most of the GHG emissions to date will find ways of using the carbon market to secure 'paper compliance', avoiding the need to take serious domestic action. Third, if this risk is to be minimized, a central legal authority with powers to establish property rights and to monitor and enforce contracts may need to be created by international agreement.

20.5 Conclusion

This chapter has discussed some of the ways in which economists think about environmental sustainability with particular reference to climate change. Ecological economists argue that there are physical limits to growth, one of which is the carrying capacity of the Earth. A sustainable economy would be one in which economic activity is organized in recognition of these limits. It is unlikely that such an economy could be constructed on the foundations of contemporary market norms and behaviour. First, an ethical dimension needs to inform economic understanding, establishing a critical distance from which reason and reflection can comment upon existing tastes and preferences. Second, markets can contribute most effectively to climate change policy by being used to achieve objectives set through the political process.

Questions for review and discussion

Question 1 Figure 20.5 shows a model of the economy embedded in the environment. Copy it and use the phrases listed below to complete the labelling.

consumption of goods and services   *low entropy*
factors of production   *high entropy*
waste   *energy*

Figure 20.5
A model of the
economy embedded
in the environment

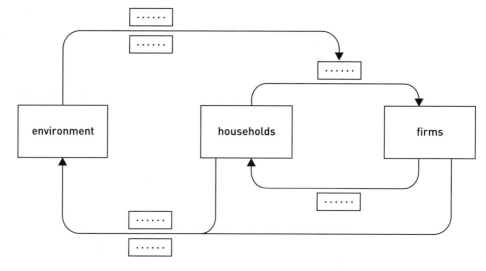

Question 2 Explain and critically discuss the statement that 'Policy interventions to try to achieve an environmentally sustainable economy see markets both as the cause of the problem and as part of the solution' (Chapter 20, Section 1).

Question 3 Explain the argument that the trading of emissions quota would cut the cost of reducing emissions of so-called 'greenhouse gases' and consider the objections to such trading.

Question 4 Comment on the extent that countries with higher levels of GDP have higher levels of carbon dioxide emissions.

(Note: While there is no fixed way to approach this question, you might find it helpful to start with the visual impression by creating scatterplots for each set of countries using SPSS, before obtaining values for the correlation coefficient and the regression equation.)

The data for Question 4 can be found on the *Economics and Economic Change* CD. A copy of this table is provided here.

Table 20.2
Comparison of
international levels
of GDP and CO_2
emissions

Country	Gross national income US$m	Carbon dioxide emissions (thousands of metric tons)
Kribati	43	6
Sao Tome	46	21
Marshall Islands	96	6
Tonga	153	32
Comoros	202	19
Vanuatu	212	17
Guinea Bissau	215	63
Samoa	236	36
Solomon Islands	275	44
St Kitts	314	28
St Vincent	333	44
Grenada	410	50
Gambia	422	62
Bhutan	487	106
Djibouti	553	100
Maldives	556	90
Cape Verde	558	33
Eritrea	608	100
Seychelles	614	54
Sierra Leone	636	143
Antigua	689	92
Burundi	689	62
St Lucia	707	54
Guyana	712	450
Belize	820	109
Surinam	846	584
Mauritian	935	796
Central African Republic	963	68
Mongolia	969	2 102
Tajikistan	991	1 395
Togo	1 219	241
Moldova	1 286	2 636
Kyrgyzstan	1 304	1 753
Equatorial Guinea	1 341	69
Chad	1 407	30
Swaziland	1 478	109
Fiji	1 495	198
Malawi	1 697	204
Laos	1 709	102
Rwanda	1 794	140
Niger	1 826	302
Armenia	1 914	936
Benin	2 168	200

▶

Country	Gross national income US$m	Carbon dioxide emissions (thousands of metric tons)
Burkina Faso	2 192	276
Mali	2 298	132
Nicaragua	2 396	935
Barbados	2 600	429
Zambia	2 911	425
Guinea	3 012	334
Georgia	3 029	1 429
New Caledonia	3 057	477
Cambodia	3 183	181
Congo	3 215	496
Namibia	3 479	3
Malta	3 565	492
Macedonia	3 573	3 378
Albania	3 752	428
Mozambique	3 754	363
Papua New Guinea	3 818	640
Madagascar	3 878	341
French Polynesia	3 929	153
Haiti	4 050	345
Senegal	4 371	900
Mauritius	4 381	471
Bosnia	4 394	1 279
Turkmenistan	4 404	7 605
Bahamas	4 818	489
Brunei	4 846	1498
Gabon	4 932	770
Ghana	5 190	1 189
Azerbaijan	5 267	10 583
Botswana	5 285	1 031
Nepal	5 497	831
Congo Democratic Republic	5 584	880
Honduras	5 932	1 396
Uganda	6 170	349
Macao	6 208	445
Ethiopia	6 391	543
Latvia	7 150	2 143
Zimbabwe	7 392	3 840
Jamaica	7 403	3 001
Paraguay	7 521	1 247
Uzbekistan	7 666	29 812
Bahrain	7 971	5 100
Bolivia	8 281	3 294
Jordan	8 340	3 799

Table 20.2
(cont'd)

Table 20.2
(cont'd)

Country	Gross national income US$m	Carbon dioxide emissions (thousands of metric tons)
Yugoslavia	8 449	13 826
Iceland	8 525	569
Yemen	8 532	3 864
Cyprus	8 698	1 615
Angola	8 828	161
Cameroon	8 879	481
Tanzania	9 027	608
Côte d'Ivoire	9 370	3 602
Panama	9 889	1 587
Kenya	10 357	2 492
Lithuania	11 314	4 259
Sudan	11 516	982
Bulgaria	11 995	12 935
El Salvador	13 211	1 653
Ecuador	13 607	7 168
Costa Rica	15 851	1 388
Sri Lanka	16 305	2 217
Lebanon	16 488	4 461
Syria	16 984	13 820
Slovenia	18 128	3 981
Kazakhstan	18 230	33 540
Luxembourg	18 892	2 096
Guatemala	18 988	2 639
Croatia	19 031	5 405
Slovakia	19 121	10 389
Tunisia	19 462	6 103
Dominica	19 669	5 529
Uruguay	19 715	1 596
Belarus	29 950	16 524
Vietnam	31 344	11 972
Ukraine	31 719	96 510
Morocco	33 345	8 743
Romania	36 719	25 211
Kuwait	37 783	13 402
Nigeria	41 085	21 413
Hungry	45 633	16 008
United Arab Emirates	46 481	24 072
Bangladesh	47 106	6 376
New Zealand	49 903	8 197
Czechoslovakia	50 777	32 293
Algeria	53 306	29 097
Peru	53 466	7 603
Pakistan	61 639	26 504

Table 20.2
(*cont'd*)

Country	Gross national income US$m	Carbon dioxide emissions (thousands of metric tons)
Chile	70 545	16 422
Philippines	74 733	20 740
Colombia	81 283	18 514
Malaysia	89 659	32 880
Singapore	92 252	22 458
Ireland	93 865	10 443
Egypt	98 725	28 864
Iran	104 940	79 119
Portugal	105 054	14 907
Israel	110 386	16 447
Greece	112 646	23 261
Venezuela	120 484	42 411
Finland	121 466	14 553
Thailand	122 166	52 523
South Africa	125 887	93 808
Indonesia	153 255	63 755
Poland	157 739	87 807
Norway	161 769	9 161
Denmark	162 343	14 563
Hong Kong	162 642	9 779
Saudi Arabia	173 287	77 237
Austria	189 029	17 431
Turkey	199 937	55 141
Belgium	226 648	27 651
Sweden	227 319	13 272
Switzerland	239 740	11 403
Russia	251 106	391 535
Argentina	284 960	37 367
Netherlands	364 766	44 713
Australia	390 113	90 470
India	456 990	289 587
Korea	457 219	61 722
Spain	558 558	67 468
Mexico	574 512	102 072
Brazil	595 458	81 578
Canada	687 882	127 517
Italy	1 073 960	113 238
France	1 294 246	100 951
UK	1 414 557	148 011
Germany	1 872 992	225 208

Source: www.worldbank.org/data

Answers to exercises

Chapter 2

Exercise 2.1 $15\,000 - 12\,000 = 3000$

$\dfrac{3000}{12\,000} \cdot 100 = 25$. The increase in 25%.

Exercise 2.2 A period of technological change that transforms the way that goods are produced and distributed is known as an 'industrial revolution'. A general purpose technology such as electricity, which stimulates constant improvements and is used widely across the economy, may initiate improvements in productivity or the efficiency of production. A further elaboration of the division of labour within the economy, exemplified by the factory system, is also likely. The result is an increase in the total output of the economy known as 'economic growth' and, usually, an increase in the wealth of producers and consumers.

Exercise 2.3 Three things that could happen in industrialized economies in the future that would go some way towards settling the debate between optimists and pessimists on the impact of IT on productivity in favour of the optimists/pessimists are:

1 the US economy endures a recession and productivity growth remains unusually high/falls back to its historical average
2 other industrialized economies with relatively inflexible labour markets experience/fail to experience a surge in productivity led by IT
3 a permanent trend rise in productivity begins/is not observed a few years after PCs reach 50 per cent market saturation in successive economies.

Exercise 2.4 Table 2.2 (completed)

Year	Actual price of product €	Price index (base 2003)
2003	12.00	100
2004	16.00	133
2005	19.00	158
2006	21.00	175

Chapter 3

Exercise 3.1 **Table 3.1 (completed)** Shifts in the market demand curve for electronic personal organizers

Change in variable	Effect on demand curve
Decrease in income	Decrease in quantity demanded at all prices Demand curve shifts to the left
Increase in income	Increase in quantity demanded at all prices Demand curve shifts to the right
Rise in price of a substitute	Demand curve shifts to the right
Fall in price of a substitute	Demand curve shifts to the left
Rise in price of a complementary good	Demand curve shifts to the left
Fall in price of a complementary good	Demand curve shifts to the right
Change in socio-economic influences in favour of electronic personal organizers	Demand curve shifts to the right
Change in socio-economic influences away from electronic personal organizers	Demand curve shifts to the left

Exercise 3.2 1 (a) Increasing returns to a factor of production occur when output increases faster than the input of a variable factor; decreasing returns to a factor of production refers to the opposite situation, in which output increases more slowly than the input of a variable factor.
   (b) Economies of scale and increasing returns to scale are used interchangeably; both refer to a decrease in long-run average costs as output increases.
   (c) Decreasing returns to scale and diseconomies of scale are used interchangeably; both refer to an increase in long-run average costs as output increases.
2 Short-run average costs differ from long-run average costs because in the short run at least one factor of production is fixed in quantity, resulting in diminishing returns to each variable factor of production above some level of output.

Chapter 4

Exercise 4.1 See Table 4.1 completed. The output numbers were of course kept unrealistically small to simplify the arithmetic.

Table 4.1 (completed)

Price (P) = average revenue (AR) €	Quantity (Q) of computers demanded	Total revenue (TR) €	Marginal revenue (MR) €
1000	1	1000	–
950	2	1900	900
900	3	2700	800
850	4	3400	700
800	5	4000	600

Exercise 4.2 1 The percentage decline in price is calculated by first working out the change in price. Subtract the old price from the new one:

$$€600 - €800 = -€200$$

The change in price is negative, since the price fell. Then calculate the percentage change. Divide the change in price by the original price and multiply by 100:

$$\frac{-€200}{€800} \cdot 100 = -\frac{1}{4} \cdot 100 = -25\%$$

2 Quantity sold rises from 5 to 9. The percentage change in quantity demanded is:

$$\frac{4}{5} \cdot 100 = 80\%$$

The change is positive since output rises.

3 The price elasticity of demand is then calculated by dividing the percentage change in quantity by the percentage change in price:

$$\text{price elasticity of demand} = \frac{80}{-25} = -3.2$$

Exercise 4.3 Figure 4.16 graphs columns 2 and 4 of Table 4.2 (completed).

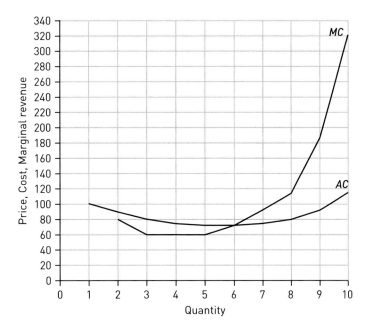

Figure 4.16
Average and marginal cost curves from data in Table 4.2

Table 4.2 (completed)

Units of output (Q)	Average cost (AC)	Total cost (TC)	Marginal cost (MC)
1	100	100	–
2	90	180	80
3	80	240	60
4	75	300	60
5	72	360	60
6	72	432	72
7	75	525	93
8	80	640	115
9	92	828	188
10	115	1150	322

Exercise 4.4 See Figure 4.17. The monopolist will now charge price P_2 and sell quantity Q_2. The firm's supernormal profits after the innovation are shown by the shaded rectangle.

Figure 4.17
A monopolist's
profit-maximizing
price and quantity
after a process
innovation

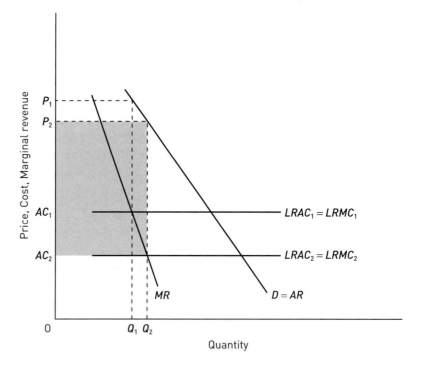

Chapter 5

Exercise 5.1   1   See Table 5.3 for marginal costs.

Table 5.3   Output, total cost and marginal cost of a shirt manufacturer

Quantity (shirts/day)	Total cost £	Marginal cost £
0	12	–
1	17	5
2	20	3
3	21	1
4	24	3
5	29	5
6	36	7
7	45	9
8	56	11

2   6 shirts per day.

Exercise 5.2   See Table 5.4.

Table 5.4   Short-run average variable cost and average total cost of a shirt manufacturer

Quantity (shirts/day)	Short-run average total cost (SRAC) £	Short-run average variable cost (SRAVC) £
0	–	–
1	17	5
2	10	4
3	7	3
4	6	3
5	5.8	3.4
6	6	4
7	6.4	4.7
8	7	5.5

See Figure 5.20. Note that the short-run *MC* curve cuts the short-run *AC* curve only approximately at its lowest point, since curves drawn from discrete points only approximate the relationships between smooth curves such as those shown on Figure 5.4.

Figure 5.20
Short-run marginal
cost, average
variable cost and
average total cost
curves from data in
Tables 5.3 and 5.4

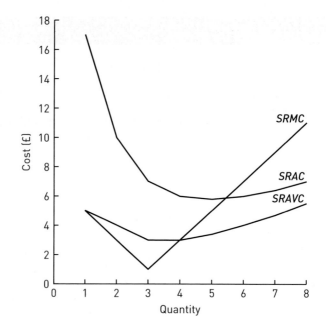

Exercise 5.3 Figure 5.21 shows the downward shift of the marginal cost curve from MC_1 to MC_2 as a result of the decline in unit costs. (The firm's average cost curves – not shown – would also shift downwards.) The profit-maximizing output of the firm at price P rises from Q_1 to Q_2. The firm's supply curve has shifted rightwards.

Figure 5.21
The effect of cost-
reducing technology
on equilibrium
output of a perfectly
competitive firm

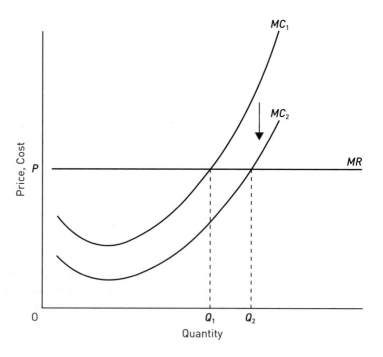

Figure 5.22
A shift to the right in
the supply curve for
orange juice

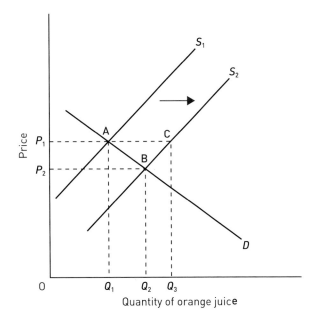

Exercise 5.4 Figure 5.22 shows the change in the equilibrium market price. The initial market equilibrium is at point A with price P_1. Unexpectedly warm weather increases the supply of orange juice at each price, hence the supply curve moves to the right from S_1 to S_2. The new market equilibrium at B will be at a lower price with a higher quantity sold. Consumers will move along their demand curve to the new price P_2 and quantity Q_2. It may help to envisage unsold orange juice piling up at the old price P_1 where supply now exceeds demand. That is, there is excess supply at P_1 measured by the distance AC. If some suppliers reduce price to clear their warehouses, others will have to follow, and demand will increase as price falls until the new equilibrium is reached. But the model only really tells us how the two equilibria A and B differ. It is a comparative static model.

Chapter 6

Exercise 6.1 If B co-operates, A does not co-operate ($4 > 3$). If B does not co-operate, A does not co-operate ($2 > 1$). Therefore, whatever B does, A does not co-operate. (Note that the sign '>' means 'greater than' and the sign '<' means 'less than'.)

   If A co-operates, B does not co-operate ($6 > 5$). If A does not co-operate, B does not co-operate ($4 > 3$). Therefore, whatever A does, B does not co-operate.

   The dominant strategy for each is not to co-operate, so the outcome is that neither co-operates with a pay-off of 2 for A and 4 for B. If each one co-operates, however, A would have 3 and B would have 5.

Exercise 6.2

Figure 6.15
General form of the
one-shot prisoners'
dilemma game

		Player B	
		co-operate	not co-operate
Player A	co-operate	P_3, P_3	P_1, P_4
	not co-operate	P_4, P_1	P_2, P_2

The structure of pay-offs takes the form $P_1 < P_2 < P_3 < P_4$. The outcome is that neither player co-operates, with pay-offs of P_2, P_2. If the players were to co-operate, the pay-offs would be P_3, P_3.

Exercise 6.3

Figure 6.16
Pay-off matrix
showing cartel
firms' pay-off

		Firm 2	
		increase output	reduce output
Firm 1	increase output	300, 300	600, 200
	reduce output	200, 600	500, 500

Although the strategy 'reduce output' would yield higher pay-offs (500 for each of the firms), collusion to reduce output would not succeed. The reason for this is that the dominant strategy for each firm is 'increase output'. For Firm 1, the pay-off is 300 to 'increase output' and 200 to 'reduce output' if Firm 2 increases output, and it is 600 to 'increase output' and 500 to 'reduce output' if Firm 2 reduces output. Thus, whatever Firm 2's strategy, Firm 1's pay-off is greater if it increases output. The same holds for Firm 2. The outcome is that each firm increases output with a pay-off of 300.

Exercise 6.4

Figure 6.17
A pay-off matrix
illustrating price
competition

		HighFlights	
		standard fare	discounted fare
FlyingHigh	standard fare	60, 60	30, 80
	discounted fare	80, 30	40, 40

The dominant strategy for each airline is to charge the discounted fare, so each one has a profit of £40 million. If HighFlights charges the standard fare, FlyingHigh has a profit of £60 million if it charges the standard fare and £80 million if it charges the discounted fare. If HighFlights charges the discounted fare, FlyingHigh has a profit of £30 million if it charges the standard fare and £40 million if it charges the discounted fare. Thus, whatever HighFlights' strategy, FlyingHigh has a better pay-off to 'discounted fare'. FlyingHigh's dominant strategy is therefore to discount its fares. The same applies to HighFlights. If both had charged the standard fare, the pay-offs would have been £60 million each.

Exercise 6.5 The 'meet competition' promise eliminates the strategy combinations in which just one airline cuts the price. This implies that the bottom-left and top-right strategy combinations are eliminated. The dominant strategy now is for each airline to charge the standard fare with a profit of £60 million.

Figure 6.18
A pay-off matrix illustrating 'meet competition'

		HighFlights	
		standard fare	discounted fare
FlyingHigh	standard fare	60, 60	
	discounted fare		40, 40

Exercise 6.6

Figure 6.19
A pay-off matrix illustrating an R&D investment decision

		FastForward	
		no R&D project	R&D project
LeadTheWay	no R&D project	100, 100	10, 180
	R&D project	180, 10	80, 80

The dominant strategy for each firm is to go for the new R&D with a pay-off of £80 million. If neither does so, the pay-off would be £100 million each. This game illustrates the risk involved in extensive innovation, as well as the potentially enormous gains for the firm that successfully innovates ahead of rivals. Strategic alliances – which help to spread the risks for firms trying to invest in R&D ahead of their rivals – are discussed in Section 6.6.

Chapter 7

Exercise 7.1 The demand for labour is derived demand, which means that it is valued for what it can be used to produce, rather than for its own sake. The marginal revenue product (*MRP*) is the extra revenue obtained by the firm from employing an extra unit of labour.

$$MRP = P \cdot MPP_L$$

Where MPP_L is the marginal physical product of labour. Diminishing marginal returns causes the MPP_L to decline, and because it is assumed that a perfectly competitive firm is a price-taker, the *MRP* is also declining. Profit maximization ensures that firms will employ labour up to the point where:

$$W = MRP$$

Hence (with labour as the only variable factor of production) the demand curve for labour is the same as the *MRP* curve, and is therefore declining as labour increases. Accordingly, a fall in wages leads a profit-maximizing firm to employ more labour.

Exercise 7.2 After the completion of the new office block, the demand curve for high-rise window cleaners shifts outwards from L_{D1} to L_{D2}, as shown in Figure 7.15, resulting in an increase in both wages and employment.

Figure 7.15
An increase in the demand for high-rise window cleaning

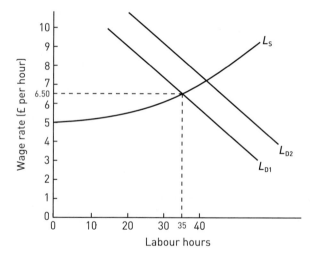

Exercise 7.3 My brief list of costs would include the following.

- Time spent studying means less potential work time and accordingly perhaps less current income. There will also be a sacrifice of domestic labour time, with, for example, less time for household responsibilities or leisure.
- There will be direct costs such as fees, stationery items and perhaps books. In addition, there may be other costs associated with the need to have somewhere quiet to study.

Perhaps we should add the mental anguish involved in having to tackle difficult material or in completing assessments – and the possible strain on family life!
My list of benefits would include the following.

- Improved future job prospects, in terms of a reduced chance of future unemployment.
- A future potential to earn higher wages.
- A future potential to do a more intrinsically satisfying job.
- In the present there is the intellectual satisfaction of studying.

One could, in principle, estimate the future wage benefits and employment prospects obtained as a result of doing the course. Perhaps you will be pleased to learn that economic research generally indicates a considerable economic return from obtaining degrees, with evidence of some increase through the 1980s compared with the 1970s. You could also estimate reasonably well the costs to you in terms of the time taken up by studying. On the other hand, it is hard to quantify the consumption benefits and costs of doing courses, even if your judgement as to whether to start the course cannot avoid taking them into account.

Exercise 7.4 Other factors sometimes preventing mobility include:

- difficulties involved in moving house (including buying and selling houses), or in travelling to where the jobs are
- family and social ties
- language and social barriers.

Exercise 7.5 If some workers offered to work for wages below the equilibrium point B on Figure 7.12, the employer would deduce that it would not be worthwhile for workers to work properly once employed. The employers would expect the workers to shirk and take the chance of being caught, since the cost of being caught is not so great with such low wages. Even if the workers would prefer to work at these wages, rather than remain unemployed indefinitely, they would find it impossible to convince the prospective employers of their intentions as, with imperfect monitoring of the workplace, the promise of 'good' behaviour could not be guaranteed. Any such promise would have to be disregarded if the employer is rational and if it is recognized that the workers are rational. All this, of course, applies strictly to a world of alienating and unsatisfying work, where unemployment is the prime disciplinary measure against shirking.

Chapter 8

Exercise 8.1 $\dfrac{£430 \text{ million}}{107.5} \cdot 100 = £400 \text{ million}$

Thus there would have been no change in real GDP. The apparent (nominal) increase would have been purely the result of inflation.

Exercise 8.2 $\dfrac{£943\,412 \text{ million}}{114.2} \cdot 100 = £826\,105 \text{ million (approximately)}$

This is not the same figure as in Table 8.5; it is about £39 million out because of rounding errors.

Exercise 8.3 Total utility rises. Total utility will always rise if marginal utility is strictly positive, that is, greater than zero.

Chapter 9

Exercise 9.1

Figure 9.18
An *ad valorem* tax on
output in a
competitive market

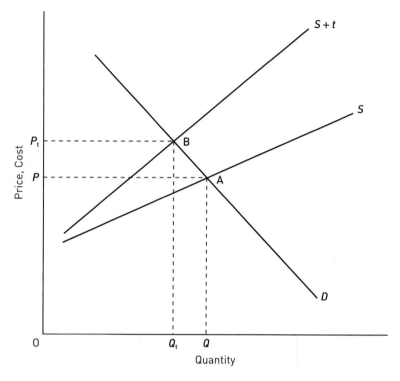

See Figure 9.18. The distance between the supply curve without the tax S and the supply curve with the tax $S + t$ will increase as output rises, instead of being constant as in Figure 9.3. The market equilibrium with the tax is again at B, with price P_t and output Q_t.

Exercise 9.2

1 See Figure 9.19. The new equipment shifts each firm's average and marginal cost curves upwards. Each firm's marginal cost curve is also its supply curve. Firms are now making a loss and some firms will leave the industry.

Figure 9.19
The effect of new
clean-up equipment
on a competitive
firm's costs

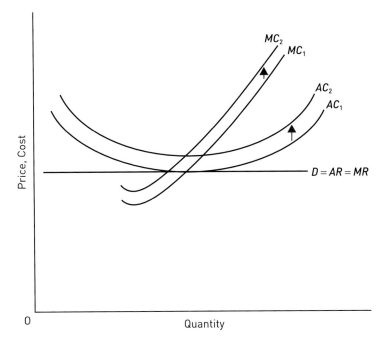

2 On Figure 9.20, the $MPC_1 = S_1$ curve is the industry supply curve before the regulations. (To simplify the diagram I have omitted the MSC curve.) After the installation
of new equipment, the industry supply curve shifts to $MPC_2 = S_2$. Equilibrium output
has fallen, and price is higher. If the equipment has reduced pollution to zero, there
will be no separate MSC curve after the installation, since the externality will have disappeared: the marginal social cost and marginal private cost curves now coincide.

Figure 9.20
The effect of a rise
in costs on the
industry supply
curve

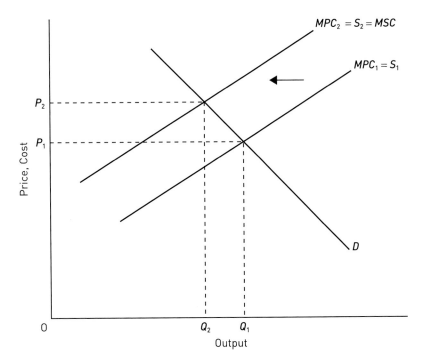

Exercise 9.3

Figure 9.21
A pay-off matrix
showing the
'tragedy of the
commons'

		Herder 2	
		moderate herd	very large herd
Herder 1	moderate herd	3, 3	1, 4
	very large herd	4, 1	2, 2

See Figure 9.21. You will probably have chosen different numbers. What matters is that the relationship between the pay-offs must be as shown in the answer to Exercise 6.2 in Chapter 6. In Figure 9.18, if Herder 2 has a very large herd, Herder 1 will have a very large herd (2 > 1). If Herder 2 has a moderate herd, Herder 1 will have a very large herd (4 > 3). So Herder 1's dominant strategy is a very large herd. The same is true for Herder 2. Each herder's dominant strategy is to maintain their herd at a level that degrades the land, with pay-offs 2, 2. The dilemma is that each herder would have preferred that both should have moderate herds, causing no overgrazing, with pay-offs 3, 3.

Exercise 9.4   There are two ways to think about this, drawing on Chapter 6. Consider Figure 9.21 (my answer). If each herder values their neighbours' benefits – and suffers from their hurts – then we might argue that in the two-person game shown it is no longer only the pay-offs that matter. Each herder will take into account the needs of the other, in addition to his own pay-off, and choose a moderate herd, rejecting the dominant strategy. Alternatively, we might amend the pay-offs themselves, to incorporate the effect of caring for neighbours. There are many ways this could be done: for example, the pay-off of 3 to having a moderate herd when the other herder does too might be increased – say to 5 – by pleasure at the benefit to the other of this outcome; similarly the pay-off of 2 to having a very large herd when the other does too might be reduced – say to 0.5 – by sadness at the other's losses. Change 3 to 5 and 2 to 0.5 in Figure 9.21 and check that the dominant strategy for each herder is now a moderate herd: the dilemma has been overcome.

Exercise 9.5   If you think that the poor are inured to their poverty while the rich feel passionately about holding on to every last penny, then you might disagree with the proposition that marginal utility declines as income rises. The conclusion concerning redistribution also depends on the assumption that people get the same utility from the same income. You might disagree that this is likely, arguing instead that people are very different. Alternatively, you might disagree with the idea of comparing utilities at all, arguing that the concept is a subjective one so people's utilities cannot be compared.

Exercise 9.6   Health-care insurance suffers from moral hazard, since insurers cannot know what treatment people need. There is more discussion of health insurance in Chapter 10. Life insurance is another example: policies do not pay out if the insurance company discovers that the policy holder committed suicide. Buildings insurance too: a company will try to establish that you have not burned down a property yourself, to claim the insurance, before paying out. As these examples show, a private insurance market may still exist in the face of moral hazard: it depends on the severity of the problem and the cost of investigation.

Chapter 10

Exercise 10.1

Figure 10.6
Market equilibrium
with a positive
consumption
externality

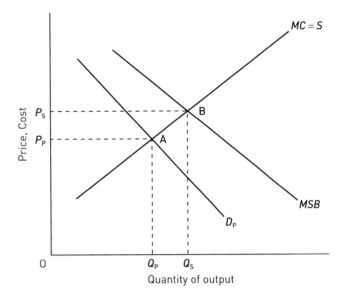

See Figure 10.6. The market equilibrium that results from private decision-making is at A, with price P_P and quantity of vaccinations purchased Q_P. The social optimum quantity of vaccinations is at B, where the marginal social benefit of the vaccinations MSB is equal to the marginal cost of producing them MC. Price would have to be higher, at P_S, to induce suppliers to supply the optimum quantity of vaccinations Q_S.

To raise the quantity of vaccinations purchased towards the social optimum, the government could subsidize the consumption of vaccinations, in order to reduce the price facing consumers at each level of output. Or the government could campaign to make people aware, through public health education, of the social benefits from vaccinations, in the hope that they might increase their own demand as they start to take into account the needs of others as well as themselves.

Exercise 10.2

Your premium is 1 per cent of £2500 = £25, plus £5 = £30 per year.

Chapter 11

Exercise 11.1

A completed version of the blank matrix in Figure 11.3 is shown in Figure 11.8. The dominant strategy equilibrium in Figure 11.7 is for both firms to invest now. If Firm A expects Firm B to invest, the pay-off to Firm A for investing now is £120 compared with £110 for waiting. If Firm A expects Firm B to wait, the pay-off to investing now is £30 as opposed to £20 for waiting. Thus, whatever Firm A expects Firm B to do, its best option is to invest now. The same reasoning applies to Firm B, and so both firms invest now.

Figure 11.8
Pay-off matrix
showing the
decision to invest
during a recession
where the
government offers
an investment grant
of £20

Firm A \ Firm B	invest now	wait and see
invest now	120 / 120	110 / 30
wait and see	30 / 110	20 / 20

Chapter 12

Exercise 12.1

(a) If households decide to save a larger proportion of their income, with unchanged aggregate investment, they would reduce their consumption expenditure $C - \Delta$, thereby causing income to fall to $Y - \Delta = C - \Delta + I$. Households find that they are saving a greater proportion of their reduced incomes, while aggregate saving is unchanged and equal to investment.

(b) If firms decided to invest less, with households committed to saving the same proportion of their income as they did initially, income would fall to $Y - \Delta = C + I - \Delta$. Households save an unchanged proportion of their lower incomes, causing aggregate saving to fall until it is equal to $I - \Delta$.

Exercise 12.2

Variable	Amount
Savings	20 000
Investment	25 000
Savings – Investment	*–5 000*
Exports	40 000
Imports	45 000
Balance of trade	*–5 000*
Government expenditure	50 000
Taxation	*50 000*
Budget deficit	*0*

In the absence of any net income from the rest of the world, it follows that:

$$(S - I) + (M - X) + (T - G) = 0$$

From the table $S - I = -5000$, $M - X = 5000$ (balance of trade $= X - M$) and hence $T - G = 0$. Thus $T = G$.

Exercise 12.3

1 In Table 12.6, the total quantity of base money (B) is depicted by the Cumulative Change in Cash plus the Cumulative Change in Reserves.

2 As a result of the central bank's action, base money increases by £1000 (£714.30 + £285.70), while the money stock increases by £3571.30.

3 The value of the money multiplier is given by:

$$\frac{1}{(1 - (1 - c)(1 - r))}$$

Substituting the values for c and r this is:

$$\frac{1}{(1-(0.8)(0.9))}$$

or 3.571

Given the £1000 increase in base money, it follows from

$$M = \frac{B}{(1-(1-c)(1-r))}$$

that

$$\frac{1000}{(1-(0.8)(0.9))}$$

$$= £3571.50.$$

Exercise 12.4 1 Recall that:

$$M = \frac{B}{(1-(1-c)(1-r))}$$

Here $B = 1000$ exes, $c = 0.10$ and $r = 0.10$. The total money supply is:

$$M = \frac{1000}{(1-(0.1)(0.9))} = 1098.90$$

2 B is now 1500 exes and we can work out as in (1) above that M is 1648.35.

Chapter 13

Exercise 13.1 1 If the marginal propensity to consume b is 0.9, the multiplier is 10:

$$\frac{1}{(1-b)} = \frac{1}{(1-0.9)} = \frac{1}{0.1} = 10$$

A decrease in investment spending of £10 billion would therefore lead to a fall in national income of £100 billion.

2 If the marginal propensity to consume b is 0.4, the multiplier is 1.67:

$$\frac{1}{(1-b)} = \frac{1}{(1-0.4)} = \frac{1}{0.6} = 1.67$$

A decrease in investment spending of £10 billion would now lead to a fall in national income of £16.7 billion.

Chapter 14

Exercise 14.1 Investment involves expenditure undertaken in the present that is intended to yield benefits in the future. Research and development expenditure by firms and government expenditure on building schools and NHS hospitals clearly fit this category, although it is worth noting that none of these expenditures is classified as investment in the national income accounts. Government expenditure on the salaries of teachers and medical staff are not investment, because the benefits of the expenditure (i.e. teaching and medical services) are enjoyed in the present. A payment into a pension fund is regarded as savings and the acquisition of financial assets that will help to pay future pensions.

Exercise 14.2 The present value of the investment over all five years would be:

$$PV = \frac{£3000}{1.15} + \frac{£3000}{(1.15)^2} + \frac{£3000}{(1.15)^3} + \frac{£3000}{(1.15)^4} + \frac{£3000}{(1.15)^5} = £10\,056$$

So the net present value of the investment is £10 056 − £10 000 = £56 and the investment is just worth doing at a 15 per cent rate of discount.

Exercise 14.3 Your present value for the investment will now be discounted by 4 per cent rather than 6 per cent.

Your returns in the first year will be $\dfrac{£700}{1.04} = £673.08$

Returns in the second year will be $\dfrac{£900}{(1.04)^2} = £832.10$

Returns in the third year will be $\dfrac{£900}{(1.04)^3} = £800.10$

Returns in the fourth year will be $\dfrac{£1000}{(1.04)^4} = £854.80$

So the present value of the sum of all returns = £3160.08. This is less than £7000. You would still not invest in the plane.

Exercise 14.4 **Table 14.2 (completed)** The multiplier and the accelerator

Period	Output	Change in output	Total capital	Net investment	Change in investment
1	100	0	200	0	–
2	110	10	220	20	20
3	140	30	280	60	40
4	200	60	400	120	60
5	290	90	580	180	60
6	380	90	760	180	0
7	380	0	760	0	−180

1 Period 2: According to the accelerator model, a rise in output of 10 units will require net investment equal to the capital–output ratio times the change in output, that is, $2 \times 10 = 20$. The desired capital stock changes to 2 times output $= 220$, and net investment has risen from 0 to 20.

2 Period 3: The increase in investment in period 2 leads to an increase in output in period 3. As the multiplier is 1.5 the increase in output is 30 (20×1.5), and this will lead to an increase in output from 110 to 140. The desired capital stock rises to 280 and net investment to 60 ($= 280 - 220$), with an increase in investment of 40.

Period 4: The increase in investment in period 3 leads to an increase in output in period 4. With a multiplier of 1.5 the increase in output is 60 (40×1.5), and this will lead to an increase in output from 140 to 200. The desired capital stock rises to 400 and net investment to 120 ($= 400 - 280$), with an increase in investment of 60.

Period 5: The increase in investment in period 4 leads to an increase in output in period 5 of 90 and output of 290. The desired capital is 580, net investment is 180 but investment increases by 60.

Period 6: The increase in investment in period 5 leads to an increase in output of 90, and a level of output of 380 in period 6. The desired capital stock rises to 760 and net investment remains at 180, and the increase in net investment is zero.

Period 7: The downturn begins! With no increase in net investment in the previous period, there is no increase in output. The desired capital stock remains unchanged, and net investment falls to zero. In the next period, output will fall to $380 - 270 = 110$.

3 This example reveals an important point about the accelerator model, that increases in investment occur only if output increases at an increasing rate. Thus, in period 6, although there is an increase in output, this increase is equivalent to the increase that occurred in period 5 and there is no change in investment.

Chapter 15

Exercise 15.1 If P_w were above P_a in Figure 15.5, domestic production at world prices (indicated by the supply curve) would be greater than domestic demand ($Q_t > C_t$ on Figure 15.10). As a result, the good would be exported by the home economy. The gain in going from autarky to free trade is C. Consumers lose $A + B$, and firms gain $A + B + C$.

Figure 15.10
The effect of a world market price that is above the domestic market price

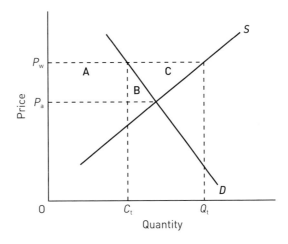

Exercise 15.2 A tariff raises the price of a good in the home economy above the world price. This reduces home demand below the quantity demanded at the world price. So the demand for imports (the gap between home demand and home supply at the world price) falls. Hence the supply of imports exceeds demand at the old world price. The world price must fall to reduce the quantity of imports supplied.

Chapter 16

Exercise 16.1 Recall the formula for the multiplier in an open economy in equation (9) from Chapter 12. This relates the change in the level of income to a change in an autonomous component of aggregate demand.

1 The first part of the question asks for the impact of new Tunisian exports of 30 000 euros on Tunisian national income when $b = 0.6$ and $m = 0$, and nothing else has changed. This latter assumption means that C, I, G, M and T are at their original levels, so the autonomous change in aggregate demand is 30 000 euros. The multiplier

$$= \frac{1}{1 - (b - m)} = \frac{1}{1 - 0.6} = \frac{1}{0.4} = 2.5$$

So change in $Y = 2.5 \cdot 30\ 000$ euros $= 75\ 000$ euros.

2 In this part of the question you know $M = 30\ 000$ euros and $b = 0.6$, but $m = 0.2$. Note that M is subtracted and so the increase in imports will cause the level of national income to fall, if nothing else changes.

Change in Y

$$= \frac{1}{(1 - (0.6 - 0.2))} \cdot -30\ 000$$

$$= \frac{1}{(1 - 0.4)} \cdot -30\ 000$$

$$= \frac{1}{0.6} \cdot -30\ 000$$

$$= -50\ 000$$

Exercise 16.2 1 See Figure 16.6.
2 The relationship between the seller concentration and foreign shares is shown by Figure 16.6. If the scatterplot shows an upward trend, this indicates a positive relationship between the four-firm seller concentration and foreign ownership.

If it appears to slope downwards, this suggests a negative relationship between seller concentration and foreign ownership.

The correlation coefficient between the two variables is 0.29. This, together with the upward slope of the scatterplot, shows a positive relationship between seller concentration and foreign ownership. That is, on average, whenever seller concentration is high, so is the share of foreign ownership in sales.

However, the correlation coefficient is rather low so this association is weak. You can also see this from the scatterplot. Some sectors have high seller concentration but low

Figure 16.6
Scatterplot of seller
concentration and
foreign shares

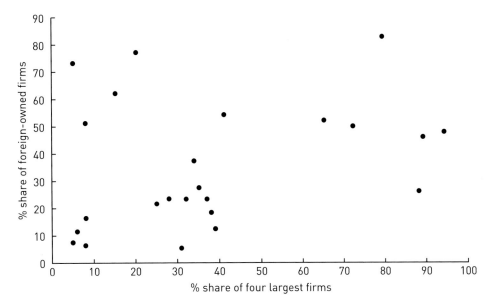

foreign shares, such as the tyres in France or textiles in the UK. Equally some countries
and sectors have high foreign shares but low seller concentration, such as electrical appli-
ances in Germany, Italy and France.

Chapter 17

Exercise 17.1   1   This is an import of goods and will appear as a debit item on the current account.
2   This is a factor income earned by residents abroad and will appear as a debit item on
the current account.
3   A UK resident buying shares abroad is a capital outflow for the UK economy. It will
be recorded as a debit item on the capital account of the balance of payments.
4   A UK student receiving a student grant from the EU constitutes a transfer of funds
from abroad. It will be recorded as a credit item on the current account.

Exercise 17.2   1   The fact that the pound's real exchange rate appreciated by more than its nominal
exchange rate implies that UK inflation was higher than inflation in the rest of the
world.
2   An appreciation of the pound's nominal exchange rate at the same time as a depreciation of its real exchange rate would imply that UK inflation was lower than inflation
in the rest of the world.

Exercise 17.3   1   If a country's income growth is consistently above that of its trading partners, its
demand for imports will outstrip its trading partners' demands for exports and its
exchange rate will therefore depreciate.
2   The experience of rapidly growing countries with customarily strong currencies, such
as Germany, might be explained in terms of the competitiveness of its internationally
traded manufactured goods, particularly, in view of the strong currency, the non-price
aspects of competitiveness.

Exercise 17.4   1 A sudden switch in tastes away from domestic exports would shift the demand curve for the domestic currency to the left, causing the exchange rate to depreciate in the absence of intervention. In order to peg the exchange rate, the authorities would have to buy the domestic currency in sufficient quantities to keep the demand curve in its original position.

2 If world inflation surged ahead of domestic inflation, the price competitiveness of internationally traded domestic output would increase and, other things being equal:

(a) foreign demand for exports would increase, shifting the demand curve for the domestic currency to the right, and

(b) domestic demand for imports would fall, shifting the supply curve of the domestic currency to the left.

Both of these changes would cause the exchange rate to appreciate without intervention. In order to peg the exchange rate, the authorities would have to sell the domestic currency in sufficient quantities to shift the supply curve to the right of its original position.

Chapter 18

Exercise 18.1   If UK policy makers had wished to reduce unemployment a little after the rise in oil prices in 1979 had shifted the Phillips curve outwards, they could have introduced expansionary monetary and/or fiscal policies. The trade-off between inflation and unemployment implies that unemployment might have been stabilized between 4 per cent and 6 per cent by allowing inflation to accelerate towards, and perhaps even beyond, the rate at which it had peaked in 1975. Instead of moving south-easterly during 1980–83, the UK economy would have moved very steeply north-westerly along the Phillips curve.

Exercise 18.2   Figure 18.17 shows the completed version of Figure 18.6. There is a discussion of the results of this exercise in the text below Exercise 18.2.

Figure 18.17
The effects of reflationary and disinflationary policies on unemployment and inflation

		Agents' expectations	
		do not change	fully anticipate policy
Government policy	Expansionary	unemployment falls, inflation rises	unemployment unchanged, inflation rises
	Contractionary	unemployment rises, inflation falls	unemployment unchanged, inflation falls

Chapter 19

Exercise 19.1

1 Whatever the public expects, it is always better for the government to have inflation. If the public expects zero inflation, then (reading down the left side) the pay-off for the government is 0 if actual inflation is zero and 1 if actual inflation is high. If the public expects high inflation, then (reading down the right side) the pay-off for the government is −2 if actual inflation is zero and −1, not so bad, if actual inflation is high. Inflation is therefore preferred by the government in both cases.

2 If the government's preferred option is to have inflation, then no one would believe a promise by the government not to create inflation, because it is always in the government's interest to break such a promise.

3 In the Barro–Gordon model, it is rational for the public to expect the government to create inflation because they know that inflation is the government's dominant strategy. In this case, the outcome is the bottom right-hand cell (−1, 0) with high expected inflation and high actual inflation.

References

Serials

Annual Abstract of Statistics, London, The Stationery Office for Office for National Statistics (annual).

Economic Trends, London, The Stationery Office for Office for National Statistics (monthly).

Labour Force Survey, London, The Stationery Office for Office for National Statistics (quarterly).

Labour Market Statistics, London, The Stationery Office for Office for National Statistics (monthly).

New Earnings Survey, London, The Stationery Office for Office for National Statistics (annual).

OECD Economic Outlook, Paris, Organization for Economic Co-operation and Development (twice yearly).

OECD Employment Outlook, Paris, Organization for Economic Co-operation and Development (annual).

Social Trends, London, The Stationery Office for Office for National Statistics (annual).

United Kingdom Balance of Payments (The Pink Book), London, The Stationery Office for Office for National Statistics (annual).

United Kingdom National Accounts (The Blue Book), London, The Stationery Office for Office for National Statistics (annual).

Other references

Abernathy, W.J., Clark, K. and Kantrow, A. (1983) *Industrial Renaissance: Producing a Competitive Future for America*, Basic Books, New York.

Abrams, F. and Astill, J. (2001) 'Story of the blues', *Education Guardian*, 29 May.

Agarwal, B. (1985) *Cold Hearths and Barren Slopes: The Woodfuel Crisis in the Third World*, London, Zed Press.

Aghion, P., Bloom, N., Blundell, R., Griffith, R. and Howitt, P. (2002) *Competition and Innovation: An Inverted U Relationship*, NBER Working Paper No. 9269, Cambridge, Mass., National Bureau of Economic Research.

Agrawal, A. (1994) 'Rules, rule making and rule breaking: examining the fit between rule systems and resource use' in Ostrom, E., Gardner, R. and Walker, J. (eds) (1994) *Rules, Games and Common-Pool Resources*, Ann Arbor, University of Michigan Press.

Akehurst, R., Brazier, J. and Normand, C. (undated) *Internal Markets in the National Health Service: A Review of the Economic Issues*, York, University of York Centre for Health Economics, Discussion Paper No.40.

Anand, P. and van Hees, M. (2001) 'Capabilities and achievements: logistic models of survey evidence', Milton Keynes, The Open University Economics Discipline, discussion paper.

Anand, P. and Wailoo, A. (2000) 'Utilities versus rights to publicly provided goods', *Economica*, vol.67, no.268, pp.543–77.

Artis, M.J. and Lewis, M.K. (1993) 'Après le déluge: monetary and exchange rate policy in Britain and Europe', *Oxford Review of Economic Policy*, vol.9, no.3, pp.36–61.

Artis, M.J. and Nixson, F. (eds) (2001) *The Economics of the European Union: Policy and Analysis*, 3rd edn Oxford, Oxford University Press.

Artis, M.J. and Taylor, M.P. (1989) 'Exchange rates, interest rates, capital controls and the European Monetary System: assessing the track record' in Giavazzi, F., Micossi, S. and Miller, M. (eds) *The European Monetary System*, Cambridge, Cambridge University Press.

Arrow, K.J. (1963) 'Uncertainty and the welfare economics of medical care', *American Economic Review*, vol.53, pp.941–73.

Arulampalam, W. (2001) 'Is unemployment really scarring? effects of unemployment experiences on wages', *The Economic Journal*, vol.111, November, pp.F585–606.

Arulampalam, W., Gregg, P. and Gregory, M. (2001) 'Unemployment scarring', *The Economic Journal*, vol.111, November, pp.F577–84.

Atkinson, A. (1999) *Is Rising Income Inequality Inevitable?: A Critique of the Transatlantic Consensus*, WIDER annual lectures 3, Helsinki, World Institute for Development and Economics Research.

Atkinson, A.B. (1999) *The Economic Consequences of Rolling Back the Welfare State*, Cambridge, Mass., MIT Press.

Axelrod, R.M. (1990) *The Evolution of Co-operation*, Harmondsworth, Penguin.

Baldwin, R.E. and Martin, P. (1999) *Two Waves of Globalization: Superficial Similarities, Fundamental Differences*, NBER Working Paper No.6904, Cambridge, Mass., National Bureau of Economic Research.

Ball, L. (1993) 'How costly is disinflation?: the historical evidence', *Business Review*, Federal Reserve Bank of Philadelphia, November–December.

Ball, L. and Mankiw, N.G. (1994) 'Asymmetric price adjustment and economic fluctuations', *Economic Journal*, vol.104, pp.247–61.

Ball, L. and Tchaidze, R. (2002) *The Fed and the New Economy*, NBER Working Paper No.8785, Cambridge, Mass., National Bureau of Economic Research.

Bank of England, *Notes on Monetary Policy*, at www.bankofengland.co.uk (accessed September 2002).

Barr, N. (ed.) (1994) *Labor Markets and Social Policy in Central and Eastern Europe: The Transition and Beyond*, Oxford, Oxford University Press.

Barro, R.J. and Gordon, D. (1983) 'A positive theory of monetary policy in a natural-rate model', *Journal of Political Economy*, vol.91, pp.589–610.

Basu, S., Fernald, J. and Shapiro, M. (2001) *Productivity Growth in the 1990s: Technology, Utilization, or Adjustment?*, NBER Working Paper No.8359, Cambridge, Mass., National Bureau of Economic Research.

Baumol, W.J. and Blinder, A.S. (1988) *Economics: Principles and Policy*, New York, Harcourt Brace Jovanovich.

Bean, C. and Crafts, N.F.R. (1996) 'British economic growth since 1945: relative economic decline . . . and renaissance?' in Crafts, N.F.R. and Toniolo, G. (eds) *Economic Growth in Europe since 1945*, pp.131–72.

Beck, U. (2000) *The Brave New World of Work*, Cambridge, Polity Press.

Becker, G. (1962) 'Investment in human capital: a theoretical analysis', *Journal of Political Economy*, vol.70, pp.9–44.

Behrendt, C. (2000) 'Holes in the safety net? Social security and the alleviation of poverty in comparative perspective', *Luxembourg Income Study Working Paper*, no.259, December.

Berg, A. (1999) *The Asian Crisis: Causes, Policy Responses and Outcomes*, IMF Working Paper No.99/138.

Bernanke, B.S. (1983) 'Non-monetary effects of the financial crisis in the propagation of the Great Depression', *American Economic Review*, vol.73, pp.257–76.

Bernanke, B.S. and Carey, K. (1996) 'Nominal wage stickiness and aggregate supply during the Great Depression', *Quarterly Journal of Economics*, vol.111, pp.853–84.

Berndt, E.R. and Rappaport, N. (2000) 'Price and quality of desktop and mobile personal computers: a quarter century of history', paper presented at the National Bureau of Economic Research's Summer Institute 2000 session on 'Price, Output and Productivity Measurement', Cambridge, Mass.

Bertola, G. (2001) 'Europe's unemployment problems' in Artis, M.J. and Nixson, F. (eds) *The Economics of the European Union*.

Bhaduri, A. (1986) *Macroeconomics: The Dynamics of Commodity Production*, New Delhi, Oxford University Press.

BIS (1992) *Annual Report*, Basle, Bank of International Settlements.

Blanchard, O.J. (1983) 'Price asynchronization and price inertia' in Dornbusch, R. and Simonsen, M. (eds) *Inflation, Debt and Indexation*, Cambridge, Mass., MIT Press.

Blanchflower, D.G. and Oswald, A.J. (2001) *Well-being Over Time in Britain and the USA*, Warwick Economic Research Paper No.616.

Blau, F.D. (2000) 'Gender differences in pay', *Journal of Economic Perspectives*, vol.14, no.4, pp.75–99.

Blomstrom, M. and Kokko, A. (1998) 'Multinational corporations and spillovers', *Journal of Economic Surveys*, vol.12, no.3, pp.247–77.

Boadway, R. and Keen, M. (2000) 'Redistribution' in Atkinson, A.B. and Bourguignon, F. (eds) (2000) *Handbook of Income Distribution, Volume I*, Amsterdam, Elsevier.

Boltho, A. (1982) 'Growth' in Boltho, A. (ed.) *The European Economy: Growth and Crisis*, Oxford, Oxford University Press, pp.9–37.

Bonacich, E. and Appelbaum, R. (2000) *Behind the Label: Inequality in the Los Angeles Apparel Industry*, Los Angeles, University of California Press.

Bordo, M. (1993) 'The Bretton Woods International Monetary System: an historical overview' in Bordo, M. and Eichengreen, B. (eds) *A Retrospective on the Bretton Woods System*, Chicago, University of Chicago Press, pp.3–98.

Borenstein, S. and Saloner, G. (2001) 'Economics and electronic commerce', *Journal of Economic Perspectives*, vol.15, no.1, pp.3–12.

Boskin, M., Dulberger, E., Gordon, R., Griliches, Z. and Jorgenson, D. (1996) 'Toward a more accurate measure of the cost of living', Final Report to US Senate Finance Committee.

Bowen, H., Leamer, E. and Sveikauskas, L. (1987) 'Multi-country multi-factor tests of the factor abundance theory', *American Economic Review*, vol.77, pp.791–809.

Bowles, S. (1985) 'The production process in a competitive economy: Walrasian, Neo-Hobbesian and Marxian models', *American Economic Review*, vol.75, pp.16–36.

Boyd, M., Mulvihill, M. and Myles, J. (1995) 'Gender power and postindustrialism' in Jacobs, J.A. (ed.) *Gender Inequality at Work*, Thousand Oaks, Calif., Sage.

Boyer, G. and Hatton, T. (2002) 'New estimates of British unemployment, 1870–1913', *Journal of Economic History*, vol.62, pp.643–75.

Boyer, R. and Savageau, D. (1981) *Places Rated Almanac: Your Guide to Finding the Best Places to Live in Americ*a, Skokie, Ill., Rand McNally.

Bresnahan, T.F. (1998) 'The changing structure of innovation in computing: sources of threats to the dominant US position', in Mowery, D. *et al.* (eds) *America's Industrial Resurgence*, Washington, DC, National Research Council.

Briault, C. (1995) 'The costs of inflation', *Bank of England Quarterly Bulletin*, February, pp.33–45.

Broadberry, S.N. (1994) 'Why was unemployment in postwar Britain so low?', *Bulletin of Economic Research*, vol.46, pp.241–61.

Broadberry, S.N. (1998) 'How did the United States and Germany overtake Britain?: Sectoral analysis of comparative productivity levels, 1870–1990', *Journal of Economic History*, vol.58, pp.375–407.

Broadberry, S.N. and Crafts, N.F.R. (1992) 'Britain's productivity gap in the 1930s: some neglected factors', *Journal of Economic History*, vol.52, pp.531–58.

Broadberry, S.N. and Crafts, N.F.R. (1996) 'British economic performance and industrial policy in the early postwar period', *Business History*, vol.38, pp.65–91.

Broadberry, S.N. and Crafts, N.F.R. (2001) 'Competition and innovation in 1950s Britain', *Business History*, vol.43, pp.97–118.

Broome, J. (1992) *Counting the Costs of Global Warming*, Cambridge, White Horse Press.

Broome, J. (1993) 'Qalys', *Journal of Public Economics*, vol.50, no.2, pp.149–67.

Brown, G. (2000) Speech given to the British Chamber of Commerce National Conference, 5 April, at http://www.hm-treasury.gov.uk/newsroom_and_speeches/press/2000/press_49_00.cfm (accessed October 2005).

Bruno, M. (1995) 'Does inflation really lower growth?', *Finance and Development*, vol.32, pp.35–8.

Bruno, M. and Easterly, W. (1998) 'Inflation crises and long-run growth', *Journal of Monetary Economics*, vol.41, pp.3–26.

Brynjolfsson, E. and Hitt, L.M. (2000) 'Beyond computation: information technology, organizational transformation and business performance', *Journal of Economic Perspectives*, vol.14, no.4, pp.23–48.

Budget Report (2000) 'The economy', Chapter B at http://www.hm-treasury.gov.uk/Budget/Budget_2000/Budget_Report/bud_bud00_chapb.cfm (accessed October 2005).

Bureau of Economic Analysis (2000) *Survey of Current Business*, Washington, US Department of Commerce.

Burnside, C., Eichenbaum, M. and Rebelo, S. (1999) *Prospective Deficits and the Asian Currency Crisis*, World Bank Policy Research Working Paper No.2174.

Cafaro, P. (2001) 'Thoreau, Leopold, and Carson: toward an environmental virtue ethics', *Environmental Ethics*, vol.23, pp.3–17.

Calomiris, C. and Wilson, B. (1998) *Bank Capital and Portfolio Management: The 1930s Capital Crunch and the Scramble to Shed Risk*, NBER Working Paper No.6649, Cambridge, Mass., National Bureau of Economic Research.

Cannan, E. (1932) 'The demand for labour', *Economic Journal*, vol.42, pp.357–70.

Capie, F. and Collins, M. (1983) *The Interwar British Economy: A Statistical Abstract*, Manchester, Manchester University Press.

Caprio, G. (1998) *Banking on Crises: Expensive Lessons from Recent Financial Crises*, World Bank Policy Research Working Paper No.1979.

Carroll, G. and Hannon, M. (2000) *The Demography of Corporations and Industries*, Princeton, NJ, Princeton University Press.

Carter, M. and Maddock, R. (1984) *Rational Expectations: Macroeconomics for the 1980s*, London, Macmillan.

Carvel, J. (2001) 'Rags or riches on the life line', *The Guardian*, Society, 10 October, p.4.

Castells, M. (2001) *The Internet Galaxy: Reflections on the Internet, Business and Society*, Oxford, Oxford University Press.

Chadha, B., Masson, P.R. and Meredith, G. (1992) 'Models of inflation and the costs of disinflation', *IMF Staff Papers*, vol.39, pp.395–431.

Chakrabati, A. (2000) 'Does trade cause inequality?', *Journal of Economic Development*, vol.25, no.2, pp.1–21.

Christian Aid (2004) 'New Year shock: millions set to lose garment jobs', 17 December, http://www.christian-aid.org

Clare, A.D. and Thomas, S.H. (1993) 'Relative price variability and inflation in an equilibrium price misperceptions model', *Economic Letters*, vol.42, pp.51–7.

Clemens, M.A. and Williamson, J.G. (2001) *A Tariff-growth Paradox?: Protection's Impact on the World Around 1875–1997*, NBER Working Paper No.8459, Cambridge, Mass., National Bureau of Economic Research.

Colecchia, A. and Schreyer, P. (2002) 'ICT investment and economic growth in the '90s: is the US a unique case? A comparative study of 10 OECD countries', *Review of Economic Dynamics*, vol.5.

Commission on Macroeconomics and Health (2001) *Macroeconomics and Health: Investing in Health for Economics and Development*, report presented to the World Health Organization, December, Geneva, WHO.

Corbett, J. and Vines, D. (1999) 'The Asian crisis: lessons from the collapse of financial systems, exchange rates and macroeconomic policy' in Agenor, P.-R., Miller, M. and Vines, D. (eds) *The Asian Financial Crisis: Causes, Contagion, Consequences*, Cambridge, Cambridge University Press, pp.67–110.

Crafts, N.F.R. (1995) 'The Golden Age of economic growth in postwar Europe: why did Northern Ireland miss out?', *Irish Economic and Social History*, vol.22, pp.5–25.

Crafts, N.F.R. (1997) 'The Human Development Index and changes in standards of living: some historical comparisons', *European Review of Economic History*, vol.1, pp.299–322.

Crafts, N.F.R. (2002) *Britain's Relative Economic Decline, 1870–1999*, London, Institute of Economic Affairs.

Crafts, N.F.R. and O'Mahony M. (2001) A perspective on UK productivity performance', *Fiscal Studies*, vol.22, pp.271–306.

Crafts, N.F.R. and Toniolo, G. (eds) (1996) *Economic Growth in Europe since 1945*, Cambridge, Cambridge University Press.

Crafts, N.F.R. and Woodward, N.W.C. (1991) 'The British economy since 1945: introduction and overview', in Crafts, N.F.R. and Woodward, N.W.C. (eds) *The British Economy Since 1945*, Oxford, Clarendon Press.

Crosse, J. (2000) 'It's a kind of magic', *VM: The Vauxhall Magazine*, London, Mediamark Publishing Ltd.

Cummins, R.A. (2000) 'Objective and subjective quality of life: an interactive model', *Social Indicators Research*, vol.52, pp.55–72.

Daly, H.E. (1973) *Towards a Steady State Economy*, San Francisco, W.H. Freeman.

Daly, H.E. and Cobb, J.B. (1994) *For the Common Good*, Boston, Mass., Beacon Press.

David, P. and Wright, G. (1999) 'General purpose technologies and surges in productivity: historical reflections on the future of the IT revolution', *University of Oxford Discussion Papers in Economic and Social History*, no.31, September.

Dawson, G. (1992) *Inflation and Unemployment: Causes, Consequences and Cures*, Aldershot, Edward Elgar.

Dawson, G. (2002) 'The costs of reducing inflation' in Vane, H. and Snowdon, B. (eds) *An Encyclopaedia of Macroeconomics*, Aldershot, Edward Elgar.

De Grauwe, P. (2003) *Economics of Monetary Union*, 5th edn, Oxford, Oxford University Press.

Department of Social Security (DSS) (2001) *Households Below Average Incomes*, London, The Stationery Office.

Disney, R., Haskel, J. and Heden, Y. (2000) *Restructuring and Productivity Growth in UK Manufacturing*, Centre for Economic Policy Research Discussion Paper No.2643.

Dixit, A.K. and Nalebuff, B.J. (1991) *Thinking Strategically: The Competitive Edge in Business, Politics, and Everyday Life*, New York, W.W. Norton.

Dollar, D. and Collier, P. (2001) *Globalisation, Growth and Poverty: Building an Inclusive Economy*, Oxford, Oxford University Press.

Dollar, D. and Kray A. (2001) *Trade, Growth and Poverty*, Policy Research Working Paper No.2199, Washington, DC, World Bank.

Driver, C. (1998) 'The case of fixed investment' in Buxton, T., Chapman, P. and Temple, P. (eds) *Britain's Economic Performance*, 2nd edn, London, Routledge.

Easterlin, R. (2001) 'Income and happiness: towards a unified theory', *Economic Journal*, vol.111, pp.465–84.

Economides, N. (2001) 'The Microsoft antitrust case', *Journal of Competition and Trade*, at www.stern.nyu.edu (accessed September 2001).

Economist, The (2000) 'Supplement: The new economy: untangling e-conomics', 23 September.

Economist, The (2001a) 'Renault's alliance with Nissan: halfway down a long road', *The Economist*, 18 August, p.59.

Economist, The (2001b) 'Corporate alliances: just good friends', Leader article, *The Economist*, 18 August, p.12.

Economist, The (2005) 'Global Agenda: Progress at last', 5 May.

Eichengreen, B. (1992) *Golden Fetters*, Oxford, Oxford University Press.

Eichengreen, B. (1996) 'Institutions and economic growth: Europe after World War II' in Crafts, N.F.R. and Toniolo, G. (eds) *Economic Growth in Europe since 1945*, pp.38–72.

Eichengreen, B. and Sachs, J. (1985) 'Exchange rates and economic recovery in the 1930s', *Journal of Economic History*, vol.45, pp.925–46.

Elton, B. (1990) *Gasping*, London, Sphere Books.

Enthoven, A.C. (1988) *Reflections on the Management of the National Health Service*, London, Nuffield Provincial Hospitals Trust.

Environmental Finance (2001) 'Trading carbon: market solutions to climate change' (Special COP 7 Supplement), October, pp.I–XX.

Epstein, R. (1928) *The Automobile Industry: Its Economic and Commercial Development*, New York, Arno Press.

Etzioni, A. (1988) *The Moral Dimension: Towards a New Economics*, New York, Free Press.

Eunjung Cha, A. (2001) 'Former Sotheby's chairman could get up to three years in prison', *Washington Post*, 6 December, p.E1.

EuroMemorandum Group (2005), www.memo-europe.uni-bremen.de/downloads/Declaration_EU-Constitution_June_2005.PDE

European Commission (1990) 'One market, one money', *European Economy*, vol.44.

Feenstra, R.C. (1999) 'Facts and fallacies about foreign direct investment' in Feldstein, M. (ed.) *International Capital Flows*, NBER Conference Report, Chicago, University of Chicago Press.

Feinstein, C.H. (1972) *National Income, Expenditure and Output of the United Kingdom, 1855–1965*, Cambridge, Cambridge University Press.

Filson, D. (2001) 'The nature and effects of technological change on the industry life-cycle, *Review of Economic Dynamics*, vol.4, pp.460–94.

Financial Times (2001) 'The Lex Column: picking and choosing', *Financial Times*, 26 June, p.22.

Finch, J. (2001) 'On the markets: laughing stock', *The Guardian*, 3 October, p.25.

Fischer, S. (2001) 'Exchange rate regimes: is the bipolar view correct?', *Journal of Economic Perspectives*, 15, Spring, pp.3–24.

Fischer, S. and Modigliani, F. (1975) 'Towards an understanding of the real effects and costs of inflation', *Weltwirtschaftliches Archive*, vol.114, pp.81–99.

Fisher, F. and Rubinfeld, D. (2000) 'United States v. Microsoft: an economic analysis', *Public Law and Legal Theory Working Paper No.30*, UC Berkeley School of Law, Calif., at http://papers.ssrn.com (accessed September 2001).

Fishwick, F. (1982) *Multinational Companies and Economic Concentration in Europe*, Aldershot, Gower.

Flores, F. and Gray, J. (2000) *Entrepreneurship and the Wired Life: Work in the Wake of Careers*, London, Demos.

Fortune International (1993) 'Toshiba pioneers new alliances with American and European partners', Advertising section: 'Global alliances', vol.128, no.4, 23 August, p.S5.

Freeman, R.B. and Medoff, J.L. (1984) *What Do Unions Do?*, New York, Basic Books.

Friedman, M. (1968) 'The role of monetary policy', *American Economic Review*, vol.58, pp.1–17.

Friedman, M. (1977) *Inflation and Unemployment: The New Dimension of Politics*, IEA Occasional Paper No.51, London, Institute of Economic Affairs.

Frey, B.S. and Stutzer, A. (2002) *Happiness and Economics*, Princeton, NJ, Princeton University Press.

Fry, M. (1995) *Money, Interest and Banking in Economic Development*, Baltimore, Johns Hopkins University.

Galbraith, J.K. (1992) *The Culture of Contentment*, Harmondsworth, Penguin.

Georgescu-Roegen, N. (1971) *The Entropy Law and the Economic Process*, Cambridge, Mass., Harvard University Press.

Gibson, C., McKean, M. and Ostrom, E. (eds) (2000) *People and Forests: Communities, Institutions and Governance*, Cambridge, Mass., MIT Press.

Giersch, H., Paque, K.-H. and Schmieding, H. (1992) *The Fading Miracle*, Cambridge, Cambridge University Press.

Gilbert, R. and Katz, M. (2001) 'An economist's guide to US v. Microsoft', *Journal of Economic Perspectives*, vol.15, no.2, pp.25–44.

Gilder, G. (1989) *Microcosm: The Quantum Revolution in Economics and Technology*, New York, Simon and Schuster.

Goldstein, M., Kaminsky, G. and Reinhart, C. (2000) *Assessing Financial Vulnerability*, Washington, DC, Institute for International Economics.

Goodman, A., Johnson, P. and Webb, S. (1997) *Inequality in the UK*, Oxford, Oxford University Press.

Goodwin, N. (1998) 'GP fund holding' in Le Grand *et al.* (1998).

Gordon, R.J. (2000) 'Does the new economy measure up to the great inventions of the past?', *Journal of Economic Perspectives*, vol.4, no.14, pp.49–74.

Graham, A. (2001) 'The assessment: economics of the Internet', *Oxford Review of Economic Policy*, vol.17, no.2, pp.145–58.

Green, F. (2001) 'It's been a hard day's night: the concentration and intensification of work in late twentieth-century Britain', *British Journal of Industrial Relations*, vol.39, no.1, pp.53–80.

Green, F. and McIntosh, S. (2001) 'The intensification of work in Europe', *Labour Economics*, vol.8, no.2, pp.291–308.

Greenaway, D., Morgan, W. and Wright, P. (1997) 'Trade liberalisation and growth in developing countries: some new evidence', *World Development*, vol.25, no.11, pp.1885–92.

Greenspan, A. (1998) 'Is there a new economy?', *California Management Review*, vol.41, no.1, pp.74–85.

Gregg, P. (2001) 'The impact of youth unemployment on adult unemployment in the NCDs', *The Economic Journal*, vol.111, November, pp.F626–53.

Gregg, P. and Wadsworth, J. (1999) 'Job tenure 1975–98' in Gregg, P. and Wadsworth, J. (eds) *The State of Working Britain*, Manchester, Manchester University Press, pp.109–26.

Gregory, M. and Jukes, R. (2001) 'Unemployment and subsequent earnings: estimating scarring among British men 1984–94', *The Economic Journal*, vol.111, November, pp.F607–25.

Greyson, J. (1996) 'The Natural Step: developing a consensus on criteria for a sustainable economy', *Renew: Technology for a Sustainable Future*, Network for Alternative Technology and Technology Assessment (NATTA)/The Open University, Milton Keynes.

Grossman, R.S. (1994) 'The shoe that didn't drop: explaining banking stability during the Great Depression', *Journal of Economic History*, vol.54, pp.654–82.

Grubb, M., Vrolijk, C. and Brack, D. (1999) *The Kyoto Protocol: A Guide and Assessment*, London, Earthscan/The Royal Institute of International Affairs.

Guerrera, F. (2001) 'Hectic year for Monti in his crusade against "cancers"', *Financial Times*, 28 December.

Haldane, A. and Quah, D. (1999) 'UK Phillips Curves and Monetary Policy', *Journal of Monetary Economics*, vol.44.

Hall, T.E. and Ferguson, J.D. (1998) *The Great Depression*, Ann Arbor, University of Michigan Press.

Hamblin, R. (1998) 'Trusts' in Le Grand *et al.* (1998).

Hardin, G. (1968) 'The tragedy of the commons', *Science*, vol.162, 13 December.

Harrison, B. and Bluestone, B. (1990) 'Wage polarisation in the US and the "flexibility" debate', *Cambridge Journal of Economics*, vol.14, no.3, pp.351–73.

Hay, D.A. and Morris, D.J. (1991) *Industrial Economics and Organization: Theory and Evidence*, Oxford, Oxford University Press.

Hayek, F. (1976, first published 1948) 'The meaning of competition' in *Individualism and Economic Order*, Chicago, University of Chicago Press.

Hayek, F.A. (1978) 'Full employment, planning and inflation', in *A Tiger by the Tail*, Institute of Economic Affairs, London, pp.53–60; originally published in *Studies in Philosophy, Politics and Economics*, London, Routledge, 1967.

Hicks, J.R. (1935) 'Annual survey of economic theory: the theory of monopoly', *Econometrica*, vol.3, no.1, pp.1–20.

Hicks, J.R. (1939) *Value and Capital*, Oxford, Clarendon Press.

Hirsch, F. (1976) *The Social Limits to Growth*, Cambridge, Mass., Harvard University Press.

HM Treasury (2003) 'The UK government's policy on Economic and Monetary Union (EMU)', http://www.hm-treasury.gov.uk/documents/the_euro (accessed October 2005).

Hobsbawm, E. (1982) *Industry and Empire*, Harmondsworth, Penguin.

Hochschild, A. (1997) *The Time Bind*, New York, Metropolitan Books.

Holtfrerich, C.-L. (1983) *The German Inflation, 1914–1923*, Berlin, de Gruyter.

Houghton, J. (1997) *Global Warming: The Complete Briefing*, Cambridge, Cambridge University Press.

Hume, D. (1906) *A Treatise of Human Nature*, Selby-Bigge, A.H. (ed.), Oxford, Oxford University Press (first published 1739–40).

Humphrey, T. (1986) *From Trade-offs to Policy Ineffectiveness: A History of the Phillips Curve*, Richmond, Va., Federal Reserve Bank of Richmond.

Hutton, W. (1995) *The State We're In*, London, Vintage.

IMF (2000) *World Economic Outlook*, Washington, DC, International Monetary Fund.

Incomes Data Services (2001) *Pay and Conditions in Call Centres*, IDS Research Report, September, London, IDS, at http://www.incomesdata.co.uk (accessed January 2002).

International Trade Administration (2005) *National Trade Data*, http://www.ita.doc.gov/td/industry/otea/usfth/top80cty/canada.html (accessed October 2005).

IPPR (2000) *Future of Work*, findings of a series of focus groups with people in low-paid jobs, funded by the Reed Academy of Enterprise, London, Institute for Public Policy Research.

Jenkins, R. (1983) 'Comparing foreign subsidiaries and local firms in LDCs: theoretical issues and empirical evidence', *Journal of Development Studies*, vol.26, no.2.

Jones, C. (2001) *Introduction to Economic Growth*, London, Norton.

Junankar, P.N. (1985) *Costs of Unemployment*, Brussels, Commission of European Community.

Kabeer, N. (2000) *The Power to Choose: Bangladeshi Women and Labour Market Decisions in London and Dhaka*, London, Verso.

Kaldor, N. (1958) 'Capital accumulation and economic growth', Chapter 10 in Lutz, F.A. and Hague, D.C. (eds) (1961) *The Theory of Capital*, London, Macmillan.

Kalecki, M. (1943) 'Political aspects of full employment' in Kalecki, M. (ed.) *Selected Essays on the Dynamics of the Capitalist Economy, 1933–1970*, Cambridge, Cambridge University Press, pp.138–45.

Kalecki, M. (1954) 'The theory of economic dynamics' in Osiatynski, J. (ed.) (1990) *Collected Works of Michal Kalecki, Volume 1: Capitalism: Business Cycles and Full Employment*, Oxford, Clarendon Press.

Kehoe, L. (2001) 'PC shipments suffer fall', *Financial Times*, 21 July, p.6.

Keynes, J.M. (1936) *The General Theory of Employment, Interest and Money*, London, Macmillan.

Klein, B. (2001) 'The Microsoft case: what can a dominant firm do to defend its position?', *Journal of Economic Perspectives*, vol.15, no.2, pp.45–62.

Klein, N. (1999) *No Logo: Taking Aim at the Brand Bullies*, New York, Picador.

Klein, R. (1983) *The Politics of the National Health Service*, London, Longman.

Krugman, P. (1989) 'The case for stabilising exchange rates', *Oxford Review of Economic Policy*, vol.5, no.3.

Krugman, P. (1991) *Geography and Trade.* Cambridge, Mass., MIT Press.

Krugman, P. and Obstfeld, M. (2003) *International Economics*, 6th edn, Boston, Mass. Addison-Wesley.

Lakin, C. (2001) 'The effects of taxes and benefits on household income, 1999–2000', *Economic Trends*, no.569, April.

Landes, D. (1972) *The Unbound Prometheus: Technological Change and Industrial Development in Western Europe from 1750 to the Present*, Cambridge, Cambridge University Press.

Landes, D.S. (1998) *The Wealth and Poverty of Nations: Why Are Some So Rich and Others So Poor?*, New York, W.W. Norton.

Layard, R., Nickell, S. and Jackman, R. (1994) *The Unemployment Crisis*, Oxford, Oxford University Press.

Le Grand, J., Mays, N. and Mulligan, J. (eds) (1998) *Evaluating the NHS Reforms*, London, King's Fund Institute.

Leontief, W.W. (1953) 'Domestic production and foreign trade: the American capital position re-examined', *Proceedings of the American Philosophical Society*, vol.97, pp.332–49.

Leopold, A. (1970) *A Sand County Almanac: With Essays on Conservation from Round River*, New York, Ballantine Books.

Lewis, S. and Brannen, J. (2000) 'Forever young? Generation X's views on gender, work and family issues' in Wilkinson, H. (ed.) *Family Business*, London, Demos.

Lindert, P.H. and Williamson, J.G. (2001) *Does Globalization Make the World More Unequal?*, NBER Working Paper No.8228, Cambridge, Mass., National Bureau of Economic Research.

Lipsey, R., Bekar, C. and Carlaw, K. (1998) 'General purpose technologies and economic growth', in Helpman, E. (ed.) *General Purpose Technologies and Economic Growth*, Cambridge, Mass., MIT Press, pp.38–43.

Lutz, M. (1999) *The Economics of the Common Good*, London, Routledge.

Lutz, M.A. (1999) *Economics for the Common Good: Two Centuries of Social Economic Thought in the Humanistic Tradition*, London, Routledge.

Machin, S. (1999) 'Wage inequality in the 1970s, 1980s and 1990s' in Gregg, P. and Wadsworth, J. (eds) *The State of Working Britain*, Manchester, Manchester University Press, pp.185–205.

McKean, M. (2000) 'Common property: what is it, what is it good for and what makes it work?' in Gibson *et al.* (2000).

Mackintosh, M. and Mooney, G. (2000) 'Identity, inequality and social class' in Woodward, K. (ed.) *Questioning Identity: Gender, Class, Nation*, London, Routledge/The Open University.

Maddison, A. (1983) *Two Crises: Latin America and Asia, 1929–38 and 1973–83*, Paris, OECD.

Maddison, A. (1987) 'Growth and slowdown in advanced capitalist economies: techniques of quantitative assessment', *Journal of Economic Literature*, vol.25, pp.649–98.

Maddison, A. (1991) *Dynamic Forces in Capitalist Development*, Oxford, Oxford University Press.

Maddison, A. (1995) *Monitoring the World Economy, 1820–1992*, Paris, OECD.

Maddison, A. (2001) *The World Economy: A Millennial Perspective*, Paris, OECD.

Makowski, L. and Ostroy, J.M. (2001) 'Perfect competition and the creativity of the market', *Journal of Economic Literature*, vol.XXXIX, no.2, pp.479–535.

Mankiw, G. (1990) 'A quick refresher course in macroeconomics', *Journal of Economic Literature*, vol.28, no.4, pp.1645–60.

Marshall, A. (1925) *Principles of Economics*, Book IV (8th edn), London, Macmillan.

Martin, W.E. and Rowthorn, R. (2004), 'Will stability last?', *CESifo Working Paper*, No.1324, CESifo GmbH.

Matthews, R.C.O. (1968) 'Why has Britain had full employment since the war?', *Economic Journal*, vol.78, pp.555–69.

Menon, A. (2005) 'The bitter truth about European sugar', *Financial Times*, 25 February.

Milburn, A. (2002) 'Redefining the National Health Service', speech to New Health Network, 15 January, *Guardian Unlimited*, http://www.guardian.co.uk/Archive/Article/0,4273,4336093,00.html (accessed May 2002).

Minford, A.P.L. and Peel, D. (1983) *Rational Expectations and the New Macroeconomics*, Oxford, Martin Robertson.

Mishkin, F.S. (1999) *Lessons from the Asian Crisis*, NBER Working Paper No.7102, Cambridge, Mass., National Bureau of Economic Research.

Mitchell, B.R. (1988) *British Historical Statistics*, Cambridge, Cambridge University Press.

Mokyr, J. (1997) 'Are we living in the middle of an Industrial Revolution?', *Federal Reserve Bank of Kansas City Economic Review*, Second Quarter, pp.31–43.

Murgatroyd, L. and Neuburger, H. (1997) 'A household satellite account for the UK', *Economic Trends*, No.527, pp.63–71.

Muth, J.F. (1961) 'Rational expectations and the theory of price movements', *Econometrica*, vol.29, pp.315–35.

Nelson, E. and Nikolov, K. (2001) *UK Inflation in the 1970s and 1980s: The Era of Output Gap Mismeasurement*, Bank of England Working Paper No.148.

Nelson, R.R. and Winter, S.G. (1982) *An Evolutionary Theory of Economic Change*, Cambridge, Mass., The Belknap Press of Harvard University Press.

Nelson, R.R. and Wright, G. (1992) 'The rise and fall of American technological leadership: the postwar era in historical perspective', *Journal of Economic Literature*, vol.30, pp.1931–64.

Newell, A. and Symons, J. (1988) 'The macroeconomics of the interwar years: international comparisons' in Eichengreen, B. and Hatton, T.J. (eds) *Interwar Unemployment in Historical Perspective*, Dordrecht, Kluwer Academic Publishers, pp.61–96.

Nickell, S. (1996) 'Competition and corporate performance', *Journal of Political Economy*, vol.104, pp.724–26.

Nickell, S., Nicolitsas, D. and Dryden, N. (1997) 'What makes rms perform well?', *European Economic Review*, vol.41, pp.783–96.

Nordhaus, W.D. (2000) 'New directions in national economic accounting', *American Economic Review Papers and Proceedings*, vol.90, pp.259–63.

Oberholzer-Gee, F., Frey, B.S., Pommerehne, W.W. and Hart, A. (1996) 'Panik Protest und Paralyse: Eine Empirische Untersuchung Uber Nukleare Endlager in der Schweiz', *Scweiserische Zeitschrift fur Volkswirtschaft und Statistik*, vol.131, pp.147–77.

OECD (1993) *Employment Outlook*, Paris, OECD.

OECD (1994) *The OECD Jobs Study: Evidence and Explanations Part II*, Paris, Organization for Economic Co-operation and Development.

OECD (1994) *The OECD Jobs Study: Facts, Analysis, Strategies*, Paris, OECD.

OECD (1998) 'The OECD Jobs Strategy: progress report on implementation of country-specific recommendations', *Economics Department Working Paper*, no.196, May.

OECD (2000) 'E-commerce: impacts and policy challenges' in *Economic Outlook No.67*, Paris, Organization for Economic Co-operation and Development.

OECD (2000) *Policy Brief: EMU One Year On*, Paris, OECD.

OECD (2001) *Labour Force Statistics*, Paris, OECD.

Office for National Statistics (2002) at www.statistics.gov.uk/statbase/TSDtimezone.asp (accessed October 2005).

Okun, A. (1970) *The Political Economy of Prosperity*, New York, Norton.

Okun, A. (1970) 'Potential GNP: its measurement and significance' (appendix) in *Political Economy of Prosperity*, Washington, DC, Brookings Institution.

Oliner, S.D. and Sichel, D.E. (2000) 'The resurgence of growth in the late 1990s: is information technology the story?', *Journal of Economic Perspectives*, vol.14, no.4, pp.3–22.

Orphanides, A. and Solow, R.M. (1990) 'Money, inflation and growth' in Friedman, B.M. and Hahn, F.H. (eds) *Handbook of Monetary Economics*, Vol. 1, Amsterdam, North Holland.

Osborn, A. (2001) 'Banks pay heavy fine for price-fixing', *The Guardian*, 12 December, p.22.

Oulton, N. (1995) 'Supply side reform and UK economic growth: what happened to the miracle?', *National Institute Economic Review*, vol.154, pp.53–69.

Parfit, D. (1984) *Reasons and Persons*, Oxford, Oxford University Press.

PartnershipsUK (2005), http://www.partnershipsuk.org.uk/information/info_viewNews.asp?newsType=3&newsID=53 (accessed October 2005).

Pearce, D.W. and Warford, J.J. (1993) *World Without End: Economics, Environment and Sustainable Development*, Oxford, Oxford University Press.

Peden, G.C. (1985) *British Economic and Social Policy: Lloyd George to Margaret Thatcher*, Oxford, Philip Allan.

Perrons, D. (2001) 'The new economy and the work–life balance: a case study of the new media sector in Brighton and Hove', *Research Papers in Environmental and Spatial Analysis No.67*, Department of Geography and Environment, London School of Economics.

Phelps, E.S. (1967) 'Phillips curves, expectations of inflation and optimal unemployment over time', *Economica*, vol.34, pp.254–81.

Phillips, A.W. (1958) 'The relationship between unemployment and the rate of change of money wage rates in the United Kingdom 1861–1957', *Economica*, vol.24, pp.283–99.

Plato (1993) *The Last Days of Socrates*, Harmondsworth, Penguin Books (translated by H. Tredennick and H. Tarrant).

Popovich, K. (2001) 'Dell predicts industry shakeout', *Eweek*, 22 January.

Pugh, P. and Garratt, C. (2000) *Introducing Keynesian Economics*, Cambridge, Icon Books.

Purdy, D. (2001) 'Social policy' in Artis, M. and Nixson, F. (eds) *The Economics of the European Union*, Oxford, Oxford University Press.

Quah, D. (1996) *The Invisible Hand and the Weightless Economy*, Centre for Economic Performance Occasional Paper No.12, London, London School of Economics.

Quah, D. (1999) *The Weightless Economy in Economic Development*, Centre for Economic Performance Discussion Paper No.417, London, London School of Economics.

Quah, D. (2001) 'Technology dissemination and economic growth: some lessons for the new economy', public lecture at the University of Hong Kong, at http://econ.lse.ac.uk/staff/dquah/ (accessed January 2002).

Quizilbash, M. (1997) 'Pluralism and well-being indices', *World Development*, vol.25, pp.2009–26.

Raff, D.M.G. and Trajtenberg, M. (1997) 'Quality-adjusted prices for the American automobile industry: 1906–1940' in Bresnahan, T.F. and Gordon, R.J. (eds) *The Economics of New Goods: NBER Studies in Income and Wealth: Vol.58*, Chicago, University of Chicago Press, pp.71–107.

Ramey, G. and Ramey, V.A. (1995) 'Cross country evidence on the link between volatility and growth', *American Economic Review*, vol.85, pp.1138–51.

Rawls, J. (1972) *A Theory of Justice*, Oxford, Oxford University Press.

Reich, R. (2001) *The Future of Success: Work and Life in the New Economy*, London, Heinemann.

Rodrik, D. (1996) 'Understanding policy reform', *Journal of Economic Literature*, vol.34, pp.9–41.

Romer, C. (1992) 'What ended the Great Depression?', *Journal of Economic History*, vol.52, pp.756–84.

Rosenbaum, E.F. (2000) 'What is a market? On the methodology of a contested concept', *Review of Social Economy*, vol.58, no.4, pp.455–82.

Rosewell, B. (2001) 'GHG trading: easier than you think', *Environmental Finance* (Special COP 7 Supplement), October, pp.I–XX.

Sadiq, A.T. and Bolbol, A.A. (2001) 'Capital flows, FDI and technology spillovers: evidence from Arab countries', *World Development*, vol.29, no.12, pp.2111–25.

Samuelson, P.A. (1969) 'The way of an economist' in Samuelson, P.A. (ed.) *International Economic Relations; Proceedings of the Third Congress of the International Economics Association*, London, Macmillan, pp.1–11.

Samuelson, P.A. and Nordhaus, W.D. (1989) *Economics* (13th edn), Singapore, McGraw-Hill.

Sargent, T.J. (1986) *Rational Expectations and Inflation*, New York, Harper & Row.

Say, J.-B. (1803) *A Treatise on Political Economy*, Philadelphia, Pa., Lippincott, Grambo.

Schneider, F. (2000) 'The increase of the size of the shadow economy of 18 OECD countries: some preliminary explanations', paper presented to the Annual Public Choice Meetings, Charleston, South Carolina.

Schneider, F. and Enste, D.H. (2000) 'Shadow economies: size, causes, and consequences', *Journal of Economic Literature*, vol.38, pp.77–114.

Schofield, J. (2000) 'Trouble at the top for PC giants', *The Guardian* online, 13 September, pp.1–3.

Schumacher, E.F. (1973) *Small is Beautiful: A Study of Economics as if People Mattered*, London, Blond & Briggs.

Schumpeter, J. (1942) *Capitalism, Socialism and Democracy*, New York, Harper.

Schyns, P. (1998) 'Cross-national differences in happiness: economic and cultural factors explored', *Social Indicators Research*, vol.43, pp.3–26.

Selzer, I.M. (2001) 'Thoughts on competition policy', *Lectures on Regulatory and Competition Policy*, London, The Institute of Economic Affairs.

Sen, A.K. (1976) 'Rational fools: a critique of the behavioural foundations of economic theory', *Philosophy and Public Affairs*, vol.6, Summer, pp.317–44.

Sen, A.K. (1985) *Capabilities and Commodities*, Amsterdam, North-Holland.

Sen, A.K. (1987) *On Ethics and Economics*, Oxford, Basil Blackwell.

Sen, A.K. (1999) *Development as Freedom*, Oxford, Oxford University Press.

Sennett, R. (1998) *The Corrosion of Character*, London, W.W. Norton.

Shipman, A. (2001) 'Privatized production, socialized consumption? Old producer power behind the new consumer sovereignty', *Review of Social Economy*, vol.LIX, pp.331–52.

Shy, O. (2001) *The Economics of Network Industries*, Cambridge, Cambridge University Press.

Smeeding, T. and Rainwater, L. (2001) 'Comparing living standards across nations: real incomes at the top, the bottom and the middle', *Luxembourg Income Study Working Paper*, no.266, May.

Smith, A. (1937, first published 1776) *The Wealth of Nations*, The Cannan Edition, New York, Modern Library.

Smith, G.D., Dorling, D. and Shaw, M. (2001) *Poverty, Inequality and Health in Britain 1800–2000: A Reader*, London, Policy Press.

Solow, R.M. (1987) 'We'd better watch out', *New York Times Book Review*, 12 July, p.36.

Sutliff, T.J. (1901) 'Revival in all industries exceeds most sanguine hopes', *New York Herald Tribune*, 6 April, p.3.

Tanzi, V. and Schuknecht, L. (2000) *Public Spending in the Twentieth Century*, Cambridge, Cambridge University Press.

Taylor, J.B. (1994) *Goals, Guidelines and Constraints Facing Monetary Policymakers*, Boston, Federal Reserve Bank of Boston.

Temin, P. (1976) *Did Monetary Forces Cause the Great Depression?*, New York, Norton.

Temin, P. (2002) 'The Golden Age of European growth reconsidered', *European Review of Economic History*, vol.6, pp.3–22.

Temple, J. (2000) 'Inflation and growth: stories short and tall', *Journal of Economic Surveys*, vol.14, pp.395–426.

Thompson, G. (2000) 'Economic globalization?' in Held, D. (ed.) *A Globalizing World? Culture, Economics, Politics*, London, Routledge/The Open University.

Timmins, N. (1995) *The Five Giants: A Biography of the Welfare State*, London, HarperCollins.

Toffler, A. (1980) *The Third Wave*, New York, William Morrow.

Tushman, M. and Anderson, P. (1986) 'Technological discontinuities and organizational environments', *Administrative Science Quarterly*, vol.31, pp.439–65.

UNCTAD (1998) *World Investment Report, 1998: Trends and Determinants*, Geneva, UNCTAD.

UNCTAD (2001) *World Investment Report, 2001: Promoting Linkages*, Geneva, UNCTAD.

US Bureau of the Census (1960) *Historical Statistics of the United States*, Washington, DC US Census Bureau.

van de Klundert, T. and van Schaik, A. (1996) 'On the historical continuity of the process of economic growth' in van Ark, B. and Crafts, N.F.R. (eds) *Quantitative Aspects of Postwar European Economic Growth*, Cambridge, Cambridge University Press, pp.388–414.

van Doorslaer, E. and Wagstaff, A. (1993) 'Equity in the finance of health care: methods and findings' in van Doorslaer, E., Wagstaff, A. and Rutten, F. (eds) *Equity and Finance in the Delivery of Health Care: An International Perspective*, Oxford, Oxford University Press.

van Doorslaer, E. *et al.* (2000) 'Equity in the delivery of health care in Europe and the US', *Journal of Health Economics*, vol.19, no.5, pp.553–83.

Van Reenan, J. (2001) 'The new economy: reality and policy', *Fiscal Studies*, vol.22, no.3, pp.307–36.

Varughese, G. (2000) 'Population and forest dynamics in the hills of Nepal: institutional remedies by rural communities' in Gibson *et al.* (2000).

Veblen, T. (1912) *The Theory of the Leisure Class*, London, Macmillan.

Veenhoven, R. (1993) *Happiness in Nations: Subjective Appreciation of Life in 56 Nations*, Rotterdam, RISBO.

Vickers, J. and Yarrow, G. (1988) *Privatization: An Economic Analysis*, Cambridge, Mass., MIT Press.

Victor, D. (2001) *After Kyoto: Politics, Economics and the Struggle to Slow Global Warming*, Princeton, Princeton University Press.

Viscusi, K. (1998) *Rational Risk Policy*, Oxford, Clarendon Press.

Voyle, S. and Edgecliffe-Johnson, A. (2001) 'Tesco exports online trading to US', *Financial Times*, 26 June, p.23.

Wade, R. (2001) 'Winners and losers', *The Economist*, 26 April.

Wagstaff, A. *et al.* (1999) 'Equity in the finance of health care: some further international comparisons', *Journal of Health Economics*, vol.18, no.3, pp.263–90.

WCED (World Commission on Environment and Development) (1987) *Our Common Future*, Oxford, Oxford University Press.

Webb, S.B. (1986) 'Fiscal news and inflationary expectations in Germany after World War I', *Journal of Economic History*, vol.46, pp.769–94.

Webb, S.B. (1989) *Hyperinflation and Stabilization in Weimar Germany*, Oxford, Oxford University Press.

Whitehead, M. (1992) 'The Health Divide' in Townsend, P., Whitehead, M. and Davidson, N. (eds) *Inequalities in Health: The Black Report and the Health Divide*, Harmondsworth, Penguin.

Women's Unit (2000) *More Choice for Women in the New Economy: The Facts*, London, Cabinet Office.

World Bank (1993) *The East Asian Miracle*, New York, Oxford University Press.

World Bank (2001) *World Development Indicators*, Washington, DC, World Bank.

World Bank (2002) *World Development Indicators* (CD-ROM), Washington, DC, World Bank.

World Health Organization (1999) *The World Health Report*, Geneva, WHO.

Wren Lewis, S. (2003) 'Estimates for equilibrium exchange rates for sterling against the euro'.

Yuengert, A.M. (2001) 'Rational choice with passion: virtue in a model of rational addiction', *Review of Social Economy*, vol.59, no.1, pp.1–21.

Zestos, G.K. (1996) *European Monetary Integration: The Euro,* Thomson, South Western.

Acknowledgements

Grateful acknowledgement is made to the following sources for permission to reproduce material in this book.

Introduction

Photo p.xi: Copyright © Ronald J. Thomas.

Chapter 1

Text

Extract on p.18: Jewson, N. (2003) 'Work changes us as people', *The Sunday Times*, 18 May 2003. Copyright © Nick Jewson.

Chapter 2

Figures

Figure 2.1: Copyright © 1997 Wasserman, *Boston Globe*, LA Times Syndicate; *Figure 2.3*: taken from www.obsoletecomputermuseum.org.

Chapter 3

Text

Extract on p.69: 'BMW wants to make internal-combustion engines that run on hydrogen', *The Economist*, 21 July 2001. Copyright © The Economist Newspaper Limited, London.

Figures

Figure 3.1: Copyright © Citroën UK Ltd; *Figure 3.2*: Copyright © IPC Media Ltd; *Figure 3.9*: Copyright © IPC Media Ltd.

Chapter 4

Text

Extract on p.76: Samuelson, R.J. (2000) 'The mystifying Microsoft case', *Washington Post*, 11 April 2000. Copyright © 2001 The Washington Post Writers Group. Reprinted with permission; *Extract on p.101*: Spiegel, P. and Abrahams, P. (2001) 'Appeals court rules against Microsoft break-up', *Financial Times*, 28 June 2001. Copyright © 2001 Financial Times Syndication.

Figures

Figure 4.1: Copyright © The New Yorker Collection from cartoonbank.com. All Rights Reserved; *Figure 4.10*: Klein, B. (2001) 'The Microsoft case: what can a dominant firm do to defend its position?', *Journal of Economic Perspectives*, Spring 2001, vol.15, issue 2, American Economic Association.

Chapter 5

Text

Extract on p.123: adapted from Finch, J. (2001) 'Body Shop buyers line up', *The Guardian*, 3 October 2001. Copyright © The Guardian.

Figures

Figure 5.14: Copyright © Fat Free Ltd/Miramax/The Kobal Collection.

Chapter 6

Text

Extract on p.167: O'Donnell, J. (2003) 'Price fixers face jail, fines and disqualification in crackdown', *The Sunday Times*, 23 February 2003. Reproduced by permission of News International Syndication Ltd.

Figures

Figure 6.10 (left): Courtesy of Mark Chilvers; *Figure 6.10 (right)*: Copyright © David Ashdown, The Independent.

Chapter 7

Tables

Table 7.1: From *The State of Working Britain*, by Paul Gregg and Jonathan Wadsworth, 1999, Manchester University Press, Manchester, UK; *Table 7.3: OECD Employment Outlook*, July 1997. Copyright © OECD.

Chapter 8

Figures

Figure 8.3: Office for National Statistics, 2001, Table 2.1, p.109. Crown copyright material is reproduced under Class Licence Number C01W0000065 with the permission of the Controller of HMSO and the Queen's Printer for Scotland.

Tables

Table 8.1: Office for National Statistics, 2001, Table 1.2, p.39. Crown copyright material is reproduced under Class Licence Number C01W0000065 with the permission of the Controller of HMSO and the Queen's Printer for Scotland; *Table 8.5*: Office for National Statistics, 2001, Table 1.2, pp.38–9 and Table 1.3, pp.40–1. Crown copyright material is reproduced under Class Licence Number C01W0000065 with the permission of the Controller of HMSO and the Queen's Printer for Scotland; *Table 8.6*: Office for National Statistics, 2001, Table 1.1, pp.36–7. Crown copyright material is reproduced under Class Licence Number C01W0000065 with the permission of the Controller of HMSO and the Queen's Printer for Scotland; *Table 8.9*: Viscusi, K. (1998) *Rational Risk Policy*, Oxford University Press, Inc.; *Table 8.11*: Oberholzer-Gee *et al.* (1996) *Schweiserische Zeitschrift fur Volkswirtschaft und Statistik*, no.131, Helbring und Lichtenhaln Verlag; *Table 8.13*: Reprinted from *World Development*, vol.25, no.12, Mozaffar Quizilbash (1997) 'Pluralism and well-being indices', pp.2009–26, Copyright © 1997, with permission from Elsevier Science.

Chapter 9

Figures

Figure 9.5: based on Tanzi, V. and Schuknecht, L. (2000) *Public Spending in the Twentieth Century: A Global Perspective*. Copyright © Vito Tanzi, Ludger Schuknecht, published by Cambridge University Press; *Figure 9.8: Luxembourg Income Study*, 10 October 2001, Copyright © LIS 2001; *Figure 9.9*: Lakin, C. (2001) *Economic Trends*, no.569, April 2001. Crown copyright material is reproduced under Class Licence Number C01W0000065 with the permission of the Controller of HMSO and the Queen's Printer for Scotland; *Figure 9.11*: adapted from *The OECD Jobs Study: Evidence and Explanations*, Part II, 1994; *Figure 9.14*: DSS (2001) *Households Below Average Income 1999/00*, p.8. Crown copyright material is reproduced under Class Licence Number C01W0000065 with the permission of the Controller of HMSO and the Queen's Printer for Scotland.

Tables

Table 9.1: DSS (2001) *Households Below Average Income 1999/00*, p.101. Crown copyright material is reproduced under Class Licence Number C01W0000065 with the permission of the Controller of HMSO and the Queen's Printer for Scotland; *Table 9.2: Luxembourg Income Study*, 10 October 2001, Copyright © LIS 2001; *Table 9.3*: Behrendt, C. (2000) 'Holes in the safety net? Social security and the alleviation of poverty in comparative perspective', December 2000. Copyright © Christina Behrendt, University of Konstanz.

Chapter 10

Text

Extracts on p.267: Carvel, J. (2001) 'Rags or riches on the life line: London reveals a widening gap in the fight against health inequalities', *The Guardian*, 10 October 2001. Copyright © 2001 Guardian Newspapers Limited.

Figures

Figure 10.2: van Doorslaer, E. and Wagstaff, A. (1993) 'Equity in the finance of health care: methods of dealings' in van Doorslaer, E., Wagstaff, A. and Rutten, F. (eds) *Equity in the Finance and Delivery of Health Care: An International Perspective*, Commission of European Communities; *Figure 10.3*: reprinted from *Journal of Health Economics*, vol.19, van Doorslaer, E. *et al.* (2000) 'Equity in the delivery of health care in Europe', p.556. Copyright © 2000, with permission from Elsevier Science.

Tables

Table 10.2: reprinted from *Journal of Health Economics*, vol.18, Wagstaff, A. *et al.* (1999) 'Equity in the finance of health care', p.268. Copyright © 1999, with permission from Elsevier Science.

Every effort has been made to trace all copyright owners, but if any has been inadvertently overlooked, the publishers will be pleased to make the necessary arrangements at the first opportunity.

Chapter 11

Text

Extract on p.315: 'Five million reasons to worry', *The Economist*, 2 February 2005. Copyright © The Economist Newspaper Limited, London.

Figures

Figure 11.1: from 'A smoother ride', © The Economist Newspaper Limited, London, 20 March 2004; *Figure 11.4*: from *The OECD Jobs Study*. Copyright © OECD 1994.

Chapter 12

Text

Extracts on p.332: 'US trade deficit hits fresh high', http://news.bbc.co.uk, 12 April 2005. Copyright © BBC; 'US Budget deficit to reach $427bn', http://news.bbc.co.uk, 25 January 2005. Copyright © BBC; *Extract on pp.332–3*: Becker, E. and Andrews, E.L. (2004) 'IMF warns that US debt is threatening global stability', *New York Times*, 8 January 2004. Copyright © 2004 by The New York Times Co. Reprinted with permission.

Chapter 14

Text

Extract on pp.385–6: 'Forestry Commission announces first PPP in the holiday sector', Partnerships UK, 2004. By kind permission of Partnerships UK.

Table

Table 14.1: from *National Income and Expenditure Blue Book 2004*, Office for National Statistics. Crown copyright material is reproduced under Class Licence Number C01W0000065 with the permission of the Controller of HMSO and the Queen's Printer for Scotland.

Chapter 15

Text

Extract on pp.411–12: 'Progress at last: World trade talks'. © The Economist Newspaper Limited, London, 5 May 2005.

Figures

Figure 15.2: Baldwin, R.E. and Martin, P., *NBER Working Papers*, January 1999, no.6904, Mohr Siebeck; *Figure 15.3*: Clemens, M.A. and Williamson, J.G., *NBER Working Papers*, September 2001, no.8459, © the authors.

Chapter 16

Text

Extract on p.439: © Christian Aid (2004). This article first appeared on Christian Aid's website www.christian-aid.org The full report 'Rags to Riches' can be downloaded at www.christian-aid.org.uk/news/media/pressrel/0401217p.htm; *Extract on p.452*: Menon, A. (2005) 'The bitter truth about European sugar', *Financial Times*, 25 February 2005. Copyright © Anand Menon.

Figures

Figures 16.1 and 16.2: © Sarah Herman, 2002; *Figure 16.3*: Atkinson, A.B., *WIDER Annual Lectures 3*, November 1999, The United Nations University, World Institute for Development and Economics Research; *Figure 16.4*: Jones, C.I. (1998) *Introduction to Economic Growth*, W.W. Norton.

Tables

Table 16.1(b): UNCTAD, 1998; *Table 16.5*: Reprinted from *World Development*, vol.25, Greenaway, D. and Morgan, W., *Trade Liberalisation and Growth in Developing Countries: Some New Evidence*, pp.1887–8. Copyright 1997, with Elsevier Science; *Table 16.6*: Dollar, D. (2001) *Globalisation, Growth and Poverty: Building an Inclusive World Economy*, World Bank.

Chapter 17

Tables

Table 17.1: Bank of International Settlements Annual Report, 1992, Bank of International Settlements, Basle; *Table 17.2: United Kingdom Balance of Payments (The Pink Book)*, 2001. Crown copyright material is reproduced with the permission of the Controller of HMSO.

Chapter 18

Illustration

Page 495: Pugh, P. and Garratt, C., *Introducing Keynesian Economics* (2000).

Chapter 19

Nicholas Crafts would like to thank Dudley Baines and Peter Law for helpful comments on an earlier draft of Chapter 19.

Tables

Table 19.1: Maddison, A., 'The world economy: a millennial perspective', *Development Centre Seminars*, OECD; *Table 19.6*: Schneider, F., 'The increase of the size of the shadow economy', *EPCS 2000*; *Table 19.12*: Oliner, S. and Sichel, D. (2000) 'Contributions to labour productivity growth in the non-farm business sector 1974–1999', *Journal of Economic Perspectives*, vol.14, no.4.

Chapter 20

Figures

Figure 20.1: Popperfoto; *Figure 20.2*: AKG; *Figure 20.4*: Courtesy of Vauxhall Magazine.

Index

Page numbers in **bold** refer to definitions given in the margin.